1987 YEARBOOK
EVENTS OF 1986

Expo Centre, a glowing symbol of Canada's popular Expo 86 world's fair.

FUNK & WAGNALLS NEW ENCYCLOPEDIA 1987 YEARBOOK

LEON L. BRAM
Vice-President and
Editorial Director

NORMA H. DICKEY
Editor in Chief

Funk & Wagnalls, Inc.

Publishers since 1876

*Funk & Wagnalls offers a 2-Album Record
Collection, "Great Music of Our Time."
For details on ordering, please write:*

Funk & Wagnalls, Inc.
P.O. Box 520
Ramsey, N.J. 07446

ISBN 0-8343-0073-7

CONTENTS

MEMBERS OF THE STAFF

SENIOR EDITOR	William McGeveran, Jr.
EDITORIAL ASSISTANT	Anne L. Galperin
CLERICAL ASSISTANT	Kay Blake
STAFF EDITORS	Richard Amdur
	Kathy Casey
	Karyn Feiden
	Inez Salinger Glucksman
	Robert Halasz
	Archibald Hobson
	Lawrence Klepp
	Kathryn Paulsen
	Gordon F. Sander
	Theodore G. Stavrou
	Wendy Svanoe
INDEXER	Vitrude DeSpain
DESIGN MANAGER	Joan Gampert
SENIOR DESIGNERS	Trudy Veit
	Marvin Friedman
DESIGNER	Emil Chendea
PHOTO EDITORS	Joyce Deyo
	Margaret McRae
	Marcia Rackow
SENIOR PRODUCTION ASSISTANT	Mynette Green
CLERICAL ASSISTANT	Valerie James
PRODUCTION EXECUTIVE	Steven G. Weinfeld

Egypt's Loss, New York's Gain

The Statue of Liberty is so thoroughly identified with the United States that it is almost impossible to imagine the Lady standing anywhere than on Liberty Island, with her gaze directed out over the Atlantic. But had historical events gone as Bartholdi originally planned, the centennial bash for the world's most impressive piece of colossal sculpture would have been held not in New York Harbor but at the mouth of the Suez Canal.

Bartholdi was a sculptor of limited talent but of grandiose vision and indefatigable energy. Living in an age that admired bigness, he revered the colossi of the past, particularly those at Thebes and Abu Simbel in Egypt, and was seized with the ambition to create some new colossus that would symbolize the values of his own time. In 1867, two years before the Suez Canal was opened, Bartholdi proposed to Ismail Pasha, the ruler of Egypt, that a lighthouse in the form of an Egyptian peasant—robed, female, and, like Liberty, carrying a torch—be constructed at the entrance of the canal. But after Bartholdi had spent two years designing the monument, the Egyptian leader, plagued with a ballooning debt and other problems, lost interest.

In 1865, however, the jurist Édouard de Laboulaye had proposed at a dinner party of fellow French

Liberty's dedication on October 28, 1886, featured much of the flamboyance of her centennial. Here, fireworks explode above a ship-filled New York Harbor in a period etching of Liberty's inaugural ceremonies.

A closeup of the statue's new gilded torch. Below, a workman plants a kiss on Liberty's forehead.

liberals—including Bartholdi—that the people of France construct a monument in the United States that would celebrate American independence and the bonds between the two nations. Laboulaye also saw the monument as a beacon to Europeans—particularly to the French, at the time under authoritarian rule—a call to them to reclaim their democratic ideals.

When the Egyptian plan fell through, Bartholdi turned with increased vigor to the idea of an American colossus. In 1871 he journeyed to the United States to find a harbor for his statue; New York, the nation's busiest port and largest city, was an obvious choice. For the site of his monument the sculptor selected Bedloe's Island (renamed Liberty Island in 1956), which had a commanding view of the harbor. Plans for the Egyptian monument were reshaped to fit Liberty, and after the Third Republic was proclaimed in France, bringing with it a liberalized political climate, fund-raising for the project began. The statue cost $250,000, ·contributed by the French people.

Copper Sheets and Curtain Walls

It takes a visionary to conceive of a colossus, but it takes an engineer to make one stand up. The bronze or

Treasury Secretary James Baker III (left) presents Lee Iacocca, chairman of the Statue of Liberty-Ellis Island Foundation, with a check for $24 million. These funds, for the restoration of both sites, were generated by the sale of gold and silver coins bearing a likeness of the statue.

stone that would have been needed for a statue 151 feet tall would have been far too heavy. For the skin of Lady Liberty, therefore, Bartholdi chose copper, shaped by a technique that required a series of molds of increasing size culminating in a full-size wooden form, against which the copper sheets were shaped by hammering. Some 300 separate copper plates were made in this way, in a process that required tens of thousands of the most painstaking measurements. The 225-ton copper skin formed by these plates was malleable and economical, but at only 3/32 of an inch (about the thickness of a penny), it was far too thin to stand up by itself on an exposed site in the middle of a windy harbor.

To design the supporting structure needed to keep Liberty from toppling, Bartholdi ultimately enlisted one of the century's true geniuses: Alexandre Gustave Eiffel, a preeminent bridge designer and engineer who is today famous for his Eiffel Tower. Eiffel designed for Liberty's interior support a central iron pylon consisting of four iron piers held together by horizontal struts and diagonal crossbracing. A secondary framework extends from this central pylon and is linked by unbraced flat iron bars to a series of iron belts that follow the

contours of the copper skin. These belts, originally separated from the skin by asbestos pads (which had deteriorated and were removed during restoration), are connected to it by riveted copper saddles. The structure is firm yet resilient, able to withstand the pressures of thermal expansion and contraction as well as the buffeting of winds and storms. As historian Marvin Trachtenberg points out in his influential study of the statue, Eiffel's design anticipates not only the stressed-skin construction of airplane wings but also the curtain-wall structure used in modern skyscrapers.

Liberty's right hand and torch were displayed at the Philadelphia Centennial Exposition in 1876, and the head, modeled after Bartholdi's mother, was ready for the Universal Exposition in Paris two years later. On July 4, 1884, ownership of the completed statue—which had been on display in the French capital—was formally transferred to the U.S. government. Because the statue proved such a popular attraction in Paris, however, it was not until May 21, 1885, that the Isère set sail from Rouen, bearing the crated Lady to her new home in the New World. On June 17, when the Isère and her escort vessel entered New York Harbor, they received a gala welcome, marred only by the fact that, after eight years of effort, Liberty's U.S. sponsors had

failed to raise enough cash to complete the pedestal the Lady was supposed to stand on.

Averting a Fiasco

Americans were not uniformly enthusiastic about having a French-made colossus on their shores, and some balked at the extravagance of the statue and its pedestal. "No true patriot can support such expenditures for a bronze female in the present state of our finances," the New York *Times* harrumphed in 1876. Repeated appeals for public support raised enough money to start the pedestal project, and the cornerstone for the pedestal, which was designed by American architect Richard Morris Hunt, was laid on August 5, 1884. But by March 1885, more than $179,000 of the funds had been spent, and only $3,000 remained. Work stopped. A fiasco was in the making.

Lady Liberty might never have been uncrated on American shores had not New York *World* publisher Joseph Pulitzer, a Hungarian immigrant, launched his own campaign to cajole the poor and shame the rich into providing money for Liberty's new home. The *World,* which prided itself on being "the people's paper," noted that the statue had been paid for "by the masses of the French people" and promised to "publish the name of every giver, however small the sum given," to help erect the pedestal. Letters poured in by the thousands, and by August 1885, Pulitzer had raised $100,000 from 120,000 contributors.

The armada of tall ships flying flags of many countries, along with the thousands of smaller craft that accompanied them through New York Harbor, was a highlight of the Liberty Weekend festivities.

Celebrations of Liberty's birthday took a few unusual forms. The Massachusetts couple above erected their own statue to welcome scarecrow "immigrants." In Washington, D.C., a building at 15th Street and New York Avenue unveiled a massive birthday greeting for the Lady which was 95 feet high and 135 feet wide.

Pulitzer's most enduring contribution, however, was his fabrication of a distinctly American meaning for the statue. The belief that the Lady was a gift of "the people" and would somehow symbolically represent them has lost little of its appeal in the 100 years since the statue was dedicated.

Central to the idea of a special bond between the Lady and the people was the perception that Liberty held out her torch not to Europe but to the millions of immigrants who had forsworn Europe to shape a new American identity. The connection between the Lady and the immigrants was made not by any of the politicians who poured forth torrents of overripe rhetoric on October 28, 1886, the day of her unveiling, but by a young Jewish woman who wrote a sonnet about Liberty in 1883 to help raise money for the pedestal. The poet was Emma Lazarus, the sonnet was "The New Colossus," and its words, later engraved on a plaque in the statue's pedestal, read in part:

> "Keep, ancient lands, your storied pomp!" cries she
> With silent lips. "Give me your tired, your poor,
> Your huddled masses yearning to breathe free,
> The wretched refuse of your teeming shore.
> Send these, the homeless, tempest-tost to me,
> I lift my lamp beside the golden door!"

Century of Corrosion

Three sour notes were sounded on dedication day. The first was a jibe by the *Times* of London, which called the unveiling "a curious festival" and wondered why "Liberty should be exported from France, which has so little thereof, to America, which has so much." The second came from the New York State Women's Suffrage Association, which, having been barred from the formal ceremonies on Bedloe's Island, noted that "in erecting a Statue of Liberty embodied as a woman in a land where no woman has political liberty, men have shown a delightful lack of consistency which excites the wonder and admiration of the opposite sex." The third was the complaint by Bartholdi that the flame of Liberty's torch, barely visible in Manhattan, gave off the "light of a glowworm."

The problem of lighting the flame has long vexed Liberty's keepers, and most attempts to enhance the Lady's role as a lighthouse only made matters worse. The torch that was lowered from the statue on July 4, 1984, had been altered in 1916 by Gutzon de la Mothe Borglum, the sculptor of Mount Rushmore. Borglum's

Complaints of overcommercializing a national treasure left many undaunted as they descended on New York City and bought thousands of specially prepared Liberty Weekend souvenirs.

solution to the lighting problem was to replace much of Bartholdi's copper with 250 panes of amber glass, so that lamps placed inside the torch could shine through. The flame burned brightly, but the torch leaked so severely that it had to be completely replaced. The Borglum flame, dubbed the "ugly teapot" by the restoration team, now stands in the pedestal, at the main entranceway to the statue.

The ugly teapot was one of several attempts to improve the statue that had to be undone in the recent restoration effort. However, much of Liberty's sagging and spotting was attributable to condensation and leaks that had triggered an entirely natural aging process—the galvanic reaction of the iron bars with the copper saddles. The iron had corroded and swollen, pulling some of the copper saddles away from the skin; some of the Lady's rivets had popped, giving the impression of a bad skin rash. In addition, the right shoulder joint had a structural flaw traceable to the improper implementation of Eiffel's support scheme.

Restoring Liberty was a massive and highly public undertaking that taxed the resources of several architectural, engineering, and construction firms and employed the skills of both French and American artisans. The project began in earnest in 1981, with the formation of the French-American Committee for the Restoration of the Statue of Liberty, a private binational group that signed a memorandum of understanding with the U.S. Department of the Interior authorizing the committee to conduct an engineering survey and to raise funds from private sources in Europe and the United States. The workings of the French-American Committee during the early 1980's remain shrouded in controversy, with allegations of excessive commercialism, favoritism, and overbilling. Gradually, many of the French originally involved in the project were eased out, and in 1984 the committee's contracts were terminated. By that time, Chrysler Corporation head Lee Iacocca had emerged as the most visible spokesman for the restoration, and the Statue of Liberty-Ellis Island Foundation, which he chairs, had become the main fund-raising body.

Rebuilding Ellis Island

Despite Lady Liberty's top billing on the Fourth of July weekend, it was Ellis Island that took the top spot on the balance sheets. The Liberty restoration absorbed only about $75 million of the funds raised by the foundation. Twice that amount was earmarked for

developing and restoring Ellis Island, a now-rundown
27-acre site nearby that served from 1892 to 1954 as a
center to process some 20 million immigrants entering
the United States from Southern and Eastern Europe.

To be sure, few of these immigrants could have
retained fond memories of the experience. Crowded
halls, harried officials, a bewildering array of languages
and peoples, inspectors who chalked letters on
immigrants' clothing to denote physical and
psychological flaws—these were the bureaucratic
obstacles with which Ellis Island welcomed the weary,
or, in about 1 or 2 percent of the cases, rejected them
as unfit and sent them back home. Nor is the Ellis
experience personally meaningful to the millions who
came to the United States, or whose ancestors came,
through other portals. Still, for many Americans, Ellis
Island, like nearby Lady Liberty, stands for an America
that welcomed peoples of widely divergent ethnic and
religious backgrounds and gave them the chance to
work and prosper.

A pressing problem in 1986 was how to develop Ellis
in a way that would preserve and call attention to its
history but prevent it from being a perpetual drain on
the federal till. There was general agreement that the
northern 10 acres, which include the Great Hall where
immigrants were processed, should be restored as a
museum site, probably at a cost of more than

*With more than the customary
fanfare, a group of immigrants
took the oath of citizenship in
the shadow of the Mt. Rushmore
National Memorial. These new
Americans were among some
15,000 to receive citizenship on
July 3.*

First Lady Nancy Reagan waves from the Statue of Liberty's crown, following the ribbon cutting ceremony on July 5 which reopened the statue. Joining her at the top are some of the 100 French and American students present at the occasion.

$1 million—a project that has already begun. For the 17 acres closest to Liberty Island, the National Park Service (which administers both Liberty Island and Ellis Island) favored an international conference center, to be financed through federal grants, bank loans, and private tax-sheltered investments under the Historic Preservation Act of 1981. An alternative proposal, favored by Iacocca, envisioned an "ethnic Williamsburg"—a kind of theme park and tourist attraction.

Early in 1986, Interior Secretary Donald P. Hodel dismissed Iacocca as chairman of the federal advisory panel charged with allocating the funds raised by the Statue of Liberty-Ellis Island Foundation (which Iacocca continued to chair). While Hodel claimed he had done so in order to avoid any possible conflict of interest, Iacocca blamed the firing on his own opposition to the idea of "a luxury hotel" that would be paid for through "a tax break for the rich" and would exclude tourists from part of the island. A 50-member advisory commission, consisting mostly of businesspeople, was appointed to make recommendations to Hodel for development of the southern part of the island.

The Grand Finale

Whatever doubts remain about the commercial arrangements the various restoration agencies entered into and whatever the eventual resolution of the Ellis Island debate, there is no question that the designers and engineers charged with rejuvenating Lady Liberty took on an excruciatingly complex task, did it well, and finished it in time for the Liberty Weekend festivities July 3-6. The most visible improvement was the new copper torch and gilded flame, now solid and lit by spotlights rather than from within, which was rekindled by President Ronald Reagan at 11:08 P.M. on July 3 in a nationally televised ceremony. Visitors hardy enough to brave the crowds and get into the statue after it reopened on July 5 found the interior completely cleaned, the weak shoulder joint refurbished, and all corroded parts of the statue's support system replaced. The renovated pedestal offers a hydraulic glass-walled elevator, improved access for the handicapped, and an expanded American Museum of Immigration.

Two of Liberty's most distinctive features were deliberately left unchanged. Because the patina on the external surface was found to have protective value, the Lady's copper skin still glows with a glorious green. And while the flow of traffic from foot to crown has been simplified, the narrow spiral staircase remains; this had not been part of Bartholdi's plan but was added years after the statue was dedicated. A new air circulation system does make the huffing and puffing up the 171 steps (where temperatures sometimes rose as high as 120°F) a little less sticky.

As for the Liberty Weekend spectaculars, millions of people watched an armada of tall ships that might have made Sir Francis Drake tremble and more fireworks than the universe has seen since the Big Bang. French President François Mitterrand was on hand, along with President Reagan, and there was a full complement of pop stars and show business luminaries. The concluding program, held at Giants Stadium in East Rutherford, N.J., had 30,000 balloons, 300 Jazzercise ladies, 75 Elvis Presley impersonators, and Hollywood notables galore. "Everything worked out like I planned it," said Hollywood producer David Wolper, who put together the four days' events at a cost of about $30 million.

The last word on the statue fittingly belongs to the tugboat captains and computer programmers, scaffold builders and photographers, engineers and metallurgists, architects and artisans who made the celebration possible. "Some structures are mute, some talk, some sing," write architects Richard Hayden and Thierry Despont, who directed the restoration of the statue. "We took one bursting with song and made it sing out even more. We have restored the statue's health without tampering with her dignity. And we are grateful, proud, and privileged to have contributed to her immortality."

Saving the Whales

by HAL WHITEHEAD

The key point is: "whether Leviathan can long endure so wide a chase and so remorseless a havoc; whether he must not at last be exterminated from the waters." So wrote Herman Melville in his epic novel *Moby Dick,* which was centered on a great white sperm whale. *Moby Dick* was published in 1851 at the height of the "Yankee era," when whaling was one of the most important and profitable industries in the United States and many were concerned about its future. Melville's worry has been pondered with increasing frequency during the 20th century, as whale populations have been systematically decimated for oil and meat.

The year 1986 was, however, an important landmark for the whales. The International Whaling Commission, which regulates the industry worldwide, declared a moratorium on all commercial whaling, to take effect that year. The ban is an imperfect one, riddled with uncertainty and loopholes, but it could mean that whales will endure for the foreseeable future.

A Long History

Whaling began in prehistory, perhaps when coastal dwellers, who used the carcasses that washed onto their beaches, tried to increase their supply of whale meat and whale oil, or when fishermen who harpooned small porpoises began to aim at larger targets. It became an important part of the economy and culture of the Alaskan and Canadian Eskimos (or Inuit), the Indians of the northwest coast of North America, and some Japanese fishermen. This whaling from small boats with harpoons and lances was generally of a

Hal Whitehead is an assistant professor of biology at Dalhousie University in Halifax, N.S. He has studied sperm whales in the Indian Ocean and off the Galápagos Islands and humpbacks near Newfoundland.

With a show of tremendous power, a sperm whale leaps clear of the water.

23

In this scene from Herman Melville's epic novel Moby Dick, *the great white whale with "both jaws, like enormous shears," bites a whaling boat "completely in twain."*

subsistence rather than a commercial nature. The meat and skin were eaten; oil from the rendered fat, or blubber, was used for lamps, and the intestines for fishing line and clothing. Small-scale, noncommercial whaling has continued to the present day among the Eskimos and a few other traditional cultures.

By the 17th century, various nations realized there was money to be made from commercial whaling. Whale oil came to be used for lighting, for lubrication of machinery, and in the preparation of soaps, cosmetics, and even margarine. Spermaceti wax from the oil reservoir, the spermaceti organ, in the sperm whale's forehead was once in great demand for candle-making. (A mistaken idea of the natural function of this oil gave the sperm whale its name.) Ambergris, a grayish substance secreted in lumps in the sperm whale's intestines, was highly prized as a perfume fixative. In the 19th century whalers received extremely high prices for baleen, which was called whalebone. A horny substance that grows down in plates from the palates of toothless whales, baleen was especially in demand for corset stays until the advent of steel stays late in the century. It was also used for buggy whips and umbrella ribs. New England whalers in the early 19th century whiled away the long hours at sea by etching designs, many quite intricate, on pieces of whalebone and the ivory teeth of sperm whales; today these carvings, known as scrimshaw, are a valuable form of American folk art.

In the late 18th century British whaling companies sent expeditions around the world to look for new stocks. The sperm whale was especially valuable for the fine grade of oil contained in the spermaceti organ. But in sperm whale hunting the British were soon overtaken by Yankee whalers. Each year during much of the 19th century, hundreds of stubby, square-rigged sailing ships left New Bedford and Nantucket, Mass.; Mystic, Conn.; and other New England whaling ports.

During their long sea voyages, whalers developed the art of scrimshaw, etching maritime scenes on the whalebones and ivory teeth of sperm whales with knives or sail needles. This tooth was carved by Frederick Myrich in 1829 while aboard the ship Susan *of Nantucket.*

For three or four years they cruised the oceans of the world, their lookouts scanning the horizon for a ''blow,'' the vapor spout of a whale.

When a whale was sighted, light whaleboats were lowered and rowed toward the quarry. A harpoon was thrown into the blubber, and the whale was played like a fish on a long rope until it could be reeled in sufficiently for the killing lance. Dead whales were towed to the whaleship, where they were ''flensed,'' or stripped of their blubber. The oil from the rendered blubber, and from the spermaceti organs of sperm whales, was stored in barrels, but most of the rest of the whale was left to float away. The whale oil unloaded in Nantucket harbor made the Quaker shipowners virtually the Texaco or Exxon of the 19th century.

The Right Whale

The Yankee whalers' primary prey were the right and sperm whales. The right whale, a slow, plump animal, got its name by being the ''right'' whale to hunt. Its slowness makes it easy to catch; it has plenty of blubber for oil and a large quantity of whalebone; and it stays afloat when killed. One-third of its 45-foot-long body constitutes an enormous mouth that has 250 plates of baleen, some up to 7 feet long, hanging from each side of the upper jaw. The right whale feeds by swimming with its mouth halfway open. Water enters at the front and leaves at the sides of the mouth after passing through the baleen plates, which form large

Thrashing and spouting blood, a harpooned sperm whale receives a mortal blow from a sailor's lance in this 1825 aquatint, thought to be the oldest whaling print in the United States. The scene is typical of the days when New England whaling ships roamed the Pacific in search of their prey.

The graceful arch of a breaching sperm whale. Whalers once thought breaching was the whale's way of playing, but now the great leaps are also taken to be displays of male sexual rivalry or vigorous ways of communicating at the feeding grounds.

sieves, straining out the plankton that is the whale's food.

During the summer months right whales are found in cooler waters, where food is abundant, steadily swimming along near the surface. In winter they gather in traditional breeding grounds in warmer waters, where the females give birth to their 15-foot calves and the males rambunctiously try to mate with as many females as possible. This promiscuous life-style has led to the evolution of an extraordinary sexual organ: the male right whale has testes which can weigh almost a ton.

Sperm Whales—Divers of the Deep

A sperm whale can often be seen lying nearly stationary at the surface, a long, battleship-gray body looking much like a log. But about once every 15 seconds, an 8-foot-high cloud of spray is blown from one end of the apparently inanimate object. This blow is the whale's exhalation. Like all whales, the sperm whale evolved from land mammals which gradually colonized the seas perhaps 70 million years ago. Despite many changes since then, they still must come to the surface to breathe.

A sperm whale usually spends about eight minutes at the surface before arching its back, throwing its flukes into the air, and beginning a vertical dive of over 1,000 feet. For about 40 minutes it will search the depths for the large squid that are its primary prey, before ascending again to breathe. Sometimes sperm whales dive to 3,000 feet, and they may stay underwater for over an hour. The squid on which they feed average about 3 pounds, but occasionally they hunt the giant squid, *Architeuthis*, which can be almost as large as the whale itself.

During our research, my colleagues and I have had the opportunity to swim with sperm whales near the surface. When we first started slipping into the water beside them, we were cautious. Melville draws a portrait of a sperm whale "so incredibly ferocious as continually to be athirst for human blood." But another 19th-century source, the English whaleship surgeon Thomas Beale, described the sperm whale as "a most timid and inoffensive animal." In our experience Beale was right.

The primary units of sperm whale society are schools of about 15 mature females with their immediate offspring. These are found in or near tropical oceans. In contrast, male sperm whales, which grow to 60 feet and are about three times the weight of the females, are found in higher latitudes and smaller schools. The larger the males, the colder the waters they inhabit and the smaller their schools, so that the largest males are usually solitary and often near the edge of the polar ice. These huge males return to the tropics to mate, but we do not know how often.

The Rorquals

By the latter part of the 19th century, Yankee whalers and their counterparts from other nations had virtually eliminated the right whale, and the sperm whale was becoming more and more difficult to find. Rising crew

The elastic ligaments on the lower jaws of humpback whales enable them to trap food by opening their mouths extremely wide, in a technique known as lunge feeding.

Below, two humpbacks in a feeding frenzy.

As the science of commercial whaling grew more sophisticated, fleets were able to deplete the whale population of an area very rapidly. Above, a Japanese sperm whaling ship. Right, an Icelandic ship hauls in its catch of whales, which have been pumped with air to keep them afloat.

wages and the increasing use of petroleum for oil were making their whaling less profitable. A good part of the Yankee whaling fleet was lost during the Civil War, and the fleet suffered another terrible blow in 1871 when most of the American vessels operating north of Alaska were crushed by the polar ice.

Still, some kinds of whale were swimming the oceans, especially near Antarctica, in considerable numbers; these were the slimmer and faster rorquals. Because they have thin blubber layers which provide comparatively little oil and because they sink after being killed, they were hard to catch using Yankee techniques and not worth the trouble. But in the 1860's a Norwegian named Svend Foyn began the modernization of an industry whose techniques had changed little over hundreds of years. He replaced the rowed wooden whaleboats with a steam-powered catcher boat and, instead of the muscled and tattooed arm of a "harpooneer," used a gun to fire a heavy metal harpoon. This harpoon had an explosive head, which usually disabled the whale quickly. Dead whales were pumped with compressed air so that they floated.

Now no whale was safe. In the early part of the 20th century, the British, the Norwegians, and other nations sent great expeditions to hunt the Antarctic rorquals. Ultimately, huge factory ships that could process the

whales onboard were sailed from Europe. Each factory
ship, attended by its flock of catcher boats, could
quickly overwhelm the whale stocks in an area and
then move on.

The principal rorqual target in the first phase of
modern whaling in the Antarctic was the blue whale.
At 90 feet long and 160 tons, the blue whale is the
largest animal that has ever lived. Blue whale calves
are born 25 feet long and grow so fast on their mothers'
rich milk that they gain about 200 pounds a day. Like
other rorquals, they are principally "gulpers"; beneath
their mouths they have a series of ventral grooves
which allow them to expand their throats and engulf a
huge mass of prey and water, often doubling their own
volume in the process.

Blue whales and other rorquals do not gather on
traditional mating grounds; instead, they seem to stay
dispersed during the winter breeding period.
Communication using low-frequency sound may help
the blues find mates. Blue whales make the loudest and
the lowest-pitched animal sound known; before the
advent of noisy propeller-driven ships they probably

The huge underside of a finback whale is about to be flensed, or stripped of its blubber.

could have heard one another's deep rumbles at hundreds, and possibly thousands, of miles.

Modern mechanized whaling is efficient, and by the late 1930's, blue whales were scarce. Other types of rorquals also became depleted over the years.

Slow Start of Whale Protection

It may seem improbable that in the 20th century a major industry could be managed with such apparent shortsightedness. But Colin Clark, a mathematician at the University of British Columbia, has shown that the whalers' strategy may have made financial sense. According to Clark's calculations, in cases where the interest rate on bank deposits is higher than the natural rate of increase of an animal population (about 5 percent a year for whales), it is generally more profitable to destroy the population and place the profits in a bank account than to manage the population on a sustainable basis, with a constant catch being available every year.

However, attempts were made to manage whaling. In the 1930's, under the auspices of the League of Nations, regulations were introduced to limit the catch of whales in order to stabilize the falling price of whale oil. After World War II, the International Whaling Commission (IWC) was formed by a group of major whaling nations to administer the industry. In some years quotas were agreed to by these nations, but they were set far above what most scientists considered the "sustainable yield"—a catch that can be taken on a continuing basis without reducing the population.

By the 1960's, it was clear to almost everyone involved that whaling and the whale populations were in deep trouble, and scientists advising the IWC had become advocates of sustained and rational management.

The whale industry was also under pressure from conservationists and the general public. People were fascinated by researcher John Lilly's speculations on dolphin intelligence (dolphins are small members of the whale family) and moved by the extraordinary songs of the humpback whale recorded by Roger Payne. Some had seen the remarkable abilities of dolphins and small whales in aquariums; others were being taken to see the great whales in their natural habitats.

Discovering Whales Firsthand

In many parts of the world, whales can be seen from shore or from boats operating near the coast. Argentineans can see right whales a few yards from the beach at Península Valdés, Californians watch the gray whales on their annual migrations between Alaska and Mexico, and in Newfoundland several whale species can be seen feeding beneath rugged cliffs during the summer months. But it is in Massachusetts, which 150

Whale-watching, sometimes sponsored by oceanographic institutes and conservation organizations, has become a popular pastime. Here, spectators near Cabo San Lucas in Baja, Calif., watch the annual migration of gray whales.

Japanese crew members set off from Yokohama Port in late October for a five-month whaling expedition to Antarctica. With the International Whaling Commission's ban on commercial whaling, this type of hunting may become a thing of the past.

years ago had been the center of the world's whaling industry, that whale-watching has shown the greatest growth. Throughout the spring, summer, and autumn, New Englanders and their visitors are taken out to watch the humpbacks of Massachusetts Bay. These whales are delightful to observe; Melville called them "the most gamesome and light-hearted of all the whales, making more gay foam and white water generally than any other of them."

During the winter humpbacks leave their cold-water feeding areas and migrate to tropical breeding grounds. Their song during breeding contains a wide assortment of sounds, whose pitch spans virtually the whole human hearing range. These sounds are arranged in a pattern which repeats about every 15 minutes, although a humpback may sing for hours. The songs are generally made by males and seem to be used to attract females, warn off other males, or both.

Another element of the humpbacks' mating system is the "rowdy group." During our research on humpback whale breeding behavior, we followed one rowdy group of about ten whales and tried to make sense of the vigorous action. In the center was a female, relatively placid. Around her, males turned and twisted and bumped, each attempting to be her closest companion. The humpbacks at their breeding grounds are also prodigious "breachers." Their tremendous leaps from the water are the most powerful, and perhaps the most spectacular, actions performed by any animal. Breaches and "flipperings," in which the humpbacks wave their long and flexible flippers in the air and slap them on the water surface, seem to be a form of communication.

Saving the Whales

In 1972 the United Nations Conference on the Human Environment recommended a ten-year ban on whaling, and "Save the Whales" movements soon sprang up. Some were parts of established conservation groups like Friends of the Earth and Greenpeace; others, such as the phenomenally effective Connecticut Cetacean Society (now called Cetacean Society International), were new and specific.

Pressured by the public and hurt by declining profits as increasingly expensive catcher boats searched for increasingly scarce whales, some countries began to stop whaling. There were some extraordinary reversals as ardent whaling nations like Australia almost overnight became exemplary preservationists. From the whales' viewpoint, progress was not uninterrupted. In 1977 the United States, which had been the major force for conservation within the IWC, found itself defending an escalating Alaskan Eskimo hunt for the few remaining bowhead whales, a relatively slow species, relentlessly hunted over the years. (Over scientists' objections, the Eskimos are still permitted to kill a certain number of bowheads each year.) But despite some setbacks, the IWC had changed relatively rapidly from an OPEC-type organization in charge of keeping whale product prices high to one sharing considerable common ground with Greenpeace.

The IWC, however, is a voluntary and toothless association of nations that cannot enforce its decisions or impose sanctions against countries that ignore them. Conservationists fear that its declaration of a moratorium on commercial whaling may trigger a

Activitists have fought for years to end all commercial whaling. Above, demonstrators at an International Whaling Conference in London. Below, members of the Greenpeace conservation group intercept a Norwegian whaling vessel.

Diving into the icy sea off Alaska, a humpback whale shows the graceful lines of its flukes. Scientists can identify an individual humpback by the distinctive black-and-white pattern on the flukes.

breakup of the commission. If whaling nations leave the IWC so that they may continue to hunt without external regulation, then the moratorium may become a disaster for the whales.

Even if the IWC holds together, the animals are not completely safe. Japan filed an objection to the moratorium; by so doing, it was allowed (under the treaty that established the IWC) to continue whaling. The United States probably could have prevented this, by the threat of further restricting Japanese fishing in U.S. waters. But Japanese whalers reached an agreement with the Reagan administration (upheld by the U.S. Supreme Court), allowing them to continue whaling until 1988. Japan, along with Iceland, Norway, and South Korea, also sought to use another IWC loophole to continue whaling. They announced that although they would be killing whales and selling the meat and oil commercially, they would be whaling "for scientific purposes" in order to learn more about whale populations. The scientific value of this whaling has been discredited by the British biomathematician Justin Cooke, who has shown that the Icelanders would have to destroy virtually the entire stock that they are hunting to learn further significant facts about it. In July 1986, to satisfy an IWC requirement and avert a threatened U.S. boycott of its fishery production, Iceland announced it would consume more than half the meat from its "scientific" whaling domestically. In November two of Iceland's four whaling ships were sunk in Reykjavik harbor when their sea valves were opened up. Environmentalists associated with the Sea Shepherd Conservation Society of Vancouver claimed responsibility; no crew members were aboard. The owners refloated the vessels, but damage was put at $2 million.

Scientific Whale-Watching

How, in fact, do we learn about whales? Traditionally, whale scientists collected samples and made measurements using carcasses provided by the whaling industry. They used catch statistics to provide population estimates. But in the last 20 years a new type of whale science has emerged—"benign research," or the study of living whales. Scientists, students, and enthusiastic amateurs sit on cliffs, go out in small boats or light aircraft, and watch, photograph, and listen to whales behaving naturally. A key to much of this research has been the ability to identify individual whales from photographs of marks and patterns on their bodies. From these and other techniques detailed findings have emerged for some whale populations—information about migration routes, population sizes, and social organization which whalers had no way of studying.

It has been my good fortune to be a part of this benign research, to sail with the whales and try to learn about them from what I see and hear. But is it too late? Are we gathering information whose only use will be to fill further chapters in the rapidly expanding catalog of extinct species?

If the IWC holds together, then the moratorium has made the whales generally safe from harpoons for the immediate future. But several populations are already down to dangerously low levels. For example, right whales, once the most common whales in the North Atlantic, have been reduced to only 200 animals. The bowhead whales were hunted nearly to extinction in Arctic waters and now number only 4,000. Small populations are particularly susceptible to a range of possible threats. Some are natural, such as inbreeding. Others arise from human activities: dangerous levels of pollutants have been found in the tissues of some marine mammals; whales and dolphins are dying gruesome deaths entangled in fishing nets set for other species; and despite their low numbers, whales are perceived in some parts of the world as threats to other fishing. Whether whales survive will depend on our attitudes not only to whaling but also to all forms of ocean life.

SPACE

Rebounding From Disaster?

by WILLIAM D. MARBACH

William D. Marbach is a general editor at Newsweek, *in charge of the magazine's Technology section.*

A cold snap gripped the Florida morning, and Cape Canaveral's launch pad 39-B was shrouded in ice when five career astronauts, an engineer, and a schoolteacher boarded the space shuttle *Challenger* shortly after 8 A.M. on January 28, 1986. The mission, 51-L (the 25th shuttle flight since 1981), was to have been NASA's latest triumph: Christa McAuliffe, a high school social studies teacher from New Hampshire and the winner of a nationwide competition to be the first teacher and ordinary citizen on such a flight, was aboard to give the children of the world their first lessons from space. *Challenger* was also carrying two satellites in its cargo bay to be launched during the seven-day mission.

But after 25 years and 55 manned space flights without an in-flight fatality, NASA's streak of successes had run out. *Challenger* and its crew perished in a fiery explosion that occurred just 73 seconds after lift-off. The tragedy was a crippling setback for the U.S. space program. And in the months that followed, while the remaining shuttles were grounded, NASA came under scathing criticism for the fateful decision to launch *Challenger*. The agency was shaken to its foundations, and the disaster sparked a national debate on the future direction of the American space program.

An Unprecedented Disaster

Before blast-off there had been no sign that anything was wrong with *Challenger*, although the flight had been delayed several times. On January 28 the lift-off was again delayed, for two hours, while NASA officials checked the ice on the launch pad. The air temperature had dropped to 28°F overnight and risen to

The seven astronauts killed in the Challenger's explosion: (top) Ellison S. Onizuka, S. Christa McAuliffe, Gregory B. Jarvis, Judith A. Resnik; (bottom) Michael J. Smith, Francis R. (Dick) Scobee, and Ronald E. McNair.

only 36°F by midmorning, the coldest temperature for any shuttle launch. After the ice check, the final countdown began, and at 11:38 A.M., as spectators cheered, *Challenger* rose past the launch tower and thundered off into the brilliant blue sky.

Seven seconds into the flight, the spaceship began rolling over, as it was supposed to, to head down-range. Fifty-three seconds into flight, as the aerodynamic forces on the spacecraft eased, the computers pushed the main engines' throttles wide open, and *Challenger* was hurtling through the atmosphere at nearly twice the speed of sound and accelerating. "*Challenger*, go at throttle up," mission control radioed. "Roger, go at throttle up," *Challenger* replied. Soon afterward, a giant fireball engulfed the ship.

To those watching the launch on television, there was no mistaking what had happened—NASA's

THE SHUTTLE CHALLENGER

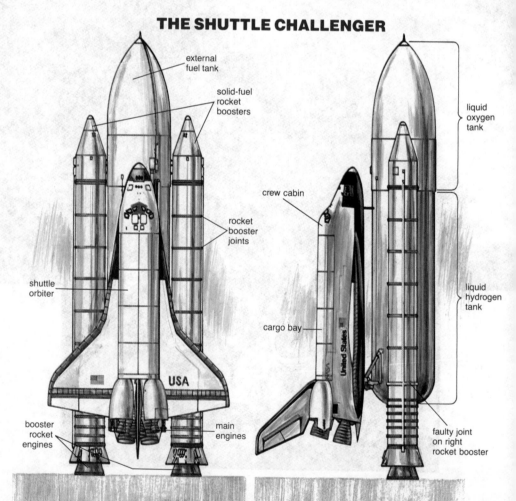

external fuel tank

solid-fuel rocket boosters

liquid oxygen tank

crew cabin

rocket booster joints

shuttle orbiter

liquid hydrogen tank

cargo bay

USA

United States

booster rocket engines

main engines

faulty joint on right rocket booster

A high-speed telephoto tracking camera caught this shot of the Challenger's crew cabin, which apparently escaped the fireball relatively intact and rose to a peak of 65,000 feet, before dropping to the ocean below.

telephoto TV cameras were trained on the spaceship when the fiery explosion occurred at 46,000 feet. Mission controllers monitoring the launch on their computer screens reacted first with stunned disbelief. The telemetry streaming in from *Challenger* had abruptly stopped, leaving their screens frozen with strings of the letter "S," for static, indicating that no new data were being received.

For those in the grandstand at Cape Canaveral's Kennedy Space Center, the cheers and tension that marked the launch suddenly gave way to doubt, then to horror and grief as it became clear that something had gone terribly wrong. NASA officials rushed to the families of *Challenger's* crew.

Once debris from the explosion stopped falling, NASA and U.S. Coast Guard search teams fanned out over the impact area in the choppy waters off the Cape. The search planes and helicopters covered thousands of square miles but found no trace of survivors. Dead in the crash were flight commander Francis R. (Dick) Scobee, 46; pilot Michael J. Smith, 40; mission specialists Ellison S. Onizuka, 39, Judith A. Resnik, 36, and Ronald E. McNair, 35; Hughes Aircraft Company engineer Gregory B. Jarvis, 41; and New Hampshire schoolteacher (Sharon) Christa McAuliffe, 37.

Husband Steven McAuliffe and son Scott mourn the death of S. Christa McAuliffe, the New Hampshire schoolteacher chosen in a nationwide contest to be the first ordinary citizen in space.

What Went Wrong?

Finding out what happened was vital to the future of the U.S. space program. The United States had made a fateful decision in the early 1970's to rely almost entirely on a new, unproven vehicle—the space shuttle—then still just a concept on the drawing boards. As a result of that Nixon-era policy, reaffirmed ever since, the space shuttles became the only way the United States could launch astronauts and many large, heavy satellites, including vital military payloads, into space. Though NASA had wanted a larger fleet, only four shuttles were built; after *Challenger* blew up, there were just three.

The search for clues, however, was daunting: the space shuttle is the most complex flying machine ever built. It is an ungainly hybrid. The winged orbiter carrying the astronauts and cargo has the structures and controls needed to land on a runway. It rides into space attached to the side of a huge, silo-like external fuel tank that carries (in two inner tanks) the highly explosive fuel (liquid hydrogen) and oxidizer (liquid oxygen) for the main engines. During the first two minutes of flight, five rockets—the two 149-foot-tall solid-fuel boosters, each attached to one side of the external tank, and the three liquid-fueled main engines of the orbiter—fire simultaneously, providing nearly 7 million pounds of thrust. Then the boosters burn out and drop to the ocean, where they are recovered for reuse. About 8½ minutes into the flight, the main engines cut off; the external fuel tank, now empty, drops away, breaking up and crashing harmlessly in the ocean.

In the days after *Challenger* exploded, search teams began recovering debris at sea, and NASA investigators examining photographs and the telemetry quickly zeroed in on the likely culprit: a fiery leak from the side of the right booster. Rather than let NASA alone determine the cause of the accident, however, President Ronald Reagan appointed a 13-member presidential commission, headed by former Secretary of State William Rogers, to conduct the formal inquiry. Congress also conducted an inquiry.

Looking Back

From the evidence, the Rogers commission and NASA investigators were able to reconstruct the accident. Unknown to anyone on the ground or in the cockpit, the first sign of trouble came less than one second into the flight. Photographs showed an ominous puff of smoke spurting from the side of the right booster near the lowest so-called field joint. A few more puffs followed. Later, at 58.788 seconds, a small flame appeared near the same joint. It immediately grew to a continuous plume and burned like a giant blowtorch at the side of the external fuel tank with its deadly cargo and on the vital strut holding the booster to the tank. *Challenger* was doomed.

There was nothing anyone could have done. Once ignited, the boosters burn like giant roman candles; there is no way to shut them off. And there was no way to escape the spacecraft, no way to jettison the boosters, no way to abort the flight and return to land. At 64.660 seconds the photographs show an abrupt change in the color and shape of the flame, and the telemetry showed a sudden change of pressure in the liquid hydrogen tank: the torch had burned through. Milliseconds later a bright glow could be seen on the underside of the orbiter. At 72.200 seconds the lower strut attaching the aft part of the right booster to the huge external fuel tank gave way. At 73.124 seconds the bottom of the hydrogen tank began to fail.

As the hydrogen tank exploded, the front end of the still firing right booster pivoted into the liquid oxygen tank in the upper section of the external fuel tank. The resulting fireball totally enveloped *Challenger*. With the fuel lines ruptured, the main engines exceeded their

President Reagan consoles bereaved relatives at a memorial service for the astronauts.

redline temperature limits and began to shut down. At the same time, violent aerodynamic forces tore the spacecraft apart. The right and left boosters soared out of the fireball, giving it an eerie Y-shape. When that happened, an Air Force range safety officer monitoring the flight on radar issued the encoded command to the boosters' self-destruct explosives that blew up the two errant rockets.

A close examination of photographs of the fireball showed huge identifiable pieces of debris raining down—including the forward fuselage containing the crew compartment. Investigators determined that the crew compartment fell relatively intact, then broke up when it slammed into the Atlantic. With the aid of sonar, underwater cameras, and a miniature submarine, search teams eventually found the wreckage of the crew cabin. U.S. Navy divers recovered the astronauts' remains and brought them aboard the U.S.S. *Preserver*, a Navy salvage ship. After pathologists identified and examined the remains, they were turned over to the seven families; those remains that could not be identified were buried in a common grave in Arlington National Cemetery.

Warnings Overruled

When investigators zeroed in on the right booster, they had taken only the first step. Still to be determined was precisely what had caused the rocket to fail. As the Rogers commission probed that question, it

The Navy salvage ship Preserver *at work near the ocean site of the shuttle wreckage. Among the debris hoisted onto the ship were the remains of the astronauts.*

discovered a startling fact: NASA officials had long known there was a potentially fatal problem with critical seals in the joints that held the boosters together. Engineers from Morton Thiokol Inc., the company that designed and built the booster rockets, as well as NASA's own engineers, had told officials at NASA headquarters that the synthetic rubber O-rings designed to contain the fiery gases produced by the burning rocket fuel were being partly eroded in flight— an indication that the joints were not sealing completely.

Worse yet, the commission learned that in a heated debate the night before launch, Morton Thiokol engineers had voted unanimously against launching *Challenger* the next morning, fearing that the cold weather would cause the O-rings to lose their resiliency, thereby increasing the likelihood of a catastrophic failure. But the NASA managers in charge of the boosters challenged that conclusion—and Morton Thiokol executives, overruling their engineers, gave NASA the green light for launch. NASA officials outside the rocket program were not told of the debate.

The discovery set off a firestorm of criticism. Commission Chairman Rogers was appalled to learn that top NASA officials had never even heard of the engineers' warnings, and he condemned the agency's convoluted decision-making process—a process which

Above, a NASA press conference with wreckage from the Challenger's main engine in the background. Below, wreckage from the space shuttle's external tanks and parts of the solid rocket booster.

KUTYNA   CHESON   RICHARD

NEIL ARMSTRONG   WILLIAM ROGERS   SALLY RIDE

William Rogers and other members of the presidential commission investigating the shuttle disaster hear evidence; their report was severely critical of NASA's management practices.

commission member and Nobel Prize-winning physicist Richard Feynman, of the California Institute of Technology, likened to a game of Russian roulette. Although neither NASA nor the commission pinned down the exact cause of the O-ring failure—whether due to the cold alone, to rainwater freezing in the joints, or to any of a number of other possible factors—one thing was painfully clear: *Challenger*'s crew had lost NASA's game of Russian roulette.

A Call for Sweeping Changes

The Rogers commission released its main report in June, calling for widespread reforms in NASA's operations. It recommended that the faulty joint and O-ring seal be redesigned, tested, and verified by independent experts and, furthermore, that NASA undertake a complete reexamination of all 748 items on the shuttles' so-called critical items list. (Failure of any one of those parts, which have no backups, could result in the loss of the spaceship and crew.)

The commission stated that a contributing cause of the disaster was NASA's "flawed" management process. It called for sweeping changes to improve communications and give NASA headquarters more control over its fiercely independent centers such as the Marshall Space Flight Center in Huntsville, Ala., the installation in charge of the shuttle rockets. The commission called as well for a separate, independent safety organization within NASA, which was

The launch pad at Cape Canaveral was shrouded in ice prior to lift-off. Engineers had warned about the possible effects of cold weather.

subsequently set up. The panel also urged that NASA include astronauts in the decision-making process.

The U.S. House Science and Technology Committee, which held hearings and numerous staff interviews in addition to studying the data and findings of the Rogers commission, agreed with many of the commission's findings but concluded that the underlying problem at NASA was "poor technical decision-making over a period of several years."

NASA also came under fire from both panels for its heavy launch schedule for 1986. The Rogers panel recommended that NASA scale back its flight rate to reduce the "relentless pressure" that had been exerted on its people and machines.

NASA faced another problem as well: Jane Jarrell Smith, the widow of *Challenger* pilot Michael Smith, filed a $15.1 million negligence claim against the agency. She said that in the seconds before the spacecraft was destroyed, Smith "knew of his impending death." (Cheryl McNair, widow of Ronald

The Atlantis, *one of three remaining shuttle spacecraft, is grounded in Florida. NASA hoped to begin flights again in 1988.*

McNair, filed suit against Thiokol.) In late July, NASA acknowledged that, on the basis of analysis of on-board tape recordings, it appeared that just before the shuttle broke up in flames, Smith had uttered the words "uh oh." The agency also said that three of the emergency air packs on the craft had been manually activated, indicating the crew may well have survived longer than originally believed. Meanwhile, in December, NASA and four of the astronauts' families, not including Smith's, agreed on a monetary settlement.

Future for the Space Program

The *Challenger* failure crippled the U.S. capability to launch spacecraft—and posed difficult policy questions. Should the United States build a new shuttle at a cost of some $3 billion to replace *Challenger,* although that would mean using essentially 1960's and 1970's technology for a spacecraft of the 1990's? Should it devote more resources instead to building a hypersonic transport plane, the so-called Orient Express, that would take off and land from a conventional runway and fly in a low earth orbit? Should the policy continue of relying almost entirely on the shuttles to launch satellites? Or should the United States build a large mixed fleet of unmanned, expendable rockets to relieve the pressures on the shuttle? After months of consideration, President Reagan announced in August that a fourth shuttle would be built over the course of the next five years. Perhaps more important, the president ordered the agency to phase itself out of the commercial launching business and concentrate on military and scientific missions.

Meanwhile, NASA dropped its long-standing objections to expendable rockets and endorsed the idea that the United States should have a more balanced rocket fleet, an idea the Pentagon had been pushing even before the *Challenger* accident. Also, the Air Force announced that it would build a large new fleet of unmanned rockets to launch military payloads.

A fleet of unmanned rockets and the development of a private space industry would somewhat relieve NASA of the huge backlog of payloads awaiting launch because of the grounding of the shuttles. Reducing the number of launches would also relieve some of the pressure that had contributed to the shuttle's heavy launch schedule. Nevertheless, the agency was still aiming at an ambitious schedule. In October, NASA said it planned to resume flights in 1988, beginning with six that year but rising to as many as 16 a few years later, when the fourth orbiter was expected to join the fleet. A panel convened by the National Research Council at the request of Congress criticized these targets as too high. NASA stressed, however, that the goals were tentative and said the agency would modify them as necessary.

The disaster at Cape Canaveral raised anew a policy question that had long been debated: should the United States rely so heavily on manned missions? Many critics believed that NASA's historic scientific role of exploring space had been compromised when the agency essentially became a space trucking firm; because of the great cost of the shuttle program, there was not enough room in the budget for an ambitious schedule of unmanned space probes, although such missions had proved extraordinarily fruitful.

The *Challenger* accident raised other doubts as well about NASA's ability to carry out its broader missions. The shuttles had been conceived originally as one element in a larger system, vehicles to ferry astronauts and payloads to a permanent, manned space station orbiting the earth. The station itself would be a laboratory and a way station for missions to the moon

NASA administrator James Fletcher testifies before the House Science and Technology Committee. He said that the Rogers commission recommendations would be implemented and that no shuttles would be launched until their safety was certain.

and beyond. But even before the *Challenger* disaster, the space station was not scheduled for launch until the early 1990's. Some 20 shuttle missions were originally projected as necessary to carry materials aloft to assemble the space station; NASA began working on plans to enable it to assemble the station with a greatly reduced number of shuttle flights.

The Soviets, meanwhile, continued to fly very long manned missions, accumulating much more experience in space than U.S. astronauts. Less than a month after the shuttle disaster, they launched their Mir ("Peace") space station. In a stinging criticism of the United States space program published in June, the editor of the London-based *Jane's Spaceflight Directory,* a noted authority on space and military technology, declared that the Soviets were ten years ahead of the United States in the space race.

In the United States, the Reagan-appointed National Commission on Space urged similar bold missions. In a report to Reagan on goals for the next 50 years, the commission offered a visionary blueprint calling for the United States to launch the orbiting manned space station, to return to the moon and establish permanent lunar bases by the year 2017, and to fly manned missions to and establish a permanent base on Mars beginning in 2027.

While some believed that such bold goals were needed to revitalize NASA, the political realities after *Challenger* were much different. Most of those directly involved in the decision to launch *Challenger* retired or were transferred. Hundreds of workers at various NASA installations and contractors' plants were laid off. Throughout the agency a difficult overhaul of flight technology and of the organization itself had begun, with many decisions to be made.

On one thing all agreed: a greater awareness of safety was vital. Senator Albert Gore (D, Tenn.) noted that NASA had cut its staff of safety inspectors by 70 percent since 1970. Jane Jarrell Smith said the Rogers commission report had revealed "incredibly terrible judgments, shockingly sparse concern for human life" on the part of NASA."I hope that from this tragedy," she said, "we have learned above all to hold allegiance to the sacredness of human life, to have the courage to place safety first, and to honor those who have the strength to honor truth." In the soul-searching after the tragedy, no one wanted it said that the *Challenger* seven had died in vain.

Despite the Challenger *disaster, which was followed by a series of unmanned rocket launch failures, the nation was determined to revive its space program. In September this unmanned Delta 180 rocket, carrying a military payload, was successfully launched from Cape Canaveral.*

1987 YEARBOOK
EVENTS OF 1986

CHRONOLOGY FOR 1986

January

1 • Spain and Portugal officially join the European Community.

13 • A massacre of rivals by South Yemen President Nasser Muhammad sets off fierce fighting that leaves thousands dead.

24 • The second of two British cabinet ministers resigns over the government's handling of the bailout of a helicopter firm.

28 • The space shuttle *Challenger* explodes shortly after launch from Cape Canaveral, killing all seven crew members.

29 • Rebel leader Yoweri Museveni is inaugurated as president of Uganda, days after his troops overran Kampala.

31 • Amid continuing rioting, Haitian President Jean-Claude Duvalier declares a state of siege.

February

4 • President Ronald Reagan's State of the Union address calls for strengthening family values and cutting the federal budget.

5 • President Reagan submits to Congress a $994 billion budget proposal, projecting a $144 billion deficit.

7 • Under pressure from massive demonstrations and protests against his rule, Haitian President Jean-Claude Duvalier flees to exile in France.

11 • Soviet Jewish dissident Anatoly Shcharansky is released in an East-West prisoner exchange.

15 • The Philippines National Assembly declares that President Ferdinand Marcos was re-elected in balloting eight days earlier.

19 • Jordan's King Hussein gives up his joint bid with the Palestine Liberation Organization for Mideast peace.

20 • President Reagan attends a Caribbean leaders' summit meeting in Grenada.

25 • Faced with widespread public protests and a lack of support from the military, Marcos flees the Philippines, and opposition leader Corazon Aquino becomes president.

28 • Swedish Prime Minister Olof Palme is assassinated on a Stockholm street.

FEB. 20

March

6 • The U.S. Senate confirms Richard Lyng as agriculture secretary, replacing John Block.

18 • French President François Mitterrand asks rightist leader Jacques Chirac to form a new government, two days after the center-right opposition won a majority in elections.

19 • President Reagan and Canadian Prime Minister Brian Mulroney complete talks in Washington, D.C., during which Reagan endorses steps to reduce acid rain.

24 • After Libya fires missiles at U.S. planes flying over the disputed Gulf of Sidra, the United

MAY 25

States launches attacks on Libyan naval vessels and a missile base.

25 • Philippine President Aquino dissolves the National Assembly and says she will rule by decree until voters approve a new constitution and legislature.

April

2 • A bomb explodes on a TWA plane flying from Rome to Athens; four Americans are killed.

5 • A bomb rips through a West Berlin disco, killing two persons outright, including a U.S. soldier, and fatally wounding another U.S. serviceman.

10 • Pakistani opposition leader Benazir Bhutto is greeted by huge rallies on her return from exile.

15 • U.S. fighter planes based in Britain, along with Navy planes from two carriers, bomb "terrorist-related" targets in Libya, including a barracks where Libyan leader Muammar al-Qaddafi's headquarters are located.

26 • An explosion at the Chernobyl nuclear power plant in the Soviet Ukraine causes a major leak of radiation into the environment and leads to more than 30 deaths in the short term.

May

2 • The Expo 86 world's fair opens in Vancouver.

3 • A bomb explodes on a Sri Lanka jetliner during boarding in Colombo, killing 16.

11 • Canadian Industry Minister Sinclair Stevens resigns amid conflict-of-interest charges.

25 • Hands Across America forms a human chain across most of the United States, in a campaign for the homeless and hungry.

APRIL 2

June

8 • Kurt Waldheim is elected as president of Austria, despite controversy over possible links to Nazi atrocities in World War II.

9 • A presidential commission report on the *Challenger* disaster criticizes NASA for management failures.

12 • South Africa imposes a nationwide state of emergency.

27 • The World Court rules that U.S. aid to Nicaraguan rebels violates international law.

30 • Prime Minister Mulroney shuffles his cabinet; 27 members depart or are reassigned, including Eric Nielsen, the deputy prime minister and defense minister.

July

7 • The U.S. Supreme Court strikes down the Gramm-Rudman-Hollings Act's automatic deficit-cutting mechanism.

14 • U.S. Army personnel and aircraft arrive in Bolivia to aid in raids against drug traffickers.

23 • Israeli Prime Minister Shimon Peres concludes meetings with King Hassan II in Morocco.

• Britain's Prince Andrew marries Sarah Ferguson in London's Westminster Abbey.

26 • An American hostage, Father Lawrence Jenco, is freed in Lebanon by the pro-Iranian Islamic Jihad.

August

4 • OPEC oil ministers, meeting in Geneva, agree to cuts in output in a bid to raise oil prices.

11 • Canadian fishing boats rescue 155 Tamil refugees from Sri Lanka adrift in small boats off the Newfoundland coast.

15 • The White House announces that NASA will phase out the launching of commercial satellites and will build a new space shuttle.

SEPT. 6

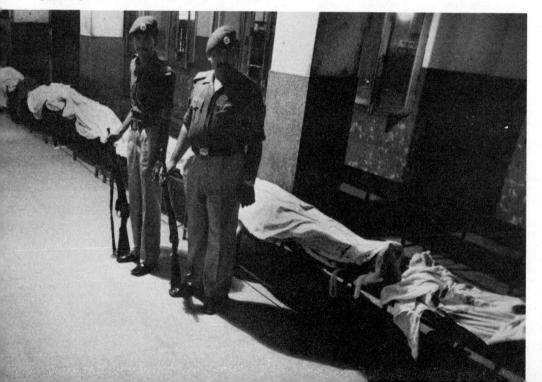

September

6 • After taking over a Pan Am jetliner at the Karachi airport in Pakistan, the hijackers open fire and throw grenades, killing more than 20 passengers.

• Arab terrorists attack a synagogue in Istanbul, Turkey, during sabbath services, killing more than 20 Jews.

7 • A state of siege is declared in Chile after President Augusto Pinochet survives an assassination attempt.

12 • Egyptian President Hosni Mubarak and Israeli Prime Minister Shimon Peres conclude a summit meeting in Alexandria, Egypt.

26 • Having been confirmed by the Senate, by a vote of 65-33, William H. Rehnquist is sworn in as chief justice of the Supreme Court. Rehnquist swears in Antonin Scalia as an associate justice.

29 • The Soviet Union frees U.S. journalist Nicholas Daniloff, arrested a month earlier and accused of espionage.

30 • The United States frees Gennadi Zakharov, a Soviet UN employee implicated in espionage activities; at the same time, a Reagan-Gorbachev summit is announced.

October

2 • U.S. economic sanctions go into effect against South Africa, after Congress overrides President Reagan's veto.

• The press accuses the Reagan administration of leaking false information in an effort to destabilize the Qaddafi regime.

6 • After shooting down a rebel supply plane, Nicaragua captures the one surviving crewman, an American named Eugene Hasenfus.

9 • Impeached federal Judge Harry Claiborne is convicted in a Senate trial and ousted from office.

OCT. 10

10 • Earthquakes rock the capital of El Salvador, killing more than 1,500 people.

12 • The U.S.-Soviet summit in Iceland concludes without agreement, breaking down in a stalemate over the U.S. Star Wars defense system.

19 • Mozambican President Samora Machel is killed in a plane crash inside South Africa.

20 • Israeli Prime Minister Shimon Peres and Foreign Minister Yitzhak Shamir exchange posts.

22 • President Reagan signs a sweeping tax reform measure.

November

1 • Millions of gallons of poisoned water enter the Rhine River when a chemical fire destroys a Swiss warehouse in Basel.

2 • American hostage David Jacobsen is freed by the Islamic Jihad in Lebanon.

4 • In U.S. midterm elections, Democrats gain control of the Senate, with a 55-45 majority,

53

and strengthen their hold on the House of Representatives.

6 • The press reports that the United States has secretly sent military equipment to Iran in an apparent effort to improve relations and help gain the release of American hostages in Lebanon.

7 • Canada imposes a heavy import duty on U.S. corn, in response to a stiff U.S. tariff on Canadian lumber.

14 • The U.S. government announces that Wall Street speculator Ivan Boesky has agreed to pay $100 million in penalties and return of profits, for illegal insider trading.

15 • Captured American Eugene Hasenfus is sentenced to 30 years in prison by a government tribunal in Nicaragua.

19 • A federal jury convicts eight men of operating a "commission" that rules organized crime activities in the United States.

23 • Philippine President Aquino dismisses Defense Minister Juan Enrile.

25 • The White House reveals that profits from arms sold to Iran were funneled to Nicaraguan antigovernment guerrillas through a Swiss bank account; U.S. national security adviser John Poindexter resigns over the affair, and Lieutenant-Colonel Oliver North, his aide, is relieved of his duties.

December

2 • A New York Times/CBS News poll shows a plunge in President Reagan's approval rating to 46 percent, from 67 percent a month earlier.

• Stock prices, responding to signs of action by the president on the Iran arms affair, surge to record levels in the third largest rally in history.

• President Reagan announces that a special prosecutor will investigate the Iran arms affair

NOV. 25

and appoints Frank Carlucci, former deputy director of the CIA, as his new national security adviser.

6 • Reagan concedes "mistakes were made" in the "execution" of the Iran operation.

8 • French Prime Minister Jacques Chirac withdraws a plan to overhaul the nation's university system, after large student protests.

10 • A 60-day cease-fire pact between the Philippine government and Communist insurgents goes into effect.

19 • The Soviet Union says that Andrei Sakharov can return to Moscow from exile.

20 • Chinese students begin massive demonstrations in Shanghai.

• Libyan troops open an offensive in Chad against guerrillas who had switched allegiance from Libya.

25 • A hijacked Iraqi jet crashes and burns on a desert airstrip in Saudi Arabia; more than 60 passengers are killed.

A

ACCIDENTS AND DISASTERS. The following were among the noteworthy accidents and disasters of 1986:

Jan. 18, Guatemala: A twin-engine jet carrying tourists to Mayan ruins crashed in a jungle as it approached an airport; all 95 aboard lost their lives.

Jan. 28, Florida: The space shuttle *Challenger* exploded shortly after lift-off, killing all seven crew members. (*See the feature article* SPACE: REBOUNDING FROM DISASTER?)

Feb. 8, Alberta: A head-on collision between a freight and a passenger train near Hinton killed 23 people.

Feb. 17, Chile: Two passenger trains collided head-on near Limache; 58 people died, and more than 500 were injured.

Feb. 28, India: At least 27 people were crushed to death in Tellichery when a train plowed into a crowd standing on the tracks to watch a predawn fireworks display.

Mar. 3, Venezuela: An explosion in a Caracas office building that housed the Chilean embassy killed the ambassador and 14 other people.

Mar. 5, Norway: An avalanche more than 100 miles north of the Arctic Circle killed 16 members of a Norwegian ski patrol.

Mar. 27, Central African Republic: A French Air Force jet based in Bangui crashed on takeoff, hitting an Islamic school building and killing 35 people, mostly children.

Mar. 30, Mozambique: A twin turboprop Air Force transport plane crashed shortly after takeoff from Pemba, killing all 49 people aboard.

Mar. 31, Mexico: In Mexico's worst air disaster yet, a Mexicana Airlines Boeing 727 caught fire and crashed into a mountain 100 miles west of Mexico City; all 167 people aboard lost their lives.

Apr. 5, South Korea: An explosion at the country's largest U.S. air base killed 15 South Koreans and 1 American.

Apr. 14, Bangladesh: Hailstones and gale-force winds battered the Dacca region and other

Officials inspect the remains of two trains that crashed May 5 near Lisbon, Portugal, killing at least 22. Human error was blamed for the accident, which occurred when a passenger train rammed into the rear of a stopped commuter train.

A suburban neighborhood near Los Angeles became a smoldering ruin on August 31, when a private plane collided in midair with an Aeroméxico DC-9, raining debris down on Cerritos. All 67 people aboard the two planes were killed, as well as at least 15 people on the ground.

areas, leaving more than 90 dead and 3,000 injured.

Apr. 14, India: In the Hindu town of Hardwar, some 50 pilgrims were trampled to death as thousands rushed to partake in ritual bathing in the Ganges.

Apr. 20, Bangladesh: A crowded double-decker ferry capsized and sank during a storm on the Shitalakhya River near Dacca, killing more than 200 people.

Apr. 20, Sri Lanka: An earthen dam near Colombo burst, flooding villages downstream and leaving more than 100 people dead and 2,000 homeless.

Apr. 26, Soviet Union: The worst accident in the history of commercial nuclear power occurred when a reactor exploded at the Chernobyl nuclear plant in the Ukraine. Two people were killed at the plant, and 29 died from radiation poisoning within the next few months. (See also Union of Soviet Socialist Republics.)

May 5, Portugal: A speeding passenger train smashed into the rear of a commuter train at a suburban station near Lisbon, killing at least 22.

May 12–15, Oregon: Nine people froze to death when their 13-member climbing party was caught in a blizzard near the summit of Mount Hood.

May 19, Solomon Islands: Typhoon Namu whipped through the islands, leaving more than 100 people dead and an estimated 90,000 homeless.

May 25, Bangladesh: A ferry capsized and sank during a storm on the Meghna River near Dacca, reportedly claiming about 600 lives, in the nation's worst river disaster yet recorded.

May 25, Taiwan: A landslide crashed into scenic Taichi Gorge 100 miles southwest of Taipei, killing at least 33 sightseers.

May 30, California: At least 20 people died when a tour bus carrying residents of a retirement home skidded off a mountain road and plunged into the Walker River.

June 18, Arizona: A twin-engine plane and a helicopter, both carrying passengers over the Grand Canyon, collided in a fiery crash, killing all 25 aboard.

July, Southeast Asia: The worst typhoon to hit southern China in 30 years smacked into Guangdong province, leaving over 200 dead and thousands homeless. It also caused floods and landslides in the Philippines, where at least 90 people died.

July–August, Southeastern United States: The worst drought in over a century, combined with a long heat wave, led to more than 120 deaths; crop and livestock damages were estimated at over $2 billion.

July 16, Australia: Twelve miners perished in Queensland's Moura coal mine when a cave-in caused by a gas explosion left them without ventilation.

Aug. 6, India: An express train smashed into a line of abandoned freight cars in northeastern Bihar, killing about 50 people.

Aug. 14, Honduras: A Honduran Air Force transport plane crashed in dense jungle about 24 miles from the Nicaraguan border, killing all 53 people aboard.

Aug. 17, Southeast Asia: Typhoon Wayne began a three-week rampage through the South China Sea that left at least 500 people dead.

Aug. 21, Cameroon: A deadly gas cloud burst from Lake Nios, a volcanic crater lake, killing over 1,700 people and thousands of animals. (See also EARTH SCIENCES: Geology.)

Aug. 31, California: A Piper Cherokee Archer collided with an Aeroméxico DC-9 jetliner approaching Los Angeles International Airport, killing all 67 aboard the planes and at least 15 on the ground.

Aug. 31, Soviet Union: At least 398 people aboard a cruise ship lost their lives when the liner was rammed by a freighter in the Black Sea and quickly sank.

Sept. 7, Nigeria: Two passenger ships collided in the Atlantic Ocean off Port Harcourt, killing some 100 people.

Sept. 16, South Africa: In the Kinross gold mine east of Johannesburg, a welder's torch ignited wiring and wall sealant, sending toxic fumes through the underground shafts; 177 miners died, most by asphyxiation.

Oct. 3, Atlantic Ocean: A Soviet nuclear submarine patrolling east of Cape Hatteras, N.C., was crippled by an explosion and fire that killed three seamen; the rest of the crew were safely evacuated before it sank.

Oct. 9, Bangladesh: About 150 people were believed killed when a severely overloaded ferry overturned in the Kajla River.

Oct. 9, India: About 70 passengers died when their bus fell off a Ganges River bridge near Kanpur after colliding with a truck.

Oct. 10, El Salvador: Two strong earthquakes leveled much of downtown San Salvador, killing about 1,500 people and leaving about 200,000 homeless. Aftershocks continued for days.

Oct. 19, South Africa: Mozambican President Samora Machel was killed when his jetliner crashed just inside South Africa under mysterious circumstances; 33 others also perished.

Nov. 1, Western Europe: Thirty tons of toxic chemicals spilled into the Rhine at Basel, Switzerland, leading to water pollution and fish kills down the length of the river. (See also ENVIRONMENT.)

Nov. 2, Iran: A military transport plane crashed in the southeastern mountains, killing all 103 soldiers and crew aboard.

Nov. 6, Scotland: In one of the worst helicopter accidents ever, a helicopter plunged into the North Sea off the Shetland Islands, leaving 45 people dead.

Nov. 11, Haiti: An overloaded coastal ferry sank near the island of La Gonâve; some 200 men, women, and children were lost.

Nov. 14, India: A snowstorm and avalanches trapped hundreds of people on a mountain road in Kashmir; around 50 people reportedly died.

Nov. 15, Taiwan: Two earthquakes measuring 6.8 and 6.3 on the Richter scale started rockslides and collapsed buildings near Taipei; 13 people were killed.

Dec. 12, East Germany: A Soviet jetliner crashed on approach to the fogbound East Berlin airport, killing at least 69 of the 81 people aboard.

Dec. 24, Soviet Union: An undisclosed number of coal miners died in a major methane explosion in the Ukraine.

Dec. 31, Puerto Rico: Fire in a San Juan beach hotel killed 96 people, mostly tourists in the casino; arson was determined to be the cause.

ADVERTISING. Patriotism was a popular theme among advertisers during 1986. Budweiser told beer drinkers, "You make America work," while Miller High Life claimed that "Miller's made the American way." The theme for Plymouth automobiles was "The pride is back, born in America." Coca-Cola Classic contributed "Red, white, and you." Another trend was foreign-language commercials with English subtitles. This technique was used in ads for Fibre Trim, Perma Soft, Oil of Olay, and Diet Coke.

Late in 1985, the search began for Herb, the fictitious man who had never been to a Burger King restaurant. The four-month campaign included teaser ads and a contest in which Burger King customers were challenged to identify the actor playing Herb, who made unannounced

Since her introduction in 1936 (left) as General Mills symbol, Betty Crocker has undergone seven transformations. Her latest image, unveiled in 1986 (right), is a younger version of the woman generations of American cooks have counted on for help.

appearances at the chain's restaurants. Although it generated considerable publicity, sales and profits were below expectations, and Herb faded as soon as he had been found.

In another contest, consumers were asked to identify the real Mikey; Mikey, now 18, was the boy who had been trying Quaker Oats' Life cereal since 1971. Meanwhile, the Merrill Lynch bull reappeared with a new theme: "Your world should know no boundaries."

Hamilton!

Under a new law debated and approved by the City Council in May, Hamilton, Ohio, received a new image. It became the first American city—as far as anyone knew—to sport an exclamation point as part of its name. The idea was the brainchild of a Cincinnati public relations firm hired to jazz up this small manufacturing city on the Miami River, previously known (to some) as the birthplace of authors William Dean Howells and Fannie Hurst and of baseball commissioner Kenesaw Mountain Landis.

Several advertisers tried unusual techniques to gain attention. NEC Computers and Communications used a 3-D ad in *Sports Illustrated;* special spectacles were bound into the magazine. Transamerica ran a pop-up ad, depicting the San Francisco skyline, in a September issue of *Time;* its cost was reported to be $3 million.

Annual U.S. expenditures for advertising were expected to exceed $100 billion for the first time in 1986, although the rate of growth in spending had slowed somewhat.

Award-winning Advertising. *Advertising Age* selected Roger Smith, chairman of General Motors, as its Adman of the Year. A GMAC Financing ad showing a bank customer's confusion with an automated teller was named best TV commercial. Hill Holliday Connors Cosmopulos was named Agency of the Year; the agency's campaign for John Hancock Financial Services won both the Grand Prix at the Cannes International Advertising Awards Film Festival and the Clio award for best national TV campaign. Mitsubishi won the Clio for best national print campaign.

Consumers. According to *Business Week,* yuppies (young urban professionals) went out of favor as the most sought-after target for advertisers. They were replaced by those 50 and older, who were valued for their high disposable income. Advertisers also began to pay more attention to children 2 to 12, the result of the recent "baby boomlet."

Media. NBC led the U.S. TV networks in ratings during prime time for the 1985–1986 season. Lower ratings and subsequent reductions in ad revenues at CBS and ABC resulted in staff layoffs at both networks.

The price of a 30-second commercial on the 1986 Super Bowl was $550,000, up from $525,000 the previous year, but in general there was lower demand for commercial time on sports programming. The price of a spot on *The Cosby Show,* the highest-rated TV program for 1985–1986, jumped from $350,000 to $400,000.

Regulation. In a decision that limited the First Amendment protection of commercial speech, the U.S. Supreme Court ruled that governments may ban truthful ads for a legal product or service. On the other hand, after the Federal Trade Commission issued a complaint against R. J. Reynolds for false and deceptive advertising in an editorial-style ad titled "Of Cigarettes and Science," an administrative law judge dismissed the complaint, ruling that the ad, as a statement of opinion rather than a promotion for a specific product, was protected speech under the First Amendment. The FTC appealed the ruling.   B.B.R.

AFGHANISTAN. In 1986, during the seventh year of war in Afghanistan, the stalemate continued between Soviet forces backing the Marxist government, on the one hand, and the Afghan resistance, the Mujahedeen, on the other.

Leadership Change. In May, Babrak Karmal resigned as effective leader of the Democratic Republic of Afghanistan. He was replaced by Najibullah (his full name, later shortened to Najib), who, with the clear support of the Soviet leadership, became general secretary of the ruling People's Democratic Party of Afghanistan (PDPA) and chairman of its Central Committee. Karmal, who had been placed in power when the Soviet Union invaded Afghanistan in December 1979, retained the mostly ceremonial post of president for a time

but was replaced in November by Haji Muhammad Chamkani. Najib's appointment did not go unchallenged. Schools in Kabul were closed after Karmal's student supporters rioted, and Soviet troops had to replace government police units until Najib was firmly installed. Late in the year there was a cabinet shakeup, apparently to strengthen Najib's control.

Increased cooperation between the major resistance parties headquartered in Pakistan made possible a formula for rotating leadership among the chiefs of the seven principal groups. This arrangement reflected a lessening of the damaging divisiveness within the resistance.

Conduct of the War. Soviet forces and their Afghan auxiliaries continued to enjoy a vast superiority in equipment, mobility, and firepower. Massive sweeps were mounted against the strongest Mujahedeen positions. More attention was paid to cities by encircling them with minefields and fortified positions. In October, Soviet officials gave wide publicity to what they said was a withdrawal of several thousand of their estimated 115,000 troops; U.S. officials described the action as a public relations move, timed to coincide with U.S.-Soviet summit talks in Iceland. A UN report in November said Soviet atrocities against civilians were increasing.

Despite Soviet efforts, Mujahedeen units generally held their own, stepping up raids against convoys and exposed installations and launching heavy rocket and mortar attacks on the capital city. Soviet air superiority remained absolute, but there was increasing evidence of the use of ground-to-air missiles by the Mujahedeen, causing heavy Soviet losses. According to some reports, rebels were receiving U.S. Stinger missiles.

International Activity. Peace talks sponsored by the United Nations between the governments of Pakistan and Afghanistan reconvened in Geneva and reportedly achieved some progress. New talks were scheduled for early 1987. U.S. support of the Mujahedeen was highlighted by President Ronald Reagan's reception of their official leaders in June—although he refused at that time to grant them diplomatic recognition and to sever ties with the Kabul government.

See STATISTICS OF THE WORLD.   N.P.N.

Africa

The confrontation between the white-minority regime in South Africa and its opponents escalated in 1986, both inside South Africa and throughout the region. Conflicts also continued in Western Sahara, Chad, Sudan, and the Horn of Africa. Low commodity prices and lessened world attention to Africa's economic problems hampered prospects for an early economic recovery.

Much attention focused during the year on confrontations between antiapartheid groups and the South African government and on the detention by the regime of thousands of activists. Pressure for action against apartheid grew substantially within international organizations, including the Organization of African Unity.

South African Conflict. In June the Pretoria government reimposed a state of emergency that had been nominally lifted in March. Human rights organizations estimated that as many as 20,000 people were newly detained. Most severely affected were local community groups affiliated with the United Democratic Front (UDF) and the growing black and nonracial trade union movement, particularly the new Congress of South African Trade Unions.

Protest actions during the year included a national stay-away strike in June, ongoing consumer boycotts, and rent strikes and school boycotts in many black townships. There were repeated incidents between security forces and young black demonstrators. However, press restrictions barred international television coverage of "unrest," and no news of any kind referring to the security forces was permitted without specific approval by the authorities. In July, the regime officially scrapped the pass laws controlling the movement of blacks, but critics said restrictions were being implemented in other ways, using new identity cards and control of access to housing and jobs.

A panel appointed by the Commonwealth of Nations visited South Africa and neighboring countries in early 1986 in an effort to encourage Pretoria to negotiate with its opponents, but concluded the regime was unwilling to discuss

diminished white control. Subsequently a number of Commonwealth countries adopted limited sanctions against South Africa, including a ban on new investment and restrictions on trade. Two of them, Zambia and Zimbabwe, dependent on South Africa for transport of their export goods, did so at potential great cost. South Africa retaliated swiftly with added duties. The other allied frontline states praised Zambia and Zimbabwe's action, but two of them, Botswana and Mozambique, noted they were too vulnerable to follow suit themselves. The European Community imposed sanctions, although a ban on coal imports from South Africa was blocked by objections from West Germany. In October the U.S. Congress overrode a veto by President Ronald Reagan to impose its own package of limited sanctions. Many foreign companies, including more than 30 U.S. firms, decided to withdraw from South Africa.

South Africa's multifaceted war against its neighbors also escalated. Economic pressures on Lesotho helped provoke a coup in January. The guerrilla war in South African-occupied Namibia (South West Africa) continued, punctuated by government raids into neighboring Angola. South Africa said the raids were aimed at guerrilla bases of the South West Africa People's Organization (Swapo); observers generally credited Angolan claims that they were also intended to boost the South African-backed Unita guerrillas fighting the Angolan government. Unita was also aided during the year by a highly publicized U.S. decision to grant it as much as $15 million in covert military aid.

The most serious escalation, however, was in South Africa's campaign against Mozam-

Mozambican President Samora Machel (inset) was among 34 people killed in a plane crash in South Africa. Seen here is wreckage at the crash site 12 hours later. Both pilot error and foul play have been suspected as possible causes of the crash.

bique, especially through the guerrilla group known as the Mozambique National Resistance (MNR). South Africa massed troops along the Mozambican border, decided to repatriate over 60,000 migrant Mozambican mine workers, and backed an MNR thrust to take over territory in Mozambique's Tete and Zambézia provinces. On October 19, Mozambique's respected President Samora Machel died in a plane crash just inside South Africa, under circumstances leading many observers to suspect South African complicity. The new Mozambican president, Joaquim Chissano, vowed to continue his predecessor's policies, and African states pledged to aid in defending Mozambique's Beira corridor, a vital outlet to the sea for inland states.

In April, Prince Makhosetive became King Mswati III of Swaziland, ending the intense political maneuvering since the death of his father, Sobhuza II, in 1982. Mswati's mother, Queen Ntombi, had been regent since August 1983.

East Africa. Yoweri Museveni took office as head of state of Uganda in January, after his National Resistance Army ousted the governing military council. Museveni promised an end to the years of polarization and violence in Uganda and was credited with making a good start, despite an apparent coup attempt involving his own vice president later in the year.

In neighboring Sudan, however, fighting between the Sudanese People's Liberation Army in the south and the central government in Khartoum reportedly led to many famine deaths, as the two sides contested the control of relief shipments to the war zone. The Eritrean guerrilla war for independence from Ethiopia continued unabated, as did disputes about the distribution of relief supplies in Ethiopia.

West Africa. There were no major political shifts in West Africa, despite reports of coup plots in Ghana and rising dissent in Liberia. Even Nigeria, the region's economic giant, was facing serious economic problems, largely as a result of the decline in oil prices. Although the military government of Ibrahim Babangida refused a formal agreement with the International Monetary Fund, it adopted austerity measures to qualify for loans from the IMF, the World Bank, and commercial banks. In Ghana, government austerity measures were reported to be taking effect, although critics charged that the poor were unfairly treated and that the regime was taking no steps toward democratization.

In Cameroon a release of toxic gas from volcanic Lake Nios in August left more than 1,700 dead. Conflict continued in Chad's long civil war, with Libyan troops still backing rebels against President Hissène Habré, who consolidated his control in the south of the country. And former Central African emperor Jean Bédel Bokassa returned from exile in October to face trial and a possible death sentence for atrocities carried out by his regime. On December 15 he went on trial, on charges ranging from embezzling state funds to killing schoolchildren.

North Africa. Tunisian President Habib Bourguiba dismissed Prime Minister Muhammad M'zali in July, raising new doubts about the succession to the 83-year-old incumbent. The continuing struggle between Morocco and Polisario Front guerrillas for control of Western Sahara received little international attention. Instead, the news focused on tensions between Libya (accused of involvement in international terrorism) and the United States, and especially on the dramatic U.S. bombing of Libya in April, which attracted wide controversy. Chad was a focus of attention late in the year, as the Libyans launched an offensive against rebels who had switched sides and no longer supported Libya.

International Organizations. The Organization of African Unity, at its annual meeting in July in Addis Ababa, Ethiopia, chose Congolese head of state Denis Sassou-Nguesso as chairman for the following year. Member nations stressed a need for stepped-up action against apartheid.

Eighteen-year-old King Mswati III of Swaziland (center) was crowned in April after four years of infighting following the death of his father, Sobhuza II.

In May a special session of the United Nations General Assembly focused on the African economic crisis. Industrial countries proved reluctant to commit the $80 billion in aid and debt relief estimated to be needed for recovery. The UN Office for Emergency Operations in Africa sounded an alarm at the falloff in world concern when nonfood development needs and even food transport requirements remained unmet, but the emergency office itself was disbanded in October.

In September the nonaligned movement met in Harare under the chairmanship of President Robert Mugabe of Zimbabwe. About half of the movement's members are African countries, and the gathering set up a fund to aid African countries under South African attack. Much of the attention focused on a flamboyant speech by Libyan leader Muammar al-Qaddafi, in which he called the movement useless in defending member nations against attack by the United States and its allies and denounced as puppets all members having ties with the United States, Britain, or Israel.

See also separate articles on many of the individual countries mentioned.   W.M.

AGRICULTURE AND FOOD SUPPLIES. World food production in 1986 was only slightly greater than in 1985, but substantial stocks of some commodities, notably grains, dairy products, meats, and sugar, assured adequate supplies for most people. U.S. agriculture continued to suffer from serious economic problems. Africa's immediate food situation took a turn for the better when timely rains boosted production in many countries, but long-term prospects remained bleak.

World Output. World grain production was forecast at 1,648 million metric tons, down 1 percent from 1985. But the total supply of grains, including stocks, was up 3 percent from that on hand in September 1985. The coarse grain harvest was projected by the U.S. Department of Agriculture (USDA) at 822 million tons, down 3 percent. Rice, on a milled basis, was put at 320 million tons, up slightly. Oilseed and soybean output showed slight increases.

Production of red meats and poultry was forecast at 128 million tons, up slightly from 1985. Pork production rose an estimated 1

percent, but beef and veal declined. Output of eggs was up only slightly; cheese production was expected to rise about 3 percent.

Sugar output was forecast at 100.5 million tons (raw basis), 4 percent above the revised 1985 estimate. Coffee production was forecast at 83 million bags, down 14 percent, largely as a result of drought-shortened production in Brazil. The world cocoa bean harvest was down slightly. The cotton crop was projected at 74.1 million bales, down from 79.0 million in 1985. Tobacco production was set at 6.6 million tons, off 4 percent, largely reflecting a substantial decrease in China, the world's largest producer.

United States. U.S. agriculture continued to be plagued by economic problems stemming from farmers' ability to produce more food and fiber than could be marketed profitably. Stores of grain continued to increase, placing strains on inadequate storage facilities. The value of farmland continued to decline. USDA estimates for net farm income in 1986 ranged from $26 billion to $30 billion, compared with $30.5 billion in 1985. Farmers' income would have been even lower had it not been for a heavy infusion of government payments. In October the USDA announced a program to pay farmers not to plant feed grains in 1987.

Exports Decline. A major factor in the depressed farm situation was a continued decline in farm product exports, attributed to two important developments: increased production in food-importing countries and higher prices for U.S. products than for those of other exporting countries. In May the USDA announced implementation of a $2 billion "export enhancement program," under which the United States offered government-owned commodities as bonuses to foreign buyers, so as to expand farm product sales in targeted markets abroad— those identified as having been taken over unfairly by foreign competitors.

Farm Credit Squeeze. Credit continued to be a major problem for farmers. The General Accounting Office reported that the Farmers Home Administration, the government agency considered the farm lender of last resort, expected to own as many as 20,000 farms through foreclosure by the end of 1987; in mid-1986 it owned only about 4,000. The Farm Credit

AGRICULTURE AND FOOD SUPPLIES

System, a network of cooperative farm banks, reported in August that it expected to post a loss of $1.8 billion for 1986; however, in October, Congress passed legislation enabling the system to refinance outstanding bonds at lower interest rates and spread its losses over the next 20 years.

Hands Across America. Despite U.S. farm surpluses, hunger continued to be a problem both in the United States and around the world. Americans' concern with persisting hunger was vividly demonstrated on May 25, when millions joined hands in a line that stretched across most of the United States. "Hands Across America" raised about $25 million by year's end, most of it for community groups fighting hunger and homelessness.

Crops. Growing conditions were generally favorable except in southeastern and mid-Atlan-

Drought and heat brought disaster to farmers in the southeastern United States in the summer. Farmers from other areas donated thousands of bales of hay to feed livestock (below, a shipment from Colorado to hard-hit Alabama), but little could be done for the acres of parched fields (above, wilted South Carolina corn).

tic states, where drought sharply curtailed harvests. Many northern farmers donated hay to farmers in drought areas. Just before harvest, bumper crops in Missouri and adjacent states were ruined by heavy rains.

From a crop production standpoint, the year was good, but not so good as 1985. Production of four feed grains (corn, sorghum, barley, and oats) was forecast at 252 million tons, down about 8 percent. The wheat harvest was put at 57.7 million tons, off 12 percent. Rice production was forecast at 5.8 million tons, up slightly, and hay at a record 153 million tons. Soybean output was set at 53.9 million tons, off 6 percent; peanuts and cottonseed were down substantially.

Cotton production was forecast at 10.5 million bales, down 22 percent. The tobacco harvest was placed at 1.22 billion pounds, 19 percent below 1985 and the smallest crop since 1936, reflecting southeastern drought damage. Commercial apple and pear production were both down moderately. The peach harvest increased 6 percent, while the grape crop decreased 12 percent.

Livestock, Dairy, and Poultry. A provision of the 1985 Food Security Act allowed the USDA to try to reduce the milk surplus, which cost the government $2.1 billion in buying and storing costs in 1985, by using a dairy herd buyout and adjustments of dairy support prices. The support price for milk remained at $11.60 per hundred-weight, but was to drop to $11.35 on January 1, 1987, and to $11.10 on October 1, 1987.

Red meat production dropped from 39.1 billion pounds in 1985 to an estimated 38.6 billion in 1986, whereas poultry meat output rose from 16.9 billion to 17.9 billion. Egg production increased slightly.

Canada. The 1986 Canadian wheat crop was estimated at a record 31.0 million tons, up 9 percent. The coarse grain harvest, also a record, totaled 27.0 million tons. Production of red meat, forecast at 1.9 million tons, was about the same as in each of the preceding two years.

Latin America and the Caribbean. Coffee production in the western hemisphere dropped from 65.1 million bags to an estimated 50.9 million, reflecting a 50 percent drop in Brazil's crop as a result of severe drought in late 1985. Sugar production in Latin America rose slightly. Combined grain production in Brazil and Argentina was up 6 percent.

Western Europe. Dry weather was a major factor in the reduced coarse grain harvest in Western Europe, down 8 percent from 1985. The projected wheat crop was off 2 percent. Milk production was forecast at about the same level as in 1985. Beef stocks, acquired under price-support operations, reached a total of 1.1 million tons in January but by September had been cut to about 640,000 tons through heavily subsidized exports.

Soviet Union. Production of wheat and coarse grains in the Soviet Union was forecast at 162 million tons, down 8 percent from 1985. Under a long-term agreement, the Soviets were to buy 4 million tons of U.S. grain through the marketing year ending September 30. Soviet purchases had fallen far short of that level by August, when the USDA announced that wheat would be made available to the Soviet Union at lower prices than before. To bring their prices down to world levels, U.S. exporters were allowed government subsidies. Nevertheless, European prices remained lower, and the Soviets purchased European grain.

The long-term effects of the Chernobyl nuclear accident on Soviet and European agricultural land remained unclear. A few weeks after the disaster, a USDA report emphasized that except for the 18-mile evacuation zone around Chernobyl, the agency had no information indicating serious radiation damage. However, the European Community temporarily banned agricultural imports from Eastern Europe, and there was wide concern.

Africa. Food production in sub-Saharan Africa improved considerably, though long-term prospects remained poor. In most countries, harvests were good to excellent. Among countries suffering from scarcity were Sudan, where rebels prevented relief food from reaching government-held towns, and Ethiopia, where the government refused to allow food aid to rebel-held areas. An international relief agency, Doctors Without Borders, charged that the Ethiopian government had used Western food aid to undertake a massive resettlement program responsible for 100,000 deaths.

Asia and Oceania. The food situation continued to be relatively favorable in the heavily populated countries of Asia. China's total grain harvest increased 5 percent over 1985, and India's crop was up 2 percent. Pakistan and Indonesia also reported gains. Australia's 1986–1987 wheat crop was forecast at 15 million tons, down 1 million tons from the previous year. Cattle and sheep numbers were up, and beef production for 1986 grew more than 3 percent. In New Zealand, beef production rose slightly, but lamb and mutton output declined 12 percent.

Fisheries. Projections for 1986 suggested that the world catch of fish and shellfish would equal or somewhat surpass the 1985 total of 84.0 million metric tons estimated by the UN Food and Agriculture Organization. The U.S. catch promised to be at least as strong as in 1985, when U.S. fishermen landed more than $2.3 billion worth of shellfish.

The International Trade Commission upheld the 5.82 percent duty on fresh whole groundfish entering the United States from Canada, but it turned down a petition to erect a similar barrier to groundfish fillets. As a result, the price gap between domestically cut fillets and fillets produced in Canada was expected to widen. The long-festering dispute over Japanese interception of U.S.-bound salmon ended in the spring, when the International North Pacific Fisheries Commission formally adopted

an accord between the two nations. (*See also* PACIFIC ISLANDS.) During the year salmon returned to the Columbia and other northwestern rivers in the largest numbers in decades, apparently because of improved environmental conditions. D.R.W. (Fisheries) & H.W.H.

ALABAMA. *See* STATISTICS OF THE WORLD.

ALASKA. *See* STATISTICS OF THE WORLD.

ALBANIA. On November 8, 1986, Ramiz Alia was elected as head of the Albanian Communist Party, at the first party congress held since the death of former party chief Enver Hoxha in April 1985. Alia had been named to the post following Hoxha's death. The Politburo's ten members were reelected to their positions, as were the five members of the secretariat headed by Alia.

There were no signs of change in Albania's long-standing policy of aloofness from both the superpowers. Albania did show indications of seeking to lessen its isolation from some other countries. Talks were held during the year between West Germany and Albania, aimed at possibly opening diplomatic ties. The talks broke down because Albania insisted on reparations for its occupation by the German Army from 1943 to 1945. Nevertheless Albanian-West German contacts were increasing.

Talks were also held with Great Britain, about the return of Albanian gold confiscated by the British, but negotiations were stalemated by the British demand (backed up by a 1949 World

Court decision) for compensation for the 1946 mining of two British destroyers in the Corfu Channel. The Greek government informally indicated a possible willingness to lift a technical state of war with Albania dating from World War II, but Greek territorial claims on Albania and concern over human rights of the Greek minority in Albania remained as obstacles to progress.

In August, Albanian and Yugoslav officials inaugurated a freight railway link—Albania's first link with the rest of Eastern Europe since the war—but Albanian media continued their invective against Yugoslavia and the Eastern-bloc countries.

Nexhmije Hoxha, Enver Hoxha's widow, was promoted in March to chairman of the Albanian Democratic Front. The move indicated the continuing strength of Enver Hoxha's adherents.

See STATISTICS OF THE WORLD.   R.A.P.

ALBERTA. See STATISTICS OF THE WORLD. See also CANADA.

ALGERIA. In 1986 tumbling oil prices dealt the Algerian economy a severe blow. President Chadli Benjedid made key leadership changes, and citizens approved a new National Charter.

After a decade of substantial energy earnings, Algeria suffered an oil countershock. Overproduction of crude oil, both by members of the Organization of Petroleum Exporting Countries (to which Algeria belongs) and by other major producers, caused prices to plummet, reducing Algeria's oil income. As a result, the government cut expenditures by 20 percent and slashed subsidies on basic consumer goods. At an OPEC meeting in August, members did agree to a temporary ceiling on oil production, which helped cause prices to rise somewhat; the agreement was essentially extended at another meeting in October, and further output cuts were adopted in December.

Alarmed by armed attacks against the police by Muslim dissidents, Benjedid moved his trusted associate Boualem Baki, formerly minister of justice, to the Ministry of Religious Affairs. He also removed General Rachid Benyelles, a potential rival, from a key Army post, leaving the military firmly under the command of General Mustapha Benloucif, who thus emerged as number-two man in the regime.

A new National Charter, approved in December 1985 by the National Liberation Front, Algeria's ruling party, was submitted to a national referendum on January 16, 1986. The document, endorsed by 98 percent of the electorate, legitimized certain policies already introduced under Benjedid, such as decentralization and a larger role for private enterprise and consumer products in the economy.

Relations with Libya improved considerably after Benjedid met with Libyan leader Muammar al-Qaddafi in southern Algeria in January. Algerian Prime Minister Abdelhamid Brahimi later visited Tripoli to cement the reconciliation, and Algeria expressed strong solidarity with Libya during its hostilities with the United States in March and April. Having visited the United States in 1985, Benjedid made a trip in March to the Soviet Union, where he signed an agreement providing Soviet aid in constructing an arms production factory.

France and Algeria signed a new cooperation agreement in March, replacing a 1966 accord. The agreement focused on technological projects in medicine, agriculture, and transportation.

See STATISTICS OF THE WORLD.   R.A.M.

AMERICAN SAMOA. See STATISTICS OF THE WORLD.

ANGOLA. Guerrillas of the National Union for the Total Independence of Angola (Unita), bolstered by South African military aid and new aid from the United States, continued to wage war against the government of President Jose Eduardo dos Santos, backed by Soviet aid and Cuban troops. The decision by the Reagan administration to openly provide $15 million in "covert" military aid to the guerrilla organization was confirmed after a February visit to Washington by Unita leader Jonas Savimbi; the U.S. move was strongly denounced by black African leaders.

As in 1985, there was a major government dry-season offensive from July through September. In August, as the Angolans pressed against Savimbi's zone of operations, South African troops allied with Unita attacked a key Angolan forward air base at the southern town of Cuito-Cuanavale. Unita also continued attacks elsewhere in Angola, making large portions of the countryside unsafe even for Red Cross relief operations. Among major incidents were a Unita attack on the town of Camabatela in February, which eyewitnesses claimed killed more than 100 civilians, and the March kidnapping of more than 170 foreigners, principally Portuguese and Filipinos, at the diamond mining town of Andrada. Both attacks were reportedly carried out by Unita guerrillas in the north who received support through neighboring Zaire. As a result of international pressure, the foreign hostages were later released in Zaire. In November, Unita rebels reportedly stepped up operations in the north.

Angola continued to depend on Soviet military aid and the presence of approximately 27,000 Cuban troops, although the Cubans apparently took little direct role in the offensive against Unita, being concentrated in rear-base and defensive positions. In June, South African commandos sank one Cuban ship and damaged two Soviet ships in the port of Namibe, also destroying the oil storage tanks in the harbor. In May, President dos Santos made his first state visit in three years to Moscow, where he received renewed pledges of support.

Angola was rated by international agencies as one of the four African countries most seriously affected by food shortages, with as many as 600,000 people severely affected. The major cause was the continuing war, which not only produced migration to urban areas but also crippled food production. A drop in world oil prices was expected to reduce revenues substantially, and the diamond mines were seriously disrupted by Unita attacks and by smuggling.

See STATISTICS OF THE WORLD. W.M.

ANTHROPOLOGY. In 1986 analysis of recent fossil discoveries appeared to place humans in northeastern South America as long ago as 32,000 years, earlier than humans are known to have lived in North America. New fossil finds also attested to early human habitation in Florida. On a more poignant note, some American Indians finally laid their early ancestors to rest.

The Earliest Americans. Anthropologists generally agree that the first people to enter the New World were Asians who crossed ice-covered Beringia (the area between present-day Siberia and Alaska) between 14,000 and 40,000 years ago (archaeological evidence places humans in Eastern Siberia no more than 40,000 years ago). Comparative studies of Eastern Asiatic and native American blood types, languages, and teeth all point to a historical link between these two populations. Anthropologists generally assume that the early Asian immigrants initially lived in North America and that some later migrated south into Central and South America.

However, the confirmed dates of known human sites do not coincide with this theory. Until recently, the Old Crow Flats site in the Yukon Territory was regarded as the oldest human habitation in North America. Among its tools was a flesher (used for fleshing hides) which archaeologists originally said yielded a radiocarbon date of 27,000 BP (before present). In the May 9 issue of *Science*, however, five Canadian scholars contend that the bone tool was incorrectly dated and is really no more than 1,500 years old. This would leave the Meadowcraft rock-shelter in western Pennsylvania, whose artifacts date back 19,500 years, as North America's oldest acknowledged human site. By contrast, findings at Boqueirao do Sitio da Pedra Furada, discovered in 1973 in Brazil, offer evidence of human habitation as early as 32,000 years ago. In their June 19 article in *Nature*, two French scholars conclude that humans repeatedly occupied the site from 32,000 to 6,000 years ago. Evidence from these and other South American sites substantially predate the known traces of human habitation in North America. Some scholars believe older North American sites will be discovered, solving this archaeological mystery.

Ice Age Bones in Florida. In January scholars from four U.S. universities announced that recent fossil finds provide evidence of human habitation in Florida about 10,000 years ago. Their excavation site near Biscayne Bay in southern Florida has already produced 40,000 bone fragments, as well as tools and a hearth. A dozen human bone fragments and the remains of 50 species of animals, including mammoth, lion, horse, bison, giant sloth, and condor, are among the key discoveries. It is one of the Southeast's oldest sites and one of the few sites in North America to yield human

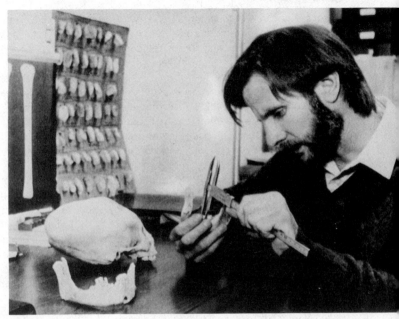

Indian activists, claiming that their religious beliefs are being violated, want ancient Indian bones now on display in museums to be reburied. However, anthropologists such as Dr. Marc Kelley, shown here, argue that reburial will cause the loss of vital clues about ancient Indian culture.

remains in direct association with extinct Ice Age animals.

American Indian Reburials. In May, Arikara Indians ceremonially reburied the bones of 3,000 of their ancestors in South Dakota. The bones had been part of the collection at the University of Tennessee. In recent years, thousands of other Indian skeletons have been recovered from museums across the United States and reburied by their living descendants, in accord with traditional Indian religious beliefs.

Over the past century, Indian skeletons uncovered by archaeologists, erosion, and construction workers were routinely given to museums and universities to be stored, analyzed, and put on display for the public. Resenting this irreverent treatment of their ancestors, many Indians are demanding control over ancestral burial grounds and the right to recover the Indian remains stored in museums and laboratories. These modern-day Indians often condemn the excavation, analysis, and display of their ancestors' bones as a form of white racism and a sign of continued white domination over native Americans.

Scientists who oppose the Indians' demands argue that their studies of the remains help reconstruct history and, in particular, help living Indians by providing information on traditional Indian diets and on genetic defects and diseases common among Indians of the past. They also deny the charge of racism, noting that many of their collections contain the bones of other races.   P.J.M.

ANTIGUA AND BARBUDA. *See* Statistics of the World.

ARAB LEAGUE. During 1986 the Arab League strongly criticized U.S. policies toward Libya. In January the league's council passed a resolution in Tunis "vigorously condemning" U.S. threats of military action against Libya for what the United States said was Libyan complicity in terrorist attacks. Following U.S. air raids on Tripoli and Benghazi in April, the league's secretary-general, Chadli Klibi, stated: "It is regrettable that a nation which for more than two centuries was the champion of freedom and democracy sees its force used in the servitude of those who can only compromise, perhaps irreversibly, U.S. relations with the Arab peoples."

Attempts were made to strengthen ties with other Western nations in a series of meetings between Secretary-General Klibi and European representatives, including talks on Swiss-Arab relations at Locarno in June and a parley with the Dutch foreign minister in Tunis in May.

In April the Arab Organization of Telecommunications by Satellite (Arabsat) general assembly met for a two-day session in Algiers. Arabsat, supervised by the Arab League, was established in 1976 to develop a satellite telecommunications network among the Arab states. By 1986 its 9,000 circuits had become sufficient to cover the Arab world, and its third satellite was ready for delivery from France.

The league faced its most serious economic crisis ever during 1986, with a $23 million deficit in a $30 million budget. The deficit arose because the 21 member countries made only 25 percent of their expected contribution. Meanwhile, several league members convened during February in Tunis to discuss the establishment of a free Arab economic zone that

Leading Maya scholar and Princeton student David Stuart works at deciphering Maya hieroglyphics in the hope of shedding light on the mysterious ancient Central American civilization.

would include inter-Arab industrial projects managed by the league's Economic Council. Explicit plans for the project were deferred.

On December 10, at an emergency meeting of the Arab League council, members called for an immediate cease-fire in the bloody "war between the camps," pitting the largest Muslim militia, the Amal, against resurgent Palestinians in Lebanon. The council met again a few days later and formed a committee to conduct a peace mission.   D.P.

ARCHAEOLOGY. Archaeological events in 1986 ranged from new interpretations of the Stone Age based on discoveries in France to fresh insights into the Maya civilization. A preliminary dig was staged at the site of a famous frontier shoot-out in New Mexico, and a major fossil find was reported in Canada.

Stone Age Cannibalism in France. Scientists working at a cave in Provence, in southern France, uncovered what they considered to be the first clear evidence of cannibalism among prehistoric people. Excavations had been going on since 1977 in the cave, called Fontbrégoua, under the direction of Jean Courtin of the French Center for Archaeological Research. Human bones were found in previous seasons, but a study of newly discovered bones, carried out with the help of an electron microscope, revealed cut marks similar to those found on the bones of butchered animals. Anthropologist Paola Villa of the University of Colorado concluded that these individuals had been butchered to be eaten like animals. Even the nutritious marrow had been removed from the bones before they were dumped into a refuse pit.

The people who inhabited the Fontbrégoua cave at the time—estimated to be nearly 6,000 years ago—were not primitive, according to the investigators. They herded sheep, grew grain on a small scale, and made pottery and jewelry. Their victims probably were captured by a raiding party and may have lived only a short distance away.

Rethinking the Maya Civilization. For the last two centuries researchers have been fascinated by the Maya, especially the developments during the so-called Classic period (A.D. 200–900) of their civilization. Recent excavations and new analyses of hieroglyphic texts were illuminating the Maya people's penchant for ritual bloodletting and self-mutilation. This new image, which emerged after years of study, was a far cry from the old stereotype of the peaceful Maya. According to Linda Schele of the University of Texas at Austin and Mary Ellen Miller of Yale University, "Blood was the mortar of ancient Maya ritual life." In preparing for battle, for example, a king would puncture his penis in a bloodletting ritual, and his queen would mutilate her tongue, thereby inducing a hallucinogenic state that led to communication with the gods. Some of the most notable examples of Maya art depict these rituals.

The recent decipherment of Maya hieroglyphic texts by archaeologists including David Stuart, a Princeton University undergraduate and the youngest expert on Maya glyphs, points to a complex writing system that included punctuation and subjects, verbs, and objects—in essence, a language. Excavations in the highlands and lowlands of the Maya region over the last several years have also provided archaeologists with firm evidence that the sites in the lowlands achieved social and political complexity in their own right, rather than solely under the influence of the highlands.

Searching for Billy the Kid. Archaeologists staged a six-week preliminary dig in Lincoln, N.M., at the site of an 1878 shoot-out involving frontier outlaw William H. Bonney, better known as Billy the Kid. The bloody three-day siege was the culmination of the so-called Lincoln County War, a long, fierce power struggle between two rival groups of cattle ranchers and businessmen. The dig began on July 19, the anniversary of the shoot-out, at the Alexander McSween House, onetime home of a leader of one of the groups. In a series of excavations, the director of the project, Thomas Caperton of the Museum of New Mexico, hopes to uncover weapons, bones, and other evidence to supplement the documentary evidence of the siege and give insight into the role played by Bonney.

Fossil Find. One of the richest North American fossil finds yet reported was made in Nova Scotia along the shore of the Bay of Fundy by a Harvard University biologist and a Columbia University geologist. The find included specimens of the tritheledont, a part-mammal, part-reptile creature whose jaw was less than an inch long, and 200-million-year-old remains of primitive crocodiles, fish, lizards, and small dinosaurs, embedded in sandstone. Many researchers believe that the sudden disappearance of these animal forms, like the mass extinction of dinosaurs about 125 million years later, may have been caused by the impact of a large meteorite or comet.

Looting in Thailand. A disturbing case of archaeological looting gained wide attention in 1986. For more than two years, scholars say, villagers in a stretch of forested mountains in western Thailand had been finding burial sites from which they removed tens of thousands of objects for sale. No scientific excavations took place, and the contexts of these well-preserved objects were lost. The artifacts being sold were mainly ceramics of high quality but also included swords and jewelry. The fact that little is known about the region added to the Thai government's concern. The eclectic mix, as well as the quantity, of the ceramics suggests an unknown culture or at least a transitional culture based on the Mon culture in Burma. More evidence, if it can be obtained before all trace of this culture is destroyed, may force a revision in our knowledge of Thai dynasties and of Thai history in general.   B.R.

ARCHITECTURE. The year marked the 100th anniversary of the birth of German-American architect Ludwig Mies van der Rohe. Several buildings of note were opened, and Expo 86 was an architectural, as well as a popular, success.

Mies van der Rohe. Various events combined to make Mies van der Rohe "architect of the year." The Museum of Modern Art in New York celebrated the 100th anniversary of his birth with a major exhibition. A show in Chicago celebrated Mies's role as educator at the Illinois Institute of Technology. Scholars weighed in with monographs on his life and works. Finally, in Barcelona, Spain, Mies's famous German pavilion of 1929 was reconstructed. Architects long familiar with black and white photographs of the pavilion, published in every history of modern architecture, were now able to study the rich colors and materials of this seminal work.

Openings. The Museum of Contemporary Art in Los Angeles, which opened its inaugural

"The Residence of the Presidents," Washington D.C.'s Willard Hotel (above) reopened in September after a long decline. The 12-story hotel, rebuilt in 1901, was restored to its turn-of-the-century splendor with the help of artisans who reproduced the look of the original mosaic tile floors, marble columns, and coffered ceilings. Reportedly the birthplace of the power lunch, the original Willard was the hangout of President Ulysses S. Grant, who coined the word "lobbyist" to describe the favor-seekers who accosted him in the Willard lobby (restored at left).

show in December, was Japanese architect Arata Isozaki's first wholly new building to be completed in the United States. Isozaki is considered by many to be the leader of a new generation in Japanese design, and the museum is a crisp, quirky composition of monumental yet simple forms. Isozaki's Okanoyama Graphic Art Museum in Nishiwaki, Japan, an equally provocative design that mimics trains passing by the site, also was inaugurated.

A long-awaited museum opened in December in the rehabilitated Gare d'Orsay in Paris. Italian architect Gae Aulenti, also responsible for the recent renovation of the art galleries at Paris's Centre Pompidou, exaggerated the differences between the 19th-century train shed, which was meticulously restored, and its new galleries, set within the shell like so many small reliquaries. The museum is dedicated to the decorative and other arts of the 19th century.

In Venice, the ubiquitous Aulenti, with Antonio Foscari, organized the restoration and conversion of the 18th-century Palazzo Grassi for use as an art center, sponsored by the Fiat Corporation and directed by Pontus Hulten, former head of the Centre Pompidou. The center opened with an exhibition on futurism.

Two long-awaited but delayed completions were celebrated in London and Washington, D.C. The new headquarters of insurance underwriters Lloyd's of London, a controversial high-tech tower designed by British architect Richard Rogers, opened in October after innumerable delays caused by its complicated construction. And Washington's Willard Hotel, once the stamping ground of President Ulysses S. Grant, reopened in September, as the Willard Inter-Continental.

In New Orleans, Riverwalk, the latest and perhaps most risky venture of the Rouse Corporation, opened in August. The city hoped this festival marketplace, sited on the Mississippi River, would revive a flagging tourist trade.

Controversies. Developer Donald Trump's extravagant plans for a seven-tower superblock on Manhattan's West Side added fuel to New York's ongoing debate over development: How much is too much? The residential, office, and television studio complex envisioned by Chicago architect Helmut Jahn and dubbed TV City was deemed by critics too big, the "givebacks" required of the developer by the city too small. Trump's controversial plan to build the world's tallest tower at TV City and reclaim for New York the title now held by Chicago's Sears Tower was immediately challenged by a developer in Phoenix and another in Atlanta; each of their towers would top that of Trump, who in any case first had to shepherd his project through New York's complicated approvals process.

In Paris, plans for a French Disneyland were greeted with a mix of delight and dismay. The theme park proposed by Walt Disney Productions for Marne-la-Vallée, a suburb of Paris, would bring tourists and 25,000 new jobs, and Disney promised further "an emphasis on French culture." But critics who opposed the proliferation of American fast-food outlets in France feared that "Mickey sur Marne" would be but one more example of what they considered American cultural imperialism.

Exhibitions. A major exhibition on the American architect Louis Sullivan opened in Chicago in September before traveling to St. Louis and

Japanese architect Arata Isozaki's trademark use of solid geometric forms is apparent in the recently completed Los Angeles Museum of Contemporary Art.

other cities. A show on the work of contemporary architect Frank Gehry opened in Minneapolis in October. And the Museum of Modern Art brought to New York a major show on Viennese design at the turn of the century.

Expo 86. Expo 86, a summer-long extravaganza in Vancouver, British Columbia, restored for many their faith in world's fairs. Following two dismal failures in recent years in New Orleans and Knoxville, Tenn., the Vancouver fair combined fine design with substantive exhibitions typified by Highway 86, an environmental sculpture/park designed by New York's SITE Projects, Inc., and constructed of real vehicles—boats, motorcycles, skateboards, and trains—immobilized on a massive highway. Plans for the 1992 world's fair in Seville, Spain, designed by New York architect Emilio Ambasz, promised an even greater success in terms of landscape design.

Awards. West German architect Gottfried Böhm was the surprise selection for the 1986 Pritzker prize, the architectural equivalent of a Nobel Prize. Böhm's style has shifted dramatically over the course of his career, from expressionistic early works such as the Neviges Pilgrim's Church and Bensberg Town Hall (both 1964) to the stricter modernism of the 1986 Zublin Company headquarters, a concrete castle in the German countryside.

Canadian architect Arthur Erickson won the Gold Medal of the American Institute of Architects; the San Francisco firm Esherick, Homsey, Dodge and Davis received the AIA Firm of the Year Award. Arata Isozaki was awarded the Gold Medal of the Royal Institute of British Architects.   D.D.B.

ARGENTINA. Argentina embarked on the third year of its return to democracy with the government of President Raúl Alfonsín facing challenges on several fronts.

Military Crimes. The trials of former military leaders continued to occupy the country's attention. In May the military supreme council found three former junta members—Generals Leopoldo Galtieri, Basilio Lami Dozo, and Jorge Anaya—guilty of the military crime of negligence in Argentina's 1982 loss in the Falkland Islands war with Great Britain; they were sentenced to prison terms of 12, 14, and 8 years, respectively, and stripped of their rank. In April the government proposed using the principle of "due obedience" to decide whether or not 300 other officers should be tried for 1,700 human rights violations committed during the so-called dirty war against dissidents and terrorists. This would prohibit prosecution of subordinates for following orders unless they "knew the illegality of the orders or carried out atrocities or aberrations." The cases were later transferred to civilian tribunals. In December, five former police officials were convicted of human rights violations and sentenced to terms of up to 25 years. However, later in the month the Congress cleared a measure (still requiring presidential signature) that would bar further prosecution of officers for human rights abuses under the former regime. The action led to protests.

Unrest. Despite divisions within its ranks, the Peronist Party-led trade union movement was able to mount a number of strikes. In July the government bypassed the General Confederation of Labor to organize direct talks between specific unions and employers. Another divisive issue in Argentina was a proposed bill to allow divorce and remarriage. Demonstrations against the measure were held around the country with the encouragement of the Roman Catholic Church, and church officials asked bishops to deny communion to legislators supporting it. The bill was approved by the lower house of Congress, but the Senate deferred consideration until 1987.

Economic Developments. A year of economic restructuring under the Austral Plan—an anti-inflation program launched in June 1985 and named after the currency it introduced—produced mixed results. Unemployment reached 8 percent in May, double the level it had been when Alfonsín took office in late 1983. However, inflation was relatively low. The second phase of the Austral Plan, unveiled in April, included a shift to more flexibly administered price controls and wage increases, as well as a currency devaluation. (There were further devaluations later in the year.) Inflation for 1986 was 82 percent, a more than fourfold drop from 1985, and gross national product grew an estimated 5 percent, after a decline in 1985.

Joyous celebrations took place throughout Argentina when the country's soccer team, captained by Diego Maradona, won the coveted World Cup; here, ecstatic fans jam Government House in Buenos Aires.

Foreign Affairs. The dispute with Great Britain over the Falkland Islands continued. Four Argentine congressmen visited Britain in February; later, UN Secretary-General Javier Pérez de Cuéllar journeyed to London on an unsuccessful mediation attempt. In October, Britain announced establishment of a 150-mile fisheries conservation area around the Falklands, a move intended to halt overfishing in the area and serve as a warning to Argentine vessels. Subsequently, Britain rejected an Argentine offer to end hostilities as a step toward negotiations on sovereignty.

Relations with Brazil showed significant improvement. In July, Argentina and Brazil signed an extensive economic agreement, under which Brazil was to buy 1.375 million tons of Argentine wheat in 1987 and Argentina was to permit more Brazilian manufactures into its protected markets. In December, Alfonsín paid a three-day visit to Brazil, and he and Brazilian President José Sarney agreed to meet regularly.

Culture and Sports. Bright spots in Argentine life were provided by a continuing cultural renaissance of films, plays, dance, literature, and art, much of which would never have been permitted under military rule. *The Official Story*—a movie about a woman who comes to believe that her adopted daughter was the natural child of a young couple killed by a right-wing death squad during the dirty war—won the Academy Award for best foreign-language film. In sports the Argentine soccer team touched off euphoric celebrations by winning the prestigious World Cup championship in Mexico City in June.

Capital Transfer. In April, Alfonsín announced plans to move the country's capital to the twin towns of Viedma and Carmen de Patagones, more than 600 miles south of the current capital, Buenos Aires. The initiative was part of a "territorial reform" program aimed at fostering economic growth, mainly through high-tech industries. In developing the plan, expected to cost an estimated $3.75 billion, the government concluded that Patagonia—a little-populated region largely devoted to sheep farming and the extraction of oil and gas—was the country's "forgotten" frontier.

See STATISTICS OF THE WORLD.   J.F.,Jr.

ARIZONA. *See* STATISTICS OF THE WORLD.

ARKANSAS. *See* STATISTICS OF THE WORLD.

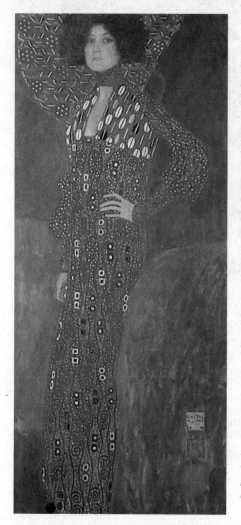

The emergence of modern art in turn-of-the-century Vienna went on display in New York during 1986. At left, Gustav Klimt's Portrait of Emilie Flöge (1902); above, Kolomon Moser's Frommes Kalender (1903).

ART. The general public will remember 1986 as the year a secret cache of paintings and drawings by Andrew Wyeth was suddenly revealed to the world. Of far greater import to art, however, were the large number of major single-artist retrospectives organized by museums across the United States and the absorption of recent contemporary art into the mainstream of museum exhibitions and corporate and private collections.

Major Exhibitions. While single-artist retrospectives dominated museum exhibition schedules, there were also several powerful survey shows. *Vienna 1900: Art, Architecture & Design* drew crowds all summer to the Museum of Modern Art (MOMA) in New York City. This was the first major U.S. survey of

Vienna's critical role in the birth of modernism. A stunning selection of paintings by Viennese artists permitted Americans to see important works rarely allowed out of Austria, but the decorative arts—the array of furniture, fabrics, glassware, silver, ceramics, jewelry, bookbinding, and posters—formed the essence of the show.

Two shows threw fresh light on the French Impressionists. *The New Painting: Impressionism 1874–1886,* organized by Charles Moffett of the Fine Arts Museums of San Francisco, was the first museum exhibition made up solely of paintings shown in the original eight Impressionist exhibitions held in Paris a century ago. *Impressionist to Early Modern Paintings From the U.S.S.R.* brought to the United States for the first time 41 masterpieces—including eight major South Seas subjects by Gauguin, Matisse's *Harmony in Red* and *Conversation,* and Picasso's *Three Women*—that are now housed in Leningrad's Hermitage Museum and the Pushkin Museum of Fine Arts in Moscow. The show, which opened at the National Gallery of Art in Washington, D.C., and traveled to Los Angeles and New York City, resulted from recently renewed cultural exchange agreements between the United States and the Soviet Union.

New York's Metropolitan Museum of Art presented *Treasures of the Holy Land: Ancient Art From the Israel Museum,* featuring 200 biblical antiquities dating from the 11th millennium B.C. to the end of the Byzantine period in the 7th century A.D. Among these rare and fragile artifacts were the matchless Dead Sea Scrolls.

Single-Artist Retrospectives. Among the most important retrospectives was *François Boucher,* jointly sponsored by the Metropolitan Museum of Art, the Detroit Institute of Arts, and France's Réunion des Musées Nationaux. The largest and most comprehensive exhibition ever devoted to this 18th-century master, it featured 86 paintings displaying the full range of Boucher's subjects, including pastoral scenes, mythologies, landscapes, and his grand portraits of Madame de Pompadour. *Diego Rivera: A Retrospective* was the first retrospective of the Mexican muralist's work to be seen in the United States and Europe. It marked two centennials: that of Rivera's birth and that of the Detroit Institute, home of Rivera's fresco series *Detroit Industry.*

Henri de Toulouse-Lautrec, at MOMA, eschewed the usual biographical look at this popular figure for a substantive, scholarly examination of the artist's technical achievements as a printmaker during the last decade of his life. Consisting of about 300 works, the exhibition illustrated the development of Lautrec's virtuoso printmaking, from spontaneously sketched motif and full-scale cartoon to lithographed image or completed poster.

The Baltimore Museum of Art organized the first major U.S. retrospective of Oskar Schlemmer, the German artist and Bauhaus teacher, composed of over 200 works in all media. The

Amon Carter Museum in Fort Worth, Texas, presented *Stuart Davis: Graphic Work and Related Paintings,* an exhibition of Davis's entire production of 26 lithographs and serigraphs with 17 related drawings and 9 oil paintings.

Two major modernists received much-needed attention. *James Rosenquist: Paintings 1961–1985,* organized by the Denver Art Museum, was the artist's first major retrospective in 15 years; it concentrated especially on Rosenquist's important contribution to the Pop Art movement. *Jasper Johns: A Retrospective,* at MOMA, covered 25 years of printmaking and included 165 of Johns's 350 prints. It displayed the artist's virtuosity with lithograph, etching, silk screen, and monotype techniques.

New York's Whitney Museum in October presented an extensive review of the oils and watercolors of John Singer Sargent that cast light on his draftsmanship and on the virtuosity with which he recorded late 19th-century European and American expatriate society.

Van Gogh in Saint-Rémy and Auvers, which opened in November at the Metropolitan, followed the artist's career from the spring of 1889, the end date of the Met's well-received 1984 Van Gogh exhibition, until his suicide in July 1890. The 89 paintings and drawings show the artist's continuing creativity in the midst of severe mental anguish.

Sculpture. The exhibition with the greatest impact consisted of just ten large-scale works created by Richard Serra since 1969 and installed at MOMA; it was the first U.S. retrospective of this controversial artist. Individual rooms were filled, dwarfed, and severed by large works of steel plates, pipes and poles, and blocks of stone and wood.

Two New York gallery shows of Anthony Caro's work revealed this sculptor moving simultaneously in vastly different directions. The André Emmerich Gallery displayed new examples of the large, abstract, welded steel works for which Caro is best known. Two months later the Aquavella Gallery offered a group of works depicting the human figure, smaller than life-size, modeled in clay and then cast in bronze.

Picasso's Sketchbooks. The Pace Gallery, in New York, sponsored one of the most important

Pierre-Auguste Renoir's vibrant Bal du Moulin de la Galette *(1876) was one of many paintings at a 1986 exhibit consisting of works first displayed at the trail-blazing Impressionist showings in Paris a century ago.*

historical shows of the year—*Je Suis le Cahier: The Sketchbooks of Picasso.* The noncommercial show consisted of 45 sketchbooks completed between 1900 and 1965, chosen from 175 that Picasso kept as working diaries throughout his career.

Contemporary Art. The art establishment embraced the Neoexpressionists, with major shows of Eric Fischl at the Whitney Museum of American Art in New York City, Enzo Cucchi at the Guggenheim, and David Salle at the Philadelphia Institute of Contemporary Art. All the works in these shows were recent and some were brand-new.

Wyeth's Secret Paintings. Wyeth's secret collection, disclosed by *Art & Antiques* magazine, consisted of 43 finished paintings, plus many preliminary sketches and watercolor studies, done between 1970 and 1985. All the pictures, many of them nudes, had a single subject—a woman identified at first only as Helga. Helga turned out to be Helga Testorf, who was the housekeeper of Wyeth's sister and who fled back to Germany rather than face the publicity. Speculation about a love affair dissipated as Wyeth's ascetic and habitually secretive methods of work became known. The works were sold to Leonard E. B. Andrews, a neighbor of Wyeth's, for an undisclosed sum said to be close to $10 million, and J. Carter Brown, director of the National Gallery of Art, agreed to exhibit the entire series in 1987.

Corporate Collections. Early in the year, the Equitable Life Assurance Society of the United States opened its much touted $200 million world headquarters in Manhattan. Not just a corporate headquarters, the Equitable Center and Art Complex was the largest example so far of the growing relationship between art and business. The street-level public spaces and

Hawke's mid-April tour of Europe and the United States, following a mission by Trade Minister John Dawkins, was overshadowed by the U.S. air raid on Libya, which took place only hours before his departure.

Hawke's main concern, however, was the potential effect of U.S. agricultural policies on Australian trade. Although President Ronald Reagan reassured Hawke that the United States would "be responsive to the extent we can to Australian interests," Australian farm concerns expressed indignation when it became known in July that the United States proposed to subsidize sales of wheat to the Soviet Union, a major Australian market, in order to aid American farmers. Both Treasurer Keating and Foreign Minister Bill Hayden suggested that the continued use of "joint facilities"—U.S. bases in Australia for satellite and submarine communications—might be reconsidered, but the threat was promptly countermanded by Prime Minister Hawke. (In the end the Soviets purchased almost no U.S. grain anyway.)

In August, Hayden and Defense Minister Kim Beazley met with their U.S. counterparts, Secretary of State George Shultz and Defense Secretary Caspar Weinberger, in San Francisco to review the Anzus military alliance involving Australia, New Zealand, and the United States. New Zealand was effectively excluded from the alliance by the United States, following the Lange government's refusal in 1985 to admit nuclear-powered or nuclear-armed U.S. vessels to its ports. In the postconference joint communiqué, both parties criticized New Zealand's stand.

Justice Murphy. Justice Lionel Murphy, on leave of absence from the High Court, was found not guilty of corruption charges in a retrial of his case concluded in April; he had previously been convicted on one of two counts in July 1985. New charges were raised, and a commission of three retired judges was formed in May 1986 to consider whether Murphy had been guilty of behavior that merited his removal from the bench, but soon afterward he became ill and the commission was dissolved. He died in October.

Australian Foreign Minister Bill Hayden speaks in San Francisco, preliminary to the annual Anzus talks. Behind him, from left, Australian Defense Minister Kim Beazley, U.S. Secretary of State George Shultz, and U.S. Defense Secretary Caspar Weinberger. New Zealand, for the second year, did not participate.

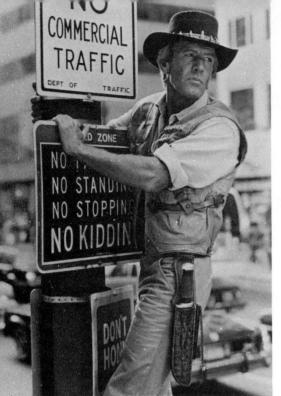

Australian actor Paul Hogan stars in "Crocodile" Dundee as a safari leader from the outback who pays a visit to New York City; the light-hearted comedy became Australia's top-grossing film ever.

State Politics. In June, New South Wales Premier Neville Wran destabilized the government by announcing his retirement. The dominant right-wing faction of the ALP selected state Health Minister Barrie Unsworth to replace him. Unsworth was subsequently sworn in; since he did not have a seat in the lower house as is traditional, he ran for a seat in a by-election, winning by a mere 57 votes.

In Queensland, Sir Johannes Bjelke-Petersen's National Party, damaged by scandals, benefited from redistricting; in November 1 elections the party won less than 40 percent of the popular vote but was thereby able to capture at least 46 of the 89 parliamentary seats.

In February elections, Brian Burke's Labor government was returned to power in Western Australia and Robin Gray's Liberal government emerged victorious in Tasmania. In the Northern Territory, the Country Liberal Party was shaken by a scandal involving Chief Minister

Ian Tuxworth, who was forced to resign; he was replaced by Steve Hatton.

Other Events. Proud possessor of the coveted America's Cup, Australia geared up nautically and commercially to defend the prize; elimination races to choose the Australian defender and the challenger extended from October 1986 through January 1987. In November, Pope John Paul paid a 6½-day visit to Australia, during which he crisscrossed the continent. Just before John Paul's arrival in Brisbane, a former mental patient carrying firebombs was arrested by police; he said he had intended to kill the pope.

See STATISTICS OF THE WORLD.   B.J.

AUSTRIA. A tumultuous political year in Austria began with dark shadows being cast over the World War II record of Kurt Waldheim (*see biography in* PEOPLE IN THE NEWS), a candidate for the presidency. Waldheim was elected despite charges of a Nazi-related past. Later in the year, the governing coalition, led by a new chancellor, broke apart, and parliamentary elections were held in late November, after which attempts to form a coalition began.

Waldheim, the former UN secretary-general, ran for the largely ceremonial post of president as candidate of the conservative opposition People's Party. He won a plurality in the first round of voting on May 4 and was elected in a runoff with Socialist Kurt Steyrer on June 8, despite mounting evidence that he had been less than candid in responding to charges of involvement in war crimes while a German army officer stationed in the Balkans from 1942 to 1945. Waldheim received 54 percent of the vote in the runoff, to Steyrer's 46 percent. Still, Waldheim had been wounded by the allegations and by his largely inadequate and even dissembling responses to them. A few days after the runoff, Foreign Minister Leopold Gratz resigned, saying he would not defend Waldheim abroad against public criticism. Israel recalled its ambassador to Vienna, while Greece and Yugoslavia, among other states, declined to tender official congratulations to the victor. President Ronald Reagan sent a message described as "correct," and the U.S. ambassador did not attend the inauguration.

The political situation became complicated when Chancellor Fred Sinowatz announced his resignation in June. The Socialists chose Franz Vranitzky to replace him. Then, in September, the Freedom Party elected rightist Jörg Haider as its new chairman. Declaring that the Freedom Party's "liberal element" had been "shoved into the background" by this action, Vranitzky ended the Socialists' coalition with that party and called a parliamentary election for November 23. In the vote, the Socialists won 80 of the 183 parliamentary seats, a decline of 10, and the People's Party won 77, a decline of 4. The environmentalist Greens (represented for the first time) took 8 seats, while the Freedom Party gained 6 new seats for a total of 18. Vranitzky began potentially lengthy negotiations in an effort to form a coalition with the People's Party.

The Austrian government rejected U.S. requests for economic sanctions against Libya, thought to have given support to the bloody December 27, 1985, terrorist attack at the Vienna airport. The two surviving terrorists, both apprehended, were to be tried for murder.

See STATISTICS OF THE WORLD.   J.O.S.

AUTOMOBILE INDUSTRY. Record sales, another rollback of federal fuel economy standards, Japanese plant expansion in North America, and a number of joint ventures highlighted the 1986 model year.

Sales. A record 16 million new cars and trucks were sold in the United States during the 1986 model year. The 11.2 million cars sold were exceeded only by the 11.7 million in 1973. Truck sales reached a record 4.9 million.

Domestic automakers sold 8.1 million cars during the model year, 3.9 percent off the 8.4 million sold in 1985. Imports accounted for 3.1 million cars, up 17 percent from the 1985 figure of 2.7 million. Imports captured a record 28 percent share of the market; the previous market-share record was 27.8 percent, set in 1982. General Motors sold 6.4 million cars and trucks in the model year, about the same number as in 1985. Ford's sales of 3.4 million vehicles represented a decrease of 1.7 percent, and Chrysler showed little change, with sales of 1.85 million. American Motors Corporation delivered 292,134 cars and trucks, off 2.6 percent. The No. 1 car was the Ford Escort. Korea's Hyundai Excel set a first-year sales record for an import.

Discount financing greatly boosted sales toward the close of the model year. Glutted with unsold vehicles, GM offered loans on all its 1986 cars and light trucks at 2.9 percent interest, the lowest rate in its history. Ford matched GM's figure, but Chrysler undercut them both with 2.4 percent financing, and AMC offered no-interest loans. Buyers were also offered rebates of up to $1,500.

Profits. The Big Three automakers reported healthy profits through the first nine months of 1986. GM reported profits of $2.31 billion, compared with $2.75 billion during the same period in 1985; Ford showed a $2.5 billion profit, up from $1.79 billion in the first three quarters of 1985; and Chrysler's profits were $1.08 billion, against $1.4 billion during the first nine months of 1985. In a rare event, Ford earned more money than GM in the second and third quarters.

GM Tremors. In November, GM said it would close 11 U.S. plants employing 29,000 people, more than 5 percent of its work force, in the "first phase" of a modernization and reorganization program. The next month, GM bought the shares of H. Ross Perot, its largest stockholder and one of its largest critics, for $700 million, twice its value when he acquired it. He left the board of directors and agreed to cease his criticism.

New Models. Chrysler introduced twin sporty subcompact hatchbacks, the Plymouth Sundance and the Dodge Shadow, giving the

---

Safety First, Wisecracks Second

A Massachusetts-based company called Safety First, Inc., recently came out with a novelty item for safety-conscious parents—bright yellow, diamond-shaped "Baby on Board" and "Child on Board" placards to be attached to a car's rear window and visible for 50 feet. The only trouble was that the relentless message began to irritate motorists. A few cynical entrepreneurs struck back with signs of their own, such as "Baby at the Wheel," "Mother-in-Law in Trunk," and "Child Carries No Cash." Companies on both sides of the battle of the placards were reportedly enjoying brisk sales.

company its first chance to compete with the Honda Accord. Ford's aerodynamically rounded Taurus was one of the major new-model successes of the year. General Motors launched the Cadillac Allante, a $50,000 personal two-seater designed by noted Italian coachbuilder Pininfarina.

Prices. Reflecting the strengthening of the yen against the dollar, Japanese cars rose in price an average of $1,331, or 14 percent, between the fall of 1985 and July 1986. During the same period, prices of U.S.-built cars rose an average of $726. Although U.S. buyers paid an average price of $12,355 for a new car in 1986, some models were available at bargain-basement rates. Cheapest of the lot was Yugoslavia's Yugo, at $3,990, followed by Korea's Hyundai Excel and Chevrolet's Chevette, both $4,995.

Fuel Economy. The U.S. Department of Transportation extended its 26 miles-per-gallon fuel economy standard for new cars through the 1988 model year. The original standard set for 1987 cars was 27.5 mpg, but this target was

The 1986 Ford Taurus, with its rounded edges and sporty shape, has boosted Ford Motor Company sales. Arch-rival General Motors is countering with its own aerodynamic car (bottom), which is still in the planning stages.

lowered to 26 mpg in 1985 after GM and Ford threatened to close their big-car factories and lay off thousands of workers. The state of California and five other plaintiffs filed suit in December to overturn the reduction. In another suit, a federal appeals court said in December that a 1985 change in the Environmental Protection Agency's methods of measuring fuel efficiency, which had brought Ford and GM higher ratings retrospectively for 1980–1984, had been in error; the ruling could cost the companies as much as $300 million.

Safety. As it marked the 20th anniversary of the passage of federal auto safety legislation, the Insurance Institute for Highway Safety reported that traffic fatalities had fallen from more than 53,000 in 1966 to fewer than 44,000 in 1985. Meanwhile, GM became the first U.S. automaker to install rear-seat shoulder safety belts as standard equipment on some 1987 models. And Ford became the first U.S. manufacturer to provide motorized self-fastening safety belts as standard equipment on some 1987 models; the belts wrap around front-seat passengers when the ignition is turned on.

Around the World. Every major Japanese automaker has now built or announced plans to build an assembly plant in the United States or Canada. Mazda, in cooperation with Ford, was currently building a plant in Flat Rock, Mich.; Mitsubishi, in conjunction with Chrysler, was building one in Bloomington, Ill.; Toyota was to begin assembling cars in Georgetown, Ky.; and Yamaha planned to manufacture community transportation vehicles near Atlanta.

Toyota was now producing its first U.S-built car, the Corolla, at the New United Motor Manufacturing (NUMMI) factory in Fremont, Calif., which is also the home of the Chevrolet Nova, the Corolla's American version. Honda began to manufacture engines in Anna, Ohio, marking the first time a Japanese carmaker has built a major component in the United States. Japan's Toyota and Honda, Korea's Hyundai, and a GM/Suzuki joint venture planned to build plants in Canada.

GM and Volvo White, a subsidiary of Sweden's Volvo, merged their heavy-truck operations to create America's second-largest truck manufacturer, the Volvo GM Heavy Truck Corporation, to be headquartered in Greensboro, N.C.

Chrysler sold its 12.5 percent ownership in France's Peugeot for $275 million to institutional investors both within and outside France. For about $3 billion a Libyan holding company sold the 14 percent ownership it had acquired in Fiat; Fiat itself put up $1.1 billion. In October, GM announced it would sell its subsidiary in South Africa to a group of investors headed by local GM managers but would continue to sell automotive components to it.

DeLorean. Automaker John Z. DeLorean went on trial in October on charges of defrauding investors in the DeLorean Research Limited Partnership of $8.9 million. He allegedly had the funds transferred from the company—which was working on a gull-winged, stainless-steel-bodied sports car—to his own bank account. DeLorean, who pleaded not guilty to a 15-count federal indictment, was acquitted in December.   D.L.L.

B

BAHAMAS. See STATISTICS OF THE WORLD.
BAHRAIN. See STATISTICS OF THE WORLD.
BANGLADESH. Parliamentary and presidential elections dominated the political scene in Bangladesh during 1986. Martial law was officially ended, but curbs remained.

On January 1 a new, progovernment political organization, the Jatiya (National) Party, was launched. Opposition parties responded with large rallies, and the main opposition party, the Awami League, joined with some smaller parties to form the National Awami League, headed by Sheikh Hasina Wazed, daughter of the late founder of Bangladesh, Sheikh Mujibur

Rahman. To combat growing restiveness, President H. M. Ershad in February named a tough "hawk," Mahmudal Hasan, to be home minister, in charge of law and order; soon thereafter, two former ministers of his regime joined the opposition.

On May 7 voters went to the polls for parliamentary elections. The final vote count gave the Jatiya Party 153 out of the 300 seats up for election. A nonpartisan delegation of observers from Great Britain reported widespread fraud, particularly by the Jatiya Party, and Wazed called a national protest strike, which paralyzed public activities for one day on May 14.

Ultimately, with 30 appointive seats for women, alliances with independents, and by-elections to fill contested seats, the progovernment forces came to hold more than 200 of the 330 total seats but fell short of the two-thirds majority needed to legitimize martial law enactments. Ershad announced a presidential election for October 15. Meanwhile, incidents of violence continued, and a security force was created to protect Ershad and other officials; members of the force were authorized to shoot to kill anyone avoiding arrest and were given immunity from prosecution.

Official tallies from the October election showed Ershad winning 90 percent of the vote against a total of 11 opponents. Most major opposition parties boycotted the election, however, and there were widespread reports of fraud. After the election, having won passage of a new law barring legal challenges to his regime, Ershad on November 10 declared an end to martial law and a restoration of the constitution suspended in 1982. However, the new law sparked an outbreak of violent protests. On November 30, Ershad reshuffled his cabinet, dismissing Hasan as home minister, removing five others, and appointing a vice president, Justice Minister A. K. M. Nurul Islam.

There was a major exodus of Buddhist Chakma refugees from the Chittagong Hill Tracts when Bangladesh army units drove tribal members out of their lands and in their place resettled Muslim peasants from the overcrowded delta plains. As Chakmas began crossing the border, New Delhi decided to install a barbed wire fence, along with checkpoints, causing resentment in Bangladesh. India and Bangladesh did, however, renew a major trade pact, and Prime Minister Rajiv Gandhi and President Ershad held cordial talks in July.

See STATISTICS OF THE WORLD.   R.I.C.

BANKING AND FINANCE. The stock market hit new highs in 1986, helped along by declining interest rates, but it also exhibited considerable volatility. An insider trading scandal shook the financial community. Internationally, the dollar fell against foreign currencies, but the U.S. trade deficit persisted. There were signs of greater economic cooperation among major industrial nations and greater flexibility on the part of the International Monetary Fund and the World Bank.

Stock Market Surge. During the first half of the year, the financial world took comfort in the strongest stock market rally in over a generation. The Dow Jones index of the stocks of 30 key industrial companies, which began the year at 1546.67, closed at 1909.03 on July 2. Analysts attributed the advance largely to the drop in interest rates. The strongest performers were the consumer-related stocks of tobacco, food, beverage, drug, and retailing companies, joined periodically by the stocks of banks and other interest-sensitive businesses. The market was also stimulated by companies that repurchased millions of shares from their stockholders. In the area of new stock issues, a record volume of nearly $9 billion was reached in the first half of the year. (The volume exceeded $9 billion in the second half.)

Falling Interest Rates. Money poured into the stock market largely in response to the dwindling return to investors on bonds and other interest-paying investments. The Federal Reserve Board eased monetary policy grudgingly during the year, caught between the periodic need to prod the stagnant economy and fears that the interest rate reductions necessary to help the economy would drag down the value of the dollar in relation to other currencies. With the economy in the doldrums, the Fed had to push to stimulate growth. In March an intense dispute over policy among the board's governors became embarrassingly public; word leaked out that Fed Chairman Paul A. Volcker had been in the minority when the board initially voted, 4-3, on February 24 to cut the discount rate, the rate the Fed charges on loans to financial institutions, from 7.5 percent down to 7 percent. This was the first time since 1978 that a Fed chairman had been outvoted on a question of monetary policy. But any doubts that Volcker remained in control were diminished later in March when Vice Chairman Preston Martin, who had been periodically at odds with Volcker over monetary policy, resigned from the board.

Any uncertainty over monetary policy did not keep interest rates from falling. The prime rate, used by banks as the benchmark for setting interest rates charged their customers, started the year at 9.5 percent; late in the year, it had declined to 7.5 percent. The rate on 30-year Treasury bonds dropped from 9.28 percent at the beginning of the year to less than 7.5 percent late in the year.

Vacillating Stock Prices. By July the markets were showing signs of investor nervousness. The Dow dropped by 61.87 points on July 7, the biggest point loss the Dow had up to that time sustained—though amounting only to a 3.25 percent loss in the average as a whole. The drop reflected fear that the decline in interest rates was bottoming out. The stock market decline continued for weeks until interest rates slipped further.

By September, the Fed had reduced the discount rate to 5.5 percent, its lowest level in nine years. A new rally returned the Dow to an even higher level of 1919.7 on September 4. On September 11, the market fell 86.6 points, a new record, and it plunged another 34.2 points the following day in record heavy trading. (The record was later exceeded, when 244.7 million shares were traded on December 19.) The market remained basically strong, however, with the Dow rising to about 1900 in early November, before it plunged again when an insider-trading scandal broke. The market recovered from the initial shock and then vacillated. After falling on December 1 out of nervousness over the Iranian arms sale scandal, the Dow staged its third best rally in history the next day, when it rose 43 points to close at a record 1955.7.

Insider Trading Scandal. On November 14 it was announced that Wall Street speculator

An exhausted trader registers a plea for help during the busiest day thus far in New York Stock Exchange history, September 12. The stock exchange lost a total of 121 points on that and the preceding day (the 86.61 point drop on the 11th was the largest ever), as share values dropped 6.5 percent; however, the market remained relatively strong.

Ivan F. Boesky had agreed to pay $100 million in a fine and a return of profits, and to plead guilty to one criminal charge of trading on inside information. He was also barred for life from the American securities business, after an 18-month phaseout period. The monetary penalty was the largest amount ever assessed by the SEC.

The Boesky agreement was a direct outgrowth of the SEC investigation of Dennis B. Levine, a 33-year-old investment banker who in June pleaded guilty to federal charges of earning $12.6 million by using inside information to trade illegally. To obtain tipoffs about upcoming corporate takeovers, Levine had secretly paid several young bankers and lawyers at prestigious Wall Street firms, most of whom subsequently pleaded guilty to stealing confidential information. Levine passed on the

information to Boesky and was to be paid a percentage of the speculator's profits; when Levine was indicted, he implicated Boesky. Boesky himself cooperated extensively with federal authorities, reportedly allowing his conversations with other senior investment industry figures to be electronically recorded.

The investigation widened, and several leading Wall Street professionals were served with federal subpoenas. On November 18 the Dow Jones average plunged 43 points under the impact of the scandal; hit especially hard were announced or rumored takeover stocks. In addition to the scandal's possible future effects on the stock market, the case gave rise to some concern over the fairness of the government's settlement with Boesky. The SEC disclosed in December that, while negotiating terms with the government, Boesky was allowed to pay off $1.4 billion of the more than $2 billion in debt carried by his principal investment fund, through the sale of stock and other transactions. SEC officials said their action helped to avoid a market panic.

Failures and Consolidations. Economic conditions, especially in agriculture and the oil industry, took a heavy toll on the banking

Korean electronics and automobile manufacturers took advantage of a currency based on the dollar to compete with higher priced Japanese goods for a share of the American consumer market. Above, Samsung advertises its wares on a busy New York City street. Below, the first shipment of low-priced Hyundai cars arrives in the United States.

system, which was plagued by loan losses; by midyear 62 banks had failed. Legislation permitting banks to operate interstate, passed in various states, stimulated new consolidation in the industry. In May, in California, Wells Fargo & Company purchased Crocker National Corporation from Midland Bank of London. Wells Fargo immediately fired 1,650 employees and planned to close 120 branches.

In November the Federal Reserve Board approved a $500 million investment by the Sumitomo Bank Ltd. of Japan in the Wall Street firm of Goldman, Sachs & Company. The deal marked the first time a giant foreign bank holding company had bought a large ownership stake in a major U.S. securities firm.

Troubled Giant. BankAmerica Corporation suffered further losses during the year. In February, Sanford I. Weill, former president of the American Express Company, offered to infuse $1 billion of new capital into the bank if its directors would elect him chief executive officer. The board turned down Weill's offer and kept on Samuel H. Armacost as chief executive until October, when he resigned and was replaced by A. W. Clausen. In July, BankAmerica had reported a $640 million loss in the second quarter, largely due to unpaid loans. However, in the third quarter the bank lost only $23 million. In October, First Interstate Bancorp of Los Angeles made a $3.4 billion takeover bid for BankAmerica; BankAmerica's board asked that the bid be withdrawn.

Falling Dollar. The United States and four major trading partners—Japan, West Germany, Great Britain, and France—kept up pressure on the dollar by selling dollars and buying yen or marks. In February, with the dollar at 181 yen and 2.4 marks, U.S. Treasury Secretary James A. Baker III said in congressional testimony that the U.S. government would not be displeased with a further decline. The dollar dropped. In March it fell to 174.3 yen, the fewest yen that could be purchased by a dollar since the inception of floating exchange rates in 1973. In May, the dollar hit 160.9 yen, after which it rallied, then fell. In late December the dollar was worth less than 160 yen and under 2 marks.

Trade Imbalances. For much of the year, the U.S. trade deficit continued to grow, even

Arbitrager Ivan Boesky was fined $100 million and faced permanent banishment from stock trading for his role in an insider-trading scandal which shook the U.S. investment community.

though many imports were more expensive because of the weaker dollar. The deficit with Japan amounted to nearly $50 billion in 1985, and most economists estimated it would be even higher in 1986. One problem was that Japanese products were deeply embedded in the U.S. market, making them relatively impervious to the effects of higher prices. Furthermore, the changes in exchange rates had an uneven impact. The rise in the yen turned out to be a boon for South Korea and Taiwan. Since their currencies were based on the value of the dollar, the drop in the dollar did not make their products more expensive in the

Convenient credit has turned into "the great credit card rip-off," according to Representative Charles Schumer (D, N.Y.). Banks are making huge profits by continuing to charge high interest rates on the cards despite a significant drop in most other interest rates.

United States; instead, it gave them a competitive advantage against Japan.

In Great Britain, meanwhile, the pound dropped 6.8 percent against a basket of currencies in the first eight months of the year. Faced with the likelihood of an international payments deficit, the British government borrowed $4 billion in September to bolster its reserves backing the pound. In mid-October, Britain's four major commercial banks raised their base lending rates from 10 percent to 11 percent in an effort to support the pound on world money markets.

In September the U.S. Commerce Department reported that the nation's trade deficit in August had fallen to $13.3 billion, a record drop of $4.7 billion from July's $18 billion deficit. Many analysts dismissed the drop as insignificant, arguing that the extraordinarily high July trade gap, itself a record, had been an aberration. The trade deficit narrowed further in September and October but widened again in November.

Earlier in the year, the trade deficit had prompted new calls to either erect or remove trade barriers. The United States and the European Community were on the verge of a trade war over farm products when they reached a truce in July. With an election coming in November, protectionist sentiment in the U.S. Congress was strong. In this volatile atmosphere, representatives from 74 nations met in Uruguay in September to launch a major new round of trade talks under the auspices of the General Agreement on Tariffs and Trade.

Coordinated Policy. The falling dollar and increasing trade tensions prompted efforts to seek a fundamental reassessment of international economic policy. The reform mentioned most prominently was one toward closer coordination of economic policies among various nations to foster a more stable environment for investment and trade. Just such a proposal was the main item on the agenda at the economic summit meeting held in Tokyo in May, attended by U.S. President Ronald Reagan and leaders of other major Western countries and Japan. The countries established themselves as a Group of Seven with plans to monitor and coordinate economic performance. Before the summit, in March, central banks of the United States, West Germany, and Japan had already cooperated to lower the interest rates they charged commercial banks. In April the United States and Japan cut their discount rates further.

When the Federal Reserve made additional cuts in its discount rate during the summer, Japan and West Germany rejected U.S. appeals for comparable reductions, fearing that new interest rate cuts might weaken their economies. In September the finance ministers of the Group of Seven sought unsuccessfully to resolve their disputes over interest rates and the dollar. However, in late October the United States and Japan announced a wide-ranging economic cooperation agreement; among other actions, the United States agreed to drop efforts to drive down the dollar against the yen, and Japan agreed to lower its interest rates.

Developing Countries. The World Bank estimated that external debts of the developing nations would reach $1.01 trillion by the end of 1986. For some of these nations, such as Brazil, the lower interest rates available in 1986 helped produce dramatic results. The Brazilian economy boomed, and its trade position improved for much of the year, leaving it in a relatively good position for debt negotiations. For oil-exporting nations the impact of falling oil prices overcame the benefit of falling interest rates. Mexico, which was expected to suffer a decline of 4 percent in its economic output on the year, was forced to seek new loans and a restructuring of old loans. In July, Mexico came to terms with the IMF, clearing the way for an agreement that required less stringent belt-tightening than usual. A sign of the IMF's new flexibility was a contingency fund that Mexico could draw on if oil prices fell below $9 a barrel in the first nine months. The final agreement also included an extra $1.7 billion in loans to be disbursed if Mexico's economic performance should falter.

The World Bank also showed signs of a new flexibility. Barber B. Conable, Jr., who became president of the bank on July 1, said the bank would make fewer loans for specific development projects and more to help countries adjust to world economic conditions. Conable predicted that the bank's loan commitments in the fiscal year ending June 30, 1987, would exceed those of the preceding fiscal year by more than $2 billion.

In March the IMF gave final approval to establishment of a $3 billion loan pool, called the Structural Adjustment Facility, to be available to 60 of the world's poorest countries. The program was to be jointly administered with the World Bank, with interest payments set at just 0.5 percent. Most of the funds were to be earmarked for sub-Saharan African countries.   G.D.W.

BARBADOS. *See* STATISTICS OF THE WORLD. *See also* CARIBBEAN BASIN.

BEHAVIORAL SCIENCES. The findings of some behavioral studies reported in 1986 had implications for the treatment of depression and for the understanding of mental skills.

Treatments for Depression. Preliminary findings released in May from an extensive study of depressed patients indicated that two forms of psychotherapy ease symptoms of depression as well as a commonly prescribed antidepressant drug and better than an inactive placebo pill.

A research team from the National Institute of Mental Health, headed by psychologist Irene Elkin, recruited 250 moderately-to-severely depressed patients who were treated at one of three major university medical centers. The subjects were divided into four groups, with most undergoing a form of "talk" therapy—either cognitive behavior therapy or interpersonal therapy. The talk-therapy patients were treated in weekly one-hour sessions for 12–16 weeks. The other subjects received drug or placebo treatments, dispensed weekly by psychiatrists who also provided about a half hour of support and encouragement per week.

The symptoms of more than half of all patients in the talk-therapy and drug groups were eliminated after 16 weeks, compared with 29 percent of the placebo group. The least depressed patients in the sample did surprisingly well in the placebo group, according to Elkin; severely depressed patients, on the other hand, did not respond well to placebos.

According to depression researcher David J. Kuffer of the University of Pittsburgh, further studies should concentrate on the effectiveness of combination of talk therapy and antidepressant drugs, now being touted as superior to either treatment alone. Other authorities cautioned that these were preliminary findings and that antidepressant drugs were still generally accepted as the most efficacious treatment for severe or persistent depression.

Mental Skills in the Elderly. It is often assumed that loss of ability to think and reason is an inevitable component of aging. But psychologists at Pennsylvania State University now say that with supervised training, the decline of two key elements of intellectual function among some elderly persons can be avoided or reversed. The same training, according to the researchers, can even boost the performance of many older adults whose intellectual capacities have not been diminished.

The researchers, K. Warner Schaie and Sherry L. Willis, tested 229 volunteers in 1970 and again in 1984. They ranged in age from 64 to 95 years by the end of the study. Both times, the volunteers were given tests to measure their inductive reasoning and spatial orientation. By 1984, the capacities of more than half the volunteers had declined significantly on one or both measures. After the second testing, all of the volunteers attended five-hour training sessions in either inductive reasoning or spatial orientation. More than 60 percent of the subjects whose scores had declined since 1970 achieved significantly higher scores after training. Interestingly, more than half the subjects whose scores had not changed between 1970 and 1984 also showed marked improvement. According to the researchers, many older adults suffer similar declines simply because they do not use reasoning and spatial abilities as much as they once did.

High Blood Pressure and Communication. Over the past several years, researchers at the University of Maryland School of Medicine have noted that blood pressure levels and heartbeat rates of many people rise merely when they speak to someone else. A wide variety of people are affected, but the rises are steepest for those with hypertension, particularly those taking antihypertensive medication. The researchers, led by psychiatrist Kenneth L. Malinow and psychologist James J. Lynch, have found that the most important determinant of how high their pressure rises is their blood pressure rate when they are at rest and not speaking. Effective treatment for hypertension may require more than drugs, according to Lynch. He and his coworkers teach deep breathing techniques, attempt to slow patients' often rapid speech, and deal with their frustrations in seeking to communicate well.

The researchers now say that deaf people show similar jumps when they use sign language. In one study the scientists recruited 38 deaf volunteers and monitored their blood pressure and heart rates for seven minutes. The volunteers relaxed during the first three minutes, then communicated with a hearing interpreter fluent in sign language for the next two minutes, then relaxed again for the last two minutes. The blood pressure and heart rates of all the test subjects increased significantly while they were signing.

Left-Brain Language. The traditional notion of a split brain in which the left hemisphere controls spoken language while the right hem-isphere regulates visual and spatial skills was being revised as a result of recent studies. Antonio Damasio of the University of Iowa College of Medicine and his coworkers found that the ability to use and understand sign language, which depends on hand movements and spatial judgments and has been considered a right hemisphere function by many researchers, is actually rooted in the left hemisphere. Thus, the left side of the brain is apparently used to comprehend both spoken and signed language.

This finding agrees with several recent studies of deaf individuals fluent in sign language who suffered brain damage following a stroke. Those with left hemisphere lesions had significant problems signing; lesions to the right hemisphere caused difficulty with several spatial skills but did not affect the ability to sign. Damasio noted that sign language might be learned in the right hemisphere, but the left hemisphere apparently controls the use and understanding of signs once they are learned.

B.B.

BELGIUM. In 1986 the four-party coalition government of Prime Minister Wilfried Martens was confronted by a major ethnic dispute as well as by opposition to its economic program.

The newest ethnic crisis arose after the militant French-speaking mayor of Fourons, in Dutch-speaking Flanders, refused to follow a court order to vacate his office because he did not speak Dutch at official functions. He argued that his constituents, though on the Dutch side of the linguistic border, were mostly French-speaking. With the government divided on how to resolve this crisis, Martens submitted his resignation to the king in October, but the king declined to accept it. When Parliament decided not to put the issue to a vote of confidence, the government gained more time to seek a resolution of the dispute.

Labor unrest broke out in the spring in protest against the government's announced plans to decrease health insurance and unemployment benefits and cut public sector jobs. Strikes briefly disrupted rail and postal services. Also, the Roman Catholic educational establishment, joined by left-wing militants, staged a march in Brussels in June to protest plans to reduce the education budget, and coal miners went on strike for two weeks to protest possible closing of mines (the government agreed to keep them open).

Belgium's gross domestic product was expected to grow 2 percent in 1986, a slight increase over the previous year. Industrial production was forecast to rise by nearly 3 percent and exports by 4 percent. Consumer prices were projected to remain fairly stable, mainly because of falling gas and oil prices during much of the year. Unemployment was forecast to remain at 13 percent, close to the 1985 level.

Police arrested and later charged three suspects believed connected with the notorious "Brabant Killers," who had launched a series of apparently motiveless attacks on Belgian supermarkets in which 16 people were killed. A fourth suspect, an ex-policeman, was also being held. An apparently unrelated radical leftist group called the Fighting Communist Cells, which claimed responsibility for more than 20 bomb attacks in 1984 and 1985, claimed authorship of an August bombing of a Socialist Trade Union Building in Antwerp. Four of its members were already in custody at the time.

See STATISTICS OF THE WORLD.   W.C.C.

BELIZE. See STATISTICS OF THE WORLD.

BENIN. See STATISTICS OF THE WORLD.

BHUTAN. See STATISTICS OF THE WORLD.

BLACKS IN THE UNITED STATES. The November 1986 elections brought mixed results for blacks. Also during 1986, the NAACP moved its headquarters, and the federal holiday honoring slain civil rights leader Martin Luther King, Jr., was observed for the first time.

Election 86. In November congressional elections, blacks expanded their ranks in the U.S. House of Representatives from 20 to 22, a record. Among the winners were Mike Espy (D), who became the first black since Reconstruction to be elected to the House from Mississippi, and John Lewis (D), who won in Georgia after having pulled off a stunning upset of state senator and civil rights leader Julian Bond in the Democratic primary runoff. Black gubernatorial candidates fared less well. Los Angeles Mayor Tom Bradley (D), seeking the governor's seat in California, was beaten soundly by the incumbent, George Deukmejian (R). In Michigan, Republican William Lucas was beaten by a resounding 2-1 margin by popular Democratic incumbent James J. Blanchard. Lucas, a Democrat until a year before the election, was one of the few GOP gubernatorial candidates for whom President Ronald Reagan campaigned.

NAACP. In October the National Association for the Advancement of Colored People offi-

Edward Perkins is sworn in as the first black U.S. ambassador to South Africa; at right is Secretary of State George Shultz.

The New York City Opera was host in October to the world premiere of X (The Life and Times of Malcolm X), *an operatic biography of the controversial black leader. Ben Holt, pictured here, sung the leading role.*

cially opened its new national headquarters in Baltimore. Among guests honored at the ceremonies were Rosa Parks, who precipitated the 1955 Montgomery, Ala., bus boycott, and the Reverend Ralph Abernathy, who with Martin Luther King, Jr., founded the Southern Christian Leadership Conference in 1957. NAACP offices had been located in New York City, in rented space, since the organization's founding in 1909. Some members had strongly opposed the move to Baltimore, saying it underscored a decline in the group's prominence. Black leaders associated with the NAACP stressed that the organization was moving in a new direction, placing greater emphasis on economic development for minority communities. During 1986 the NAACP Economic Development Corporation was formed as a nonprofit subsidiary for this purpose.

Court Decisions. In *Batson* v. *Kentucky,* the Supreme Court ruled that blacks could not be excluded from juries out of concern that they would be more likely to favor a defendant of their own race. The case involved the use of peremptory challenges, those in which lawyers can reject a prospective juror without explanation. The defendant claimed he had been denied his Sixth Amendment right to a fair and impartial jury when the prosecutor used peremptory challenges to remove other blacks from potentially serving as trial jurors. A 7-2 Court majority held that attorneys must explain peremptory jury challenges when these appear to be motivated by racial considerations alone. The decision, which reversed a ruling by Kentucky's highest court, was called a major victory for blacks, civil libertarians, and defense lawyers.

For other Supreme Court decisions affecting blacks, see CIVIL LIBERTIES AND CIVIL RIGHTS *and* UNITED STATES: Supreme Court.

Troubling Statistics. Statistics continued to paint a generally bleak picture of blacks' economic status in the United States. Unemployment for blacks remained very high, at around 14 percent, double the rate for whites. In July the Census Bureau released a study showing that white households on the average owned 11 times more assets—such as housing, automobiles, stocks, and savings—as black households. The study also indicated that Hispanics were accumulating assets faster than blacks were. Black leaders, including Benjamin L. Hooks, executive director of the NAACP, criticized the Reagan administration for allowing strong white-black economic disparities to persist. However, there were indications of black economic progress in a study by the United States Commission on Civil Rights, released in September. It concluded that in 1980 the average earnings of black men were 69 percent of those of white men, up from 42 percent four decades earlier.

King Holiday. January 20 marked the first observance of the federal holiday in honor of slain civil rights leader Martin Luther King, Jr. All federal government offices were closed, as were many state and local government offices and schools, but most businesses remained open. On January 16, a bust of King was placed in the Capitol Rotunda in Washington, D.C.; he was the first black to be so honored.

South Africa. King's widow, Coretta Scott King, sparked controversy during her September visit to South Africa for the installation of Desmond Tutu as archbishop of Cape Town. She met with Winnie Mandela, wife of imprisoned African National Congress leader Nelson Mandela, and with the Reverend Allan Boesak, president of the World Alliance of Reformed Churches, two of the country's most prominent black activists, but only after having canceled scheduled meetings with South African President Pieter W. Botha and with KwaZulu leader Chief Gatsha Buthelezi, whom many blacks consider too cooperative with the white-minority regime. Mandela and Boesak had said they would not see King if she went ahead with the meetings.

In November, Edward J. Perkins, a veteran black diplomat, was sworn in as U.S. ambassador to South Africa. Earlier, the Reagan administration had selected other black nominees, who declined for various reasons.

M.Gr. & R.A.

BOLIVIA. In an attempt to bring new life to his economic stabilization plan, President Victor Paz Estenssoro shuffled his cabinet at the end of January 1986, placing business leaders in key ministries. Paz Estenssoro also invited the Nationalist Democratic Action party (ADN), the strongest opposition group, with which he had previously formed an alliance, to join the restructured cabinet, but the ADN declined.

Austerity measures introduced under the plan reduced the annual inflation rate to less than 50 percent by early in the year, from a level estimated at more than 8,000 percent a year earlier. Implementation of the plan removed a major obstacle to further credit from the International Monetary Fund, and a $3.5 billion standby loan was received from the IMF in late August. Meanwhile, negotiations with governmental creditors produced a debt rescheduling agreement in June.

In August seven mines operated by Comibol, the state mining company, were ordered closed and several others ordered leased to miners' cooperatives, to help offset heavy losses from low world prices for tin. The action provoked 20,000 Comibol miners to stage a two-day strike; several thousand of them marched on La Paz, where the government declared a 90-day state of siege, saying the march had been infiltrated by extreme leftists. Miners were subsequently trucked to their homes, and over 150 opponents of the regime were detained.

In April former President Luis García Meza and about 30 others involved in a 1980 coup that overthrew the elected government went on trial on a variety of charges, ranging from misuse of public funds to murder and genocide.

Some 250 U.S. troops arrived in Bolivia at the end of April to conduct war games with 1,000 Bolivian troops in coca-growing areas around Cochabamba. The presence of U.S. troops was opposed by local farmers, as well as by drug traffickers, who reap nearly $600 million a year in illegal coca sales abroad. An antidrug operation was launched with the assistance of U.S. forces who arrived in Santa Cruz on July 14. The four U.S. cargo planes carried about 160 U.S. army personnel and six transport helicopters, along with auxiliary equipment necessary for search-and-destroy missions against hundreds of cocaine-produc-

A U.S. Army Black Hawk helicopter, one of six brought in as part of a controversial joint U.S.-Bolivian military operation to fight the cocaine trade in Bolivia, sits at a base camp.

ing jungle laboratories. While Bolivian police raided the laboratories, the U.S. troops provided support. After 60 days, the Bolivian government asked the United States to extend the tour of the soldiers. The last U.S. troops left in mid-November, but the Bolivian operation was continuing on its own.

See STATISTICS OF THE WORLD.   L.L.P.

BOTSWANA. See STATISTICS OF THE WORLD.

BRAZIL. Brazil's new civilian president, José Sarney, took bold measures early and late in 1986 to deal with the nation's economic problems.

The Cruzado Plan. On February 28, responding to record inflation rates, President Sarney announced a set of sweeping economic measures that came to be called the Cruzado Plan. The cruzeiro was replaced by a new currency, the cruzado, at 1,000 old cruzeiros for one cruzado, with the cruzado initially set at 13.8 to the U.S. dollar. Taxes and prices of goods and services were frozen indefinitely; rents and mortgage payments were frozen for a year. Brazil's complex 20-year-old system of automatically indexing wages to the inflation rate was ended. The government also introduced unemployment insurance for workers out of a job for more than one month and increased the minimum wage. Sarney warned that businesses violating the price freeze would be closed down, and he invited the country's 135 million people to act as monitors.

Sarney's bold economic measures and his accompanying appeal to fellow Brazilians to make sacrifices in a "life or death struggle against inflation" appeared to work. The inflation rate fell precipitously early in the year. The economy was expanding very rapidly, with the growth rate projected at 10–11 percent for the year as a whole.

Elections and Cruzado Plan II. As November congressional and gubernatorial elections approached, however, it was felt that, despite the Cruzado Plan's successes, the economy would have to be cooled. Growing consumption was attracting imports and cutting sharply into the trade surplus Brazil counted on to reduce the foreign debt. There were fears that the country's industries could not keep up with demand.

On November 15, Sarney's party swept to victory in all 23 state gubernatorial elections and in both houses of Congress. The landslide was regarded as a strong popular endorsement of the government's economic program. Six days later, however, major changes in the economic plan were unveiled; prices were raised on many products and taxes increased, in order to slow consumption. The new policies, informally dubbed the Cruzado Plan II, brought violent demonstrations by workers and students. However, a general strike called on December 12 achieved only limited success. The country's powerful finance minister, Dilson Funaro, submitted his resignation, but it was rejected. The government insisted that poorer Brazilians would be protected by a broad price freeze until inflationary pressures eased.

Later, the government was relieved when public-sector creditors agreed to renegotiate Brazil's debt without demanding agreement from the International Monetary Fund. Efforts to reschedule the debt to commercial banks were planned.

Drought. As a consequence of drought-reduced agricultural production, Agriculture Minister Pedro Simon announced in February that Brazil would need to import over 3 million tons of corn, about 1 millon tons of rice, and 20,000 tons of beans. It was predicted that the 1986–1987 coffee harvest might fall to 11 million 132-pound bags, about one-third the number produced in 1983–1984.

Agrarian Reform. The land reform program continued to be a focus of violence and controversy. Budgetary constraints and opposition from landowners led to goals being radically revised; only 4.2 million acres were to be distributed in 1986, to some 45,000 landless peasants in seven states.The land reform plan, as enacted in October 1985, envisioned the redistribution of 106.5 million acres over a four-year period. In late June, hundreds of peasants from the central state of Goías camped out on the lawn of the presidential palace in Brasília in an unsuccessful effort to meet with Sarney, while 250 other peasants in Rio Grande do Sul walked nearly 300 miles and occupied the Legislative Assembly in Porto Alegre.

Opposition from other government agencies, as well as from landowners, led to the resignation in June of Nélson Ribeiro as minister of agrarian reform and development. He was replaced by Dante de Oliveira, a former army colonel and leftist deputy.

Foreign Affairs. Foreign Minister Roberto de Abreu Sodré and his Cuban counterpart, Isidoro Malmierca, announced on June 25 that their two governments had reestablished relations. On July 29 in Buenos Aires, President Sarney signed economic accords with Argentina's President Raúl Alfonsín that laid the foundation for possible greater regional political and economic integration. In September, Sarney met with President Ronald Reagan and addressed a joint session of Congress, during a three-day visit to the United States.

Priestess Dies. On August 13, Mother Meninha, high priestess in the Afro-Brazilian cult of spiritism known as Candomblé, died in Salvador at the age of 92. The city's mayor declared three days of official mourning, and tens of thousands lined the streets during the funeral procession for the prestigious cult leader, whose real name was Maria Escolástica de Conçeicão Nazaré.

See STATISTICS OF THE WORLD.   N.J.P.

BRITISH COLUMBIA. *See* STATISTICS OF THE WORLD. *See also* CANADA.

BRUNEI. *See* STATISTICS OF THE WORLD.

BULGARIA. Party and state chief Todor Zhivkov, who turned 75 in September 1986, continued to play a key role in Bulgarian politics. The National Assembly, on January 27, approved the establishment of three new bodies—an Economic Council, a Social Council, and a Council for Science, Culture, and Education—to oversee the relevant ministries. This reorganization illustrated Zhivkov's policy of repeatedly amending the structures of government, often in an effort to remedy cited failures in the economic system.

At a March plenum of the Bulgarian Communist Party in Sofia, Georgi Atanasov was appointed prime minister and promoted to full membership in the Politburo. Grisha Filipov, whom Atanasov replaced as prime minister, retained membership in the Politburo and was made a secretary of the Central Committee. Overall responsibility for the economy was given to Ognyan Doinov, a deputy prime minister and chairman of the powerful new Economic Council. At the same time, Zhivkov was singled out for extravagant praise. At the subsequent party congress in April, he was reelected secretary-general of the party; upon his reelection, he received a warm message of congratulations from Soviet leader Mikhail Gorbachev.

Bulgaria's economic performance declined in 1985 and prospects for 1986 did not appear better. The regime continued to divert attention from the economy by encouraging Bulgarian chauvinism, especially against Turkish and Macedonian minorities. In February, Bulgarian news media accused the Turkish government of "pan-Turkish designs on Bulgarian territory" and reaffirmed Bulgaria's intention "to obliterate the remnants of Ottoman rule."

Among social reforms, the use of alcohol was prohibited in government ministries, public enterprises, and other places of work, and the omission of alcohol at weddings and funerals was strongly recommended. Also, rules were issued forbidding discotheques to play American, Western European, Greek, Yugoslav, or Gypsy music. Only music from Bulgaria and other "socialist" countries was to be allowed.

See STATISTICS OF THE WORLD.   R.A.P.

BURKINA FASO. See STATISTICS OF THE WORLD: *Upper Volta.*

BURMA. Military strongman Ne Win, in his mid-70's and seemingly in improving health, dominated Burmese politics in 1986 as much as ever since coming to power in 1962. His supposed designated successor, President San Yu, on the other hand, appeared in poor health,

and other figures were being named as more likely prospects to succeed Ne Win.

Burma continued to be plagued by various insurrections. During the year, Communist leaders met with representatives of nine different insurgent groups, offering to share power with them in exchange for cooperation. The regime took such potential cooperation seriously and stepped up military activity against rebels.

The Burmese government, with U.S. assistance and a controversial U.S.-supplied herbicide, undertook a spraying program in an effort to destroy the opium crop in the northeastern Shan states—part of the so-called Golden Triangle, which is the world's largest opium-producing area. Shan rebels, who have used trade in opium and sometimes heroin to help finance their rebellion, accused the government of genocide. Officials acknowledged that they had used 2,4-D, a herbicide that has raised questions as to a possible risk of increased cancers.

Burma's economy worsened during the year; exports were down, imports were cut back, the external debt remained high, and inflation was up. Rice, despite increased production, lagged behind teak and hardwood among the country's leading exports.

See STATISTICS OF THE WORLD.   R.L.B.

BURUNDI. See STATISTICS OF THE WORLD.

C

CABINET, UNITED STATES. See UNITED STATES OF AMERICA: *The Presidency.*

CALIFORNIA. See STATISTICS OF THE WORLD.

CAMBODIA. In 1986, as economic progress slowed down, the guerrilla war between the Vietnamese-backed Phnom Penh regime, led by Heng Samrin, and its Cambodian foes escalated, and a major government shuffle was announced.

The resistance forces, made up of the Communist Khmer Rouge and its two non-Communist allies, stepped up attacks deep inside Cambodia during the first four months of the year. In February they attacked the southeast-

ern provinces of Prey Veng and Svay Rieng, both previously considered safe areas. Battalion-size units swept through Prey Veng, hitting villages and military installations. In an attempt to strengthen the army, the government stepped up its recruitment of men 18 to 45 years old and extended military service from three to five years.

The leadership rift within one of the non-Communist resistance groups, the Khmer People's National Liberation Front, grew wider in January. Opponents of the leader of the Front, Son Sann, accused him of meddling in military affairs and refusing to allow any cooperation with the other non-Communist faction, headed by Prince Norodom Sihanouk, who leads the Cambodian government-in-exile in Peking. The United States induced the Front to settle the dispute and, together with China and the Association of Southeast Asian Nations, put pressure on the three resistance groups to carry out joint operations. In March the three groups mounted a cooperative large-scale attack on Vietnamese military facilities, food warehouses, and a Soviet-staffed hospital.

In February the National Assembly postponed new elections until 1991, by which time the Vietnamese proposed to have their troops withdrawn from the country. In December the ministers of defense and planning were removed from their posts, and Prime Minister Hun Sen lost his positions as foreign minister and head of a party foreign affairs commission.

The government appealed to the international community in July for massive donations of rice to meet an anticipated food shortage. A drought in several provinces was said to be ravaging the current rice crop. The government also amended the constitution to allow small-scale private enterprise.

See STATISTICS OF THE WORLD.   L.G.H.

CAMEROON. See STATISTICS OF THE WORLD. See also EARTH SCIENCES: Geology.

CANADA. In 1986 the most prominent issue on the national agenda in Canada was the controversial question of opening free-trade negotiations with the United States. The Progressive Conservative administration of Prime Minister Brian Mulroney (see biography in PEOPLE IN THE NEWS) struggled through midterm difficulties and tried to restore its popular appeal. It presented its second budget, along with other key elements of its legislative program, and coped with the foreign policy challenge of South Africa. Regional political developments were highlighted by four province-wide elections.

Free Trade. Preliminary talks between Canada and the United States over the issue of free trade began in May, with a meeting in Ottawa between Canadian negotiator Simon Reisman and his U.S. counterpart, Peter Murphy. By fall, substantive bargaining had begun.

In principle, a free-trade treaty appealed to the free-market instincts of both Mulroney and President Ronald Reagan. It was easy, as well, for each to see their common interests in a free-trade deal. The Reagan administration understood that Canada was the largest single U.S. trading partner—a rich market and an important source of raw materials. The Mulroney government saw that fully three-fourths of all Canadian exports flowed to the United States, leaving Canada especially vulnerable to the protectionist tides that repeatedly rise in Congress.

Even as Reisman and Murphy were meeting in Ottawa, however, the U.S. administration

The Canadian cedar shingles industry, which depends on exports to the United States, was hard hit by an unexpected U.S. tariff (later changed to an export tax). The move posed problems for the negotiations on free trade that were just then beginning in Ottawa.

inauspiciously slapped a 35 percent tariff on Canadian red cedar shakes and shingles. Canada retaliated by imposing new tariffs on books, computer parts, and such miscellaneous goods as Christmas trees and rolled oats. Bad as the tariff on shingles appeared to Canadians, there was a worse peril on the horizon. The U.S. International Trade Commission held hearings on U.S. industry complaints against imports of Canadian softwood lumber, valued at more than $3 billion annually (Canadian dollars used here and throughout). U.S. producers argued that low Canadian stumpage fees paid by timber companies to Canadian governments amounted to an export subsidy; Canada denied the allegation. The ITC made a preliminary determination that the U.S. industry had suffered injury, and the U.S. Commerce Department made a preliminary determination that the injury had been caused by an unfair export subsidy. In October the Reagan administration imposed a 15 percent import duty (also preliminary) on Canadian softwood lumber. The following month, the Canadian federal government countered by imposing a duty on imports of U.S. corn that amounted to more than 70 percent of the current price. Under a controversial settlement reached in December, the U.S. lumber tariff was replaced with a 15 percent Canadian export tax.

During a visit to Canada in June, U.S. Vice President George Bush said ongoing trade disputes had "demonstrated further the need for a comprehensive trade agreement." Not everyone agreed. Reagan won consent for the negotiations from the Senate Finance Committee only after intense lobbying, and only by a tie vote. In Canada, labor leaders and many others worried that abolishing import barriers would cost thousands of Canadian jobs and cause Canada to be overwhelmed by the powerful U.S. economy.

Domestic opposition to the Mulroney free-trade policy led the government to adopt an agreement with the provincial premiers providing for continuing federal-provincial consultation as negotiations proceeded. And Mulroney vowed, in his first national television address since taking office in 1984, that there would be no trade treaty that did not serve Canadian interests.

Legislative Program. In Parliament, meanwhile, the government was assembling its legislative program and trying to cope with a decline in support as measured by public opinion polls. Among important bills passed before summer recess were: a controversial law making it easier for police to win soliciting convictions against prostitutes, a Competition Act with new antitrust provisions and other rules for corporations, a measure compensating depositors in two failed Alberta banks, and the final dismantling of the previous Liberal government's National Energy Program. The government also introduced a bill to promote competition in the transportation industry and Patent Act amendments restoring market protections for makers of brand-name drugs.

Political Turmoil. By the end of its first session in August, the Commons had passed about 100 bills since the Mulroney government was elected in September 1984. Yet the Conservatives were clearly laboring through the sagging middle of their term in office. By midyear they were trailing the opposition Liberals in the polls and appeared wounded by a series of small scandals and embarrassments. One member of Parliament from Québec left the Conservative caucus to sit as an independent, and a minister from Québec quit the cabinet.

Industry Minister Sinclair Stevens resigned amid charges that he had been guilty of a conflict of interest. A newspaper reported that Stevens's wife, an executive and partner in his business interests, had sought loans from firms that, in turn, did business with Stevens's government department.

The government was also drawn, unexpectedly, into another conflict-of-interest controversy—this one in Washington. When Michael Deaver, a former White House aide (see biography in PEOPLE IN THE NEWS), came under congressional investigation for allegedly abusing his presidential contacts as a lobbyist, one of his clients was the Canadian embassy. In Ottawa the Commons external affairs committee rebuked External Affairs Minister Joe Clark for hiring Deaver to help the embassy deal with the U.S. government on the question of acid rain. Canada subsequently allowed its contract with Deaver to expire.

As one way of repairing his party's fortunes,

Expo 86, with its theme "Transportation and Communications," was the Canadian success story of the year. Above, British Columbia's host pavilion, B.C. Place Stadium, capable of housing 60,000 spectators, is a permanent structure for the city of Vancouver. At left, a spaceship and its horde of aliens was a popular attraction, squirting any child within range. Below, Highway 86, the creation of architect and artist James Wines, featured more than 200 vehicles frozen in place on a 235-yard-long concrete highway.

Mulroney performed a major cabinet reorganization in late June. He added 8 new people to his circle of ministers, dropped 6, and reassigned 21 others in his 40-member cabinet. Among the departures was Erik Nielsen, a 28-year veteran of the Commons who had served as Mulroney's hard-nosed deputy prime minister. Nielsen informed Mulroney that he wished to step down. His successor was Don Mazankowski, a popular Alberta member of Parliament. The former energy minister, Pat Carney, took over the trade portfolio.

In another move to regain political initiative, Mulroney prorogued Parliament, a procedural device allowing him to open a fresh session October 1 with a speech from the throne outlining a new legislative agenda. Among his proposals were reduction of the deficit, tax reform, and a review of regional development policies. The overall theme of the speech was fiscal restraint.

Economy. Canada's economy as a whole continued to expand robustly through midyear, continuing a long recovery, but in the third quarter economic growth plunged to an annual rate of only 1.2 percent, a four-year low. Inflation also worsened in the third quarter, to an annual rate of 4.9 percent, from around 2 percent in the preceding quarters. The unemployment rate remained high. Personal savings flagged in the third quarter.

Finance Minister Michael Wilson, in his February budget, took advantage of the country's healthy growth in the early part of the year to impose a 3 percent surtax on corporate and personal income taxes, raise the federal sales tax, and reduce the rate of growth in government spending (partly by cutting the size of the public service).

Acquisitions and Mergers. Among major company mergers was the buyout by Gulf Canada and British-based Allied-Lyons (Teacher's scotch, Baskin-Robbins ice cream) of Hiram Walker Resources Ltd. The federal government itself was active in the acquisition market, selling several crown corporations. Canadair Ltd. was sold to Bombardier of Montréal, and another aircraft manufacturer, de Havilland Aircraft Company of Canada, was taken under Boeing's wing.

Toronto realty magnate Robert Campeau took over New York's Allied Stores Corporation, whose assets included Brooks Brothers, Jordan Marsh, and many other chains of stores in the United States. Toronto's troubled Continental Bank announced it would be taken over by Lloyds Canada, an affiliate of Britain's huge Lloyds Bank. In still another deal, retailer and cigarette maker Imasco Ltd. took over conglomerate Genstar Corporation, including Genstar's rich subsidiary Canada Trust.

Expo 86. On May 2 the Prince and Princess of Wales officially opened Expo 86, the world transportation and communication fair, on the banks of False Creek in downtown Vancouver. By the time the fair closed, on October 13, some 22 million visitors had seen its more than 50 international exhibits. Among the most ambitious pavilions was that of the Canadian federal government, which occupied a spectacular site on Vancouver harbor.

Regional Review. General elections were held in four provinces during the year. In Alberta on May 8, the ruling Progressive Conservative party, led by Premier Donald Getty, retained firm control, winning 61 of the expanded legislature's 83 seats; however, the opposition parties increased their total strength from 4 seats to 22. In British Columbia, the charismatic William Vander Zalm, a former cabinet minister, succeeded retiring Premier Bill Bennett in August, after having been chosen by the governing Social Credit Party as its leader. Vander Zalm then led the government to victory in elections on October 22. In Prince Edward Island, on April 21, the Liberal Party, under Joseph Ghiz, a Harvard-trained lawyer of Lebanese descent, won 21 seats in the 32-member legislature to upset Premier James Lee and his Conservatives. In Saskatchewan the governing Progressive Conservatives, led by Grant Devine, suffered losses but retained a comfortable majority in October 20 elections. Meanwhile, in Québec a by-election on January 20 gave Premier Robert Bourassa a legislative seat, following December 1985 general elections in which he had led the Liberals to victory over the long-incumbent Parti Québécois.

Canada's regional economies turned in a varied performance. British Columbia, enjoying the fruits of Expo 86, looked toward a growth rate of around 5 percent, but the big

A group of 155 Hindu Tamils fleeing from Sri Lanka were picked up from lifeboats by Newfoundland fisheries in August. Originally claiming to have sailed from India, the Tamils finally acknowledged that they had been brought to the coast of Canada from West Germany in the hope of gaining refugee status.

fair, and the $3 billion it was expected to generate in tourism, seemed to be benefiting the Vancouver area at the expense of northern and interior sections of the province. In Alberta the collapse in world oil prices—as well as in the grain trade—was devastating; total output fell by as much as 2 percent, at the cost of tens of thousands of jobs. Saskatchewan's economy grew only by about 2 percent, hampered by low grain prices. Manitoba took advantage of its increasingly diverse economy to offset a struggling farm sector.

Central Canada experienced a genuine boom. Ontario's consumer-led growth rate, projected at about 4.5 percent, was buoyed by vigorous business investment, as was Québec's. In much of the Atlantic region, however, there was virtual stagnation. Offshore oil and gas development in Nova Scotia and Newfoundland stalled, as oil prices fell.

In other news, fossil remains believed to be nearly 200 million years old were found along the shores of the Bay of Fundy, in Nova Scotia. On August 31, three Dutch balloonists—Captain Henk Brink; pilot Evelien Brink, his wife; and copilot Willem Hageman—left St. John's, Newf., for a balloon trip across the Atlantic.

They arrived in the Netherlands on September 2, in a record time of 51 hours, 15 minutes. Finally, in a controversy that received considerable publicity, the Supreme Court of Canada upheld a widely defied Ontario law requiring most retail stores to remain closed on Sundays.

Foreign Relations. The acid rain issue dominated two days of talks in March between Prime Minister Mulroney and President Reagan. Mulroney had been pressing the United States to reduce industrial emissions of sulfur dioxide and other pollutants that were said to be producing acid rain over Canada. At the summit, in Washington, Reagan endorsed a report on the subject that called for the expenditure by the United States and U.S. industry of $6.9 billion to develop technology to burn coal more cleanly.

Mulroney and External Affairs Minister Clark stressed the need for tougher Commonwealth action against the apartheid regime in South Africa. At the same time they sought to avoid isolating Great Britain as the single Commonwealth country refusing to join a consensus on sanctions. However, at a meeting of seven Commonwealth leaders in London in August, Prime Minister Margaret Thatcher largely rejected the sanctions adopted by the others. Canada, along with other Commonwealth countries, promptly announced new measures, including bans on agricultural imports and on new Canadian investments in South Africa.

In August, 155 Tamil refugees from Sri Lanka were found adrift in lifeboats off Newfoundland. After first claiming to have come by ship from India, they admitted that they had sailed from West Germany. The government granted them temporary residence while authorities heard their claims for refugee status. The ship's captain, who, it appeared, had accepted about $500,000 from the refugees, was by then back home in West Germany. He was charged with breaking Canadian immigration regulations, but could not be extradited.

In November five soldiers who had deserted

Citing ill-health, Montréal Mayor Jean Drapeau (shown here with his wife) ended a legendary career in Canadian politics when he announced his retirement effective in November. Drapeau, who won seven consecutive elections, was the longest-serving mayor of any North American city.

from the Soviet Army in Afghanistan were brought to Canada under a secret government mission and offered asylum. Overall relations with the Soviet Union were nevertheless improving, and Canada announced plans to lift sanctions it had imposed on the Soviet Union after the 1980 invasion of Afghanistan.

New National Park. A new national park was dedicated on Ellesmere Island, North America's most northerly chunk of land. The park encompasses more than 15,000 square miles, making it three times larger than Yellowstone and Yosemite parks combined. Conservation and the desire to assert Canadian sovereignty over the country's northern reaches were cited as the primary reasons for the park's establishment. Tourists to this remote, rugged, and frigid area were expected to number only about 50 a year.

Transitions. Tommy Douglas, the former national leader of the New Democratic Party who had governed Saskatchewan as the country's first socialist premier, died at the age of 81. Jean Chrétien, a Trudeau cabinet minister who lost a bid to become Liberal leader in 1984 to John Turner, resigned from the Commons to practice law. Jean Drapeau retired as mayor of Montréal, the city he had ruled for more than 25 years; he was succeeded by Jean Doré, a labor lawyer, who defeated Drapeau's chosen successor in an election on November 9.

See STATISTICS OF THE WORLD.   J.H.

CAPE VERDE. *See* STATISTICS OF THE WORLD.

CARIBBEAN BASIN. The region suffered from a stagnant economy in 1986 but benefited from a worldwide fall in energy prices. Several countries elected new leaders.

Regional Developments. The Caribbean Basin Initiative (CBI), extended by the United States in 1983 to 27 Caribbean states (Cuba and Nicaragua were excluded), continued to have a mixed impact. During a February meeting in Grenada with nine Caribbean leaders, President Ronald Reagan promised an extension of the CBI and an increase in scholarships for study in the United States. However, because of budgetary pressures U.S. aid to the region was leveling off. Tourism increased modestly, but Caribbean exports to the United States were declining. U.S. business leaders, when discussing problems of trade with the Caribbean, tended to emphasize red tape, a lack of infrastructure, and arbitrary exchange rates as the primary obstacles; Caribbean leaders pointed to U.S. quotas placed upon such important exports as sugar and rum.

Aid from other sources also declined. Mexico and Venezuela were phasing out their sales of oil at discount prices. Aid and technical assistance from Britain and Canada remained steady, however, and the European Community provided $7.9 million for agricultural development and loans to Barbados and Jamaica. Also, most Caribbean countries benefited from the worldwide decline in energy prices. Trinidad and Tobago, as an oil exporter, was a notable exception.

Drug trafficking remained a major problem. U.S. funds, pressure, and training were active in inducing Caribbean governments to increase their antidrug law-enforcement efforts.

Barbados. The opposition Democratic Labor Party (DLP), led by former Prime Minister Errol Barrow, won a stunning 24 out of 27 seats in Barbados parliamentary elections held on May 28. Out of office since 1976, the DLP capitalized on growing unemployment and a decline in government expenditures on social services.

Dominican Republic. The major political event in the Dominican Republic was the return to power of former President Joaquín Balaguer, standard-bearer of the conservative Social Christian Reform Party. For 30 years a leading figure in the dictatorship of General Rafael Trujillo, Balaguer had been the country's elected president for three terms ending in 1978. The lackluster economy played a prominent role in his election victory in May. It was a narrow victory according to official results, and his nearest rival, Jacobo Majluta Azur of the Dominican Revolutionary Party, charged fraud. After negotiations following the election, Balaguer agreed to form a "government of national unity."

Grenada. In December, 14 people were convicted and sentenced to death for the 1983 killing of Prime Minister Maurice Bishop. Bishop, a leftist, was shot to death during a coup attempt by hard-line elements in his government; his deputy was among those sentenced

to hang. Six days after the killing the Reagan administration mounted a successful invasion of Grenada to restore order and prevent the island from moving any further to the political left.

Guyana. In December, Larry Layton, a former member of the People's Temple cult, was convicted of conspiring to murder Representative Leo J. Ryan (D) of California, who was killed while visiting Guyana to investigate conditions at the jungle camp set up by the Reverend Jim Jones, the group's leader. Shortly after Ryan's death, 913 cult members, at Jones's urging, committed suicide; Jones was said to have been shot to death. Jones, apparently worried that Ryan would issue negative reports on the group upon returning to the United States, was said to have ordered the attack on Ryan, in which four people in addition to Ryan were killed.

Jamaica. In July elections for local government offices in Jamaica, the leftist opposition People's National Party, led by former Prime Minister Michael Manley, won 57 percent of the vote, confirming an erosion of support for the government of Prime Minister Edward Seaga. Since the PNP had boycotted the 1983 national elections, its victory prompted calls for new elections ahead of schedule. Seaga resisted the idea. In October he announced he would resign in 1987 as prime minister and party leader, but he changed his mind and said in November that he would stay.

Suriname. In July, 14 people were arrested by U.S. authorities in Louisiana and charged with violating the U.S. Neutrality Act by conspiring to overthrow the regime of Lieutenant Colonel Dési Bouterse, Suriname's de facto head of state. The arrests took place as most were being driven to a small airport where they reportedly expected to fly to Suriname and join in a rebellion against the government. In September, the suspects pleaded guilty to reduced charges or declined to contest the charges in U.S. district court; four of the defendants received prison sentences of up to 2½ years.

Trinidad and Tobago. The People's National Movement (PNM), in office since 1956, was soundly defeated by the opposition National Alliance for Reconstruction, led by A. N. R. Robinson, in general elections held on December 15. Both parties are pro-Western. The outcome hinged on economic issues; recession and high unemployment had eroded support for the government.

See also STATISTICS OF THE WORLD; CUBA; HAITI; PUERTO RICO.

CENTRAL AFRICAN REPUBLIC. See STATISTICS OF THE WORLD.

CEYLON. See SRI LANKA.

CHAD. Chad's civil war erupted again early in 1986, prompting the return of French troops.

For most of the year, the main antagonists in the civil war were Goukouni Oueddei and Hissène Habré, both Muslims and members of the Tubu ethnic group in northern Chad. Goukouni, as head of the Libyan-backed GUNT (Transitional Government of National Unity) alliance, had been president of Chad from 1979 until the GUNT was overthrown by Habré in 1982. In early February 1986, GUNT rebel forces moved south from their bases and launched ground attacks along and south of the 16th parallel, which divides the northern third of Chad, controlled by rebels and Libyans, from the rest of the country. Habré's FANT (Chad National Armed Forces) decisively repelled the attacks and inflicted heavy casualties. France sent about 1,000 troops, plus weapons and aircraft, to assist in Chad's defense. The troops did not engage in actual ground fighting, however. On February 16, French planes bombed a Libyan-built airstrip in northern Chad; the next day, a Libyan bomber attacked N'Djamena, the capital. Sporadic fighting continued into March; then an uneasy quiet returned.

The Habré government made progress in promoting reconciliation. Members of several opposition groups and thousands of southern rebels had rallied to the government late in 1985, and formal agreements were worked out. In March several opposition figures received positions in a newly reorganized cabinet. The Organization of African Unity also invited Habré and Goukouni to meet in the Congo's capital in March, but Goukouni refused, reinforcing his image as a puppet of Libya. Later in the year, however, Goukouni did offer to open peace talks with Habré. He was subsequently reported to have been wounded when he resisted arrest by Libyan soldiers in Tripoli, and in November a new rebel leader, Acheikh Ibn Oumar, was named to replace him.

Most of the rebels who had supported Goukouni switched sides and began attacking the Libyans, who launched operations against them in late December. The Chadian Army joined in the anti-Libyan resistance; France sent in military supplies and the United States authorized $15 million in aid.

Chad remained one of the world's poorest nations. Since half of government revenues and 80 percent of Chad's export earnings come from cotton farmed by southern Chadians, a decline in cotton prices caused hardship.

See STATISTICS OF THE WORLD. J.D.

CHEMISTRY. The development of polymers that can release insulin in response to the body's need and new drugs to combat hypertension and memory loss were among highlights in chemistry in 1986.

Polymers for Drug Release. Scientists are developing polymers that release drugs at rates dependent upon conditions in the body. (Polymers consist of large molecules containing atoms arranged so that a certain repeating pattern occurs again and again.) The chief advantage of these polymers, most of which have been studied for use with insulin, is that they mimic the activity of the pancreas, which releases increased quantities of insulin when the body needs it.

For example, Robert Langer of the Massachusetts Institute of Technology has attached the enzyme glucose oxidase to the interior of tiny beads of polysaccharide—a sugar polymer—that are also filled with crystalline insulin. Normally, the polymer would release insulin at a slow, constant rate. However, when the level of glucose outside the beads rises—as it would in blood after a meal—the glucose oxidase within the beads converts some of the glucose to gluconic acid. This makes the interior of the bead more acidic, which in turn makes the insulin more soluble, so that more of it dissolves and escapes from the device. Because the gluconic acid is also released, the bead returns to its normal state as external sugar levels are reduced. Langer reported in July on tests of polymer implants placed under the skin of rats. When the rats were injected

Some two dozen people died in Italy early in the year after drinking low-quality red wine that had been adulterated with toxic amounts of methyl alcohol. Here, a laboratory worker in Asti tests wine samples.

with glucose, the implants doubled their release of glucose into the rats' blood. These and other polymers could eventually be tried in human diabetics.

Chemicals and Health. *Hypertension Drugs.* Chemists at Abbott Laboratories in North Chicago have formulated several compounds that may reduce hypertension, or high blood pressure. The compounds inhibit the action of renin, an enzyme that plays a key role in regulating blood pressure. Renin triggers a series of enzymatic reactions by cleaving a specific bond in the circulating protein angiotensinogen, producing a peptide—a chain of amino acids—known as angiotensin I. Another enzyme, called angiotensin-converting enzyme, or ACE, converts angiotensin I to angiotensin II, which causes blood vessels to shrink, thereby increasing blood pressure.

Existing antihypertension drugs, such as captopril and enalapril, reduce blood pressure by inhibiting ACE. However, ACE has other functions in the body, and drugs that inhibit it produce several undesirable side effects. Renin, in contrast, is believed to act only on angiotensinogen, and drugs that inhibit it should have few side effects.

More Oxygen From Blood. Pharmacologist Murray Weiner of the University of Cincinnati has devised a way to treat blood so that hemoglobin, the oxygen-carrying component of red blood cells, will release more oxygen. During times of physical stress hemoglobin holds on to oxygen too tightly. Blood stored in banks for more than a day or two also holds on to oxygen too tightly.

Scientists have long known that phytic acid, a sugarlike compound obtained from plants, can force hemoglobin to release more oxygen, but the chemical is too big to fit through the membrane of red cells. Weiner has overcome this problem by treating the red cells with a chemical called DMSO. Cells treated with DMSO absorb water and swell up, allowing the phytic acid to pass through the enlarged membrane. When the DMSO is washed away, the cells shrink back to normal size, trapping the phytic acid inside. The process, which takes only a few seconds, is similar to dialysis.

Weiner reported in April that the treated blood releases oxygen more efficiently than normal blood and that the treated cells persist in chimpanzees for as long as untreated red cells, without producing ill effects.

CHEMISTRY

Memory Drug. A new drug that may help people with certain types of memory disorders could become available in the United States. The drug, called vinpocetine, was originally developed in Hungary and appears both to restore damaged memories and to improve an individual's ability to acquire new memories.

Scientists from Ayerst Laboratories in New Jersey began testing the drug on patients suffering from multiple infarct dementia, a brain disorder resulting from a series of small strokes. Previous tests had found that 60 to 70 percent of patients receiving vinpocetine showed some improvement of memory; for 20 to 30 percent of them it was a significant improvement. Ayerst hoped to sell the drug for use in multiple infarct dementia.

Dioxin and Immunity. Long-term exposure to 2,3,7,8-tetrachlorodibenzo-*p*-dioxin (TCDD), the most potent of the many dioxins found in hazardous wastes, may depress certain parts of the human immune system, according to a study by epidemiologists at the U.S. Centers for Disease Control, St. Louis University, and the Missouri Department of Health. The researchers studied 154 people who lived in a mobile home park near St. Louis where soil had been contaminated with TCDD. Among harbingers of future health problems were impaired functioning of white blood cells vital to the immune system and indications of liver damage.

Methanol in Wine. About two dozen Italians died and more than 50 were blinded in early 1986 as a result of drinking cheap wine laced with methyl alcohol, also known as methanol. Toxic methanol occurs naturally in wine, but only at safe concentrations—below about 0.15 percent. Apparently, the methanol was added to the wine, whose price depends on alcohol content, by unscrupulous distributors trying to boost the alcohol content. Inexpensive Italian wines were removed from U.S. stores for testing, although there were no reports of health problems in the United States, and large quantities were dumped in Italy and elsewhere in Europe.   T.H.M.

CHESS. Gary Kasparov retained the world chess championship by defeating Anatoly Karpov in 1986 for the second time in a year. The intensely contested 24-game match, which began in London in July and ended in Leningrad in October, was the third championship match between the two Soviet citizens and had its share of dramatic moments; at one point Karpov, apparently hopelessly behind, won three games in a row to draw even before Kasparov recovered the momentum.

Judith Polgar of Hungary, who says she shows "no mercy" for her opponents, became the youngest player ever to achieve the ranking of master (she was nine) after her stunning first place finish among unrated players in the New York Open Chess Tournament.

Karpov, the original titleholder, had retained the championship in February 1985 when the grueling but inconclusive first match with Kasparov was terminated—after more than five months of play—by International Chess Federation President Florencio Campomanes. Kasparov then took the title from Karpov, 13-11, in a match played in Moscow late in 1985.

The new champion rejected an attempt by Campomanes to schedule a rematch with Karpov almost immediately. Eventually, however, Kasparov and Karpov, who had not been on speaking terms, worked out an agreement to start play in July 1986, with the first 12 games to take place in London and the remaining games—up to a total of 12 more—scheduled for Leningrad. A total of six victories or 12½ points was required to win the match (each victory counting for one point and each draw for one-half). In the event of a 12-12 tie, the champion would retain the title.

In the match, Kasparov took the lead in Game 4, exploiting an endgame advantage, but Karpov drew even by winning Game 5. Kasparov won Game 8 with an aggressive mating attack; it so puzzled Karpov that he overran his time limit and had to forfeit. Kasparov led, 6½-5½, after Game 12.

Kasparov won the 14th and 16th games with fiercely aggressive, complicated attacks, but his seemingly insurmountable 9½-6½ lead evaporated as Karpov won the 17th, 18th, and 19th games with solid performances that exploited what appeared to be overconfident carelessness in Kasparov's play. Nevertheless, after a day's rest, Kasparov seemed to regain control. The even score still left him with the advantage of a prospective tie, and he edged closer to victory with two draws before clinching it with a brilliant win in the 22nd game and a draw in the 23rd. The 24th game, which Karpov had hoped to win so as to salvage his honor with a tie, also ended in a draw, leaving the final score 12½-11½ in favor of Kasparov.

The cycle to determine the next challenger for the world championship was dominated by Soviet players, including Artur Yusupov and Andrei Sokolov. In October Sokolov defeated Yusupov, 7½-6½, in Riga, Latvia, and won the right to play Karpov to determine Kasparov's challenger for the title.   J.T.S.

CHILE

CHILE. The 13-year-old regime of President Augusto Pinochet Ugarte came under increasing pressure to move toward democracy in 1986, but Pinochet continued to firmly resist any relaxing of his grip on power.

A political coalition called the Asamblea de la Civilidad was formed by 20 organizations in April. Claiming to represent 3 million Chileans, it included representatives of workers, professionals, students, human rights groups, peasants, and Indians. The Asamblea issued a 50-point "Demand of Chile" calling for an end to the state of emergency, a democratically approved constitution, freedom of expression, cuts in military spending, public works to alleviate unemployment, and renegotiation of Chile's foreign debt.

The Chilean fall and winter saw four months of protests. In May more than 15,000 persons were detained in raids on the shantytowns of Santiago, and in June the government detained hundreds of students and instructors who supported the Asamblea. The Asamblea called a general strike on July 2 and 3; eight people were killed during the strike and 50 were wounded.

On September 7, Pinochet's motorcade was attacked with bombs, machine guns, and bazookas by members of the Manuel Rodríguez Patriotic Front, a Communist group. The president survived, but five of his bodyguards were killed. That night, a 90-day state of siege was declared; six opposition publications were suspended and dozens of opposition figures were arrested. In the first week of the state of siege, four people were murdered, apparently by death squads. In late October, police arrested five suspects in the September 7 attack. They were charged with murder and could receive the death penalty, which was upheld by a Supreme Court ruling in November. Seven others were charged as accomplices.

The recession of 1982–1985 was reversed in 1986, with a projected 3 percent growth rate. The trade surplus was expected to rise to around $860 million, led by copper, but 50 percent of export earnings went to service Chile's $21 billion foreign debt.

Under an experienced new ambassador, Harry G. Barnes, Jr., U.S. pressure on the Pinochet government tended to increase. In

CHILE

March the United States for the first time condemned the Chilean human rights situation at the United Nations by sponsoring a motion, which passed 43-0, that called on Chile to end torture and to investigate political killings and kidnappings.

In July, Ambassador Barnes attended the funeral of Rodrigo Rojas de Negri, a 19-year-old Chilean-born resident of the United States who had died as a result of burns received during the general strike. According to witnesses, he and a companion were sprayed with gasoline and set on fire by soldiers. U.S. Senator Jesse Helms, who made a three-day visit to Chile at that time, criticized the ambassador's attendance at the funeral, which he charac-

terized as a gathering of extreme leftists, but the Reagan administration hastened to affirm its support of the ambassador. (A civilian judge absolved 24 members of an army patrol of any guilt in Rojas's death but ordered its commander to be tried in a military court for criminal negligence in not seeking medical help for the victims. The military court instead increased the charge to homicide.)

In November the World Bank approved a $250 million loan to Chile, despite strong objections from human rights groups. The Reagan administration, which had reportedly considered blocking the action with a "no" vote, instead abstained.

See STATISTICS OF THE WORLD.   J.F., Jr.

Chilean President Augusto Pinochet survived a September 7 assassination attempt by leftist guerrillas who ambushed his motorcade, killing five bodyguards. Afterward, Pinochet appeared on television to show he had survived (inset) and had the burnt-out cars displayed in Santiago's Central Plaza (below).

CHINA. The year 1986 was marked by the continuing political ascendancy of Deng Xiaoping and his colleagues, by anticorruption efforts, and by a gradual but limited liberalization of political and cultural life in China. Late in the year, massive student demonstrations broke out in Shanghai and other cities. Peking maintained a cautious course in relation to the two superpowers.

Politics and Society. Deng appeared to be turning over increasing responsibilities to his colleagues, while still retaining a high degree of authority. On the other hand, Communist Party General Secretary Hu Yaobang and Premier Zhao Ziyang were regarded by many observers as transitional figures, in part because of their age. Considerable attention was focused instead on a group of younger men, also protégés of Deng. Among them was Hu Qili, a member of the Secretariat, who appeared to be a leading candidate for eventual succession to the post of party general secretary.

There were repeated efforts by the top leadership to improve party efficiency and morale, especially through exhortation; a good example was a conference of party officials on January 9, which was addressed by Hu Yaobang and others. In September the Central Committee of the Communist Party held a meeting and reaffirmed the program for economic modernization and higher living standards through increased trade and contacts with foreigners. But it also warned against corruption and the tendency to "blindly worship bourgeois philosophies and social doctrines."

The government's crackdown against official corruption and other kinds of misbehavior continued vigorously. A disproportionate number of offenders were the sons of senior or mid-level officials, a group sometimes referred to as China's "new class" because of its access to special privileges, including education abroad. A few cases involving especially serious crimes, such as multiple rape, resulted in execution of the offenders. An anticorruption campaign was also launched within the People's Liberation Army.

Nevertheless, the political climate in recent years has generally been somewhat freer. Some strikes took place in 1985 and 1986 without known reprisals. The subject of political reform and liberalization remained a favorite one among many younger officials and intellectuals. The official view was stated in July by Vice Premier Wan Li, who limited "democratization" to the seeking of objective advice from experts by policy-makers. But there was real progress toward liberalization in March when the National People's Congress passed legislation providing a guaranteed place for private enterprise and a legitimate status for contracts between private individuals.

In early December, sporadic student demonstrations broke out in several cities, and on December 20, students marched in Shanghai, in the largest demonstration since the end of the Cultural Revolution, calling for democracy, freedom of the press, and protection of the right to protest. The number of demonstrators in Shanghai later reached about 50,000, before a ban issued by city authorities had a dampening effect. Large protests also broke out in Peking. The government, while condemning the mass protests, appeared to take a generally tolerant approach.

Unification. China reached an accord in October providing for the eventual return of the Portuguese settlement of Macao to Peking. A working group was to be set up to arrive at a detailed agreement.

A significant development in relation to Taiwan took place after the pilot of a Boeing 747 cargo aircraft belonging to China Air Lines, Taiwan's flag carrier, defected to Peking in May. The rest of the crew wanted to return to Taiwan, and Taipei was eager to recover the plane. Peking tried to use the situation to bring about direct, formal negotiations on Chinese territory, but Taipei agreed only to talks in Hong Kong, which led to return of the airplane and crew. Regardless of Taipei's interpretation and reservations, the fact remained that, for the first time since 1949, the two sides had engaged in open negotiations.

Economy. Although the Chinese economy was clearly making progress, it continued to suffer from serious problems. One was the country's huge economic bureaucracy, which was inept and cumbersome. Another was a series of bottlenecks and shortages in the fields of energy and infrastructure, partly as a result of overexpansion. A huge hydroelectric project long

Student protesters in Shanghai throng the streets under banners calling for human rights and an end to oppression.

contemplated for the middle Yangtze River and known as the Three Gorges Project appeared stalled by problems and objections, including environmental considerations and a desire on Peking's part not to get too closely entangled with the United States, the principal foreign source of hydroelectric technology. A large offshore oil exploration program in the South China Sea involving foreign (including U.S.) firms had thus far yielded little but natural gas. Peking's ambitious plans for nuclear power plants in the coastal region were cut back—apparently now providing for only three new plants, two near Shanghai and one near Hong Kong—in part because of a general retrenchment and in part, it seemed, as a result of the Chernobyl nuclear power-plant disaster in the Soviet Union.

China's economic policy took an "open" approach to the outside world, especially with respect to the technology of the advanced industrial countries, and aimed at export-led growth. Imports in 1985 had risen sharply (54 percent over 1984), mainly because of greatly increased purchases of foreign (principally Japanese) capital equipment and consumer durables, while exports were up only 5 percent. Drastic measures were taken in 1986 to curb imports.

China's leading trading partner continued to be Japan. In 1985, Sino-Japanese trade had registered a $5.9 billion gap in Japan's favor; this imbalance was eased somewhat in 1986 by the strengthening of the yen, which made exports from Japan more expensive. In a move intended to promote Chinese exports, Peking devalued the yuan in July. Because of a foreign exchange crisis, resulting largely from the import surge of 1985, the yuan remained inconvertible.

Foreign Affairs. Although Chinese leaders spoke in private of their nation's "equidistance" between the two superpowers, what China really sought was to avoid extremes—either undue closeness or dangerous confrontation—in its relations with the superpowers; in that way,

executed in the United States for an offense committed as a juvenile. Despite widespread clemency pleas, Roach was electrocuted at South Carolina state penitentiary in Columbia for a murder he had committed at age 16.

Civil Rights Commission. In October, Congress slashed the budget of the U.S. Civil Rights Commission by almost 40 percent. As a result, the commission planned to cut its staff and close most of its regional offices. The budget cut was sponsored by liberal Democrats who charged the Reagan administration had gutted the commission's traditional functions by stacking it with conservative appointees. In November, John H. Bunzel, one of the commission's eight members, announced that he did not want to be reappointed when his term expired in December; he charged that the commission had lost its "credibility" and "moral strength."

Court Appointments. President Reagan's nomination of Supreme Court Justice William H. Rehnquist (see biography in PEOPLE IN THE NEWS) to succeed retiring Chief Justice Warren Burger and of Judge Antonin Scalia to replace Rehnquist drew major attention from civil liberties groups. Both nominees were regarded as strong ideological conservatives who were unsympathetic with the liberal civil liberties agenda. Both were approved by the Senate, but Rehnquist received the most negative votes ever for a justice confirmed to the Court.   M.Gr.

COINS AND COIN COLLECTING. The year 1986 went down in numismatic history when, on October 20, the U.S. government introduced the American Eagle, America's first new gold coin in 50 years. Demand for the coin proved unexpectedly heavy. The coins, an alternative to the South African Krugerrand (now banned from import into the United States), had face values of $5, $10, $25, and $50 but were sold according to their weight and at a 6 percent premium over the current price of gold. Initial sales estimates for the year were more than doubled.

The obverse side of the Eagle, the same on all four coins, resurrects the handsome Saint-Gaudens design of Liberty that appeared on U.S. $20 gold pieces from 1907 to 1933. Miss Liberty, however, is much slimmer. The reverse on each of the new coins features a "family of eagles"—a male eagle, carrying an olive branch, flies above a nest containing a female eagle and hatchlings. The design symbolizes the unity and family tradition of America.

The U.S. Mint also introduced a silver Liberty $1 bullion coin, slightly larger than a regular silver dollar and containing 1 troy ounce of fine silver, to trade at the value set by the silver market.

When the refurbished Statue of Liberty was unveiled on July 3, collectors stood proud knowing that a major share of the restoration funds came from the sale of a three-piece commemorative coin set struck by the Mint. U.S. coin sales raised more than $40 million for the Statue of Liberty-Ellis Island Foundation.

The American Numismatic Association modified its standards for uncirculated coins. The new standards recognize 11 numerical grades, from MS-60 to MS-70 (perfect). On some silver dollars, a grade point difference could mean several hundred dollars in the marketplace.

The new "American Eagle" gold bullion coins, the first to be issued as legal tender, are intended as an alternative to the banned Krugerrand. The obverse shows a decidedly slim Lady Liberty, and the reverse features a domestic scene of eagle family life.

COLOMBIA

A unique exhibit by the British Royal Mint at the American Numismatic Association's 95th anniversary convention in Milwaukee traced the mint's 1,100 years of continuous operation, from the year 886, when Alfred the Great occupied London and ordered a famous penny hammered, to the modern issues it strikes today for some 70 countries at Llantrisant, Wales. Meanwhile, in France, a 100-franc piece honoring the 100th anniversary of the Statue of Liberty was released in both gold and silver, marking the inauguration of an annual series that will culminate with the bicentennial celebration of the French Revolution in 1989.

E.C.R.

COLOMBIA. Colombian voters elected a new president in 1986, and an economic growth

Colombia's newly elected President Virgilio Barco Vargas acknowledges the cheers of his supporters after his landslide victory on May 25; the success of his Liberal Party was widely attributed to the failure of Conservative President Belisario Betancur to arrange a lasting peace with rebels.

rate of 6 percent was projected, double that of the previous year.

Virgilio Barco Vargas was installed as president of Colombia on August 7, succeeding Belisario Betancur Cuartas. A Liberal, Barco had defeated Conservative Alvaro Gómez Hurtado in a general election on May 25, with an unprecedented majority of 58 percent of the popular vote. The Conservative rout was generally attributed to Betancur's inability to arrange a lasting peace with Colombia's various rebel groups. The Conservatives declined to join in the new administration with the Liberals, thus ending a 28-year experiment in power sharing.

Barco, a member of a wealthy oil-producing family from northeastern Colombia, had previously served in key political posts, including that of ambassador to the United States. He promised significant economic reforms and pledged to negotiate with the guerrilla groups, combat drug trafficking, and create jobs. In December, after a prominent journalist was killed apparently by drug traffickers, he issued a decree making it easier for the military to crack down on drug traffic.

President Betancur's failure to bring about more than a partial cease-fire in the 40-year-old civil conflict reflected his inability to get promised reforms through an opposition-dominated Congress and the resistance of military leaders, right-wing paramilitary groups, and some political leaders to the reconciliation effort. Both the April 19 Movement (M-19) and the Popular Liberation Army had withdrawn in 1985 from a previous cease-fire agreement with the government. In early 1986 only the bulk of the pro-Moscow Colombian Revolutionary Armed Forces and the extreme leftist Workers' Self-Defense Movement continued to honor the truce. By July, though, five detachments of the Cuban-oriented National Liberation Army had negotiated a truce with the government.

Carlos Pizarro León Gómez became the head of M-19 after its leader, Alvaro Fayad, was assassinated in March in Bogotá; meanwhile, the second in command, known as Commandante Boris, was killed in northern Colombia in July while under detention by police.

The economy's growth resulted from a substantial increase in coffee exports and coal shipments. Colombia also exported oil for the first time in a decade; daily shipments were expected to reach 180,000 barrels by the end of the year. Total exports were expected to net $6.5 billion in 1986, and coffee sales alone were forecast at $3.6 billion. High unemployment persisted, however, with close to 15 percent of the workforce lacking jobs.

Pope John Paul II visited Colombia in July and addressed such issues as the maldistribution of wealth, the urgency of land reform, and the protection of workers from exploitation.

See STATISTICS OF THE WORLD.   L.L.P.

COLORADO. See STATISTICS OF THE WORLD.

COMMONWEALTH OF NATIONS. The controversial issue of economic sanctions against South Africa, a former member of the Commonwealth of Nations, threatened to split the 49-member organization in 1986. Most of the Commonwealth countries favored stiff measures to protest South Africa's continued apartheid policies. India, Canada, and Australia were among prominent members favoring strong steps. But Prime Minister Margaret Thatcher of Great Britain, mindful of her nation's close economic ties to South Africa, among other considerations, resisted the call for harsh sanctions. (Britain was the largest foreign investor in South Africa, earning nearly $6 billion from trade, investments, and services in 1985.) She said sanctions were "immoral" and would only "lead to starvation, poverty, and unemployment" among black South Africans.

In the face of Thatcher's opposition, many feared that Britain's leadership of the organization was at stake. It was even reported in the Sunday Times of London that Queen Elizabeth II herself, who is titular head of the Commonwealth and acknowledged queen of 17 of its member states, was dismayed by the government's position on sanctions. (The report, attributed to sources "close to" the queen, was denied by Buckingham Palace.)

The whole issue of sanctions came to a head in early August, when a minisummit of seven Commonwealth leaders convened in London. Thatcher reiterated her general opposition to sanctions but agreed to a "voluntary ban" on new investments in, and the promotion of tourism to, South Africa. The remaining six

leaders slapped a total ban on Commonwealth air links and government contracts with South Africa. They also proscribed all trade of farm goods, coal, uranium, and iron and steel with the Pretoria government. The leaders were also harsh in their postsummit criticism of Thatcher, who, commented Zambian President Kenneth Kaunda, "cut a very pathetic figure at the summit." Indian Prime Minister Rajiv Gandhi flatly stated, "Britain is not the Commonwealth leader any more." Meanwhile, South Africa responded by imposing import levies on all goods from Zimbabwe and Zambia.

Political strife spilled over into the world of sports, as 31 countries boycotted the Commonwealth Games, held in Edinburgh, Scotland, in July. Swimmer Annette Cowley and runner Zola Budd, both born in South Africa but carrying British passports, were prevented from competing by the Commonwealth Games Federation because, according to the federation, they did not meet residency requirements.

J.O.S.

COMMUNIST WORLD. The members of the Communist movement were generally no more successful in 1986 at resolving the serious cleavages that separated some of them than they had been in recent years. However, prospects for a normalization of relations between the Soviet Union and China appeared better than at any time since the rift between the two countries developed in the early 1960's.

Soviet Union. General Secretary Mikhail Gorbachev worked to consolidate his power as head of the Soviet Communist Party—both by replacing key personnel within the party apparatus and by continuing to push for greater economic efficiency and responsibility. By year's end, nearly all of the 12 full members of the party Politburo, other than Gorbachev, were new figures, rather than being holdovers from the Brezhnev period. At the provincial level, more than 50 percent of party first secretaries had been replaced by the time of the Soviet Communist Party Congress in February. Extensive changes were made in structure and in high-level personnel within the Foreign Ministry, setting a new tone for Soviet foreign relations.

Gorbachev called for major reforms to encourage increased economic productivity, and he attacked those opposed to change, accusing them of attempting to deceive the Soviet people. In his efforts to foster increased responsibility and efficiency, Gorbachev pushed for more open public discussion of economic problems facing the Soviet Union. The result was a substantial expansion of coverage of such items in the Soviet mass media.

The devastating accident in late April at the Chernobyl nuclear reactor in the Soviet Ukraine resulted, in the near term, in more than 30 deaths and hundreds of serious radiation injuries. The Soviet failure to provide information immediately on the disaster, which spread radioactive contaminants across much of Eastern Europe and Scandinavia, was strongly criticized abroad. The accident also called into question the long-term safety of the entire Soviet nuclear energy program.

Eastern Europe. Gorbachev called for reform in Eastern Europe as well as in the Soviet Union, as the only means to deal effectively with the serious economic problems facing all of the European Communist countries. Although he emphasized the need for renewed efforts at economic and political integration within the region, the Soviets at the same time approved continued East European efforts to acquire Western goods and technology.

A proclamation signed by 122 prominent dissidents from Hungary, Poland, Czechoslovakia, and East Germany, and issued simultaneously in the four countries' capitals a few days before the 30th anniversary of the October 23, 1956, Hungarian uprising, commemorated the revolt as "our common heritage and inspiration." The boldly worded statement was issued by writers, scientists, professionals, workers, and human rights activists from four of the six Warsaw Pact allies of the Soviet Union. There were no signers from Bulgaria or Romania, where organized opposition groups were lacking. The declaration concluded with a pledge of mutual support for efforts to develop political democracy and "pluralism based on the principles of self-government."

In Poland all political prisoners were released in September in a general amnesty, though deep political and economic conflicts persisted. In Albania the new leadership of Ramiz Alia moved toward closer economic and political ties with several countries in both Eastern and Western Europe.

Comecon. Soviet efforts to "streamline" the trade-cooperation bloc known as Comecon (Council for Mutual Economic Assistance) included advocating an increased Comecon role in the domestic economic planning of each member country. In November, at a meeting of the prime ministers of the ten Comecon countries in Bucharest, agreements designed to increase economic integration and joint productive enterprises were signed. A week later, a meeting in Moscow brought together the Communist Party leaders of the member nations for the first such Comecon summit since June 1984. The leaders vowed to raise living standards by means of more direct and comprehensive economic and technological cooperation, including factory-to-factory and ministry contracts across national borders.

In Geneva, during late September, Comecon officials had held the first substantive talks in more than five years with their European Community (EC) counterparts on the possibility of establishing mutual diplomatic relations—an idea spurned by both blocs in earlier years. EC representatives were willing to establish such a tie provided there was a parallel establishment of formal relations—and separate trade pacts—individually with each of the six Eastern European Comecon members. (Cuba, Mongolia, and Vietnam, as well as the Soviet Union, were also Comecon members.) EC imports from Eastern European Comecon nations have far exceeded EC exports to those countries, and it was considered unlikely that the situation could change appreciably. Observers did think, however, that the initiation of diplomatic relations between the two blocs might somewhat reduce the influence of Moscow and Washington on members of their respective blocs.

Warsaw Pact. At a Warsaw Pact summit meeting in Budapest in June, members of that Soviet-bloc military alliance proposed substantial reductions in the manpower and armaments of conventional military forces in Europe, from the Urals to the Atlantic. The proposal called for mutual NATO and Warsaw Pact reductions in several phases, with total conventional forces 25 percent lower than present levels by the early 1990's.

Significant changes in leadership were evident at the 27th Congress of the Communist Party of the Soviet Union, held at the Palace of Congresses in Moscow. By the end of the sessions, fewer than half of the Central Committee members were holdovers from the previous congress, which met in 1981.

Asia. Despite concerns in China about the impact of wide-ranging economic reforms, including the acceptance of some free enterprise, the Chinese leadership continued to push ahead with its experiments. The Chinese responded positively to overtures made by Gorbachev in a speech at Vladivostok in July. Gorbachev indicated a Soviet willingness to be more flexible on at least two of the major issues that divide the two nations—Soviet support for the Vietnamese occupation of Cambodia and the maintaining of a large number of Soviet troops in Mongolia and elsewhere along the Chinese border. China signed a consular treaty with Mongolia in August, and it was reported at that time that some Soviet troops had been withdrawn. Despite an improved climate in Sino-Soviet relations and a substantial increase in trade between the two countries, the Chinese still questioned whether the Soviets were willing to put pressure on their

Vietnamese allies and continued to condemn the Soviet military occupation of Afghanistan. Meanwhile, China was making progress in improving its long cold relations with Eastern Europe. In November, Polish leader Wojciech Jaruzelski paid a working visit to Peking; the following month, East German leader Erich Honecker paid the first formal state visit to China by the leader of a Warsaw Pact nation since the early 1960's.

In December, at a Vietnamese Communist Party conference in Hanoi, there was a wide shakeup of Vietnam's top leaders. The impact of the changes on Vietnam's foreign policy remained to be determined.

In May the Soviets installed Najibullah as the new leader of the Communist party in Afghanistan, replacing Babrak Karmal. The Soviets announced a modest troop withdrawal in late summer, but the struggle for control of Afghanistan remained largely stalemated.

COMOROS

Nonruling Parties. Communist parties in many Western European countries were on the verge of becoming little more than political sects. In French national elections in March, the Communist Party attracted less than 10 percent of the vote—down from more than 20 percent at the start of the decade. In Portugal, support for the strongly pro-Soviet Communist party dropped to 15 percent of the electorate, while in Spain the party received less than 5 percent of the vote in June elections. In the Netherlands the Communists ended up with no seats in Parliament after the May elections—for the first time since 1922. In Greece, one of the two competing Communist parties disbanded to try to form a broader-based coalition of the left. Only in Italy, where the party had abandoned much of its Leninist rhetoric, was the Communist Party still relatively robust, with about 30 percent of the popular vote. Even there, the membership was aging, as the party had difficulty attracting young people.

See also articles on individual countries.

R.E.K.

COMOROS. *See* STATISTICS OF THE WORLD.

COMPUTERS. In 1986, Compaq Computer Corporation took the lead in introducing a personal computer that uses a new breed of microprocessor. Apple enjoyed brisk sales for its Macintosh, while IBM was running into difficulties.

New Chip. Compaq, a very successful manufacturer of personal computers compatible with the IBM PC, became the first major vendor to bring out a personal computer—the Deskpro 386—based on Intel Corporation's powerful new 80386 microprocessor. The 386, as the chip is familiarly known, can handle data in chunks of 32 "bits" at a time. The Deskpro 386 can run popular software written for the IBM PC, but its 32-bit chip has a much faster processing speed than the IBM PC's 16-bit chip. This means the new machines can run the software written for the IBM PC or AT-class computers significantly more rapidly. The 386 chip also allows vast increases in memory size—more, in fact, than mainframe computers. As a result, developers can design more complex and powerful software for office, scientific, and engineering applications.

Apple. In the home and school markets, Apple Computer boosted the power of Apple II by replacing its 8-bit microprocessor with a 16-bit chip. The new top-of-the-line computer,

Weighing in at 30 tons and programmable with the help of 6,000 dials and switches, ENIAC (Electronic Numerical Integrator and Computer) was the world's first electronic digital computer. In February computer enthusiasts celebrated the 40th anniversary of its dedication.

the Apple IIgs, was designed to run 90 percent of the software written for the 8-bit Apple family (but was not compatible with Apple's Macintosh). Meanwhile, after a slow start, Macintosh sales to large corporations increased, and Apple successfully promoted a new market for "desktop publishing" using personal computers. With the Macintosh's graphics capability, special software, and a laser printer, it was possible for users to produce their own reports, newsletters, and other documents without having to obtain larger, more expensive computers or turn to costly printing contractors. The company was certain to encounter growing competition because of the enhanced graphics capabilities of the 386 machines and other computers. However, Apple was expected to introduce a new, more powerful version of the Macintosh, based on the next generation of its microprocessor, the 32-bit Motorola 68020.

IBM. IBM's share of the personal computer market declined, as a flood of IBM-compatible machines, primarily from Asia, led to repeated price-cutting. In the market for larger computers—long IBM's stronghold—IBM also suffered a slump in demand. The company sought to reduce its work force through attrition and early retirement incentives. Still, despite a 27 percent drop in third-quarter income, IBM remained the most profitable U.S. corporation.

Unisys. Burroughs Corporation and the Sperry Corporation agreed to merge into a single company, which was named Unisys after a contest among employees of both companies. The merged company hoped to compete more effectively with IBM in the mainframe market. Both lines of computer products were to be marketed under the brand name Unisys, while keeping their individual product designations.

International Purchases. In September the Honeywell Corporation announced that it was negotiating with the NEC Corporation of Japan and Groupe Bull S.A., France's state-owned computer maker, over the purchase of a large stake in Honeywell's computer operations, afflicted by declining sales. In October it was announced that, subject to U.S. government approval, the Japanese electronics company Fujitsu Ltd. would buy a controlling interest in Fairchild Semiconductor Corporation, a former

Programmed Prose

No longer content simply to process the words we write, computers are now helping us write them. Some software now on the market will actually evaluate your style and offer hints for improvement. But if a computer program tears apart your prose, don't throw in the towel just yet. Given the Gettysburg Address to critique, one of the new style-checking programs condemned Abraham Lincoln's use of the passive voice in such classic phrases as "Now we are engaged in a great civil war." Another program balked at the former president's "wordy writing style" and took strong offense at the famous sentence "The world will little note nor long remember what we say here, but it can never forget what they did here" (too many negatives). The overall rating for "strength of delivery": zero. It seems the new style-checking programs, though possibly helpful to the novice writer, don't know when to break a general rule.

Silicon Valley leader, from Schlumberger Ltd., an oilfield services firm.

Computers of the Future. In the Pentagon-sponsored VHSIC (Very High Speed Integrated Circuits) program, semiconductor firms competed to create chips that would have the power of a supercomputer. Other researchers sought to lay the groundwork for a generation of 21st-century optical computers that would use light instead of conventional electronics for computation.

Still others worked on radically new computer architectures. From the beginning of the computer age the machines have been built with a central processing unit (CPU), which does the calculating, and a stored memory. At very high speeds, however, the link between the CPU and memory can be a bottleneck. Thinking Machines Corporation in Cambridge, Mass., unveiled a computer that overcomes this problem: the Connection Machine. Instead of operating on a problem in serial fashion, the Connection Machine's 65,536 processors (each with its own memory) operate in parallel, greatly boosting the machine's speed. While the initial market was small, future prospects were intriguing. W.D.M.

CONGO. See Statistics of the World.

CONGRESS OF THE UNITED STATES. See United States of America: *Congress.*

CONNECTICUT. See Statistics of the World.

CONSTRUCTION. See Economy and Business.

COSTA RICA. Oscar Arias Sánchez, candidate of the incumbent National Liberation Party, was elected president of Costa Rica on February 2, 1986. He won a surprise victory over Social Christian Unity Party leader Rafael Angel Calderón Fournier; it was only the second time since the revolution of 1948 that the incumbent party's candidate had triumphed. Calderón's denunciation of Costa Rica's neutrality policy and his embrace of the hawkish U.S. stand toward the Sandinista regime in Nicaragua had apparently alarmed a number of voters. Arias also benefited from fears of a return to the economic chaos associated with the last Social Christian Unity administration, in which Calderón had been a prominent figure.

Before his inauguration on May 1, Arias declared his opposition to any further U.S. aid to the contras fighting to overthrow the Sandinistas. However, in June the U.S. House approved aid to the contras, and although official Costa Rican policy remained that of expelling all contra forces, its ability to enforce such a policy in the face of U.S. opposition remained a question mark. Arias himself appointed a cabinet on the basis of perceived merit, with no great consideration of past party associations and ideology; thus the new foreign minister, Rodrigo Madrigal, was a former opposition whip deeply suspicious both of the Sandinista regime and of the so-called Contadora peace process.

Costa Rican economic performance during the final years of the previous administration had been quite respectable, thanks to a rise in coffee prices, massive U.S. aid, and some austerity measures, but the economy began to unravel around election time, and the public sector deficit rose. One of Arias's first and most unpopular acts as president was to increase corn, rice, and bean prices. Also, a new austerity package, announced in July, limited central bank financing of public sector deficits, called for a 15 percent spending cut, and held down private-sector wage increases.

See Statistics of the World.   L.W.G.

CRIME AND LAW ENFORCEMENT. Developments in 1986 included the handing down of convictions in major espionage and organized crime cases and a growing national concern about drug abuse. Violent crime continued to make news when 14 employees of an Oklahoma post office were killed by a fellow worker.

Espionage. On August 28, former navy radioman Jerry A. Whitworth, 47, was sentenced to 365 years in prison and fined $410,000 for his role in a Soviet spy ring. Whitworth had been paid for passing stolen classified Navy cryptographic data to John A. Walker, Jr., a retired naval officer who has said he headed the spy ring. Walker had pleaded guilty to espionage in October 1985 and agreed to testify against Whitworth in exchange for a life sentence for himself and a reduced prison term for his son, Michael, a Navy yeoman also indicted in the case. Despite lie-detector tests that raised doubts about whether John Walker had testified truthfully, on November 6 he was sentenced accordingly, while his son received a 25-year term.

On July 14 a federal judge sentenced Richard Miller to two concurrent life sentences for spying for the Soviet Union. Miller, the first FBI agent ever convicted of espionage, was found guilty of plotting to exchange information about the bureau's counterintelligence operations. A federal jury found Ronald W. Pelton, a former employee of the National Security Agency, guilty on June 5 of selling highly sensitive intelligence secrets to Moscow. The day before Pelton's conviction, Jonathan Jay Pollard, a former U.S. Navy intelligence analyst, pleaded guilty to spying for Israel. His wife, Anne Henderson Pollard, pleaded guilty to lesser offenses. Federal prosecutors claimed Israeli officials had asked Pollard to gather intelligence material related to Israel's defense.

In February a federal jury convicted retired CIA analyst Larry Wu-Tai Chin, a naturalized American citizen, on charges of having spied for the Chinese government for more than 30 years. Chin committed suicide while in a Virginia county jail awaiting sentencing.

War on Drugs. Efforts to halt drug trafficking and drug abuse were in the forefront of the news. A major cause for concern was the

The war against drugs proceeded on all fronts, as the Reagan administration made the halting of drug abuse a top announced objective. Above, special Navy radar planes are used to track drug smugglers' planes at the southern border of the United States. Below, Los Angeles police raid a "crack house" in an effort to curb the spread of this highly addictive form of cocaine.

increased popularity of crack, a potent and highly addictive form of cocaine.

In September the U.S. House of Representatives passed a sweeping bill that provided substantially increased federal fines and jail penalties for producing or distributing drugs, with a mandatory fine for drug possession in any federal jurisdiction and a mandatory life sentence for anyone aged 21 or over convicted a second time of selling drugs to an individual under 21. Provisions were also made for the use of U.S. military forces to intercept drugs

entering the country by ship or airplane. The bill that eventually passed Congress in October allocated $1.7 billion to step up enforcement efforts and fund education and treatment programs. Using authority provided by the new law, the Forest Service announced that it would deploy special agents to combat the illicit cultivation of marijuana in national forests.

As part of its drug-fighting campaign, the Reagan administration issued an executive order in September requiring the heads of federal agencies to implement widespread drug testing programs. Controversial testing programs were also announced by athletic associations and already were mandated by many corporations for their employees.

In July a special detachment of U.S. forces was sent to Bolivia to aid Bolivian authorities in operations against narcotics processing laboratories based in mountainous areas of the country. Mexico was criticized publicly by some U.S. officials for inadequate efforts to control drug trafficking, and the Mexican government agreed to closer cooperation on antidrug efforts. However, serious problems continued. In August, U.S. Drug Enforcement Administration agent Victor Cortez was arrested in Guadalajara by members of the Jalisco state police and allegedly tortured before being released. Members of the Jalisco police were suspected of involvement in drug trafficking.

Singer Cathy Evelyn Smith, who gave comedian John Belushi an injection of heroin and cocaine the night he died from a drug overdose, pleaded no contest in June to involuntary manslaughter in the incident and was sentenced in August to three years in prison.

White-Collar Crime. On July 22 the U.S. House of Representatives voted to impeach U.S. District Judge Harry Claiborne of Nevada because of his conviction on two counts of federal income tax evasion. He was found guilty by the Senate on October 9 and was removed from office.

In February, Cook County Circuit Court Judge Reginald J. Holzer was found guilty in Chicago of extortion and mail fraud. Holzer was one of ten judges indicted in a corruption investigation of the county court system. He was sentenced to an 18-year prison term, the harshest sentence yet handed down in the probe; as of late 1986, five other judges had received terms of 10 to 15 years, while one had been acquitted.

Violent Crime. Early in the morning on August 20, mail carrier Patrick Henry Sherrill, 44, opened fire in a crowded post office in Edmond, Okla., killing 14 workers and injuring 7 others before killing himself with a bullet in the head. The police said Sherrill, a former weapons expert in the Marine Corps, had been criticized by his supervisor the day before the shootings and threatened with dismissal.

On May 16, David Young, a former police officer, and his wife, Doris, walked into a Cokeville, Wyo., elementary school brandishing handguns, rifles, and gasoline bombs. They herded about 150 children and adults into a classroom and asked for a ransom of $2 million for each hostage. One of the bombs went off accidentally, injuring some 70 children. During the incident Doris Young was apparently shot to death by her husband. David Young also shot and wounded the school's bandleader, before fatally shooting himself.

On December 18 a Rwanda court convicted U.S. wildlife researcher Richard McGuire in absentia of the December 1985 murder of gorilla expert Dian Fossey at her research camp. McGuire denied involvement and had returned to the United States, from which he could not be extradited.

Product Tampering. Diane Elsroth, of Peekskill, N.Y., died in February after taking an Extra-Strength Tylenol capsule contaminated with cyanide. Johnson & Johnson, Tylenol's manufacturer, recalled all capsule products and ended production of all nonprescription capsule medicine. In June the Bristol-Meyers Company also halted the sale of all nonprescription capsules, after Sue Snow Webking and Bruce Nickell, both residents of Auburn, Wash., died from taking cyanide-tainted capsules of the company's Extra-Strength Excedrin painkiller.

In March, SmithKline Beckman Corporation recalled three of its nonprescription medicines, after traces of rat poison were found in about half a dozen capsules. Edward Arlen Marks, who was convicted of tampering with the products and sentenced in October to 27 years in prison, had sought to create a public scare in order to make money on stock market transactions. In September, Louis Denber of Runnemede, N.J., died after tasting Lipton's chicken noodle Cup-A-Soup. Authorities said the soup packet had been slit open and loaded with cyanide.

Organized Crime and Racketeering. Major trials involving New York's five reputed organized-crime families got underway in the summer. The indictments, made under the federal Racketeer-Influenced and Corrupt Organizations Act (RICO), were aimed at a "commission" of top crime leaders alleged to rule the Mafia. Reputed crime bosses Anthony Salerno of the Genovese clan, Anthony Corallo of the Lucchese family, and Carmine Persico of the Columbos were among eight defendants convicted of racketeering in November in the Mafia commission trial. Persico, his son, and several others had been convicted in June in a separate case against the Columbo family; they received long prison sentences. Late in the year, John Gotti, reputed boss of the Gambino family, was on trial for racketeering charges. In October,

Philip Rastelli, the alleged Bonanno clan leader, was convicted on racketeering charges in another case.

During September, in the first trial to prosecute members of United Bamboo, a Taiwan-based international gang, under RICO provisions, 11 defendants were convicted on various charges ranging from racketeering and murder to drug dealing. Most received prison sentences ranging from 10 to 25 years. In January, Joseph

On August 20 part-time mailman Patrick Sherrill shot to death 14 workers at the Edmond, Okla., post office where he was employed, injured 7 others, then shot himself in the head. Known to his neighbors as "Crazy Pat," Sherrill was an apparently mentally disturbed ex-Marine who had been told to improve his work. At right, a shaken survivor is comforted by his wife and daughter. Below, victims of the tragic massacre are removed from the scene.

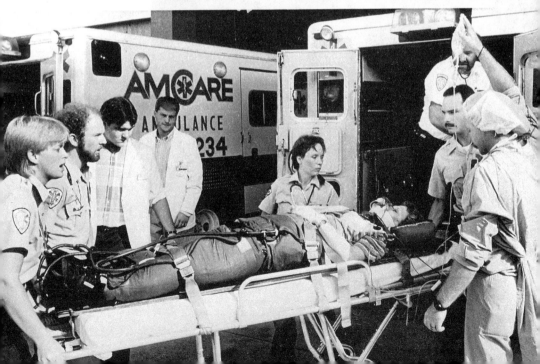

CRIME AND LAW ENFORCEMENT

J. Aiuppa and four other reputed organized-crime figures were convicted in Kansas City, Mo., of conspiring to skim profits from Las Vegas gambling casinos; they received prison terms of up to 28½ years. In April a federal jury sentenced Gennaro J. Angiulo, alleged Boston crime boss, to 45 years on racketeering charges; four others drew lesser sentences.

Arms Sales Conspiracy. A plot to sell more than $2 billion in U.S.-made weapons to Iran was unveiled by the Justice Department in April, and a federal grand jury indicted 18 defendants, including a London-based American lawyer and a retired Israeli general, on conspiracy charges. Prosecutors said the defendants had forged documents to sell the Iranians fighter and transport planes, tanks, missiles, and other armaments. In light of later developments linking the federal government to the sale of arms to Iran, a court delay was granted to reexamine the case.

Prison Riots. During a three-day-long siege in January at the West Virginia Penitentiary in Moundsville, 15 guards and a food-service worker were held hostage, and three inmates were killed by fellow prisoners. The crisis ended after West Virginia Governor Arch Moore agreed to hear prisoners' grievances. Later in

the year at the Lorton, Va., prison complex near Washington, D.C., rioting prisoners set fire to dormitories; over 500 inmates had to be transferred to other facilities.

Domestic Terrorism. Ten members of a neo-Nazi group known as the Order were sentenced in February to prison terms ranging from 40 to 100 years for a range of violent crimes aimed at inciting racist revolution. In May, six members of the so-called United Freedom Front were sentenced to prison terms ranging from 15 to 33 years for planting bombs at military reserve centers and corporate buildings in New York City to protest U.S. policies.   L.S.G.

CUBA. After a long period of stable leadership, Cuba in 1986 witnessed a major political shake-up. The purge of so-called old Communists (members of the prerevolutionary Popular Socialist Party) continued with the "retirement" of PSP founder Blas Roca from the Politburo and the removal of Lionel Soto as ambassador to the Soviet Union. They were replaced by prominent Castro loyalists. Meanwhile, the ouster of three of Castro's closest guerrilla commanders—Ramiro Valdés, Guillermo García, and Sergio del Valle—from both ministerial and Politburo posts reflected deeper dissatisfactions. The changes also strengthened the

A joyous reunion with his wife was Ricardo Montero Duque's welcome to Newark, N.J., after 25 years in Cuban prisons. Montero, a military commander in the failed Bay of Pigs invasion of 1961, had received a 30-year sentence.

position of Defense Minister General Raúl Castro as heir apparent to his brother.

At the Third Congress of the Communist Party, held in February, 9 of the Politburo's 24 members were ousted, along with half of the Central Committee's 225 members. Their replacements reflected Castro's intention of putting more women, blacks, and youth in leadership positions.

A major task of the party congress was to review progress under the 1981–1985 five-year plan. Castro's assessment was that overall growth had exceeded goals and that basic needs had been met in food, housing, health, and education. But he noted that growth had been insufficient in key export sectors and imported substitution industries, where it was most needed. Among other factors, Castro blamed planning failures, labor indiscipline, and "bourgeois liberal" tendencies for Cuba's economic problems, along with low world prices for sugar and Western restrictions on Cuban trade and credits. He also cited low sugar production, partly attributable to drought. For the future, Castro called for a return to tight central planning.

In June the Cuban government announced that its six-year experiment in economic liberalization had come to an end: the "free markets" in which peasants had sold their surplus produce were closed, the nascent private sector of builders, artisans, and street vendors was restricted, and the private sale of housing was banned.

Cuba continued to remain heavily dependent on subsidies from and trade with the Soviet Union; the two countries signed a five-year aid package in April.

Talks with U.S. officials aimed at reviving a suspended 1984 agreement, for regulated migration of Cubans to the United States and repatriation of "undesirable" Cuban refugees held in U.S. prisons, broke down amid mutual recriminations. However, the United States agreed to admit some Cuban political prisoners; 67 such prisoners arrived in Miami on September 15, after as long as 25 years in Cuban jails. In June the regime freed Ricardo Montero Duque, a senior officer in the abortive 1961 Bay of Pigs invasion by U.S.-sponsored Cuban exiles. In October, Ramón Conte Hernández,

last imprisoned member of the invasion force, was freed. Both went to the United States.

At the same time, human rights activists reportedly continued to be jailed and, in some cases, beaten and possibly murdered. In one such instance, a 17-year-old activist was arrested in August by security officials in Havana; hours later, his body was delivered to his parents with the explanation that he had committed suicide.

See STATISTICS OF THE WORLD.   P.W.

CYPRUS. In March 1986, a new proposal to reunite Cyprus was presented by United Nations Secretary-General Javier Pérez de Cuéllar. It called for the creation of a federated republic with a Greek Cypriot and a Turkish Cypriot state, each with its own official language. The federal government would control foreign affairs, currency and banking, communications, a federal judiciary, and defense. The lower chamber of the legislature would be 70 percent Greek and 30 percent Turkish, while Greeks and Turks would be equally represented in the upper chamber. The president would be Greek and the vice president Turkish. Each would have the power to veto legislative decisions.

Although the Turkish Cypriot government accepted the UN proposal, Greek Cypriot President Spyros Kyprianou said it needed major changes. His position, worked out in consultation with Greek Premier Andreas Papandreou, called for the evacuation of all Turkish troops, agreement on the right of Greek refugees to resettle in the North, and guarantees against any future Turkish military intervention prior to the creation of a transitional federated government. Both the conservative Democratic Rally Party and the Communist AKEL party criticized Kyprianou for rejecting the proposal.

Turkey's Premier Turgut Özal paid a visit to northern Cyprus in July to demonstrate support for the Turkish Cypriot government, prompting objections not only from the Greek Cypriot government but also from the UN, the United States, the Soviet Union, and several European governments. Calling the Greek Cypriot and UN objections insults, Turkish Cypriot President Rauf Denktash retaliated by temporarily closing all five crossing points between the Turkish and Greek sectors, an action viewed by diplomats as a serious challenge to the UN peacekeeping mission on Cyprus.

In September, Turkish Cypriot Prime Minister Dervis Eroglu formed a new coalition government between his National Unity Party and the small New Birth Party.

On August 3 three terrorists launched a rocket and mortar attack on Britain's Akrotiri Air Base in southwest Cyprus, wounding two people. A group calling itself the United Nasserite Organization claimed responsibility. A Lebanese suspect was convicted of involvement and sentenced to seven years in prison.

The Turkish Cypriot economy remained weak, suffering from large trade deficits and annual inflation exceeding 50 percent. The Greek Cypriot economy was reportedly doing well.

See STATISTICS OF THE WORLD.   P.J.M.

CZECHOSLOVAKIA. The 17th congress of the Communist Party of Czechoslovakia opened in Prague on March 24, 1986. In a three-hour keynote address, party chief Gustáv Husák indicated that although planning would have to be "improved" and economic growth accelerated, the party would stand firm on its principles of ideology and on nonreformist policies. The eighth five-year plan, in preparation since 1983, was still incomplete when the congress began. Covering the period 1986–1990, it envisioned an 18–19 percent increase in national income to be achieved mainly through greater labor productivity, despite the resistance of conservative managers reluctant to change the habits of almost 40 years of Communist rule.

Meeting at Karlovy Vary in February, the Czechoslovak and West German foreign ministers tried to improve relations between the two countries, but no real progress was reported. Government reaction to the April accident at the Chernobyl nuclear power plant in the Soviet Union was guarded. Officials said that no change had taken place in the atmosphere over Czechoslovakia and that there was no need to take any special measures to protect the population.

In September, Karel Srp, the leader of an independent cultural organization called the Jazz Section, was arrested along with six members of the group. The government had already banned concerts sponsored by the 8,000-member group, cut off its phones, and seized its mailing lists, but it still was able to put out a newsletter that reached as many as 80,000 readers.

It was an all-Czechoslovak final at the U.S. Open tournament in New York City in September, as Martina Navratilova, originally from Revnice and now a U.S. citizen, defeated Helena Sukova of Prague in the women's final, and Ivan Lendl, originally from Ostrava and now living in Connecticut, beat Miloslav Mecir of Prievidza in the men's final. In July, Navratilova, returning to her native country for the first time since she defected to the United States in 1975, got a warm reception from the Czech public despite official neglect, as she led the U.S. team to victory in the international Federation Cup tournament in Prague.

See STATISTICS OF THE WORLD.   R.A.P.

D

DAHOMEY. See STATISTICS OF THE WORLD.

DANCE. The year 1986 was notable for the return of several dance companies to North America after long absences, as well as for some important anniversaries.

Soviet Companies. The Kirov Ballet was back in North America for the first time in 22 years. The company performed at Canada's Expo 86 in May and then headed for a quick U.S. tour,

hastily arranged after the signing of a new cultural exchange agreement by President Ronald Reagan and Soviet leader Mikhail Gorbachev in late 1985. Much had happened to the Kirov since its last visit, from defections by Natalia Makarova and Mikhail Baryshnikov to administrative changes.

On its U.S. stops, the company presented *Swan Lake* and the "Shades" scene from *La*

Bayadère, among other classics. Canadian audiences also had the opportunity to see *The Knight in the Tiger's Skin,* a recent ballet by the company's new artistic director, Oleg Vinogradov. The current crop of male principals was disappointing, but the women principals boasted such formidable technicians as Olga Chenchikova, Tatiana Terekhova, and Lubov Kunakova. The female corps continued to exhibit a superb classical style. Among promising young male soloists were the powerful Alexander Lunev and the elegant Sergei Vikharev; among the women was the extraordinary new ballerina Altinai Asylmuratova.

The Moiseyev Dance Company was also back, in its first visit to the United States since 1974. The premiere performance at New York City's Metropolitan Opera House had to be cancelled after tear gas was released in the hall, causing 4,000 patrons to flee. Security was beefed up for subsequent performances, and the rest of the tour proceeded without trouble. Enthusiastic audiences once again enjoyed the bravura, virtuosity, and charm of the company's dancers in director Igor Moiseyev's cannily theatrical versions of Russian, Moldavian, Ukrainian, and Asian folk dance forms.

The Bolshoi ballet toured Vienna, Rio de Janeiro, Dublin, London, and Paris, dancing with all its vaunted drive and vitality. The company was to visit the United States in summer 1987.

In June, Soviet dancers competed for the first time in the International Ballet Competition in Jackson, Miss., taking many of the top honors. Copping the grand prix was the team of Nina Ananiashvili and Andris Liepa, both Bolshoi principals.

Other Visiting Companies. The Paris Opera Ballet, whose only previous visit to the United States was in 1948, played seasons in July at the Met and at Washington's Kennedy Center for the Performing Arts. Both the critics and the public found much to admire in the technique and style of the dancers but little in the productions of Rudolf Nureyev, ballet master since 1983. Neither his stagings of *Swan Lake* and *Raymonda* nor his baroque adaptation of Henry James's *Washington Square* was well received. The talents of such stars as Elisabeth

The exquisite Soviet ballerina Altinai Asylmuratova, seen here performing in La Bayadère, *had a stunningly successful North American debut when the Kirov Ballet of Leningrad made its first visit in more than 20 years.*

Platel, Sylvie Guillem, Charles Jude, and Laurent Hilaire could be better appreciated in Serge Lifar's *Les Mirages* and in George Balanchine's *Palais de Cristal* (created for the Paris Opera Ballet and later remounted by Balanchine for New York City Ballet as *Symphony in C*). At age 48, Nureyev revealed little of the splendid dancing form that had made him the most exciting male dancer of the 1960's.

In July, Expo 86 hosted Britain's Royal Ballet, in its first North American season in five years. The company presented Kenneth MacMillan's *Romeo and Juliet,* the first performance outside of London of MacMillan's new version of *Le Baiser de la Fée,* and the world premiere of *Galanteries* by the Royal's new resident choreographer, David Bintley. Sadler's Wells Royal Ballet, the junior branch of Britain's Royal Ballet, made its first visit to the United States since 1951. On tour in Boston, New York, Cleveland, and other cities early in the year, it performed a new production of *The Sleeping Beauty* by its artistic director, Peter Wright, as well as works by Bintley.

DANCE

The Central Ballet of China embarked on its first U.S. tour in March. The influence of Soviet training was evident both in the Western classical showpieces, like the *Don Quixote* pas de deux, and in the more ordinary choreography of the native repertory. The dancers, although somewhat weak in technique, showed a winning modesty and charm.

In July, New York audiences got the chance to see the National Ballet of Canada perform Glen Tetley's *Alice,* a new ballet commissioned by the company's artistic director, Erik Bruhn, not long before his death on April 1. Inspired by David Del Tredici's *In Memory of a Summer Day,* a composition for mezzo-soprano and orchestra based on Lewis Carroll's *Alice's Adventures in Wonderland* and *Through the Looking Glass,* the ballet was widely acclaimed upon its debut in Toronto but did not quite duplicate its success in New York.

U.S. Troupes. The Joffrey Ballet, which has home seasons in both Los Angeles and New York, celebrated its 30th anniversary in 1986, and to cap it off staged its first production of Frederick Ashton's evening-length *La Fille Mal Gardée.*

The level of dancing continued to be high at New York City Ballet and showed marked improvement at American Ballet Theatre. Both companies, however, experienced difficulty in finding worthy additions to their repertories. Neither Jean-Pierre Bonnefous's *Shadows* nor Peter Martins's *Songs of the Auvergne* aroused much interest during NYCB's winter season. Equally uninspiring in the spring season were two Jerome Robbins pieces: *Piccolo Balletto* and *Quiet City* (a memorial to Joseph Duell, the principal who committed suicide in February). At ABT, David Parson's *Walk This Way* and John Taras's *Francesca da Rimini* failed to

The ballet Alice, *created by Glen Tetley for the National Ballet of Canada, retained Lewis Carroll's haunting mood of childlike wonder in its sensitive exploration of love and memory. Its Canadian debut was a big success.*

excite critics and audiences, while Mac-Millan's *Requiem*, set to Andrew Lloyd Webber's score, was described by one critic as an "endless panorama of tortured, suffering, dying flesh." More successful were NYCB's revival of Balanchine's *Slaughter on Tenth Avenue*, after a 17-year hiatus, and the reconstruction by Paul Taylor of the solo choreographed for him by Balanchine in the 1959 *Episodes*. *Slaughter's* resurrection was justified by Suzanne Farrell's enchanting performance as the Strip Tease Girl.

The Martha Graham Dance Company's three-week run at City Center in May and June commemorated the founder's 60th anniversary as an independent artist. In addition to two new works by the 93-year-old choreographer (*Tangled Night* and *Temptations of the Moon*), the season was notable for a number of significant reconstructions, including the 1929 *Heretic* and five early solos by Graham and her artistic mentors, Ted Shawn and Ruth St. Denis. Preceding Graham into City Center was the Paul Taylor Dance Company, which featured a major new work by Taylor, *A Musical Offering*, set to the contrapuntal Bach score of the same name. Also at City Center, the Merce Cunningham Dance Company presented two premieres: *Arcade*, originally choreographed for the Pennsylvania Ballet in 1985, and *Grange Eve*, a work whose square dance motifs may be a recollection of their creator's rural boyhood.

The biggest news on the modern dance scene was the emergence of 30-year-old Mark Morris, whom *Time* magazine called "the hottest young choreographer in the country." Blessed with an extraordinary and eclectic musicality and a wide-ranging, offbeat imagination, Morris, with his Seattle-based group of 13 dancers, was in heavy demand across the United States and abroad.　　　　　　　　　　K.F.R.

DELAWARE. See STATISTICS OF THE WORLD.

DEMOCRATIC PARTY. See UNITED STATES OF AMERICA: *Political Parties.*

DENMARK. The long-brewing controversy over Danish participation in the European Community came to a head early in 1986 when the minority nonsocialist coalition government of Prime Minister Poul Schlüter lost a bid for parliamentary acceptance of proposed treaty reforms strengthening the Community's powers. Schlüter responded by putting the issue to a referendum on February 27; voters endorsed the changes by a margin of 56 percent to 44 percent.

During the month-long public debate before the referendum, government leaders argued that popular rejection would mean a potential end to Denmark's membership in the European Community. That was precisely the intention of many domestic critics, who remained unreconciled to membership, largely because they preferred cooperation with the other Scandinavian countries to that with continental Europe and Britain. Social Democrats and other opponents had been strengthened in their resolve by opinion polls indicating that a majority of the citizens would vote against membership if the question were once again put to them, as it was in 1972. Most Danes then favored joining, but an economic slump followed later in the decade. After the February 27 vote, Danish officials signed the treaty, enabling the reforms to be implemented in March.

Social Democrats and various left-center parties had scored a clear victory in November 1985 local elections. Trying to articulate a more sharply defined national policy, Schlüter appointed a few private-sector representatives to the cabinet in March. Simultaneously, he unveiled an austerity budget, with new taxes on alcohol, tobacco, luxury goods, and energy consumption. In October, Schlüter introduced a new austerity plan—the fourth in 18 months. It sought to control consumer spending and reduce the balance-of-payments deficit by taxing consumer loans, increasing interest on individual savings, and boosting exports.

Denmark, Sweden, and Norway agreed in April to coordinate steps to reduce the flow of Third World political refugees into the Scandinavian region via East Germany. Government officials vowed to work through the UN and other international organizations.

See STATISTICS OF THE WORLD.　　M.D.H.

DISTRICT OF COLUMBIA. See STATISTICS OF THE WORLD.

DJIBOUTI. See STATISTICS OF THE WORLD.

DOMINICA. See STATISTICS OF THE WORLD.

DOMINICAN REPUBLIC. See STATISTICS OF THE WORLD. See also CARIBBEAN BASIN.

E

EARTH SCIENCES. In 1986 drought conditions in the Southeast, emissions of toxic gas from an African crater lake, and new equipment for exploring the ocean depths attracted the interest of earth scientists.

CLIMATOLOGY

A devastating heat wave and drought, the worst to hit the southeastern United States in over a century, caused widespread suffering and agricultural damage during the summer. Long-term developments such as global warming and depletion of the ozone layer were a cause of concern.

Heat Wave and Drought. The Southern drought and heat wave resulted from a persistent high pressure system that blanketed the area, drawing in warm air but inhibiting cloud formation. Daily temperatures in many areas exceeded 100°F, and scores of deaths were attributed to the heat. The weather also proved disastrous to agriculture. Heavy rains in mid-August helped increase surface moisture but could not restore underground water levels or help most crops already planted; the U.S. Department of Agriculture designated more than 420 counties in 10 states agricultural disaster areas.

Tornadoes and Hurricanes. Tornadoes, hailstorms, and high winds pounded Indiana, Kentucky, and Ohio on March 10, causing six deaths and widespread damage in the worst such outbreak to hit the region so early in the season. The hurricane season also began early, when Bonnie struck the Texas Gulf Coast in June, causing at least two deaths and forcing the evacuation of 20,000, including thousands of oil rig workers in the Gulf. In August, Hurricane Charley hit the eastern United States with 100-mph winds, bringing at least five fatalities.

Rains and Flooding. Devastating storms containing rain and hurricane-force winds from the subtropical Pacific struck the western United States and British Columbia in mid-February. California was particularly hard hit. Avalanches, landslides, and floods accompanied the area's worst rain in 30 years; there were at least 18 deaths and considerable damage.

Heavy precipitation in late 1985 and early 1986 swelled the Great Lakes to record levels, flooding basements and destroying property along Lake Michigan's 1,400-mile shoreline. Precipitation brought some Great Lakes to even higher levels in the fall. Heavy rainfall also saturated the lower midwestern states in the fall, causing severe flooding.

Water levels in Utah's Great Salt Lake continued to rise from their record low of 1963; a study by the National Climatic Data Center linked the rise to a precipitation pattern that could be expected to occur once in about every 120 years.

Ozone Depletion. A major study coordinated by NASA concluded that, by the year 2050, stratospheric ozone could decrease by more than 9 percent if emissions of chlorofluorocarbons continued at their 1980 levels. Scientists traveled to Antarctica to study a worrisome continent-sized hole that has recently appeared in the ozone layer over the South Pole each September and October.

Global Warming. According to testimony before a congressional subcommittee, there was a growing consensus among scientists that a gradual small rise in temperatures could be expected over the coming decades, caused by the entrapment of carbon dioxide and other gases within the earth's atmosphere, in the so-called greenhouse effect. The resulting melting of polar ice could cause a rise in sea levels around the world; agriculture could also be seriously affected. One scientist predicted that global temperatures would rise 1 degree Fahrenheit before the year 2000, with further increases thereafter.

Liability for Forecasts? U.S. officials were temporarily relieved when a federal appeals court reversed a lower court decision and found that the National Weather Service did not have to pay $1.25 million to the families of three Cape Cod, Mass., fishermen. The men had been lost in heavy seas after heeding an inaccurate Weather Service prediction of fair weather. The decision was appealed to the Supreme Court. **N.M.R.**

A surge in water levels, brought on in part by above average levels of precipitation over the winter, threatened waterfront homes in the Great Lakes; shown here, the eroding shoreline of Lake Michigan.

GEOLOGY

In 1986 a deadly cloud of gas rose from a lake in Africa and a devastating earthquake shook Central America. Researchers constructed the first three-dimensional maps of the earth's core.

Killer Lake. On August 21, in northwestern Cameroon, a volcanic crater lake, which local villagers had dubbed the good lake because of its shimmering blue color, became a killer. A deadly cloud of gas exploded from Lake Nios, killing more than 1,700 people and thousands of animals in the surrounding valley. According to medical examiners sent by the U.S. Agency for International Development (AID), the victims became unconscious within seconds of exposure to the cloud and died shortly thereafter of suffocation or cardiac failure. The examiners tentatively fingered asphyxiating carbon dioxide as the lethal gas.

The AID researchers suspected that the carbon dioxide originated from an underlying source of magma. If so, the cloud probably was not generated by a sudden volcanic eruption—the floor of the lake was found to be flat and smooth. The carbon dioxide most likely leaked slowly into the lake. It could build up to very high levels in the bottom waters over a long period of time because the surface of Lake Nios, like that of other volcanic lakes in the tropics, is perennially warmed. This warm top layer of water effectively caps the lake, leaving the colder and denser bottom waters undisturbed.

What upset this stratification and triggered the release of the carbon dioxide? One possibility, among many, is that a landslide caused the bottom waters, rich in carbon dioxide under high pressure, to rise toward the surface. The sudden change in pressure might have set off a runaway release of gas similar to what happens when a soda bottle is opened after being shaken.

Volcanoes. The Nevado del Ruiz volcano in Colombia, Mount St. Helens in Washington state, and Pavlof Volcano on the Alaskan peninsula were active during the year, and Alaska's Augustine Island volcano awakened with a series of powerful eruptions starting on March 27, sending ash and gas clouds into the stratosphere and disrupting air traffic. On Jan-

On August 21 a deadly cloud of poisonous gases escaped from the volcanic Lake Nios in Cameroon. More than 1,700 people and thousands of animals in the surrounding area were killed.

Hawaii's Kilauea changed pattern in July after years of periodic eruptions that sent lava fountains 1,000 feet into the air. A new vent opened on its side, allowing a steady flow of lava that reached the sea in November. Kilauea did not then stop, as Hawaiian myth said it would, but continued to produce lava at a steady rate. By late December, more than two dozen homes had been destroyed.

Earthquakes. During the year, earthquakes caused fatalities in Cuzco, Peru; in Turkey and Soviet Georgia; in Kalamai, Greece; in Taiwan; and off the coast of Venezuela. A quake measuring 5.9 on the Richter scale, the strongest to shake southern California in seven years, struck an area about 12 miles north of Palm Springs on July 8, injuring 29 persons. But by far the worst disasters were the two earthquakes estimated at 5.4 magnitude that shook El Salvador on October 10, killing about 1,500 people. These were the latest in a series of devastating quakes since 1965 in Central Amer-

uary 18 a submarine volcano in the Pacific near Japan began erupting, giving birth to a small island that, however, had eroded below sea level by the end of March. Residents of O-Shima, an island south of Tokyo, fled November 21 when Mount Mihara erupted, accompanied by continuous earthquakes; a few days later the volcano was quiet and residents began returning, despite a small eruption on December 18.

ica, where three major tectonic plates come together.

Mapping the Inner Earth. Earth scientists have been probing the deepest reaches of the planet with seismic waves generated by earthquakes. Two research groups recently constructed the first three-dimensional maps of the earth's core, with a technique similar to the CT (computerized tomography) scans used in medicine. They show that the earth's molten metal core is not a smooth sphere but has peaks and valleys much more extreme than those on the earth's surface. These and future maps will help scientists decipher the mysterious swirlings of liquid iron in the outer core that are thought to create the earth's magnetic field. And they may shed light on how heat from the heart of the planet escapes, ultimately firing up volcanoes, generating earthquakes, and building mountains.   S.A.W.

OCEANOGRAPHY

In 1986, state-of-the-art underwater technology allowed oceanographers to probe the secrets of the sunken *Titanic*. And researchers examined new evidence to explain the mass extinction of dinosaurs millions of years ago.

Probing the *Titanic*. Using the submersible *Alvin* and a new underseas robot, called *Jason, Jr.*, scientists descended nearly 13,000 feet into the North Atlantic to inspect and photograph the wreck of the *Titanic*. The British luxury liner, billed as unsinkable, struck an iceberg in the frigid seas southeast of Newfoundland on its maiden voyage in 1912 and sank, drowning more than 1,500 people.

Robert Ballard of the Woods Hole Oceanographic Institute, who had located the wreck in September 1985, returned in July aboard the research vessel *Atlantis II*. His expedition team made 11 dives in 22 days at sea to explore and photograph the wreck. *Alvin* landed on the *Titanic*'s deck; its operators controlled the highly maneuverable robot *Jason, Jr.*, as it explored the ship's interior, at depths that would crush ordinary equipment, and took 57,000 still photographs, along with hours of videotape. The expedition team found no evidence of a gash in the *Titanic*'s side, thought to have been the cause of the sinking. Ballard speculated that the ship's exterior steel plates had buckled when the *Titanic* hit.

Oceanographers were very interested in the newly developed equipment used to explore the *Titanic*. With the new generation of 20,000-foot submersibles, 97 percent of the ocean floor was now accessible to exploration, opening up new possibilities for unraveling its mysteries. The new technology could also help the U.S. military to conceal submarines in ocean trenches and track Soviet equipment.

Ancient Crater. About 65 million years ago, around the end of the Cretaceous Period, there were worldwide mass extinctions of plants and animals. The disappearance of dinosaurs and other reptiles that had dominated the earth permitted mammals to evolve rapidly and eventually led to the development of humans. Scientists have theorized that the extinctions came after an asteroid about 6 miles in diameter hit the earth, creating a cloud of dust so dense that it blocked the sun for years, killing plants and the animals that fed on them. From an examination of ocean-bottom topography, C. J. H. Hartnady of the University of Cape Town suggested in May that the Amirante Basin, in the Indian Ocean north of Madagascar, might be the missing impact crater made by that

The first extensive exploration of the wreck of the Titanic was conducted by a Woods Hole Oceanographic team. A variety of newly developed oceanographic research devices were used; shown here is the three-man submersible Alvin.

asteroid. The Amirante Basin is nearly circular and has an elevated margin, similar to craters formed by meteor impacts on land. The unusual features of this basin are not easily explained by the geologic processes that normally act on the ocean floor. Among other evidence, intriguing support for his theory came from indications of a large mass of very dense material below the Amirante Basin; this might be the remains of a meteor.   M.G.G.

ECONOMY AND BUSINESS. During 1986 the U.S. economy remained sluggish, but prospects for the future were difficult to assess. Oil prices were lower, inflation was very mild, and interest rates fell. But the federal budget deficit and heavy consumer debt caused concern, as did the huge trade deficit. Liability insurance was increasingly costly and difficult to obtain. Passage of a major federal tax reform bill had at least one immediate effect: it accelerated the already brisk pace of mergers and acquisitions activity. On the international scene, the United States, Japan, and West Germany cooperated in economic policy moves, international trade talks were launched, and some corporate giants announced a withdrawal from South Africa.

Trade Deficit, Oil Prices, Interest Rates. A plan to drive down the dollar's value, engineered in late 1985 by Treasury Secretary James A. Baker III with the finance ministers of Japan, West Germany, Great Britain, and France, achieved its immediate purpose; by September 1986 the dollar was more than 40 percent lower relative to other major currencies. The plan's underlying aim—cutting the record-high U.S. trade deficit—proved more difficult to accomplish. In the first half of 1986 the trade deficit continued to widen. From August through October figures showed improvement, but the November deficit hit a new record. Despite improvement in December, the year's deficit was a record $170 billion.

The decline in oil prices during the year was generally good for the U.S. economy; however, the impact on economic activity in the nation's energy patch, chiefly Texas and Oklahoma, was devastating. Oil industry investment came to a virtual halt, and ripple effects spread to other areas of the regional economy, depressing jobs and income. Many in the oil patch

breathed a sigh of relief when OPEC agreed to output reductions in August. The price of oil was up to around $15 a barrel in October; at that price American consumers still enjoyed lowered gasoline prices in the range of 75 cents to 85 cents a gallon.

Another reason for optimism was a decline in interest rates, caused by several factors. One was the 1985 Gramm-Rudman-Hollings balanced-budget law, which mandated progressively smaller budget deficits each year—and a balanced budget by 1991. This legislation seemed to reassure the financial markets that something was being done to tame huge federal deficits, which put upward pressure on interest rates. (Even though the Supreme Court threw out the enforcement mechanism for automatic cuts under the law, a "fallback" provision required Congress to follow the deficit-ceiling targets anyway.) At the same time, demand was not especially strong, because of the general sluggishness of the economy. Finally, the Federal Reserve Board made several cuts in its discount rate, the interest rate it charges member banks for borrowing. The prime lending rate charged by commercial banks, the lowest rate offered to their most creditworthy customers and a barometer of other short-term interest rates, also fell. The decline in inflationary pressures in particular also led to a drop in long-term interest rates. Adjustable rate mortgages fell below 10 percent early in the year; by November, uncapped adjustable rate mortgages had fallen to 8.55 percent. As rates declined, many home owners chose to refinance their mortgages.

Slow Growth. Economic growth was generally slow, with considerable variations from one quarter to the next. In the first quarter, real GNP rose at an annual rate of 3.8 percent, but in the second quarter it slowed to a 0.6 percent annual rate. Economic growth rebounded somewhat in the third quarter, to 2.8 percent; but growth slowed in the last quarter. The year's rate was 2.5 percent.

Consumers spent vigorously in the first half of 1986, boosting their purchases after inflation at an annual rate of 3.6 percent, faster than the growth of the GNP itself. One reason for the slow GNP growth rate was that domestic firms, especially automobile companies, re-

Automobile manufacturers' incentives, including rebates and uncommonly low finance rates, drove consumers to showrooms in record numbers during the late summer and led to a record one-month rise in retail sales.

duced their inventories. In the third quarter General Motors announced it would offer 2.9 percent financing on selected models, and other automakers followed suit with similar or more generous incentives. This triggered a stampede to auto showrooms and led to a 4.6 percent increase in overall retail sales for September, the sharpest one-month rise in nearly 20 years. However, retail sales for the whole year were up only a modest 5.2 percent over 1985.

In general, industrial production was torpid. Businesses told the government they would increase their spending on new plants and equipment by only 2.5 percent in 1986. Energy companies, hard hit by lower oil prices, reduced their investment plans, while other companies said they were scaling back because of reduced tax incentives contained in the new tax reform measure. Total industrial production rose only 0.9 percent in 1986. Construction did well, with housing starts up 3.7 percent for the whole year, to a total of 1.807 million units.

Inflation and Social Security. Inflation slowed down. As measured by the Consumer Price Index (CPI), inflation actually declined at an annual rate of 0.2 percent through July. From August through December there were small rises of less than 0.5 percent a month, leaving inflation for 1986 at 1.1 percent, the lowest in a quarter-century. On the basis of CPI measurements a 1.3 percent increase in social security benefits was set for 1987; the maximum wage subject to social security tax was set to rise to $43,800.

New Tax Law. Some economists were concerned about the short-term economic impact of the new tax legislation. Under its provisions, individuals would be taxed in 2 brackets rather than 15, with the top tax rate reduced from 50 percent to 28 percent. Many individual deductions were removed or tightened, but the standard deduction and personal exemptions were liberalized. The average individual taxpayer enjoyed a slight net tax cut; to compensate, total taxes paid by businesses would rise by about $120 billion over the next five years. Some economists believed the new law, by removing the investment tax credit for businesses, which was worth up to 10 percent of the cost of machinery and equipment, and scaling back of business investment incentives for plants and equipment would damage the economy at least in the short run; others believed that because companies would be forced to make decisions on economic rather than tax grounds, capital would flow to the

In a market that now favors either upscale stores or massive discount chains, there are fewer customers left for middle-of-the-road department stores like Gimbels; in September all but one of the Gimbels stores closed down—including the 76-year-old flagship store in New York City's Herald Square.

most efficient producers, which would ultimately help the economy. (*See also* UNITED STATES: Congress.)

Mergers and Acquisitions. Mergers and acquisitions continued to proceed at a feverish rate and were given a further stimulus late in the year, with the passage of the tax reform measure. The giant Beatrice Companies accepted a final $6.2 billion buyout early in the year from the investment firm of Kohlberg Kravis Roberts & Co., which itself acquired Safeway, the third-largest U.S. retailer, for $4.2 billion. PepsiCo Inc. paid $850 million for Kentucky Fried Chicken Corporation, thus becoming the second-largest fast-food company after McDonald's. MidCon Corporation accepted a $3 billion offer from the Occidental Petroleum Corporation in the first merger between a major pipeline and a leading oil company. Among other mergers and acquisitions, May Department Stores acquired Associated Drygoods; Delta Air Lines agreed to purchase Western Airlines; Burroughs Corporation acquired Sperry Corporation; and Citicorp won its long battle for Quotron Systems Inc. After passage of the new tax law, Time Inc. purchased SFN Companies Inc., an educational publishing company. Doubleday was sold to Bertelsmann AG, the largest West German publishing company.

Allied Stores Corporation, which operates such chains as Bonwit Teller and Brooks Brothers, agreed to be acquired by the Canadian Campeau Corporation for $3.6 billion. Unilever N.V., a British consumer products company, agreed to pay $3.1 billion for Chesebrough-Pond's Inc., manufacturer of such products as Vaseline and Ragu spaghetti sauce. Texas Air, which already owned Continental Air Lines and New York Air, purchased Eastern Air Lines for at least $600 million and paid close to $300 million for People Express; these acquisitions made Texas Air the largest U.S. airline operation under a single corporate entity.

Corporate raiders attacked, and in some cases "greenmail" was paid—that is, the target company repurchased its own stock at a premium price from a raider who had acquired a sizable stake. Sir James Goldsmith lost the Goodyear Tire and Rubber Company but won about $93 million, in one instance of alleged greenmail. Late in the year, the rate of mergers and acquisitions was running ahead of 1985 and was about 35 percent above 1983 levels.

Insurance Crisis. U.S. liability insurance rates jumped alarmingly, by as much as 1,000 percent for some risks; and some insurance protection was unavailable at any price. Physicians, board directors, and municipalities withdrew services when liability protection was canceled or became too expensive to justify the cost. To meet the crisis, federal legislation was enacted allowing business, government, and professional associations to form risk retention groups that could write all forms of liability insurance. The insurance industry condemned the new law as unfair for giving such groups a competitive advantage by exempting them from state insurance taxes and payments to state guaranty funds (reserves mandated by state law to protect against insolvency of insurance companies).

Employment. For the first six months of the year, the civilian unemployment rate averaged slightly over 7 percent, virtually unchanged from the 7.1 percent rate for 1985. Civilian unemployment decreased in the summer, to 6.8 percent in August, edged back up to 7 percent, then dipped to 6.9 percent and 6.7 percent in November and December. Partly because of the increased number of women in the work force, the nation experienced a record percentage of Americans holding jobs. Another factor that may have increased this percentage was the return of many older Americans to the work force. A good number found jobs in the fast-food industry, where declining numbers of teenagers in the work force had left a void.

Trade Relations. With the United States facing import problems, Federal Reserve Board Chairman Paul Volcker made a major issue of economic growth in Japan and West Germany, saying that too much of it relied on exports to other countries, chiefly to the United States. West Germany and Japan cooperated with the United States in economy-stimulating interest rate cuts early in the year, but they resisted when the Federal Reserve dropped the discount rate in late summer. Officials in West Germany pointed to a resumption of economic growth there, and Japan said its interest rates were already low. In October, however, the United States and Japan announced a plan to coordinate economic policies. The former agreed to stop efforts to push the dollar down further against the yen; Japan agreed to cut its discount rate from 3.5 to 3 percent.

GATT Talks. After several years of delay, 74 nations agreed to start a new round of comprehensive talks to liberalize the rules governing international trade. The agreement, reached

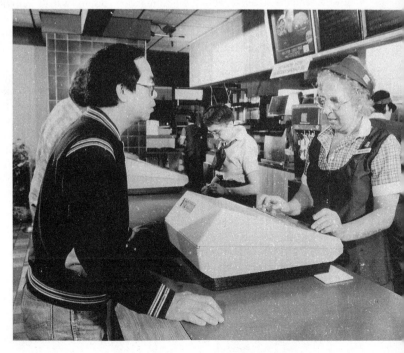

Older fast food workers, like these women at a Massachusetts Burger King, are filling a gap created by declining numbers of teenagers in the employment pool.

on September 20 at Punta del Este, Uruguay, called for establishing new rules for conducting trade in services and for reducing export subsidies for agricultural products, a politically explosive subject. In general, the agreement would overhaul the world's trade rules under the General Agreement on Tariffs and Trade, which polices unfair trade practices. The decision to put agricultural subsidies on the agenda required a great deal of negotiating. Reduction of the subsidies was expected to proceed very slowly because of the political power of agriculture in almost all countries. Trade in services was included in the agenda for new talks despite the opposition of several developing countries led by Brazil and India, which felt that their own developing service industries would be damaged if they could not protect them in the early stages. Significantly, however, the new round apparently was not to include talks on ending the restrictions on foreign investment that many developing countries had put in place.

The Soviet Union created a stir when it made a bid to gain observer status at GATT. GATT and Reagan administration officials reacted coolly, indicating they did not believe the Soviets would make available the information required to join the organization. The request was consistent with Soviet leader Mikhail Gorbachev's efforts to increase trade ties with the West and modernize industry. It was not granted for the GATT conference in September.

United States and Canada. A trade dispute broke into the open between the United States and Canada when President Ronald Reagan imposed a tariff on Canadian red cedar shakes and shingles used in home building. The Canadian government retaliated by imposing tariffs on U.S. books, magazines, and computer products. In October the United States imposed a duty on Canadian softwood lumber imports, citing Canadian government subsidies as unfair and damaging to the U.S. lumber industry. Canada placed a tariff on U.S. corn, in apparent retaliation. After negotiations, the softwood lumber duty was replaced with a 15 percent Canadian export tax.

Trade Agreements. The Reagan administration was very active on the trade front, announcing a number of cases involving unfair trade practices and signing several market agreements. It reached an agreement with Taiwan, South Korea, and Hong Kong to limit textile and apparel exports from those countries and signed a new multifiber agreement which regulates textile imports on a worldwide basis. The multifiber pact covers 38 bilateral agreements and nearly 1,000 individual quotas. Also, Taiwan agreed to raise the value of its currency and to open its markets to U.S. beer, wine, and cigarettes. Reagan's veto of a textile import quota bill was sustained in Congress, signaling that the White House stood a good chance of defeating further protectionist legislation that might be proposed by Congress.

South Africa. In October, General Motors and IBM announced their withdrawal from South Africa; both companies planned to continue selling products and services there through agreements with former subsidiaries. The following month, Eastman Kodak said it would halt all shipments of its products to South Africa in addition to selling off its assets there. Also in November, Barclays Bank of Britain announced plans to sell its South African interests to the Anglo American Corporation, in another expression of foreign concern over South Africa's inability to solve its racial crisis.

See also AUTOMOBILE INDUSTRY; BANKING AND FINANCE; COMPUTERS; MANUFACTURING INDUSTRIES; PUBLISHING; TELEVISION AND RADIO BROADCASTING; TRANSPORTATION; and separate articles on individual countries.   W.N.

ECUADOR. Ecuadorean voters dealt the government of President León Febres Cordero a setback in June 1986 elections. Febres lost his majority in the unicameral Congress to a center-left bloc dominated by the Democratic Left and Popular Democratic parties. Also soundly defeated was a proposal calling for a constitutional change that Febres had supported. The election was viewed as a referendum on his presidency; his detractors saw him as a high-handed violator of the constitution and as authoritarian in his conduct of public affairs. The results led Febres to shuffle his cabinet, bringing in nine new members.

Following the elections, FUT, the largest trade-union organization, demanded that Febres act to reduce prices and increase the minimum wage. Students took to the streets to protest economic policies, and two were killed in clashes with police. FUT also called a mass illegal strike in September.

In March, General Frank Vargas Pazos, armed forces chief of staff and air force commander, attempted to foment a rebellion against the regime by exploiting the issue of corruption in the military forces, but the services generally remained loyal to Febres. Dismissed from his post on March 7, Vargas seized an air base in Manta. On March 14 he was apprehended and turned over to a special military tribunal for trial. In September the president vetoed a congressional resolution that would have given him amnesty. Meanwhile, Defense Minister Luis Piñeiros and Manuel Albuja, the army commander, resigned amid accusations they had fraudulently misused public funds.

See STATISTICS OF THE WORLD.   L.L.P.

EDUCATION. Illicit drugs and academic standards were two issues of concern in education during 1986.

Len Bias Death. On June 19, Len Bias, a University of Maryland basketball star, died of a cocaine overdose in his dormitory room, just two days after the Boston Celtics had made him their first pick in the National Basketball Association draft. Bias's death generated increased public concern about drug use at all levels of education. It was also revealed that Bias had not passed a single course in the spring semester and was far short of the credits needed for graduation. In addition, 5 of the 12 players on the Maryland team flunked out during the year. In what he called an "emergency" move, university chancellor John Slaughter canceled the team's basketball games for the fall semester. Three persons were indicted on charges relating to Bias's death. Charges against two of them—both teammates of Bias—were dropped. A third individual, Brian Tribble, was to go on trial in 1987 on a variety of charges; he was accused of having given Bias the cocaine that killed him.

The Drug Problem. In the annual Gallup Poll of attitudes toward education, released in August, drugs were most frequently cited as the foremost problem in the schools, for the first time ever in this survey. Much of the concern over drugs centered on cocaine, which was growing in popularity in both high schools and

colleges, according to polls by the National Institute on Drug Abuse. A survey of colleges and universities found that an increasing proportion—30 percent—of the seniors questioned had used cocaine in the past year, although the number of students using marijuana had decreased and heroin had been tried by only 0.2 percent of the 1,100 college students questioned. Cocaine use by high school seniors also was on the increase, according to another report released by the NIDA, but three out of four seniors surveyed said they now regarded marijuana as a dangerous drug, compared with about one in four seniors in 1978.

Amid signs of increased public concern, government officials, legislators, and others announced highly publicized efforts to combat drug abuse among the general public and in schools and colleges. President Ronald Reagan took a visible and prominent role in advocating a national crusade against illegal drugs; first lady Nancy Reagan had already been highly active in efforts to deter young people from the use of drugs. Meanwhile, school districts, parents' groups, and others were making increased efforts to develop full-fledged drug education programs, aimed at providing real-

Slime 'Em, Slugs!

Bulldogs? Tigers? Wolverines? These are only some of the aggressive creatures that spring to mind when one thinks of college athletic teams. But Banana Slugs?? Students at the unconventional University of California at Santa Cruz voted overwhelmingly in April to adopt as their official school mascot that lowly, slime-exuding yellow mollusk that abounds in the nearby Santa Cruz Mountains. "The slug represents our uniqueness and our resolve to stay that way," said one student, referring to a school where fraternities and athletic scholarships are unknown and letter grades are given only by request. Chancellor Robert Sinsheimer long resisted the idea, favoring the "more majestic" sea lion, but after the April referendum he reluctantly bowed to the popular will. "The students," he conceded with ill-concealed disgust, "are entitled to a mascot . . . with which they can empathize."

EDUCATION

istic information and motivation to resist peer pressure.

At a news conference in September, Education Secretary William Bennett called upon schools to exercise greater discipline and offer more thorough education on drug abuse. He also released a manual, *What Works: Schools Without Drugs,* outlining strategies intended to combat drug use in schools.

A wide-ranging antidrug bill approved by Congress in October included more than $400 million in fiscal year 1987 for education programs to be operated by federal, state, and local governments, as well as by education agencies and colleges and universities. The measure also provided penalties for an adult convicted of selling, producing, or possessing an illegal substance within 1,000 feet of a school or college.

Taking advantage of Duquesne University's unique "pay now, study later" plan, Robert and Catherine Walker have already paid full college tuition for their young children. Innovative payment plans have become popular as college costs continue to rise.

Jan Kemp Suit. The University of Georgia was rocked by a scandal when Jan Kemp, a remedial English instructor at the university, filed a successful suit against university officials, claiming she had been dismissed in 1983 for speaking out against a university policy of preferential treatment for athletes. Testimony at the trial early in the year indicated that many athletes were given easy courses and special tutoring and even had failing grades changed so that they could continue to participate in intercollegiate competition. In February, Kemp was awarded $2.57 million in damages by a jury; after a reviewing judge had reduced the award, she settled for $1.1 million and reinstatement on the faculty. In March, university President Fred Davison resigned in the wake of the scandal.

Academic Standards for Athletes. The National Collegiate Athletic Association approved a new set of academic standards for incoming college athletes. The move had divided college officials, with many black leaders saying the new requirements were discriminatory. Under the rules as finally adopted, freshmen entering college in 1986, in order to be eligible for intercollegiate sports, had to have earned at least a 1.8 grade point average (GPA), just below a "C," in high school academic courses and have a total combined score of at least 740 (on a scale of 400 to 1600) on the Scholastic Aptitude Test (SAT), or else have at least a 2.2 GPA and a 660 on the SAT. Stricter requirements were to be phased in in subsequent years.

The concern about athletes and academics extended to high schools as well. California became the third state, after Texas and West Virginia, to require that a student have a 2.0 grade point average in order to participate in sports or other extracurricular activities.

Reform Efforts. Only 28 percent of those polled by Gallup in 1986 said the nation's public schools deserved an "A" or "B" grade for performance. Meanwhile, a major report issued in May by the Carnegie Forum on Education and the Economy recommended a restructuring of the schools as part of a plan to elevate teaching to a profession on a par with medicine and law. Subsequently, the National Governors' Association said in a report that,

Teachers in Texas were required to take a competency test in March, despite a bitter dispute about its significance and about the effect it would have on professional morale.

while schools should have flexibility in how they did their jobs, they should be more accountable. The report favored a plan for declaring "educational bankruptcy" in schools that produced consistent failure and for taking over their operation from local officials.

State efforts to upgrade the teaching profession were having mixed results. Florida dropped its "master teacher" program, as schools found it too difficult to devise a selection process for "master teachers" that would satisfy educators. Texas, in a controversial move, gave a competency test to all teachers; 97 percent passed all three sections of the test—reading, writing, and math.

Student Achievement. Despite the wide public and political concern about school reform, some test results released during the year suggested that American public schools were not making great progress. In March the U.S. Department of Education reported that American students scored near the bottom in a 17-nation study of mathematics achievement. Eighth-grade students from Japan, the Netherlands, France, Belgium, and Hungary were the top scorers, while U.S. students ranked 14th, ahead of those from Swaziland, Nigeria, and Thailand. The new findings came from testing that took place in 1982, the first results of which appeared in 1986 in an Education Department publication titled *What Works*.

A separate study of the top high school seniors in math found U.S. students on the bottom. Among students from ten industrial nations, the top 5 percent of the seniors from Japan, Finland, Canada, and Sweden had the best average scores, while Americans had the lowest. Also, the federally funded National Assessment of Educational Progress reported what it called "disappointing" results in a nationwide test of writing. Only 20 percent of high school seniors could write a persuasive paragraph, and only 38 percent could manage "a detailed and well-organized informative" piece of writing, according to the report, released in April.

One group of students seemed to do well regardless of the odds: those of Asian ancestry. For the first time in its 45-year history, the top five winners of the Westinghouse National Science Talent Search were all either born in Asia or of Asian parentage. Secretary Bennett noted the success of Asian students and said other children should follow their example. His department's publication *What Works* urged parents to read to their children and stress the value of hard work and personal responsibility.

In September, Secretary Bennett released another special report, entitled *First Lessons*. It concluded that America's grade schools were in better shape than that depicted in the 1983 report of the National Commission on Excellence in Education, which had described a "rising tide of mediocrity." In particular, the

Helping Harvard University celebrate its 350th anniversary in 1986 was Britain's Prince Charles (extreme right), who delivered a keynote speech about the importance of the moral spirit in education. Here he sits with Harvard faculty members.

1986 report noted improvement in basic skills but less progress in applying these skills to more complex tasks in the later grades.

Textbooks. In October the California Board of Education voted to reject all of the mathematics textbooks submitted by publishers for use in the state's public schools for kindergarten through eighth grade. The board complained that rather than focusing on learning by understanding concepts, the books continued to emphasize rote memory. The 14 publishers were given one year to revise the materials, which included more than 150 textbooks. California is a major purchaser of textbooks, and in the past its textbook standards have often become national standards.

In two highly publicized lawsuits, Christian fundamentalists contended that textbooks their children used in public schools subjected them improperly to anti-Christian and "secular humanist" views. (*See* RELIGION.)   D.G.S.

EGYPT. In 1986, Egypt's economic problems reached crisis proportions, giving rise to serious strains in the social fabric.

Economic Woes. Revenues from oil exports were expected to plummet to less than half of the $2.1 billion level attained in 1985. The oil-based economies of Egypt's Arab neighbors were similarly affected by the worldwide oil glut, and the resulting contraction of economic activity sent hundreds of thousands of Egyptian migrant laborers back home. This development undercut economic growth, previously stimulated by the massive foreign remittances of the migrant workers, and gave rise to serious employment problems. Public understanding of the economic situation gave the government greater freedom to implement price hikes for transportation, water, electricity, and gasoline. Price controls on fruits, vegetables, meat, and other products were gradually abandoned, with resulting price increases placing many commodities beyond the means even of middle-class families. In October, Prime Minister Ali Lutfi, an economist named in 1985 to deal with Egypt's financial problems, was replaced by economist Atef Sedki.

Domestic Unrest. In February a rumor spread among soldiers of the Central Security Forces that budgetary pressures would bring a government decision to extend their duty by one year. Poorly treated by their superiors and forced to subsist on low salaries, the conscripts mutinied, setting fire to hotels and nightclubs near the Giza pyramids. Security forces in other parts of Cairo also went on a rampage, and Muslim radicals apparently exploited the breakdown in order to wreak havoc on their own. President Hosni Mubarak summoned the regular army to restore order; the official toll was 107 dead and more than 700 wounded. More than 1,300 alleged rioters were arrested; many were released pending trial. One trial of 106 conscripts was postponed late in the year when the judge withdrew from the case because the court had not provided relevant documents to the defense.

148

Increases in the cost of living helped trigger illegal strikes by public-sector textile workers in February and railroad engineers in July. Although not responsible for the direction of these strikes, the National Progressive Unionist Party and the Socialist Labor Party benefited from the opportunity to present themselves as representatives of working-class interests.

In December, 33 people—some of them said to have links to the Muslim fundamentalist group implicated in the 1981 assassination of President Anwar al-Sadat—were indicted on charges of plotting to overthrow the government. Four military officers were among the accused. Also in December, more than 40 suspects were arrested for involvement in what the government maintained was a conspiracy to oust Mubarak and install a Communist regime in Egypt.

Foreign Affairs. There were some signs of a thaw in the "cold peace" with Israel. Negotiations over the disputed border area of Taba yielded results in September when both parties agreed to submit the issue to binding international arbitration. Subsequently, Mubarak and Israel's Shimon Peres held a summit meeting in Egypt to discuss efforts to promote peace in the region.

Mubarak's upholding of the 1979 Camp David peace treaty with Israel and his quiet diplomacy throughout the region had continued to yield political dividends. The July meeting between Peres and Morocco's King Hassan II left Egypt somewhat less isolated as regards its relations with Israel. In the same month, Saudi Arabia's King Fahd made a significant overture for the restoration of normal ties with Egypt. Finally, Mubarak's numerous cordial meetings with Jordan's King Hussein, PLO leader Yasir Arafat, and the new regime in Sudan, as well as his support for Iraq in its war with Iran, placed Egypt on the verge of normal ties with most other Arab nations. Relations with the more radical Arab states, such as Libya and Syria, remained cool.

See STATISTICS OF THE WORLD.   K.J.B.

In the first Egyptian-Israeli summit since 1981, President Hosni Mubarak of Egypt (left) and Prime Minister Shimon Peres of Israel met in Mubarak's summer palace in Alexandria on September 11 and 12.

ELECTIONS IN THE UNITED STATES. The midterm elections on November 4, 1986, left the U.S. political landscape significantly altered. In 1987, for the first time since taking office, President Ronald Reagan would be facing a Congress in which both houses were controlled by the opposition Democrats. Not only did the Democrats reclaim control of the Senate, which they had lost in 1980, but they did so by a surprisingly comfortable 55-45 margin, with the aid of victories in a few tight races. Reagan thus faced the prospect of spending the last years of his presidency embattled in conflict. (His prospects were further darkened after the election by revelations of scandal involving arm sales to Iran.) On November 5, in upbeat remarks to his staff, the president challenged aides to "complete the revolution that we have so well begun." But retiring House Speaker Thomas P. ("Tip") O'Neill, Jr. (D, Mass.), saw matters differently. "If there was a Reagan revolution, it's over," he said.

One thing was clear: Reagan had undertaken a personal crusade to maintain Republican control of the Senate, and he had fallen short. He had traveled thousands of miles and raised millions of dollars for GOP senatorial candidates, only to find that his popularity, though still strong at this point, was his alone.

A counterpoint to the Republicans' loss of the Senate was their exceptionally strong showing in statehouse races. They elected 12 new governors, including 11 in states where the governorship had previously been held by Democrats, for an overall net gain of 8. That left the Democrats with an edge of 26-24, down from 34-16 before the election. Moreover, the GOP elected governors in Florida and Texas and reelected one in California, three big states that party officials hoped would anchor their drive to hold onto the White House in 1988. Republicans also held their losses in the House to five seats.

But the Democrats scored significant gains in less nationally visible state legislative races, picking up 150 to 160 more seats and control of 4 more legislative chambers. Going into the election, Democrats had controlled 63 of 98 chambers (excluding Nebraska's nonpartisan one-house legislature) and occupied 4,304 of the 7,461 legislative seats.

No analysis of the election was complete without a look at the strange arithmetic of 1986. In the Senate, where 34 seats were at stake, the GOP was forced to defend 22, compared with only 12 for the Democrats. With the Democrats needing a shift of only 4 seats to overcome the GOP's 53-47 edge (a 50-50 split would leave control with the Republicans, since Vice President George Bush would be the tiebreaking vote), the Republicans' vulnerability was so great that they could have won a majority of the races and still lost control of the Senate. Conversely, the numbers in the statehouse races worked in favor of the GOP, as Democrats found themselves defending 27 governorships to only 9 for the Republicans. Moreover, the closest gubernatorial races were expected in the 19 states where no incumbent was running, and 15 of those had Democratic governors going into the election.

Huge amounts of money were poured into the 1986 elections—more than $340 million into the congressional races alone, the majority of it going as usual to Republicans and incumbents.

Senate. The battle for the Senate was the centerpiece of the political year, with Reagan telling political audiences that he would be reduced to a caretaker in his final two years in office if deprived of the leverage the GOP-controlled Senate had given him against the overwhelmingly Democratic House. Tapping into the partisan emotions of his 1984 reelection campaign, he said, "I'm asking you to win one more for the Gipper." Reagan undertook what was regarded as the most prodigious personal effort ever made by a sitting president on behalf of his party. Most of the effort was for Senate candidates, for whom he raised nearly $14 million, made 38 visits to 18 states, and traveled nearly 25,000 miles between early September and Election Day.

Fifteen states emerged as the main Senate battlegrounds, and Reagan visited each of them at least once, some three times. In general, the most vulnerable Republicans were 9 of the 16 who had swept into office on Reagan's coattails in 1980, many of them elected by narrow margins in states where he had piled up large majorities. Another of the 16, John East of North Carolina, committed suicide earlier in

Among winners in the November elections were incumbent Senator Alan Cranston (D, Calif.), above left, and Representative Barbara Mikulski (D), above right, who captured a Maryland Senate seat. Also a winner was the Democratic Party, which took control of the Senate. Below, Senators Robert Byrd (D, W.Va.), right, and George Mitchell (D, Me.) celebrate the party's 55-45 edge.

Presidential Hopeful?

Since his electrifying keynote speech at the 1984 Democratic National Convention, New York Governor Mario Cuomo has been considered a possible 1988 presidential candidate. His Republican opponent in the 1986 gubernatorial race, Andrew P. O'Rourke, tried to make this a campaign issue, but Cuomo won reelection in a landslide with a record 65 percent of the vote. A former New York City lawyer, Cuomo captured the statehouse in 1982. During his first term the thriving economy allowed him to cut taxes and raise spending. His *Diaries of Mario M. Cuomo: The Campaign for Governor* (1984) became a best-seller; he was also a sought-after speaker nationwide. The son of Italian immigrants, Mario Cuomo was born in the New York City borough of Queens in 1932. He earned his bachelor's and law degrees from St. John's University. In 1954 he married Matilda Raffa; the couple have five children.

Mario Cuomo

the year, and his GOP replacement, former Representative James Broyhill, faced a tough battle. Of the open seats for which no incumbent was running, four—in Missouri, Colorado, Nevada, and Louisiana—were considered good targets for either party. And in California, three-term Democrat Alan Cranston, a longtime Reagan critic in the president's home state, faced a potentially stiff GOP challenge. But Reagan's campaigning was of little help—Republicans lost in 11 of the 15 crucial contests.

The Democratic trend was evident early on election night when reports from Florida showed popular Democratic Governor Bob Graham had unseated first-term incumbent Senator Paula Hawkins. Three other GOP Senate seats fell in the South. Senator Mack Mattingly of Georgia was ousted by Representative Wyche Fowler, Jr. Senator Jeremiah Denton of Alabama, a crusader for New Right moral causes and a former prisoner of war in Vietnam, was beaten by Representative Richard Shelby. (Another ex-POW, Republican Representative John McCain of Arizona, did win a Senate seat.) Broyhill's tenure in North Carolina proved short, as former Governor Terry Sanford, 69, staged a comeback to defeat him.

Republican freshman senators in both Dakotas fell to the Democrats, as did the hotly contested open seats in Louisiana and Colorado. In Nevada, incumbent Senator Paul Laxalt (R) was defeated by U.S. Representative Harry Reid. In Washington, Republican Slade Gorton was defeated by Brock Adams, President Jimmy Carter's transportation secretary, while in California, Cranston staved off the challenge of moderate GOP Representative Ed Zschau despite two appearances by Reagan in the final three days of the campaign.

House. The Democrats went into the 1986 House elections with a safe 253-180 margin (two formerly GOP seats were vacant). Big changes were not anticipated, and they did not materialize; the Republican losses were below the average for a party holding the White House in a midterm election. Two members of a new generation of Kennedys sought to begin congressional careers. In Massachusetts, Democrat Joseph P. Kennedy II, son of the late Senator Robert F. Kennedy, was elected to the House seat being vacated by Speaker O'Neill (and formerly held by John F. Kennedy). But in Maryland, his sister, Kathleen Kennedy Townsend, lost her House race against Republican incumbent Helen Delich Bentley.

Statehouse Elections. Despite the Republicans' loss of four southern Senate seats, the emergence of an increasingly two-party South was ratified by the election of GOP governors in Florida, South Carolina, Alabama, and Texas. In the especially bitter Texas race, incumbent Democrat Mark White was turned out of office by the man from whom he had taken the job, crusty Republican William Clements. In Florida the new chief executive, former Tampa Mayor and ex-Democrat Bob Martinez, was also the state's first Hispanic governor. And in a major GOP victory, farmer Guy Hunt was elected to succeed the retiring George Wallace in Alabama, to become the first Republican governor of Alabama since Reconstruction.

Other gubernatorial highlights included the nation's first all-woman gubernatorial race, in Nebraska, in which Republican state Treasurer Kay Orr defeated former Lincoln Mayor Helen Boosalis. In Idaho, onetime Interior Secretary Cecil Andrus (D), a former two-term governor, captured the statehouse by less than 4,000 votes. And Neil Goldschmidt (D)—like Adams, a former transportation secretary—was elected governor of Oregon.

Tactics and Turnout. Despite Reagan's efforts in the final weeks to "nationalize" the election by making it, in effect, a referendum on his presidency, the key races turned largely on local issues and personalities. The turnout of 37.3 percent of eligible voters was the lowest since 1942.

The 30-second television commercial became the major weapon in the arsenal of many candidates, who often used it to assail their opponents. While some attacks focused on the candidate's record or positions, others questioned his or her character. Republicans and Democrats appeared to embrace negative campaigning with equal vigor. In Florida, where 18 percent of the population is over 65 years old, senatorial candidates Hawkins and Graham each aired commercials questioning the other's commitment to social security benefits. In Maryland, advertisements run by Republican senatorial candidate Linda Chavez accused her unmarried opponent, Barbara Mikulski, of being an "anti-male, San Francisco-style Democrat." (Mikulski still won the election.)

See also BLACKS IN THE UNITED STATES; STATE GOVERNMENT REVIEW; WOMEN. R.T.

Señor Governor

In November former Tampa Mayor Bob Martinez became the first Hispanic-American ever elected governor of Florida, and only the second Republican in this century. Martinez became a Republican only in 1983, when he switched party affiliations because the political philosophy of President Ronald Reagan appealed to him. In 1986 he campaigned on a conservative platform, stressing the need to fight crime—the number-one concern of the state's large elderly population. Martinez owed much of his victory to a bitter Democratic primary and runoff battle that left the opposition divided. He was also strongly supported by the Miami area's Hispanic communities. Born in Tampa in 1934, he is the grandson of immigrants from Spain. Before becoming the city's mayor in 1979, he worked as a teacher, a teacher's union representative, and the proprietor of a café popular among politicians and journalists. In 1984 he delivered the keynote address at the Republican National Convention.

Robert Martinez

GOVERNORS, U.S. SENATORS, AND U.S. REPRESENTATIVES ELECTED IN 1986

Governors

ALABAMA
Guy Hunt (R)
ALASKA
Steve Cowper (D)
ARIZONA
Evan Mecham (R)
ARKANSAS
Bill Clinton (D)
CALIFORNIA
George Deukmejian (R)
COLORADO
Roy Romer (D)
CONNECTICUT
William A. O'Neill (D)
FLORIDA
Robert Martinez (R)
GEORGIA
Joe Frank Harris (D)
HAWAII
John D. Waihee (D)
IDAHO
Cecil D. Andrus (D)
ILLINOIS
James R. Thompson (R)
IOWA
Terry Branstad (R)
KANSAS
Mike Hayden (R)
MAINE
John R. McKernan (R)
MARYLAND
William Donald Schaefer (D)
MASSACHUSETTS
Michael S. Dukakis (D)
MICHIGAN
James J. Blanchard (D)
MINNESOTA
Rudy Perpich (D)
NEBRASKA
Kay Orr (R)
NEVADA
Richard H. Bryan (D)
NEW HAMPSHIRE
John H. Sununu (R)
NEW MEXICO
Garrey Carruthers (R)
NEW YORK
Mario M. Cuomo (D)
OHIO
Richard F. Celeste (D)
OKLAHOMA
Henry Bellmon (R)
OREGON
Neil Goldschmidt (D)
PENNSYLVANIA
Robert P. Casey (D)
RHODE ISLAND
Edward DiPrete (R)
SOUTH CAROLINA
Carroll A. Campbell, Jr. (R)
SOUTH DAKOTA
George Mickelson (R)
TENNESSEE
Ned Ray McWherter (D)
TEXAS
William P. Clements, Jr. (R)
VERMONT
Madeleine Kunin (D)

WISCONSIN
Tommy G. Thompson (R)
WYOMING
Mike Sullivan (D)

Senators

ALABAMA
Richard C. Shelby (D)
ALASKA
Frank Murkowski (R)
ARIZONA
John McCain (R)
ARKANSAS
Dale Bumpers (D)
CALIFORNIA
Alan Cranston (D)
COLORADO
Timothy W. Wirth (D)
CONNECTICUT
Christopher J. Dodd (D)
FLORIDA
Robert Graham (D)
GEORGIA
Wyche Fowler, Jr. (D)
HAWAII
Daniel K. Inouye (D)
IDAHO
Steven D. Symms (R)
ILLINOIS
Alan J. Dixon (D)
INDIANA
Dan Quayle (R)
IOWA
Charles Grassley (R)
KANSAS
Robert Dole (R)
KENTUCKY
Wendell H. Ford (D)
LOUISIANA
John B. Breaux (D)
MARYLAND
Barbara A. Mikulski (D)
MISSOURI
Christopher S. Bond (R)
NEVADA
Harry Reid (D)
NEW HAMPSHIRE
Warren B. Rudman (R)
NEW YORK
Alfonse M. D'Amato (R)
NORTH CAROLINA
Terry Sanford (D)
NORTH DAKOTA
Kent Conrad (D)
OHIO
John Glenn (D)
OKLAHOMA
Don Nickles (R)
OREGON
Robert Packwood (R)
PENNSYLVANIA
Arlen Specter (R)
SOUTH CAROLINA
Ernest F. Hollings (D)
SOUTH DAKOTA
Thomas A. Daschle (D)

UTAH
Jake Garn (R)
VERMONT
Patrick J. Leahy (D)
WASHINGTON
Brock Adams (D)
WISCONSIN
Robert W. Kasten, Jr. (R)

Representatives

ALABAMA
1. Sonny Callahan (R)
2. William L. Dickinson (R)
3. William Nichols (D)
4. Tom Bevill (D)
5. Ronnie G. Flippo (D)
6. Ben Erdreich (D)
7. Claude Harris (D)
ALASKA
At large: Donald E. Young (R)
ARIZONA
1. John J. Rhodes III (R)
2. Morris K. Udall (D)
3. Bob Stump (R)
4. Jon Kyl (R)
5. Jim Kolbe (R)
ARKANSAS
1. Bill Alexander, Jr. (D)
2. Tommy F. Robinson (D)
3. John P. Hammerschmidt (R)
4. Beryl F. Anthony, Jr. (D)
CALIFORNIA
1. Douglas H. Bosco (D)
2. Wally Herger (R)
3. Robert T. Matsui (D)
4. Vic Fazio (D)
5. Sala Burton (D)
6. Barbara Boxer (D)
7. George Miller (D)
8. Ronald V. Dellums (D)
9. Fortney (Pete) Stark (D)
10. Don Edwards (D)
11. Tom Lantos (D)
12. Ernest L. Konnyu (R)
13. Norman Y. Mineta (D)
14. Norman D. Shumway (R)
15. Tony Coelho (D)
16. Leon E. Panetta (D)
17. Charles Pashayan, Jr. (R)
18. Richard H. Lehman (D)
19. Robert J. Lagomarsino (R)
20. William M. Thomas (R)
21. Elton Gallegly (R)
22. Carlos J. Moorhead (R)
23. Anthony C. Beilenson (D)
24. Henry A. Waxman (D)
25. Edward R. Roybal (D)
26. Howard L. Berman (D)
27. Mel Levine (D)
28. Julian C. Dixon (D)
29. Augustus F. Hawkins (D)
30. Matthew G. Martinez (D)
31. Mervyn M. Dymally (D)
32. Glenn M. Anderson (D)
33. David Dreier (R)
34. Esteban Edward Torres (D)
35. Jerry Lewis (R)
36. George E. Brown, Jr. (D)

37. Alfred A. McCandless (R)
38. Robert K. Dornan (R)
39. William E. Dannemeyer (R)
40. Robert E. Badham (R)
41. Bill Lowery (R)
42. Dan Lungren (R)
43. Ron Packard (R)
44. Jim Bates (D)
45. Duncan Hunter (R)

COLORADO
1. Patricia Schroeder (D)
2. David Skaggs (D)
3. Ben Campbell (D)
4. Hank Brown (R)
5. Joel Hefley (R)
6. Dan Schaefer (R)

CONNECTICUT
1. Barbara B. Kennelly (D)
2. Samuel Gejdenson (D)
3. Bruce A. Morrison (D)
4. Stewart B. McKinney (R)
5. John G. Rowland (R)
6. Nancy L. Johnson (R)

DELAWARE
At large: Thomas R. Carper (D)

FLORIDA
1. Earl Hutto (D)
2. Bill Grant (D)
3. Charles E. Bennett (D)
4. Bill Chappell, Jr. (D)
5. Bill McCollum (R)
6. Buddy MacKay (D)
7. Sam Gibbons (D)
8. C. W. Bill Young (R)
9. Michael Bilirakis (R)
10. Andy Ireland (R)
11. Bill Nelson (D)
12. Tom Lewis (R)
13. Connie Mack (R)
14. Dan Mica (D)
15. E. Clay Shaw, Jr. (R)
16. Lawrence J. Smith (D)
17. William Lehman (D)
18. Claude Pepper (D)
19. Dante B. Fascell (D)

GEORGIA
1. Robert Lindsay Thomas (D)
2. Charles Hatcher (D)
3. Richard Ray (D)
4. Patrick L. Swindall (R)
5. John Lewis (D)
6. Newt Gingrich (R)
7. George Darden (D)
8. J. Roy Rowland (D)
9. Ed Jenkins (D)
10. Doug Barnard, Jr. (D)

HAWAII
1. Patricia Saiki (R)
2. Daniel K. Akaka (D)

IDAHO
1. Larry E. Craig (R)
2. Richard H. Stallings (D)

ILLINOIS
1. Charles A. Hayes (D)
2. Gus Savage (D)
3. Martin A. Russo (D)
4. Jack Davis (R)
5. William O. Lipinski (D)
6. Henry J. Hyde (R)
7. Cardiss Collins (D)
8. Daniel Rostenkowski (D)
9. Sidney R. Yates (D)
10. John Edward Porter (R)
11. Frank Annunzio (D)
12. Philip M. Crane (R)

13. Harris W. Fawell (R)
14. J. Dennis Hastert (R)
15. Edward R. Madigan (R)
16. Lynn Martin (R)
17. Lane Evans (D)
18. Robert H. Michel (R)
19. Terry L. Bruce (D)
20. Richard J. Durbin (D)
21. Melvin Price (D)
22. Kenneth J. Gray (D)

INDIANA
1. Peter J. Visclosky (D)
2. Philip R. Sharp (D)
3. John P. Hiler (R)
4. Dan Coats (R)
5. James Jontz (D)
6. Dan Burton (R)
7. John T. Myers (R)
8. Frank McCloskey (D)
9. Lee H. Hamilton (D)
10. Andrew Jacobs, Jr. (D)

IOWA
1. James A. S. Leach (R)
2. Thomas J. Tauke (R)
3. David Nagle (D)
4. Neal Smith (D)
5. Jim Lightfoot (R)
6. Fred Grandy (R)

KANSAS
1. Pat Roberts (R)
2. Jim Slattery (D)
3. Jan Meyers (R)
4. Dan Glickman (D)
5. Robert Whittaker (R)

KENTUCKY
1. Carroll Hubbard, Jr. (D)
2. William H. Natcher (D)
3. Romano L. Mazzoli (D)
4. Jim Bunning (R)
5. Harold Rogers (R)
6. Larry J. Hopkins (R)
7. Carl D. Perkins (D)

LOUISIANA
1. Bob Livingston (R)
2. Lindy Boggs (D)
3. W. J. Tauzin (D)
4. Buddy Roemer III (D)
5. Jerry Huckaby (D)
6. Richard H. Baker (R)
7. James A. Hayes (D)
8. Clyde C. Holloway (R)

MAINE
1. Joseph E. Brennan (D)
2. Olympia J. Snowe (R)

MARYLAND
1. Roy Dyson (D)
2. Helen Delich Bentley (R)
3. Benjamin Cardin (D)
4. Thomas McMillen (D)
5. Steny H. Hoyer (D)
6. Beverly B. Byron (D)
7. Kweisi Mfume (D)
8. Constance Morella (R)

MASSACHUSETTS
1. Silvio O. Conte (R)
2. Edward P. Boland (D)
3. Joseph D. Early (D)
4. Barney Frank (D)
5. Chester G. Atkins (D)
6. Nicholas Mavroules (D)
7. Edward J. Markey (D)
8. Joseph P. Kennedy II (D)
9. Joe Moakley (D)
10. Gerry E. Studds (D)
11. Brian J. Donnelly (D)

MICHIGAN
1. John Conyers, Jr. (D)
2. Carl D. Pursell (R)
3. Howard Wolpe (D)
4. Fred Upton (R)
5. Paul B. Henry (R)
6. Bob Carr (D)
7. Dale E. Kildee (D)
8. Bob Traxler (D)
9. Guy Vander Jagt (R)
10. Bill Schuette (R)
11. Robert W. Davis (R)
12. David E. Bonior (D)
13. George W. Crockett, Jr. (D)
14. Dennis M. Hertel (D)
15. William D. Ford (D)
16. John D. Dingell (D)
17. Sander M. Levin (D)
18. William S. Broomfield (R)

MINNESOTA
1. Timothy J. Penny (D)
2. Vin Weber (R)
3. Bill Frenzel (R)
4. Bruce F. Vento (D)
5. Martin Olav Sabo (D)
6. Gerry Sikorski (D)
7. Arlan Stangeland (R)
8. James L. Oberstar (D)

MISSISSIPPI
1. Jamie L. Whitten (D)
2. Mike Espy (D)
3. G. V. (Sonny) Montgomery (D)
4. Wayne Dowdy (D)
5. Trent Lott (R)

MISSOURI
1. William Clay (D)
2. Jack Buechner (R)
3. Richard A. Gephardt (D)
4. Ike Skelton (D)
5. Alan Wheat (D)
6. E. Thomas Coleman (R)
7. Gene Taylor (R)
8. Bill Emerson (R)
9. Harold L. Volkmer (D)

MONTANA
1. Pat Williams (D)
2. Ron Marlenee (R)

NEBRASKA
1. Douglas K. Bereuter (R)
2. Hal Daub (R)
3. Virginia Smith (R)

NEVADA
1. James Bilbray (D)
2. Barbara F. Vucanovich (R)

NEW HAMPSHIRE
1. Robert C. Smith (R)
2. Judd Gregg (R)

NEW JERSEY
1. James J. Florio (D)
2. William J. Hughes (D)
3. James J. Howard (D)
4. Christopher H. Smith (R)
5. Marge Roukema (R)
6. Bernard J. Dwyer (D)
7. Matthew J. Rinaldo (R)
8. Robert A. Roe (D)
9. Robert G. Torricelli (D)
10. Peter W. Rodino, Jr. (D)
11. Dean A. Gallo (R)
12. Jim Courter (R)
13. Jim Saxton (R)
14. Frank J. Guarini (D)

NEW MEXICO
1. Manuel Lujan, Jr. (R)
2. Joe Skeen (R)
3. Bill Richardson (D)

NEW YORK
1. George J. Hochbrueckner (D)
2. Thomas J. Downey (D)
3. Robert J. Mrazek (D)
4. Norman F. Lent (R)
5. Raymond J. McGrath (R)
6. Floyd Flake (D)
7. Gary L. Ackerman (D)
8. James H. Scheuer (D)
9. Thomas J. Manton (D)
10. Charles E. Schumer (D)
11. Edolphus Towns (D)
12. Major R. Owens (D)
13. Stephen J. Solarz (D)
14. Guy V. Molinari (R)
15. Bill Green (R)
16. Charles B. Rangel (D)
17. Ted Weiss (D)
18. Robert Garcia (D)
19. Mario Biaggi (D)
20. Joseph J. DioGuardi (R)
21. Hamilton Fish, Jr. (R)
22. Benjamin A. Gilman (R)
23. Samuel S. Stratton (D)
24. Gerald B. H. Solomon (R)
25. Sherwood L. Boehlert (R)
26. David O'B. Martin (R)
27. George C. Wortley (R)
28. Matthew F. McHugh (D)
29. Frank Horton (R)
30. Louise M. Slaughter (D)
31. Jack F. Kemp (R)
32. John J. LaFalce (D)
33. Henry J. Nowak (D)
34. Amory Houghton, Jr. (R)

NORTH CAROLINA
1. Walter B. Jones (D)
2. Tim Valentine (D)
3. Martin Lancaster (D)
4. David E. Price (D)
5. Stephen L. Neal (D)
6. Howard Coble (R)
7. Charles Rose (D)
8. W. G. Hefner (D)
9. J. Alex McMillan (R)
10. Cass Ballenger (R)
11. James McClure Clarke (D)

NORTH DAKOTA
At large: Byron L. Dorgan (D)

OHIO
1. Thomas A. Luken (D)
2. Willis B. Gradison, Jr. (R)
3. Tony P. Hall (D)
4. Michael G. Oxley (R)
5. Delbert L. Latta (R)
6. Bob McEwen (R)
7. Michael DeWine (R)
8. Donald Lukens (R)
9. Marcy Kaptur (D)
10. Clarence E. Miller (R)
11. Dennis E. Eckart (D)
12. John R. Kasich (R)
13. Donald J. Pease (D)
14. Thomas C. Sawyer (D)
15. Chalmers P. Wylie (R)
16. Ralph S. Regula (R)
17. James A. Traficant, Jr. (D)
18. Douglas Applegate (D)
19. Edward F. Feighan (D)
20. Mary Rose Oakar (D)
21. Louis Stokes (D)

OKLAHOMA
1. James Inhofe (R)
2. Michael Lynn Synar (D)
3. Wes Watkins (D)

4. Dave McCurdy (D)
5. Mickey Edwards (R)
6. Glenn English (D)

OREGON
1. Les AuCoin (D)
2. Robert F. Smith (R)
3. Ron Wyden (D)
4. Peter DeFazio (D)
5. Denny Smith (R)

PENNSYLVANIA
1. Thomas M. Foglietta (D)
2. William H. Gray III (D)
3. Robert A. Borski (D)
4. Joe Kolter (D)
5. Richard T. Schulze (R)
6. Gus Yatron (D)
7. Curt Weldon (R)
8. Peter H. Kostmayer (D)
9. Bud Shuster (R)
10. Joseph M. McDade (R)
11. Paul E. Kanjorski (D)
12. John P. Murtha (D)
13. Lawrence Coughlin (R)
14. William Coyne (D)
15. Don Ritter (R)
16. Robert S. Walker (R)
17. George W. Gekas (R)
18. Douglas Walgren (D)
19. William F. Goodling (R)
20. Joseph M. Gaydos (D)
21. Thomas J. Ridge (R)
22. Austin J. Murphy (D)
23. William F. Clinger, Jr. (R)

RHODE ISLAND
1. Fernand J. St Germain (D)
2. Claudine Schneider (R)

SOUTH CAROLINA
1. Arthur Ravenel, Jr. (R)
2. Floyd Spence (R)
3. Butler Derrick (D)
4. Liz Patterson (D)
5. John M. Spratt, Jr. (D)
6. Robin Tallon (D)

SOUTH DAKOTA
At large: Tim Johnson (D)

TENNESSEE
1. James H. Quillen (R)
2. John J. Duncan (R)
3. Marilyn Lloyd (D)
4. Jim Cooper (D)
5. William Hill Boner (D)
6. Bart Gordon (D)
7. Don Sundquist (R)
8. Ed Jones (D)
9. Harold E. Ford (D)

TEXAS
1. Jim Chapman (D)
2. Charles Wilson (D)
3. Steve Bartlett (R)
4. Ralph Hall (D)
5. John Bryant (D)
6. Joe Barton (R)
7. Bill Archer (R)
8. Jack Fields (R)
9. Jack Brooks (D)
10. J. J. Pickle (D)
11. Marvin Leath (D)
12. Jim Wright (D)
13. Beau Boulter (R)
14. Mac Sweeney (R)
15. E. de la Garza (D)
16. Ronald D. Coleman (D)
17. Charles W. Stenholm (D)
18. Mickey Leland (D)
19. Larry Combest (R)

20. Henry B. Gonzales (D)
21. Lamar Smith (R)
22. Tom DeLay (R)
23. Albert G. Bustamante (D)
24. Martin Frost (D)
25. Michael A. Andrews (D)
26. Richard K. Armey (R)
27. Solomon P. Ortiz (D)

UTAH
1. James V. Hansen (R)
2. Wayne Owens (D)
3. Howard C. Nielson (R)

VERMONT
At large: James M. Jeffords (R)

VIRGINIA
1. Herbert H. Bateman (R)
2. Owen B. Pickett (D)
3. Thomas J. Bliley, Jr. (R)
4. Norman Sisisky (D)
5. Dan Daniel (D)
6. James R. Olin (D)
7. D. French Slaughter, Jr. (R)
8. Stanford Parris (R)
9. Frederick C. Boucher (D)
10. Frank R. Wolf (R)

WASHINGTON
1. John R. Miller (R)
2. Al Swift (D)
3. Don Bonker (D)
4. Sid Morrison (R)
5. Thomas S. Foley (D)
6. Norman D. Dicks (D)
7. Mike Lowry (D)
8. Rod Chandler (R)

WEST VIRGINIA
1. Alan B. Mollohan (D)
2. Harley O. Staggers, Jr. (D)
3. Robert E. Wise, Jr. (D)
4. Nick Joe Rahall II (D)

WISCONSIN
1. Les Aspin (D)
2. Robert W. Kastenmeier (D)
3. Steve Gunderson (R)
4. Gerald D. Kleczka (D)
5. Jim Moody (D)
6. Thomas E. Petri (R)
7. David R. Obey (D)
8. Toby Roth (R)
9. F. James Sensenbrenner, Jr. (R)

WYOMING
At large: Richard Bruce Cheney (R)

ELECTRONICS. Despite the ongoing battle over video formats and the sharp increase in the value of the Japanese yen against the U.S. dollar (making Japanese imports more expensive), 1986 was another very strong year for sales of consumer electronics products in the United States. Color television sets, videocassette recorders (VCR's), camcorders (video camera-recorders for home use), and compact disk players (CD's) were selling at a record pace.

Video recording technology was once again a battlefield of competing formats. Sony promoted the 8-millimeter-tape video format introduced in 1985, against the dominant VHS format. Most of the battle took place in the fast-growing market for video camcorders. Sony touted its lightweight 8-mm video camcorder as the superior technology, with its smaller tape and cassette and compact electronics. JVC countered with a lightweight, compact camcorder using the so-called VHS-C format, which consists of the standard VHS tape in a smaller cassette and requires an adaptor for playback.

In the television market, hand-held TV's and jumbo-sized screens were popular. And stereo television continued to gain converts: a growing number of stations broadcast programming in stereo, and stereo videocassettes also grew in popularity. Manufacturers also offered digital TV sets, a new technology introduced in 1985. In a digital TV, the analog broadcast signal is converted from wave form to a digital format. Once the signal has been converted, special digital electronic circuits can cancel out ghost images, for example, or store the video image in memory, just as a computer does. To provide similar features manufacturers brought out the first digital VCR's.

In the audio market, compact disk players continued to sell extraordinarily well. Manufacturers brought out jukebox-style CD players that can load and play more than one disk.

Canon, the Japanese camera maker, brought out a filmless still camera, that takes pictures on a 2-inch magnetic floppy disk. The disk can be hooked to a special ink-jet printer in the home that produces two sizes of color prints, or can be inserted into a compact recorder-player that transmits the image to a TV screen.

The slump experienced by U.S. semiconductor manufacturers continued, with several of the largest companies reporting record losses and new plant closings and workforce reduc-

Digital TV sets, featuring sharper reception, freeze-frame capability, and screens that can show more than one channel at a time, were a hit in a specialized consumer market.

Two devastating earthquakes struck El Salvador one day in October; here, residents of the capital, San Salvador, pick their way through wreckage.

tions. In May the United States and Japan signed a trade agreement that required Japan to grant U.S. firms greater access to Japanese semiconductor markets, but the immediate effect was merely to raise prices in the United States.   W.D.M.

EL SALVADOR. Continuing armed conflict, a controversial austerity plan, and a natural disaster contributed to unrest in El Salvador during 1986.

Civil War. In January and February the government of José Napoleón Duarte won a significant victory in the protracted conflict, driving opposition forces from the slopes of Guazapa volcano, just outside San Salvador. In order to further strengthen its position prior to projected peace talks, the military command deployed 30,000 troops in a counterinsurgency drive during July. That same month, the commander of the army announced a collaborative effort of government, army, church, businesses, and unions to rebuild areas of the country damaged by the war.

Rebel forces, stymied in part by the military's acquisition of 75 helicopters, relied increasingly on economic sabotage and urban terrorism. Rebels also pursued some battlefield operations, including an assault on a major government base in San Miguel, in which the government lost 57 troops.

Peace Talks. In May, President Duarte reiterated his offers of amnesty to rebels who laid down their arms, and the following month, under pressure from labor unions, he called for a peace summit with rebel forces. The rebels agreed, and a date and place were finally set. However, the talks were later canceled as a result of rebel demands for the withdrawal of all government troops from the area.

Economy. The Reagan administration increased its aid request for El Salvador by 25 percent for fiscal 1987, to $513 million. The gross domestic product had risen by about 1.5 percent in 1985, and some growth was expected in 1986. However, inflation of 50 percent was forecast for the year. In early

January, the government came out with a long-awaited economic austerity plan that provided for tax hikes and a 100 percent devaluation of the colón. It also introduced a 15 percent export tax on coffee, increased the price of gasoline and diesel fuel by 50 percent, and imposed restrictions on imports of luxury items and automobiles. To cushion the impact on the poor, price controls were placed on basic consumer goods, and some rents were frozen.

There was a marked increase in labor unrest in response to the new austerity package, and new labor alignments developed. The Popular Democratic Union, traditionally centrist, pro-Duarte, and Christian Democrat, joined with left-of-center groups to form a National Union of Salvadoran Workers (UNTS). Claiming the UNTS was backed by the rebels, 20 unions loyal to President Duarte formed a progovernment National Worker-Farmer Union (UNOC).

Human Rights. After being promised unrestricted access to information and to human rights activists, the Inter-American Human Rights Commission of the Organization of American States came to El Salvador on August 11, marking its first visit in five years. Five leaders of the nongovernmental Salvadoran Human Rights Commission (CDHES), accused of links with guerrillas, were in prison at the time of the visit. Earlier in the year, in an effort to gain release of the CDHES and other activists, about 100 women took over the San Salvador cathedral for six days. However, the New York-based Americas Watch Committee concluded in May that human rights violations were generally decreasing under President Duarte.

In February two former members of the National Guard were convicted of the 1981 murders of José Rodolfo Viera, head of El Salvador's land distribution program, and two U.S. citizens, Mark D. Pearlman and Michael P. Hammer, advisers on land reform. However, U.S. officials said that the verdicts still did not bring to justice those who bore the ultimate responsibility. Another American, Peter S. Hascall, was mysteriously murdered by an unidentified gunman on February 15.

Earthquakes. Two earthquakes struck El Salvador on October 10, leaving about 1,500 dead and 200,000 homeless. The capital, San Salvador, was especially hard hit. Several downtown office buildings collapsed, and shanties in surrounding slum areas were leveled. The U.S. government sent 16 planeloads of aid, including medicine, medical teams, and food.

See STATISTICS OF THE WORLD.   L.L.P.

ENERGY. An unprecedented price war rocked international oil markets in 1986. In April the worst disaster in the history of nuclear power occurred at Chernobyl, in the Ukraine region of the Soviet Union.

Oil. A drop in world oil prices that began in 1985 accelerated in 1986 into the steepest oil price slide in history. The average price of world export crude oils dropped from $27 a barrel in early 1986 to around $10 by midyear. The price of some oil produced by members of the Organization of Petroleum Exporting Countries (OPEC) fell even lower. However, by the end of the year, oil prices were up, to above $16 a barrel, as production cuts were being made. Most analysts believed that world production in the first half of 1986, which averaged 55.39 million barrels per day (up about 5 percent from the first half of 1985), exceeded the demand for $24-a-barrel oil by 2 million to 3 million b/d.

The price drop was a boon to oil-importing countries and U.S. motorists alike. The average city retail price for leaded gasoline in the United States fell from an average of $1.12 a gallon in 1985 to $0.82 a gallon by April 1986 and remained close to that level. But the plunge proved little short of disastrous for the U.S. petroleum industry, as oil companies slashed research and exploration budgets, idled drilling equipment, and laid off workers. Particularly hard hit were drilling contractors and the oil field service industry. With the decline in production came an increased reliance on imports, prompting fears that the United States could become vulnerable to an "oil shock" in the 1990's similar to those that occurred in the 1970's. The decline in oil prices also sharply reduced the federal government's revenue from the windfall profits tax—the tax on increased oil company profits that resulted from price decontrol begun in 1979.

OPEC countries convened in Geneva in late July to try to raise world oil prices and restore some stability to international oil markets. It

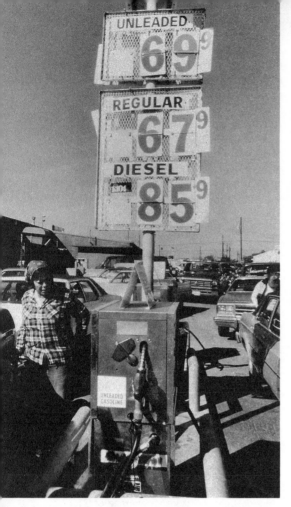

The plunge in world oil prices was good news for consumers (at left, prices at a Dallas gas station), but bad news for oil producers. The number of rigs in operation in the United States was down, and at an auction in Texas (above) oil-drilling equipment sold for 20¢ on the dollar.

was agreed to change strategy and cut production, by restoring all but one of the individual production quotas set in October 1984 and abandoned in 1985 after rampant cheating by member countries. Iraq was exempted from adherence to a quota. The agreement limited total OPEC output to 16.8 million b/d (about 14.8 million b/d not counting Iraq), a decrease from the actual 20.5-million-b/d output at the time of the meeting. In response to the quotas, crude oil prices rose quickly. In October, OPEC oil ministers met again and agreed to essentially maintain their production quotas, though increasing some slightly.

Apparently, several members of OPEC had believed the price war strategy was working too slowly and hurting OPEC producers more than the non-OPEC producers in the North Sea. In late October the Saudi Arabian oil minister, Sheikh Ahmed Zaki Yamani, the major proponent of the price war strategy, was dismissed by the Saudi government. At a final, acrimonious OPEC meeting in Geneva in December, 12 of the 13 oil ministers agreed on production cuts for the first half of 1987 of about 7 percent from existing actual production, with the goal of bringing the price of oil toward $18 a barrel. The meeting was stalemated for a time by Iraq's refusal to accept a cut in its output, and the final agreement excluded Iraq. The total output quota, including an estimate for Iraqi production, came to 15.8 million b/d. (See also ORGANIZATION OF PETROLEUM EXPORTING COUNTRIES.)

Natural Gas. Falling oil prices led to lower natural gas prices in the United States. The average wellhead price declined from $2.63 per thousand cubic feet in January 1985 to

$2.31 in December. By May 1986 it had dropped to $1.92, and by November, the spot market price was about $1.45. Marketed production and dry gas consumption declined during 1985 and 1986, but not because of any shortage. Indeed, the United States had a natural gas surplus, stemming primarily from greatly accelerated drilling activity after the removal of wellhead prices for some categories of natural gas on January 1, 1985. However, rising gas prices coupled with falling oil prices in more recent years led some industrial consumers to switch from natural gas to fuel oil. Because of the steep drop in oil prices in 1986, many experts expected the natural gas surplus to vanish by 1988.

In June, six Western European gas companies announced a provisional agreement to bring in natural gas, beginning in 1993, from Norway's North Sea fields, to be conveyed by pipeline to Belgium. If implemented, the agreement, approved by the Norwegian Parliament in December, would make Norway the principal source of Western European gas supplies.

Chernobyl Nuclear Accident. Early on April 25, operators at the Soviet Union's Chernobyl nuclear power station 80 miles north of Kiev began a test at the No. 4 reactor to determine how long one of the turbine generators could continue to generate electricity after an emergency shutdown of the reactor. In order to conduct the test, plant operators reduced the reactor's power level and committed several safety violations. They shut off the reactor's emergency cooling system, disengaged a mechanism designed to automatically shut the reactor down when steam no longer reaches the turbine, and reduced the number of control rods (which keep the nuclear chain reaction in check) inside the reactor core. At about 1:22 A.M. on April 26, the reactor's power level surged suddenly, and at 1:24 two explosions shattered the 1,000-ton concrete lid of the reactor and blew hot graphite and fragments of reactor fuel through the roof of the containment building. After the initial explosions, the graphite in the reactor core burned for days before the Soviets were able to extinguish the fire by dropping sand and other materials from helicopters onto the disabled reactor.

The explosions and fire spewed a cloud of radioactive debris into the atmosphere that subsequently passed over most of Europe. Traces of radioactive iodine-131 were detected at altitudes of 30,000 feet over the United States about two weeks after the accident.

The full impact of the Chernobyl disaster on the environment, on public health, and on the future of nuclear power may not be known for decades. By late in the year, at least 31 people had died in the explosion or from acute radiation poisoning. A 382-page report released by the Soviet Union in August indicated that the explosions and the graphite fire sent 12 million curies of radioactivity into the environment during the first 24 hours and another 38 million curies during the subsequent 10 days. The accident also reportedly released 45 million curies of radioactive xenon, an inert gas that decays quickly and so is not considered a serious long-term problem. In contrast to these enormous radiation emissions, the 1979 Three Mile Island accident in Pennsylvania released only about 15 curies. Radiation levels rose quickly in the immediate vicinity of the Chernobyl plant, and 135,000 people living within an 18-mile radius were evacuated during the ten days after the explosion. Soviet officials indicated that most of those evacuated would probably not be able to return home for at least four years.

Estimates of the number of cancer deaths likely to occur over the next few decades as a result of exposure to the Chernobyl fallout vary from about 5,000 to 500,000. The Soviet report estimated that exposure to external radiation among Soviet citizens in the path of the fallout would lead to about 5,000 cancer deaths over the next 70 years and that ingestion of radioactive iodine-131 in contaminated food would cause perhaps 1,500 deaths. The most serious long-term concern is over cesium-137. Half of a sample of that radioactive substance takes 30 years to decay into a nonradioactive form. Because soils in the affected region have a low organic matter content, uptake of cesium-137 by plants is expected to be high. The Soviet report estimated that as many as 40,000 cancer deaths might occur as a result of exposure to cesium-137.

On September 26, at a conference of the International Atomic Energy Agency in Vienna,

ENVIRONMENT

50 governments signed two conventions, in response to Chernobyl, agreeing to give prompt, detailed information on any civilian nuclear accident affecting other nations and to provide emergency aid to a nation suffering such an accident. The Soviet Union ratified both conventions but declared that it would not be bound by the requirement to submit disputes to outside arbitration. At the end of September, the Soviet Union restarted the first of the remaining three Chernobyl reactors.

U.S. Nuclear Power. In the aftermath of Chernobyl, some experts raised questions about the possibility of a similar disaster in the United States. Certainly U.S. reactor designs are inherently safer than the one at Chernobyl. In the Chernobyl unit, the moderator, which slows neutrons given off in the fission process, was graphite, a combustible material that can react with steam at high temperatures to produce explosive hydrogen. (All U.S. commercial reactors except the Fort St. Vrain plant in Colorado use water instead of graphite as the moderator.) One of the main problems with the Chernobyl reactor design is that the power level increases if cooling water is lost from the reactor core; water-moderated reactors are designed so that a loss of cooling water causes the reactor power to decrease. Still, although a Chernobyl-type disaster in a U.S. nuclear plant seems improbable, there are no existing safety systems that cannot be circumvented either deliberately or accidentally by plant operators.   D.F.A.

ENVIRONMENT. While the accident at the Soviet Union's Chernobyl nuclear power plant dominated headlines for much of 1986, the United States grappled with the disposal of nuclear and toxic wastes and the regulation of pesticides and acid rain. New studies further confirmed the threats posed by radon.

Chernobyl. On April 26, two explosions ripped through the building containing the No. 4 reactor at the Chernobyl nuclear power station in the Soviet Ukraine and resulted in the world's worst nuclear power plant accident to date. More than 30 people died from direct exposure to the radiation released. Estimates varied widely as to the number of people expected to die over the next several decades from cancers caused by radioactive isotopes that were in the

For the Birds

In a traditional wedding, the bride and groom feed each other wedding cake and the bride tosses her bouquet, but the event isn't complete without a shower of rice for the departing newlyweds. This tradition brings unexpected hazards, though. People tend to slip on the sturdy rice grains. Also, if birds eat the rice after the ceremony, it may expand in their stomachs so much that it kills them. Now both problems can be solved by ordering Feather & Lace Authentic Nuptial Birdseed from Kel-Lee Enterprises of Newtown, Conn. For $25, the company sends 25 plastic champagne glasses, each decorated with lace, ribbon, and paper hearts and filled with off-white birdseed. The seed can be easily crushed underfoot and is good for birds. The festive champagne glasses are an added touch dreamed up by the company's founders, Lisa Mae Schmidje and Robert Keller, after "drinking a little too much champagne while trying to think of ways the idea could be promoted." Traditionalists can take heart—in midair the birdseed looks just like rice.

air or that worked their way into food and water sources. (See ENERGY and UNION OF SOVIET SOCIALIST REPUBLICS.)

Bhopal. U.S. attorneys representing individual victims of the disastrous 1984 chemical gas leak from a Union Carbide plant in Bhopal, India, agreed in March to a $350 million settlement offered by the company, but the settlement was rejected by the Indian government, which claimed to be the victims' sole legal representative. Several months later, the Indian government filed suit against Union Carbide in Bhopal, after a U.S. district court ruled the suit could not be tried in the U.S. courts. Indian courts were also to decide the issue of victim representation. In November, Union Carbide denied any responsibility for the disaster, saying that its Indian subsidiary was in charge of the plant and that sabotage had caused the leak. India subsequently announced that it would seek at least $3 billion in compensation. At least 2,000 people were killed in the Bhopal accident; many survivors were still unable to work and experienced such symptoms as eye and lung problems, behavioral disorders, and muscle fatigue. In April the India Council on Medical Research reported that methyl isocyanate (MIC), the primary chemical released, has been found to remain highly toxic for much longer than had been anticipated. Other studies showed how MIC produces long-term lung-tissue damage that reduces the capacity of the lungs and increases susceptibility to respiratory diseases.

Rhine Calamity. One of Western Europe's worst chemical spills occurred on November 1, when 30 tons of toxic chemicals, including 440 pounds of mercury, entered the Rhine river in water used to douse a fire at a chemical warehouse near Basel, Switzerland, owned by the Sandoz corporation. Environmentalists feared that much of the river's ecosystem had been destroyed, reversing gains achieved in a decade of conservation work. In the four countries through which the contaminated water flowed—Switzerland, France, Germany, and the Netherlands—fishing was banned, plants processing Rhine water for drinking were shut down, and sluices and locks were closed to prevent the river's water from polluting streams and underground water.

As protests were held in Basel and other locations, a second, smaller discharge of chemicals from the plant took place on November 7. At a November 13 meeting of environment ministers from the affected countries, Switzerland accepted responsibility for the chemical contamination and agreed to indemnify other governments. Switzerland also agreed to consider action to tighten its anti-pollution safeguards.

Reactor Shutdown. In December the Department of Energy announced that a reactor at the Hanford nuclear complex in the state of Washington would be shut down for a six-month, $50 million upgrading of its safety systems. A permanent shutdown was ruled out, the department said, because the Hanford nuclear plant—called the "centerpiece" of the Hanford nuclear reservation in Richland—is a "key source" of plutonium for the nation's nuclear weapons. The reactor was said to bear some design similarities to the Soviet Union's Chernobyl reactor, but federal officials said

that a "Chernobyl-type accident is not possible" at Hanford. The Chernobyl accident had prompted a review of the Hanford operation by panels of consultants.

Radioactive Waste. On January 15, President Ronald Reagan signed a bill setting 1993 as the deadline for 47 states to have designated sites for the disposal of low-level radioactive wastes. Nevada, Washington, and South Carolina, the only states with dumps open, ultimately received additional funding to let other states use these facilities until the 1993 deadline.

A policeman pulls dead eels from the Rhine, after tons of toxic chemicals were washed into the river during a fire at the Sandoz chemical plant in Basel, Switzerland, in November. The Rhine's entire ecosystem, from plankton to waterfowl, was endangered by the disaster.

ENVIRONMENT

In May the Department of Energy named Nevada, Washington, and Texas as the final Western candidates for one of the nation's first two high-level nuclear waste repositories, to hold spent nuclear-reactor fuel. The department postponed the naming of three possible Eastern sites for the other repository.

A study published by the nonprofit Environmental Policy Institute criticized the Energy Department for mishandling radioactive waste and exposing workers to radioactivity at South Carolina's Savannah River Plant, which provides most of the plutonium and uranium for U.S. nuclear weapons. Close to 30 million gallons of liquid radioactive waste were stored at the facility in aging underground tanks. In 1983, under pressure from Congress, the Energy Department had begun a program to move the waste to a high-level radioactive waste storage facility by the end of the century.

Radon. New studies indicated that radon, the odorless, colorless gas produced by the radioactive decay of uranium, is a pervasive and hazardous pollutant. In August the Environmental Protection Agency (EPA) said that as many as 8 million U.S. homes contained a level of radon high enough to produce the same cancer risk as smoking ten cigarettes a day. The agency, which issued new radon safety standards, estimated that the radiation might cause up to 20,000 lung cancer deaths in the United States each year.

Kerr-McGee Accident. A cylinder containing 14 tons of uranium hexafluoride ruptured on January 4 at a Kerr-McGee Corporation uranium-processing plant in Gore, Okla., as a result of a procedure barred by federal regulations. On contact with air, uranium hexafluoride, used in the manufacture of nuclear-reactor fuel, breaks down to form a highly corrosive gas, which caused one death and a number of injuries in the accident. Several suits amounting to millions of dollars in damages were filed, and in October the Nuclear Regulatory Commission fined Kerr-McGee $310,000 for safety violations. The plant resumed operations in November.

Silkwood Case. After a decade of litigation in the Karen Silkwood nuclear contamination case, Kerr-McGee agreed in August to pay the Silkwood estate $1.38 million. Silkwood, a laboratory analyst at a company plutonium plant in Oklahoma, died in an automobile accident on November 13, 1974; she was on her way to meet a newspaper reporter to discuss alleged safety problems at the plant, where she had been contaminated by radioactivity.

Toxic Waste Cleanup. On January 27 the U.S. Supreme Court ruled that trustees of bankrupt companies could not avoid responsibility to clean up toxic waste sites. Cleanup under the federal Comprehensive Environmental Response, Compensation, and Liability Act (Superfund) slowed, primarily because Congress bogged down in debate over the level of funding and over renewing the law, which had expired in September 1985. Finally, House and Senate conferees agreed on an expanded, $9 billion program, which Reagan approved.

In September, W. R. Grace & Company settled out of court, reportedly for over $8 million, in a suit by several Woburn, Mass., families claiming that well water contaminated by toxic waste from a Grace plant caused six deaths and many illnesses.

Acid Rain and Air Pollution. According to a report released by the National Academy of Sciences in March, sulfur dioxide emissions

---

Cash for Trash

The City Council of Rockland, Ill., found a new way to encourage residents to recycle newspapers and aluminum cans, thus cutting down on the recyclable trash that goes to the landfill. In the Cash for Trash program, one family is selected at random each week to have their refuse searched in order to determine whether "good trash" was separated from the rest. If so, the lucky person gets at least $1,000. If not, the forfeited money goes into the pot for next week's prize. So far, Cash for Trash has been a big success. In June 1986, Rockland collected three times as much separately bagged recyclable material as it had a year earlier, and in August the City Council voted to renew the program for six months and increase its budget. In answer to those concerned about the privacy of their rubbish, promoters point out that once it's put out on the street, it belongs to the city. Besides, if refuse can bring you money, why refuse?

At a summit meeting in The Hague in June, British Prime Minister Margaret Thatcher, together with West German Chancellor Helmut Kohl, led the opposition to economic sanctions but agreed to dispatch British Foreign Secretary Sir Geoffrey Howe on a mission in August to persuade the South African government to make certain concessions. Howe met with no success, and as a result the pressure for sanctions mounted within the EC. In September a sanctions package was adopted, banning imports of South African iron and steel and gold coins and prohibiting any new EC investment in South Africa. Coal was excepted from the package on the insistence of West Germany.

The Community was cool to the request of President Ronald Reagan for economic sanctions against Libya because of its involvement in terrorism. However, EC countries did order the expulsion of some Libyan diplomats; in reaction, the Libyan government expelled 36 embassy staff members from seven EC countries.

In April, for the ninth time in its seven-year history, the European Monetary System was realigned. The French franc was devalued an average of 4.7 percent against the EMS's other currencies, as part of the economic strategy of the French government aimed at encouraging growth and curbing inflation. Both the West German mark and the Dutch guilder rose 3 percent in value; other currencies were somewhat less affected.

Also in April, after prolonged negotiations, EC farm ministers agreed in April to a virtual price freeze on agricultural products. The accord also imposed a 3 percent cut in EC milk quotas to curb the further growth of the Community's large surplus output. There was also agreement on strategies for reducing the general food surplus, including a cut in storage payments. Nonetheless, by late in the year the food surplus was said to have brought the Community to the brink of bankruptcy, with subsidies to farmers and storage costs accounting for an estimated two-thirds of the $26 billion annual budget.

Early in May the EC placed a temporary ban on Eastern European food and animal exports, which authorities feared might be contaminated by fallout from the reactor accident at Chernobyl in the Soviet Union. The ban lasted until May 31, when permanent EC standards for acceptable radiation levels in food were established.

Gathering in London in December for their semiannual meeting, EC leaders found themselves unable to make progress on crucial agricultural issues but agreed that the Iran arms controversy facing President Ronald Reagan could also harm the Western alliance, particularly as regards arms negotiations between the United States and the Soviet Union. The Community also called for further action to fight terrorism and for a withdrawal of Soviet troops from Afghanistan.   J.O.S.

F

FASHION. The commitment of women to proper diet and overall fitness continued to exert a strong impact on fashion in 1986, and there was a return to greater femininity. Menswear emphasized rugged American style.

Shapely and Comfortable. The overall demand in women's spring fashions was for clothing that emphasized and flattered a trim but well-developed female form. Shapely, figure-defining, yet tailored silhouettes were in the forefront, while camouflaging flounces and frills were rare. While the trend was toward body-hugging clothes, they had the freedom of movement desirable in an outdoor-oriented season. The result was a hybrid of classic, easy-to-wear sportswear, natty menswear polish, and curvaceous feminine allure.

The colors of the season tended overwhelmingly toward white, navy, khaki, and black, with bright color in accessories. Denim was

Donna Karan's collection featured her trademark body-conscious styling; above left, clothes are softly draped but revealing. The Dior look, at right, emphasized detailing at the waist, strong-shouldered jackets, and skirts stopping above the knee.

used in more seriously styled clothing, such as Fendi's short, strapless, body-hugging dress set off by gold buttons. Donna Karan distinguished herself with a number of classically simple yet stylish pieces, including sarong-draped skirts that could also be worn over pants.

Despite an emphasis on femininity, the influence of menswear remained strong, surfacing in the selection of such fabrics as tropical-weight worsted wool in solids (especially nautical navy and white) and haberdashery plaids and checks. Also adapted from menswear was the use of such details as gold buttons on blazers, broadly defined shoulders, and wide lapels. At the same time, some designers moved further away from the menswear look. In Rome, Valentino presented an array of feminine knit

day dresses cut close to the body, belted, and trimmed in contrasting piping.

Rugged Men's Look. Classic clothes were the rule for men's spring fashions, with a generous, easy cut for an unconstricted fit and ample air circulation. Navy and a variety of grays were still the backbone of suit colors, but ice cream pales, which were cool on the eyes in the face of the long, hot summer ahead, offered a welcome relief. In a surprising twist, dark suits with a more formal air became an important look on the West Coast, usually noted for its more casual and colorful dress code. The California look in sportswear—loud plaids, bright colors, bold graphics, surfer trunks, and all-white separates with the loose, easy fit of pajamas—was another menswear hit for the summer season.

Femininity Reigns. For fall, women's wear designers produced some of the most assertively feminine styles to appear since the 1950's, which was exactly where many of them found their inspiration. The clothes were on the whole confident and poised and bore a subtle air of luxury. Silhouettes were sleek and smooth; the shapes were body-conscious but simple, comfortable, and classic. Shoulders were broadened but rounded, and waists were nipped, tucked, peplumed, or belted for emphasis. Most skirts slid intimately over the hips, either opening slightly to soft hemlines barely reaching the knee or swirling voluptuously into full circles that ended below the calf.

Muted fall colors predominated, along with black and healthy shots of vibrant hues, especially reds and oranges. To balance the simplicity of the styling, fabrics were often sumptuous, relying heavily on cashmere, silk, leather, and suede. Evening looks were as spare and devoid of unnecessary decoration as their daytime counterparts.

Classic daytime dresses were an important part of the season. The best had small, easily fitted tops and narrow sleeves (often pushed up to three-quarter lengths), belted waistlines, and hemlines that either ended at the knee or swirled to the calf. The dominant fabric was jersey, of either wool or cashmere.

Suits showed not the slightest masculinity. Jackets were either longer and defined at the waist over knee-length skirts or shorter and paired with long flowing skirts. Pantsuits were a comfortable and practical alternative, with equally chic styling.

Sweater sets, such as those by Calvin Klein, were a key element of the season, revived from the 1950's in soft, luxurious cashmere and lamb's wool. Coats were also an important element: they were either short, square-shouldered, and straight, or else ultra-long, polo-styled or nipped at the waist, and flaring almost to the ankle.

Easygoing Menswear. Menswear for fall gained from the subtle richness of its fabrics—houndstooth wools overshot with rich jewel-toned yarns, vibrant yet subliminal patterns, and Harris (and other) tweeds flecked with nubs of gold, turquoise, plum—and layers of complementary textures. Not surprisingly, the cut of

The tuxedo was a radical new design in 1886 (above); its most recent incarnation (below) retains some of the old formality while following a newer trend toward soft pastels.

FASHION

the season's suits was easygoing, less confining, and less reliant on fusings and paddings. The country-gentleman look dominated weekend clothing. Suede and leather remained important, as did rugged-looking textural sweaters.

Death of Perry Ellis. Designer Perry Ellis died on May 30. Ellis, 46, had been producing collections in New York City under his own name for a decade and was best known for his hand-knit sweaters, baggy pleated pants, and oversized jackets in natural fabrics and neutral colors, epitomizing the outdoorsy American look. According to Manhattan Industries, which owns Perry Ellis Sportswear, the company was continuing under the direction of Ellis's two former design assistants, Jed Krascella and Patricia Pastor.   E.J.G.

The house of Chanel displayed its usual classic style in an easy fitted top paired with a doubled-breasted detailed skirt.

FIJI. *See* STATISTICS OF THE WORLD

FINLAND. Finland was the first nation to detect high levels of radiation after the Chernobyl nuclear disaster in the Soviet Union in April. Subsequently, Finnish government officials postponed construction of a fifth Finnish nuclear reactor, and in May the Rural Party, a member of the governing coalition in Parliament, moved to dismantle existing nuclear plants by the year 2000. A government crisis ensued, as Prime Minister Kalevi Sorsa of the Social Democrats, the largest party in the coalition, angrily threatened to resign. Rural Party leaders backed down and withdrew their motion.

Finland suffered its most serious labor disputes in 30 years, with one strike involving 250,000 industrial workers and another, ultimately involving 55,000 government employees, that virtually shut down air and rail traffic as well as most government offices. Even the staff of the presidential palace joined in for a time, forcing President Mauno Koivisto to move temporarily to a guest house. Both conflicts were ultimately settled by compromise agreements covering two years.

The split between moderate "Eurocommunist" and Stalinist factions in the Finnish Communist Party resulted in two separate parties, as the Stalinist dissidents formed a party called the Democratic Alternative in order to run candidates in the general election scheduled for March 1987.

After 25 years of associate membership in the European Free Trade Association, Finland became a full member on January 1. It had originally assumed associate status to avoid provoking the Soviet Union, which regarded membership in the organization as a violation of Finnish neutrality. But Finland had gradually acquired the full benefits of free industrial trade with other members, so the elevation to full membership was largely symbolic.

See STATISTICS OF THE WORLD.   M.D.H.

FISHERIES. *See* AGRICULTURE AND FOOD SUPPLIES.

FLORIDA. *See* STATISTICS OF THE WORLD.

FORMOSA. *See* TAIWAN.

FRANCE. The conservative opposition to President François Mitterrand's Socialist government won a slim majority in the National

Right-wing National Front supporters celebrate on the Champs-Elysées after the neofascist party won nearly 10 percent of the vote in France's general election in March—its largest share ever.

Assembly elected on March 16, 1986. As a result, Mitterrand was forced to share power with a conservative cabinet headed by Prime Minister Jacques Chirac. The divided leadership created a climate of political uncertainty heightened by the continued success of the extreme right-wing National Front party and by Mitterrand's statement in October that he did not intend to run for reelection in 1988. Student unrest and incidents of terrorism posed difficult problems for the government.

Electoral Change. Three years of economic uncertainty and increasing austerity produced the expected result in the elections: the opposition coalition of the Rassemblement pour la République (RPR), led by Chirac, and the Union pour la démocratie française (UDF), led by former President Valéry Giscard d'Estaing and former Prime Minister Raymond Barre, returned the French National Assembly to its pre-1981 center-right majority. Although the coalition won 42 percent of the vote, it gained only 277 seats of 577 in the newly enlarged Assembly and thus fell short of an absolute majority, which it was forced to make up through alliances with deputies from small right-wing parties. The Socialist Party (PS) won 32 percent of the popular vote and gained 215 seats, down from its absolute majority of 286 (out of 491) in the previous Assembly. Of the two other major parties, the Communist Party (PCF) continued its slide of recent elections

and gained only 9.8 percent of the vote, losing primacy in its traditional working-class strongholds. The neofascist National Front (FN) came in at virtually the same level as the Communists (winning its largest vote yet). For the first time in the history of the Fifth Republic, the president and the parliamentary majority (hence the prime minister) were of different, and opposite, political tendencies.

A new voting system, proportional representation—in which the number of seats won by a party was proportional to its vote in each department—limited the extent of the Socialist defeat but was also responsible for the election of 35 National Front deputies.

Party Politics. Denationalization was the most hotly debated campaign issue among the parties, with the center-right coalition committed to returning state-owned industrial and banking groups to private ownership and selling at least one public television network. The Socialists had promised to accelerate the upward indexing of the guaranteed minimum wage and to use fiscal policy to promote equality. The conservatives were committed to a balanced budget, reduced state expenditures, the elimination of price controls, and a sharp reduction of taxes on the wealthy.

Recently, the growing number of immigrants of African and Middle Eastern origin had grown into a major political issue. Coupling a hard line against immigration with an equally hard

171

Embattled Marriage Partner

With the center-right coalition's victory in French parliamentary elections in March, Jacques Chirac, 54, the mayor of Paris and a former prime minister under Valéry Giscard d'Estaing, was invited to form a new government by Socialist President François Mitterrand, in an unlikely marriage of two political rivals with opposing philosophies. There were fears that this unusual "cohabitation," as the French called it, would lead to political paralysis. But Chirac pressed forward energetically, effectively opposing Mitterrand to win parliamentary approval of a bill denationalizing key French government firms. Chirac had less success later in the year, as he sought to deal with a wave of terrorist bombings and with violent student protests against his plan (subsequently withdrawn) for reforming French universities.

Jacques Chirac

line on law and order issues and anti-Communism, the FN, only three years after it first emerged into prominence, had scored a meteoric electoral success. Its vote was greatest in the areas of greatest immigrant concentration and of high unemployment—the south, the Rhône valley, the Mediterranean coast, and the Paris region. The FN's charismatic leader, Jean-Marie Le Pen, a millionaire ex-Foreign Legionnaire who had fought in Indochina and Algeria, became a media star in the campaign.

"Cohabitation." Two days after the election, President Mitterrand invited Chirac to form a new government. Chirac accepted, and both men vowed to make a serious effort at power sharing—which the French immediately labeled "cohabitation."

Besides differing in politics, the two had opposite styles. Chirac had developed a new, relaxed informality that contrasted with Mitterrand's studied aloofness and was yet another potential source of friction between them. Nevertheless, they maintained basic cooperation for a few months, until Chirac began to press his denationalization program.

Denationalization Battle. In June the Chirac government announced its intention to move ahead with the denationalization of 24 of the 65 state-owned businesses, including 9 massive industrial groups accounting for 20 percent of total manufacturing sales in France. Chirac's original plan was to push through denationalization by decree, avoiding the procedural snarls associated with parliamentary action, but he was faced with the requirement that he obtain Mitterrand's signature on every decree, which Mitterrand said he would withhold. The Chirac government then won passage in the National Assembly of a bill authorizing the privatization of state-owned companies; Finance Minister Edouard Balladur subsequently initiated the program, naming a bank, an insurance company, and a glass and construction enterprise to be sold to the public.

Devaluation. The fourth devaluation of the franc since 1981 was the keystone of a realignment of currencies among the eight members of the European Monetary System, undertaken in early April. The West Germans and the Dutch agreed to revalue their strong currencies upward 3 percent while the French devalued the franc by 3 percent (other revaluations were smaller). The government hoped thus to reduce France's competitive disadvantage in European and world markets. Finance Minister Balladur also announced a series of deflationary measures, including a tight monetary policy, a sharp reduction in government spending, a balanced budget by 1989, and dismantling of price and currency controls.

Strikes. A 24-hour strike by millions of civil servants on October 21 disrupted public service throughout France. The strike was called in protest against declining salary purchasing power and a proposed cut of 17,000 civil service jobs. New strikes were called by railroad engineers, as well as by dockworkers, seamen, and transit workers late in the year; the strikes severely hindered domestic transit and port traffic.

Terrorism in Paris. A series of terrorist bombings shook Paris during the year. Three department stores were bombed in February; in March there was an explosion on a high-speed train near the capital. On March 20, 2 persons were killed and nearly 30 wounded when a bomb exploded in a crowded shopping mall off the Avénue des Champs-Elysées. Responsibility for these attacks was attributed to a group calling itself the Committee for Solidarity with Arab and Middle Eastern Political Prisoners. In July, four blasts shattered the Parisian summer; the worst demolished part of an annex of police headquarters, killing a police inspector.

On September 8, a blast at the Paris City Hall post office killed 1 person and injured 18 others. It was the first in a series of Paris bombings that killed 11 persons and injured about 200. The worst, on September 17, killed 5 people outside a popular department store. The Committee for Solidarity, which claimed responsibility for all but the September 17 bombing, said that its aim was the release of a convicted Lebanese terrorist being held in a French prison, Georges Ibrahim Abdallah. On September 25, four Lebanese and five radical French leftists believed to be linked to Direct Action were arrested in connection with the investigation. It was speculated that the Abdallah issue was only a façade for a campaign by Iran or Syria to force the French out of their prominent role in the Middle East. During the summer several French soldiers attached to UN peacekeeping forces in Lebanon had been killed, and on September 18 the French military attaché in Beirut was assassinated.

Direct Action also claimed responsibility for several Paris bombings in November and was linked to the assassination, on November 17,

of Georges Besse, president of the state-owned automaker Renault, in front of his Paris home. The following month, the murder trial of three Direct Action members was postponed indefinitely, after five jurors dropped out, apparently because of a threat made in the courtroom by one of the defendants; the postponement raised wide concern. The government indicated it would seek retroactive legislation permitting

Ambulances swarm to the scene after a terrorist bomb exploded outside the popular Paris department store Tati, killing 5 people and wounding 53. Five such attacks occurred during a ten-day period in September, making Paris a city under siege.

terrorism suspects to be tried by special courts without juries.

Student Revolt. The Chirac government faced a serious challenge to its authority when a bill to overhaul the university system and tighten admissions policies touched off two weeks of widespread, often violent student demonstrations and rioting in the streets of Paris, beginning in late November. One student died, apparently of a heart attack, after being beaten by police during a demonstration. Chirac gave in on December 8 and announced that the bill would be withdrawn. The next day, he also canceled a special parliamentary session in which he had hoped to push through restrictive naturalization measures, legalization of private prisons, and a new military spending program opposed by Mitterrand. The backdown was seen as a serious loss of authority for Chirac. He appeared to regain some of his leverage later in the month, however, when, after a bitter battle, he won enactment of a new measure, opposed by Mitterrand and the Socialists, allowing more flexible working hours in French offices and factories. The measure was pushed through at the very end of the regular legislative session.

Foreign Affairs. In the months after the elections, Mitterrand appeared to be asserting the primacy of the president in foreign affairs. Heading France's delegation to the Tokyo summit of major industrial nations in May, he arrived on board a Concorde the day before Chirac flew in on an ordinary Air France 747. In July, Mitterrand traveled to the United States to take part in the Statue of Liberty centennial; because he was to visit the Soviet Union soon after, Reagan sent with him a personal message to Soviet leader Mikhail Gorbachev; in talks with Gorbachev, Mitterrand focused on arms control and other major elements of East-West relations. Later in the year, however, Chirac began to take a leading role in foreign affairs, while Mitterrand was less conspicuous.

In July the governments of France and New Zealand reached agreement on the final disposition of the Greenpeace case. (*See* NEW ZEALAND.) In December, France parachuted supplies into northwestern Chad shortly before Libya launched its expected offensive in an effort to regain portions of the area from forces that had switched allegiance to the Chadian government. (*See* CHAD.)

Channel Tunnel. On January 20, Mitterrand and Prime Minister Margaret Thatcher of Britain announced plans for a double railway tunnel under the English Channel to run 30 miles between the areas of Calais and Dover. On the tunnel's completion in 1993, motor vehicles would make the 30-minute trip under the channel on special trains. A separate motor tunnel was to be built by the end of the century.

Mickey on the Marne. Plans for Europe's first Disneyland, in the Paris suburb of Marne-la-Vallee, drew protests from local farmers who would lose land to eminent domain proceedings. The government agreed to extend mass transit lines to the site; 15,000 hotel rooms, 7,000 luxury apartments, and 6 million square feet of office space were to be provided to accompany the amusement park.

See STATISTICS OF THE WORLD.　　　　S.E.

G

GABON. *See* STATISTICS OF THE WORLD.
GAMBIA, THE. *See* STATISTICS OF THE WORLD.
GEORGIA. *See* STATISTICS OF THE WORLD.
GERMAN DEMOCRATIC REPUBLIC, *or* **EAST GERMANY.** In April 1986 the 11th Congress of the Socialist Unity Party met for five days in East Berlin and elected Erich Honecker to his fourth five-year term as general secretary. The tone of the congress was one of enormous self-congratulation for what the German Democratic Republic (GDR) had achieved: in the economy, for example, a doubling of real national product in 15 years and a 125 percent increase in industrial production. Prime Min-

ister Willi Stoph spoke of "a dynamism that has reaped international acclaim."

The new five-year plan adopted by the congress offered nothing in two areas of need—increased pensions and a shorter work week. It did call for an increase in real income of 20 percent to 23 percent over the five years, enough new housing to finally solve the perennial housing shortage in the GDR, and—to encourage a higher birthrate—a sweetening of the government's already generous benefits to families.

Labor productivity in the GDR is, at best, about 60 percent of that in West Germany, and a major emphasis in the new five-year plan was to increase economic production by applying the latest scientific and technological methods to save on labor. In the first six months of 1986, real national income was 4.3 percent higher than in the same time period in 1985, while production inputs per unit of national income fell by 2 percent. Industrial labor productivity grew by 8.6 percent. As has been the case for a quarter of a century, there was no unemployment in the GDR, and there was no inflation with respect to consumer necessities, such as bread and potatoes, mass transit fares, and rents.

On August 13, leaders of both East and West Germany commemorated the 25th anniversary of the construction of the concrete-and-steel wall that surrounds the city of West Berlin. East German propaganda claims the wall prevented the fascist West from invading the GDR through West Berlin. In truth, the wall prevented East Germans from "voting with their feet"—exiting from the GDR through the once-uncontrolled border into West Berlin and then by air into the free and more prosperous Federal Republic. The wall pressured young, well-educated East Germans with no easy way out to devote their energies to building a more prosperous East Germany.

See STATISTICS OF THE WORLD.   R.J.W.

GERMANY, FEDERAL REPUBLIC OF, *or* **WEST GERMANY.** Buoyed by successes in important state elections during 1986, the governing coalition headed by West German Chancellor Helmut Kohl, leader of the Christian Democratic Union (CDU), was looking forward to victory in national elections scheduled for

January 1987. West German economic growth increased, and prices remained stable.

Politics. On June 15 in Lower Saxony, the CDU lost its absolute majority in the state legislature, as its share of the vote dropped to 44.3 percent (down from 50.7 percent in 1982). However, the incumbent premier, Ernst Albrecht, was able to form a new government with a one-seat majority in the 155-member chamber, by adding to the 69 seats taken by the CDU the 9 won by the Free Democratic Party (FDP). The FDP, already in coalition with the CDU at the national level, had won 6.0 percent of the vote, up slightly from 1982. The overall victory for these parties, though narrow, came despite strong recent controversy over allegedly confusing guidelines issued by the federal government regarding fallout from the disaster at the Soviet nuclear plant in Chernobyl.

In Bavarian state elections in October, the conservative Christian Social Union (the second-largest party in Kohl's coalition) won a solid 55.9 percent of the vote. The opposition Social Democratic Party (SPD) took just 27.4 percent of the vote, its poorest performance since World War II. Then, in November elections in Hamburg—traditionally a Social Democratic stronghold—the SPD suffered a stunning defeat, dropping from 51.3 percent to 40.9 percent of the vote and losing its parliamentary majority to the CDU, which took 41.9 percent. An all-female slate of candidates run by the leftist opposition Greens took an unexpected 10.4 percent of the popular vote.

At the SPD congress in August, delegates overwhelmingly chose Johannes Rau, 55, minister-president of North Rhine-Westphalia, as their nominee for chancellor in the 1987 elections. Rau, a moderate, lacked a personal following among the party leadership, and the platform adopted at the congress seemed likely to make his task even more difficult. It called for a total phase-out of nuclear energy, the withdrawal of NATO missiles from West Germany, and the reorganization of the army to "render it incapable of offensive action." On the other hand, the Greens' congress a month later saw an apparent shift of strength toward the Realo, or "realistic," wing of the party, which favors forming coalitions with the SPD.

175

Terrorism. The leftist Red Army Faction claimed responsibility for the assassination of a top West German industrialist and his driver in July on the outskirts of Munich. Three RAF members were later arrested in connection with the crime. In October a senior official of the West German Foreign Ministry was killed outside his home near Bonn; the RAF again claimed responsibility.

On April 5 a terrorist bomb exploded in a West Berlin discotheque frequented by American troops. It killed a U.S. serviceman and a young Turkish woman and wounded over 200 others. (Another American soldier died in June from injuries received in the explosion.) Libya was thought to be behind the bombing, and Britain, France, and the United States took measures to prevent Libyan diplomats from crossing into West Berlin. In December two Arabs were convicted for another West Berlin bombing, a March attack on an Arab social club that severely wounded nine Arabs. Evidence of Syrian complicity in the bombing was heard during the trial; after the verdict, Bonn expelled three Syrian diplomats and downgraded its relations with the regime of President Hafez al Assad.

East German Relations. East German officials agreed to ease another border-crossing problem—a flood of Asians and Africans pouring into West Berlin as applicants for political asylum. Asylum is offered with few restrictions under the West German constitution, and the West Germans want their constitutional rights to hold in West Berlin as well. The problem is that most of the applicants are not genuine political refugees. They are attracted by the rich West German economy. In the first half of the year, asylum applicants numbered 42,000, and 23,000 of them came in by way of West Berlin after being flown into East Berlin on Soviet and East German transport planes. The asylum seekers are not prevented from entering West Berlin, because the Western allies, considering Berlin a single city, do not normally check credentials at city border crossings. In September, however, East Germany announced that beginning October 1, passengers arriving at the East Berlin airport would be allowed to pass through only if they held valid entry visas for their country of destination.

In May the two German states signed a cultural agreement under negotiation since 1973. The pact represented a concession on the part of East Germany and the Soviet Union inasmuch as it included West Berlin as a recognized part of the Federal Republic. Earlier in the year, Horst Sindermann, the third-ranking political figure in East Germany, visited the Federal Republic, becoming the highest-ranking East German official ever to do so.

Foreign Relations. A major issue in U.S. relations was policy toward Libya. Kohl refused to follow the lead of President Ronald Reagan in imposing economic sanctions against Libya after terrorist attacks in December 1985 at the Rome and Vienna airports. After the West Berlin discotheque bombing in April, Kohl responded to U.S. requests for pressure against Libya with only a minor measure, the expulsion of two diplomats from the Libyan embassy in Bonn. Only after an April 21 resolution by European Community foreign ministers to reduce the number of Libyans in their countries did Kohl move farther, by expelling 22 of 41 Libyan diplomats in Bonn. Kohl was also cool toward U.S. military action against Libya.

In March, Kohl appeared to be acceding to a major request of the U.S. president by signing agreements on Reagan's Strategic Defense Initiative, the "Star Wars" plan for a defensive shield against Soviet nuclear missiles. But the Federal Republic would not be an official participant in Star Wars research; the agreements simply allowed West German private firms interested in research contracts to bid for them. Public monies were committed instead to Eureka, a high-technology research effort on the part of 19 European countries, sponsored originally by the French as an alternative to Star Wars. West Germans were also upset by Reagan's decision to exceed the SALT II agreement limiting nuclear arms—a step taken without consulting European allies.

Soviet leaders were disappointed in the West German response; Kohl also created a stir when, in an interview for *Newsweek*, he appeared to compare Mikhail Gorbachev's public relations skills to those of Joseph Goebbels, the Nazi propaganda chief.

Economic Trends. U.S. officials made repeated appeals to the West Germans to lower interest

Contrasting ceremonies marked the 25th anniversary of the famous Berlin Wall. On the west side, protesters joined hands in a human chain along the "wall of shame." On the east side, Communist Party leader Erich Honecker praised the "antifascist protective rampart."

rates, in the hope that a resulting increase in economic growth would stimulate demand for U.S. exports. In 1985 the West German surplus of exports over imports was up 36 percent from the record surplus in 1984, whereas the United States in 1985 posted its greatest trade deficit ever. After making one interest rate cut in March, the West Germans resisted later U.S. appeals, believing that enough help was being given to U.S. trade by an upward movement of the mark against the dollar (it rose 50 percent in the period June 1985 to September 1986) and by progress in the fight against inflation. In late 1986, because of declining energy costs, West German consumer prices were actually lower than a year earlier. Unemployment continued to be a problem, however. The jobless rate late in the year stood at 8.7 percent.

See STATISTICS OF THE WORLD. R.J.W.

GHANA. *See* STATISTICS OF THE WORLD.

The first day of the "Big Bang" saw traders at the London Stock Exchange adjusting to the new roles and the technology that accompanied deregulation.

GREAT BRITAIN. In 1986, Great Britain entered the magnetic field of the next general election, which had to be held by June 1988. The Conservative government of Prime Minister Margaret Thatcher (*see biography in* PEOPLE IN THE NEWS) contended with ministerial infighting and economic problems, but the opposition was also beset by weaknesses and divisions. Despite problems, the country was in a holiday mood for the summer wedding of Queen Elizabeth's second son, Prince Andrew.

The Government's Program. The news that inflation had come down to just below 2.5 percent by the middle of the year, from over 20 percent six years previously, was widely appreciated. But there had been no parallel reduction in unemployment, and the annual rate of increase in unit labor costs had not abated. Parliamentary by-elections in April and May, at Fulham in London and in Derbyshire and Yorkshire, went badly for the government, as did local council elections in May. Polls suggested that many voters found Thatcher divisive and valued public services, especially in healthcare and education, above cuts in

taxes, thus contradicting the government's order of priorities.

The difficulty for the government was partly of its own making. The proclaimed thrust of its policy had been the reduction of public spending and the enlargement of private responsibility. The medical queues, the down-at-heel hospitals and schools, the disaffected teachers were thus commonly attributed to government cutbacks. But figures could be assembled to show that the Thatcher government had spent more in those directions than any government before it. In the case of education, the dilemma was eased by a change of minister. Sir Keith Joseph, the chief theorist of neoconservatism in the cabinet, bowed out as education minister. His place was taken by Kenneth Baker, who immediately settled a long and unpopular dispute with schoolteachers by the method, abjured by Sir Keith, of finding more money for the purpose.

The Thatcher cabinet was divided over whether to press on vigorously with tax cuts and spending cuts or go more slowly, watching out for voters' uneasiness. In part, this dilemma could be avoided by stressing the agreed importance of "popular capitalism." Nigel Lawson, chancellor of the Exchequer, moved in this direction in his budget on March 18 by introducing personal equity plans, under which a person could enjoy a limited exemption from tax on capital gains and reinvested dividend income from equity shares. The popular capitalism line was tied in with the government's continuing privatization program and with unprecedented deregulation of the investment industry.

Much of the excitement in the City was directed to the "Big Bang" on October 27, when massive deregulation of the London Stock Exchange brought no-holds-barred competition to financial markets. The Big Bang abolished fixed commissions on stock and bond trading— the result was lower, negotiated commissions. In addition, the old precautionary separation of jobber, who trades stock, and broker, who sells it, was abandoned. Newly merged, more powerful, and increasingly transnational groups now had the freedom of the markets under untried regulatory arrangements.

On November 12, Queen Elizabeth opened Parliament with her annual speech from the throne. The queen outlined the government's proposed new legislative program, which contained no basic change of direction in policy; it called chiefly for law and order measures and for a continuation of selling off government-owned companies.

The Opposition. The opposition Liberal/Social Democratic Alliance continued to do better in by-elections than national opinion polls suggested. It was handicapped, however, by a difference of opinion on nuclear defense policy between the two Alliance leaders, David Owen of the Social Democrats and David Steel of the Liberals. Both agreed that the Trident nuclear submarine system, which the government intended to purchase, should be dropped. They did not agree about what to do when Britain's present nuclear deterrent, the submarine-borne Polaris, became obsolete. The two tried to bridge their differences by promoting the concept of nuclear cooperation with France to create a "minimum European deterrent." But the Liberal Assembly, which determines official party policy, narrowly voted in September to call for a collective European "defense capability" that would be "nonnuclear." This policy was unacceptable to Owen and most of the Social Democrats.

In Neil Kinnock, the Labor Party had a personable leader aware of the need to jettison much of his party's vote-losing baggage from the past. He had some success in persuading the Laborites to accept the most popular feature of the Tories' trade union legislation—compulsory ballots for strikes and election of officers—and in clipping the wings of the party's extreme Militant Tendency. Labor's annual party conference in September was unusually harmonious. However, it adopted, with Kinnock's support, a defense policy that many saw as an election loser: abandoning British nuclear arms on the understanding that the Soviet Union would make a similar reduction, removing from Britain all U.S. nuclear bases and facilities, and opting out of NATO's nuclear strategy.

The Westland Affair. The financial troubles of Westland P.L.C., Britain's only manufacturer of helicopters, posed a divisive problem for the government. Disagreement within the cabinet over whether to allow a U.S. helicopter

---

Toad Patrol

Bumper stickers begging travelers to "Help a Toad Across the Road" sprouted all over England in the spring, in a compassionate campaign to prevent the annual flattening of hordes of "Britain's best-loved amphibians." Thousands of migrating British toads are run over each year on warm, rainy evenings (their most active time), as they scurry across roadways to the low-lying ponds where they breed. The British Department of Transport tried to help by putting up roadside warning signs, showing an endangered toad inside a red triangle. The Fauna and Flora Preservation Society went further, dispatching squads of raincoated animal-lovers to carry the creatures across in buckets. It may not be everyone's idea of fun, but as one amphibian expert put it, "Toads are our friends. They eat lots of pests, and if there were more of them, we wouldn't need so much chemical spraying."

company, Sikorsky Aircraft, to bail out Westland led to infighting that resulted in the resignation of Defense Secretary Michael Heseltine and of Trade and Industry Secretary Leon Brittan in January. Heseltine had favored a bailout by a Western European consortium, with a view to preserving a European helicopter capability independent of the United States. (The decision was left to the Westland shareholders, who approved the Sikorsky arrangement in February.)

The Archer Affair. The Conservatives also suffered embarrassment when Jeffrey Archer, deputy chairman of the party, resigned in October after a Sunday tabloid printed the text of a conversation he reportedly had with a prostitute. The paper quoted him making arrangements for an intermediary to deliver money to the woman so that she could leave Britain to escape reporters who were harassing her about her connection to the politician-novelist.

Roger Tomkys, the British ambassador to Syria, leaves for home after the British government broke diplomatic relations with Syria late in October over that country's suspected involvement in a recent terrorist incident.

Anglo-American Relations. The balancing of British foreign policy between continental Europe and the United States was tested by the use of U.S. fighter-bombers based in Britain to bomb Libya on April 15. President Ronald Reagan had sought British consent for the use of the planes. Thatcher received an assurance that action would be limited to clearly defined targets; she also learned that the F-111 aircraft in Britain (18 were used) were the only ones available and that without their use the risk of civilian casualties would have been greater. There was a sharp hostile reaction in Britain to the strike against Libya and the government's part in facilitating it.

The Thatcher government and the Reagan administration were in general accord in the matter of economic sanctions against South Africa. Thatcher continued to declare her disbelief in the efficacy of sanctions as a means of bringing down apartheid. However, Foreign Secretary Sir Geoffrey Howe was sent to South Africa to urge the Pretoria government to release Nelson Mandela, the black leader, from prison and lift the ban on the the black nationalist African National Congress. When this mission failed, Howe, at a European Community foreign ministers' meeting in Brussels, voted for limited sanctions, which banned imports of iron and steel and gold coins and prohibited new investments in South Africa by European companies.

Thatcher visited the United States in November and met with Reagan. A major topic of discussion was arms control priorities in the wake of the Iceland summit between Reagan and Soviet leader Gorbachev. Thatcher apparently succeeded in reaching an understanding that the United States would not press for elimination of offensive strategic forces or a banning of all ballistic missiles. Such proposals were reportedly a cause of concern for Britain and other NATO allies.

Awacs Purchase. In December, after long and controversial deliberation, the Thatcher government announced it was purchasing Boeings instead of Britain's own Nimrod aircraft for its airborne early warning defense system. The Labor opposition strongly protested the $1 billion decision, which, it said, would cost thousands of British jobs.

A one-day general strike was called by Protestant Unionists in Northern Ireland on March 3 to protest the 1985 Anglo-Irish agreement; here picketers line up outside Stormont Castle in Belfast, home of the Northern Ireland Assembly.

Break With Syria. On October 24 the government broke off relations with Syria after a jury convicted a Jordanian of attempting to bomb an Israeli airliner at Heathrow by getting his unsuspecting pregnant Irish fiancée to place the explosive device in her carry-on luggage. (The bomb was discovered before she boarded the plane.) Foreign Secretary Howe told Parliament that Syrian diplomats, including the ambassador to Britain, had aided the Jordanian.

Northern Ireland. The treaty of cooperation signed by Thatcher and Irish Prime Minister Garrett FitzGerald in late 1985 did not reduce the violence in Northern Ireland. Just after midnight on January 1, the Irish Republican Army exploded a remote-controlled bomb in the center of Armagh, killing two policemen. The leaders of both main Unionist parties pledged themselves to work for the cancellation of the Anglo-Irish agreement. Denied a plebiscite in Ulster, all 15 Unionist members of Parliament arranged one for themselves by resigning and offering themselves up for re-election; in the by-elections that followed, on January 23, Unionists won 14 seats, losing 1.

A one-day general strike called by the Unionists in March was accompanied by widespread violence, as Protestants attacked the police trying to control the routes and behavior of marchers. The IRA, for its part, had developed a profitable tactic—blowing up police stations and threatening with death any building contractor who repaired them. In Belfast the number of random sectarian killings increased. Meanwhile, the Northern Ireland Assembly, dominated by Unionists, ceased to carry out its statutory functions, and the government dissolved it on June 12. The Thatcher government attached much importance to a revised extradition treaty reached with the United States, intended to facilitate the return of fugitive IRA suspects.

Royal Family. Prince Andrew and Sarah Ferguson, the daughter of Prince Charles's polo

In a ceremony full of down-home majesty on July 23, Prince Andrew, the second son of Queen Elizabeth II and Prince Philip, married Sarah Ferguson, known to the royal-loving British as Fergie. As a wedding gift, the queen named them the duke and duchess of York.

manager, were married in Westminster Abbey on July 23. The couple, created duke and duchess of York prior to the ceremony, spent their honeymoon in the Azores aboard the royal yacht *Britannia*.

On April 21, the queen celebrated her 60th birthday. Earlier in the year, she had visited Nepal, New Zealand, and Australia. In Australia, she signed a proclamation dissolving all remaining legislative and judicial links between the former colony and the United Kingdom; the British monarch remained, however, queen of Australia. In October the queen made a fortnight's visit to China and Hong Kong. It was the first time a reigning British sovereign had set foot in China.

On July 20 the *Sunday Times* of London printed a story, attributed to impeccable sources at Buckingham Palace, that the queen had become increasingly dismayed by Prime Minister Thatcher's policies. In the queen's reported view, the prime minister was threatening the cohesion of the Commonwealth by her opposition to sanctions against South Africa and the social order at home by her lack of compassion for the underprivileged. The queen's private secretary, Sir William Heseltine, denied the story.

The duchess of Windsor, who made history in the 1930's when King Edward VIII abdicated in order to marry her, died in Paris on April 24 at the age of 89. She was buried beside her husband at Frogmore, near Windsor Castle, as he had wished.

New Words. The editors of the *Oxford English Dictionary* completed the fourth and final volume of their work updating the original 12-volume dictionary, which came out between 1884 and 1928. The OED is widely regarded as the definitive English-language dictionary. The update recorded changes in the language as they had occurred throughout the world. Appearing for the first time were such words as *wimp, yuppie,* and *yuck.*

See STATISTICS OF THE WORLD. *See also* COMMONWEALTH OF NATIONS. T.J.O.H.

GREECE. During 1986 the Greek Parliament approved major constitutional reforms, and there were mass protests against the austerity program instituted by the Socialist government of Prime Minister Andreas Papandreou.

Constitutional Reform. On March 7, Parliament gave final approval to the first major revision of the country's constitution since its enactment in 1975. The revision removed the president's power to seek reconsideration of legislation already passed, to dissolve Parliament over policy issues, to call referendums, to suspend articles of the constitution in a national emergency, and to appoint or dismiss prime ministers without parliamentary backing. If no party had a majority in Parliament, the president had to offer the premiership successively to the leader of each of the four largest parties until a government could be formed; if none of the leaders could do so, he could assemble an all-party government. Deputies of the opposition party New Democracy walked out before the vote, contending that the reform would lead to parliamentary dictatorship.

Political Problems. Protests were organized against the Socialist government's new austerity program, particularly its wage policy designed to keep average earnings from growing more than 15 percent annually. On February 27 an estimated 700,000 trade unionists staged a 24-hour strike. On April 7, 800,000 strikers, including business and salaried people, paralyzed activities in more than 30 cities and towns.

Papandreou also had to contend with leftist dissent within his own party; he did so both by making tactical bids for leftist support and by imposing discipline. In April it was reported that 300 trade unionist and regional party officials had been expelled for opposing the austerity program. In addition, Papandreou and his ruling Panhellenic Socialist Movement (Pasok) suffered a major setback in October municipal elections when the Socialist mayors of Athens, Salonika, and Piraeus were defeated by New Democracy candidates. Communists and other leftists, angry over both the austerity program and the government's refusal to enact an electoral law to benefit smaller parties, had refused to give their usual support in the runoff to the Socialist candidates. To present a new image following the election losses, Papandreou reorganized his cabinet.

Foreign Affairs. As part of a continuing thaw in Greek-U.S. relations, U.S. Secretary of State George Shultz visited Greece in March. He apparently failed to obtain a firm Greek commitment on preserving U.S. military bases beyond the current expiration date of December 1988. (Papandreou denied speculation that a secret deal had been made.) However, Shultz said that bilateral relations had taken "a real turn for the better," and within a week of his departure, the U.S. State Department issued an export license for the sale of 40 F-16 fighter aircraft to Greece.

The Papandreou government quietly cooperated with the Reagan administration in tightening security in Greece, while it pursued an independent course within the Western alliance. Athens expressed strong reservations about U.S. actions against Libya and opposed limited actions taken by the European Community against Libya and, later in the year, against Syria (for apparently aiding terrorists).

See also CYPRUS and STATISTICS OF THE WORLD.   J.A.B.

GRENADA. See STATISTICS OF THE WORLD. See also CARIBBEAN BASIN.

GUAM.   See STATISTICS OF THE WORLD.

GUATEMALA. On January 14, 1986, Guatemala inaugurated its first civilian president in almost 20 years. In his inaugural address, President Marco Vinicio Cerezo Arévalo vowed to attack corruption and other abuses by the military and police. Warning that Guatemala faced a period of austerity and sacrifice because the national treasury was empty, the Christian Democrat, elected in December 1985, said he would seek foreign loans to implement an emergency economic plan. He also promised to work to find a regional solution to the conflict in Central America—a promise he later made good on when he hosted the first summit of Central American heads of state in a decade.

On another issue, the Cerezo government indicated it did not expect to open a dialogue with Guatemalan guerrilla groups. A spokesman for the National Guatemalan Revolutionary Unity, a guerrilla front, said the government's position violated campaign promises and reflected the continued hegemony of the military.

The Mutual Support Group of relatives of missing persons marched outside the National Palace in January, prior to Cerezo's inauguration, to demand that the military account for the disappearances of their loved ones, attributed by guerrilla groups to security forces. Continued killings and disappearances soon led the new government to abolish the Technical Investigations Department (DIT), a plainclothes secret police force. Some members were retrained as national police; others resigned or were fired.

Several governmental officials and others involved in the land redistribution program were killed in a series of incidents during May and June. Atrocities such as these increased pressure on the government to repeal an amnesty law, signed by outgoing President Humberto Mejía Victores, that had absolved the military of responsibility for murders, disappearances, and other crimes.

A devaluation of the quetzal, increased coffee revenues, and lower oil prices combined with the start-up of the Chixoy hydroelectric complex and other factors to help improve Guatemala's economic outlook. Nevertheless, the budget deficit was projected to reach 3.5 percent of the gross domestic product, and a 30 percent inflation rate was projected.

In May, President Cerezo met with the presidents of El Salvador, Honduras, Nicaragua, and Costa Rica at the religious shrine of Esquipulas, east of Guatemala City. The five leaders signaled interest in accepting a regional peace treaty but remained divided over various provisions. A commission was authorized to draft a charter for an elected Central American parliament. In late June, the Foreign Ministry announced that diplomatic relations with Great Britain, severed in 1963 in a boundary dispute over claims to British Honduras (now Belize), would be restored gradually.

See STATISTICS OF THE WORLD.   L.L.P.

GUINEA. See STATISTICS OF THE WORLD.
GUINEA-BISSAU. See STATISTICS OF THE WORLD.
GUYANA. See STATISTICS OF THE WORLD. See also CARIBBEAN BASIN.

H

HAITI. The central event in Haiti in 1986 was the flight of Jean-Claude ("Baby Doc") Duvalier and the end of the Duvalier family's 28-year dictatorship.

Fall of the Duvalier Dynasty. Jean-Claude Duvalier, who succeeded to power at 19 on the death of his father, François ("Papa Doc") Duvalier, in 1971, had been under increasing pressure to improve human rights and undertake basic reforms. But the young president continued to rule in a corrupt manner, often appearing the puppet of stronger figures in his family and dependent upon U.S. political and economic backing. Having lost the support of Haiti's poor blacks and facing opposition from the Roman Catholic Church, Duvalier, by late 1985, was running scared, alternately placating and repressing his critics.

Events came to a climax in January 1986, after Washington cut its financial aid and popular protests multiplied, prompting Duvalier to unleash his feared secret militia, the Tontons Macoutes. On January 31 the White House mistakenly announced that Duvalier had fled the country. Popular celebrations turned to widespread protests when it became clear Duvalier had not left, and he imposed a state of siege. On February 7, the 34-year-old president-for-life, apparently incapable of retrieving his position, fled the country on a U.S. plane, and riotous celebrations broke out again, leading to the sacking of Duvalier's palace and the killing of a number of Tontons Macoutes.

France, following a plan worked out with the United States, provided Duvalier with temporary refuge. When no other offers came, Duvalier was allowed to stay on in France.

The Namphy Regime. A six-person military-civilian council under Lieutenant General Henri Namphy assumed power as soon as Duvalier fled. Although the council, which included four veteran Duvalier officials, released political prisoners, suspended the Duvalier constitution, dissolved his hand-picked National Assembly, and disbanded the Tontons Macoutes, its composition and its willingness to let some of Duvalier's associates flee the country led to criticisms that it represented "Duvalierism without Duvalier." These perceptions and the council's own inactivity fueled a renewal of popular protests that led to new deaths and arrests. On March 20, Justice Minister Gérard Gourgue, the one council member without ties to the old regime, resigned. The next day,

Namphy ousted three former Duvalier aides and formed a three-man council with a close associate, Colonel Williams Regala, and Foreign Minister Jacques François. Violent protests ensued.

On June 7, warning that Haiti was at "the edge of anarchy," Namphy announced a timetable for transition to democracy over 17 months, beginning with the registration of political parties and the election in October 1986 of a special assembly to draft a new constitution and culminating with the inauguration of a civilian president on February 7, 1988. Protests continued, though the government bowed to demands for the dismissal of a Duvalier cabinet holdover and began to prosecute Duvalier aides. In demonstrations on November 17 in Port-au-Prince, two people were shot and killed by soldiers.

The October election to choose drafters of a new constitution took place as scheduled. Turnout was sparse. It was Haiti's first democratic election in nearly 30 years.

Economic Problems and Prospects. Economic conditions worsened in the turmoil after Duvalier's fall. By July, 40 of 230 U.S. firms that had been doing business in Haiti had halted operations there. New investment was conspicuous by its absence, and tourism all but ceased. Food and fuel were scarce, prices were soaring, and distribution of food aid was impaired.

Corruption under Duvalier had cost the treasury an estimated $1 billion and left Haiti virtually without foreign reserves. Hundreds of millions of dollars in capital had fled overseas; much of the money was removed by the Duvaliers themselves.

See STATISTICS OF THE WORLD.   P.W.

HAWAII. *See* STATISTICS OF THE WORLD.

Twenty-eight years of oppression under Duvalier family rule ended February 7 when Haiti's President Jean-Claude Duvalier fled the country. Inset, Duvalier and his wife arrive at the airport, where a U.S. Air Force plane waits to fly them to France. Below, jubilant Haitians celebrate outside the presidential palace.

Health and Medicine

The growing AIDS epidemic and continuing widespread use of illicit drugs, especially a popular form of cocaine known as crack, were focuses of increased concern in health and medicine during 1986.

During 1986 there were small gains in knowledge about acquired immune deficiency syndrome (AIDS), and an experimental drug was found to prolong the life of some patients afflicted with the disease. The scientific community warned nevertheless that AIDS represented a health crisis, demanding immediate stepped-up programs in education and research. Meanwhile, an epidemic of crack (a

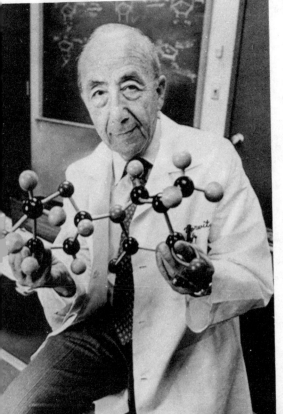

An experimental drug called azidothymidine (AZT) that can prolong the lives of some AIDS patients, though not cure the disease, showed good results in clinical tests. The drug was first developed by Dr. Jerome P. Horwitz in the 1960's.

smokable, or freebase, widely available modification of cocaine) spread through the United States with alarming speed. Some scientists warned that the war on cancer was being lost and urged greater emphasis on prevention efforts.

AIDS Developments. As of December 1986, according to the U.S. Centers for Disease Control (CDC), over 28,000 cases of AIDS (acquired immune deficiency syndrome) had been diagnosed in the United States, and more than 16,000 AIDS patients had died. Since it was first recognized in 1981, the syndrome has become the leading cause of death for males age 30–39 in New York City. By the end of 1991, the U.S. Public Health Service estimated, there would be a cumulative total of 270,000 U.S. cases and 179,000 deaths; the annual cost of caring for patients was projected at up to $16 billion by that time.

AIDS Breakthrough? The U.S. Department of Health and Human Services announced in September that an experimental drug called azidothymidine (AZT) had been shown to block the action of the basic AIDS virus in patients with a form of pneumonia called *Pneumocystis carinii,* one of the common manifestations of AIDS. Scientists emphasized that AZT was not a cure and could actually harm some patients, but it was the first drug that clearly prolonged the lives of some AIDS victims. A national telephone line established to provide more information was swamped with calls asking about the drug, which was to be made available to patients with the form of pneumonia it affects. AZT was first synthesized by Dr. Jerome P. Horwitz in the 1960's as part of an unsuccessful search for an anticancer drug.

Transmission of the Disease. AIDS has been largely confined in North America to three high-risk groups: homosexual males, intravenous drug abusers, and hemophiliacs and other recipients of blood and blood products. Several studies reported evidence that transmission among the heterosexual population does not occur through casual contact. Dr. Gerald H. Friedland and colleagues at Montefiore Medical Center in New York conducted interviews, physical examinations, and blood tests of 101 people who lived in the households of 39 AIDS patients for at least three months. Many shared dishes and other household goods and helped to feed, bathe, and take care of the AIDS patients. Of these people, only one—a five-year-old child—tested positive for exposure to the basic AIDS virus. Both of her parents were intravenous drug abusers, and her mother had been diagnosed as having AIDS, making it likely that the child was infected before birth. According to Friedland, the study supported the view that infection with AIDS can only be transmitted through injection of blood or blood products or intimate sexual contact.

In Africa, AIDS has shown a predilection for spreading through intimate heterosexual contact. Researchers' concern that intimate heterosexual contact might eventually become a significant mode of transmission among Americans increased when it was reported in March that AIDS viruses had been found in vaginal and cervical secretions in women.

Healthcare workers have been concerned that they could be infected while taking care of AIDS patients, but this happens very rarely, a monitoring project by the CDC found. Of the 938 healthcare workers studied who had been exposed to AIDS, usually because of injuries with needles or cuts with sharp instruments, only two developed serum antibodies for the virus. None had developed symptoms of AIDS.

Dire Warnings. Despite evidence that casual transmission of AIDS does not take place, a report issued in late October by the U.S. National Academy of Sciences warned that unless "wide-ranging and intensive efforts" were made, the disease could still cause a medical catastrophe. The 390-page report, by a panel of experts, stated that AIDS represented a national health crisis and could be checked only by immediate action, including greatly increased expenditures on education and re-

search and steps to bring more scientists from universities and private industry into the fight.

AIDS and Transfusions. Blood transfusions pose a small but real risk of AIDS, a panel of experts convened by the U.S. National Institutes of Health reported in July. The experts estimated that a small number of contaminated units of blood would slip into the nation's blood supply because of false negative test results; all blood donations are tested, but the available tests are not 100 percent accurate. The panel recommended continued research to develop better tests.

For those who might need blood during planned surgery, the NIH panel said that the safest procedure of all would be donating their own blood in advance. However, both the panel and the Red Cross opposed the private stockpiling of blood for possible, unspecified emergencies.

More on the AIDS Virus. Scientists also improved their understanding of the major AIDS virus and its mechanisms. CDC researchers identified the molecules that bind the virus to lymphocytic cells as glycoprotein—a protein on the virus's coat, or envelope—and the T4 molecule of the "helper-inducer" white blood cells. The finding was said to suggest the possibility of developing either a vaccine against the glycoprotein or drugs that interfere with the binding of the virus to the cell.

Antibodies against a human hormone involved in the activity of the cells targeted by an AIDS virus could prevent the virus from replicating, National Cancer Institute researchers found in laboratory experiments. The hormone, thymosin alpha-1, acts on helper T cells. The scientists obtained antibodies against the hormone by injecting it into rabbits and then adding the antibodies the rabbits developed to cell cultures infected by an AIDS virus. For reasons that remain unknown, the hormone antibodies were found to protect the cells against the virus.

Scientists also reported the discovery of at least two new AIDS viruses—LVA-2, found in Portugal among West Africans; and SBL, identified in West African patients in Sweden. Both viruses would escape detection by the existing AIDS blood test; neither virus, however, had yet been reported in the United States.

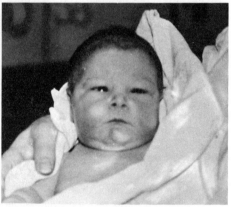

Denied a heart transplant for their newborn baby, a young unwed couple appeared on the Phil Donahue television show to deliver an emotional plea for a heart donation that could save the child's life. Amid audience tears and applause, a telephone call, prearranged by the show, came from a Michigan hospital, saying that the parents of a brain-dead baby were donating a heart to Baby Jesse (shown above). Bypassed was another infant who had been next on the national list to receive a heart. Both babies did eventually receive hearts, and were reportedly doing well, but the issues that were raised remained unresolved: the role of the communications media in publicizing individual cases and the responsibility of hospitals and the medical profession in a still-experimental process.

Worldwide Developments. Scientists from France and Zaire began the first human experiments for potential immunization of people already infected with an AIDS virus but not yet ill. Experts pointed out, however, that development of an effective vaccine was a long way in the future. Meanwhile, late in the year, the World Health Organization announced the first coordinated global effort to combat AIDS. Calling the disease "a health disaster of pandemic proportions," WHO estimated that 100,000 people around the world had contracted the disease thus far and that as many as 10 million now carried an AIDS virus and were presumably capable of infecting others.

AIDS Fallout. The AIDS catastrophe was further complicated by an ongoing international controversy—reflected in a lawsuit filed by the Pasteur Institute in Paris against the U.S. government over recognition as the discoverer of the major AIDS virus. U.S. researchers under Robert Gallo, at the U.S. National Cancer Institute, had discovered essentially the same virus as the French scientists. At stake was not only scientific prestige (and the possibility of a Nobel Prize) but also millions of dollars in royalties from blood tests for detecting antibodies to the virus. In July the American research team of the U.S. National Cancer Institute won the first legal round in Washington, D.C., when a claims court dismissed the Pasteur Institute suit, on the ground that it was based on a prior research agreement between the French and U.S. teams over which the court had no jurisdiction. The French were also pursuing a patent issue before the U.S. Patent and Trademark Office; at stake was an AIDS antibody test for which the American team had been granted a patent.

War Against Cancer. A controversial study that appeared in the *New England Journal of Medicine* in May argued that "we are losing the war against cancer." While conceding that progress had been made in certain areas, the report noted that between 1950 and 1982 (the most recent year for which reliable data were available) the overall age-adjusted cancer mortality rate—the number of cancer deaths for every 100,000 Americans—increased. Particularly marked was the rise in deaths due to lung cancer. The death rate from breast cancer in women was stable, despite improvements in detection and treatment. The authors of the report called for more stress on prevention as opposed to treatment.

Genes and Cancer. Many cancers are believed to have a genetic component. The most clear-cut example of this is retinoblastoma, a cancer of the eye that develops early in childhood and tends very strongly to run in families. If caught in the early stages, the cancer can be treated; in later stages, the affected eye must be removed. Researchers at the University of Cincinnati and other institutions identified a genetic marker that predicts which infants in the group at risk will develop the disease. Late in the year, another research team, headed by Dr. Robert A. Weinberg, of the Massachusetts Institute of Technology, reported discovery of a gene that prevents the development of retinoblastoma. It was the first time a gene had been identified that blocked the growth of a human cancer.

Birth Control Pills and Breast Cancer. Long-term use of birth control pills does not increase the risk of breast cancer, a new government study reported. The study compared the contraceptive use of 4,711 women between the ages of 20 and 54 years of age who had been diagnosed recently as having breast cancer with that of 4,676 healthy women. The researchers looked at all formulations of birth control pills, the duration of use, and the interval since the women had last taken the pills. None of these factors affected the risk of breast cancer. The study did confirm other risk factors, however: women who had never been pregnant, who had had their first child at a late age, who had a history of benign breast disease, or who had a family history of breast cancer were all more likely to develop the disease, whether or not they had ever used the pill.

Smoking and Health. In his annual report on smoking and health, Surgeon General Dr. C. Everett Koop cited evidence that smoke from others' cigarettes increases the risk of lung cancer and other diseases in nonsmokers. The surgeon general concluded that smoke-free workplaces ought to be available to nonsmokers. (In December the federal government acted by ordering all agencies to provide a "reasonably smoke-free environment for workers.") Meanwhile, the American Cancer Society reported that, while the number of adult smokers in the United States declined by nearly a fifth in the last decade, the number of women smokers increased. Statistics also show that lung cancer has now passed breast cancer as a leading cause of death in women.

For those who have tried and failed to quit smoking, a group of University of California at San Francisco researchers reported, smoking the "ultralow" cigarettes introduced in the past few years may reduce the risks. Dr. Neal L. Benowitz and his colleagues compared the amounts of tar, nicotine, and carbon monoxide that smokers were exposed to from high-yield, low-yield, and ultralow cigarettes. High-yield and low-yield cigarettes were found to expose the smokers to the same amounts of nicotine, tar, and carbon monoxide. But when the smokers switched to ultralow cigarettes, exposure to these substances was signficantly lower, even though they smoked a greater number of the weaker cigarettes.

Cocaine Epidemic. The rapidly increasing abuse of the smokable, or "freebase," form of cocaine called crack was threatening to become as serious a health and social problem as AIDS. National attention was focused on crack in June when two prominent athletes—Len Bias, an All American basketball player at the University of Maryland, and Don Rogers, a defensive back for the Cleveland Browns and a former University of California All American football player—died after using the drug. Their deaths came as a surprise to many, who incorrectly thought of cocaine as a relatively safe drug. Meanwhile, the use of crack spread with wildfire speed, especially along the East Coast (particularly southern Florida and a wide area around New York City), in parts of the West Coast, especially Los Angeles, and in such inland cities as Detroit.

Crack is a slight chemical modification of the cocaine hydrochloride powder that has long been snorted (or, occasionally, injected) recreationally in the United States. This freebase modification is easily inhaled when heated. Many authorities believe crack is the most highly addictive and dangerous of all illicit drugs.

Crack became a serious problem within a short time because of recent innovations in its production and marketing. In the past, freebase cocaine was made from cocaine powder by using ether in a complex and dangerous process. But a simpler method was discovered that could be used in any kitchen. Thus, drug pushers could now make crack themselves, and, by marketing the drug in various-sized packages, they could sell it in "vials" to fit everyone's pocketbook and habit. The user gets an extremely pleasurable "high" from inhaling freebase cocaine, but unless more of the drug is available, the high is followed in a few minutes by an equally extreme "low," or "crash," of depression and later by anhedonia (a state in which nothing,except more cocaine, can give pleasure). Users tend to go on "binges" alternating with exhaustion and sleep. After weeks or months of this pattern, they usually develop such symptoms as malnutrition from poor appetite, depression, seizures, hallucinations, and antisocial behavior.

Treatment for crack addiction is not markedly successful unless the addict wants badly to get off the drug. Prevention efforts have involved mostly educating the public on the dangers of cocaine, testing athletes and other groups to discourage drug use and to detect users early in order to start rehabilitation, and

Growing use of the highly addictive smokable form of cocaine known as crack posed a major health problem in the United States. Pictured here are crack crystals.

interdicting the importation, as well as interrupting the manufacture and sale, of the drug. These efforts, however, seemed to make little headway.

Alzheimer's Progress. Scientists from New York City's Albert Einstein College of Medicine reported identification of what could prove to be the first accurate diagnostic indicator of Alzheimer's disease: an abnormal protein called A-68 that appears in the brain and spinal fluid of living patients thought to have the disease. If further trials prove satisfactory, a routine test for Alzheimer's could become available. Meanwhile, preliminary studies conducted in Pasadena, Calif., showed improvement in the memories of a small group of patients with Alzheimer's disease who were treated with the experimental drug tetrahydroaminoacridine (THA).

Artificial Hearts and the Auxiliary Pump. The longest surviving recipient of a permanent artificial heart died in August, 620 days after he became the second person to receive the device. William Schroeder, a retired civil servant,was near death when the Jarvik-7 mechanical heart was implanted by Dr. William C. DeVries in November 1984. Schroeder recovered quickly at first, then suffered a series of debilitating strokes from which he never fully recovered. But even with these setbacks, he became the only artificial-heart recipient who recovered sufficiently to move to an apartment outside Humana Hospital in Louisville, Ky. (In June, Murray Haydon, who had lived 16 months on the device, died at the hospital.) A total of five permanent artificial hearts had been implanted by late 1986, and others used as temporary "bridges" until human hearts became available for transplant. All of the recipients of permanent hearts suffered severe complications.

Prime candidates for the artificial heart, and for human heart transplants, are victims of chronic congestive heart failure, whose own hearts cannot pump enough blood. Dr. Larry W. Stephenson and colleagues at the University of Pennsylvania reported a new experimental technique, tested on dogs, that might eventually help such patients. It involves inserting an auxiliary pump made from the patient's back muscle and operated by an implanted electronic pacemaker. The new system would avoid the need for an external power supply and virtually eliminate the risk of rejection, it was said, besides reducing the risks of infections and blood clots.

Month-After Pill. Late in the year, a team of French researchers reported that a substance known as RU 486 had proven effective in terminating pregnancies when taken within ten days of a missed menstrual period. The drug works by blocking the action of the hormone progesterone, causing the lining of the uterus to be sloughed off, so that an embryo, if present, would be detached and expelled. Of 100 women given RU 486 up to a month into their pregnancies, 85 aborted within four days, and no major side effects were encountered. There was no information on how the substance might affect the fetus when it fails to induce abortion, since all 15 women whose pregnancies survived the use of the drug later received clinical abortions. The drug was expected to be approved in France and Italy in 1987.

Exercise and Long Life. Regular exercise can strengthen the heart and lungs, improve muscle tone, and enhance mental outlook. A 1986 study that monitored the life-styles of 16,936 Harvard alumni found that those who exercise regularly also live longer. With freshman physical examinations as a point of comparison, Dr. Ralph S. Paffenbarger, Jr., and others at the Stanford University School of Medicine and the Harvard University School of Public Health conducted follow-up surveys of the alumni over a period of 12 to 16 years. Those men who expended 2,000 or more calories weekly in physical activity had a 28 percent lower death rate than those who were less active. Much of the reduced mortality was due to lower death rates from cardiovascular and respiratory diseases.

Running and Arthritis. Some experts have argued that running causes the type of arthritis called degenerative joint disease, or osteoarthritis, through repeated heavy pounding of the joints. However, in a study published in March, Dr. Richard S. Panush and his colleagues at the University of Florida and the Veterans Administration Medical Center in Gainesville compared 18 male nonrunners with 17 men age 50 or over who had been running at least

Five-year-old Brent Meldrum shows how he saved playmate Tanya Branden from choking on a piece of candy with his quick use of the Heimlich maneuver, which he had seen demonstrated on a television show. Dr. Henry Heimlich himself looks on.

20 miles weekly for at least the last five years. The two groups reported about the same number of joint aches and pains, and X-ray exams further confirmed that the runners had no greater evidence of arthritis.

A second study compared 41 long-distance runners between the ages of 50 and 72 with 41 nonrunners in the same age group. Dr. Nancy E. Lane and her colleagues at the Stanford University School of Medicine examined the two groups both for bone and joint damage and for bone density, a measure of osteoporosis. They too found that runners seemed no more prone to osteoarthritis.

Genes and Obesity. Obesity affects millions of Americans; two studies led by the University of Pennsylvania's Dr. Albert J. Stunkard suggested that a disposition to obesity may be genetic in origin. In the first study, Stunkard and his group compared the weights of 540 adult Danish adoptees, their adoptive parents, and their biological parents. This allowed the researchers to judge how much a person's weight was the product of environment and how much of heredity. Adopted children and their biological parents were likely to be close to the same weight relative to height, whether they were fat or thin. Of the children with two obese biological parents, 80 percent became obese, compared with only 14 percent of the children whose biological parents were of normal weight for their height. In contrast, there was no statistically significant relationship between the weight of the adoptees and of their adopted parents, suggesting that environment played only a small role.

In the second study, Stunkard and his colleagues compared the weight of identical and fraternal twins. In general, identical twins— who are more closely related genetically— were twice as likely to share the same level of overweight as their nonidentical counterparts. In a 25-year follow-up of the twins, the same relationship held. Scientists concluded that prevention should be aimed at those most at risk—people with fat parents.

Sickle-Cell Anemia and Antibiotics. Sickle-cell anemia is one of the major killers in black children. Those born with the disorder, which is characterized by abnormal red blood cells, are very prone to bacterial infections: pneumonia, meningitis, and other infections are major causes of death among young children with sickle-cell anemia. A study designed to see whether regular doses of oral penicillin could prevent infections proved so successful that the researchers ended the trial early and began treating all the study subjects with the life-saving antibiotics. The researchers recommended that infants with sickle-cell anemia start receiving penicillin by four months of age.

Recombinant Vaccine Approved. The first human vaccine made using recombinant DNA techniques went on the market, following its licensing by the U.S. Food and Drug Administration. Recombivax HB, manufactured by Merck, Sharp & Dohme, provides protection against hepatitis B, an inflammation of the liver that can lead to liver cancer, and was said to be safer than a similar vaccine derived from

the serum of chronically infected patients, available since 1982.

Fetal Surgery on Twins. Surgeons at Baltimore's Sinai Hospital made medical history when they successfully drained water off the brain of a fetus with hydrocephalus, whose rapid head growth was endangering the health of the normal twin. (Hydrocephalus is a circulatory system malfunction causing cerebrospinal fluid to build up in the brain; the drainage procedure had been done before, but never on unborn twins.) The surgery carried the risk of inducing premature labor, but the condition of the hydrocephalic twin could have had the same effect. Neurosurgeon Phillip Goldstein performed the procedure on the sedated mother using ultrasound to pinpoint the location of the fetuses and inserting a newly developed device that functioned for about two weeks. After that time, the twins, both girls, were delivered by cesarean section.

Preventive Medicine and Cholesterol. It was reported in May that Americans' efforts to maintain good health were generally improving. *Prevention* magazine's third annual survey of health and safety practices, conducted by Louis Harris & Associates, Inc., yielded a "prevention index" of 64.1 for 1985, up from 63.2 in 1984 and 61.5 in 1983. One of the most striking findings was a dramatic rise of respondents who said they always wear seat belts when sitting in the front seat of a car. More Americans were trying to get enough calcium in their diets, and more were having blood tests for cholesterol and blood pressure. More women were doing self-examinations for breast cancer. Fewer people were driving after drinking, and more adults were taking steps to reduce stress. On the other hand, while the same number of Americans exercised strenuously three days a week, fewer exercised six or seven days a week. Over half of Americans were still overweight, and fewer drivers obeyed highway speed limits.

Other sources also indicate that cholesterol remains a serious health problem; an eight-year government study found 80 percent of all middle-aged men at risk of premature death from heart disease because of unhealthy cholesterol levels in their blood. Two other studies late in the year found an apparent link between high cholesterol levels and increased risk of colon cancer.

Animal Rabies. The Middle Atlantic states suffered the worst outbreak of animal rabies in 40 years. The epidemic, originally carried by raccoons, spread to cows, horses, dogs, and cats and reached as far north as Pennsylvania from the Appalachian Mountains, where it began. Although many persons were bitten by rabid animals, by late in the year no human cases of the disease had been reported, apparently because of the effective rabies vaccine available.

See also BEHAVIORAL SCIENCES.

S.W. & J.F.J.

HONDURAS. José Azcona del Hoyo, inaugurated as president of Honduras on January 27, 1986, faced formidable problems, including a mounting deficit, a politically powerful military dependent on U.S. aid, and the impact of a continuing war between the Sandinista regime in neighboring Nicaragua and the contras, guerrillas fighting against that regime, with bases inside Honduras.

The November 1985 election results, which gave Azcona about 28 percent of the vote, meant that his faction of the Liberal Party was allotted only 46 of the 134 seats in Congress. The president subsequently struck a deal with his National Party opponents, which gave them control of the Supreme Court and half of all other judicial appointments, as well as certain other positions. In return, Azcona was allowed to choose his own cabinet—although it had to include two National Party members—and name the president of Congress.

The president's power was further affected by conflicts within the military. The U.S. Central Intelligence Agency was said to be involved in an effort to weaken and isolate a group of young officers who opposed the presence of contras in Honduras and sought a more independent role for Honduras in the region. Meanwhile, General Walter López Reyes, long a thorn in the side of the United States, resigned as commander of the armed forces; Humberto Regalado Hernández, the senior officers' nominee, was elected by Congress to replace him. In September, three high military officers were dismissed on charges of plotting to oust Regalado.

After a period of improvement in 1985, the human rights situation showed signs of deterioration. One bright spot was an amnesty for political prisoners, mandated by Congress over the objections of the military. By summer, however, it seemed clear that the military was determined to silence dissent. General Regalado spoke of a "Communist plot" against Honduras, which he said sought to discredit the contras and force the withdrawal of U.S. troops, about 1,200 of which maintained a year-round presence.

In March, Sandinista forces attacked contra base camps inside Honduras; the Honduran government denounced the invasion and requested U.S. assistance, reportedly after the United States had exerted pressure for it to do so. After the U.S. Congress voted to send $100 million in aid to the contras, the Azcona administration indicated, as it had before, that it would not allow the United States to train contra forces on Honduran soil.

Fighting in the border region intensified late

A joint Honduran-U.S. ribbon-cutting ceremony in June marked the opening of a 13-mile road built by the U.S. military (left, General Humberto Regalado Hernandez; right, General John Galvin).

in the year, as Nicaraguan forces allegedly made new forays into Honduran territory against contra forces there, also clashing with Honduran troops. U.S. helicopters ferried additional Honduran troops to the region, and Honduran planes bombed Sandinista positions. Meanwhile, contra leaders agreed to a Honduran demand that they move their forces into Nicaragua by the spring of 1987.

In December, U.S. and Honduran forces began a planned four-month joint military exercise involving about 3,000 U.S. troops; separate maneuvers involving about 4,500 U.S. National Guardsmen were slated to start in January 1987.

A state of economic and social crisis continued, with an estimated 40 percent of the work force unemployed. The declining production of key foodstuffs, especially maize, brought famine conditions to the department of Choluteca. Any economic growth that occurred was more than offset by soaring birthrates. The coffee harvest was only half that of 1985. Capital flight continued, and labor and peasant groups complained that Azcona did not have a coherent economic plan.

See STATISTICS OF THE WORLD.   D.E.S.

HOUSING AND CONSTRUCTION. *See* ECONOMY AND BUSINESS.

HUNGARY. October 23, 1986, marked the 30th anniversary of the inception of the Hungarian uprising, crushed by Soviet tanks after 12 days of street fighting. A proclamation signed by 122 prominent East Europeans and extolling the revolt was issued in October in Budapest and three other Eastern European cities. The document said that those who joined in the revolt had destroyed "the credibility of the regime" and showed that the Hungarian people wanted "independence, democracy, and neutrality."

Possibly because of the anniversary, Hungarian authorities appeared anxious to clamp down on dissent. Early in the year, Budapest police attacked and beat a group of about 20 Hungarian and Austrian environmentalists protesting the construction of a joint Hungarian-Czechoslovak hydroelectric dam on the Danube. Also, several hundred police dispersed a demonstration that was trying to proceed across the Chain Bridge on the Danube.

Public concern mounted over the plight of ethnic Hungarians in Romania. In January, Romanian authorities suspended the Hungarian-language magazine *Muvelodes* (Culture). These and other instances of alleged oppression led to bitterly worded commentary in the Hungarian media, but the Kádár regime was careful to avoid open confrontation with Romania. Relations with Yugoslavia, by contrast, were cordial. Agreements were worked out for sharing hydroelectric resources and conducting joint exploration for oil and natural gas in border areas.

Progress in implementing the seventh five-year plan (1986-1990) was disappointing. The country's 2.3 million pensioners were hard hit by inflation, and a program was announced to provide interest-free state loans to help them buy fuel for the winter.

Cardinal Laszlo Lekai, the archbishop of Esztergom and primate of Hungary since 1976, died on June 30 at the age of 76.

See STATISTICS OF THE WORLD.   R.A.P.

I

ICELAND. Reykjavík was the site of the summit meeting between U.S. President Ronald Reagan and Soviet leader Mikhail Gorbachev on October 11-12, 1986. The meeting attracted a throng of journalists, protestors, and U.S. and Soviet security personnel to the city and focused world attention on the national placidity that the attention itself momentarily interrupted. Reykjavík also celebrated its bicentennial in mid-August.

A reshuffle of the Independence-Progressive coalition cabinet was completed in January,

Hoefdi House, Reykjavík's official guest house, undergoes preparations for October's summit meeting between U.S. President Ronald Reagan and Soviet leader Mikhail Gorbachev.

when Geir Hallgrímsson, minister of foreign affairs, resigned at his own suggestion, with former Minister of Commerce Matthías Matthiesen succeeding him. Another important change was the entry into the cabinet of Independence party leader Thorsteinn Pálsson as minister of finance.

In the May elections for members of 23 town councils and 36 district councils, the Independence and Progressive parties lost some support throughout the country, except in Reykjavík, where the Independence Party increased its majority. The left-wing People's Alliance remained the second-ranking party, while the Social Democrats scored a major gain, winning 16 percent.

An anti-inflationary wage settlement agreed to by employers and unions in February and implemented by the government led to the first drop in the cost-of-living index in 15 years. Government efforts to reduce prices during the year included the lowering of import duties on automobiles and other consumer items, as well as cuts in local taxes and rates for electricity and heating.

See STATISTICS OF THE WORLD. *See also the feature article* SAVING THE WHALES.　　E.J.F.

IDAHO. *See* STATISTICS OF THE WORLD.

ILLINOIS. *See* STATISTICS OF THE WORLD.

INDIA. Prime Minister Rajiv Gandhi's leadership of the Congress-I Party was challenged by dissidents in 1986. Communal violence escalated in several states.

Gandhi's Second Year. Rajiv Gandhi, critical of Congress-I Party's leadership, had launched a program of high-level personnel changes late in 1985 that troubled many old-time party regulars. In a letter to the prime minister, the octogenarian Congress politician Kamalapati Tripathi subsequently charged that Gandhi had become inaccessible and was surrounding himself with sycophants and persons hostile to his late mother, former Prime Minister Indira Gandhi. A few days after the Tripathi letter reached Rajiv Gandhi, in April, expulsions from the Congress Party began. Tripathi was ultimately denied the chance to run again for a seat in the upper house of Parliament. Also, Gundu Rao, the former chief minister of Karnataka and a strong Indira loyalist, was expelled from the party for public criticisms.

The dissidents' disaffection partly reflected political fears, fueled by recent electoral losses in Punjab, Assam, and West Bengal and by the growing strength of the Assam People's Party. The Congress Party also lost ground in 1986 state elections in Karnataka. In addition, price increases for foods, fertilizers, and other items

195

led to demonstrations and to increased disaffection on the part of farmers and of poor and middle-class consumers.

Punjab and the Sikhs. The most intractable problem of Gandhi's second year in office was the continuing Sikh agitation in Punjab. Under a 1985 agreement, Chandigarh, the capital city shared by Punjab and the neighboring Hindu-majority state of Haryana, was to be transferred on January 26 to Punjab while a special commission was to recommend territorial compensation for Haryana. But the deadline was extended to June 21, and at the end of January, the commission announced it could not decide the compensation issue. Clashes broke out at the Golden Temple in the holy city of Amritsar, the most sacred Sikh shrine, between moderates and extremists among Sikhs. By February the extremists were in control of most of the temple complex, and by early April a Sikh terrorist campaign in Punjab had left 60 dead, mostly Hindus.

On April 30, a seven-hour operation by the state police and paramilitary forces resulted in the temporary expulsion of militant elements from the Golden Temple, but the temple's management committee seemed unable to keep the militants out. With the leaders of Punjab and Haryana unable to agree on a territorial exchange in line with the pact, the transfer date for Chandigarh was tentatively reset for July 15. That deadline also passed without action.

On July 25, Sikh extremists boarded a Punjab bus near the Pakistan border, singled out 14 Hindu passengers, and shot them dead one by one. (One Sikh was also killed.) This led to Hindu-instigated reprisals against Sikhs in New Delhi. By the following month, more than 500 people had been killed by terrorists in Punjab since the beginning of the year. Another attack on a Punjab bus occurred in November; at least 24 passengers were killed, and riots again ensued.

On October 2, a lone Sikh gunman fired several shots at Gandhi as the prime minister attended a prayer service in New Delhi. Gandhi was unhurt, but the breakdown in security was a cause for alarm. Later in October, a senior Sikh official of the Congress Party was murdered in Punjab, along with eight others.

One encouraging sign was an agreement reached in December between India and Pakistan, calling for coordination of security efforts to prevent Sikh extremists from using Pakistan as a base for attacks inside India.

Sikh extremists raided the Golden Temple complex in Amritsar on June 5, stabbing a volunteer guard to death.

Three Sikhs were convicted in January and sentenced to hang for the October 1984 assassination of Indira Gandhi; the death sentences were confirmed by India's High Court late in 1986, but an appeal to the Supreme Court was planned.

Communal Violence. In early March, following Hindu-Muslim communal riots, the state government of Jammu and Kashmir was dismissed, and governor's rule was imposed. (In November, Gandhi appointed a political foe, Faroq Abdullah, as chief minister.) In Gujarat, birthplace of Mohandas K. Gandhi, a week of violence in mid-July left at least 72 people dead and more than 400 wounded. Communal violence also infected other states.

Mizoram. On a more positive note, the Mizo tribe agreed to end a 20-year insurgency against the federal government, and Parliament approved a bill in August making the territory of Mizoram India's 23rd state.

Economy. A positive economic sign was the domestic investment boom, augmented by foreign investment, particularly from Indians living abroad. Agricultural and industrial production remained at a modest level. The negative trade balance (projected at $5 billion for 1986) emerged as the main economic problem—other than poverty—faced by the Indian government. Reforms designed to stimulate exports were unveiled in October. Despite additional taxes announced during the February budget session of Parliament, the budget deficit remained at the $3 billion level.

U.S. Relations. Early in the year, the U.S. Defense Department approved the release of the General Electric F404 jet engine for use by India to build its first indigenous light combat aircraft. Also encouraging was the fact that India was running a trade surplus with the United States. On the other hand, the Indian government was distressed when the Reagan administration announced its intention to seek a new six-year aid package for Pakistan when the present one expires in 1987.

On October 29, after a trial in closed sessions that had gone on (with various adjournments) for nine years, six defendants, including five former Indian government officials, were convicted of spying for and passing on military secrets to the United States.

Other Foreign Relations. Relations with Pakistan deteriorated. India's offer to Pakistan of a no-war pact was withdrawn in February, and Gandhi's planned trip to Islamabad was canceled when Indian intelligence claimed to have evidence that Pakistan was training and arming Sikh extremists. In September terrorists seized a Pan American airliner in Karachi after it had landed on the first leg of a flight from Bombay to New York. The incident ended in a wild shootout and grenade-throwing spree, as hijackers killed 21 people and wounded over 100, many of them Indians; Gandhi charged that Pakistan had bungled a rescue attempt.

In June, one month before the seventh round of Sino-Indian border talks, China again laid claim to 35,000 square miles of territory in northern India. The Peking talks were held as scheduled in July but ended after three days without success. In November, Gandhi played host to Soviet leader Mikhail Gorbachev for four days of talks.

See STATISTICS OF THE WORLD. M.C.C.

INDIANA. *See* STATISTICS OF THE WORLD.

INDIANS, AMERICAN. Sophisticated lobbying and careful negotiation succeeded in keeping Indian concerns before Congress in 1986. However, many Indian leaders opposed the legislated settlement of Chippewa land claims. Reservation bingo remained largely unregulated.

Indian Rights Legislation. In a significant achievement for Indian rights activists, Congress cleared a bill restoring federal tribal status to the Klamaths of Oregon; the bill was signed by President Ronald Reagan in August. The Klamaths were seeking to reestablish their government-to-government relationship with the United States, a relationship severed in 1954 when Congress "terminated" the group's tribal status as part of a general effort to reduce federal responsibility for Indian affairs.

Less popular among Indian leaders were companion federal and state laws enacted in March authorizing payments of land and money to the White Earth Chippewa of Minnesota as compensation for 100,000 acres of land that passed out of Indian hands under dubious circumstances early in this century. The Minnesota Supreme Court had ruled in 1977 that the land had been taken illegally. The new

Bingo games are an important source of revenue for Indian reservations, which are exempt from state gambling laws; however, federal legislation has been proposed to regulate Indian gambling operations. Shown here is an Otoe Missouria bingo game.

laws were intended to give the present owners of the land clear title by paying cash to former Indian owners of the disputed property and awarding the tribe about $7 million and 10,000 acres of state-owned forest. Some of the Chippewa who were dissatisfied with the settlement filed a class action suit in federal district court in Minnesota seeking to overturn it.

Reservation Gambling. Bingo and other forms of gambling continued to be important sources of tribal revenue for the more than 100 tribes that operate games of chance. Because such gambling has become a $100 million enterprise and because of fears that organized crime would become involved, both the Reagan administration and members of Congress pressed—unsuccessfully—for legislation to regulate Indian gambling operations. Indian groups opposed such regulation by federal or state government.

In a related legal decision, the U.S. Court of Appeals for the Ninth Circuit ruled that neither the state of California nor Riverside County could regulate bingo and card games operated by the Cabazon and Morongo Indian communities. The Supreme Court announced it would hear an appeal of the decision.

Hopi-Navajo Land Dispute. Fueled by an Academy Award-winning documentary film, public interest in the Hopi-Navajo land dispute in Arizona rose to the point where Indians involved began to resent the sympathy they received. The film, *Broken Rainbow,* presented a moving case against the relocation of the Navajo families who continue to live in the portion of a 1.8 million-acre tract awarded to the Hopis in a 1974 land settlement act. Even as public sympathy swelled for these Navajos, members of both tribes began calling on white activists to stop "meddling" in the intertribal controversy. The Navajo tribal newspaper urged non-Indian sympathizers to "find a whale to save and move on." The Hopis started their own newspaper in May to counteract what their tribal chairman called "misinformation" disseminated by outsiders. Other Indians, including Russell Means of the American Indian Movement and Ross Swimmer, assistant secretary of the interior for Indian affairs, urged the parties involved to work out a negotiated solution. When the July 6 deadline for final relocation of the Navajos came, the Bureau of Indian Affairs announced that none of the remaining Navajos who refused to relocate would be forcibly removed. In August the BIA estimated that 240 dwellings on Hopi land were still occupied by Navajos.

Health Problems. On May 1 the congressional Office of Technology Assessment released a report on Indian health that contained a grim evaluation of current conditions. Among the report's findings was that 37 percent of Indian and Alaskan native deaths occurred before age 45, compared to 12 percent for the general population. According to the Indian Health Service, the leading causes of premature death among Indians are accidents, homicide, suicide (more than double the national rate for those aged 15 to 24), and cirrhosis of the liver. Alcoholic cirrhosis of the liver occurs among Indians at up to 18 times the overall U.S. rate, and significant numbers of deaths from this condition occur as early as ages 15 to 24. Such statistics have caused the BIA to announce that it will place greater emphasis on health promotion and disease prevention.

Indian Achievements. On March 17, Charles Cloud, a Cherokee from Oklahoma, became a judge in. the Norfolk, Va., general district court. Cloud, a former chief deputy attorney for the state, was the first Indian to serve as a judge in the Virginia court system. In May, Donald E. Pelotte became bishop coadjutor of Gallup, N.M. Pelotte was the first American Indian to become a bishop in the Roman Catholic Church.

Bald Eagles. In June the U.S. Supreme Court dismissed an appeal by a member of the Yankton Sioux tribe of his conviction for shooting bald eagles in violation of the Endangered Species Act. Federal law does permit Indians to kill bald eagles to collect ceremonial feathers, but the Court ruled that this case did not involve any religious issues.   F.E.H.

INDONESIA. President Suharto, in office since 1967, announced in October 1986 that he would run for a fifth term in early 1987. Meanwhile, his government coped with economic troubles and brought to trial suspects implicated in riots and sedition.

Indonesia's budget and plans for economic development were hard hit by the rapid fall for much of the year in the price of oil. The growth rate in gross domestic product was only about 1 percent, far below the 5 percent called for in current development planning, forcing the government, for the first time in 17 years, to announce cuts (amounting to 7 percent) in the national budget. The development budget was pared by 22 percent, a hold being placed on all new projects, and in September the gov-

ernment announced a 45 percent devaluation of the rupiah. Authorities expressed concern over repercussions of the adverse economic climate, especially the likelihood of higher unemployment. Still, Indonesia earned respect from creditor nations for its conservative management, reflected in the country's $10.7 billion foreign exchange reserve and its exercise of restraint in the use of concessional loans.

In the wake of a rash of violent incidents, many involving Islamic and other opposition to the government, subversion trials filled court agendas during the year. The most prominent defendant, retired General H. R. Dharsono, was sentenced to ten years for publicly challenging the government's account of the Tanjong Priok riots of 1984; his published defense statement was promptly banned.

The toppling of Ferdinand Marcos and the rise of Corazon Aquino as president of the Philippines attracted much interest, although for a variety of reasons. Some government figures expressed pride that no comparable situation existed in Indonesia; critics, however, said that Marcos's fate gave Indonesians "food for thought" and suggested that there were indeed similarities between Marcos and Suharto. An article in the Australian press, suggesting such an analogy, led to strained relations between Indonesia and Australia. During a state visit by Aquino to Indonesia, government officials expressed concern over what they viewed as a continued serious Communist threat in the Philippines, which they believed might be underestimated by Aquino.

See STATISTICS OF THE WORLD.   W.F.

INTERNATIONAL CONFERENCES. A variety of international conferences were held in 1986. For some not covered below, see AFRICA; BANKING AND FINANCE; COMMONWEALTH OF NATIONS; ECONOMY AND BUSINESS; EUROPEAN COMMUNITIES; NORTH ATLANTIC TREATY ORGANIZATION; ORGANIZATION OF AMERICAN STATES; ORGANIZATION OF PETROLEUM EXPORTING COUNTRIES; UNION OF SOVIET SOCIALIST REPUBLICS; UNITED NATIONS; UNITED STATES OF AMERICA.

Helsinki Accords. After three years of protracted negotiations, diplomats from the NATO and Warsaw Pact nations agreed on terms for a major new security pact, as the Conference on Confidence and Security Building Measures

The 19th annual meeting of the Association of Southeast Asian Nations took place in Manila in June, with Philippine President Corazon Aquino hosting. Besides meeting among themselves, the foreign ministers conferred with representatives of the United States and other so-called dialogue nations.

and Disarmament in Europe came to a close on September 22. Regarded as an important first step, the new pact requires each side to give advance notification of large-scale military land exercises in Europe and allows for periodic inspections of the other side's forces. Thirty-five nations attended the Stockholm conference, one of the follow-up meetings established to advance the 1975 Helsinki accords.

On November 4, the third full review meeting of the 35 signators to the Helsinki accords opened in Vienna. This session of the Conference on Security and Cooperation in Europe was to evaluate the progress to date toward obligations assumed at previous follow-up meetings in Belgrade and Madrid.

Nonaligned Movement. At the triennial summit conference of the nonaligned, representatives from 101 nations and national movements met in Harare, Zimbabwe, in September. The keynote address was given by Zimbabwe's Prime Minister Robert Mugabe, but much of the attention went to a more dramatic speech by Libyan leader Muammar al-Qaddafi, in which he criticized the concept of nonalignment and

said other nations should have come to Libya's aid after the U.S. bombing raid in April. A declaration issued at the end of the conference cited the problem of Third World debt and called for more equitable trading practices and reform of the international monetary system. Also issued were demands for increased international pressure on South Africa and an end to U.S. "unprovoked aggression."

Asean Meetings. Foreign ministers representing six Asian nations attended the 19th annual meeting of the Association of Southeast Asian Nations in Manila in June. They called for a draft treaty creating a nuclear-free zone in the Pacific and criticized Japan for reducing its investments in the region. An energy conservation and petroleum securities pact was signed, and plans for a summit of Asean heads of states were announced. The foreign ministers also met with representatives from the United States, Canada, the European Community, Australia, New Zealand, and Japan. Complaints about protectionist trade policies dominated those sessions. K.F.

IOWA. *See* STATISTICS OF THE WORLD.

IRAN. As the war with Iraq continued in 1986, Iran made a significant gain with its capture of the strategic port of Fao (al-Faw) at the mouth of the Persian Gulf, and Iranian morale appeared to be improving. However, Iraq maintained overwhelming superiority in the air. Late in the year, it was reported that Iran had secretly been buying arms from the United States.

War With Iraq. In February, Iranian forces crossed the Shatt al-Arab waterway and overran the port of Fao to achieve an important strategic advantage. Iraq's efforts over the next few months to regain territory in this region were unsuccessful. In February, Iran also mounted a less successful offensive into northern Kurdistan, ultimately holding on to only some of the territory, according to reports.

Iran continued its practice of stopping foreign ships in international waters to search for military goods bound for Iraq. An American freighter—the *President Taylor*—was boarded and searched by Iranian personnel in January. Iran also began intercepting oil tankers in the Strait of Hormuz, and in September, Iran for a time detained two freighters belonging to the Soviet Union, Iraq's main arms supplier.

Because Iran's main oil terminal at Kharg Island was heavily attacked by Iraqi fighters, the Iranians sought to cushion the impact on exports by shuttling oil to makeshift loading facilities at Sirri Island and other locations farther south in the Gulf. However, Iraqi jets did manage to strike at Sirri Island and other loading facilities as well. In October, Iraqi planes struck the refinery city of Bakhtaran in two days of heavy raids, killing over 30 people. Iran bombed the port of Basra in retaliation. Later in the year, Iraqi warplanes continued to conduct heavy bombing raids on Iranian targets. Among other events, Iran reported that more than 300 people were killed in Iraqi raids on Bakhtaran and other industrial targets in late December.

In the summer, it was reported that Iran had massed more than half a million troops along the border, possibly in preparation for a massive offensive, but no such offensive emerged. Late in the year, Iranian forces did overrun four Iraqi islands in the Shatt al-Arab waterway, but after a bloody battle, the Iranians were repulsed. According to one report, Iranians suffered heavy casualties.

Iranian forces occupy the Iraqi port of Fao, formerly a major oil terminal, located at the mouth of the Persian Gulf—a strategic gain that caused concern among other Gulf states.

IRAN

U.S.-Iranian Relations and Arms Controversy.
Iranian relations with the United States remained tenuous. In February the U.S. delegate to the UN Security Council clearly blamed Iran for the continuation of the war. In April the United States charged 18 defendants with conspiring to sell over $2 billion worth of American weaponry to Iran. However, the disposition of that case, and other cases involving smuggling of U.S. arms to Iran, was called into question in November when it was revealed that the U.S. government itself had, in secret, sold arms to Iran. The operation was an apparent bid to improve relations and gain the freedom of American hostages held by a pro-Iranian group in Lebanon. Two of those captives—Father Lawrence Jenco and David Jacobsen, director of the American University hospital in Beirut— were released in 1986, each shortly after arms shipments were said to have reached Iran.

News of the secret arms dealings emerged after a Lebanese publication reported that Reagan administration emissaries had traveled to Tehran for negotiations. The shipments appeared to violate the administration's policy not to supply arms to countries it deemed supporters of terrorism. Reaction was negative in the United States, in Europe—the Reagan administration had urged members of the Western alliance not to sell arms to Iran—and in the Middle East, where many Arab countries were already concerned about Iranian advances in the war with Iraq. Afterward, President Ronald Reagan ordered a stop to the dealings but did not repudiate the policy. Iran's leader, Ayatollah Ruhollah Khomeini, denounced so-called moderates in Iran—to whom the Reagan administration said the arms sales were intended as a gesture—for seeking U.S. ties, but he defended obtaining arms from the country he normally calls the "great Satan." Public statements of other Iranian leaders varied in tone. One of the key "moderates," Speaker of Parliament Hojatolislam Hashemi Rafsanjani, indicated that Iran would still be willing to intercede for the hostages in return for weapons. Meanwhile, the United States and Iran were negotiating the planned return to Iran of $500 million in frozen assets.

Other Foreign Relations. Iran and the Soviet Union remained at odds, largely over the Soviet presence in neighboring Afghanistan and the Soviet Union's role as arms supplier to Iraq. But Iran announced that it would resume gas exports to the Soviet Union, a move which would provide badly needed income.

Iran's relations with France improved; this was perceived as largely the result of French efforts to obtain the release of French hostages held by pro-Iranian groups in Lebanon. Relations with Syria remained strained.

Oil and the Economy. In April the government announced plans to put up 10 percent of an estimated $400 million to build an oil refinery in Zimbabwe; the project was part of Iran's general attempts to find new outlets for crude oil exports. Iran was also considering alternate pipeline routes, including a twin pipeline from Pars to Ahwaz that would allow Iran to export the full quota permitted by the Organization of Petroleum Exporting Countries without using Kharg Island at all.

Tehran's oil income was expected to decline significantly, in large part because of Iran's decision to cut exports in reaction to weak international demand and low prices. The situation shifted somewhat in early August, when OPEC oil ministers reached agreement on an Iranian proposal that cut overall OPEC production but set Iran's quota at 2.3 million barrels per day, above Iran's previous level of production. Another OPEC meeting in October essentially extended the August quota agreement. In December, Iran joined 11 of the other 12 OPEC nations in an agreement to cut production further; Iraq refused to participate. Oil revenues were not keeping up with the cost of damage incurred by the oil industry because of the war. In the face of this disparity, the Iranian government introduced austerity measures and planned to cut import spending by $2 billion for the year.

Domestic Trends. The domestic situation was dominated by the needs of the war effort. Women university graduates were told they must do one year's nursing before they could take up state jobs in any sector, with the exception of engineering, education, or the medical field itself. In April, Ayatollah Khomeini called for all able-bodied men to go to the front.

See STATISTICS OF THE WORLD.   J.S.I.

Iraqi street scene following an Iranian bombing east of Baghdad in September. The Iran-Iraq war entered its seventh year that month.

IRAQ. The Iran-Iraq war escalated in 1986 with the Iranian capture of the strategic port of Fao (al-Faw) at the mouth of the Persian Gulf. The war continued to place a heavy burden on Iraq's economy.

War With Iran. In the ground struggle along the border, Iran launched its most serious offensive in over five years by crossing the Shatt al-Arab waterway in February and taking the nearly abandoned Iraqi port of Fao (al-Faw) once the site of Iraq's major oil terminal. The Iranian success threatened the city of Basra and Iraq's access to the Gulf. February also saw the launching of a major Iranian ground offensive into Kurdistan in northeastern Iraq. Portions of this territory were reportedly later regained by Iraq, but a six-week counteroffensive launched in response to the Iranian success at al-Faw was turned back in July.

In February, Iraq shot down what it claimed was a military plane; 46 passengers died, among them members of the Iranian Parliament and a close associate of Ayatollah Ruhollah Khomeini, Iran's leader. The Iraqi Air Force continued to bombard Iran's principal oil export facilities at Kharg Island and also mounted air raids on Iran's Sirri Island and Larak Island oil terminals; Iran retaliated with air raids of its own against Iraqi oil facilities in and around the city of Kirkuk. Late in the year, among other bombardments, the two countries traded attacks on each other's capital cities. In November, 48 people were killed when an Iranian

missile struck a residential neighborhood of Baghdad, and in December, Iraqi warplanes bombed Tehran, reportedly destroying a power plant and military installations.

Iraq appeared to have resigned itself to a war of attrition, declaring that outright military victory was impossible for either side. But Iran's religious leaders continued to promise a "final offensive" that would achieve victory. After devastating Iraqi air raids on industrial centers killed over 300 people in late December, Iranians temporarily overran four Iraqi islands but were repulsed, in what Iraq sought to portray as a major victory.

Foreign Relations. After the so-called Fao offensive, members of the Gulf Cooperation Council—Saudi Arabia, Kuwait, the United Arab Emirates, Qatar, Bahrain, and Oman—reportedly were reviewing their anti-Iranian position on the war in light of Iran's improved strategic position. There were also indications that Iraq and Syria, its long-time archenemy, were considering an easing of tensions.

Iraq's relations with the Soviet Union were generally good, with the two countries signing a five-year oil and gas industry cooperation protocol in May and the Soviet Union continuing to supply Iraq with arms. France, also one of Iraq's major arms suppliers, maintained close ties.

Diplomatic relations between Iraq and the United States continued to develop but were seriously strained by revelations late in the year that the United States had, in secret, sold arms to Iran in an apparent attempt to improve relations with Iran and win the release of American hostages. It was uncertain whether the arms shipments would significantly help Iran's war effort against Iraq. At the same time, the United States, in what was said to be an effort to avert an Iranian victory in the war—which Reagan administration officials said would be disastrous to U.S. interests—had also reportedly been secretly supplying Iraq with military intelligence about Iran since 1984.

Economy. As oil prices dropped, agreements reached by the Organization of Petroleum Exporting Countries in August and October imposed production cuts from which Iraq was exempted. The overall decline in oil revenues and the heavy cost of the Iran-Iraq war put mounting pressure on the Iraqi economy, and at a December OPEC meeting, Iraq stalemated the talks by resisting pressure to join in new output cuts designed to raise prices. (The final agreement was reached by excluding Iraq.)

President Saddam Hussein called for austerity measures, in conjunction with a move away from the country's dependence on oil and toward agricultural and industrial self-sufficiency. On a more optimistic note, Iraq predicted that its export capacity would be increased substantially with the completion of new expansions of pipelines to Turkey and Saudi Arabia. In May the first deliveries of Iraqi-associated gas to Kuwait began and the construction of the first stage of an Iraqi-Kuwaiti gas pipeline system was commissioned.

See STATISTICS OF THE WORLD.   T.I.

IRELAND, NORTHERN. See GREAT BRITAIN.

IRELAND, REPUBLIC OF. The government of Prime Minister Garrett FitzGerald was occupied during 1986 with implementing the 1985 Anglo-Irish treaty, which had provided a consultative role for Irish ministers on Northern Ireland through an Anglo-Irish Intergovernmental Conference. However, as of the pact's first anniversary in November, FitzGerald had little to show for his efforts. The treaty had also been intended to enhance cross-border security, partly through readier extradition of suspected terrorists to Britain. There was therefore much embarrassment in London and annoyance in Dublin when British authorities failed

to complete the formalities correctly in the highly publicized cases of two suspects, who, as a result, had to be freed by the courts.

FitzGerald's efforts in realizing the treaty's intentions were impeded indirectly by his stunning failure to persuade the Irish electorate to back divorce law reform. In April, after consultation with church leaders of all denominations, the prime minister—long committed to ridding the Irish constitution of elements based on the teachings of the Roman Catholic Church—announced a referendum to remove the constitutional bar to divorce, as well as an intention to promote legislation allowing civil divorce on the sole ground of failure (after at least five years) of the marriage. Opinion polls at the outset had suggested a comfortable majority in favor of the constitutional change. The Catholic bishops said they sought no veto but warned against the moral and social consequences of what was proposed. Opponents of a divorce law were also able to arouse anxieties about entitlement of the divorced to pension rights and social benefits as well as to rights of property and inheritance. Thus, on June 21, the proposition was defeated by almost two to one—a severe blow to FitzGerald's prestige, particularly north of the border, where unionists used the vote to deride what they considered to be the priest-ridden nature of the republic.

In June, FitzGerald's coalition lost one Labor member in Parliament, but retained its majority. However, its chances of being returned to power at the next general election, due before the end of 1987, were seen to be fading, as popular resentment against high taxes and unemployment increased. In November, Sinn Fein, the political wing of the Irish Republican Army, voted to end its long-standing policy of abstention from the Dáil. Some party members objected and said they would break away to form a new party to continue the old policy.

The budget presented on January 29 brought some relief for hard-pressed earner-taxpayers and was another small step in reducing government borrowing, which remained a heavy burden on the economy. Unemployment continued at around 17 percent of the work force. Inflation came down into low single figures. In August the Irish pound was devalued by 8 percent within the European Monetary System; the fall in value of the U.S. dollar and pound sterling over the summer months had left Irish goods dangerously uncompetitive.

See STATISTICS OF THE WORLD.　　T.J.O.H.

ISRAEL. Israel scored a number of foreign policy successes in 1986; at home, the economy stabilized and the national unity government completed a transfer of power.

U.S.-Israeli Relations. Israel's ties with the United States remained strong despite some tension. One source of friction was the case of Jonathan Jay Pollard, a former U.S. Navy intelligence analyst who pleaded guilty in June to spying for Israel. His wife pleaded guilty to lesser charges, and four Israelis were named as unindicted conspirators. Prime Minister Shimon Peres apologized publicly for the incident.

The disclosure of Israel's role as a middleman for secret U.S. arms sales to Iran—reportedly aimed at least in part at securing the release of American hostages in Lebanon from their pro-Iranian captors—also produced possible strains in U.S.-Israeli ties. As details of the controversial transactions were revealed, the Israeli government indicated it had transferred U.S. arms to Iran on an understanding (reached in 1985) that the stocks would be replenished, without any funds passing through Israel. Israel said it had acted at the behest of the United States and had not known about the use of profits from the deals to fund the "contra" rebels in Nicaragua. Other sources suggested that Israel may have sought to promote the U.S.-Iranian arms sales. It was also reported that Israel had previously been supplying arms to Iran in secret on its own, as a way of protecting Jews in that country and of putting pressure on Iraq so as to reduce its capacity for anti-Israeli hostilities.

Shcharansky Release. In February, Anatoly Shcharansky, the leading Soviet Jewish "refusenik"—a Soviet citizen denied permission to emigrate—was released as part of an East-West prisoner exchange. He had been imprisoned since his 1978 conviction on spying charges. Shcharansky went to Israel, where his wife had emigrated in the 1970's; other family members were later allowed to join them. Overall, however, the number of Jews permitted to leave the Soviet Union continued to decline.

In a surprise summit meeting in July, Prime Minister Shimon Peres (right) and King Hassan II of Morocco (left) attempted to revive the long-dormant peace process in the Middle East.

Mideast Affairs. Relations with Egypt improved, after a chill dating back to the 1982 Israeli invasion of Lebanon. Hanging over the entire relationship was the question of Taba, a tiny Israeli-controlled stretch of beach near Elat that was claimed by Egypt. In January, after prolonged debate, the Israeli inner cabinet, prodded by Prime Minister Shimon Peres, agreed to Egypt's demand that the dispute be settled by an international arbitration panel. Talks between Israeli and Egyptian negotiators dragged on for eight more months, until an agreement was reached on September 10 covering terms of arbitration. During the next two days, in Alexandria, Peres and Egyptian President Hosni Mubarak held the first Israeli-Egyptian summit meeting in five years. Mubarak subsequently announced that he was upgrading Egypt's chargé d'affaires in Israel to the status of full ambassador.

In July, Prime Minister Peres and King Hassan II of Morocco held a surprise summit meeting in Morocco. While there was no breakthrough in the peace process, it was the first time since Egypt concluded a peace treaty with Israel in 1979 that an Arab leader had invited an Israeli prime minister for a public visit.

Tension in the Israeli-occupied West Bank and Gaza Strip continued to run high. In March, Peres's plan to "devolve" a certain amount of self-rule onto the West Bank was dealt a blow when the Israeli-appointed mayor of Nablus was murdered, apparently by a faction of the Palestine Liberation Organization. Despite the setback, three more Arab mayors were appointed. On October 7 an Israeli cab driver from Ashkelon was killed in Gaza when he stopped to have his car repaired; he was the second Ashkelon resident to be stabbed to death in Gaza in two weeks. Thousands attended the driver's funeral, which turned into an emotional anti-Arab demonstration. On December 4 two Palestinian students were killed by Israeli soldiers during a demonstration at Bir Zeit University; a day later, a 14-year-old Palestinian boy was shot to death during a confrontation with Israeli troops.

Tension with Syria also mounted. In February, Israel intercepted a Libyan jet flying from Tripoli to Damascus, following Israeli intelligence reports that PLO terrorist leaders were aboard. After forcing the plane to land in Israel and conducting a five-hour search, the Israelis allowed the jet, carrying a group of Syrian politicians and Lebanese militia officials, to proceed. Syria was later implicated in unsuccessful attempts to plant bombs on Israeli El Al planes in Britain and Spain.

In Lebanon, Israel continued to mount periodic air attacks on Palestinian positions. During an October raid near Sidon, launched in retaliation for a grenade assault by Palestinians during a military ceremony near Jerusalem's Western Wall, an Israeli jet was downed and its pilot captured by Shiites.

Other Foreign Relations. In January, Spain and Israel established full diplomatic relations. The Ivory Coast and Cameroon also resumed diplomatic relations with Israel. Relations with Austria deteriorated when it was revealed by the World Jewish Congress that Kurt Waldheim, the former UN secretary-general who was running for the presidency of Austria (see biography in PEOPLE IN THE NEWS), had concealed his Nazi past. Following Waldheim's election in June, the Israeli Foreign Ministry expressed regret and the Israeli ambassador to Vienna was twice recalled for consultations. In October, Austria recalled its envoy to Israel.

Israel's national unity government successfully completed the transition agreed upon two years earlier; in October, Likud coalition leader Yitzhak Shamir (left) and Labor Party leader Shimon Peres traded roles, the former becoming prime minister, the latter foreign minister. Here they are shown at a parliamentary debate.

Domestic Politics. The transfer of power from Peres of the Labor Party to Likud coalition leader Yitzhak Shamir took place on October 20, delayed almost a week by disputes on cabinet appointments. A number of crises had threatened the government's existence during the year, but none was deemed significant enough to break up the partnership, especially given public opinion polls indicating that a majority of Israelis wanted the rotation agreement to be implemented.

In June, Avraham Shalom resigned as head of the Shin Beth, Israel's internal security organization, after evidence was amassed suggesting he had ordered the killing of two Arabs arrested for the 1984 hijacking of a bus. (One Israeli passenger and two other hijackers died during the incident.) In exchange for resigning, Shalom was granted a presidential pardon, an action widely denounced as a whitewash. Shalom was later quoted as saying that his political superiors—meaning Yitzhak Shamir, who was prime minister at the time—had known and approved of the killings. However, a Justice Ministry inquiry completed in late 1986 concluded that Shamir had not known.

Economic Upturn. Israel's economy made a remarkable turnaround in 1986, helped by U.S. economic aid and the dramatic drop in world oil prices. Before an austerity program was instituted in July 1985, Israel's annual inflation rate was more than 400 percent and rising rapidly, and the currency was steadily deteriorating against the dollar; by July 1986 the inflation rate had dropped below 18 percent, and the shekel was remaining steady.

See Statistics of the World.   R.O.F.

ITALY. In August 1986, Prime Minister Bettino Craxi completed his third year in office—easily a record for postwar Italy, known for its short-lived governments. Craxi, leader of the Socialist Party, headed a five-party coalition composed of his own small party, the Christian Democrats (still Italy's largest party), the Social Democrats, the Liberals, and the Republicans. His days in office appeared to be numbered, however, as a result of a compromise reached after a government crisis broke out in June.

Government Crisis. On June 27 the lower house of Parliament was debating a measure on government finance and decided to attach

Nearly 500 alleged members of the Sicilian Mafia, including reputed boss Luciano Liggio (shown here), went on trial in Palermo in February. The trial was expected to last at least a year.

a vote of confidence to its approval because of the uncertain political situation. When the text of the bill was put to a secret vote, as is the procedure, it was defeated, 293-266. Upon hearing of the government's defeat, Craxi returned from a European Community meeting in the Netherlands and, after a brief cabinet meeting, met with President Francesco Cossiga to offer his government's resignation.

Cossiga faced a difficult task in resolving the situation. At first he asked Senate President Amintore Fanfani to take on an "exploratory mandate" in negotiating between Christian Democrats and Socialists. When Fanfani's effort yielded no firm results, Cossiga asked Foreign Minister Giulio Andreotti, the country's most eminent Christian Democratic politician, to try to put together a government, but Craxi refused to join a government led by Andreotti or any other Christian Democrat. Cossiga then asked Craxi to try to form a government. On July 25, Craxi reported having worked out a compromise with the Christian Democratic Party, under which he would continue as prime minister until March 1987, when a Christian

A controversial addition to Rome's picturesque Piazza di Spagna, a McDonald's restaurant—the first in Italy—opened in March to crowds of curious teenagers and the outraged protests of much of the Roman citizenry.

Democrat would take over until the end of the current Parliament in June 1988. Craxi's new government—the same coalition as before, with most cabinet posts unchanged–was sworn in on August 1 and received a vote of confidence from Parliament soon after.

Organized Crime and Terrorism. The massive trial of 474 Sicilians, charged with trafficking in cocaine and heroin, arms trading, and over a hundred murders, opened under very heavy security in Palermo on February 10. Those appearing in court included Luciano Liggio, head of the Corleone Mafia, and the brothers Salvatore and Michele De Greco, the last considered to be the top Mafia leader in Sicily. About 100 of the defendants were fugitives being tried in absentia.

The year's first killing by the Red Brigades took place in Palermo on February 10, the day of the Mafia trial's opening, when a former mayor of Florence was shot dead, in what some interpreted as an attempt by the now-fading Brigades to demonstrate their continued presence. On June 16 the trial of 174 Red Brigaders opened in Rome.

Sicilian financier Michele Sindona, sentenced to 15 years in prison by a Milan court in 1985, was sentenced to life imprisonment on March 18 after being convicted of ordering the murder of Giorgio Ambrosoli, the lawyer appointed to liquidate his failed Italian bank. Four days later, Sindona died, after having drunk coffee that was found to have contained traces of cyanide. A seven-month investigation concluded Sindona had committed suicide.

Economic Improvements. The 1986 budget was approved, two months late and after 950 amendments, on February 26. By then the generally favorable conditions for the economy were making themselves felt. Italy, heavily dependent on imported energy, was beginning to profit from the fall in crude oil prices and the decline in the value of the dollar. By the end of October, inflation had fallen to 5.9 percent; the balance-of-payments deficit for the year's first half was less than half that for the corresponding period of 1985, and the balance of trade showed a similar improvement.

Toxic Wine Scare. In mid-April it was reported that wine contaminated with methanol, or methyl alcohol, had been found to be the cause of about two dozen deaths. The toxic substance had been added to boost the alcohol content (and therefore the price) of cheap wine. The ministries of health and agriculture instituted stringent measures to check wine for contamination; out of 1,103 samples of wine they examined, 7 percent were found to contain methyl alcohol in amounts above the permitted level. Some arrests were made among distillers and wholesalers.

Chernobyl Aftermath. Radiation reached Italy after the Chernobyl nuclear power plant accident in late April, and some agricultural products were affected. The Italian government temporarily banned the sale of leafy green vegetables and halted imports of fresh food from Eastern Europe. An antinuclear march attended by about 100,000 took place in Rome on May 10. The government did not take steps to abandon its nuclear power program.

Tourist Decline. There was a sharp decline in the number of foreign tourists visiting Italy during the high season. Owing to a combination of factors, chief among them the falling value of the U.S. dollar and a fear of terrorist attacks, luxury hotels in Rome were said to be only one-third full in August. Florence and Venice were similarly affected.

Foreign Affairs. On April 15, after U.S. planes bombed targets in Benghazi and Tripoli, Libya attacked radar installations on the Italian island of Lampedusa, but no damage was done. Craxi was critical of the U.S. bombing raid but did support moves by the United States and the European Community for sanctions against Libya, which was suspected of involvement in the December 1985 terrorist attack at Rome's airport in which 16 people died. On April 21, Italy and other EC members agreed to reduce the number of Libyan diplomats in their countries to a minimum.

***Achille Lauro* Aftermath.** In June, 15 of the hijackers and coconspirators implicated in the *Achille Lauro* hijacking of October 1985 went on trial in Genoa (five were in custody; ten, including Muhammad Abbas, the alleged mastermind of the plot, were tried in absentia). On July 10 the court sentenced Abbas and two others to life imprisonment and three hijackers in custody to prison terms of 15-30 years.

Papal Assassination Plot. Another trial, concerning an alleged international conspiracy behind the attempt on the life of Pope John Paul II in 1981, came to an end in Rome during March. Mehmet Ali Agca, the Turk convicted in 1981 of actually shooting the pope, contended that the assassination plot was contrived by the Soviet and Bulgarian security services and a right-wing Turkish group. Agca's conspiracy theory was not accepted by the court as proved, and three Bulgarian and three Turkish defendants were acquitted. However, a court document later indicated that the judge had found, at least, indications that Agca had not acted alone. Agca himself was found guilty of smuggling a gun into Italy.

See STATISTICS OF THE WORLD. M.C.

IVORY COAST. See STATISTICS OF THE WORLD.

J

JAMAICA. See STATISTICS OF THE WORLD. See also CARIBBEAN BASIN.

JAPAN. Japanese domestic politics in 1986 centered on the question of whether Prime Minister Yasuhiro Nakasone would be able to extend his term in office. Nakasone's Liberal Democratic Party (LDP) has had a majority in the Japanese Diet (parliament) for three decades, which has ensured that the party president would be prime minister. Party rules, however, state that the president may serve only two consecutive two-year terms. Nakasone's second term ended in October, and he could therefore continue as prime minister

JAPAN

only if LDP rules were amended by a two-thirds vote of the party's elected representatives. After the tremendous success of the party in July 6 elections, the LDP membership unanimously voted in September to alter the rules and allow Nakasone to remain in office. But instead of a full two-year term, LDP members, several of whom wanted to become prime minister themselves, voted Nakasone only a one-year extension.

Election Results. The July elections were a major success for both Nakasone and the LDP. The ruling party reversed its decline in popularity over the last two decades, a decline that had reached its low point in 1983 when the party lost its majority in the Diet and was forced to form a coalition government. As a result of the election, the LDP had a record 304 members in the lower house (300 elected LDP candidates and 4 independents who joined the LDP after being elected); this represented a gain of 54 seats and a clear majority in the 512-member body. The party maintained its control of the much less powerful upper house, where only half the seats were up for election, raising its majority in the 252-seat body from 131 to 142.

The election was a severe blow especially to the largest opposition party, the Japan Socialist Party (JSP), which suffered its worst defeat ever in a national election. While retaining its 41 seats in the upper house, the JSP suffered a disastrous defeat in the lower house, dropping from 111 seats to 86. The smaller and more right-wing Democratic Socialist Party (DSP) suffered a similarly precipitous defeat in the July elections. The party's totals dropped from 14 seats to 12 in the upper house and from 37 to 26 in the lower house.

Other opposition parties fared better. The well-financed and well-organized Japan Communist Party kept its 27 seats in the lower house. Kōmeitō, the Clean Government Party, which relied on strong support from the Sōka Gakkai, a militant Buddhist religious organization, suffered only minor losses.

New Cabinet. Nakasone, who campaigned vigorously for LDP candidates across the country, got much of the credit for his party's victory. Afterward, he appointed Kiichi Miyazawa, his most vocal economic critic, as minister of finance, a move expected to strengthen his own position within the party. He also named Tadashi Kuranari, a member of his own faction with almost no diplomatic experience, as minister of foreign affairs; this action suggested that Nakasone would continue to maintain a strong personal role in foreign policy.

Nakasone chose Masayuki Fujio as education minister, a surprising decision in view of

Prime Minister Yasuhiro Nakasone paints an eye on a daruma doll, an act that symbolizes victory, after the July elections brought his Liberal Democratic Party its biggest gains in 26 years.

Women security officers demonstrate their technique (above) before the Tokyo summit meeting of industrial democracies. Despite government precautions, radicals fired five homemade rockets from an apartment 2 miles away (inset); no one was hurt.

Fujio's strongly nationalistic and conservative views. Indeed, Fujio quickly became involved on the nationalistic side of an ongoing dispute about changes in Japanese history textbooks. China and South Korea have been particularly critical of changes that glorified Japan's imperial past and ignored or excused Japan's actions in World War II. Fujio's further insistence that Japanese schools fly the national flag and play the national anthem, his attempt in an interview to justify Japanese atrocities in China in 1937, and his insistence that Korea had agreed to its annexation by Japan in 1910 also led to both domestic and foreign criticism. When Nakasone asked Fujio to retract his statements or resign, he refused to do either, and the prime minister dismissed him. This was the first ouster of a cabinet member in 34 years, and it outraged many of Nakasone's conservative supporters. Conservatives were also angry over Nakasone's refusal to revisit the Yasukuni Shrine in Tokyo, dedicated to Japan's war dead, and his request that cabinet ministers also refrain from doing so (16 min-

isters defied him and visited the shrine in August).

Economic Developments. The Japanese economy grew at an inflation-adjusted rate of 4.6 percent in fiscal year 1985 (ending March 31, 1986). This falling off from the previous year's 5.1 percent rate reflected the slowing growth of exports. Real gross national product (GNP) grew still more slowly in the first half of fiscal 1986, making it unlikely that the government's target of 4 percent could be achieved for the whole fiscal year.

At a September 1985 conference with four other major industrial countries, Japan had agreed to use its reserves to force the value of the yen up against the dollar. By September 1986 the yen had risen in value by more than 50 percent; the increase made Japanese exports more expensive, reducing demand for them.

211

A new island rose above the waters of the Pacific Ocean, south of the Japanese island of Iwo Jima, when an underwater volcano erupted in January. The island had a two-month fling with open-air existence, then slowly eroded away.

In December government leaders agreed to a 1987 military budget of $22 billion, equal to 1.004 percent of projected GNP. It was the first departure from a ten-year policy limiting military spending to 1 percent of GNP. The government also adopted a tax reform plan.

Foreign Relations. Friction over the large Japanese trade surplus continued to mark Japan's relations with the United States. The 1985 U.S. trade deficit of $50 billion with Japan was approximately one-third of the total U.S. trade deficit. However, during 1986 the two countries did reach agreements on trade disputes involving telecommunications, pharmaceuticals, and computer microchips. Declines in Japan's total trade surplus and in its surplus with the United States were being reported late in 1986, although the total surplus for the whole fiscal year was expected to reach new records.

Japan announced new sanctions against South Africa in September. These included a ban on imports of South African iron and steel and a halt to tourist visas for South Africans. In January, Soviet Foreign Minister Eduard Shevardnadze paid a visit to Japan, the first by a Soviet foreign minister in ten years. Agreements were made to resume negotiations on a peace treaty and have regular meetings between foreign ministers.

Radicalism and Protest. Nakasone hosted the 12th annual summit meeting of the seven major industrial powers in Tokyo in May. Almost overshadowing the event itself was a rocket attack by Japan's dominant radical group, the left-wing Middle Core Faction. Despite the 30,000 police officers mobilized to provide security, several homemade rockets were fired at the state guest house during the welcoming ceremonies there; however, the rockets overshot their target, and no one was hurt. In October attackers presumed to be left-wing radicals fired rockets at the prime minister's residence and government buildings; the rockets again missed their targets. Also in October, farm families and large numbers of radicals launched demonstrations at Narita airport, protesting airport expansion plans.

See STATISTICS OF THE WORLD.   M.S.B.

JORDAN. King Hussein's joint peace initiative with Palestine Liberation Organization Chairman Yasir Arafat collapsed in 1986, and relations with the PLO deteriorated. After meeting with a U.S. State Department official in London, Hussein had held a series of critical meetings with Arafat in Amman in late January, to try to meet U.S. conditions for support of the initiative. But the talks broke down when Arafat would not give written acceptance of two UN resolutions which implicitly accept Israel's right to exist but do not refer to Palestinian statehood. On February 19, Hussein said he was ending the effort with Arafat and blamed the PLO leadership for the collapse.

The king's attack on Arafat was denounced throughout the Arab world and on the Israeli-occupied West Bank. Zafir al-Masri, the pro-Jordanian, moderate Palestinian mayor of Nablus, was assassinated on March 2 by radical Palestinians—an act widely interpreted as demonstrating Palestinian rejection of Hussein. Masri's funeral provided the occasion for anti-Hussein and pro-PLO demonstrations on the West Bank. Responding, the king closed PLO liaison offices in Amman and deported about 100 PLO military and civilian personnel. He also suspended PLO publications, blacklisted pro-PLO West Bank journalists, and confiscated the passports of prominent West Bank PLO supporters crossing into Jordan.

In July the Jordanian government ordered the closing of the offices of al-Fatah, a PLO group cofounded and still headed by Arafat, and expelled Arafat's deputy Khalil Wazir (Abu Jihad). Jordanian officials claimed the actions were taken in response to al-Fatah's interference in Jordanian parliamentary by-elections and to its instigation of riots at Yarmouk University in May, in which three students were killed. However, Hussein proclaimed that he still recognized the PLO as the sole legitimate representative of the Palestinians.

King Hussein's campaign to gain support on the West Bank continued in September, when it was announced that the Cairo-Amman Bank would reopen its Nablus branch, closed since 1967. On September 28, in a move applauded by Hussein, Israel appointed three Arabs considered to be pro-Jordanian as mayors of Hebron, al-Birah, and Ram Allah.

After Hussein's December 1985 visit with Syrian President Hafez al-Assad in Damascus, Assad reciprocated in May with his first visit to Amman since 1979. The rapprochement between the two leaders was motivated by, among other things, Hussein's desire to please Saudi Arabia, his major financial backer, and put pressure on Arafat, who is opposed by Assad. However, major differences still divided Jordan and Syria.

Jordan's relations with the United States continued to deteriorate. Early in the year, President Ronald Reagan withdrew a long-delayed proposed $1.9 billion U.S. arms sale, when it became apparent that the U.S. Senate would reject it overwhelmingly.

A prolonged drought contributed to the country's economic woes. Grain production was expected to be at an all-time low. Because of the slump in the petroleum industry throughout the Middle East, remittances of Jordanians working abroad dropped 17 percent in 1985, and were expected to fall further during 1986.

See STATISTICS OF THE WORLD.   C.H.A.

KAMPUCHEA. See CAMBODIA.
KANSAS. See STATISTICS OF THE WORLD.
KENTUCKY. See STATISTICS OF THE WORLD.
KENYA. In 1986 the Kenyan government encountered an upsurge of criticism from religious leaders, as it appeared to move closer to totalitarianism. Economically, the year began with promise; the Brazilian drought boosted Kenyan coffee prices, and good rains generated bumper food harvests. The coffee boom faded,

however, as prices tumbled when Colombia lowered its prices drastically.

Pastors at a September conference of the National Council of Churches of Kenya denounced a decision by the ruling party to eliminate secret ballots in the next presidential election. President Daniel arap Moi sought to defuse criticism by these and other religious leaders by announcing that church leaders and senior civil servants would still be allowed to vote by secret ballot. In December, Parliament unanimously approved a constitutional amendment removing tenure for the attorney general and auditor general, thus making them subject to dismissal by the president. Religious leaders objected strongly to the move.

Public pressure mounted for information regarding AIDS (acquired immune deficiency syndrome), which, according to an article in the *New England Journal of Medicine*, was found in over half the female prostitutes in Africa tested in a recent study. In July the government embarked on a health education program to help curb the spread of AIDS. The government also tried to come to grips with population control. (Kenya leads the world in its rate of population growth.) A program to provide contraceptives and family planning education was stepped up but met stiff resistance from the Roman Catholic Church and the Muslim community.

The Kenyan financial world was shaken by the failure of two banks and four credit companies as a result of mismanagement and fraud. The ensuing investigation and shakedown of the banking system had serious political implications. All the failed banks were Kikuyu-controlled, and some believed the scandal was being used in an effort to loosen the Kikuyu grip on banking.

See STATISTICS OF THE WORLD.   P.S.

KHMER REPUBLIC. See CAMBODIA.

KIRIBATI. See STATISTICS OF THE WORLD.

KOREA, DEMOCRATIC PEOPLE'S REPUBLIC OF, or **NORTH KOREA.** President Kim Il Sung's son, Kim Chong Il, received prominent media attention in North Korea in 1986 and was presumed to be in charge of party and state affairs. His role as the heir to power seemed well established. There were reports later in the year that his father had died, but these

proved false (see KOREA, REPUBLIC OF). Kim Il Sung was reelected by Parliament in December, and a new prime minister was named.

The national budget, as passed by the Supreme People's Assembly, reportedly allocated 14 percent of outlays to defense. Western sources believed the defense percentage was actually higher. Large increases in outlays were reported for the chemical, mining, and power industries—all apparently problem areas in the economy.

Early in the year, North Korea suspended political and economic talks with South Korea, in protest against the annual South Korean-U.S. joint military exercise.

Relations with the Soviet Union continued to improve. In January the Soviet foreign minister visited Pyongyang. In February the two countries signed a five-year agreement on commodity delivery and payments, and in July the 20th anniversary of the North Korean-Soviet friendship treaty was celebrated with fanfare. July also marked the 20th anniversary of North Korea's mutual assistance treaty with China, but observances in both capitals seemed in much lower key. Cuban President Fidel Castro visited North Korea in March and signed a 20-year friendship and cooperation pact. Chinese President Li Xiannian came in October.

See STATISTICS OF THE WORLD.   D.S.M.

KOREA, REPUBLIC OF, or **SOUTH KOREA.** A dominant political issue in South Korea was the opposition's demand for direct election of the president. South Korean-U.S. relations were clouded by a growing trade imbalance between the two countries.

Politics and Government. Early in the year, the opposition, led by the New Korea Democratic Party (NKDP), launched a petition campaign for constitutional reform, which gained the support of many students, educators, and religious groups. The government and its Democratic Justice Party, while not ruling out eventual changes, reasserted the intention to carry out the 1988 presidential election through a 5,000-member electoral college, under the existing constitution.

The NKDP sponsored a series of generally peaceful rallies that drew large crowds, and by May the party claimed 700,000 signatures on petitions supporting constitutional change.

On May 3, however, a planned rally in Inchon was called off at the last minute, after violent demonstrations were begun by radical student-worker groups. Police detained hundreds of people.

President Chun Doo Hwan had met with opposition leaders in April and indicated a willingness to accept some constitutional revision before 1988. In July the Democratic Justice Party presented a draft constitution calling for a parliamentary system with a symbolic president elected by a one-chamber legislature. The NKDP was not satisfied by such a proposal. In mid-October an NKDP legislator was arrested for remarks on unification that the government said were a violation of national security laws. Parliament must approve the arrest of a lawmaker, but police were called to the legislature to prevent NKDP members from entering the hall where the vote was taking place.

Meanwhile, protests from a minority of university students were growing increasingly militant and anti-American. On October 28, students from some 25 universities occupied buildings at a university in Seoul. On October 31, after a two-hour battle in which the occupiers hurled gasoline bombs at riot police and set fires, police stormed the occupied buildings and arrested 1,500 protesters.

In an attempted compromise, opposition leader Kim Dae Jung announced in November that he would abandon plans to run for president in 1988 if the government agreed to direct elections. The regime's opposition to direct elections was said to be due in part to a fear that Kim might emerge the winner. Nevertheless, the stalemate continued. A scheduled opposition rally on November 29 in Seoul was stymied by the government, which sent large numbers of police (estimated at 70,000) to disperse crowds and prevent protest activity.

Economic Developments. As a result of the "three lows"—low petroleum prices, low value of the Korean won against other currencies, and low international interest rates—projec-

Demanding democratic constitutional reform, thousands of South Koreans, led by a flag-carrying contingent of New Korea Democratic Party members, marched through the streets of Taegu in early April.

tions of real economic growth for 1986 were revised upward in the spring, to 9 or 10 percent. Exports for the first six months exceeded those for the same period of 1985 by 23 percent. Automobile exports were booming. The surging trade surplus with the United States was not expected to be much affected by Seoul's decision late in the year to let the won rise against the dollar.

Foreign Affairs. In April the United States announced reduction of preferential tariff treatment for imports from South Korea and some other countries. However, agreement was reached in midyear on removal of insurance sales restrictions against U.S. firms and on the sale of American tobacco products (long forbidden) in South Korea. In August the U.S. House upheld a presidential veto of a bill that would have rolled back textile imports from South Korea by 30 percent. South Korea promised legislation protecting U.S. copyrights on computer software and audio materials and patents for pharmaceuticals and chemicals.

Asian Games. An Olympic park, with facilities for housing the events of the 1988 Olympics, was completed in time to host the 1986 Asian Games. Sixteen nations competed, including the People's Republic of China (but not North Korea). On September 14, nearly a week before the games opened, a bomb exploded at Kimpo International Airport in Seoul, killing 5 persons and wounding 30. No one claimed responsibility.

Kim Il Sung Muddle. In late November the South Korean government reported that North Korean leader Kim Il Sung had apparently died. The report was based on announcements allegedly made by North Koreans through loudspeakers along the border, picked up by South Korean military personnel. The broadcasts were not recorded by the military. Kim subsequently appeared in public to greet a Mongolian delegation. It remained uncertain whether he actually had been reported dead by North Koreans and, if so, why.

See STATISTICS OF THE WORLD. See also KOREA, DEMOCRATIC REPUBLIC OF. D.S.M.

KUWAIT. In February 1986, an Iranian thrust into southern Iraq brought the Iran-Iraq war within miles of the Kuwaiti border; Iran also occupied the Iraqi port of Fao (al-Faw), near the Kuwaiti island of Bubiyan. Saudi Arabia declared that it would defend Kuwait if the latter was attacked by Iran; Kuwait, in turn, offered to provide airborne surveillance for Oman and Qatar, but they declined. Kuwait also ordered its troops to shoot on sight any intruders trying to cross its border.

In September shells fired by an Iranian gunboat set ablaze a Kuwaiti supertanker loaded with oil. In June four bombs exploded at an oil complex in southern Kuwait, damaging two pipeline networks and an oil well; opponents of Kuwait's support for Iraq were thought responsible. Because of fears that some foreign residents were involved in terrorist attacks, the government attempted to make it more difficult for expatriate laborers to remain. By late in the year, around 30,000 foreigners had been deported.

On July 3, Sheikh Jabir al-Ahmad al-Jabir al-Sabah dissolved the National Assembly because of its frequent clashes with the government. The sheikh also decreed press restrictions. In October, the government placed five Iraqis on trial (four of them in absentia) in connection with a 1985 attempt to assassinate Sheikh Jabir, in which four persons were killed. The single defendant present, a pro-Iranian radical, was sentenced to death; one other was sentenced to life in prison, and the remaining defendants were acquitted.

After increasing oil production to its highest level since 1981 in an attempt to boost oil revenues in the face of plunging prices, Kuwait, with other OPEC members, accepted temporary production quotas worked out at an August meeting; Kuwait's represented a 43.7 percent cut in production. At an October OPEC meeting, Kuwait held up renewal of the temporary arrangement by insisting on an increase in its quota, which it was granted, in modified form, for November and December. Kuwait's oil minister was on the three-member pricing committee, which recommended in November that OPEC raise prices by $3 a barrel and return to a fixed price system. The recommendation was not followed, and at December's OPEC meeting, Kuwait accepted a reduction of its quota to 948,000 barrels per day, as against an estimated output capacity of 2.3 million b/d.

See STATISTICS OF THE WORLD. L.A.K.

L

LABOR UNIONS. A continuation of sluggish economic growth, intense foreign competition, and massive trade deficits resulted in another dismal year for labor unions in 1986. Employers pursued tough bargaining stances, resulting in reduced labor costs and a further breakdown of industry bargaining patterns.

Deregulated Telecommunications. The telecommunications industry, still suffering shocks from the 1984 breakup of the American Telephone and Telegraph Company and deregulation, experienced its first round of bargaining in the tough new competitive environment. Instead of bargaining over a single national agreement on wages and benefits involving one big corporation, the industry saw bargaining in more than 20 separate companies.

The first agreement, reached between the Communications Workers of America (CWA) and GTE Corporation early in April, was hailed as a "no concessions" pact by the union. It provided a 3 percent wage increase in the first year and 2 percent increases in 1987 and 1988. Obtaining a settlement with AT&T required contract extensions and a strike that began on June 1 and lasted most of the month. The new three-year contract did not provide cost-of-living adjustments but granted a 2 percent wage increase the first year and 3 percent in each of the next two years. Pacts were subsequently signed with various former components of AT&T.

Bitter Meat-Packing Struggle. Since 1983, intensified competition from lower-cost, non-union meat-packing companies, changes in processing and distribution methods, and cuts in consumption of red meat had hurt many firms and forced members of the United Food and Commercial Workers Union (UFCW) to accept a reduction in pay from more than $10 an hour to around $8.25. Following this concession, the union set a goal of restoring the rate to about $10 per hour over the next few years, and it was successful in some 1986 settlements.

The real struggle took place in Austin, Minn., between UFCW Local P-9 and the flagship plant of George A. Hormel & Co. In August 1985 some 1,500 workers of Local P-9 had gone out on strike over wages and other contract provisions. After closing the plant for a time, the company reopened it in mid-January 1986, with replacement workers and members of the local willing to cross picket lines. Wages for returning workers were the same as outlined in the company's final offer to the union—a base of $10 an hour in the first year, with a freeze for the second and third years. Replacement workers started at $8 per hour. Reopening of the plant resulted in violence on the picket line and calls to the Minnesota National Guard to keep the peace. When Local P-9 sent pickets to other Hormel plants, the company fired the workers who refused to cross the picket lines outside the plant. The local leadership hired a consultant to help launch a corporate campaign against Hormel, but P-9 soon lost the support of the international union, which sought an accommodation with Hormel in harmony with its larger strategy for dealing with the industry.

In May the international union placed the local in trusteeship and filed suit in federal court to prevent militant local officers from interfering with the trusteeship order. The courts upheld the international union, and negotiations were reopened between the international union and Hormel. An agreement was reached in August and approved by local union members the following month. The new contract provided for a base wage of $10.25, with an increase to $10.70 after two years. About 800 workers who had not returned to their jobs were to be allowed back only as needed, and on the basis of seniority.

Unabated Air Turbulence. Continuing upheavals in the airline industry caused trouble for workers at Eastern, Trans World, and other airlines. Talks between flight attendants and TWA, which financier Carl Icahn had bought in 1985, became strained when he demanded wage cuts of 20 percent or more. They struck in March but became frustrated as the airline hired replacements and some strikers returned

Billy clubs in hand, National Guardsmen take up positions in late January outside the George A. Hormel meat-packing plant in Austin, Minn., where employees had been on strike over wage and benefit cuts since August 1985. Governor Rudy Perpich, at the request of Austin officials, sent in the Guard to prevent outbreaks of violence, following Hormel's decision to reopen the plant with newly hired workers.

to work. In mid-May the strikers set a date (May 21) for a vote on the proposed contract but offered to return to work regardless of the outcome. Although the contract was rejected, Icahn agreed to hire from the ranks of prestrike workers, since they were no longer withholding services. He said, though, that fewer than 200 places would be available. The union sued in a federal district court, and the judge ruled that 463 senior workers must be reinstated. More than 4,600 other prestrike workers remained without jobs with the airline.

The ongoing financial travail at Eastern Air Lines placed demands on workers for new wage concessions. In January, Eastern cut 1,010 flight attendants from the payroll, reduced wages of the remaining attendants by 20 percent, and increased their work load. The Air Line Pilots and Transport Workers unions agreed to further concessions, but bitter animosity between Charles E. Bryan, president of the International Association of Machinists' District 100, and Frank Borman, Eastern's chairman, eventually resulted in the sale of the airline to Frank Lorenzo's Texas Air Corpora-

tion. Lorenzo had been instrumental in eliminating the unions at Continental Air Lines during a Chapter 11 bankruptcy proceeding in 1983. The need to stem losses at Eastern resulted in the layoff early in September of more than 1,500 workers.

Other Industries. In the copper industry, heavily battered by foreign competition, a coalition of 14 unions signed contracts with major firms, providing for pay cuts of around $3 an hour. Woodworkers in the Pacific Northwest struck Weyerhaeuser Co. for six weeks in June and July; they eventually settled for a $4.30-an-hour rollback in pay and benefits, in return for a profit-sharing plan. Workers at Deere & Company went on strike in late August when the company refused to meet UAW pension and job security demands.

Work at Home. The issue of work at home emerged in 1986 when the Department of labor ordered a North Carolina manufacturer to stop hiring women employed in making gloves in their homes, because such work at home was banned by the federal Fair Labor Standards Act. The federal ban, strongly supported by unions (since most work at home is nonunionized work for low wages), has been only sporadically enforced over the years. Conservative legal groups took up the cause of the glove workers, and the secretary of labor formally proposed lifting the federal ban on six kinds of work at home; measures to repeal the regulations also were introduced in Congress. These developments brought strong protests from union leaders.

Legal Developments. A 1985 bankruptcy ruling, which allowed the Wheeling-Pittsburgh Steel Company while in Chapter 11 bankruptcy proceedings to abrogate a collective bargaining agreement and unilaterally slash wages and benefits for a five-year period, was overturned in May by a federal appeals court.

The U.S. Supreme Court set minimum standards for public sector unions that collect a fee from nonmembers, saying they must provide advance justification for the amount of the fee, hold a prompt impartial hearing for nonmembers who object to it, and set up an escrow arrangement that preserves the funds of dissenting payers while their objections are being adjudicated.

Organized labor was heartened when National Labor Relations Board general counsel Rosemary Collyer dismissed unfair labor practice charges stemming from the Saturn Corporation agreement in 1985 between the United Automobile Workers and General Motors Corporation. The pact—which covers the plant being built in Spring Hill, Tenn., to produce the new Saturn automobile—had been challenged by the National Right to Work Legal Defense Foundation, on the grounds that it granted an unlawful hiring preference to UAW members from other plants and prematurely recognized the UAW as the bargaining agent for Saturn employees.

Union Organization and Affiliation. In April the United Transportation Union pulled out of the AFL-CIO in a dispute over the federation's procedures for resolving interunion disputes over organizing workers, among other causes. Leaders of the United Mine Workers, which faced tough negotiations with coal mine operators during 1987, were considering merging with another union—most likely with one that would bring them back into the AFL-CIO.

Jay Mazur was elected president of the International Ladies' Garment Workers' Union at a convention in June, succeeding Sol Chaikin, who retired after 45 years as an ILGWU organizer and officer. Albert Shanker stepped down as president of the American Federation of Teachers Local 2, to devote more time to his job as national president of the AFT.

See also MANUFACTURING INDUSTRIES.

G.B.H.

LAOS. Prince Souphanouvong, who became president of Laos with the abolition of the monarchy in 1975, resigned the largely ceremonial post in October 1986, citing ill health. He was temporarily replaced by Deputy Prime Minister Phoumi Vongvichit.

A major problem facing the government of Prime Minister Kaysone Phomvihan was the tense relationship with neighboring Thailand, as Lao refugees continued to cross the Mekong River into that country. According to the UN High Commissioner for Refugees, by mid-1986, more than 90,000 Lao refugees were in Thai camps in the river valley. Late in the year, Thailand indicated plans to phase out all refugee camps.

Security continued to be disturbed by guerrillas, who attacked remote military posts, ambushed vehicles, blew up bridges, and disrupted development projects. Some of the rebels were based in or near refugee camps in Thailand; others may have come from China.

Laos remained in Vietnam's orbit; according to Western sources, there were about 50,000 Vietnamese troops and 6,000 Vietnamese advisers in the country. Signs of a thaw in the relationship between Laos and China appeared when Prime Minister Phomvihan received a favorable response from Peking to his call for stronger ties.

Early in the year, a U.S. congressional delegation went to Vientiane to discuss the 556 Americans still listed as missing in action in Laos during the Vietnam war. Laos continued to insist there were no living U.S. servicemen there, and the talks produced no new information. In February a joint U.S.-Laotian excavation of a Vietnam-era crash site led to the recovery of human remains; the remains of four U.S. servicemen were later identified.

See STATISTICS OF THE WORLD.   J.J.Z.

LEBANON

LEBANON. Lebanon's 11th year of civil war, in 1986, was marked by the growing influence of extremist elements, by the return of Palestinian guerrillas, and, in general, by persistent chaos and political paralysis.

Syrian Peace Plan Fails. In January intra-Christian strife brought about the collapse of a Syrian-brokered peace plan that had been signed in late December. Christians opposed to what they saw as a sellout of Lebanon's sovereignty to Syria, including President Amin Gemayel and Samir Geagea, a hard-line militant, launched a revolt against Elie Hobeika, leader of the Lebanese Forces and the only Christian who had signed the pact. Hobeika was routed and fled for a time to Damascus.

War in South Lebanon. In February a radical group known as the Islamic Resistance, which included members of the radical Shiite organization Hezbollah (Party of God) and Palestinian guerrillas loyal to the mainstream Palestine Liberation Organization headed by Yasir Arafat, stepped up operations against Israel and its local ally, the predominantly Christian "South

Lebanon Army" (SLA), in the "security zone" maintained by Israel in Lebanese territory adjacent to the international frontier. In one action Islamic Resistance managed to capture two Israeli soldiers; the Israelis, in retaliation, made a large sweep through several Shiite villages, giving rise to bitterness among the Lebanese.

During the summer, Hezbollah increased its attacks, firing rockets into Israel proper and at the SLA. Hezbollah was also believed responsible for attacks against the United Nations Interim Force in Lebanon in September that left 5 soldiers dead and 35 wounded.

War Against Westerners. Clandestine militant groups, foremost among them the pro-Iranian Islamic Jihad (Holy War), continued efforts to rid the country of Western influence. In March, Michel Seurat, a Frenchman abducted in 1985, was reportedly slain by his captors, though no body was found. In April, Lebanese authorities recovered the bodies of Peter Kilburn, an American kidnapped in 1985, and two British teachers at the American University of Beirut. They

A massive car bomb exploded in a Christian suburb of Beirut on July 28, killing 33 people, injuring more than 100 others, and initiating a series of retaliatory car bombs on both Christian and Muslim sides of the divided city.

had been killed, the abductors said, in reprisal for that month's U.S. air raid on Libya, which was mounted in part from U.S. bases in Britain. Also in April, a British television journalist was kidnapped. The next month, a Lebanese Christian professor at American University was seized, and on July 19, militants ambushed a bus carrying university doctors to East Beirut, killing four of the physicians.

A few months later, in September, two more Americans were kidnapped—Frank Reed, the director of a school, and Joseph James Cicippio, the comptroller at American University, while the French military attaché was murdered in Beirut. Around the same time, it was revealed that a Frenchman named Marcel Coudari was being held. In October an American writer, Edward Austin Tracy, was abducted.

There were a few encouraging developments, in some cases apparently influenced by controversial secret negotiations involving the sale of U.S. arms to Iran. (See also UNITED STATES OF AMERICA.) One American captive, Father Lawrence Jenco, was released on July 26 by Islamic Jihad. Another U.S. captive, David Jacobsen, director of the American University Hospital, was freed by Islamic Jihad on November 2. However, the group still held Thomas Sutherland, of American University, and journalist Terry Anderson, as well as three Frenchmen. Islamic Jihad claimed to have executed U.S. embassy officer William Buckley in 1985, though his body was never found.

In June, two members of a four-person French television crew abducted earlier in the year were freed by a group called the Revolutionary Justice Organization. A third member was released just before Christmas. In November, Coudari and another French hostage were freed, after being released by the same group to Syrian authorities. The group still reportedly held two American hostages and the remaining member of the French TV crew.

In late December an underground Shiite Muslim group known as the Organization of the Oppressed on Earth claimed it had killed three Lebanese Jewish hostages kidnapped in West Beirut over the past two years. No bodies were found. The same group had claimed responsibility for killing five other Jews in Beirut.

After 18 months in captivity, Father Lawrence Jenco, who had served as the head of Catholic Relief Services in Lebanon, was freed by the pro-Iranian Islamic Jihad organization; here he is shown in Wiesbaden, West Germany.

Return of Palestinian Guerrillas. Pro-Arafat Palestinian fighters made a gradual reappearance in Lebanon, taking advantage of the partial vacuum left by Israel's troop withdrawal from southern Lebanon. By September the Palestinians were estimated to number around 8,000. The resurgence of the increasingly formidable PLO alarmed both the Syrians and the Syrian-supported Amal (the main Shiite Muslim organization). Clashes between Shiites and the Palestinians occurred throughout the year. Especially fierce battles began breaking out in early autumn, at refugee camps in the Beirut area and in southern Lebanon, among other areas, claiming close to 600 lives by December. By this time, the Palestinians had established a 6-square-mile "liberated zone" outside Sidon. Israel mounted periodic air strikes against reemergent Palestinian positions; in one such attack in November, near Sidon, an Israeli jet was shot down and one of its pilots captured. Meanwhile, in late December, Muslim fundamentalists hostile to Syria were overpowered by Syrian tanks and armored cars, in a heavy outbreak of fighting in Tripoli.

Security Plan and Other Fighting. In early July, Syria announced a new security plan for West Beirut. Though President Gemayel rejected the legality of the plan, West Beirut enjoyed a brief respite from violence. Then, on July 28, a huge car bomb exploded in a Christian suburb of East Beirut, killing 33 people. In response the next day, another massive car bomb exploded, this one in West Beirut, killing 25. Five more bombs went off within two weeks, leaving over 40 more noncombatants dead.

September saw a resurgence of intra-Christian fighting and a reportedly Syrian-backed attempt by Elie Hobeika to wrest control of East Beirut and pressure Gemayel to step down. Hobeika's forces were repulsed in bloody street fighting, and 60 of his followers were found slain in Christian areas in East Beirut, believed to be victims of a Geagea-inspired purge.

Economic Collapse. The decline of the Lebanese economy continued, as evidenced by the falling value of the Lebanese pound. As inflation soared and industrial and agricultural production plummeted, perhaps the only bright spot was that the armed militias apparently had less money at their disposal.

See STATISTICS OF THE WORLD.   M.C.H.

LESOTHO. *See* STATISTICS OF THE WORLD.

LIBERIA. *See* STATISTICS OF THE WORLD.

LIBRARIES. Funding for collections, staff, and services continued to be a primary concern for U.S. libraries in 1986, as the impact of federal efforts at deficit reduction began to be felt.

Legislation and Funding. Legislation favorable to libraries was identified as the top priority in the 1985 American Library Association (ALA) Member Opinion Survey, and in 1986 librarians sought to ensure continued funding from federal, state, and local sources. Librarians and their supporters also worked to increase financial assistance through foundation grants, fund-raising campaigns, and special programs designed to heighten community support.

A reduction in congressional appropriations and a further cut mandated under the Gramm-Rudman-Hollings "balanced-budget" act reduced the Library of Congress budget for fiscal 1986 by $18.3 million, and in March the library implemented cuts in acquisitions, cataloging, preservation, and hours of service. The shortened hours sparked a protest lasting three nights by some 100 readers, who refused to leave the main reading room when the library closed. The protesters were later tried and convicted of unlawful entry. The former hours were restored in July.

The Las Vegas Public Library raised $67,000 in its fourth annual Bucks for Books direct mail campaign, bringing the four-year total to $200,000. Other efforts for municipal support had uneven success. In Boston libraries won a 30 percent increase in operating funds and a $22 million capital budget to restore the city's historic central library. As declining oil prices created a critical shortage of state and local tax revenue, staff salaries were cut and branch libraries closed in Dallas and Houston.

Library of Congress. Daniel J. Boorstin, the Librarian of Congress for almost 12 years, announced in December that he would resign his post in June 1987, to devote more time to writing. As a departing gift, he and his wife indicated they would donate $100,000 to the Library of Congress to establish a Daniel J. and Ruth F. Boorstin Publication Fund.

Personnel. An ALA survey reported that among public, academic, and school libraries, the average starting salary paid to beginners with a master's degree in library science was $18,263. The job market for librarians continued to open up; there were shortages of qualified personnel especially in cataloging and children's and young adult services. Public employee strikes affected library and other services in many U.S. cities.

Pornography Report. The report of the Attorney General's Commission on Pornography, issued in July, sparked controversy among libraries, publishers, the press, and other groups. Its assertion that exposure to pornography is related to the level of sexual violence and sexual coercion in society differed from the conclusion of a 1970 presidential commission on pornography, and was criticized by some as unsupported by scientific evidence.

Technology. Many libraries joined the growing trend toward computer-based catalogs in place of the card catalog. The technology that most dazzled librarians with its potential for storage and retrieval of huge quantities of information was the CD-ROM (compact disk-read only memory). CD-ROM publications on the market include massive databases of catalog records for books and periodicals, indexes to business and news journals, an encyclopedia, and interactive book ordering systems.

Fires and Floods. In one of the largest library fires in history, the Los Angeles Public Library burned for seven hours in April, causing about $20 million in damage to its collection. Many of the 600,000 water-damaged books were saved by freeze-drying. Another fire broke out in September in the same library, causing $2 million in damage and destroying 25,000 volumes. Both fires were believed to have been caused by arson.

On July 11 a broken water main exposed during construction of an annex to the Chicago Historical Society flooded the building's basement, soaking priceless newspapers, documents, and paintings. Salvage efforts were believed to have preserved 95 percent of the damaged items.

Celebrations. A year of celebrations began in 1986, commemorating the January 1887 opening of the first U.S. library school, by Melvil

Donning top hat and bow tie, a normally staid guardian of the New York Public Library (inset) went formal in May for a gala celebration of the Library's 75th anniversary. Welcoming celebrity guests— some of them straight from the pages of literature—to the fund-raising party in the library's marble halls were library president Vartan Gregorian and his wife, shown below with Hester Prynne, Merlin, and Cleopatra.

In the wake of the U.S. bombing raid on Libya, in April, Colonel Muammar al-Qaddafi's wife, Safia, flanked by two of her sons, held a press conference in which she defended her husband and railed angrily against the United States. She gave no explanation for her crutches.

Dewey at Columbia University. The school moved in 1889 to the New York State Library at Albany. The New York Public Library, while continuing with its $77 million renovation project and launching a new $300 million fund-raising campaign, celebrated its 75th birthday.   J.M.L.

LIBYA. On more than one occasion Libya and the United States engaged in armed hostilities in 1986. The decline in the price of oil added to Libya's problems.

Americans Ordered Out. On January 7, President Ronald Reagan called Libya "a threat to the national security and foreign policy of the United States." Citing "irrefutable evidence" of Libya's involvement in Palestinian guerrilla

attacks at the Rome and Vienna airports on December 27, 1985, that left 20 people dead and more than 100 wounded, he ordered the 1,000 to 1,500 Americans still in Libya to leave and announced plans to cut virtually all economic ties with the country. However, U.S. oil companies, which accounted for virtually all U.S. economic interests in Libya, were given an extension until June 30.

Gulf of Sidra Showdown. On January 24 the U.S. Navy began a week-long exercise off the Libyan coast, prompting Libyan leader Muammar al-Qaddafi (see *biography in* PEOPLE IN THE NEWS) to accuse the United States of "aggressive provocation." The Libyan leader boarded a patrol boat the following day and sailed into the Gulf of Sidra to "confront" the U.S. Sixth Fleet if it crossed what he described as the "line of death" marking Libya's self-proclaimed internal waters. Qaddafi claimed all°of the gulf south of parallel 32.5, an area that in places is more than 100 miles wide. Most nations claim territorial waters no more than 12 miles wide.

No U.S.-Libyan confrontation took place in January, but on March 23 a 30-ship U.S. Navy task force led by three aircraft carriers began new maneuvers in the Mediterranean Sea off Libya. The next day, Libya fired several missiles after American planes and vessels entered the Gulf of Sidra. Two U.S. Navy planes and a cruiser then attacked three Libyan naval vessels and a missile site. A Libyan ship and the missile site were struck again on March 25. U.S. officials said at least two Libyan vessels had been sunk.

Raid on Libya. Four Americans were killed on April 2 when a bomb exploded on a TWA airliner flying from Rome to Athens. Qaddafi said he was "completely against any action like this," but the Reagan administration would not rule out Libyan involvement. On April 5 a U.S. serviceman and a Turkish woman were killed and over 200 people, including 60 Americans, were wounded when a bomb exploded in a West Berlin discotheque. (One of the wounded Americans later died.) The United States accused Libya of complicity. It reportedly had intercepted incriminating communications between the Libyan mission in East Berlin and Libya, which denied involvement.

On April 15, 18 U.S. F-111 fighter-bombers based in Britain struck three targets around Tripoli: a barracks, also the site of Qaddafi's headquarters and home; a port, reportedly a training area for terrorists; and the military side of the city's major airport. Navy warplanes from two carriers bombed Benghazi, hitting a military airfield and a barracks. Some bombs fell on a residential area of Tripoli. Libya said that Qaddafi's 15-month-old adopted daughter was killed and that two of his sons were wounded in the attack. The government reported that 37 people had been killed and 93 injured. One U.S. F-111 was lost, apparently shot down by antiaircraft fire, and its two crewmen were presumed killed.

Aftermath. Several terrorist incidents followed. On April 21, European Community foreign ministers agreed to reduce the number of Libyan diplomats in their countries; in the next three weeks almost 300 Libyans, mostly students, were expelled from Western Europe, and many Europeans were deported from Libya in response. Leaders of the seven largest industrial democracies, meeting in Tokyo in May, singled out Libya as a major source of terrorism but rejected imposing sanctions.

In the aftermath of the raid, there was speculation that dissident officers might attempt to overthrow Qaddafi. Severe shortages and mounting economic problems were reported. Qaddafi was said to have been shaken by the raid and severely critical of the performance of the armed forces. When he failed to make a major announced appearance, at a rally on June 11, and delivered a speech on television instead, speculation about his physical and psychological health mounted. By late summer, however, he appeared firmly in control. On September 1 he reviewed a military parade marking the 17th anniversary of the coup that brought him to power.

The credibility of reports about Qaddafi's precarious position was called into question after the Washington *Post* reported on October 2 that the Reagan administration, in a highly controversial action, deceived the press and public, leaking false information designed to persuade Qaddafi that another U.S. attack was imminent and that he was about to be overthrown by domestic opponents.

Oil Slump. A global oversupply of crude oil led to a plunge in oil prices and created problems in oil-producing countries, including Libya. When the Organization of Petroleum Exporting Countries met in Tripoli in February, Libya led an unsuccessful campaign for lower production quotas in order to force up prices. In August, OPEC members did agree to establish reduced country-by-country production quotas—and prices did rise. Ironically, OPEC monitors discovered that Libya was among three countries cheating on their quotas; Libya's quota was raised slightly for November and December. It was reduced for the first half of 1987, under a December OPEC agreement.

Libya in Chad. On December 20, thousands of Libyan troops, backed by tanks and aircraft, launched a major attack in northern Chad to crush resistance there by anti-Libyan forces. The region had been occupied by Libya and Libyan-backed rebels, but most of the rebels switched support in October to the Chadian government and drove out the Libyans from many northern towns. Their leader, former Chadian President Goukouni Oueddei, who was then in Libya, was shot and wounded in a fight with Libyan supporters and was put under virtual house arrest.

Breach With Morocco. In August, Morocco canceled its 1984 treaty of unity with Libya. The move followed Libyan condemnation of a meeting between Morocco's King Hassan and Israeli Prime Minister Shimon Peres.

See STATISTICS OF THE WORLD.   A.D.

LIECHTENSTEIN. *See* STATISTICS OF THE WORLD.

LIFE SCIENCES. Genetic engineering research made headlines in 1986. Other reported advances included new discoveries about rain forest ecology, lake algae, zooplankton, and the behavior of herons.

BIOLOGY

Biotechnologists made great strides during the year developing new products with important agricultural and medical uses, but the field-testing of genetic engineering products encountered legal obstacles.

Biotechnology. *Environmental Release.* The first release of a genetically engineered microorganism into the environment occurred in October 1985 but was not revealed publicly until the following April. A flock of piglets was injected with a genetically engineered vaccine designed to combat pseudorabies, a viral disease that costs the U.S. pork industry as much as $60 million per year. The vaccine, developed by a Baylor University virologist, was licensed to the Biologics Corporation of Omaha, Neb., which received approval to market it from the U.S. Department of Agriculture in January. Because of protest the USDA briefly suspended Biologic's license, but the agency restored it after concluding that no rules had been violated in the licensing procedure. Antibiotechnology activist Jeremy Rifkin filed suit in an attempt to prevent marketing of the vaccine, but it remained commercially available late in the year.

Activists also challenged two proposed tests of an engineered bacterium designed to retard frost formation. Steven Lindow of the University of California at Berkeley and Advanced Genetic Sciences, Inc. (AGS) of Oakland, Calif., had both developed strains of the bacterium *Pseudomonas syringae* which are unable to produce a protein that catalyzes ice formation at temperatures near freezing. The researchers believed spraying this "ice-minus" bacteria on plants should prevent the growth of the normal bacteria, which do catalyze frost formation, and thereby should minimize frost damage to crops.

After three years of delays caused by litigation, the Environmental Protection Agency (EPA) gave Lindow permission in May to test the ice-minus bacteria on potato plants at the University of California's experimental farm in Tulelake. But the test was blocked by new lawsuits spearheaded by Rifkin. The university then agreed to assess potential environmental effects before allowing Lindow to proceed.

The EPA also authorized AGS to test the ice-minus bacteria, but revoked its permission temporarily and fined AGS $13,000 on learning that AGS scientists had already injected the engineered bacteria into trees on the roof of the company's headquarters. Rules require that such tests be conducted in a greenhouse. In August the agency reinstated the field test permit.

Crop Engineering. U.S. scientists made progress with an approach that could help revolutionize farming through a new method of weed killing. Developing chemical weed killers that eliminate weeds but not crop plants is very expensive. A better approach is to take an effective herbicide and engineer resistance to it in the crop plant; spraying would then eliminate all competing weeds cheaply, without damaging the crop.

Scientists from the Monsanto Company of St. Louis developed a technique to engineer resistance to Monsanto's herbicide glyphosate (sold under the name Roundup), a commonly used weed killer. The scientists used cultured petunia cells to isolate a resistant strain, then identified and cloned the gene giving that resistance. They inserted the gene sequence back into petunia cells; the grown plants were then resistant to glyphosate. Meanwhile, researchers at Agracetus of Middleton, Wis., planted in an open field 200 seedlings genetically modified to make them resistant to infection by a certain bacterium. Later, scientists with the Ciba-Geigy Corporation planted tobacco plants in North Carolina that were genetically modified to be resistant to the herbicide atrazine.

In another area of experiment, Rohm & Haas Company of Philadelphia began in October to field-test plants that had been genetically altered to be toxic to insects.

In April a team of biologists headed by Roger Beachey of Washington University in St. Louis announced that they had incorporated a gene from the destructive tobacco mosaic virus into plant cells and had then grown plants with the protein for which the added gene had been coded. The new protein protected the tobacco plants from infection by the virus. Later in the year, scientists at the University of California in San Diego reported the successful genetic alteration of tobacco plants so that they emitted light on orders from a gene transplanted from fireflies. The ability to make cells light up when a certain gene is activated was expected to be a valuable aid in genetic research.

Medical Applications. The year saw government approval of new genetically engineered products designed for medical uses. These included alpha-interferon, used to battle a rare leukemia and under study as a potential weapon against AIDS; a safer hepatitis B vaccine (*see also* HEALTH AND MEDICINE); and an antibody

Lawsuits by activist Jeremy Rifkin (inset) created difficulties for the biotechnology industry. One experiment halted by his efforts was a test by University of California scientists of a new ice-minus bacteria for frost-resistant crops.

against tissue rejection, for use in kidney transplant patients. Other products were being studied in humans, including an antitumor protein, known as tumor necrosis factor (TNF), and a new malaria vaccine.

For the first time, scientists cured a genetic defect in animals by inserting a new gene into the animal's DNA. Columbia University researchers reported that they had cured a hereditary defect in the synthesis of a crucial blood protein in mice; the defect was similar to a form of human anemia known as beta-thalassemia. They inserted a human gene coding for the missing protein into mouse reproductive cells. Many of the recipient mice and their descendants were then able to produce the protein at the proper time and place—in fetal and adult red blood cells, but not in embryonic red blood cells.

A different use of biotechnology was de-scribed in July by a group of French and Belgian researchers. Rabies is still spreading in Europe and North America and is almost always fatal to humans who are not treated by the time symptoms develop. In Europe the natural reservoir of the disease is the fox, and elimination of rabies in foxes could halt the spread and prevent transmission to dogs and people. A new vaccine developed by the researchers was based on vaccinia, a harmless virus used successfully to protect humans from smallpox. A gene coding for only the protein coat of the rabies virus was added to the vaccinia virus genes. Although the modified vaccinia was unable to cause rabies, it was able to give effective protection against the disease when injected into foxes or fed to them.

Meanwhile, some research scientists conducted field trials of gene-altered vaccines outside the United States, to avoid the complex approval process for genetic engineering products. Wistar Institute of Philadelphia reported participation in tests on cows in Argentina involving a genetically altered living rabies vaccine, without the knowledge or approval of the Argentine or U.S. government. Oregon State University researchers tested a genetically engineered viral vaccine on farm animals in New Zealand, in this case with permission of the New Zealand government.

Archaeopteryx Vindicated. So far several fossils of *Archaeopteryx lithographica*, the earliest known species of fossil bird, have been found in the limestone formations of Solnhofen in Bavaria. *Archaeopteryx* is one of the most familiar examples of a fossil spanning the evolutionary gap between two modern groups— in this case, reptiles and birds. The scientific community reacted with consternation when it was alleged in 1985 that the best-known specimen, found in 1861, was a fake. It was contended that the feather impressions on the slab containing the fossil were made by those of a modern bird pressed into a thin layer of an artificial cement around the skeleton of a small dinosaur. In May 1986 the journal *Science* carried a detailed defense of the *Archaeopteryx* fossil, written by Alan Charig and associates at the British Museum, where the accused specimen was housed. Charig and his colleagues made a detailed study of the main limestone slab and its counterslab, which provides the mirror image of the fossil that resulted when the original block containing the fossil was split. Even the most minute details corresponded perfectly on both surfaces, indicating to them that the fossil could not have been faked. *Archaeopteryx*, reinstated, remains a superb evolutionary link between advanced dinosaurs and early birds.

Vanishing Species. Calling for worldwide action to slow the accelerating mass extinction of animal and plant species, scientists at a September conference sponsored by the National Academy of Sciences and the Smithsonian Institution warned that habitat destruction, toxic substances, and climatic changes caused by human activity were dangerously reducing earth's biological diversity. Edward O. Wilson, of Harvard University, observed that, while over 1.6 million organisms of various kinds had been classified by science, an estimated 5 million to 30 million had not yet been described. Meanwhile, he estimated, 10,000 or more species were vanishing each year. Biologist Paul Ehrlich, of Stanford University, noted that disappearing species might provide important food sources or cures for cancer and other diseases and that their disappearance might even disrupt the entire ecological system upon which human life depends.

S.M.H. & T.H.M.

BOTANY

Scientists cast fresh light on the richly diverse ecology of the Peruvian Amazon, as well as on some food-manufacturing and reproductive patterns of organisms.

River Erosion and Rain Forest Ecology. The lowland rain forests of the Peruvian Amazon are dense, rich, and very diverse, with countless different plant and animal species growing among many species of tall forest trees. The fossil record suggests the community as a whole may be of great geological age. Scientists have traditionally considered the Amazon forest to be relatively stable, with regrowth and regeneration taking place only in gaps left where a giant dying tree has fallen. But if this is the case, it is difficult to explain the staggering diversity. If the habitat is very stable, why do some species not come to dominate the community, reducing the diversity?

A team from the University of Turku, Finland, headed by Jukka Salo and working with Phyllis D. Coley of the University of Utah, has pointed out a simple explanation. The tributaries of the upper Amazon run in giant meanders over the floodplain. Over the years they continually erode one bank and deposit new sediment on the other, so that the meanders slowly migrate until the rivers cut off as oxbow lakes. The forests growing along the river banks are therefore a patchwork or mosaic of different ages; this patchwork pattern of different communities must contribute substantially to maintaining a high diversity of species. In addition, since each patch is separated from others of the same community type, the isolated small populations of organisms within each patch are in a favorable position to evolve into new species. The upper Amazon must therefore be in a state of dynamic stability, changing fast at the local level within certain constant overall patterns. This new understanding could alter the ways in which conservation of this unique habitat is approached.

Lake Algae Break the Rules. The most important difference between green plants and animals is that the plants are autotrophic—making their own food from sunlight, water, and simple chemicals—while animals depend on plants or other animals for food. Until 1986, the known exceptions, such as insectivorous plants, were few and unimportant, but in a paper published in January, David Bird and Jacob Kalff of McGill University revealed that in some abundant lake algae, animal-like nutrition can be very important.

Tests were carried out using radioactively labeled bacteria and bacteria-sized latex beads. Four species of the abundant lake algae *Dinobryon* were found to consume bacteria at a rapid rate (as measured by their consumption of the beads). Each algal cell could eat three bacteria every five minutes, equivalent to almost 30 percent of its own weight in bacteria each day. The scientists calculated that *Dinobryon* could obtain half its daily food requirements from bacteria. They also noted that the algae removed more bacteria than all the animal plankton organisms together.

Heat Shock Turns on Alga. *Volvox*, a common pond alga that forms small spherical colonies composed of large numbers of similar cells, usually reproduces asexually during most of the year, but it can also reproduce sexually in response to a potent hormone-like inducer chemical normally released only by mature male colonies. In research published in January, David and Marilyn Kirk, of Washington University in St. Louis, disclosed that the reproduction of *Volvox* is well-geared to its ecology. They found that a two-hour heat shock at up to 45°C caused normally asexual males and females to produce the sexual inducer immediately, resulting in a subsequent sexual generation. High temperatures must be common in the small freshwater ponds or puddles in which *Volvox* thrives, especially in late summer, when ponds start to dry up in strong sunlight. The ability to switch rapidly to sexual reproduction at such times may be critical to the survival of the species, because only the

sexually produced zygospores have the ability to withstand extremes of heat, cold, and desiccation found in late summer and through the winter. In spring, when ponds are full and conditions ideal for growth, sexual reproduction is not needed, and the faster asexual method dominates until conditions begin to deteriorate again.   S.M.H.

ZOOLOGY

In 1986 scientists reported the discovery of a new animal group, gained insight into zooplankton feeding patterns, and studied an ingenious Japanese heron that fashions its own fishing bait. An "extinct" woodpecker reappeared.

Zooplankton Ecology. Zooplankton, the animal component of plankton, form a vital link in aquatic food chains between microscopic photosynthesizing algae and the fish we eat. Although these tiny animals are very important and interesting, they are difficult to study, and much of their ecology remains mysterious. Many zooplankton engage in vertical migration: with bodies as short as a tiny fraction of an inch, they swim daily through hundreds of feet of water, feeding in rich, warmer surface waters at night, and diving to the much less productive depths by day. Why do they expend so much energy in, presumably, restricting the efficiency of their feeding?

New studies in a group of mountain lakes in

Return of "Jaws"

A true-life adventure story was played out off the coast of Montauk, N.Y., in August, when fishermen brought in a shark they called "Big Guy"—at 3,427 pounds the largest fish ever caught with rod and reel. The mighty great white shark was landed by charter-boat captain Donald Braddick, with the help of Long Island shark hunter Frank Mundus, reportedly the model for Quint in the novel and movie *Jaws*. Mundus and Braddick had spotted "Big Guy" among a group of sharks feeding on a dead whale. It took over four hours to lure the shark away from his feast, and once he bit the hook, baited with whiting and butterfish, it took another two hours to land him.

For the first time since the 1970's, Cuban and American ornithologists have sighted at least one male and one female ivory-billed woodpecker in a Cuban forest. Experts remain uncertain whether the nearly extinct birds can reestablish themselves in Cuba, and debate the woodpeckers' introduction to the swamp forests of southeastern United States.

Poland have shown that vertical migration is directly related to the avoidance of predators that hunt by sight. Maciej Gliwicz of the University of Warsaw studied populations of the tiny copepod crustacean *Cyclops abysso-* *rum* in alpine lakes left without predatory fish populations after the last glaciation. Some of these lakes have remained without fish, others were naturally colonized millennia ago, and still others are known to have been artificially stocked within the past three centuries. Gliwicz found that *Cyclops* populations in fish-free lakes did not migrate, but those in lakes with fish showed strong vertical migration patterns. Significantly, the phenomenon was best developed in lakes with the longest established fish populations, suggesting that copepod migration is a response to predation and that it evolves through natural selection over many generations.

Sea Daisies. Although many animal species remain to be described, it is very unusual for a major new animal group to be discovered. Alan Baker and Helen Clark of the National Museum of New Zealand and Francis Rowe of the Australian Museum were fortunate to find nine tiny specimens of a previously unknown class of animals in pieces of driftwood sunk in deep waters off New Zealand. The "sea daisies," formally named *Xyloplax medusiformis* by their discoverers, look rather like small jellyfish but lack a mouth or gut. They probably absorb dissolved food through their thin undersurface, possibly aided by bacteria digesting the decaying wood of their only known habitat. The creatures have calcite skeletons, fivefold symmetry, and special appendages marking them as echinoderms, but they cannot be classified with the known starfish, sea urchins, or other echinoderms and have been placed in a class of their own, the Concentricycloidea.

Wasp Defender Larvae. The tiny parasitic wasp *Copidosomopsis tanytmemus* lays its eggs inside eggs of the flour moth. Each wasp egg divides to form many larvae, which eat the tissue of the moth larva as it grows. There are many such wasp parasites; if two species parasitize the same egg, they will compete and may die. Y. P. Cruz at the University of California at Berkeley discovered an extraordinary adaptation that gives *Copidosomopsis* a major competitive advantage. As the parasite wasp's egg divides and forms larvae, some develop precociously and abnormally. Their mouths, guts, and nervous systems develop typically, but other organs do not, and the precocious larvae all die before reaching maturity. This bizarre situation was explained when Cruz allowed moths to be parasitized by other species in competition with *Copidosomopsis*. In almost all cases the precocious larvae destroyed the competitors. Apparently the precocious larvae are a competitive adaptation to ensure survival of *Copidosomopsis*. But the adaptation means that the precocious larvae are doomed and will not reproduce. How could the genes transmitting the adaptation be passed on to later generations? Being produced from one egg, they are genetically identical to their slower-growing siblings that survive to adulthood. Their sacrifice helps to preserve their genes just as well as if they themselves survived to reproduce.

Tool-using Heron. Herons, which are among the most primitive of modern birds, sometimes throw bait items like worms, bits of bread, and insects on to the water to attract fish to catch. Hiroyoshi Higuchi of the University of Tokyo found that Japanese green-backed herons, as they grow older, improve their ability to catch fish with bait, in part by learning to use appropriately sized bait items. To his surprise, Higuchi found that some adult herons would select long twigs, then deliberately break off short lengths to form successful lures. Construction of tools by birds is very unusual; the only previously known example is a Galápagos finch that breaks off cactus spines to help it extract grubs from wood.

"Extinct" Woodpecker. A handsome bird that had been thought extinct emerged for a reappearance during the year. In March and April, U.S. and Cuban scientists, including Lester L. Short of the American Museum of Natural History, made definite sightings of at least two ivory-billed woodpeckers (an adult male and an adult female) in the forests of Cuba's Guantánamo Province. Once common in the southeastern United States, ivorybills (*Campephilus principalis*) disappeared as their forest habitat dwindled. The last confirmed U.S. sighting was in 1941 and the last Cuban one in the 1970's.   S.M.H.

This rare Himalayan snow leopard is one of 17 housed in a special habitat at New York City's Bronx Zoo. The habitat features caves, meadows, and ravines, plus an artificial heated rock. Fewer than 1,000 snow leopards remain in the wild.

LITERATURE

LITERATURE. Among the major literary developments of 1986 were those that follow.

AMERICAN

Big was better than ever in American publishing, with several mammoth novels—by Tom Clancy, Stephen King, and others—making their way up the best-seller lists. Ernest Hemingway and critic Edmund Wilson reappeared in important posthumous works. A handful of veteran writers, such as Donald Barthelme, Peter De Vries, and John Updike, proved as expert as ever.

Fiction. Upon his death, Hemingway left a number of incomplete manuscripts, but the one that seems to have mattered most to him was a novel about a ménage à trois in southern France, rendered in the understated, softly declarative sentences that were a trademark of his style. *The Garden of Eden,* finally published in 1986, was a work of great interest and became a best-seller.

Robert Stone's new novel, *Children of Light,* took on Hollywood with its depiction of freaked-out, revved-up characters on the set of a major film. Newspaperman Jimmy Breslin produced an expert slice-of-life portrait of the working class in the New York City borough of Queens in his novel *Table Money.* George V. Higgins, the man with the golden ear for the lingo of the Boston Irish, checked in with a complex novel called *Impostors.* In a similar vein, John D. MacDonald's *Barrier Island* portrayed a crooked real-estate deal in Florida.

Perfectly reproduced bureaucratese made Christopher Buckley's satiric novel *The White House Mess* a special success. Donald Barthelme's novel *Paradise* offered both humor and pathos in its story of a 53-year-old architect who, having left his wife and job, lives in an apartment with three women who had given away all their money to fight hunger in Africa. Peter de Vries's *Peckham's Marbles* dealt with the impossible love of a highbrow novelist for the author of steamy historical romances. In *Bigfoot Dreams,* Francine Prose imagined the life of a writer for a sleazy tabloid who finds that one of her fantastic stories comes true. Paul Rudnick's *Social Disease* took on the New York club scene.

Pat Conroy's *The Prince of Tides,* which

America's Poet Laureate

The only writer to have won Pulitzer Prizes for both poetry and fiction, Robert Penn Warren, 81, has added another honor to his long list of achievements—in February 1986 he was named the first poet laureate of the United States, a post established by Congress in 1985.

The South, where Warren was born and educated—though he also studied at Yale and at Oxford as a Rhodes scholar—has always influenced Warren's literary output. Best known of his work is the Pulitzer Prize-winning *All the King's Men* (1946), a novel about a ruthless demagogue, inspired by Louisiana politician Huey Long. Warren considers himself primarily a poet and has twice been awarded the Pulitzer Prize for poetry; his work is richly colored by American history and the American scene. In 1981, he was among the first to receive the MacArthur Foundation's "genius" award, a generous five-year stipend given to "exceptionally talented individuals" to encourage them to pursue their creative work.

Robert Penn Warren

In The Golden Gate, *Vikram Seth (above) gives unusual drama to the ordinary lives of San Francisco yuppies by setting their lives to verse. In his modern-day epic some stanzas reach lofty heights of emotion and religious speculation, but others place the book firmly in California, with computerese and the latest pop-culture slang.*

immediately hit the best-seller list, chronicled the complexities of a Southern clan, while Richard Yates's *Cold Spring Harbor* examined the pressures on a young family during World War II. Louise Erdrich confirmed her narrative expertise with *The Beet Queen,* a moving, madcap story of two unconventional North Dakota families, one white, one Indian.

Peter Taylor's *A Summoning to Memphis* demonstrated his talent for evocative description and his fascination with Southern social strata, as it traced the impact on a family of a move from Nashville to Memphis. Another Southerner, Reynolds Price, displayed his talents in the story of *Kate Vaiden,* a kind of Dixie-style *Moll Flanders.* Mightily praised T. R. Pearson continued his tales of small-town life in *Off for the Sweet Hereafter,* as did Ellen Gilchrist in her latest collection, *Drunk With Love.* Scott Spencer's *Waking the Dead* portrayed an ambitious young politico haunted by his dead wife. National Book Award laureate

Thomas Williams's *The Moon Pinnace* was a classic love story of separation and reunification.

John Updike's contribution was *Roger's Version,* which focuses on the rivalry and erotic entanglements of a hypocritical professor of theology and a computer wizard hoping to prove the existence of God through programming. Another master of word music is Steven Millhauser, who brought out two books: *In the Penny Arcade,* a collection of stories ranging in subject from automatons to snowmen, and *From the Realm of Morpheus,* a novel offering a gallery of mermaids, giants, and paintings that come alive. Gene Wolfe in *Soldier of the Mist* set down the adventures of Latro, a fighting man in archaic Greece.

Specialties. Stephen King's best-seller *It* focused on a group of misfits who must confront a nameless horror, first as children, later as adults. Some critics found the book bloated, despite its great power and vivid writing. Tom

LITERATURE

Clancy's new thriller *Red Storm Rising* described the moves and countermoves that occur as the Soviet Union and the West escalate toward World War III—and the war that follows.

Another genre that has done well of late is the western. Among the year's best, Pete Dexter's *Deadwood*—an account of Wild Bill Hickok and friends—earned plaudits from reviewers far and wide. Edward Hoagland offered *Seven Rivers West,* the adventures of a group of men and women out West at the turn of the century.

The crime wave continued with Ed McBain's thriller about lawyer Matthew Hope, the much-admired *Cinderella.* Joe Gores returned with *Come Morning,* the crisply told story of a professional thief. Charles Willeford confirmed his mastery of the sleazy Florida scene in *New Hope for the Dead.*

In science fiction, William Gibson brought out a novel, *Count Zero,* and a short-story collection, *Burning Chrome.* Other outstanding collections of science-fiction stories included Michael Bishop's *Close Encounters With the Deity,* Kim Stanley Robinson's *The Planet on the Table, In Alien Flesh* by Gregory Benford, *Howard Who?* by Howard Waldrop, and Robert Silverberg's *Beyond the Safe Zone.*

Poetry. A novel-length poem became one of the most talked-about books of the year; Vikram Seth's *The Golden Gate,* chronicled the life, loves, ambitions, and religious crises of a group of San Francisco yuppies. Charles Simic, Stanley Kunitz, Hayden Carruth, and Robert Bly all gathered some of their best work. Short-story writer Raymond Carver brought out a collection of poems, *Ultramarine,* and Richard Wilbur produced his version of Racine's *Phaedra.*

In February, prolific poet, novelist, and critic Robert Penn Warren was named the first poet laureate of the United States. Warren had already won two Pulitzer Prizes for poetry and one for fiction.

Nonfiction. Anthony Hecht's *Obbligati* included significant essays on Shakespeare, a first-rate appreciation of Robert Lowell, and important pages on Emily Dickinson, Richard Wilbur, and the pathetic fallacy. James Merrill's *Recitative: Prose* reflected the virtues of his poetry—easy colloquial speech and a seriousness about poetry leavened with witty gossip

about its practitioners. *The Collected Prose of Marianne Moore* gathered everything by this much-loved poet, from essays to dust jacket blurbs to her correspondence with the Ford Motor Company.

Novelist Ralph Ellison collected his essays and speeches—on jazz, the black contribution to American culture, and other topics—in *Going to the Territory.* In *The Mechanic Muse,* Hugh Kenner focused on the modernists, Beckett being a favorite, and their relationship to modern technology. *The Selected Essays of R. P. Blackmur* makes available some of this demanding but rewarding critic's major work. The sequence of Edmund Wilson's diaries that began with *The Twenties* continued with *The Fifties,* the most appealing volume yet.

In biography, *Capote: Dear Heart, Old Buddy,* by John Malcolm Brinnin, was a personal memoir by an old friend. Other literary figures to attract new biographies included Willa Cather, Emily Dickinson, Theodore Dreiser, Robert Frost, Langston Hughes, and Wallace Stevens. Among nonliterary biographies to attract attention were studies of Red Smith, Edward R. Murrow, Lillian Hellman, Dwight D. Eisenhower, and Martin Luther King, Jr., as well as two volumes in Kenneth Davis's complex biography of Franklin D. Roosevelt.

Awards. The National Book Critics Circle selected Anne Tyler's *The Accidental Tourist* for its fiction award, Leon Edel's monumental *Henry James: A Life* for biography, Louise Glück's *The Triumph of Achilles* for poetry, and William Gass's *Habitations of the Word* for criticism. The PEN/Faulkner Award for fiction, perhaps the most austere of any of the prizes, went to Peter Taylor's *The Old Forest and Other Stories.*

See also PUBLISHING. *For Pulitzer Prizes, see* PRIZES AND AWARDS. M.D.

AUSTRALIAN

Australian women writers continued to win critical acclaim and popular success at home and abroad. Twelve of them were featured in interviews by Jennifer Ellison published in *Rooms of Their Own,* a collection of talks with female Australian writers.

Fiction. Elizabeth Jolley's *The Well* was a comic horror story distinguished by the author's perceptive, witty, and readable style. Kate Grenville's novel *Dreamhouse* was an entertaining contemporary Gothic tale. The heroine in Blanche D'Alpuget's *Winter in Jerusalem,* as in her earlier novels, was an emotionally disoriented Australian woman in an exotic setting. Two promising novelists made their debut. *Tilly's Fortunes,* by Helen Asher, was concerned with the role of women, while Suzanne Falkiner's *Rain in the Distance* was a skilled examination of youth. A unique collaboration between Jean Bedford and Rosemary Cresswell resulted in a humorous exploration of the feminist generation after the revolution, titled *Colouring In: A Book of Ideologically Unsound Love Stories.*

Patrick White's novel *Memoirs of Many in One,* with the author himself as a character, received critical acclaim as his best comic work. David Foster wrote a clever, funny novel set in the late Middle Ages—*The Adventures of Christian Rosy Cross.* Youthful Tim Winton, already the winner of three Australian fiction awards for earlier works, published *That Eye the Sky,* a perceptive novel about childhood and the nature of love and frustration. Peter Corris's seventh thriller, *Deal Me Out,* featuring private eye Cliff Hardy, again displayed his intimate knowledge of the city of Sydney, as well as a wonderful ear for dialogue. Alan Wearne demonstrated a similar love affair with the city of Melbourne in a highly original verse novel, *The Nightmarkets.*

Other Works. Two welcome volumes of plays were David Williamson's *Collected Plays: Volume 1,* containing five early plays by Australia's most popular dramatist, and Patrick White's *Collected Plays: Volume 1,* featuring four plays by the Nobel Prize laureate.

Two excellent general surveys for newcomers to Australian literature were Ken Goodwin's *A History of Australian Literature* and *The Oxford Companion to Australian Literature,* a wide-ranging reference work.

Awards. The winner of the Miles Franklin Literary Award was Christopher Koch's novel *The Double-Man.* Helen Garner won the National Fiction Award for *The Children's Bach.* A collection of her short stories, *Postcards From Surfers,* received the New South Wales Premier's Award for fiction; the poetry award went to Robert Gray's *Selected Poems, 1963-*

Nobelist Patrick White, Australian novelist and playwright, won critical acclaim for his new novel, Memoirs of Many in One.

1983, which also received the National Poetry Award. Peter Carey's *Illywhacker* was named joint winner of the important Barbara Ramsden Award, along with *Ocean of Story,* a collection of short stories by Christina Stead, published posthumously. The Gold Medal of the Australian Literature Society went to the novelist Thea Astley for her continuing contribution to Australian literature. At the Victorian Premier's Literary Awards, the Vance Palmer Prize for Fiction went to Carey's *Illywhacker.* The award for poetry was shared by John A. Scott for *St. Clair* and Rhyll McMaster for *Washing the Money,* while the drama award went to Janis Balodis for *Too Young for Ghosts.*   I.K.

CANADIAN

Politics dominated Canadian publishing in 1986. The commercial success of former Liberal minister Jean Chrétien's political memoirs, published simultaneously in French and in English in 1985, seemed to have prompted other political figures to indulge in autobiography, a genre that has never been prevalent in Canada.

LITERATURE

Fiction. English Canada witnessed the appearance of fine collections of short fiction. Preeminent was Alice Munro's sixth anthology, *The Progress of Love,* which focuses on her characters' struggles with love, often in a rural Ontario setting. Alistair MacLeod's *As Birds Bring Forth the Sun* confirmed this Maritimer's singular power in the short-story form. Audrey Thomas published some of her best short fiction in *Goodbye, Harold, Good Luck.* Among other notable collections were Austin Clarke's *Nine Men Who Laughed,* Janette Turner Hospital's *Dislocations,* John Metcalf's *Adult Entertainment,* H. R. Percy's *A Model Lover,* and Ray Smith's *Century.* Margaret Atwood and Robert Weaver edited *The Oxford Book of Canadian Short Stories.*

Alice Munro confirmed her standing as one of the finest contemporary short story writers with her collection The Progress of Love. *Set mostly in rural Ontario, the stories show her characters' sense of the precariousness of life and love.*

Timothy Findley's sixth novel, *The Telling of Lies,* stood at the top of the novels in English. Matt Cohen's *Nadine* followed a Jewish woman's journey to self-discovery in France, Israel, and Canada, and Scott Symons's *Helmet of Flesh* traced a similar journey by a homosexual in Morocco. Hugh Hood brought out *The Motor Boys in Ottawa,* the sixth in his projected 12-volume epic.

The finest fiction from Québec included a variety of novels with complex narratives. In Jacques Godbout's *Une histoire américaine* ("An American Story"), the protagonist accepts an invitation to deliver a series of talks at Berkeley on the subject of Québec within Canada. He presents a journal within the novel, and his California is far from paradise. Robert Lalonde's third novel, *Une belle journée d'avance* ("One Fine Day Long Ago"), is a breathtaking evocation of a single day (June 2, 1946) and passionate love, as the narrator holds himself and his reader poised between past and present; the novel won the 1986 Prix Québec-Paris. Other interesting novels were Roch Carrier's *L'Ours et le kangourou* ("The Bear and the Kangaroo"), Claude Jasmin's *Alice vous fait dire bonsoir* ("Alice Tells You to Say Good Night"), Louise Leblanc's *Popcorn,* Jean-Robert Sansfaçon's first novel, *Loft Story,* and *Les Cormorans* ("The Cormorants") by Suzanne Paradis.

Poetry. New and interesting volumes of poems included Claude Beausoleil's *Il y a des nuits que nous habitons tous* ("We All Have Nights Like This"), Don Domanski's *Hammerstroke,* Christiane Frenette's *Indigo nuit* ("Indigo Night"), Seymour Mayne's *Children of Abel,* and John Newlove's *The Night the Dog Smiled.* There were major retrospectives of Margaret Atwood, Douglas Lochhead, Al Purdy, and Wilfred Watson.

Nonfiction. René Lévesque's *Memoirs,* published simultaneously in French and in English, captured vividly the turbulent career of the retired Québec nationalist leader. Keith Davey, who engineered many of Pierre Elliott Trudeau's campaigns, reflected on his own career and on Canadian political life in *The Rainmaker: A Passion for Politics.* Trudeau's former press secretary, Patrick Gossage, contributed *Close to the Charisma: Between the Press and* the Prime Minister, and former Liberal cabinet ministers Donald Johnston, Roy MacLaren, and Eugene Whelan published reminiscences.

Among other biographies, Claude Bissell's *The Imperial Canadian: Vincent Massey in Office* was an exemplary sequel to *The Young Vincent Massey*. John Coldwell Adams explored the life of the first English Canadian man of letters in *Sir Charles God Damn: The Life of Sir Charles G. D. Roberts*. Meanwhile, in *The Forty-ninth and Other Parallels: Contemporary Canadian Perspectives*, edited by David Staines, two former cabinet ministers, as well as other political and social figures, addressed a variety of public issues.

Awards. The Governor General's Awards for 1985 went to Margaret Atwood for *The Handmaid's Tale* and Fernand Ouellette for *Lucie ou midi en novembre* ("Lucy, or Noon in November") in the fiction category; to Fred Wah for *Waiting for Saskatchewan* and André Roy for *Action Writing* in poetry; to George F. Walker for *Criminals in Love* and Maryse Pelletier for *Duo pour voix obstinées* ("Duo for Persistent Voices") in drama; and to Ramsay Cook for *The Regenerators: Social Criticism in Late Victorian English Canada* and François Ricard for *La Littérature contre elle-même* ("Literature Against Itself") for nonfiction. D.S.

ENGLISH

The historical novel continued to flourish in 1986, as British writers applied to it a refreshing variety of tone and treatment. Some dramatists also looked back to the past.

Fiction. Bamber Gascoigne's *Cod Streuth* concerned the experiences of a prim 16th-century French Calvinist captured by Brazilian cannibals—who, mistaking the tattered remains of his Rabelais for holy writ, elected him their priest-king. In *The Seven Ages*, Eva Figes took a more earnest approach to history in her view of England since the Middle Ages from the standpoint of woman, perennial victim of the predatory male.

Timothy Mo's *An Insular Possession* was a substantial, meticulously documented chronicle of the mid-19th-century Opium Wars between Britain and China, seen mainly through the eyes of an Irish painter and two American newspaper editors. *The Fisher King*, Anthony Powell's first full-length novel in 11 years,

traced parallels between the personalities of the Grail legend and a group of modern passengers on a cruise to the Orkneys.

In Fay Weldon's *The Shrapnel Academy*, a weekend party at a military training establishment ended in annihilation for the quarrelsome assembled representatives of modern society. Hilary Mantel in *Vacant Possession* combined acute observation of current welfare-state ironies with an ingenious, chilling black comedy about an ex-mental patient's sinister revenges.

The Innocents, by Carolyn Slaughter, a compassionate novel of whites and blacks agonizing over racial identity, reflected with painful immediacy the contemporary situation in South Africa. In Stanley Middleton's 25th novel, *An After-Dinner's Sleep*, a retired educator, prompted by the unexpected renewal of a past love, reassessed his outwardly successful career.

Margaret Forster's *Private Papers* depicted the conflict between a mother and the daughter who discovered her hidden memoir; it cleverly communicated their antagonism by interspersing pages from the journal with the daughter's caustically contradictory version of events. Patricia Barrie's moving first novel *Devotions* also employed the device of alternating narrators in her portrayal of a daughter nursing without rancor a fiercely embittered widowed father crippled by a stroke. In *Last Dance With You*, by Grace Ingoldby, a son who returns home after his father's suicide becomes remorsefully imprisoned by the past.

Barbara Pym's final posthumous novel, *An Academic Question*, observed with candor and wry wit the humors and unrest of life at a provincial university. Meanwhile, Anthony Burgess came out with yet another comic novel, a lively, well-received opus entitled *The Pianoplayers*.

Biography. Richard Mabey's well-informed portrait, *Gilbert White*, assessed, in the context of his time, the merits of the man who "studied the natural world like a scientist but was involved with it like a romantic." In *The Bondage of Love: The Life of Mrs. Samuel Taylor Coleridge*, Molly Lefebure set out successfully to rescue the reputation of "the most maligned of great men's wives." Michael Ffinch, in his substantial, diligently researched biog-

raphy *G. K. Chesterton,* celebrated an engagingly ebullient personality and his many-sided literary achievement. And Robert Skidelsky won credit for the first volume in his biography of economist John Maynard Keynes, also bringing to life the social and intellectual world of Cambridge University and the Bloomsbury group.

Two eminent woman novelists were commemorated in Robert Liddell's double portrait *Elizabeth and Ivy.* The liveliest glimpses of Ivy Compton-Burnett came from her friend and admirer, Elizabeth Taylor, who emerged as vividly as her subject in her anecdotes of visits and conversations. In *Helen Waddell,* by Dame Felicitas Corrigan, the author of such classics as *The Wandering Scholars* and *Peter Abelard* was revealed as a character as memorable as her work: exuberantly generous and unspoiled by success.

Drama. Over the past year some important British playwrights were noticeably preoccupied with the past, and with relating historical backgrounds and events to our own time. Parallels between the present situation in Northern Ireland and that of Saxon farmers in Roman Britain were implicit in a strange, dark allegory, *The Saxon Shore,* by David Rudkin, himself an Ulsterman. The scene and themes of John Clifford's *Lucy's Play,* set in Sicily, again evoked familiar echoes.

In the wake of *Amadeus* came two more plays about composers. Julian Mitchell's *After Aida* concentrated on the end of Verdi's unproductive nine-year exile on his farm following the opera's opening, and on the strenuous efforts of family and friends to lure the morose master back to the theater. *Café Puccini,* by Robin Ray, depicted another gloomy musical hero, dramatizing the woes of his professional career and the unhappy deterioration of his love affair.

Anthony Minghella's *Made in Bangkok* skillfully assembled an assorted group of tourists on a package holiday to show the impact on their lives, characters, and hidden desires of a distant country shamefully exploited by tourism.   M.W.

WORLD

During 1986 increased attention was paid to topical matters and to their roots in social and political history.

Latin American, Spanish, Portuguese. Augusto Roa Bastos evokes the Paraguay of the mid-19th century in *I The Supreme (Yo, el supremo,* 1974), a newly translated novel portraying the tumultuous emancipation of that country from colonialism. The poet Armando Valladares, speaking for many Cuban artists accused by Fidel Castro of "ideological weakness," recounts his 22 years of imprisonment and torture in *Against All Hope (Contra toda esperanza).* The Peruvian writer Mario Vargas Llosa mixes fact and conjecture in probing the dynamics of contemporary revolutions and the mentality of their leaders in his novel *The Real Life of Alejandro Mayta (La historia de Mayta,* 1984). Also emerging in translation was the author's critical study *The Perpetual Orgy: Flaubert and Madame Bovary.* Writing in Portuguese, the late Brazilian novelist Clarice Lispector directed a blend of realism and sharp wit against a male-dominated society in her novel *The Hour of the Star (A hora da estrela,* 1984).

Austrian, German, Swiss. Elias Canetti, the Bulgarian-born Nobel Prize winner who writes in German and resides in London, has been publishing volumes of his autobiography at intervals. The most recent volume, *The Play of the Eyes (Das Augenspiel,* 1985), covers the years between 1931 and 1937 and consists largely of personal anecdotes, with little to say about the ominous political atmosphere of the time, in contrast to Thomas Bernhard's memoirs *Gathering Evidence.* The latter were published serially beginning in 1975 with *Die Ursache* ("The Cause") and continuing through *Ein Kind* ("A Child"). Bernhard's memoirs are a graphic recollection of the "descent of darkness" that lasted into the postwar years.

Siegfried Lenz has yet to match the wide appeal of his novel *The German Lesson (Deutschstunde,* 1968). In *Exerzierplatz* ("Parade Ground"), advocates of turning an old military training field into a tree-cultivating area fight a losing battle against a chauvinistic bureaucracy, but Lenz's message cannot save a chaotic narrative. Yet to be translated was the late Heinrich Böll's final novel, *Frauen vor Flusslandschaft* ("Women by a Countryside River"), in which the wives and mistresses of powerful men in Bonn somberly reflect on the materialistic environment that is strangling their lives. Though better known as a playwright, Volker Braun has written a wickedly satiric novel, *Hinze-Kunze-Roman* ("Ordinary People"), in which the political sloganeering of the divided Germanies is ridiculed. In his

Master Literary Performer
Peruvian writer Mario Vargas Llosa loomed large on the American literary scene as his novel *The Real Life of Alejandro Mayta* appeared in English translation to wide (if not universal) critical acclaim. Set amid the decay and unrest of Lima in the 1950's, *Mayta* is the narrator's search for the true story behind an aging, failed revolutionary; ultimately, in elusive Vargas Llosa fashion, the narrator admits to having falsified much of the account. Like Vargas Llosa's other novels—including *The Time of the Hero, The Green House, Conversations in the Cathedral,* and *Aunt Julia and the Scriptwriter*— *Mayta* aroused varied responses, partly because of its complexity and stylistic experimentation. Later in the year, Vargas Llosa's highly original critical study *The Perpetual Orgy* was published in English translation; in it he confesses his undying love for the heroine of Flaubert's classic *Madame Bovary.*

Mario Vargas Llosa

provocative idea-novel *Justiz* ("Justice"), the great Swiss writer Friedrich Dürrenmatt steers the reader through an intricate murder case and the conflict between absolute and manipulated justice.

French. The wounds incurred by the divisive reactions of the French to the German occupation during World War II are still unhealed, and Marguerite Duras's searing and sorrowful memoir *The War: A Memoir (La Douleur,* 1985) impressively deepens the human dimensions of this bitter historical episode. Duras also won a major prize, the $50,000 Ritz Paris Hemingway award, for her acclaimed novel *L'Amant* ("The Lover"). The biography *Sartre* by Annie Cohen-Solal has been acclaimed as the most complete exposition of Jean-Paul Sartre's life and thought. It will also help readers wend their way through his posthumous *Critique de la raison dialectique* ("Critique of Dialectical Reason"), an elaborate, two-volume study of Marxist philosophy.

Ali Ghanem was born into the Muslim culture of Algeria and in time became an internationally renowned filmmaker in France. His novel *The Seven-Headed Serpent (Le Serpent à sept têtes,* 1984) richly captures the cultural contrasts and the agonizing years of warfare between the Algerians and the French. Similar notes of historical authenticity are struck in Conrad Detrez's novel *Zone of Fire (La Ceinture de feu,* 1984), about a French scientist who becomes closely involved with the Nicaraguan Sandinistas during the 1970's.

Italian. Umberto Eco's *Travels in Hyperreality* features brilliant, slyly humorous essays on topics ranging from the ancient Greek belief in divinities to the modern devotion to the anonymous divinity of technology. The success of Leonardo Sciascia's Sicilian stories in *The Wine-Dark Sea* prompted the publication of *Sicilian Uncles (Gli zii di Sicilia,* 1958), three humane, wry novella-length narratives about Sicily's revolutionary history and its people's responses to foreign ideologies and conflicts. In *The Monkey's Wrench (La chiave a stella,* 1978), Primo Levi conveys a sense of the human dignity of work through an undignified character—a profane, boastful rigger of derricks who is elevated by the risk and craft of his profession.

Russian. Vasily Grossman, a prodigiously talented Soviet war correspondent, wrote the memorable novel *Life and Fate,* a panorama of the Battle of Stalingrad and war-ravaged Eastern Europe. Soviet censors confiscated the manuscript, but a microfilm copy was smuggled to the West by Vladimir Voinovich. Now an émigré, Voinovich, in his collection of essays *The Anti-Soviet Soviet Union,* reflects with grim humor on the prejudices that lubricate the Soviet political machinery.

Hebrew and Yiddish. Two resonant autobiographies received new translations. *The Selected Poetry of Yehuda Amichai,* culled from works published between 1955 and 1985, speaks in a language "torn from its sleep in the Bible" and serves to express the discrepancies between the dreams and the harsh realities of Israeli life. Rachel Korn (1898–

French writer Marguerite Duras displays a token quill pen after winning the $50,000 Ritz Paris Hemingway award for her novel The Lover.

1982), a Polish émigré, left an oppressive life and settled in Canada, where "Fate doled out happiness/with a miser's hand," and old memories lingered. She aided her translator in the bilingual rendering of selections from a 30-year harvest of Yiddish verse called *Paper Roses (Papierene Roisen,* 1985).

Nobel Prize. Wole Soyinka (Akinwande Oluwole Soyinka), a Nigerian novelist, poet, critic, and playwright whose dramas have been performed around the world, became the first African to win a Nobel Prize in Litèrature. Cited for his "wide cultural perspective," he draws on both English and African traditions in his work, most of which is written in English.

S.M.

BOOKS FOR CHILDREN

Among favorite children's books to be reissued in 1986 were four Freddy the Pig books by Walter R. Brooks and a Beatrix Potter story entitled *The Two Bad Mice.* Freddy, the star of 25 books first published in the 1940's, is a pig detective who lives on a farm in New York. The reissue marked the centennial of the author's birth. The four adventures, which appeared in paperback, were *Freddy and the Perilous Adventure, Freddy Goes Camping, Freddy the Pilot,* and *Freddy the Politician* (Alfred A. Knopf). Beatrix Potter's tiny classic was reissued as a pop-up book from Frederick Warne; it was described by *Publishers Weekly* as "a genuine charmer in a very crowded field."

Two notable sequels were Robert Kraus's *Where Are You Going, Little Mouse?* (Greenwillow), about a mouse character last seen 15 years earlier in *Whose Mouse Are You?,* and *Racso and the Rats of NIMH* (Harper & Row), by Jane Leslie Conly, who picks up the story of the rats where her father, Robert C. O'Brien, left off at the end of his Newbery-winning *Mrs. Frisby and the Rats of NIMH.*

Maureen Daly, whose celebrated *Seventeenth Summer* was published 44 years earlier to rave reviews, finally penned another novel for teenagers: *Acts of Love* (Scholastic Hardcover), a story of young love and of heritage, family, and growing up.

Books About Child Abuse and Abduction. A small flood of materials, from toddler books to board games, were published to help children

An all-time favorite, 82-year-old Dr. Seuss, whose real name is Theodor Geisel, stands by while a 22-foot replica of his most famous creation, the Cat in the Hat, is hoisted on top of the San Diego Museum of Art, where the retrospective exhibition "Dr. Seuss: Then and Now" opened in May.

answer such questions as: What should you do if someone wants to touch you? asks you to get in a car? offers you candy? Among the new books were *Berenstain Bears Learn About Strangers,* a much praised volume by Stan and Jan Berenstain (Random House), and *You Can Say "No,"* by Betty Boegehold (Golden Books). *Be a S.A.F.E. Kid!* by the Safety and Fitness Exchange (Children's Creative Safety Program) is a workbook that defines situations where abuse can occur and instructs children in ways to be safe. It comes with a poster, an audio tape, decals, and an identification tag. Scholastic published *Close to Home* by Oralee Wachter, which uses appealing vignettes to warn children about abduction and is a companion volume to the author's *No More Secrets for Me* (1983).

Business News. With the recent strength of juvenile book sales came the creation of new children's lines, the expansion of the Book of the Month Club's continuity program for children, and an expansion of *Publishers Weekly's* reviews and coverage of children's books.

In the fall Walker and Company initiated Millennium Books, a science fiction series of hardcovers for young adults. Harper & Row announced the creation of two rack-size paperback imprints—Keypoint, to publish general-interest books for young adults, and Starwanderer, a collection of science fiction and fantasy titles. Farrar, Straus & Giroux revived its Sunburst imprint in the fall to issue a line of children's paperbacks and to reprint backlist titles. William Morrow had similar plans for Mulberry Books, which was to reprint picture books from its three children's divisions as trade paperbacks. In July, Simon and Schuster launched Minstrel Books, which was to issue both original and reprint titles as digest-size paperbacks geared to children aged 7 to 11.

Contests. Delacorte Press held its third annual writing contest open to American and Canadian writers who have not yet published a young adult novel. The winner of the 1984–1985 Delacorte Press Prize for an Outstanding First Young Adult Novel was Ray Maloney for *The Impact Zone,* which was published in the spring. Louise Plummer was awarded an honorable mention for *The Romantic Obsessions and Humiliations of Annie Sehlheimer,* to be published in the spring of 1987.

Avon/Flare held its second biennial writing contest, in which teenagers are invited to submit manuscripts, with publication of the winning novel as the prize. The winner of the 1985 Avon/Flare Young Adult Novel Competition was Tamela Larimer for *Buck,* which was published in the fall.

In May, E. P. Dutton announced its first picture-book competition to encourage and attract new illustrators. The contest was open to anyone enrolled in college-level art or design courses, as well as to recent graduates. The winner, Janet Stoeke, received a $1,500 cash prize. In July, G. P. Putnam's Sons, a member of the Putnam Young Readers Group, promised a cash prize and publication for "the most distinguished submission of a first novel with a contemporary setting in North America suitable for ages 8–12."

Prizes. In January the prestigious Newbery Medal was awarded by the American Library Association to 1985's "most distinguished contribution to American literature for children published in the United States." The winner was Patricia MacLachlan for *Sarah, Plain and Tall* (Harper & Row). MacLachlan is the author of several other books for children, including *Arthur, for the Very First Time.* The 1985 Honor Books were *Dogsong,* by Gary Paulsen (Bradbury), and *Commodore Perry in the Land of the Shogun,* by Rhoda Blumberg (Lothrop, Lee & Shepard). The Caldecott Medal for 1985, awarded by the ALA to the illustrator of the best American picture book of the year, went to Chris Van Allsburg, for *The Polar Express* (Houghton Mifflin). Selected as Caldecott Honor Books were *King Bidgood's in the Bathtub,* by Audrey Wood, illustrated by Don Wood (Harcourt Brace Jovanovich), and *The Relatives Came,* by Cynthia Rylant, illustrated by Stephen Gammell (Bradbury).   A.M.M.

LOUISIANA. See STATISTICS OF THE WORLD.

LUXEMBOURG. In 1986 the Christian Social-Socialist government of Premier Jacques Santer benefited from positive economic developments and a generally tranquil social and political climate. As a result of the healthy position of state finances, Santer was able to announce in April that the budget proposal for 1987 would provide individual and corporate tax relief amounting to about $50 million. However, the new tax package would require strict budgetary discipline, and public spending would be allowed to increase by less than 1 percent.

Santer also announced that Luxembourg's successful economic restructuring program would be continued as a government priority. The financial restructuring of the steel industry, already completed, was accompanied by favorable prospects for the industry. Government aid to encourage industrial diversification was to be continued, including programs aimed at modernizing the industrial sector and increasing public investment for the establishment of new enterprises and the expansion of existing ones.

Gross domestic product was projected to increase by 2 percent for 1986. Exports were forecast to increase 1.7 percent, continuing a four-year trend of growth, and private consumption was expected to increase substantially. Unemployment was projected at 1.4 percent, the lowest level of any country in the European Community, and the external account surplus was expected to reach as high as 31.5 percent of gross domestic product in 1986.

See STATISTICS OF THE WORLD.   W.C.C.

M

MADAGASCAR. See STATISTICS OF THE WORLD.
MAINE. See STATISTICS OF THE WORLD.
MALAWI. See STATISTICS OF THE WORLD.
MALAYSIA. National elections in August 1986 saw Malaysia's ruling National Front, led by Prime Minister Mahathir Mohamed, convincingly defeat Islamic fundamentalists to capture 148 out of the 177 seats in Parliament. Expected gains by the Islamic Party failed to materialize, and its chief opponent in the National Front coalition, the United Malays National Organization, lost only 1 of the 84 seats it contested. Despite the Front's victories, the opposition Democratic Action Party increased its seats from 10 to 24, with the Chinese parties in the Front the major losers. The Democratic Action Party also made substantial gains in state government races in the August elections, but the

Malaysia's strict narcotics laws claimed their first non-Asian victims, as two Australians (Kevin Barlow in foreground and Brian Chambers in back with sunglasses) were hanged on July 7 for heroin smuggling. They are shown here after their convictions in 1985.

National Front retained large majorities in all of the states. Overall, the Democratic Action Party won 37 state assembly seats, and the Islamic Party 14—compared to 300 for the National Front parties. The Malaysian Chinese Association (MCA) won barely half of the seats it contested in the August elections, compared to over 80 percent in 1982.

In Sabah and Sarawak, the state elections were held in May, separately from the national elections. The United Sabah Party easily swept them, winning 34 out of the 48 seats. The United Sabah National Organization (USNO) captured most of the rest. The United Sabah Party's showing prompted the National Front to admit the 15-month-old party to the Front as well as to readmit USNO, assuring a National Front state government and a Front victory in the national elections in the state.

The plunge in international oil prices virtually erased prospects for economic growth for 1986. With the sharp weakening in international commodity prices for such exports as palm oil and cocoa and the cessation of international trading in tin owing to a glutted market, even revised estimates of 3 percent growth now seemed optimistic. The fragile state of the economy was evidenced in August by the collapse of 23 savings cooperatives.

Malaysian narcotics laws provide for mandatory execution of persons convicted of possessing substantial amounts of heroin, and in July two Australians were hanged for heroin smuggling, despite pleas from the Australian and British prime ministers and worldwide attention. The previous executions of 38 Singaporean and Malaysian citizens for the same charges had been largely ignored. In October the government moved to make its laws even tougher on drug traffickers, enacting legislation that allowed confiscation of their assets.

In December, Parliament enacted a measure making jail sentences mandatory for anyone convicted of unauthorized possession of a wide range of government documents. The law, sharply protested by journalists, also allowed government ministers discretion to label any document as restricted or secret.

See STATISTICS OF THE WORLD.   K.M.

MALDIVES. See STATISTICS OF THE WORLD.

MALI. See STATISTICS OF THE WORLD.

MALTA. A tense atmosphere in the Mediterranean influenced Malta's relations with other countries in 1986. Before U.S. aircraft bombed targets in Libya in April, Malta's prime minister, Carmelo Mifsud Bonnici, offered to act as a mediator between the United States and Libya. He also proposed a regional conference on terrorism, but according to Maltese officials, the U.S. government rejected both ideas. Bonnici called the American bombing of Libya unjustified; he also claimed the Maltese had spotted the attacking U.S. planes on radar and had warned Libya of their approach.

Despite Malta's apparent support for Libya, its relations with that country weakened. Libya's financial difficulties, stemming from reduced oil prices and demand, adversely affected almost all joint Maltese-Libyan economic ventures. Malta's exports to Libya dropped sharply, as did the number of Maltese workers employed in Libya and in Libyan-supported companies in Malta.

The government refused Egypt's request that it extradite the only surviving suspect in the November 1985 hijacking of an Egyptian airliner forced to land in Malta. Sixty innocent people were killed in the hijacking and rescue attempt. The suspect, Omar Muhammad Ali Rezaq, was to be tried in 1987.

Malta settled its dispute with Great Britain over financial responsibility for clearing wartime shipwrecks from the Valletta harbor; in March, Britain paid Malta $2 million for wreckage removal.

See STATISTICS OF THE WORLD.   P.J.M.

MANITOBA. See STATISTICS OF THE WORLD.

MANUFACTURING INDUSTRIES. Slow, lackluster growth of the U.S. economy during 1986, the passage of sweeping tax reform legislation, and a massive U.S. trade deficit had experts divided between fears of recession and guarded optimism over the future of U.S. manufacturing. The new tax law, with slower depreciation of business equipment, plants, and machinery and repeal of the investment tax credit, appeared likely to hit an already slumping sector. Prospects of a shrinking trade gap fueled by the decline of the American dollar offered hope to domestic manufacturers battling foreign competition. However, the U.S. trade deficit, though moderating in some months, soared to a new record of nearly $170 billion for the year as a whole, with the future prognosis uncertain.

American factories, mines, and utilities late in the year were operating at a low level, about 79 percent of capacity. Industrial production was generally slow, although figures for August through November showed improvement and some of the blame for lags could be placed on strikes and other work stoppages. Orders to factories were variable, but generally slow. Durable goods orders reached $109.68 billion in November, rising 5.9 percent after a 4.7 percent decline the previous month; the gain was attributed to a surge in military spending and to last-minute efforts to get tax breaks. Manufacturing inventories, which slipped in the third quarter, rose sharply in October, but the increase was attributed to temporary factors and so was not a cause for general concern.

Steel. The leading U.S. steel producers—U.S. Steel (renamed USX), LTV Corporation, Bethlehem Steel, and Wheeling-Pittsburgh—experienced a broad spectrum of crises. The heaviest impact was felt by the biggest U.S. producer, industry giant USX. The firm's steel operations had a working loss of $978 million over five years; during that time, it had closed over 150 plants and facilities, cut steelmaking capacity by more than 24 percent, and reduced its steel work force by 50,000 workers. In 1986, USX steel production accounted for less than 30 percent of sales, with heavier emphasis placed on oil and gas holdings and a diversified group that includes such activities as chemical engineering, consulting, and real estate. Adding to USX's woes was a shutdown, begun August 1, involving more than 20,000 members of the United Steelworkers of America. (Union leaders called it a lockout, management a strike.) In October, USX also began efforts to shore up defenses against corporate raider Carl Icahn's attempt to acquire the company.

On July 17, the number-two U.S. steelmaker, LTV Corporation, asked for court protection from its 20,000 creditors and suspended payments on its $4 billion debt. LTV represents a collection of such steel producers as Jones & Laughlin, Youngstown Sheet & Tube Co., and Republic Steel. Meanwhile, Bethlehem Steel announced a second-quarter loss of $238 mil-

lion and omitted the quarterly dividend on its two preferred stocks; the slide continued in the third quarter. In a climate of weak capital spending, Bethlehem had allocated about 60 percent of its output to heavy structural and plate products used in construction and machinery. Wheeling-Pittsburgh posted a $60.3 million loss at the close of 1985, attributable in part to an only limited recovery from a 98-day strike and to management changes. After an uneven three quarters in 1986, the company, still operating under Chapter 11 protection, reported a nine-month loss in net income of $37.1 million and was closing down a number of facilities. Inland Steel showed signs of life with a $15.7 million net income for the second quarter, although net income fell slightly in the third quarter.

The year's upheavals forced steelmakers to reassess attitudes toward capital investment in new technology. Chief among new cost-cutting technologies is continuous casting of molten steel into 10-inch slabs that can be cut for processing as they cool. Expenses to refit conventional mills to continuous casting were estimated at $100 million, and late in the year U.S. steel producers had just reached the halfway mark in changing over. On the other hand, 90 percent of Japan's factories use this method, as do two-thirds of the facilities in Western Europe.

One expected target for technological improvement in 1987 was the quality of molten steel. Increasingly stringent requirements were forcing steel producers to adopt a new technology to provide high surface, internal, and micro cleanliness. However, such technology requires heavy capital investment.

Paper. The American Paper Institute estimated that total paper and paperboard production would reach a record high—70 million tons—for the year, almost 5 percent above depressed 1985 levels. Gains reflected large differences in various grades of paper, with printing and writing papers, newsprint and tissue papers, and major grades of paperboard showing greatest strength. There was a rising demand in particular for computer and office copier papers, while demand for coated paper declined. Paperboard production recovered sharply and was expected to close out the year in excess

245

out against fear of initiating a general protectionist war.

Industry spokesmen were bitter over the president's veto in the face of rising U.S. textile imports. In November, after a flurry of negotiations aimed at undercutting possible protectionist moves in the new Congress, Japan agreed to sharp reductions of both textile and machine tool exports to the United States. The significance of the move was debated, however.

Mill fiber consumption showed little growth in the first half of 1986; second-quarter figures were up less than 1 percent. Natural fiber consumption leveled during the second quarter after recording heavy gains in the first quarter. Artificial fibers were running only slightly ahead of the previous year.

Machine Tools. Gloom pervaded the U.S. machine tool industry, as new orders for both metal-cutting and metal-forming units continued a downward slide. By November 1986, new orders were down 32 percent from levels a year earlier. Losses in the industry were attributed to a sluggish economy and uncertainty over the effects on capital spending of the new tax bill.   L.R.H.

MARYLAND. *See* STATISTICS OF THE WORLD.

MASSACHUSETTS. *See* STATISTICS OF THE WORLD.

MAURITANIA. *See* STATISTICS OF THE WORLD.

MAURITIUS. *See* STATISTICS OF THE WORLD.

MEXICO. Contentious relations with the United States, a worsening economic situation, and internal political difficulties marked 1986 in Mexico.

Foreign Relations. President Ronald Reagan and Mexican President Miguel de la Madrid Hurtado met in January, at Mexicali on the U.S. border, then again in August in Washington, D.C. It was the first time the two leaders had met twice in a year.

The August meeting was seen as an attempt by the Reagan administration to smooth Mexican feathers, ruffled by a series of so-called Mexico-bashing congressional hearings held in May by U.S. Senator Jesse Helms (R, N.C.). In the sessions, U.S. commissioner of customs William Raab testified that he believed most Mexican officials were open to bribes, and the recently departed U.S. ambassador to Mexico, John Gavin, stated that at least two Mexican

A breakdown in contract negotiations between troubled steel industry giant USX (formerly U.S. Steel) and the United Steelworkers of America led to a work stoppage in August involving more than 20,000 employees—union leaders called it a lockout—that continued through the year.

of 35 million tons, compared to 33 million tons in 1985. The declining value of the dollar internationally caused export levels to rise sharply in the latter part of the year.

The new tax reform bill was expected to impact strongly on the capital-intensive paper industry in 1987. Executives remained cautious about industry prospects, citing increasing foreign competition, especially in the lucrative specialty papers.

Textiles. In August the U.S. House of Representatives narrowly failed to override presidential veto of a bill placing strict limits on imports of textiles from 12 countries, most of them in Asia. Deep concern in the textile industry over the loss of thousands of mill worker jobs lost governors were involved in the drug trade. (Gavin, a controversial figure, had resigned in March.) Helms said the United States should not continue to help Mexico economically until it did more to combat narcotics smuggling across the border, eradicate corruption, and eliminate dishonest elections.

Drugs were the main point of contention between the two countries. On his visit to Washington in August, de la Madrid was accompanied by Mexican Attorney General Sergio Garcia Ramirez, who discussed the drug problem with U.S. Attorney General Edwin Meese III and Vice President George Bush. Meese and Bush announced a joint U.S.-Mexican drug operation, entitled "Operation Alliance." Just as this news was being announced, however, U.S. officials said that Victor Cortez, a U.S. Drug Enforcement Administration agent working in Guadalajara, had been seized the day before by Mexican state police, detained overnight for questioning, and tortured and threatened with death before being released. (In 1985, another DEA agent, Enrique Camarena Salazar, had been killed in Mexico; Mexican police officers and drug traffickers were implicated in the crime, and in late 1986, two suspects were arrested in Los Angeles in connection with it.) In October the State Department released a survey which said that Mexico was "the largest single-country source of heroin and marijuana imported into the United States."

A bright spot in U.S.-Mexican relations was the appointment of a new U.S. ambassador, Charles J. Pilliod, Jr., who reportedly took steps to stress the positive in reports to the U.S. government and dealings with Mexican officials.

A Troubled Economy. Having borrowed heavily during the oil boom to finance developments, Mexico found itself in the grip of a recession as oil prices fell. Automobile sales dropped, and in the summer the Renault automotive plant was permanently closed. Credit, even at interest rates of 100 percent, was virtually unavailable. By October the peso, which had been trading at 450 to the dollar when the year began, had slipped to 800. The Reagan administration assisted Mexico with its continuing economic problems by negotiating a $12 billion loan package for the country, enabling it to avoid defaulting on interest payments on its $100 billion foreign debt.

A key obstacle to the U.S.-negotiated aid package was overcome when U.S. Secretary of the Treasury James Baker and Federal Reserve Board Chairman Paul Volcker persuaded the International Monetary Fund to agree to a $1.68 billion standby credit, thereby clearing the way for more credits from commercial banks. For its part, Mexico agreed to adopt a growth-oriented economic reform plan approved by the IMF, which included spending cuts and tax increases.

Political Unease. At home, the loan package was greeted without enthusiasm. At the opening of the World Cup soccer championships, the president was hooted and booed—an almost unheard-of insult in Mexico. During the previous few years, workers had seen their buying power cut almost in half. Subsidies on everything from tortillas to public transportation had already been eliminated or sharply reduced, and the minimum wage in 1986 was a little over $2 a day. A year after the devastating earthquakes that hit Mexico City in September 1985, thousands were still homeless, while the financial damage was calculated at $4 billion.

With resentment growing, it was expected that the Institutional Revolutionary Party, which had governed the country since 1929, would suffer setbacks in local and state elections. Instead, the party was accorded victory in all but a few obscure municipalities. This, in turn, led to charges of fraud.

In November, de la Madrid proposed a package of changes in the electoral laws and Parliament that he claimed would allow greater democracy. The changes provided for an electoral tribunal controlled by the governing party, with representation from two opposition parties, and an expansion of Parliament from 400 to 500 seats, with the additional seats going to opposition parties. However, the majority party would never have less than 51 percent of the seats, regardless of popular vote. Opposition parties criticized the proposals as intended to perpetuate control by the ruling PRI.

See STATISTICS OF THE WORLD.　　　J.H.B.

MICHIGAN. See STATISTICS OF THE WORLD.

MICRONESIA. See PACIFIC ISLANDS.

Middle East

The Middle East peace process was stalemated during 1986, as terrorism, continued violence, and shifting allegiances overwhelmed potentially promising contacts between the Israeli and Arab camps. The Iran-Iraq war dragged on, as the United States became implicated in a major scandal involving the secret sale of arms to Iran.

Israeli Prime Minister Shimon Peres's summit meetings with the leaders of Morocco and Egypt raised hopes about chances for peace in the Middle East. But progress was frustrated by terrorist incidents, associated with various factions in the Mideast, and by continued hostilities in the region. Revelations late in the year that the United States had secretly supplied arms to Iran, in what was said to be an attempt to sway a pro-Iranian group in Lebanon to free American hostages, angered many Arab leaders already concerned about earlier Iranian advances in its war with Iraq.

U.S.-Libyan Hostilities. In January and February the U.S. Navy conducted air and sea maneuvers off the Libyan coast near the Gulf of Sidra, claimed by Libya as its territorial waters. By March the U.S. task force in the area had grown to 30 warships, and on March 23, American planes and vessels entered the gulf, prompting a limited military confrontation. President Ronald Reagan meanwhile had announced economic steps against Libya, including a freeze on its U.S. assets. These measures, in response to what the administration said were Libyan-backed terrorist incidents in Europe, were intended to isolate Libyan leader Muammar al-Qaddafi and lay the groundwork for possible military action should the United States decide Qaddafi was continuing his involvement in terrorism.

On April 15, U.S. F-111 fighter-bombers based in Britain and other planes launched from U.S. carriers bombed targets in Tripoli and Benghazi, killing 37 people, according to the Libyan government. President Reagan said that the air raids had been aimed at "terrorist installations" and that he had "irrefutable proof" of Qaddafi's "direct responsibility" for the April

5 bombing of a West Berlin discotheque frequented by American servicemen. The Arab League and most individual Arab states condemned the U.S. raid. European reaction was ambivalent, with several nations disapproving and a few supporting the action.

In October it was reported that the United States had waged a "disinformation" campaign aimed at Qaddafi's overthrow. The plan was said to consist of "a series of closely coordinated events involving covert, diplomatic, military, and public actions." Secretary of State George Shultz later said he did not object to "a little psychological warfare against Qaddafi," but others said the United States had seriously damaged its credibility.

Terrorism. Among terrorist incidents of note was an abortive attempt to detonate explosives aboard an Israeli El Al flight from London in April. A British court later convicted a Jordanian of the attempted bombing and sentenced him to 45 years in prison; evidence presented at the trial implicated Syria in the plot, leading London to sever relations with Damascus. Other events included bombing attacks on civilians in central Paris, for which Lebanese terrorists were thought accountable, an attack on a synagogue in Istanbul in which 22 worshipers were killed (various Islamic and Palestinian groups claimed responsibility), and the hijacking of a TWA airliner in Karachi, in which 21 passengers were killed by gunmen alleged to be Palestinians. In late December, hijackers armed with grenades sought to take over an Iraqi airliner shortly after takeoff from Baghdad; explosions and fire ensued, and the plane made a forced landing at an airstrip in Arar, Saudi Arabia, where it crashed and burned. Over 60 passengers were killed.

248

Striking against Libyan-supported terrorism, U.S. planes bombed installations in Libya on April 15. Above, a US. F-111 bomber at its base in Great Britain a day before the raid; at right, Libyans survey the damage done to planes at Benghazi's airport.

Lebanon. Syria's attempts to contain hostilities among and within the diverse factions in Lebanon collapsed again. In January, Lebanese President Amin Gemayel refused to support a Syrian-brokered peace agreement signed the previous month in Damascus by Druze leader Walid Jumblatt, Nabih Berri of Amal (the main Shiite Muslim organization), and Elie Hobeika, a rival Christian leader. Amid intra-Christian fighting, Hobeika was quickly routed and forced to flee to Damascus. During the year, joint Syrian and Lebanese Army peacekeeping forces deployed in Beirut failed to put a stop to intermilitia combat, as fighting continued not only across the Green Line dividing the capital into Christian- and Muslim-controlled sectors but within each sector, among Christians and among a variety of Muslim factions. A series of car bombings in late July and August claimed about 100 lives, and fierce fighting between Palestinians and Amal, which broke out in early autumn and lasted for the remainder of the year, saw hundreds of people—many of them noncombatants—killed. Amal, with Syrian backing, was trying to prevent the Palestinians from reestablishing the strong military presence they had in Lebanon before Israel's 1982 invasion.

The violence in Lebanon was also directed at Westerners. French forces in the country—an observer force and a contingent in the United Nations Interim Force in Lebanon (Unifil)—were caught in the fighting between rival Shiite factions—those of Amal, which wanted France to maintain its presence, and those of Hezbollah (Party of God), militant fundamen-

249

United Nations trucks loaded with supplies and medicine enter a Palestinian refugee camp in Lebanon on July 2. The camp had gone without food or supplies during a month-long siege by the Shiite Amal militia, which was seeking to prevent the Palestinians from reestablishing a presence in Lebanon. Similar fighting erupted in September and lasted through December.

talists who wanted to remove the French forces and, indeed, any trace of Western influence in Lebanon. In April, Paris ordered the withdrawal of its 45-member observer force but allowed the French contingent in the 5,800-member, multinational Unifil force to remain.

Militant groups continued to abduct American, British, French, and other civilian hostages. Some of those who had been abducted were killed, and a few were released unharmed. Among the latter were Father Lawrence Jenco, an American set free in July by the pro-Iranian Islamic Jihad, and David Jacobsen, the director of the American University of Beirut Hospital, freed on November 2 by the same group, as well as three French hostages.

Iran Arms Controversy. Within days of Jacobsen's release, a Lebanese periodical revealed that the U.S. government had apparently attempted to win the hostages' freedom by selling arms to Iran. The Reagan administration denied that an actual trade was involved, stressing that the arms sales were intended as an overture to strengthen relations with moderate elements in Iran. In any event, both Jenco and Jacobsen

had been released shortly after secret shipments of arms apparently' reached Iran. The U.S. action contravened Washington's general policy of not selling arms to countries considered to support international terrorism; the United States had also urged other countries not to do so. (It was later disclosed that the United States had, at the same time, been supplying Iraq with military intelligence about Iran.) Iran was implicated in several terrorist incidents, among them the 1983 bombing of U.S. Marine barracks in Lebanon, which killed 241 people.

Israel was reported to have acted as a middleman in the complicated series of transactions. Israel, whose relations with Iran date back to the days of the shah, when the two non-Arab nations in the region often found themselves with a confluence of interests, also had reportedly been supplying some arms to Iran on its own in the early 1980's. The Israeli government apparently hoped to gain protection for Jews living in Iran and to keep Iraq focused on the Iranian threat and therefore less able to mount hostilities against Israel. Arab leaders were said to be furious over the arms sales, particularly because of Iran's war with

Iraq. Many Arab states feared a wider spread of the Iranian brand of Islamic fundamentalism throughout the region if Iran won the war. (*See also* UNITED STATES: The Presidency *and* UNITED STATES: Foreign Affairs.)

Iran-Iraq War. It was unclear what effect the U.S. arms shipments to Iran had or would have on the course of the Iran-Iraq war. As the combatants entered their seventh year of hostilities in September, Iran appeared to have an edge in morale and on the ground, but Iraq maintained its substantial advantage in the air and in virtually all categories of military equipment. In February, Iranian forces captured the abandoned yet strategic Iraqi oil port of Fao (al-Faw), tightening the stronghold Iran held in the southern sector near Basra, Iraq's second largest city, and bringing the war to the border of Kuwait. However, Iraq continued its air war against Iranian oil shipping sites and targets in the Persian Gulf, and on Iranian industrial targets elsewhere. Casualties on both sides escalated, reaching over 100,000 Iraqi and 250,000 Iranian dead and more than half a million wounded, according to some estimates. By year's end, Iran had yet to launch its long-promised massive offensive, and a smaller action against four Iraqi islands in late December ended in an Iranian defeat.

Peres-Hassan Summit. In July, Israeli Prime Minister Shimon Peres flew to Morocco for secret talks with King Hassan II that were seen as the most important public contact between an Arab leader and an Israeli prime minister since Egyptian President Anwar Sadat's historic visit to Jerusalem in 1977. After a two-day meeting at the king's palace, the two leaders issued a joint communiqué. It said their talks had been "marked with frankness" and were "purely exploratory" in nature.

Appraisals of the meeting differed. Peres called the parley a success, while Hassan focused instead on the two leaders' divergent views, saying that Israel's refusal to evacuate territories seized in the 1967 Arab-Israeli war and its refusal to negotiate with the Palestine Liberation Organization remained major obstacles to peace. Some Arab countries, including Egypt, approved the meeting, but most condemned it. Syria broke diplomatic ties with Morocco over the issue. In response to hostile Arab reaction, King Hassan resigned from his titular role as president of the Arab League and cancelled Morocco's 1984 treaty of union with Libya.

Palestine Liberation Organization. In February, Jordan's King Hussein announced that he was ending a year-long peace initiative with PLO leader Yasir Arafat. He blamed the collapse of the effort on Arafat's refusal to endorse UN resolutions 242 and 338, which implicitly recognize Israel's right to exist while calling for it to return all occupied territory. The rift between Arafat and Hussein widened in the summer, when the monarch, continuing his challenge to Arafat's leadership, closed the Jordanian offices of al-Fatah, the largest group within the PLO.

Following the break with the PLO, Hussein seemed intent on creating alliances that would protect him against dangers growing out of the strong pro-PLO sentiment among his largely Palestinian population. Accordingly, he improved relations with Syrian President Hafez al-Assad, who also opposed Arafat's leadership. Improved relations with Assad encouraged Hussein to act as an intermediary between Syria and Iraq in an attempt to end the deep hostility between the two neighboring Arab states, but little progress was made toward that goal.

The crackdown on the PLO in Jordan highlighted the deep-rooted differences among the diverse Palestinian guerrilla organizations over allegiance to Arafat. The Palestine National Salvation Front, a bloc of six groups backed by Syria, continued its opposition to Arafat, accusing him of forsaking armed struggle in favor of "capitulationist designs favoring the Israeli enemy." In October, Arafat said he would move his military command posts to Yemen and Iraq, both countries far removed from the mainstream of Arab politics and Palestinian interests. At the same time, intense internal organizational pressures apparently influenced Arafat to decide upon a shift in strategy—away from a stress on international diplomacy and toward a greater emphasis on armed struggle against Israel. Thus, a PLO spokesman claimed responsibility for an October attack on Israeli soldiers near Jerusalem's Western Wall.

Meanwhile, in Lebanon pro- and anti-Arafat Palestinian fighters fought together against Amal. To some, this development offered promise of an eventual reconciliation within the PLO, but the increased Palestinian success was a cause of concern to other groups.

Israeli-Egyptian Relations. Improvement in the "cold peace" between Israel and Egypt came in September when the two countries agreed to resolve through arbitration their dispute over Taba, the tiny enclave on the Gulf of Aqaba that is controlled by Israel but claimed by Egypt. This agreement, reached after more than a year of arduous negotiations, cleared the way for a summit in Alexandria between Prime Minister Peres and Egyptian President Hosni Mubarak, the first meeting between leaders of the two countries since 1981. Although the two men failed to resolve their differences, they issued the so-called Alexandria Declaration, which stated that the September conference marked "a new era in bilateral relations between Egypt and Israel as well as in the search for a just and comprehensive peace in the Middle East." Egypt announced that it was upgrading its chargé d'affaires in Israel to the status of full ambassador; the previous envoy had been withdrawn in 1982.

Israeli "Rotation." In October, Prime Minister Peres and Likud coalition leader Yitzhak Shamir, the foreign minister, traded posts in accordance with their agreement on a government of national unity, which had been reached after inconclusive elections in 1984. Noting that Shamir was more hard-line than Peres and the Labor Party—particularly in his stated policy of stepping up Jewish settlement of the Israeli-occupied West Bank—analysts said that the change might affect the chances for movement in the generally stalemated Middle East peace process.

See also articles on individual countries

Iraqi air raids on Iranian military and civilian targets resumed in July after a three-month lull; here, residents of Sanandaj, about 250 miles west of Tehran, survey the damage. The Iran-Iraq war entered its seventh year in September.

mentioned and other Middle Eastern countries.   D.P.

MILITARY AND NAVAL AFFAIRS. After considerable progress had apparently been made in arms control negotiations, an October 1986 summit meeting between U.S. and Soviet leaders ended in failure. The United States carried out bombing raids against Libya; meanwhile, late in the year, it was revealed that the Reagan administration had secretly sold military arms to Iran, with profits being used to aid antigovernment rebels in Nicaragua. The Middle East remained volatile, with continuing violence among warring factions in Lebanon. Civil war resumed in Chad (see CHAD), while warfare continued in Afghanistan. In the United States, Congress and the Reagan administration battled over the military budget, and a sweeping military reorganization program was approved.

Arms Control. The United States and Soviet Union engaged in intensive negotiations aimed at reducing the size of their respective nuclear arsenals, and a landmark agreement was nearly concluded during a summit meeting in October between President Ronald Reagan and Soviet General Secretary Mikhail Gorbachev in Reykjavík, Iceland. But the talks foundered in a dispute over Reagan's Strategic Defense Initiative (SDI), popularly known as Star Wars, and the year ended with little apparent progress in arms control.

The two-day Iceland summit had been anticipated by both sides as preparatory to a meeting in Washington between the two leaders in early 1987. Instead, more than a dozen hours of detailed negotiations resulted in both sides tentatively accepting dramatic mutual reductions in their nuclear weapons arsenals. The tentative agreements included a limit of 100 medium-range missile warheads on each side, with both sides agreeing to remove all such missiles from Europe, and a 50 percent reduction in strategic weapons, including the complete elimination of ballistic missiles, over ten years. But the agreement collapsed when Reagan and Gorbachev could not settle their differences over SDI. Reagan was willing to guarantee that SDI would not be deployed for ten years; but he did not accept Gorbachev's condition that research and testing of the system be very sharply restricted.

After the summit, the United States carried out its previous threat to exceed the limits of the 1979 Strategic Arms Limitation Treaty (SALT II), signed by both nations but never ratified by the U.S. Senate. Reagan had announced in May that two Poseidon ballistic missile submarines would be dismantled to keep the United States within the limits of the treaty, but declared that the United States would exceed those limits later if Soviet arms control policies did not change significantly in the meantime. The United States exceeded SALT II in November, when the Air Force deployed its 131st strategic bomber armed with nuclear cruise missiles. In December, Soviet officials announced plans, outlined in a book published in both Russian and English, for measures to counter SDI, which they claimed would be far more cost-efficient than SDI technology. The Pentagon asserted in response that the proposed U.S. system could be adequately protected.

Middle East. Violence continued in Lebanon between Israeli and United Nations forces and Palestinian guerrillas. Israeli troops remaining in a security zone in southern Lebanon after the 1985 Israeli withdrawal came under heavier sporadic attacks by guerrillas, and the United Nations Interim Force in Lebanon (Unifil) came under direct attack for the first time since being deployed in 1978. Several Unifil soldiers died in attacks by Shiite Muslim troops in August and September. Israeli jets made sporadic raids on Palestinian bases in response to terrorist actions. Palestinian forces increased their presence and made gains in bloody battles with Shiite Muslims.

Iran-Iraq War. The war between Iran and Iraq entered its seventh year of stalemate. The Iranians made an important gain by capturing the Iraqi port of Fao (al-Faw), formerly a major oil terminal, in February; late in the year, Iranian officials reportedly were massing troops and continued to insist that a major new offensive would be launched. But no major offensive emerged by year's end. Heavy air attacks were made by both sides, with Iraq demonstrating superiority in its air power. Casualties in the war were estimated to have reached well over half a million.

In November it was disclosed that the United States had been secretly providing military arms

Nature's Early Warning System

It may not be the last word in technology, but the U.S. Army came up with a new way—more accurately, an old way—to bolster security at military installations in West Germany. Starting in September, some 900 squawking geese, in gaggles of 6 to 40, began auxiliary guard duty at 30 sites run by the 32nd U.S. Air Defense Command. A bird-brained idea? Not really. Geese have keen hearing and, at the slightest disturbance, will begin hissing, honking, and flapping about in tumultuous dismay. That's why the Romans used them more than 2,000 years ago to guard the Palatine Hill, and why Ballantine maintains goose patrols today outside its whisky distillery in Scotland. Furthermore, at a cost of about $30 each plus all the grass they can eat, these web-footed sentinels are a lot cheaper than guard dogs.

to the Iranian armed forces—apparently, at least in part, in an effort to win the release of American hostages held by pro-Iranian militants in Lebanon. (Two of these hostages were released during the year.) Published reports also indicated that, in the course of the war with Iraq, Iran had spent billions of dollars buying arms from a wide variety of other nations; besides China and North Korea (the major suppliers) and Iran's Mideast allies (Libya and Syria), some Western allies were cited as sources for Iranian arms. The Soviet Union, Iraq's main supplier, also reportedly had shipped arms to Iran. As controversy over the Iranian arms affair escalated, President Reagan stated that there would be no further such sales to Iran. Meanwhile, the Reagan administration said it had learned that Iranian arms-sale profits, amounting to perhaps $30 million, had been diverted via Swiss bank accounts to U.S.-backed "contra" rebels opposing the leftist Sandinista government in Nicaragua.

Central America. The Reagan administration's campaign to undermine the Sandinista government had achieved a major victory on June 25 when the Democratic-controlled House of Representatives narrowly approved $100 million in aid for the contras. The Republican-controlled Senate approved the aid package, by a 53-47 vote, on August 13. In addition to $70 million in military aid and $30 million in humanitarian aid to the contras, the package included $300 million in economic assistance to four friendly nations in Central America (Costa Rica, El Salvador, Guatemala, and Honduras). The legislation also removed congressional restrictions on the involvement of the Central Intelligence Agency in the anti-Sandinista effort. The congressionally approved military aid was to be used for training and more sophisticated weapons, including ground-to-air missiles designed to shoot down Soviet-built helicopter gunships in the Nicaraguan Air Force.

The Pentagon disclosed in February that it intended to build $50 million in additional facilities in Honduras over five years. Approximately 1,200 U.S. troops were stationed in Honduras and several thousand others participated in training exercises there during 1986. Late in the year, there were increased clashes in the border region, involving Nicaraguan forces, contra rebels, and Honduran Army troops.

Libyan Raids. In April, in the largest American military action since the invasion of Grenada in 1983, U.S. aircraft carried out intensive bombing raids against targets in two Libyan cities. The raids, which followed a smaller military confrontation in March, were in retaliation for alleged Libyan involvement in international terrorist activities and escalated a continuing war of nerves with the Libyan regime of Muammar al-Qaddafi.

The year's first confrontation occurred on March 24 and 25, shortly after an American naval task force began "freedom of navigation" training exercises in the area of the Gulf of Sidra, an arm of the Mediterranean claimed as territorial waters by Libya but considered international waters by other nations. After U.S. planes flying over Libyan-claimed waters were attacked by surface-to-air missiles fired by Libyan ground batteries, American jets sank at least two Libyan naval vessels and attacked missile batteries on the Libyan coast. The U.S. task force reported no losses.

More intensive operations against Libya were ordered by President Reagan three weeks later,

U.S. sailors make friends with four-year-old Yu Hao, after three U.S. naval vessels sailed into China's Qingdao port, in the first such visit by an American warship since 1949.

after U.S. intelligence reported evidence that Libyan agents were responsible for the April 5 bombing of a West Berlin discotheque that killed two American servicemen. On April 15, in a joint attack code-named Eldorado Canyon, planes from the aircraft carriers *Coral Sea* and *America* joined U.S. F-111 bombers from Royal Air Force bases in Great Britain in attacking military targets in Libya. The Navy jets bombed a military airfield and a barracks near Benghazi, while the Air Force bombers struck port facilities, a barracks, and airport military installations at Tripoli. The raids were carried out at night, to reduce the risk of American casualties; the only U.S. losses were a single F-111 bomber and its two-man crew, apparently shot down by Libyan antiaircraft fire. A Pentagon spokesman termed the raids "a near-flawless operation." Some bombs, however, landed in a residential area of Tripoli (the French embassy was party destroyed, and civilian casualties were reported), and it was later disclosed that nearly one-fourth of the attacking aircraft had aborted their mission.

Afghan War. The Soviet military occupation of Afghanistan entered its eighth year in December. An estimated 115,000 Soviet troops in Afghanistan continued to hold major population centers, but several Soviet offensives failed to crush the insurgency. In October the Soviets withdrew several thousand troops from Afghanistan, although many Western observers claimed the move was a propaganda ploy related to the Reykjavík talks. UN-mediated indirect peace talks between the Soviet Union and Afghanistan recessed with no agreement, but timetables for a future withdrawal of Soviet troops were to be discussed at new talks scheduled for February 1987. U.S. Secretary of Defense Caspar Weinberger disclosed in October that the United States was considering deploying surveillance aircraft near the Pakistani-Afghan border until Pakistan was able to obtain its own airborne radar system. In December, U.S. officials said Afghan rebels had begun using newly furnished Stinger antiaircraft missiles against Soviet and Afghan government aircraft.

Military Coups. A military coup in Lesotho overthrew the government of Prime Minister Chief Leabua Jonathan in January; General Justin Lekhanya headed the junta, which replaced two decades of autocratic rule by Jonathan. The military government in Uganda was overthrown the same month by rebel troops calling themselves the National Resistance Army; the rebels installed NRA leader Yoweri Museveni as the country's new president. In late September, the government of Togo put down an attempted coup, which it blamed on Togolese dissidents in Ghana; in the aftermath of the incident, France sent in paratroopers at the government's request.

More notable than various coups and coup

Former Navy communications specialist Jerry A. Whitworth leaves the San Francisco Federal Building on the second day of his espionage trial. Whitworth, a member of the Walker spy ring, was sentenced in August to 365 years in prison for supplying naval secrets to the Soviet Union.

attempts during the year were the "people power" revolution in the Philippines and the change of government in Haiti. In both cases, strongmen relinquished power under popular pressure, rather than being overthrown by a positive exercise of military power.

Arms Sales. According to an analysis by the Congressional Research Service, the Western European nations in 1985 made 31.3 percent of all arms sales to Third World nations, surpassing the Soviet Union (30.4 percent) and the United States (17.8 percent), which had previously ranked first and second, respectively.

Aside from the Iranian arms deal, there were few major U.S. arms sales of particular note. China signed an agreement in November to buy $550 million worth of American radar and electronics gear for its fighter planes, and U.S. officials indicated that the Reagan administration would be willing to sell computers and some military hardware to India if safeguards could be established to keep sophisticated technology secrets from the Soviet Union. The Reagan administration announced in October that it was willing to sell Honduras F-5 jets to replace its aging fleet of French-built fighter planes, but Honduras, foreseeing difficulty in obtaining U.S. congressional approval for the sale, elected instead to buy Israeli Kfir jets with U.S. aid funds. A $1.9 billion sale of arms to Jordan was withdrawn by the administration in January, in the face of overwhelming opposition in the U.S. Senate. The White House had previously removed $400 million in sophisticated surface-to-air missiles from the package in hopes of winning congressional approval, but the modified deal was vigorously opposed by the Israeli government.

Congressional opposition also caused the administration, with Saudi agreement, to withdraw 800 shoulder-fired Stinger antiaircraft missiles from a $354 million arms sale (already scaled down in scope) to Saudi Arabia. The modified deal went through when President Reagan vetoed measures in both houses opposing the sale. Meanwhile, the first of five Awacs planes, which had been contracted for in 1981 and for which the Saudis had paid some $3 billion in advance, was finally delivered in June, with the rest scheduled to follow by March 1987.

Naval Affairs. The United States and Soviet Union continued their race for worldwide naval supremacy. Both fleets proceeded with substantial fleet modernization programs, but the Soviet lead in warships began to shrink as the U.S. Navy moved nearer its goal of a 600-ship fleet by the end of the decade. Another World War II-era battleship, the *Missouri*, was taken out of mothballs and recommissioned in June, while a 15th aircraft carrier, the nuclear-powered *Theodore Roosevelt*, was commissioned in October. Two U.S. Navy ships sailed into the Black Sea in March, provoking a protest from the Soviet Union, which claimed the ships had invaded Soviet territorial waters. A Soviet Yankee-class nuclear-powered missile submarine sank in the Atlantic Ocean 600 miles east of Bermuda in October; the vessel had been crippled when one of its 16 ballistic missiles exploded and caught fire.

Three U.S. Navy ships paid a port call to the Chinese city of Qingdao in November, becoming the first American warships to visit China since the Communist takeover in 1949. Relations between the United States and New Zealand deteriorated after Prime Minister David Lange refused to change his government's year-old policy of refusing to allow U.S. ships to make port calls if they were nuclear-powered or carried nuclear weapons.

U.S. Developments. Despite growing opposition to escalating military spending after five years of unprecedented peacetime budgets, the Reagan administration, on February 5, submitted a budget requesting $320.3 billion for defense, a 12 percent increase over fiscal 1986. The largest Defense Department budget item was a $4.8 billion request for SDI. Even many longtime supporters of the Pentagon complained that the spending levels were unrealistic in a time of growing pressure to cut the federal deficit. Despite several appeals by Reagan, including a nationally televised address, Congress voted sizable cuts in the military budget. The final appropriations amounted to $289.2 billion, including $3.5 billion for the SDI. In December the Defense Department asked Congress for $2.8 billion in supplemental funds, including about $500 million more for SDI.

Although critics complained that SDI was technologically dubious and too expensive, and Congress was unwilling to grant the administration all the funds it wanted for testing and research, SDI research actually accelerated during the year. The Pentagon reported several successful tests of experimental weapons—demonstrating, it claimed, the technological viability of the program. The United States signed agreements allowing Great Britain, West Germany, Israel, and Italy to participate in SDI research and development activities.

In December, U.S. helicopters carried Honduran troops to the border to repel a reported invasion of Nicaraguan government troops searching for contra rebel bases in Honduras. Military action along the border was intensifying late in the year.

Soviet troops about to leave Afghanistan participate in a predeparture ceremony in the Shindand desert; the October pullout of about 8,000 soldiers was regarded by the West as only a token gesture from Moscow.

Weapons Systems. On December 23, eight years after development began, the MX intercontinental ballistic missile was declared operational, as the first ten missiles moved to full-alert status in Wyoming. Their deployment marked the first addition to the U.S. land-based nuclear arsenal in 16 years. Deployment of 50 missiles has been authorized by Congress; Reagan announced he would pursue his request for another 50, with the latter to be based on rail cars instead of in silos like the others. The chances of approval were considered doubtful.

More B-1B strategic bombers and Trident ballistic missile submarines were delivered by manufacturers in 1986. The first batch of B-1B's received by the Air Force, however, had to undergo repairs for fuel leaks, and it was not until early autumn that a B-1B went on full-alert status. Testing continued on the single-warhead mobile missile nicknamed Midgetman, on submarine-launched cruise missiles, and on the so-called ASAT system for destroying enemy satellites in outer space.

In August the Pentagon gave preliminary approval to Army plans to develop an $11 billion battlefield air-defense system. The new program, termed Forward Area Aid Defense, would use heavy missiles carried on an armored chassis and lighter missiles on trucks. FAAD would replace the Sergeant York, or

Divad, antiaircraft gun program that was canceled in 1985 after tests showed it ineffective.

In October the Air Force awarded General Dynamics Corporation a contract, worth billions of dollars, to update U.S. air defenses against attacking bombers. Northrop Corporation was selected, along with McDonnell Douglas, to form one of two teams that would develop and build prototypes for the next generation of combat aircraft, known as the Advanced Tactical Fighter. The other team was to consist of Lockheed Corporation, General Dynamics, and Boeing. Development proceeded on a laser-guided bomb and on a new class of nuclear submarines. In May, NATO defense ministers approved a Reagan administration plan to resume production of nerve gas weapons for the first time since 1969. (Congress in 1985 had conditioned its approval of the resumption on NATO endorsement.)

The Washington *Post* reported in August that 50 "Stealth" jet fighters had become operational and were hidden in hangars in the Nevada desert, flying only at night to escape detection. The Stealth project was one of the Pentagon's most closely guarded secrets; the plane reportedly had the ability to avoid detection by enemy radar systems through its ungainly shape and special design features incorporating state-of-the-art technology. An Air Force jet that crashed in California on July

11 under mysterious circumstances was later reported to be a Stealth fighter on a training mission.

The Army's Bradley armored troop carrier came under severe criticism during the year. A House Armed Services Committee report released in May, by which time the Army had already received nearly 2,500 of the vehicles, said that Army tests of the Bradley in 1985 were poorly supervised and may have failed to reveal potential vulnerabilities. In September an engineer who had been dismissed by the vehicle's manufacturer, FMC Corporation, sued FMC for allegedly falsely certifying that the Bradley met specified requirements for crossing deep water. The Army admitted that the Bradley had sunk on several occasions while crossing streams.

Military Reform. The most sweeping reorganization of the U.S. military in 40 years was passed by Congress in September. The legislation significantly strengthened the chairman of the Joint Chiefs of Staff, created a new vice chairman of the Joint Chiefs of Staff, and gave more authority to field commanders in combat situations. The legislation had been opposed by the chiefs of the military services and the civilian service secretaries because their authority would be diluted. But proponents argued that the changes were necessary to increase cooperation between the branches of the armed forces and improve the chain of command. This, they said, could prevent the kinds of operational mistakes that contributed to the failure of the mission to rescue U.S. hostages in Iran in 1980 and failure to prevent the 1983 terrorist bombing of a U.S. Marine barracks in Lebanon, in which over 240 servicemen were killed.

Efforts to reform the military procurement system were strengthened by a critical report issued in February by a presidential commission headed by former Deputy Secretary of Defense David Packard. The commission blamed the problems more on faulty procedures and bureaucratic complexities than on "fraud and dishonesty" and recommended centralizing the Pentagon's procurement system under a new undersecretary of defense for acquisition. The panel also urged that the military budget be drawn up every two years instead of annually to provide more stability to the procurement process.

Personnel. A major reform of the military retirement system was signed into law on July 2. The new law would eventually reduce pension benefits by approximately 20 percent annually but would apply only to personnel who joined the armed forces after August 1, 1986. The Army instituted a major crackdown on smoking on July 7, prohibiting smoking in all Army vehicles and aircraft and "in all Department of Army-occupied space, except for designated smoking areas."

Russell A. Rourke resigned as secretary of the Air Force in the spring and was replaced by Edward C. Aldridge, Jr., who had been undersecretary. Rear Admiral Grace Hopper was honored with a farewell ceremony on August 14 aboard the U.S.S. *Constitution* in Boston Harbor, as she retired from the Navy after 43 years of service. At 79, she was the country's oldest active-duty officer.

Espionage. Perhaps the most notable espionage conviction of the year was that of Jerry A. Whitworth, a former Navy communications specialist. He was sentenced on August 28 to 365 years in prison and fined $410,000 for his involvement in a spy ring that supplied naval secrets to the Soviet Union for well over a decade. Navy officials reported in June that the damage done to naval security by the spy ring had been repaired at an estimated cost of $100 million in new cryptographic and communications equipment.

See also UNITED STATES: Foreign Affairs *and articles on individual countries.*   T.D.

MINNESOTA. *See* STATISTICS OF THE WORLD.

MISSISSIPPI. *See* STATISTICS OF THE WORLD.

MISSOURI. *See* STATISTICS OF THE WORLD.

MONACO. *See* STATISTICS OF THE WORLD.

MONGOLIAN PEOPLE'S REPUBLIC. *See* STATISTICS OF THE WORLD.

MONTANA. *See* STATISTICS OF THE WORLD.

MOROCCO. King Hassan II received Israeli Prime Minister Shimon Peres for a 48-hour visit on July 21–23, 1986. Hassan urged Peres to accept the terms of the 1982 Fez plan, which called for an Israeli withdrawal from all occupied territories and the creation of a Palestinian state, among other provisions. Peres rejected the proposal. His visit, applauded by the United States and Egypt, was sharply criticized in the Arab world, and Syria immediately broke relations with Morocco. On August 27, Syria and Libya issued a communiqué denouncing the meeting as an "act of treason" by Morocco and a "violation of the Arab consensus." Hassan responded by canceling the treaty of union that Morocco had signed with Libya in 1984.

The focus of the 11-year-old conflict over the Western Sahara, between Morocco (which had annexed it) and the guerrilla forces of the Polisario Front, shifted to diplomacy in 1986. Morocco agreed to hold indirect talks with the front; the first round, held in April at the United Nations, centered on UN proposals for a cease-fire in the Western Sahara and the organization of a referendum in the territory. After a second round of talks revealed irreconcilable differences, the UN secretary-general went to Morocco in July. At that time Morocco agreed to his proposal for an international inquiry to determine the consequences of confining the Moroccan armed forces and administration to their quarters during a referendum, but the Polisario Front refused to agree to this inquiry and continued to press for direct negotiations with Morocco.

Morocco's close relations with Spain suffered because of a new Spanish law threatening the residency rights of Moroccans in the Spanish enclaves of Ceuta and Melilla, on Morocco's Mediterranean coast. The funeral of a Moroccan killed by Spanish police sparked a demonstration against the law. Spain promised that the law would be applied with restraint, but Moroccan residents in the enclaves organized another round of demonstrations, hoping to establish a new political status inside the Spanish state—a position opposed by Hassan.

Morocco showed signs of modest progress in coping with the severe economic difficulties of the past several years. Factors that contributed to this included an exceptionally good cereal harvest, a drop in oil prices, and lower interest rates. The balance-of-payments deficit declined, and the economic growth rate was projected at 4 percent. On the negative side, the budget deficit was expected to rise by more than 80 percent.

See STATISTICS OF THE WORLD.   J.D.

MOTION PICTURES. Despite a weak summer season and complaints from some critics and moviegoers about the paucity of good fare coming from Hollywood, the public was able to enjoy many worthy American and foreign movies during 1986.

Allen and Ivory. The first half of the year brought two major treats—Woody Allen's *Hannah and Her Sisters* and James Ivory's *A Room With a View*. Allen wrote and directed the mature romantic comedy about three sisters, luminously played by Mia Farrow, Dianne Wiest, and Barbara Hershey, and their complications with men and careers. Allen also starred, in an excellent cast that included Michael Caine, Sam Waterston, Max Von Sydow, Maureen O'Sullivan, and the late Lloyd Nolan in his final role. *A Room With a View,* latest of the modestly budgeted works stemming from the 20-year partnership of director Ivory and producer Ismail Merchant, was based on E. M. Forster's 1908 novel. Merchant-Ivory films have generally earned high praise but a limited audience. This one, the story of a chaperoned English girl and her awakening to passion on an Italian holiday, topped the $1 million box-office mark at a single New York theater, besides entertaining audiences in many other cities.

British Films. Other highlights in the first half of the year reflected a renaissance of British filmmaking. *A Letter to Brezhnev* examined with charm and vitality the frustrations and dreams of two young working-class women in Liverpool, while *My Beautiful Laundrette* depicted the struggle of Pakistanis to become entrepreneurs in London. *Mona Lisa* was an original and sensitive thriller starring the dynamic Bob Hoskins as an ex-convict who falls in love with a prostitute he chauffeurs. A later import, *No Surrender,* was a dark comedy set in Liverpool, with rival groups of pensioners supporting different sides in the Northern Ireland conflict.

Autumn Harvest. The fall season brought some generally distinguished films. Roland Joffe's *The Mission,* winner of the Golden Palm at the Cannes Film Festival in May, starred Robert De Niro and Jeremy Irons in a beautifully photographed epic dramatizing the futile efforts of 18th-century Jesuits to save their Indian

The intertwined, often tangled lives, loves, and aspirations of three sisters (played by Mia Farrow, Barbara Hershey, and Dianne Wiest) formed the heart of the comedy-drama Hannah and Her Sisters, *Woody Allen's most acclaimed film since* Annie Hall. Hannah *featured Michael Caine in a pivotal male role and Allen himself playing the part of a hypochondriac.*

missions in Latin America from destruction by Spanish and Portuguese authorities. William Hurt and Marlee Matlin were outstanding in *Children of a Lesser God,* the adaptation of Mark Medoff's play about the relationship between a teacher and the deaf young woman with whom he falls in love. The theater was also the source for *'night, Mother,* based on Marsha Norman's Pulitzer Prize-winning play, with Sissy Spacek as the daughter who announces her intention to commit suicide and Anne Bancroft as the mother who desperately tries to stop her. Screen versions were made of two hit stage comedies: Beth Henley's *Crimes of the Heart,* directed by Bruce Beresford and teaming actresses Jessica Lange, Sissy Spacek, and Diane Keaton, and Neil Simon's *Brighton Beach Memoirs.*

The film of Umberto Eco's best-selling novel *The Name of the Rose,* a murder mystery set in a monastery during the 14th century, was directed by Jean-Jacques Annaud and starred F. Murray Abraham and Sean Connery. Writer-director Blake Edwards offered *That's Life,* in which an architect (Jack Lemmon) plunges into depression when he turns 60, and his wife (Julie Andrews) nervously awaits the results of a biopsy. The year also brought two films based on novels by Paul Theroux: Peter Weir's *The Mosquito Coast,* starring Harrison Ford, and Robert Swaim's *Half Moon Street,* starring Sigourney Weaver and Michael Caine.

Major Directors. Among other directors, Sidney Lumet turned out an entertaining murder

mystery, *The Morning After,* starring Jane Fonda and Jeff Bridges. Martin Scorsese succeeded in making a powerful sequel, *The Color of Money,* to the 1961 hit *The Hustler;* Paul Newman brilliantly reprised his role as Fast Eddie Felson, with Tom Cruise outstanding as his new-generation costar. Francis Ford Coppola's *Peggy Sue Got Married,* starring Kathleen Turner as a woman who goes back in time, was chosen to close the New York Film Festival.

Among directors from abroad, Franco Zeffirelli brought Verdi's opera *Otello* to the screen with Placido Domingo in the role of the Moor. Federico Fellini was represented by *Ginger and Fred,* pairing Marcello Mastroianni and Giulietta Masina as rediscovered old vaudevillians. In *Summer,* Eric Rohmer told the affecting story of a Parisian secretary facing a lonely vacation. Bertrand Blier's farce *Ménage* starred Gérard Depardieu as a thief who becomes part of an unusual romantic triangle.

Subjects Heavy and Light. Some of the year's best films dealt with serious subject matter. Oliver Stone followed up his gritty *Salvador,* released earlier in the year, with *Platoon,* a powerful film about American soldiers in Vietnam. Undercurrents of violence and sex in society were probed in David Lynch's drama *Blue Velvet.* In addition to *The Mission,* films with spiritual themes included *Thérèse,* based on the life of the 19th-century Carmelite nun who became Saint Theresa of Lisieux, and *Mother Teresa,* a documentary about the con-

MOTION PICTURES

temporary Nobel Peace Prize-winning nun.

On the lighter side, *Star Trek* addicts enjoyed the latest addition to the movie series, *Star Trek IV: The Voyage Home*. Veteran actors Burt Lancaster and Kirk Douglas found lively material in *Tough Guys,* about two just-released convicts trying to adjust to old age and the modern world after 30 years in prison. John Cleese starred as a tardy headmaster in the daffy British comedy *Clockwork*. Comic talents Steve Martin, Chevy Chase, and Martin Short appeared in *The Three Amigos,* and *The Golden Child,* starring Eddie Murphy, was the hit of the Christmas season, despite mixed reviews.

Jonathan Demme directed a lively, original comedy, *Something Wild*. Richard Gere starred in Richard Pearce's thriller *No Mercy*. In *Heartbreak Ridge,* which he directed and produced, Clint Eastwood portrayed a marine sergeant whose men take part in the U.S. invasion of Grenada. And the man-eating plants of Roger Corman's low-budget cult classic *Little Shop of Horrors* (1960) came to life again in a screen musical based on the long-running musical stage adaptation.

One of the year's biggest hits was an Australian import, *"Crocodile" Dundee,* about an innocent's first brush with New York City life. This pleasant comedy, starring Australian television personality Paul Hogan, already had broken all box-office records in Australia before it came to the United States in September.

New Talent. Jim Jarmusch, who previously made a splash with *Stranger Than Paradise,* demonstrated that the achievement was no fluke. His stature rose with the New York Film Festival's choice of his *Down by Law,* an idiosyncratic comedy about three losers who escape from a Louisiana prison, as its opener. Writer-director Spike Lee received major media attention for *She's Gotta Have It,* a spirited comedy about a black woman and her three boyfriends. Donna Deitch attracted attention with her *Desert Hearts,* about a love affair between two women.

Playwright Beth Henley made inroads as a screenwriter; in addition to scripting the adaptation of her *Crimes of the Heart,* she wrote *Nobody's Fool,* about the relationship between a small-town girl and a man passing through with a theater company, and with David Byrne of the Talking Heads cowrote *True Stories,* which debuted at the New York Film Festival.

Among new or relatively new faces on screen, special promise was offered by Laura Dern, daughter of actor Bruce Dern and actress Diane Ladd, who was praised for her breakthrough performance as the precocious but vulnerable teenager in *Smooth Talk*. Italian comedian Roberto Benigni proved original and funny in

William Hurt carries on an impassioned conversation in sign language with Marlee Matlin, in Children of a Lesser God, *an adaptation of the Tony Award-winning play about the relationship between a teacher and a young deaf woman.*

Ageless screen idol Paul Newman and Tom "Top Gun" Cruise teamed up in The Color of Money, *a long-awaited sequel to Newman's 1961 hit,* The Hustler. *In a scene from* Money, *mentor Fast Eddie Felson attempts to convince the kid, Vincent, of pool hustling's payoffs.*

his American film debut in *Down by Law.* Oprah Winfrey, the talk-show hostess who made her acting debut in *The Color Purple,* took another movie career step in *Native Son,* based on Richard Wright's explosive novel about black-white relations. And with her success in *Pretty in Pink,* a John Hughes film about teenagers, Molly Ringwald, at 18, achieved the status of a "bankable" star.

Summer Doldrums. Although offset by improvements later on, the summer months stood out as a dismal period. *Heartburn,* starring Jack Nicholson and Meryl Streep and directed by Mike Nichols, was one of the few summer releases aimed at an adult audience, but it was a disappointment. The biggest box office hit of the season, and the year, was *Top Gun,* a slickly made but clichéd Navy pilot yarn featuring dogfights with the latest planes; it had grossed $119 million by Labor Day and was still going strong. Other box-office winners included *The Karate Kid II; Back to School,* starring Rodney Dangerfield as a wheeler-dealer who enrolls in college along with his son; *Aliens,* a suspenseful sequel to the 1979 hit *Alien,* starring Sigourney Weaver; and *Ferris Bueller's Day Off,* starring Matthew Broderick as a high school senior who plays hookey. Jeff Goldblum turned in a noteworthy performance in a remake of the 1958 film *The Fly,* which also did well.

Howard the Duck was an expensive failure, as were Roman Polanski's *Pirates* and George Lucas's and Jim Henson's *Labyrinth.* Other duds included *Shanghai Surprise,* with Madonna and Sean Penn, and Prince's *Under the Cherry Moon.* A worthier film that also flopped was Marshall Brickman's *The Manhattan Project,* about a high school student who builds a nuclear bomb for his science project.

Cobra, the violent movie starring Sylvester Stallone, grossed in the vicinity of $50 million by Labor Day, but was still regarded as a flop because it hadn't lived up to the projected figures and made the kind of money that Stallone's *Rambo* did.

Disney Hits. The revamped Disney studio showed continued strength with two big adult-oriented hits. *Down and Out in Beverly Hills* starred Nick Nolte in a remake of Jean Renoir's *Boudu Saved from Drowning* (1932); and *Ruthless People,* indebted to O. Henry's "The Ransom of Red Chief," featured Bette Midler as a kidnapped wife whose husband doesn't want her back. A new animated movie, *The Great Mouse Detective,* was in the tradition of the Disney classics.

Colorization. Because of the resistance of television programmers to black and white films, film marketers have begun using computer technology to color films for television showing and for videocassettes. Among films being colorized have been such classics as *Casablanca* and *The Maltese Falcon.* The process destroys effects that were often created with great care in black and white, and even the most sophisticated touch-ups are those of someone other than the original director. Because of the commercial inducements and the lack of control by filmmakers, however, it seemed unlikely that the trend could be reversed.

Awards. In March the Academy Award for best picture of 1985 went to *Out of Africa,* which garnered a total of seven awards, including one to Sydney Pollack for best director. Best actress honors went to Geraldine Page for her performance in *A Trip to Bountiful.* It was her first Oscar after having received seven previous nominations. William Hurt was named best actor for his work in *Kiss of the Spider Woman;*

Anjelica Huston, best supporting actress for *Prizzi's Honor;* and Don Ameche, best supporting actor for *Cocoon.* The overlooking of *The Color Purple,* despite 11 nominations, generated controversy, particularly since its director, Steven Spielberg, had not been nominated for best director. However, he was chosen best director by the Directors' Guild of America. Also overlooked was Terry Gilliam's black comedy *Brazil,* set in an Orwellian city of the future; contrary to expectations, it received only two nominations.

Canadian Film. It was a banner year for Canadian cinema. The success of such films as Sandy Wilson's *My American Cousin* proved that Canadians could break away from Hollywood formulas and produce good films on modest budgets. A bittersweet story of a young girl's coming-of-age in rural British Columbia,

Breathtaking special effects, white-knuckle suspense, and a powerful performance by Sigourney Weaver as she fights to save a little girl from extraterrestrials made Aliens, *the multimonstered sequel to the 1979 hit* Alien, *a top-grossing summer movie. Here, in the tense moments before the alien attack, a cool and competent Weaver prepares the troops for battle.*

Teen Superstar

Molly Ringwald, the 18-year-old actress with the trademark orange coif and pouty lips, was widely hailed as "Hollywood's new teen princess," as she deftly executed her latest star turn in the hit film *Pretty in Pink.* The precocious daughter of a Sacramento, Calif., musician, Molly recorded her own album at six and became a successful child actor. At the age of 13 she landed a part in Paul Mazursky's 1982 film of *The Tempest,* and then was catapulted to teen movie stardom in 1984, as the winsomely frustrated birthday girl of *Sixteen Candles.* In *The Breakfast Club* (1985), her second collaboration with teen-film author-director John Hughes, she played a high school student at a Saturday detention. In *Pretty in Pink,* also by Hughes, she again played a teenager, this time a girl from the wrong side of the tracks who is caught between the rich boy she loves and the goofy but good-hearted boy who loves her. This fall, sated with teen roles, Molly tried her hand at a New York stage production of Horton Foote's *Lily Dale.* She also signed a development deal with United Artists aimed at enabling her to create and direct her own projects.

Molly Ringwald

Cousin was produced by Toronto's Peter O'Brian (*The Grey Fox*) for just Can$1.2 million. At the Academy of Canadian Cinema and Television's annual Genie Awards in April, it took six prizes—including those for best film, best director, and best actor.

Decline of the American Empire, a Can$1.8 million movie written and directed by Montréal's Denys Arcand, took the International Critics Prize at Cannes and won distribution in 25 countries. It also broke box-office records in Québec and lured Hollywood producers into negotiations to shoot an English-language remake. *Decline* is a comedy-drama consisting of a protracted dialogue among a group of affluent intellectuals, who discuss their sexual adventures in graphic detail while preparing for a dinner party. It was part of a major revival in Québec filmmaking. Léa Pool won international acclaim for *Anne Trister,* an intimate drama about a Swiss artist searching for her identity in Montréal. *Pouvoir Intime* (*Intimate Power*), a sleek psychological thriller, marked an impressive debut for its 30-year-old director Yves Simoneau. All three films were coprod-

uced by the National Film Board, which has helped support a shift in Québec cinema toward personal films accessible to international audiences.

In English Canada, critics hailed Martha Henry's electrifying performance In Leon Marr's first feature, *Dancing in the Dark,* a sensitive adaptation of Joan Barfoot's novel about the collapse of a marriage. Anne Wheeler made a strong impact with her first fictional feature, *Loyalties,* set in a remote village in northern Alberta. And the NFB's John N. Smith directed *Sitting in Limbo,* a funny and touching documentary-style drama about a West Indian couple struggling to survive in Montréal.

B.D.J. (Canadian films) & W.W.

MOZAMBIQUE. On October 19, 1986, Samora Machel, who had been president of Mozambique since the country's independence from Portugal in 1975, was killed, along with 33 others, including some of his top aides, in a mysterious plane crash in South Africa. Machel was returning from Zambia, where he had been conducting talks with other African leaders. South African authorities said the Soviet-built plane had strayed into South African air space and faltered because of bad weather and possible pilot error. Others, noting a simultaneous escalation of South Africa's support for the antigovernment forces of the Mozambique National Resistance (MNR), suspected foul play. South Africa, Mozambique, and the Soviet Union began inquiries into the crash. Meanwhile, South Africa produced documents said to have been taken from the wreckage, suggesting that Mozambique and Zimbabwe had been plotting to overthrow the pro-South African government of Malawi.

On November 6, Joaquím Chissano, foreign minister since 1975, was installed as Mozambique's new president. The year had already seen a series of government shake-ups. In March, in response to charges of administrative inefficiency and unresponsiveness, key party leaders were assigned to take over various sectors of the government. In April there was a cabinet reshuffle; in addition, six of the ten provincial governors were replaced. In July, Mário de Graça Machungo was appointed to the newly created post of prime minister, taking over direction of the cabinet from President Machel, who had decided to concentrate on his duties as head of state and on defense.

The MNR insurgency continued with mixed results. In the central area, MNR guerrillas recaptured, then lost again, their strategic Gorongosa base. In the south, government forces managed to confine the MNR to small attacks, and the northern province of Cabo Delgado was mostly secure. But in areas adjoining South Africa, constant MNR infiltration made road travel unsafe, and fighting led to the flight of thousands of refugees to the South African homeland of Gazankulu. A similar insecurity plagued areas adjoining Malawi, which was said to serve as a base for MNR attacks. There were reports late in the year that very large numbers of people had fled into Malawi to escape rebel attacks.

Despite an easing of drought conditions, Mozambique was still listed as seriously affected by food shortages. Mozambican officials estimated that 4 million people would go hungry unless emergency assistance was received. The major reason for the problem was a shortage of foreign exchange and a disruption of food production caused by the civil war. Matters were made worse when South Africa announced it would expel Mozambican workers in retaliation for Mozambique's alleged harboring of guerrillas fighting the South African government.

See STATISTICS OF THE WORLD.   W.M.

MUSIC. In popular music there were albums by Madonna, Bruce Springsteen, Paul Simon, and Cyndi Lauper, among others, and plaudits for Whitney Houston and Aretha Franklin. The music world was saddened by the passing of jazz great Benny Goodman. In classical music, performances and recordings commemorated the 100th anniversary of the death of Franz Liszt, and pianist Vladimir Horowitz made a triumphal concert tour, returning to his native land.

POPULAR MUSIC

Censorship appeared to threaten American popular music in 1986, as fundamentalist Christians and concerned parents pushed their attacks on the lyric content of records and performances. Rap music acts continued to attract substantial audiences, although their shows were often marred by violence. American record labels began rediscovering jazz as a potential commercial entity.

Thoroughly Modern Minnie

Minnie Mouse, the Walt Disney character who made her debut with Mickey Mouse in the 1928 cartoon "Steamboat Willie," has undergone startling changes. Now a frenetic, fashion-crazed teenager, she wears a lime-green minidress, bangle bracelets, and high-top sneakers, and she slips on red lace fingerless gloves over her proper white ones. Minnie may take out her old polka-dot dress and bloomers occasionally, but she'll never again take a backseat to Mickey. As part of a new Disney Productions campaign, she stepped out on her own in 1986, cutting a record, "Totally Minnie," which includes a song describing Minnie as "so outrageous—still dancing when the band goes home." The new Minnie has also starred in music videos, hosted her own TV special, and enjoyed star billing in Disney theme park parades and stage shows. Can a new Mickey be far behind?

African sounds and rhythms are making inroads into American popular music, with a South African Zulu a cappella group, Ladysmith Black Mambazo, singing backup on a track from Paul Simon's new album Graceland. *Here they perform with the songwriter on NBC's* Saturday Night Live.

Popular. Rock and roll came under attack from seemingly everywhere. Most intense were the assaults of the religious right, which found satanism, hidden messages, and encouragement of suicide and drug use in rock lyrics and stage performances. The city of San Antonio banned attendance at rock shows by those under age 13, and several other cities were considering following suit. The Parents' Music Resource Center, a procensorship lobbying group, pressured some record companies into putting "parental advisory" notices on albums. Soul great Smokey Robinson surprised some by putting a procensorship single on his latest album. And, heeding the advice of television evangelist Jimmy Lee Swaggart, the Wal-Mart chain of stores began pulling allegedly offensive albums of all genres from its shelves, along with rock magazines.

Drug use by musicians themselves also continued to be an issue, as Boy George, lead singer of Culture Club, finally confirmed rumors of heroin addiction and was arrested for drug possession. Also, a member of his entourage died of an overdose in George's living room while the singer was away.

Apart from such extra-musical issues, there wasn't much happening in the world of rock and roll. Heavy metal seemed to have peaked. Only a few groups continued to sell well, including Van Halen (with Sammy Hagar replacing original lead singer David Lee Roth, who had embarked on a solo career), and Metallica, which was sidelined by the accidental death of bassist Cliff Burton in late September.

Independent groups continued to do well. Southern rock bands, led by REM from Athens, Ga., remained strong sellers, as did Los Angeles-based country-flavored bands like the Long Ryders, EIEIO, Green on Red, and the Rave-Ups.

In Britain the biggest noise of the year was made by the outrageously dressed Sigue Sigue Sputnik. EMI was reputed to have shelled out close to $6 million for the act before the band

Rosanne Cash is all smiles as she poses with her Grammy for Best Female Country Vocalist of 1986.

even recorded, but their record, a mishmash of electronic effects, bombed, and was one of the first to bear a parental advisory notice. Most Britishers opted for simplicity, with a strong folk and acoustic tinge noticeable in groups like the Pogues, Lloyd Cole and the Commotions, the Smiths, and James. An Anglo-Irish band, Simply Red, managed a nice soul-rock fusion that found favor on both sides of the Atlantic.

Madonna's new album, *True Blue,* put her once again in the midst of controversy, despite her protestations, as pro-lifers seized as an anthem the first single, "Papa Don't Preach." The song told of an unmarried pregnant teen-ager approaching her father with the news that she intends to keep her illegitimate baby. Among other stars, Bruce Springsteen released a mul-tirecord set of live recordings, eagerly pur-chased by fans. The Police temporarily reunited for the "Conspiracy of Hope" tour, a traveling benefit for Amnesty International (which also featured Peter Gabriel, Bryan Adams, and Lou Reed). Paul Simon gathered raves for his album, *Graceland,* based on tracks he had recorded

in South Africa with black artists. Cyndi Lauper came out with her first album in nearly three years, *True Colors;* its title song was an instant hit.

The Whitney Houston phenomenon (*see biography in* PEOPLE IN THE NEWS) was confirmed as her 1985 pop-soul debut album, *Whitney Houston,* continued to dominate the charts; the singer also won the 1986 Grammy Award for Best Female Pop Vocalist. Other honored pop performers included Phil Collins (Album of the Year, Best Male Pop Vocalist), Don Henley (Best Male Rock Vocalist), Sade (Best New Artist), and Tina Turner (Best Female Rock Vocalist). *We Are the World,* of 1985 Live-Aid fame, was declared Record of the Year.

Richard Manuel, a founding member of the famed Band (when it was still Bob Dylan's back-up group), committed suicide in March after a Florida reunion. Others in the rock music world who died included Albert Gross-man, flamboyant manager of such 1960's fig-ures as Joan Baez, Bob Dylan, and Janis Joplin; as well as pioneering 1950's Nashville radio host John ("John R") Richbourg and Gordon ("the old Scotsman") McClendon, who used Fort Worth's station KLIF to build a Top 40 radio empire.

Soul. Probably the biggest news in black music in terms of sales was named Jackson—but she wasn't one of the boys. After making several indifferent records in recent years, Janet Jack-son hit the top of the charts with her album *Control,* and stayed there.

Rap continued to be the voice of the young black city dweller. Leading the rap pack was the trio Run-D.M.C., whose *Raising Hell* album was one of the year's top sellers—and the first rap album to go platinum. Newcomers Joeski Love, U.T.F.O., and L.L. Cool J. came to the fore, while veterans Fat Boys and Kurtis Blow remained popular. Sadly, some rap concerts—and Run-D.M.C.'s otherwise successful tour—were marred by outbursts of youth gang vio-lence which made major headlines.

In general, soul music continued its back-ward drift. Anita Baker, blessed with a great voice and minimal production, took produc-tion values back 15 years as part of a trend called "retronuevo." In many ways this was a reaction to both the highly electronic hip-hop producers and overproduced string-heavy productions of recent years. Prince's second movie, *Under the Cherry Moon,* flopped, as did the accompanying soundtrack; audiences were not responding to his live shows either. Another black-music based movie, *Good to Go,* attempted unsuccessfully to start a new craze for Washington, D.C.'s heavily percussive "go-go" music. From Chicago came "house," another stripped-down cross between rap and regular singing.

Aretha Franklin's great comeback was certified by her winning the 1986 Grammy for Best Female Rhythm and Blues Vocalist, while perennial favorite Stevie Wonder took the equivalent male honor.

Black pop lost at least two major figures: the highly influential blind blues harmonica player Saunders ("Sonny Terry") Terrill, long-time partner of guitarist Brownie McGee; and O'Kelly Isley, founding member of the Isley Brothers—one of soul's true dynasties.

Country. Country music continued to stagnate, with the majority of records released being indistinguishable from soft-pop. About the only bright moment in an otherwise moribund scene was Farm Aid II, a giant benefit concert held on July 4 under Willie Nelson's auspices in Manor, Texas, drawing a virtual who's who of country. Nelson, undaunted by poor organization and attendance, promised a Farm Aid III. Rosanne Cash was named Best Female Country Vocalist at the 1986 Grammys, and Ronnie Milsap was Best Male Country Vocalist.

Jazz. The good news in the world of jazz was largely overshadowed by the passing of a titan. Benny Goodman, the clarinetist who had made jazz respectable in the 1930's, died in his sleep in New York City in June. Goodman straddled the worlds of pop and jazz for nearly his entire career, but when he wanted to play serious jazz, he won the respect of critics and fans alike. Unlike many of his era, he never stinted on thanks and praise for the black musicians who founded jazz, and he made the daring move of integrating his band well before anybody else did when he introduced pianist Teddy Wilson, vibraphonist Lionel Hampton, and guitarist Charlie Christian into his band. At the end of July, Teddy Wilson also passed away. Wilson had been accused of playing cocktail

music, not serious jazz, by various critics who were deceived by his light touch. But his work with Goodman and later with Billie Holiday assured him of a place in the jazz pantheon.

The good news was that record labels were taking a new look at jazz and finding it worthy of commercial consideration. In part, this was because of the astonishing success of "new age" music, improvised instrumental music similar to jazz. Several of the new jazz labels, like RCA's Novus imprint, straddled the jazz and new age categories, releasing records in

Run-D.M.C., shown here in performance, led the rap music pack in 1986, with their top-selling album Raising Hell. *Unfortunately, youth gang violence marred some of their concerts.*

both styles in the hope that consumers might find one a pleasant entrée into the other. But there was also activity in the straight-ahead jazz world as longtime San Francisco disk jockey Herb Wong started up the Black-Hawk label, named after the legendary Chicago jazz club. He released several albums to immediate critical acclaim, thanks to his skillful melding of contemporary and classic styles.

Jazz lost other significant performers during the year. Among these, Curley Russell, a bassist who had been an integral part of the bebop movement of the early 1940's and who had played with nearly all of the important instrumentalists of that time, died in July. Trumpeter and arranger Thad Jones, best known for leading, with Mel Lewis, a jazz orchestra that once played each week at the Village Vanguard in New York City, died in August. Jimmy Lyons,

Soul singer Janet Jackson was the latest of her legendary family to seize the limelight, with her hit album Control.

whose strong saxophone playing was essential to the Cecil Taylor Unit's uncompromising avant-garde music, but who was also capable of a lyricism that was rarely heard in the confines of Taylor's music, succumbed to lung cancer at the end of the summer. And Sippie Wallace, a classic blues singer and songwriter of the 1920's nicknamed the Texas Nightingale, died in November.   E.W.

CLASSICAL MUSIC

Highlights of the year included a triumphal visit to his native Soviet Union by pianist Vladimir Horowitz and performances celebrating the 200th birthday of Carl Maria von Weber and marking the centennial of Franz Liszt's death.

Horowitz Tour. Pianist Vladimir Horowitz triumphantly returned in April to his native Soviet Union for a performance in the Moscow Conservatory that made the world gasp, applaud, and weep for joy. His program was vintage Horowitz: Scarlatti, Mozart, Schubert, Chopin, Liszt, Scriabin, and Rachmaninoff. For the two-hour event, telecast by satellite, Soviets waited all night in freezing weather to buy tickets. In Moscow, Horowitz also visited Scriabin's home and played two Scriabin études for the composer's 86-year-old daughter.

Subsequently, Horowitz performed in Leningrad, Berlin, Hamburg, London, and Tokyo. At his last appearance in Tokyo three years earlier, critics had been merciless, calling him "a cracked antique." His decision to return there netted him a high-paying audience, as well as accolades as "an incomparable magician."

Opera. Some of the year's significant opera performances did not take place in an opera house at all, but in New York's Carnegie Hall, where concert versions of three seldom-performed operas by Richard Strauss—*Capriccio, Intermezzo,* and *Daphne*—were welcomed back as prodigal sons early in the year.

Carmen, performed with some innovations, came in for rough treatment from audiences and critics. At New York's Metropolitan Opera, Maria Ewing was "a cool street urchin in need of psychiatric help," according to *Opera News.* A Vancouver Opera version set in a circus was "irreverent, jeering, and iconoclastic," in the opinion of *Musical America.*

A nearly full staging of *Oberon* at Tanglewood commemorated the bicentennial of Carl Maria von Weber's birth. Conducted by Seiji Ozawa, the production moved on to the Edinburgh Festival and the Frankfurt Alte Oper. Ozawa also led the Boston and New York premieres of three of the eight tableaux of Olivier Messiaen's opera *Saint François d'Assise*.

Wagner's *Ring* cycle was staged in Seattle with Linda Kelm as Brünnhilde, Edward Sooter as Siegfried, and the much-admired newcomer Roger Roloff as Wotan. Directed by François Rochaix and conducted by 82-year-old Manuel Rosenthal, the operas were sung only in German but were presented with supertitles for the first time. (Supertitles, or surtitles, allow an opera to be sung in the original language while keeping the audience tuned in to the story.)

The Met began its season with a traditionally romantic staging of *Die Walküre*, with Simon Estes as Wotan and Hildegard Behrens as Brünnhilde, and put on a production of Handel's oratorio *Samson*, in which Jon Vickers was well received. Also at the Met, Joan Sutherland celebrated the 25th anniversary of her debut there with a performance of Bellini's *I Puritani*. An ear infection forced her to cancel a series of concerts with Luciano Pavarotti, also celebrating the 25th anniversary of his operatic debut; he performed without her. The Washington Opera's world premiere of Gian Carlo Menotti's *Goya*, with Placido Domingo in the title role, was presented at the Kennedy Center. The Des Moines Metro Opera offered the world premiere of American composer Lee Hoiby's *The Tempest*, based on Shakespeare's play.

The Santa Fe Opera, celebrating its 30th season, gave the American premiere of Finnish composer Aulis Sallinen's *The King Goes Forth to France*. Peter Maxwell Davies's *The Lighthouse* had its Canadian premiere at Ontario's Guelph Spring Festival. The New York City Opera gave the world premiere of Anthony Davis's *X (The Life and Times of Malcolm X)*.

New Music. Pierre Boulez, former conductor of the New York Philharmonic, toured the United States with his Paris-based Ensemble InterContemporain in a performance and speaking series called "Boulez Is Back." The

Australian opera star Joan Sutherland celebrated the 25th anniversary of her Metropolitan Opera House debut in November, with a performance there as the tragic Elvira in Bellini's opera I Puritani. The world-famous coloratura soprano, now 60 years old, was hailed by music critics for her still-brilliant bel canto technique.

New York Philharmonic's Horizons Festival, entitled "Music as Theater," used live visual accompaniment including ballet and other dance; the seven concerts included the world premiere of Morton Feldman's *Coptic Light*. In June the Detroit Symphony premiered Ellen Zwilich's *Piano Concerto*, with Canadian Marc-André Hamelin as soloist. Tanglewood's Festival of Contemporary Music included concerts devoted to electronic and computer music from around the world.

A concert on October 28 at New York's Avery Fisher Hall commemorated the 100th anniversary of the Statue of Liberty's dedication. Included on the program was the world premiere of William Schuman's *On Freedom's*

MUSIC

Ground: An American Cantata, commissioned for the occasion.

Publications and Discoveries. American Music Week was highlighted by the publication of the *New Grove Dictionary of American Music*. Besides classical music, the four-volume set's 5,000 articles included entries on jazz, pop, rock, and Indian music, as well as biographies of performers and composers.

Of importance to organists was the discovery of a trove of Mendelssohn manuscripts in a library in Kraków, Poland. They included four previously unknown works. A discovery of another kind occurred during the Tanglewood festival, when a Japanese violinist received a great deal of attention for her youthful poise under trying conditions. The 14-year-old Midori broke two E strings in succession. She coolly exchanged violins twice with the con-certmaster, finishing the piece while Boston Symphony Orchestra members quickly jock-eyed violins to keep up with her.

Liszt Anniversary. The centennial of Franz Liszt's death was marked in July with a week-long festival in Washington, D.C. Participants included pianists Jorge Bolet, widely considered today's leading Liszt interpreter, and festival organizer Jerome Rose. Earl Wild gave three recitals in Carnegie Hall meant to display Liszt as poet, transcriber, and virtuoso, respectively; Wild toured the United States with the programs and performed in England as well. An unpublished Liszt work received its world premiere in Utrecht, the Netherlands, and then was put on in Chicago and New York City. The 21-minute piece, based on Mendelssohn's "Song Without Words," is the only Liszt work written for two pianos.

New York's Carnegie Hall was reopened in grand style in mid-December, after a seven-month hiatus for renovations; long a favorite with musicians, the auditorium was refurbished carefully in an effort to retain its famous acoustics.

A Triumphant Homecoming

After an absence of 61 years, the 81-year-old pianist Vladimir Horowitz went home to the Soviet Union, where he received a tumultuous welcome at his recital in the Great Hall of the Moscow Conservatory. He went on to win accolades and bedazzle audiences in Hamburg, Berlin, and Tokyo, among other places. The trip was an enormous personal triumph for Horowitz, who had been thought on the verge of retirement. The pianist had sworn he would never return to the Soviet Union (he left in 1925 and settled in the United States in 1940), but after several successful concerts in 1985, he changed his mind. In July, President Ronald Reagan awarded him the Medal of Freedom, the nation's highest civilian honor, praising his Soviet trip as a "pilgrimage of peace." In October he performed at the White House.

Vladimir Horowitz

Carnegie Hall Reopening. On December 15, New York's Carnegie Hall was reopened in gala ceremonies, after a seven-month shutdown for renovation. For the occasion, Leonard Bernstein led the New York Philharmonic in the world premiere of his *Opening Prayer.* Zubin Mehta conducted the Philharmonic in selections from Haydn, Bach, Wagner, and Mahler. Vladimir Horowitz made a surprise appearance, and Frank Sinatra performed, as did other luminaries.

Appointments and Honors. Morton Gould, who was unanimously elected president of the American Society of Composers, Authors, and Performers, also replaced the late Roger Sessions on the American Institute of Arts and Letters. Edo de Waart replaced Neville Marriner as music director of the Minnesota Orchestra, and André Previn replaced Carlo Maria Giulini in Los Angeles.

The Pulitzer Prize for music went to George Perle for his Wind Quintet IV, commissioned by the Dorian Wind Quintet. Toscanini Achievement awards went to James Levine, Jon Vickers, Marilyn Horne, Nathan Milstein, Rudolf Serkin, Janos Starker, and the Juilliard Quartet. The St. Louis Symphony won the Ascap award for "strongest commitment to American music." In competitions, a pianist from Northern Ireland, Barry Douglas, won Moscow's Tchaikovsky, the Paganini was swept by Soviet contestants, and the Franciscan String Quartet won Alberta's Banff International.

Composer Virgil Thomson, who celebrated his 90th birthday on November 25, was honored by a program of his works at the Saratoga Festival.   L.K.

RECORDINGS

In 1986 the compact disk (CD) consolidated its hold on the classical record market. Many veteran collectors decided to give up black vinyl (long-playing records, or LP's) in favor of the CD when making new purchases, and beginners tended to bypass the older medium altogether. Prerecorded tape cassettes continued to be popular, however, particularly for in-car use, and they were far more attractively priced than the CD.

CD Reissues. Anticipating some consumer resistance to the continuing high cost of the CD, and seeking to attract new converts, many classical labels offered greater value per dollar in the form of extended playing time—extended, that is, over the maximum playing time of the LP. The CD is capable of a little over 70 minutes of playing time, so that two or three works by a particular composer or related works by different composers might occupy a single disk or fill out a multidisk package. Often this coupling procedure leads to the reappearance of a recording otherwise deleted on LP. Such was the case, for instance, with the CD reissue by Philips Records of Mahler's *Kindertotenlieder,* sung by baritone Hermann Prey with the Concertgebouw Orchestra of Amsterdam under Bernard Haitink, to fill out the second of the two CD's required by Mahler's Ninth Symphony.

The wide acceptance of the CD encouraged major labels to brush off some vault treasures, upgrade the sound by digitally remastering the original tapes or acetates, and give them a new lease on CD. Angel/EMI went back to 1950 for a recital of Chopin waltzes recorded by pianist Dinu Lipatti. London/Decca returned to 1953 for an album of arias by Bach and Handel sung by English contralto Kathleen Ferrier under Sir Adrian Boult's direction. Among the CD reissues was the path-breaking Mahler symphony cycle recorded by Leonard Bernstein for CBS Masterworks.

New Artists. Meanwhile, the Frankfurt Radio Orchestra was being led through the Mahler cycle by a virtually unknown young Israeli conductor, Eliahu Inbal, with great success. The year also saw recordings by at least two new U.S. artists with artistic and commercial promise—pianist Bennett Lerner, with a winning collection (his second) of out-of-the-way U.S. repertoire for Etcetera, and soprano Aprile Millo, with a debut album for Angel devoted to Verdi arias. Other new artists included the British-born, Juilliard-trained violinist Nigel Kennedy (EMI), the Swedish conductor Esa-Pekka Salonen (CBS), and a trio of talented Russian pianists—Vladimir Feltsman (CBS), Sergei Edelmann (RCA), and Alexander Toradze (Angel).

Mainstream Repertoire. Distinguished recordings of mainstream repertoire by established artists included a Beethoven Piano Concerto No. 5 ("Emperor") by Claudio Arrau (Philips), launching the veteran pianist's third integral recording of the five concertos; a number of Beethoven's piano sonatas recorded by the late Emil Gilels (Deutsche Grammophon); three recitals by pianist Vladimir Horowitz, including the one he played on his return visit to Moscow in 1986 (Deutsche Grammophon); a set of the complete symphonies of Mendelssohn performed by the London Symphony under Claudio Abbado (Deutsche Grammophon); and the never-ending tide of monumental recordings

by Herbert von Karajan, led by a Brahms *Requiem* (Deutsche Grammophon).

First Recordings. First recordings by major artists included the Brahms Concerto for Violin and Cello, which Yehudi Menuhin recorded for the first time with the equally veteran French cellist Paul Tortelier (Angel), and Bizet's *Carmen,* conducted by Karajan (Deutsche Grammophon). Probably the operatic sleeper of the year was the first recording of Rossini's *Il viaggio a Reims.* The recording was derived from a revival of the little-known opera performed at Pesaro, Rossini's birthplace, with a cast of world-class singers under Abbado's direction (Deutsche Grammophon).

Other Operatic Highlights. Another operatic entry of historic importance was the release by Denon on CD of a performance of Richard Strauss's *Der Rosenkavalier* recorded at the opening in 1985 of the newly restored Semper Opera House in Dresden. Other highlights included Verdi's *Rigoletto* conducted by Giuseppe Sinopoli (Philips); Cavalli's *Xerse* with René Jacobs conducting and singing the title role (Harmonia Mundi); an "authentic" Mozart *Così fan tutte* recorded under Arnold Österman's direction (L'Oiseau-Lyre); a sparkling Offenbach *Belle Hélène* starring Jessye Norman (Pathé Marconi/EMI); a compelling Purcell *Dido and Aeneas,* also with Norman (Philips); and a rousing Verdi *Ballo in maschera* sung by Luciano Pavarotti, Margaret Price, Kathleen Battle, Christa Ludwig, and Renato Bruson under Sir Georg Solti (London/Decca).

Anniversaries. Centennial tributes to Franz Liszt were led by a collection of miscellaneous piano pieces played by the dean of Liszt specialists, Georges Cziffra (Pathé Marconi/EMI); two other French pianists, Cécile Ousset (EMI) and François-René Duchable (Erato), made outstanding contributions, as did the American pianist André Watts, (Angel).

The Statue of Liberty, which was 100 years old in 1986, was honored musically by a symphonic work composed by Broadway's Richard Adler, entitled *The Lady Remembers (Statue of Liberty Suite).* It was recorded by the Detroit Symphony under its new music director, the East German conductor Gunther Herbig, with the U.S. mezzo-soprano Julia Migenes-Johnson as soloist (RCA).   C.B.

N

NAMIBIA. *See* SOUTH WEST AFRICA.
NAURU. *See* STATISTICS OF THE WORLD.
NEBRASKA. *See* STATISTICS OF THE WORLD.
NEGROES IN THE UNITED STATES. *See* BLACKS IN THE UNITED STATES.
NEPAL. *See* STATISTICS OF THE WORLD.
NETHERLANDS, THE. Despite controversy over its economic and nuclear policies, the ruling center-right coalition prevailed again in May 1986 general elections. The Christian Democrats and Liberals, partners in the coalition government, had achieved a combined vote of only 50 percent in local elections in March, and pollsters had predicted doom in May. However, a strong showing by the Christian Democrats enabled the coalition to retain its 81-seat majority in the 150-member lower house of the States General, or Parliament. Led by Prime Minister Ruud Lubbers, the Christian Democrats took 54 seats, 9 more than in the 1982 election, and replaced the opposition Labor party as the largest party in the legislature. However, the right-wing Liberals, the junior partners in the coalition, dropped from 36 to 27 seats, largely because of public disenchantment with the party's leadership and its pre-

sumed responsibility for an unpopular austerity program. Fringe parties on both the left and right lost ground.

The new Lubbers cabinet, formed in July, worked out an austerity program representing a compromise between Christian Democrats, who wanted smaller cuts, and Liberals, who wanted larger ones. The economy continued a slow recovery with real gross domestic product forecast to rise 1.7 percent. Private consumption was expected to increase by 3.1 percent, spurred by rising wages and stable prices. However, unemployment remained at around 14 percent.

The Soviet nuclear disaster at Chernobyl heightened concerns about the safety of nuclear power. Two weeks before the general election in May, the government suspended plans for two new nuclear power plants, pending further research.

In February, Parliament narrowly approved a U.S.-Dutch treaty providing for stationing 48 U.S. cruise missiles in the Netherlands in 1988. The vote climaxed a six-year national debate. To mollify opposition, the government said that in 1988 its fighter-bomber and antisubmarine

A new, technologically advanced dike, designed to guard against flooding caused by storm surges along the Netherlands' Eastern Scheldt River, was inaugurated in October. Unlike traditional dikes, which permanently block waterways and destroy fragile ecosystems, the new dike permits the river to flow unimpeded until a flood threatens—at which time 62 hydraulically operated gates drop into position along the structure's 1.5-mile span.

aircraft would no longer be equipped with nuclear weapons, though nuclear-capable artillery and the short-range Lance missile would be retained.

See STATISTICS OF THE WORLD.   W.C.C.

NEVADA. See STATISTICS OF THE WORLD.

NEW BRUNSWICK. See STATISTICS OF THE WORLD.

NEWFOUNDLAND. See STATISTICS OF THE WORLD.

NEW HAMPSHIRE. See STATISTICS OF THE WORLD.

NEW JERSEY. See STATISTICS OF THE WORLD.

NEW MEXICO. See STATISTICS OF THE WORLD.

NEW YORK. See STATISTICS OF THE WORLD.

NEW ZEALAND. Continuing disputes with France over the Greenpeace affair and with the United States over New Zealand's antinuclear policies were major issues in 1986.

In January, Prime Minister David Lange announced that his government was powerless to force France to pay reparations for its complicity in bombing the Greenpeace protest vessel *Rainbow Warrior* in July 1985. A photographer for the international environmentalist group was killed in the explosion, which occurred shortly before the ship was to sail for Mururoa Atoll to protest French nuclear testing in the Pacific. Two French intelligence agents were later jailed in New Zealand after pleading guilty to manslaughter and arson. In February 1986, Lange accused the French government of economic retaliation. In July, however, the two governments announced a settlement of their differences. New Zealand would release the agents, who would spend three years at France's military garrison on the Pacific atoll of Hao. In return, France agreed to pay New Zealand US$7 million in reparations, tender a letter of apology, and stop blocking New Zealand's food imports.

U.S. Defense Secretary Caspar Weinberger said during a visit to Australia in April that New Zealand's ban on nuclear-involved ships from its waters threatened to break the Anzus alliance that commits Australia, New Zealand, and the United States to mutual defense in case of attack. A few months later, U.S. Secretary of State George Shultz said that, because of the ban, the United States would no longer be bound by the defense agreement with New Zealand, and in August the United States announced a formal suspension of its military obligations to New Zealand. Lange reiterated his antinuclear position.

In March the opposition National Party selected Jim Bolger, a former minister of labor, to replace Jim McLay as party leader. The change appeared to presage a move away from the free market economic policies backed by McLay.

In May, 10,000 angry farmers marched to the Parliament grounds in Wellington, New Zealand's capital, in protest over the plight of the farming industry, hit hard by falling prices and the government's economic restructuring policies.

On February 26, at ceremonies marking the traditional opening of Parliament, Britain's Queen Elizabeth II delivered an address prepared by the Lange government that sparked controversy because it defended the government's antinuclear policy. The nine-day royal tour prompted street protests as well; at least six people were arrested.

See STATISTICS OF THE WORLD.   F.D.S.

NICARAGUA. In 1986 the Sandinista regime continued its state of emergency and sought to cope with a deteriorating economy as it battled against the so-called contra rebels who—with U.S. support—sought the regime's overthrow.

State of Emergency. At the turn of the year, under a state of emergency and suspension of civil liberties imposed late in 1985, the government of President Daniel Ortega Saavedra shut down the Roman Catholic radio station for violating censorship laws and failing to broadcast Ortega's annual speech to the nation. In June, after the U.S. Congress approved a $100 million Reagan administration aid request for the contras, Ortega announced that his regime would enforce the state of emergency more strictly. The regime closed down *La Prensa,* the opposition newspaper. Soon afterward, a Catholic cleric accused of lobbying for contra aid was expelled, and another was prohibited from returning home from abroad. However, Ortega did meet with the Catholic primate of Nicaragua, Miguel Cardinal Obando y Bravo, and a bilateral commission was established to work on "normalizing" church-state relations.

Enforcing a state of emergency, Nicaragua's Sandanista government in June closed down "indefinitely" the country's only opposition daily newspaper, La Prensa.

Economic Crisis. The Nicaraguan economy was worse off than in any year since the Sandinistas came to power in 1979. The country was expected to export barely $250 million worth of goods, in contrast to $660 million in 1978. Sugar prices remained extremely low. The coffee crop was slow to recover from rebel attacks, and the cotton harvest was plagued by disease. Drought struck. Mining output hit an all-time low.

The trade deficit was expected to run about $400 million, in part because of economic pressure by the United States. Worsening consumer shortages and skyrocketing inflation led to widespread complaints.

War Against the Contras. During the first half of the year, the fortunes of the contras varied. In the south, the Sandinista Army virtually obliterated the forces of rebel leader Eden Pastora Gomez. After his senior commanders deserted to join the U.S.-sponsored United Nicaraguan Opposition (UNO), Pastora gave up the military struggle in May. In the north, the government was less successful against the larger and better trained and equipped Nicaraguan Democratic Force (FDN), the primary beneficiary of U.S. aid. Nevertheless, FDN forces were weakened by the government's

increasing military power and its relocation of peasants from vulnerable areas, to deprive rebels of recruits. Allegations of widespread contra human rights violations and corruption also undermined the efforts of the rebel groups.

In June, after an intense lobbying effort by the Reagan administration and a unity accord among UNO leaders designed to increase the power of civilian moderates, the U.S. House of Representatives narrowly approved $100 million in contra aid, including $70 million in military aid. It was the first time the House had approved overt military aid to the contras. Bolstered by the prospect for renewed U.S. aid (which won final congressional approval in October), rebels launched a new offensive, bringing the number of contras operating inside Nicaragua back to 1984 levels.

On October 5, a cargo plane based in El Salvador was shot down by the Sandinistas as it was carrying arms and supplies to the contras. Only one of its four crew members, a U.S. citizen named Eugene Hasenfus, survived; he was captured the next day. He at first implicated the CIA in the supply mission, but later said he was uncertain. Hasenfus was placed on trial in a revolutionary people's tribunal; his American attorney, former U.S. Attorney

Eugene Hasenfus (right), an American, is taken prisoner after Nicaraguan Army forces shot down a cargo plane carrying arms and supplies for U.S.-backed contra rebels. Hasenfus, the only survivor, was sentenced to 30 years in jail by a people's tribunal but was later pardoned.

General Griffin Bell, worked with a Nicaraguan defense lawyer but was barred from actively taking part in the courtroom. He was convicted on November 15 and sentenced to 30 years in prison. Meanwhile, in a widening U.S. scandal, it was learned that, with the knowledge of some U.S. officials, money from the surreptitious sale of U.S. arms to Iran had been diverted through a Swiss bank account to the contras. The U.S. government also reportedly solicited money for the contras from other sources, including the sultanate of Brunei. (*See* UNITED STATES: Foreign Affairs.)

On December 12, Sam Nesley Hall, another American, was arrested in a restricted area of Nicaragua and detained on suspicion of espionage. He was said to be carrying concealed maps and sketches of military targets. Meanwhile, on December 17, Hasenfus was pardoned by the government and set free, in what the regime described as a humanitarian gesture. He was expected to testify in 1987 before U.S. investigative committees.

In March the Sandinista Army attacked a rebel training camp in Honduran territory, encountering heavy resistance. In early December, Nicaraguan troops reportedly made attacks across the border, as they also stepped up their pressure along the border against contra incursions; in response, Honduras mounted air strikes against Sandinista positions. (*See* HONDURAS.)

World Court Decisions. On June 27 the International Court of Justice, or World Court, ordered the United States to cease arming and training the rebels and pay reparations to Nicaragua. The United States refused to recognize the court's jurisdiction.

See STATISTICS OF THE WORLD.   D.E.S.

NIGER. *See* STATISTICS OF THE WORLD.

NIGERIA. In 1986, Nigeria's military regime sought to quell unrest, improve the economy, and plan for civilian rule.

Politics. On January 13, President Ibrahim Babangida inaugurated a 17-member Political Bureau to coordinate a national dialogue on how to move to a civilian form of government. The bureau, composed of civic and academic leaders, was given a year to solicit proposals from the public and offer its own recommendations. Babangida said the military government would hand over power to a democratically elected civilian government by October 1, 1990. The debate over the proper structure and ideology for a new democratic system dominated the news media.

In March, following a trial by a military tribunal, ten officers were executed for their part in an alleged military coup attempt discovered by the government in December 1985. Five others were given prison terms, one was dismissed from the army, and three were acquitted.

Two judicial tribunals formed to review the

sentences given to officials of the former Second Republic reduced or rescinded many of the sentences but ordered other people to be tried by a new tribunal. Former President Shehu Shagari was among those freed, but he was banned from politics for life. Babangida himself announced that all office-holders in the Second Republic would be automatically banned from new political office for ten years. Meanwhile, in October a Nigerian journalist questioned by police and accused of plotting a socialist revolution was killed by a parcel bomb he subsequently opened at his home. Public suspicion pointed to state security forces.

A student protest at Ahmadu Bello University in Zaria in May ended in violence when police were summoned to suppress it. As many as 23 students were killed, according to some sources. The killings provoked sympathy demonstrations at other universities, leading to further violence.

Economy. The emphasis of the government's economic program was to reduce the role and cost of government. The budget was balanced for the first time in several years. Defense spending was cut sharply, while spending on health, primary education, and police was increased. New taxes on corporate profits, dividends, and rents and a 30 percent levy on all imports increased government revenues, and government employees received pay cuts.

The government planned steps to reduce its involvement in the economy and stimulate market forces. It planned to turn over more than 100 state enterprises to private owners, to end its direct role in agriculture, and to abolish commodity marketing boards, which had kept farmers' prices down and thus retarded their productivity. It also instituted a "realistic exchange rate policy" that allowed the value of the naira to find its own level. Late in the year, preliminary agreements were reached on debt rescheduling.

Yellow Fever. More than 500 people died during the year in a yellow fever epidemic afflicting the eastern part of the country. Some 3,000 others were reportedly treated for yellow fever and associated diseases, and the government paid $1.5 million to purchase vaccine for fighting the disease.

See STATISTICS OF THE WORLD.   L.D.

NORTH ATLANTIC TREATY ORGANIZA-TION. There were strains between the United States and other NATO members in 1986. One reason was President Ronald Reagan's decision to cease observing the limits of the unratified 1979 Strategic Arms Limitation Treaty (SALT II). The U.S. bombing of Libya and the Reagan administration's secret arms sales to Iran also met with disapproval in NATO. At the same time, after the collapse of the Iceland summit meeting between Reagan and Soviet leader Mikhail Gorbachev, there was concern over any proposed sharp cuts in strategic nuclear forces while Soviet conventional arms remained superior.

SALT II. In late May, President Reagan, complaining of frequent Soviet violations of arms treaties, threatened that unless they ceased the United States would abandon the framework of the SALT II treaty and deploy B-52 strategic bombers armed with cruise missiles, thus pushing beyond the missile launcher limit set by the accord. The Reagan stance evoked strong protest from the NATO defense ministers, who met in Halifax, Nova Scotia, soon afterward. Even those allies usually most supportive of American arms decisions were highly critical. British Foreign Secretary Sir Geoffrey Howe said that adhering to the treaty was "in the West's best interest," and other allies noted that European public opinion would be adversely affected by a U.S. repudiation of the treaty. The Reagan administration nevertheless kept to its plan and exceeded the treaty limits in November.

Southern Flank. The various measures taken by the United States against the Qaddafi regime also met with protests in NATO, particularly by "southern flank" members. Italian Premier Bettino Craxi commented, "Italy does not want wars on its doorstep." During his March trip to Turkey and Greece, U.S. Secretary of State George Shultz failed to come away with new, extended agreements to maintain vital military bases in both countries. The existing base agreement with Greece was to expire at the end of 1988. In the case of Turkey, which of all the NATO members has the longest border with the Soviet Union, a five-year agreement to allow U.S. use of 15 bases had already expired in December 1985. In return for re-

279

newal, Turkey was seeking greatly increased U.S. aid. However, further negotiations finally produced an agreement in December permitting U.S. use of Turkish bases until 1990, without the specific commitments to increased aid that Turkey had wanted.

French-German Agreement. In February, the French and German governments reached an agreement in what some felt was a turning point in French security strategy. France pledged that, in the event of war with a Warsaw Pact nation, it would consult the West Germans before using its tactical nuclear weapons based in German territory. The West Germans had long been anxious about a French strategy which seemed to regard West Germany as no more than a buffer zone if war occurred.

Chemical Weapons. In another area of agreement, NATO defense ministers, meeting in Brussels in May, approved a U.S. plan to resume production of chemical weapons in 1987, after an 11-year hiatus. These weapons would be "binary"—that is, composed of two chemicals lethal only when mixed together in bombs and shells. The chemicals were to be stored in the United States and transported to Europe only in response to a crisis. The Americans had produced evidence indicating that the Warsaw Pact stockpiles were ten times greater than those of NATO. The agreement was not unanimous, however; the ministers of Norway, Denmark, Iceland, Luxemburg, the Netherlands, and Greece opposed the resumption of production. The Soviet Union criticized the decision.

Arms Control. A proposal to reduce military force levels in Europe emerged from the June Warsaw Pact summit, held in Budapest. The discussions, led by Gorbachev, linked cuts in nuclear weapons to reductions in conventional air and ground forces. The proposed goal was to scale down to 500,000 troops on both sides by the 1990's and to eliminate chemical warfare capability by the end of the century. Effective verification measures were to exist at each step along the way. Although there was some skepticism in NATO about the verification procedures, NATO Secretary-General Lord Carrington said he welcomed the proposal and promised it would be studied by a special NATO task force.

Any hopes for deep cuts in intermediate range missiles stationed in, or targeted on, Europe were stymied, at least for the present, when President Reagan and Soviet leader Gorbachev failed to reach agreement at their summit meeting in Iceland in October. American determination to push on with work on its Strategic Defense Initiative (SDI) technology, in the face of Soviet objections, precluded agreement on arms reductions. The attitudes of the NATO allies toward cuts in "Euromissiles" remained complex. Most would like to see an agreement made but were afraid that reduction or elimination of NATO's intermediate range missiles would leave Western Europe vulnerable to the Warsaw Pact's more powerful conventional forces.

The final communiqués from two December NATO meetings, one of defense ministers and the other of foreign ministers, conspicuously avoided mention of President Reagan's proposal at Reykjavík for the eventual elimination of all ballistic missiles, with some leaders expressing reservations about any such plan. The NATO foreign ministers did put forth a plan to replace the stalemated, 13-year-old Vienna talks on conventional arms reduction in Central Europe with negotiations in two forums: meetings of the 35-nation group of signators to the Helsinki Accords of 1975 and conferences between NATO and the Warsaw Pact.

See also INTERNATIONAL CONFERENCES; MILITARY AND NAVAL AFFAIRS.   J.O.S.

NORTH CAROLINA. See STATISTICS OF THE WORLD.

NORTH DAKOTA. See STATISTICS OF THE WORLD.

NORTHWEST TERRITORIES. See STATISTICS OF THE WORLD.

NORWAY. In May 1986, Labor Party leader Gro Harlem Brundtland replaced Conservative Party chairman Kaare Willoch as prime minister of Norway. The change of government came seven months after Willoch and his nonsocialist parliamentary alliance had narrowly won national elections. Government revenues dropped sharply in late 1985 and early 1986, as a result of falling oil prices, and nonsocialist leaders had sought to recoup some of the government's losses by proposing a measure to cut public spending and raise taxes on consumer goods. When the measure was defeated by Parliament in late April, Willoch tendered his resignation to King Olav V, who then invited Brundtland (previously prime minister during 1981 and the first woman to serve in that post) to form a new government.

Once in office Brundtland immediately devalued the krone by 12 percent in an effort to stimulate exports. In mid-June her Labor-led minority coalition government submitted an austerity package similar to the one proposed by the nonsocialist coalition, and this time the measure passed. The cabinet's immediate goal was to save money. Its longer-term strategy was to continue to promote development of the country's rich offshore oil and gas deposits.

Several catering unions struck the country's oil rigs in early April demanding wage increases, and the owners promptly locked out some 3,000 workers. The nation's entire oil production was shut down for nearly three weeks while negotiators sought an end to the impasse. In late April, the government ordered the dispute settled by compulsory arbitration, and the strikers returned to work.

During the same month, a breakdown in wage negotiations prompted employer groups to lock out 100,000 workers in several major industries. The conflict was further provoked by union efforts to reduce the work week and simultaneous attempts by employers to lower the minimum wage. An agreement was reached with the help of the state Wages Board: the work week was reduced, hourly wages were increased, and the minimum wage was unchanged.

The government initiated sweeping health precautions in late April after nuclear fallout from the Chernobyl nuclear disaster in the Soviet Union reached dangerous levels. Radiation contaminated meat, produce, and dairy products and posed a serious threat to the livelihood and culture of the region's nomadic Lapp population. By late summer government authorities determined that many of the Lapps' reindeer herds were dangerously radioactive and unfit for human consumption.

See STATISTICS OF THE WORLD.   M.D.H.

NOVA SCOTIA. *See* STATISTICS OF THE WORLD.

NUCLEAR POWER. *See* ENERGY.

Gro Harlem Brundtland (center), the leader of the Labor Party, replaced Conservative Party chairman Kaare Willoch as the prime minister of Norway after the Conservative coalition lost a vote of confidence in Parliament. Brundtland is pictured here with women members of her cabinet.

O

OBITUARIES. Each entry below contains the name of a notable person who died in 1986. It also contains a brief description of the accomplishments and events that contributed to making the person notable.

Adams, (Llewellyn) Sherman, 87, crusty, blunt New Hampshire Republican who served as President Dwight Eisenhower's White House chief of staff from 1953 until resigning under fire in 1958 for having accepted gifts, including a vicuña coat, from a favor seeker. October 27 in Hanover, N.H.

Addabbo, Joseph P(atrick), 61, Democratic U.S. representative from Queens County, N.Y., since 1961 and chairman of the influential House Appropriations Subcommittee on Defense since 1979; he was known for his staunch opposition to heavy military spending. April 10 in Washington, D.C.

Aherne, Brian, 83, handsome British-born actor who played the quintessential English gentleman in Hollywood films. He was an accomplished stage actor who made his memorable 1931 Broadway debut with Katharine Cornell in *The Barretts of Wimpole Street.* February 10 in Venice, Fla.

Alda, Robert (Alphonse d'Abruzzo), 72, veteran American stage, screen, and television actor (and father of actor Alan Alda), best known for his Tony Award-winning portrayal of gambler Sky Masterson in *Guys and Dolls* (1950) and for the film *Rhapsody in Blue* (1945). May 3 in Los Angeles.

Arlen, Harold (Hyman Arluck), 81, American popular composer who produced such classics as "Get Happy" (1929), "Stormy Weather" (1933), "It's Only a Paper Moon" (1933), "That Old Black Magic" (1942), and the Oscar-winning "Over the Rainbow" (1939), sung by Judy Garland in *The Wizard of Oz.* April 23 in New York City.

Arnaz, Desi(derio), 69, Cuban-born musician, actor, and producer; with Lucille Ball, his wife from 1940 to 1960, he created the innovative and immensely popular *I Love Lucy* television series and launched Desilu Produc-tions, which owned the largest motion picture and television studio in the world. December 2 in Del Mar, Calif.

Baddeley, Hermione (Hermione Clinton-Baddeley), 79, British actress best known as the maid in the TV series *Maude;* she earned an Oscar nomination for her role in the film *Room at the Top* (1959). August 19 in Los Angeles.

Bandy, Way, 45, American celebrity makeup artist and author of the 1977 best-seller, *Designing Your Face;* his clients included Nancy Reagan, Elizabeth Taylor, and Raquel Welch. August 13 in New York City.

Bernardi, Herschel, 52, American character actor best remembered for his more than 700 starring performances as the milkman Tevye in the Broadway musical *Fiddler on the Roof* during the late 1960's. May 9 in Los Angeles.

Bias, Len, 22, University of Maryland basketball star forward, honored as Atlantic Coast Conference Player of the Year. June 19 in Riverdale, Md., of cocaine intoxication, two days after being chosen first by the Boston

Basketball star Len Bias's shocking death by cocaine poisoning focused national attention on the problem of drugs in sports.

Celtics and second overall in the professional draft of college players.

Borges, Jorge Luis, 86, Argentine short story writer, poet, and man of letters regarded by many as the greatest Latin American author of the century. Known at first for his vivid, heavily metaphorical verse and for his literary essays, Borges began in the late 1930's to write the offbeat, paradoxical, often fantastic stories that became his trademark. In 1979 he received the Cervantes Award, highest literary award of the Spanish-speaking countries. June 14 in Geneva, Switzerland.

Bowles, Chester, 85, American statesman who served as U.S. representative, Connecticut governor, ambassador to India, and adviser to four Democratic presidents, from Franklin D. Roosevelt to Lyndon Johnson. Starting out as a copywriter, he founded the Benton & Bowles advertising agency in 1929 and left it as a multimillionaire to enter public service in the 1940's. May 25 in Essex, Conn.

Braine, John, 64, British novelist and playwright; a leading figure among the "Angry Young Men" of the 1950's whose writings reflected their disenchantment with the country's class system. October 28 in London.

Bricker, John W(illiam), 92, Republican governor of Ohio (1939–1945), vice presidential candidate (1944), and U.S. senator (1947–1959); he introduced the controversial Bricker Amendment (to the U.S. Constitution), which would have restricted the president's treaty-making powers. March 22 in Columbus, Ohio.

Bruhn, Erik (Belton Evers), 57, Danish-born ballet star whose brilliant performances with American Ballet Theatre in the 1950's and 1960's established him as one of the finest classical dancers of the 20th century; also an innovative choreographer, he directed the Royal Swedish Ballet from 1967 to 1972 and later was artistic director of the National Ballet of Canada. April 1 in Toronto.

Bubbles, John (John William Sublett), 84, American singer and dancer who created the role of Sportin' Life in George Gershwin's *Porgy and Bess* and invented the syncopated heel-toe sound of rhythm tap dancing. May 18 in Baldwin Hills, Calif.

Caesar, Adolph, 52, American stage and screen actor nominated for an Academy Award

For his role as showman George M. Cohan in the film Yankee Doodle Dandy, James Cagney won an Oscar in 1942.

for his portrayal of the bitter Sergeant Waters in *A Soldier's Story* (1984). March 6 in Los Angeles.

Cagney, James (Francis, Jr.), 86, versatile American movie actor celebrated for the scrappy vitality and explosive energy of his portrayals in over 60 films. He made his movie debut in 1930 and became a star the next year with his leading role as a gangster in *The Public Enemy,* the first of many memorable roles. He won an Oscar for his portrayal of showman George M. Cohan in the film musical *Yankee Doodle Dandy* (1942). Retiring from the screen in 1961, Cagney returned to play the feisty police commissioner in *Ragtime* (1981). March 30 in Stanfordville, N.Y.

OBITUARIES

Canfield, Cass, 88, American publisher, editor, and author who spent more than six decades with Harper & Row (formerly Harper & Brothers); among the writers he published were James Thurber, J. B. Priestley, and Julian Huxley. March 27 in New York City.

Cecil, Lord (Edward Christian) David (Gascoyne), 83, British literary historian, biographer, and Oxford don whose lectures and writings helped revive interest in Victorian life and literature. January 1 in London.

Chase, Lucia (Mrs. Thomas Ewing, Jr.), 88 (?), American ballet dancer who helped found the American Ballet Theatre in 1940 and served as its codirector for 35 years. January 9 in New York City.

Childress, Alvin, 78, American actor who was one of television's first black stars as cabdriver Amos Jones in the 1950's comedy series *Amos 'n' Andy.* April 19 in Inglewood, Calif.

Aggressive and often controversial lawyer Roy Cohn was disbarred shortly before his death.

Ciardi, John (Anthony), 69, American poet, professor, and poetry editor of the *Saturday Review* (1956–1972). His works include an acclaimed translation of *Dante's Inferno* (1954), the well-known textbook *How Does a Poem Mean?* (1959), and several collections of poetry for children. March 30 in Edison, N.J.

Cohen, Myron, 83, Polish-born comedian who drew on his early life as a salesman in New York City's garment district for his gentle ethnic jokes and dialect stories. March 10 in Nyack, N.Y.

Cohn, Roy M(arcus), 59, controversial American attorney who gained notoriety as relentless chief counsel to Senator Joseph McCarthy's investigations subcommittee during the senator's 1950's campaign against alleged Communist infiltration. Cohn later became a powerful New York lawyer known for his aggressive—and successful—courtroom tactics but accused of shady legal dealings. He was acquitted of various charges in three federal trials but was disbarred in New York in 1986 for "unethical" conduct. August 2, in Bethesda, Md.

Colonna, Jerry (Gerardo Luigi), 82, American comic actor who, with his trademark walrus mustache and rolling eyes, appeared in films and on tours with comedian Bob Hope for 25 years. November 21 in Woodland Hills, Calif.

Cooper, Lady Diana (Manners), 93, British socialite and actress of the 1920's and 1930's known for her beauty, quick wit, and amusing eccentricities; touring for years as the Madonna in Max Reinhardt's play *The Miracle,* she became one of the world's most photographed women. June 16 in London.

Crawford, Broderick, 74, American actor who won an Academy Award for his portrayal of corrupt politician Willie Stark in the 1949 film *All the King's Men.* He also earned wide acclaim for his 1937 Broadway performance in *Of Mice and Men* and starred in the 1950's TV series *Highway Patrol.* April 26 in Rancho Mirage, Calif.

Crothers, Scatman (Benjamin Sherman), 76, American actor and musician who began performing in speakeasies in the 1920's and later appeared in numerous films and television series, including a featured role in *Chico and*

Character actor Broderick Crawford is perhaps best remembered as the police chief in the 1950's TV series Highway Patrol.

the Man from 1974 to 1978. November 22 in Los Angeles.

Crowley, James H. (Jim), 83, American football player who was left halfback and last surviving member of the Four Horsemen, the legendary backfield of Notre Dame's team in 1923 and 1924. January 15 in Scranton, Pa.

Da Silva, Howard, 76, American stage and screen actor, producer, and director, possibly best known for his role as Benjamin Franklin in stage and screen versions of the musical *1776.* February 16 in Ossining, N.Y.

Dassault, Marcel, 94, French aircraft designer and manufacturer celebrated for his brilliant aeronautical innovations; with such best-selling planes as the Mystère and Mirage fighter jets, he established France as a leader in the aeronautics industry. April 18 in Paris.

De Beauvoir, Simone (Bertrand), 78, French writer, intellectual, and leftist activist whose 1949 treatise on women in Western culture, entitled *The Second Sex,* became a cornerstone of the feminist movement. She was a longtime companion of philosopher Jean-Paul Sartre. Among her novels was the roman à clef *The Mandarins;* she also wrote four volumes of autobiography, as well as *The Coming of Age* (1970), which protested the impoverishment and neglect of the elderly in contemporary society. April 14 in Paris.

Deferre, Gaston, 75, tough-minded French Socialist who was mayor of Marseilles since 1953, held a number of cabinet posts, and played a major role in the growth of the Socialist Party. May 7 in Marseilles.

Dionne, Elzire, 77, French-Canadian farm woman who gave birth to identical female quintuplets on May 28, 1934. The quints, all of whom survived to adulthood, were treated as sensations and grew up in a glare of publicity. November 22 in North Bay, Ontario.

Douglas, Thomas Clement (Tommy), 81, Scottish-born Canadian socialist leader; he headed the first socialist government in a Canadian province, serving as premier of Saskatchewan from 1944 to 1961, then became the first national leader of the newly formed New Democratic Party. February 24 in Ottawa.

East, John P., 55, Republican U.S. senator from North Carolina since 1981 and a staunch philosophical conservative and ally of the state's senior senator, Jesse Helms. In ill health, he had announced he would not seek a second term. Committed suicide June 29 in Greenville, N.C.

Eastland, James O(liver), 81, longtime U.S. senator from Mississippi who served 6 years as president pro tem of the Senate and 22 as chairman of the Judiciary Committee; he stubbornly opposed desegregation and what he saw as Communist penetration of U.S. society. February 19 in Greenwood, Miss.

Eliade, Mircea, 79, Romanian-born American religious scholar whose works analyzed the meaning and symbolism underlying religious experience, past and present, in varied cultures and traditions. April 22 in Chicago.

Ellin, Stanley (Bernard), 69, critically acclaimed and much-translated mystery writer whose works included the classic short stories "The Specialty of the House" and "The Blessington Method." July 31 in New York City.

Ellis, Perry, 46, leading American fashion designer whose casual style of sportswear increased acceptance of American designs in the late 1970's. May 30 in New York City.

Goodman, Benny (Benjamin David), 77, American clarinetist and bandleader known as the King of Swing. With a repertory of innovative jazz-based arrangements by Fletcher Henderson, Goodman and his orchestra began drawing throngs to nightclubs and theaters in the mid-1930's, also attracting a wide audience for radio broadcasts, recordings, and films. Goodman provided a training ground for other bandleaders like Harry James, Gene Krupa, Teddy Wilson, and Lionel Hampton; by featuring Wilson and Hampton, he also broke the color barrier between white and black groups. Still active as a big bandleader in the 1940's, he later formed small groups for concerts and tours around the world. June 13 in New York City.

Grant, Cary (Archibald Alexander Leach), 82, debonair English-born actor who became one of Hollywood's greatest stars. After working as an acrobat, he made his screen debut in 1932 and went on to partner some of Holly-

The epitome of romantic elegance in more than 70 films, actor Cary Grant will long be remembered as Hollywood's quintessential leading man.

The immortal King of Swing, bandleader and clarinetist Benny Goodman raised jazz to an art form and brought it into the mainstream of American music.

Genet, Jean, 75, influential, revolutionary French playwright, novelist, and poet. He began writing while in prison for male prostitution and theft; in autobiographical novels such as *Our Lady of the Flowers* (1943) and absurdist plays such as *The Maids* (1947), *The Balcony* (1956), and *The Blacks* (1958), he graphically celebrated the seamy side of life while condemning traditional values. April 15 in Paris.

Glubb, Sir John Bagot, 88, British army officer who as the legendary Glubb Pasha commanded Jordan's Arab Legion from 1939 to 1956; his troops were the only Arab force to win a substantial victory over the Israelis in the 1948 Palestine war. March 17 in Mayfield, England.

wood's grandest leading ladies in his 72 films, which included such classics as *Bringing Up Baby* (1938), *His Girl Friday* (1940), *The Philadelphia Story* (1940), *None But the Lonely Heart* (1944), *To Catch a Thief* (1955), and *North by Northwest* (1959). November 29 in Davenport, Iowa.

Greenberg, Hank (Henry Benjamin Greenberg), 75, American Hall of Fame baseball player; he compiled a lifetime batting average of .313 and hit 331 home runs in his 13 major league seasons, spent mostly with the Detroit Tigers. September 4 in Beverly Hills, Calif.

Halleck, Charles A(braham), 85, Republican U.S. congressman from Indiana from 1935 to 1968; a conservative who described himself as "100 percent Republican," he served as both majority and minority leader in the House. March 3 in Lafayette, Ind.

Halop, Florence, 63, gravel-voiced character actress who played the bailiff on the TV series *Night Court* (1985–1986) and Mrs. Hufnagel on the series *St. Elsewhere* (1984–1985). July 15 in Los Angeles.

Harriman, W(illiam) Averell, 94, American statesman and financier who inherited millions but served in government for decades, holding key posts under four Democratic presidents, from Franklin Roosevelt to Jimmy Carter. He coordinated the Marshall Plan recovery program after World War II and at various times was secretary of commerce, ambassador to the Soviet Union, and governor of New York. He made two unsuccessful bids for the Democratic presidential nomination. July 26 in Yorktown Heights, N.Y.

Hayden, Sterling (Sterling Relyea Walter), 70, handsome American actor-author who won acclaim as the petty hoodlum in *The Asphalt Jungle* (1950) and the crazed general in *Dr. Strangelove* (1964); his private life as an amateur sailor inspired his autobiographical book *Wanderer* (1963) and his epic novel *Voyage* (1976). May 23 in Sausalito, Calif.

Heidt, Horace, 85, American bandleader whose radio and television talent shows boosted the careers of such stars as Art Carney, Gordon MacRae, and trumpeter Al Hirt. December 1 in Los Angeles.

Hemingway, Mary, 78, journalist and author who was a foreign correspondent for *Time* and

In key diplomatic posts under four Democratic presidents, statesman Averell Harriman helped shape 20th-century American foreign policy.

Life magazines during World War II and was married to novelist Ernest Hemingway from 1946 until his suicide in 1961; she published an autobiography, *How It Was*, in 1976. November 26 in New York City.

Herbert, Frank (Patrick), 65, American science-fiction writer best known for the novel *Dune* (1965) and its five sequels, which together sold 35 million copies. February 11 in Madison, Wis.

Hobson, Laura Z(ametkin), 85, American writer best known for her 1947 novel *Gentleman's Agreement*, which explored U.S. anti-Semitism; her 1975 novel *Consenting Adult* dealt with another controversial issue, homosexuality. February 28 in New York City.

Hubbard, L(afayette) Ron(ald), 74, American science-fiction writer who founded the Church of Scientology, a "new religion" based on his 1950 book *Dianetics: The Modern Science of Mental Health;* at his death the group, though charged with fraud, harassment of opponents, and tax violations, reportedly had assets of nearly $300 million. January 24 in Creston, Calif.

OBITUARIES

Isherwood, Christopher (William Bradshaw), 81, British-born writer best known for his quasi-autobiographical stories set in decadent pre-World War II Berlin, including those in *Goodbye to Berlin* (1939), which served as the basis for the play and film *I Am a Camera* and the musical *Cabaret*. He later became a Hollywood scriptwriter. January 4 in Santa Monica, Calif.

Isley, O'Kelly, 48, American rhythm and blues singer and member of the popular Isley Brothers group, who recorded such hits as "Twist and Shout" (1962), selling 12 million records over a period of 25 years. March 31 in Englewood, N.J.

Jacuzzi, Candido, 83, Italian immigrant to the United States who in 1949 invented the Jacuzzi whirlpool bath to help treat his 15-month-old son's rheumatoid arthritis. October 7 in Scottsdale, Ariz.

Jarvis, Howard (Arnold), 83, retired California business leader who sparked a nationwide tax revolt in 1978 by leading a successful campaign for the passage of Proposition 13, a referendum to slash the state's soaring property taxes. August 12 in Los Angeles.

Javits, Jacob K(oppel), 81, four-term U.S. senator from New York; a liberal Republican, he became one of the nation's most respected and influential politicians. Javits served in the House of Representatives from 1947 to 1954 and was elected to the Senate in 1956. He later played a major role in the passage of the War Powers Act, which limits the president's authority to wage war. Although struck by a nerve and muscle disorder, he remained an active speaker and writer until his death. March 7 in Palm Beach, Fla.

Jones, Thad, 63, self-taught American jazz trumpeter, composer, and arranger noted for his syncopated style and complex harmonizations; a onetime soloist with the Count Basie Orchestra, he led a well-known band with drummer Mel Lewis in the 1960's and 1970's. August 20 in Copenhagen, Denmark.

Kantorovich, Leonid V(italiyevich), 74, Soviet economist and mathematician ridiculed under Stalin for his innovative approaches to problems of economic planning, work for which he later shared the 1975 Nobel Prize for economics. April 7 in the Soviet Union.

Kaplan, Lazare, 102, legendary Russian-born diamond dealer who helped make New York City a center of the world diamond trade; an artisan as well as a businessman, he cut the famous 726-carat Jonker diamond in 1936. February 12 near Roscoe, N.Y.

Kekkonen, Urho Kaleva, 85, Finnish political leader who in a quarter century (1956–1981) as president adroitly pursued a foreign policy of "active neutrality" enabling Finland to preserve its political system through conciliatory moves toward its neighbor, the Soviet Union. August 31 in Helsinki.

Klinghoffer, Marilyn, 58, national symbol of American outrage over terrorism after her husband, Leon, was killed by terrorists in 1985 on the hijacked Italian liner *Achille Lauro*. February 9 in New York City.

Knight, Ted (Tadeus Wladyslaw Konopka), 62, American comic actor best known for his Emmy Award-winning portrayal of pompous anchorman Ted Baxter on *The Mary Tyler Moore Show* (1970–1977) and for his starring role in *Too Close for Comfort* (1980–1986). August 26 in Pacific Palisades, Calif.

Kraft, Joseph, 61, syndicated American political columnist whose independent views and access to government leaders made him both widely respected and widely read. January 10 in Washington, D.C.

Krishnamurti, Jiddu, 90, Indian-born religious philosopher; hailed in his youth as virtually a messiah by the Theosophical Society, he renounced this claim and embarked on a worldwide mission to teach unflinching self-awareness as the path to spiritual liberation. February 17 in Ojai, Calif.

Lanchester, Elsa, 84, British stage and film actress best known for her character roles, among which was that of the monster's bride in *The Bride of Frankenstein* (1935). She won two Academy Award nominations, for *Witness for the Prosecution* (1957) and *Come to the Stable* (1949). December 26 in Woodland Hills, Calif.

Lartigue, Jacques-Henri, 92, innovative French photographer who, starting as a child, took over 250,000 pictures, many recording the fashions and foibles of the privileged class in unposed images foreshadowing the art of candid photography. September 12 in Nice.

288

Layne, Bobby, 59, American Hall of Fame football quarterback who led the Detroit Lions to two National Football League titles in the 1950's. December 1 in Lubbock, Texas.

Le Duan, 78 (?), secretary general of the Vietnamese Communist Party since the death of Ho Chi Minh in 1969 and an architect of Hanoi's victory in the Vietnam war. July 10 in Hanoi.

Lerner, Alan Jay, 67, American lyricist and screenwriter who collaborated with composer Frederick Loewe to create such legendary Broadway musicals as *Brigadoon* (1947), *Paint Your Wagon* (1951), *Camelot* (1960), and, most successful of all, *My Fair Lady* (1956), as well as the Oscar-winning film musical *Gigi* (1958); he also teamed up with Kurt Weill for the innovative 1948 musical *Love Life* and wrote the award-winning screenplay for *An American in Paris* (1951). June 14 in New York City.

Called "the father of streamlining" for his sleek reshaping of everything from cars and toasters to Air Force One, industrial designer Raymond Loewy radically altered the look of American life.

Lifar, Serge, 81, colorful Russian-born dancer and choreographer who, as ballet master at the Paris Opera for many years, played a key role in the development of modern French ballet. December 15 in Lausanne, Switzerland.

Loewy, Raymond, 92, French-born American industrial designer whose sleek reshaping of everyday objects radically altered the look of American life and earned him the title "Father of Streamlining." His designs include the familiar eagle logo of the U.S. Postal Service and the presidential jet, Air Force One. July 14 in Monte Carlo.

MacDonald, John D., 70, award-winning American suspense novelist and short story writer whose 70 books sold millions of copies; he was best known for those featuring the hardboiled adventurer Travis McGee. December 28 in Milwaukee.

Machel, Samora Moïses, 53, charismatic president of Mozambique since its independence from Portugal in 1975 who was both a committed Marxist and pragmatic nationalist. Under Machel a liberal foreign investment law was enacted, and, despite his opposition to apartheid, an accord with South Africa was signed in an effort to end the latter's support of Mozambican rebels. Killed October 19 in a plane crash in South Africa.

Macmillan, (Maurice) Harold, 92, British statesman and publisher who, as Conservative prime minister (1957–1963), helped Britain adapt to a diminished role in the world, while strongly favoring negotiations between East and West. He resigned his post in 1963, following a scandal involving War Secretary John Profumo, and later wrote six volumes of memoirs. December 29 in Sussex, England.

MacRae, Gordon, 64, American baritone singer and actor who starred in such popular film musicals as *Oklahoma!* (1955) and *Carousel* (1956) and had a successful stage, TV, and nightclub career; a recovered alcoholic, he became a crusader against alcoholism. January 24 in Lincoln, Neb.

Malamud, Bernard, 71, acclaimed American novelist and short-story writer who, often utilizing fable and allegory, explored the moral rebirth of ordinary people through suffering and struggle; Jewish characters were the focus of many, but not all, of his works. His first novel,

OBITUARIES

The Natural (1952), was the basis for a 1984 film. His 1966 novel *The Fixer* won a Pulitzer Prize and a National Book Award, and his short-story collection *The Magic Barrel* (1958) earned a National Book Award. March 18 in New York City.

Malone, Dumas, 94, American historian, professor, and editor whose definitive, multivolume biography of Thomas Jefferson won a 1975 Pulitzer Prize. December 27 in Charlottesville, Va.

Marchenko, Anatoly T., 48, imprisoned Soviet political dissident who spent much of his life in prison or labor camps and wrote of his experiences in *My Testimony,* published in the United States in 1970. December 8, at a prison hospital in Chistopol, Soviet Union, after a long hunger strike.

McAuliffe, (Sharon) Christa, 37, Concord, N.H., high-school teacher chosen from among 11,000 applicants to become the first ordinary U.S. citizen in space; she died with her fellow crew members—Gregory Jarvis, Ronald McNair, Ellison Onizuka, Judith Resnick, Francis (Dick) Scobee, and Michael Smith—when the space shuttle *Challenger* exploded shortly after its launch from Cape Canaveral, Fla., on January 28.

McKenna, Siobhan, 63 (?), renowned Irish actress who portrayed Joan of Arc in her own Gaelic translation of G. B. Shaw's play *Saint Joan* and interpreted the role to great acclaim in English in Ireland, London, and New York. In 1971 she had a New York triumph with a one-woman show, *Here Are the Ladies.* November 16 in Dublin.

Milland, Ray (Reginald Truscott-Jones), urbane Welsh-born actor who appeared in more than 120 films, including *The Lost Weekend* (1945), in which his portrayal of an alcoholic writer won an Oscar, *Beau Geste* (1939), *The Big Clock* (1948), *Dial M for Murder* (1954), and *Love Story* (1970); on television he starred in *The Ray Milland Show* (1953–1955) and the detective series *Markham* (1959–1960). March 10 in Torrance, Calif.

Miller, Merle, 67, American writer best known for his controversial oral histories of U.S. Presidents Harry Truman and Lyndon Johnson, based on extensive taped interviews. June 10 in Danbury, Conn.

Massive human figures with tiny heads and unexpected holes were trademarks of British sculptor Henry Moore.

Minnelli, Vincente, 76 (?), Oscar-winning American film director whose sweeping use of color, and skillful blending of music, dance, and plot produced such classic Hollywood musicals as *Meet Me in St. Louis* (1944), *An American in Paris* (1951), and *Gigi* (1958). From 1945 to 1951 he was married to Judy Garland; Liza Minnelli is their daughter. July 25 in Los Angeles.

Molotov (Skryabin), Vyacheslav Mikhaylovich, 96, longtime Soviet Communist Party and government figure closely associated with Joseph Stalin; he was a humorless, unbending negotiator as foreign minister (1939–1949 and 1953–1956) and signed the 1939 nonaggression pact with Nazi Germany. He was expelled from the party leadership for his role in a 1957 bid to depose party head Nikita Khrushchev. November 8.

Moore, Henry (Spencer), 88, leading British sculptor of the 20th century whose monumental works—often human figures with unexpected holes and tiny heads atop huge body masses—adorn parks and buildings around the world. He was also known for his World War II "shelter" drawings of Londoners in the subway during the blitz. August 31 in Much Hadham, England.

Mulliken, Robert S(anderson), 90, University of Chicago physicist and chemist who won the 1966 Nobel Prize in chemistry for his seminal research on chemical bonds and the electronic structure of molecules. October 31 in Arlington, Va.

Myrdal, Alva (Reimer), 84, Swedish sociologist, writer, and diplomat who shared the 1982 Nobel Peace Prize for her efforts to promote disarmament, both as cabinet minister and as private citizen. She was married to Nobel economics laureate Gunnar Myrdal. February 1 in Stockholm.

Nakian, Reuben, 89, acclaimed American sculptor whose energetic, powerful works, ranging from small pieces to mammoth sculptures, generally drew their inspiration from classical mythology. December 4 in Stamford, Conn.

Narain, Raj, 69, Indian opposition figure who defeated Indira Gandhi in her home constituency in 1977 and later led a revolt against her successor Morarji Desai. A lifelong political activist, Narain was part of the independence movement and later was frequently jailed for opposition activities. December 30 in New Delhi.

Neagle, Dame Anne (Florence Majorie Robinson), 81, leading British stage and screen actress who starred in such films as *Victoria the Great* (1937) and *Spring in Park Lane* (1948); she was listed in the *Guinness Book of World Records* as "most durable leading actress" after 2,062 performances in the musical *Charlie Girl* from 1965 to 1971. June 3 in Surrey, England.

Norgay, Tenzing, 72, Nepalese-born Sherpa guide who accompanied Sir Edmund Hillary in 1953 in the first successful ascent of Mount Everest, the world's highest peak. May 9 in Darjeeling, India.

O'Keeffe, Georgia, 98, American painter of remarkable originality and power who was a central figure in American art; much of her work evoked the desert landscape of the West, with images of flowers and of bleached bones prominent in her clear, colorful paintings. March 6 in Santa Fe, N.M.

Known for her bold, clean style and her focus on the American Southwest, painter Georgia O'Keeffe was a central figure in 20th-century American art.

OBITUARIES

Palme, (Sven) Olof Joachim, 59, prime minister of Sweden since 1982 and from 1969 to 1976; a socialist and egalitarian from an aristocratic background, he played an active role in the international arena, advocating disarmament and a nuclear-free Europe. Assassinated February 28 on a Stockholm street.

Palmer, Lilli (Lillie Marie Peiser), 71, sophisticated German-born actress who appeared on Broadway and in numerous films, including *Cloak and Dagger* (1946) and *The Pleasure of His Company* (1961). January 27 in Los Angeles.

Pears, Sir Peter, 75, renowned British tenor who interpreted a wide range of musical forms and had many works written for him by his longtime companion, composer Benjamin Britten. April 3 in Aldeburgh, England.

Perkins, (Richard) Marlin, 81, American zoo director and zoologist who hosted two award-winning television programs—*Zoo Parade,* which he originated in 1949, and *Wild Kingdom,* from 1962 to 1985. June 14 in St. Louis.

Picasso, Jacqueline Roque, 60, second wife of painter Pablo Picasso and chief inspiration of his later work. October 15, of a self-inflicted gunshot wound, in Mougins, France.

Plante, Jacques, 57, Canadian star goaltender who played 17 seasons in the National Hockey League, including ten with the Montréal Canadiens, during which the team won five straight Stanley Cups (1956–1960). He introduced the face mask and was one of the first goaltenders to range away from the goal. February 26 in Geneva, Switzerland.

Preminger, Otto L(udwig), 80, Austrian-born producer and director of such Hollywood classics as *Laura* (1944), *Anatomy of a Murder* (1959), and *Exodus* (1960). He was notorious for his dictatorial manner. Through such films as *The Moon Is Blue* (1953) and *The Man With the Golden Arm* (1955) he hastened liberalization of film industry morality codes. April 23 in New York City.

Rainwater, (Leo) James, 68, American physicist who shared a Nobel Prize in 1975 for helping to show that, contrary to accepted scientific theory, some atomic nuclei are asymmetrically shaped. May 31 in Yonkers, N.Y.

Ram, Jagjivan, 78, Indian political leader active in India's struggle for independence from Britain during the 1930's and 1940's; he subsequently served in nearly every important cabinet post and was an ardent champion of the nation's more than 100 million "untouchables"—the once outcast class into which he had been born. July 6 in New Delhi.

Reed, Dean, 47, American pop singer who became a superstar in the Communist bloc after leaving the United States in 1962. Reportedly drowned June 17, near his home in East Germany.

Reed, Donna (Donna Belle Mullenger), 64, American actress who symbolized the quintessential wife and mother in such films as *It's a Wonderful Life* (1946) and in television's *Donna Reed Show* (1958–1966); she won an Academy Award as best supporting actress for a part played against type—that of a prostitute—in the 1953 film *From Here to Eternity.* January 14 in Beverly Hills, Calif.

Although she won an Oscar for the role of a prostitute in From Here to Eternity *(1953), actress Donna Reed is best remembered as the screen's stereotypical wife and mother.*

Rickover, Hyman G(eorge), 86, U.S. naval officer responsible for the design and construction of the *Nautilus,* the world's first nuclear-powered submarine, and known as the father of the modern nuclear navy. Born in Russian Poland, he emigrated to the United States as a child, later earning an advanced degree in electrical engineering. His 63-year naval career was marked by frequent clashes with the naval bureaucracy, which opposed his often unorthodox methods. Rickover was promoted to admiral in 1973 and was allowed to remain on active duty until the age of 82. It was learned later that he had received gifts valued at $68,000 from General Dynamics, a military contractor. July 8 in Arlington, Va.

Ritz, Harry (Harry Joachim), 78, American comedian, youngest of the zany Ritz Brothers, who brought vaudeville routines to the screen in such 1930's musical comedies as *Sing, Baby, Sing, One in a Million,* and *The Goldwyn Follies.* March 29 in San Diego.

Rogers, Don, 23, American football player who was defensive back for the Cleveland Browns and an All American at the University of California at Los Angeles in 1983. Died June 27, the day before he was to be married, of cocaine poisoning in Carmichael, Calif.

Ruffing, Charles ("Red"), 81, American baseball pitcher and pinch hitter who played 22 major league seasons, including 15 with the New York Yankees, for whom he won seven World Series games; by the time he retired he had a regular season record of 273-225 and had hit over .300 in eight seasons. February 17 in Mayfield, Ohio.

Rulfo, Juan, 67, Mexican writer; one of the creators of the "magic realism" school of Latin American fiction. January 7 in Mexico City.

Santmyer, Helen Hooven, 90, American author whose novel of small-town life ". . . And Ladies of the Club" became a best-seller in 1984, making her a celebrity at the age of 88. February 21 in Xenia, Ohio.

Schroeder, William J., 54, American who was the world's second permanent artificial heart recipient and the first to live for some periods outside the hospital; he survived a record 620 days on the device before succumbing to strokes and other complications. August 6 in Louisville, Ky.

A U.S. naval officer for six decades, feisty Hyman Rickover earned praise for creating the modern nuclear navy—and a reputation for cutting through naval red tape.

Seifert, Jaroslav, 84, Czechoslovak poet who won the 1984 Nobel Prize for literature for his lyrical freehearted investigations into the human spirit. January 10 in Prague.

Sindona, Michele, 65, Sicilian-born international financier whose holdings reached an estimated $450 million before his empire, including Franklin National Bank in New York and Banca Privata Italiana, collapsed in 1974, leading to his conviction for fraud in both the United States and Italy; in 1986 a Milan court sentenced him to life imprisonment for arranging a murder. March 22 in Voghera, Italy, of cyanide poisoning, ruled a suicide.

Smith, Kate (Kathryn Elizabeth), 79, American singer and show business legend who recorded close to 3,000 songs and introduced the song "God Bless America." In 1931 she launched the first of some 15,000 radio broadcasts, opening with the song that became her

Adored by millions of radio and television fans, singer Kate Smith recorded some 3,000 songs, including her classic God Bless America.

theme, "When the Moon Comes Over the Mountain." She later starred in her own television program. June 17 in Raleigh, N.C.

Stockwell, Sir Hugh, 83, British army officer who commanded British land forces during the 1956 Anglo-French invasion of the Suez Canal Zone and led an airborne division in Palestine when Arabs and Jews were battling over what is now the State of Israel. November 27 in Wroughton, England.

Szent-Györgyi Von Nagyrapolt, Albert, 93, Hungarian-born biochemist who won the 1937 Nobel Prize in physiology or medicine for his discoveries on the role of certain organic compounds, particularly vitamin C, in the cell's oxidation of nutrients; he moved to the United States in 1947. October 22 in Woods Hole, Mass.

Tan, Le Trong, 72, Vietnamese Army chief of staff since 1978 and a key leader in the 1975 offensive that resulted in the Communist takeover of South Vietnam. December 5 in Hanoi.

Tarkovsky, Andrei, 54, Russian émigré director whose abstract, highly symbolic films received critical acclaim in the West, though they were often banned in his homeland. December 29 in Paris.

Ullman, Albert Conrad (Al), 72, Oregon Democrat who served 12 terms in the U.S. House of Representatives until his 1980 election defeat; he chaired the House Ways and Means Committee for six years. October 11 in Bethesda, Md.

Vallee, Rudy (Hubert Prior), 84, American singing idol of the 1930's and 1940's who thrilled a generation of female fans with such hits as "My Time Is Your Time" and "I'm Just a Vagabond Lover," crooning over the airwaves on such popular radio programs as the *Fleischmann Hour*. He enjoyed a revival in the 1960's, starring in Broadway and film versions of the musical *How to Succeed in Business Without Really Trying*. July 3 in Los Angeles.

Veeck, Bill (William Louis Veeck, Jr.), 71, flamboyant American baseball executive and former owner of the Cleveland Indians, St. Louis Browns, and Chicago White Sox; his innovations included such practices as season tickets and putting players' names on their uniforms. January 2 in Chicago.

Wallis, Hal (Harold Brent Wallis), 88, American film producer associated with over 400 movies, including, *Little Caesar, The Maltese Falcon, Casablanca, Becket,* and *True Grit;* his films earned more than 30 Oscars, and he discovered such stars as Burt Lancaster, Kirk Douglas, and Shirley MacLaine. October 5 in Rancho Mirage, Calif.

White, Theodore H(arold), 71, American journalist and historian whose account of the 1960 U.S. presidential campaign and election, entitled *The Making of the President 1960*, sparked a new trend in political journalism. Later, after turning out three more *Making of the President* books, he wrote *Breach of Faith:*

Best known for his *Making of the President* books, journalist and historian Theodore White pioneered the investigative style of modern journalism.

The Fall of Richard Nixon (1975) and *In Search of History: A Personal Adventure* (1978). May 15 in New York City.

Wilson, Theodore (Teddy), 73, legendary American jazz pianist who broke through the

American divorcée Wallis Warfield Simpson became the Duchess of Windsor after Britain's King Edward VIII gave up his throne to marry her.

color barrier as a member of the Benny Goodman trio in the late 1930's and accompanied such singing greats as Billie Holiday and Ella Fitzgerald. July 31 in New Britain, Conn.

Windsor, Duchess of (Wallis Warfield Simpson), 89, elegant American divorcée for whose hand in marriage King Edward VIII of Britain abdicated his throne in December 1936. The couple were married in June 1937 and became fixtures on the international social circuit; the Duke died in 1972. April 24 in Paris.

Wynn, Keenan, 70, versatile American character actor whose roles in over 250 TV shows and 200 movies included the gung ho Colonel Bat Guano in *Dr. Strangelove* (1964). October 14 in Brentwood, Calif.

Ye Jianying, 90, Chinese head of state from 1978 to 1983; a veteran of the epic Long March of 1934–1935, he held major Communist Party posts for many years. October 22 in Peking.

Zorin, Valerian Aleksandrovich, 84, Soviet diplomat who, as chief delegate to the United Nations, engaged in a dramatic Security Council confrontation in 1962 with his U.S. counterpart, Adlai Stevenson, over the presence of Soviet missiles in Cuba. January 14 in Moscow.

OHIO. See STATISTICS OF THE WORLD.

OKLAHOMA. See STATISTICS OF THE WORLD.

OMAN. See STATISTICS OF THE WORLD. See also PERSIAN GULF STATES.

ONTARIO. See STATISTICS OF THE WORLD. See also CANADA.

OREGON. See STATISTICS OF THE WORLD.

Newly appointed Saudi oil minister Hisham Nazer shares a laugh with other delegates at the start of a critical OPEC meeting in December.

ORGANIZATION OF AMERICAN STATES. The Organization of American States devoted new attention in 1986 to drug problems, while continuing to be preoccupied with issues of war and peace.

At an OAS conference on narcotic drugs, held in Rio de Janeiro in April, member nations signed an agreement to set up an Inter-American Drug Control Commission, aimed at curbing drug abuse and trafficking in the region. The new organization, when ratified and created, would coordinate drug enforcement, eradication, and prevention programs. The meeting marked the first attempt at a hemispheric approach to drug problems.

The Falklands/Malvinas Islands sovereignty controversy dominated early sessions of the annual OAS General Assembly at Guatemala City in November; the OAS called for Great Britain and Argentina to settle the protracted dispute by negotiation. The General Assembly received an annual report that named Chile, Cuba, El Salvador, Guatemala, Haiti, Nicaragua, Paraguay, and Suriname as human rights abusers. The OAS also passed a resolution calling on the Contadora group (Colombia, Mexico, Venezuela, and Panama) to press its efforts to negotiate a peaceful solution to ongoing Central American conflicts.

In December representatives of the Contadora governments and four other Latin American nations—Brazil, Argentina, Peru, and Uruguay—agreed to meet regularly as the so-called Group of Rio de Janeiro. These countries also agreed to send a delegation to Central American capitals to encourage new peace negotiations.   L.L.P.

ORGANIZATION OF PETROLEUM EXPORTING COUNTRIES. During 1986, OPEC met more frequently and in meetings of greater length than at any other time in its history, in order to deal with the drastic plunge of world oil prices from $30 a barrel in late 1985 to below $10 by mid-1986. This decline had resulted in part from a dramatic increase in Saudi Arabian production—from 2 million barrels a day (b/d) during 1985 to some 5.5 million by early 1986—which followed the decision by OPEC in December 1985 to cease attempting to limit production in defense of the organization's official price. The "price war" strategy, undertaken at Saudi initiative, had been aimed at recapturing a "fair share" for OPEC of the world oil market, driving weaker competitors from the market, and ultimately forcing worldwide cutbacks of production, which would be needed in order to stabilize prices and bring supply into balance with demand. In the face of downward spiraling prices, however, OPEC sought to return to a strategy of limiting production in order to raise prices. Members had trouble achieving agreement on specific quotas.

The first conference, an emergency meeting in March of OPEC's 13 oil ministers, included discussions with representatives of five non-OPEC oil-producing countries—Egypt, Mexico, Malaysia, Angola, and Oman. The meeting did not succeed in working out common policies, but both OPEC and non-OPEC countries did agree to seek eventually to return to a price of $28. At a second emergency meeting, during April, the ministers reached an accord to impose a production quota of 16.7 million b/d on annual output, but again failed to parcel out quotas among members. Three members—Libya, Iran, and Algeria—who had advocated a lower ceiling on output denounced the agreement recommended by the majority. Iran's representative called it part of a "conspiracy" between Washington and Saudi Arabia to undercut Iran's war effort against Iraq by eliminating its oil revenues.

A minority of at least four—Libya, Iran, Algeria, and Gabon—kept the regular June meeting, at Brioni, Yugoslavia, from producing agreement on a ceiling of 17.6 million b/d, which was supported by the majority. However, there was greater success at the fourth meeting, beginning July 28 in Geneva, when all 13 ministers voted to adopt an Iranian plan to reinstate for September and October a 1984 quota system, limiting production to some 14.8 million b/d by all OPEC members except Iraq, which was exempted from restrictions. In order to obtain agreement, Iran dropped its demand that it be allowed a quota twice that of Iraq's. Mexico, Egypt, Malaysia, and Oman volunteered to support the OPEC agreement with quotas of their own. Oil prices rose appreciably following the August agreement.

An October meeting in Geneva, the longest in OPEC's history, lasted 17 days, partly because of the demand by Kuwait, one of the more affluent OPEC members, for a 10 percent increase in its quota. A compromise was finally reached over the Kuwaiti demand, and the basic production agreement was extended to the end of the year.

On December 11, OPEC oil ministers met again, in an effort to work out production cuts. The meeting was stalemated for some time because of Iraq's refusal to accept output cuts. Ultimately, on December 20, an agreement was reached that excluded Iraq. It called for total OPEC production of 15.8 million b/d for the first half of 1987, representing about a 7 percent reduction from current actual levels. The total figure included a "postulated production ceiling" for Iraq of just under 1.5 million b/d, below its current level of 1.6 million b/d. Partly because of the optimistic figure for Iraqi production, there were some doubts as to whether the agreement would succeed in its goal of raising oil prices to an average of $18 per barrel.   D.P.

P

PACIFIC ISLANDS. In 1986 both the Soviet Union and the United States were involved in negotiations on fishing rights in the Pacific region. Progress continued toward dissolving the U.S. Trust Territory of the Pacific Islands.

In October, 16 Pacific island nations reached an agreement over U.S. tuna fishing in the area. Waiving previous arguments that tuna, as a migratory species, could be freely fished anywhere, the United States agreed to pay the islands $60 million over the next five years, including $2 million by the tuna industry.

The Soviet Union, which continued to vie for influence in the region, was reportedly deadlocked with Kiribati over renewal of a fishing agreement that expired in October. Meanwhile, the Soviets announced the establishment of diplomatic relations with Vanuatu.

PAKISTAN

The Northern Marianas, whose residents had voted in 1975 to become U.S. citizens, got their wishes in November when the islands formally became a U.S. commonwealth under a proclamation signed by President Ronald Reagan. The proclamation also put into effect compacts of "free association" with two of the other trust regions, the Federated States of Micronesia and the Republic of the Marshall Islands, under which the territories had the right of self-government, with the United States assuming defense responsibilities.

A compact of free association with the Republic of Palau, the remaining trust area, was being held up because its provision for the passage of U.S. nuclear ships and storage of nuclear materials had been found unconstitutional by Palau courts. In December a plebiscite aimed at removing the constitutional ban failed for the fourth time to win the required 75 percent approval from Palau's voters.

In December, three men were found guilty of the 1985 assassination of Palau's President Haruo Remeliik and sentenced to long jail terms.

On September 3, Guam's Governor Ricardo J. Bordallo was indicted on charges of bribery, extortion, wire fraud, and other crimes. He handily won the Democratic primary three days later, but was defeated in November by the Republican candidate, Joseph Ada.

On May 19, Typhoon Namu battered the Solomon Islands with winds of up to 140 miles an hour. Over 100 people were killed, and some 90,000 left homeless. Officials speculated that full recovery could take a decade. Guadalcanal, hardest hit of the main islands, was estimated to have lost up to 30 percent of its cash crops.

In Papua New Guinea the new government of Prime Minister Paias Wingti cut overall spending and won passage of a law banning the introduction of television until 1988, so as to allow time to formulate broadcasting guidelines and controls.

See STATISTICS OF THE WORLD.

K.P. & R.J.M.

PAKISTAN. During 1986, the government of President Muhammad Zia ul-Haq sought to deal with a vocal but often disorganized opposition.

Government and Opposition. Although Zia had lifted the state of martial law in December 1985, he continued to publicize his belief that parties were unnecessary in an Islamic state. In January the government announced that all parties must register with the Election Commission and that their right to participate in politics would be determined on the basis of their loyalty to the ideology and unity of the country. Meanwhile, a government party to be known as the Muslim League of Pir Pagaro was taking form in the National Assembly, under the leadership of Prime Minister Muhammad Junejo. On January 28 a new federal cabinet was named.

On January 30 the opposition Movement for the Restoration of Democracy (MRD) convened a mass meeting demanding Zia's resignation. However, the MRD, which was dominated by the Pakistan People's Party (PPP), remained disunified, even as political groups on the far left were uniting. In March, Zia said that Benazir Bhutto (see biography in PEOPLE IN THE NEWS), the PPP leader and daughter of former President Zulfikar Ali Bhutto, would be allowed to return from London; the PPP called on all opposition groups to unite behind her leadership.

When Bhutto arrived on April 10, acclaimed by hundreds of thousands of supporters, she launched a nationwide speaking tour. On August 14, major demonstrations were initiated by the MRD, despite a ban imposed by the government; Bhutto and hundreds of supporters were arrested, and about 25 people were killed in clashes with security forces. Turnout for the protests did not meet the organizers' expectations. Bhutto was released from custody on September 8 and vowed to resume the drive against Zia.

Violence and Unrest. Bombings in Karachi and Peshawar caused fatalities during the year. Clashes between Islamic fundamentalist and secular leftist groups, as well as between police and students, led to closings of colleges and universities. In September, troops used force against curfew violators in Lahore; 12 people were killed.

On September 5 a Pan American 747 was seized at the Karachi airport by four armed Palestinians, who had driven up to the plane

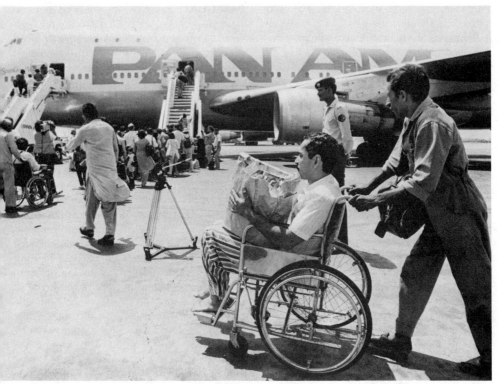

Survivors of a massacre on a hijacked Pan Am 747 jetliner at the Karachi airport board a relief plane sent by the airline. Palestinian terrorists had opened fire on the passengers, mostly Indians or Pakistanis, as Pakistani commandos stormed the jet in darkness on September 6. Twenty-one passengers were killed and more than 100 wounded in the incident.

disguised as security officers. When the plane's auxiliary generator failed the next day and the craft was plunged into darkness, terrorists started firing indiscriminately. Twenty-one passengers were killed and more than 100 wounded. Zia announced that the hijackers would be tried for murder and, later, that the security command would be disciplined and reorganized because of lapses that had allowed the incident to occur.

In December, fierce fighting between Pathans and Muslim refugees from India (Mohajirs) broke out in Karachi, causing over 160 deaths. The Pathans set fire to shops and houses and, according to witnesses, brutally stabbed, hacked to death, or threw into burning buildings many of their victims, who included women and children. In the wake of these riots, all the cabinet ministers except the prime minister handed in resignations, but many were reappointed to the new cabinet.

Foreign Relations. India continued to accuse Pakistan of supporting Sikh militants; Pakistan countered that India was training Afghan troops for attacks on the Afghan rebels, whom Pakistan supports. (The two nations did, however, agree on coordinating efforts to prevent Sikh extremists from using Pakistan as a base.) In May, Pakistani jets shot down an attacking Afghan jet. A preliminary U.S. decision to provide Pakistan with Awacs aircraft to warn against future Afghan attacks occasioned protests from India.

See STATISTICS OF THE WORLD.   L.Z.

PALESTINE LIBERATION ORGANIZATION. *See* MIDDLE EAST.

PANAMA. Political life in Panama was dominated in 1986 by discussion of the alleged extensive involvement of the Panamanian military, led by strongman General Manuel Antonio Noriega, in drug-smuggling and other illicit activities.

U.S. unhappiness with Noriega—already evident at February Senate confirmation hearings for a new ambassador to Panama—grew after Guillermo Sanchez Borbon, a prominent columnist, was jailed for articles linking the Panamanian defense forces with the September 1985 murder of Hugo Spadafora, a leading military critic. In March, Ruben Darío Paredes Rios, son of an ex-National Guard commander, was reported killed in Colombia; the Panamanian press linked the assassination to the seizure of cocaine on Paredes's luxury yacht by Colombian officials. In April, U.S. Drug Enforcement Administration officials told a U.S. Senate subcommittee that more than $600 million was being laundered each year by Panamanian banks; meanwhile, a Panamanian banking official refused to loosen banking secrecy in order to expedite U.S. antidrug efforts.

Criticism of the Noriega regime reached a new pitch when the New York *Times* in June published an article, based on evidence collected by U.S. intelligence agencies, detailing Noriega's alleged participation in major drug and arms trafficking activities, money laundering, and intelligence gathering for both the United States and Cuba. American officials had already been unhappy with Panama for its refusal of U.S. requests early in the year to grant asylum to exiled presidents Jean-Claude Duvalier of Haiti and Ferdinand Marcos of the Philippines.

On June 14, Panamanian naval authorities seized over 200 tons of machine guns, rocket launchers, and military trucks aboard the Danish ship *Pia Vesta*. The vessel, which had sailed from an East German port, went through the Panama Canal on June 2, heading for Callao, Peru. Mysteriously, it later changed course and returned to Panama, where its captain and crew were arrested. Authorities were uncertain as to the intended destination of the arms.

See STATISTICS OF THE WORLD.   N.J.P.

PAPUA NEW GUINEA. See STATISTICS OF THE WORLD. See also PACIFIC ISLANDS.

PARAGUAY. Paraguay experienced unusual signs of growing unrest in 1986, as the government of President Alfredo Stroessner faced economic difficulties at home and political pressures for a transition to democracy from abroad.

In January the Acuerdo Nacional, a coalition of opposition parties, called for church-mediated dialogues between all parties as a first step toward democratizating the 32-year-old Stroessner regime. The Paraguayan Bishops Conference expressed support for the proposal; the government rejected the invitation but left room for negotiation.

From mid-February to May an unprecedented series of protests and demonstrations were held. As many as 5,000 people attended rallies in Asunción and Caraguatay. In April police used tear gas and batons to disperse a crowd demonstrating in front of the home of Domingo Laíno, exiled leader of the Authentic Liberal Radical Party. When Laíno himself later tried to return to Paraguay, he was beaten by plainclothes police and forced to flee the country.

At the beginning of the year a corruption scandal surfaced when 29 Central Bank officials and businessmen were jailed in connection with a $100 million fraud involving falsified import invoices. Other economic problems included a sharp drop in export earnings as a result of drought and lower world market prices for cotton and soya. An ultimatum by the World Bank to devalue the guaraní or lose $160 million in loans for 15 projects passed unmet in June, and the World Bank carried through its threat to withhold the funds. After the guaraní was devalued in August, transfer of loan funds was resumed.

More difficult relations with Washington were signaled when the new U.S. ambassador, Clyde Taylor, met with opposition leaders in January to discuss their plans for democratization; the Paraguayan government accused Taylor of "open interference" in domestic affairs. The U.S. government was also considering possible suspension of preferential tariff treatment for Paraguayan exports, pending greater trade union freedom.

See STATISTICS OF THE WORLD.   J.F., Jr.

PENNSYLVANIA. See STATISTICS OF THE WORLD.

People in the News

The parade of new and familiar celebrities continued in 1986, as the great, the near-great, and the not-so-great all staked their claims on the popular imagination.

It's normal in American life for the first family to dominate the headlines, and 1986 was no exception. While President **Ronald Reagan,** 75, led the fight for tax reform, campaigned for Republican candidates, discussed arms control with Soviet leader **Mikhail Gorbachev** in Reykjavík, and grappled with the Iranian arms sales scandal, his wife, **Nancy Reagan,** 63, pursued a dual agenda. In public the first lady led the administration's antidrug crusade; in private, according to White House sources, she fought to protect her husband's interests and, especially, to quell the spreading Iran-contra scandal by urging that some of his top aides be dismissed.

The first family reportedly viewed with mixed emotions the publication by 33-year-old **Patti Davis** (née Patricia Ann Reagan) of *Home Front,* a novel portraying a fiercely independent young woman whose father just happens to become governor of California and then president of the United States. The Reagans first learned about the book not from their daughter but from a news item in *Time* magazine. "Of course there's bound to be some hurt," said a close family friend. "Would you want to see all your warts in public, exposed by somebody in your family?"

Another family member, **Ron Reagan,** was also a published author, although the White House—and the Attorney General's Commission on Pornography—may have viewed his publisher, *Playboy* magazine, with some disfavor. And in February, as host of television's *Saturday Night Live* comedy romp, the 28-year-old Ron, formerly a dancer with the Joffrey Ballet, pranced around in a pink shirt and skimpy briefs as he played broom-guitar and lip-synched to **Bob Seger**'s "Old Time Rock and Roll." The takeoff on **Tom Cruise**'s solo in the 1983 film *Risky Business* drew raves from the first parents, who after seeing the show on tape declared, "He was at ease. We enjoyed it." Ron made another barely dressed appearance in a photo story in the July issue of *Vanity Fair*. His half-brother **Michael,** 41, also got the chance to appear in front of cameras. The former fundraiser and radio talk show host, who had been studying acting for 18 months, landed a bit part as a truck driver in a new **Sylvester Stallone** movie, *Over the Top.*

Reagan's immediate White House predecessor, **Jimmy Carter,** had his moment of glory when the $25 million Carter Presidential Center

Former President Jimmy Carter officially unveiled the Carter Presidential Center in October. Built in Atlanta at a cost of $25 million, the center features an extensive library of Carter administration documents, a historical museum, and an office complex for public policy organizations.

Caroline Kennedy, daughter of the late President John F. Kennedy and Jacqueline Onassis, was married to Edwin Schlossberg in Centerville, Mass., on July 19. Despite the family's attempts to avoid publicity, the wedding received international attention.

Gerald Ford, 73, who sponsored a seminar on White House comedy at the Ford Presidential Museum in Grand Rapids, Mich. Honored guests included Chevy Chase, Art Buchwald, and Pat Paulsen, all of whom had poked fun at President Ford in the mid-1970's. Political Comeback of the Year honors go to Richard Nixon, 73, credited in a Newsweek cover story in May with exercising renewed influence in the White House and in Republican Party circles. "People see me and they think, 'He's risen from the dead,' " the former president was quoted as saying. Among the year's many reminders of the Nixon era were the retirement of Watergate trial judge John J. Sirica, 82, and the opening to public view by the National Archives of the first 1.5 million pages of documents from the Nixon presidency.

Literary news of a different sort was made by the former president's daughter Julie Nixon Eisenhower, who published Pat Nixon: The Untold Story, a memoir of her mother. Her husband, David Eisenhower, brought out Eisenhower at War: 1943–1945, the first volume of a trilogy chronicling the career of David's grandfather, former President Dwight D. Eisenhower. Both books were best-sellers. Another political family fared less well. John Zaccaro, Jr., the 22-year-old son of 1984 Democratic vice presidential nominee Geraldine A. Ferraro, was arrested in February for attempting to sell cocaine to an undercover policeman. In the fall, Ferraro's husband, John Zaccaro, was reportedly charged in a sealed indictment in connection with a bribery scheme.

More than any other first family, the Kennedys have been continuously in the public eye. In 1986 the two eldest children of the late Senator Robert F. Kennedy ran for the House of Representatives. Joseph P. Kennedy II won election to the seat being vacated by House Speaker Thomas P. ("Tip") O'Neill, Jr. (D, Mass.), but Kathleen Kennedy Townsend, the first Kennedy woman to seek public office, lost her race in Maryland. In the first of two weddings celebrated by the Kennedy clan, CBS anchorwoman Maria Shriver, 29, daughter of Sargent and Eunice Kennedy Shriver, married the Austrian-born Arnold Schwarzenegger, 38, a muscleman, actor, and entrepreneur. Attending the April wedding, which was billed

was formally dedicated in Atlanta on his 62nd birthday, October 1. The guest of honor, President Reagan, who attended with the first lady, took the occasion to call Carter's life and career "distinctively and gloriously American." Also in attendance were former Vice President Walter F. Mondale and numerous Georgia notables. Home for the ceremony was Brown University sophomore Amy Carter, 19. An emerging political activist, she was arrested in March while protesting IBM involvement in South Africa, and again in November while taking part in a demonstration against CIA recruiting on the campus of the University of Massachusetts at Amherst.

If there were a Good Sport award for former presidents, the 1986 winner would surely be as a private affair, were Maria's uncle Senator **Edward M. Kennedy** (D, Mass.); former first lady **Jacqueline Kennedy Onassis;** newspersons **Barbara Walters, Tom Brokaw,** and **Diane Sawyer;** and the always newsworthy **Grace Jones** and **Andy Warhol,** among others. The Kennedys gathered again in July for the marriage of Columbia University law student **Caroline Bouvier Kennedy,** 28, the daughter of former President **John F. Kennedy,** to **Edwin A. Schlossberg,** 41, president of a company that designs museum exhibitions.

Considerably more elaborate was the wedding on July 23 of the dashing **Prince Andrew,** 26, second son of **Queen Elizabeth II,** and the vivacious **Sarah Margaret Ferguson,** also 26. Sarah told her father, "I want everyone to have a wonderful time." And so they did—the beaming couple; the hundreds of thousands of Londoners who thronged the processional route between Buckingham Palace and Westminster Abbey; and a guest list that included not only British royalty but also Nancy Reagan, British Prime Minister **Margaret Thatcher,** pop star **Elton John,** and 17 representatives of foreign royal houses. Later in the year, the plucky Sarah, now formally known as the Duchess of York, completed her maiden flight after several weeks of pilot lessons given her as a wedding present by the Oxford Air Training School.

The British also celebrated the 60th birthday of Queen Elizabeth II and the 65th birthday of her husband, **Prince Philip. Prince Charles** and **Diana, Princess of Wales,** maintained a heavy schedule of foreign travel that included North America, the Persian Gulf, and Japan. The prince was the main Foundation Day speaker at ceremonies honoring Harvard University's 350th birthday, and the usually sophisticated Diana displayed a carefully self-effacing wardrobe when visiting the Muslim states.

In other royal doings, **Crown Prince Makhosetive,** 18, took leave from his studies at England's Sherborne School to return to Swaziland, where in secret ceremonies he was crowned **King Mswati III.** Jordan's **King Hussein** and **Queen Noor,** the former Lisa Halaby, became the parents of their fourth child, Princess **Ralyah al-Hussein.** Monaco's **Princess Caroline** gave birth in August to a daughter, **Charlotte Marie Pomeliné Casiraghi.** Caroline's younger sister, the flamboyant **Princess Stephanie,** took the No. 1 spot on the French pop charts with "Ouragan" (Hurricane); the successful model, renowned for her unisex clothing, also had the dubious distinction of

Accepting bouquets from admiring children, Diana, Princess of Wales, begins a week-long royal visit to British Columbia, where she and Prince Charles helped open Expo 86.

topping **Mr. Blackwell**'s Worst Dressed List of 1986.

In August, **Prince Frederick von Anhalt, Duke of Saxony** (born Robert Lichtenberg), 45, who sells knighthoods for a living, married **Zsa Zsa Gabor,** said to be 67. According to most calculations, the wedding was his fifth and her eighth. Other celebrity nuptials included those of ABC-TV newswoman **Barbara Walters,** 54, who wed Lorimar Telepictures chairman **Merv Adelson,** 56 (her second, his third); and tennis star **John McEnroe,** 27, and actress **Tatum O'Neal,** 22, who were parents of a baby son. In November former heavyweight boxing champion **Muhammad Ali,** 44, married **Lonnie Williams,** 28, in Louisville, Ky., where the two had once been neighbors. It was her first marriage and Ali's fourth.

The sometimes involuntary travels of the rich and famous also claimed public notice. Exiled from Haiti in February, former dictator **Jean-Claude Duvalier,** his wife, **Michèle,** and their two children set up housekeeping in France, at a villa near Cannes. Forbidden to leave the area by the French government and unable to touch $124 million in frozen assets, Michèle reportedly whiled away the time watching television, doing crossword puzzles, and giving her husband a twice-monthly manicure. Also deposed in February, Philippine President **Ferdinand Marcos** and his wife, **Imelda,** set up housekeeping in Hawaii; a personal fortune valued at up to $5 billion and thousands of pairs of Imelda's shoes now appeared tantalizingly beyond their grasp. Another famous traveler was **Svetlana Alliluyeva,** daughter of Soviet dictator **Joseph Stalin.** Alliluyeva, who had defected to the West in 1968 and then returned to the Soviet Union in November 1984, again left her homeland in April in order to join her 14-year-old American-born daughter, **Olga Peters,** in Great Britain.

In the pop world, **Madonna** held center stage, although her *Shanghai Surprise,* filmed in Macao with husband **Sean Penn** (who had several well-publicized scuffles with the press during the filming), opened in late summer to critical scorn and public apathy. Among Madonna's hits was the single "Papa Don't Preach," which tells the story of a pregnant 15-year-old who insists on "keeping" her baby; the song drew outcries from pro-choice activists and praise from conservative commentators who in the past had denounced the Material Girl for the sexy allure of her songs and image.

Culture Club lead vocalist **Boy George** (born George O'Dowd) pleaded guilty in London to heroin possession—for which he was fined $370—and checked into a treatment center. His brother David had earlier revealed that George was saddled with a $1,600-a-day heroin habit. **Frank Sinatra** tried but failed to halt publication of *His Way,* Kitty Kelley's tell-all biography, which portrays him as having behaved with little gallantry toward **Judy Garland, Ava Gardner, Elizabeth Taylor,** and others. The 70-year-old singer recovered from emergency surgery on a perforated colon in time to perform at the gala reopening of New York's Carnegie Hall in December. Meanwhile, the ever-more-reclusive **Michael Jackson** left the womblike comfort of his hyperbaric chamber

Proud papa John McEnroe, in London to play in the Benson and Hedges tennis tournament, poses with his wife, Tatum O'Neal, and their six-month-old son Kevin. The wedding was in August.

Clint Eastwood, whose on-screen characters achieved renown for their unique brand of justice, is sworn in as mayor of Carmel, Calif., after winning 72 percent of the vote.

to put the finishing touches on *Captain EO,* a 17-minute space fantasy produced with George Lucas for the Walt Disney Company, at a cost of about $20 million.

Reunions joined together the **Everly Brothers,** the **Monkees,** and the Canadian duo of **Ian** and **Sylvia Tyson.** *Miami Vice* heartthrob **Don Johnson** had a hit single with "Heartbeat," and rock 'n' roll pioneer **Chuck Berry** celebrated his 60th birthday at a gala concert in St. Louis with guests like **Eric Clapton, Keith Richards, Linda Ronstadt,** and **Julian Lennon. Bob Geldof,** lead singer of the Boomtown Rats and a driving force behind rock's famine relief efforts, did not get the Nobel Peace Prize his supporters had hoped for, but he was named an honorary Knight Commander of the British Empire.

Television filled the airwaves with talk, talk, talk, as **Oprah Winfrey** squared off against longtime leader **Phil Donahue** for daytime talk-show supremacy, and **Joan Rivers,** once regarded as heir apparent to NBC's *Tonight Show,* went head-to-head against **Johnny Carson** with her own syndicated night-owl program. Two casualties of the late-night talk wars, **Jimmy Breslin** and **Dick Cavett,** saw their new shows canceled by ABC. (Breslin, however, claimed to have fired ABC first.) And veteran talk-show

Refusing to come unstrung even when two violins did, 14-year-old prodigy Midori dazzled conductor Leonard Bernstein (right) and the audience during a Boston Symphony concert. She finished the difficult piece on a third violin, losing neither the beat nor her aplomb.

Dith Pran, whose harrowing escape from Cambodia was the basis for the movie The Killing Fields, *takes the oath of U.S. citizenship in New York City, along with his wife.*

host **Merv Griffin** retired. Dubbed "America's Favorite Father," comedian **Bill Cosby** not only had the nation's most-watched weekly television program but also was the proud author of one of its biggest best-sellers, *Fatherhood.*

The talk of Hollywood was **Debra Winger,** 30, who married **Timothy Hutton,** 25, and continued to nettle her costars. In an interview in *Esquire* she labeled **Richard Gere** "a brick wall" and revealed that on the *Legal Eagles* set she had tagged **Robert Redford** "the Unnatural." Generally known in his movie roles as a man of few words, **Clint Eastwood** captured the mayoralty of Carmel, Calif., in a campaign that attracted political reporters and Eastwood fans from Fiji to Finland. The Hollywood superstar unburdened himself of his $200-a-month mayoral responsibilities long enough to play, in *Heartbreak Ridge,* a gunnery sergeant heavily addicted to profanity.

Every year has its winners and losers. Among the former was Tennessean **Kellye Cash,** the 21-year-old grandniece of country music star **Johnny Cash,** who became Miss America 1987. Winner of the Supermodel of the World contest

Pilots Dick Rutan and Jeana Yeager made aeronautic history late in the year when they flew around the globe in their experimental plane Voyager without stopping or refueling.

Jubilant team members of the Steger International North Pole Expedition reach their destination, after a grueling 55 days of dogsledding through hundreds of miles of frozen terrain and below-zero temperatures; they were the first group to reach the North Pole without mechanical transportation since Admiral Robert Peary's 1909 expedition.

was 14-year-old **Monika Schnarre** of Scarborough, Ontario, who stands 6 feet tall and claims to have "the hugest, ugliest feet you've ever seen—size 10!" Size was no liability for two Maryland Democrats, 6'11" **Tom McMillen,** a former pro basketball player who was elected to the House of Representatives in November, and 4'11" **Barbara Mikulski,** a five-term congresswoman who won election to the Senate. Another diminutive champion, 4'9" Olympic gold medalist **Mary Lou Retton,** announced her retirement at age 18 from active gymnastics. Meanwhile, though not competing at all, Japanese violinist Midori, 14, won cheers at a Boston Symphony concert; despite breaking two violin strings in a row, she kept on with aplomb, deftly exchanging violins with the concertmaster.

Big winners in other fields included Chicago Bears quarterback **Jim McMahon,** who followed up a Super Bowl victory with the modestly titled *McMahon!,* a top-selling autobiography; University of Miami signal-caller **Vinny Testaverde,** awarded the Heisman Trophy as the nation's outstanding college football player; **Greg LeMond,** the first North American ever to pedal to victory in the Tour de France cycle race; **Gary Kasparov,** confirmed as world chess champion after a grueling series of matches with **Anatoly Karpov;** and **Mike Scott,** whose no-hitter to clinch the National League West title for the Houston Astros also cinched his chances for the Cy Young Award. **Ray Knight,** winner of Comeback of the Year honors and Most Valuable Player in the Mets' World Series triumph, saw it all turn sour in December when the team cut him loose in a contract dispute. Baseball set a classier example by choosing a distinguished scholar, Yale University President **A. Bartlett Giamatti,** to head the National League, and by having Holocaust survivor **Elie Wiesel,** winner of the 1986 Nobel Peace Prize, throw out the first ball at a Series game.

Dith Pran, another survivor, whose ordeal in Cambodia under the Khmer Rouge was depicted in the 1984 film *The Killing Fields,* was sworn in as an American citizen in New York City, where he works as a photographer.

307

PEOPLE IN THE NEWS

Intrepid adventurers scored new triumphs in 1986. Six hardy members of a polar expedition—five men and a woman—completed a two-month, 900-mile trek to become the first explorers since Admiral Robert Peary in 1909 to reach the North Pole assisted only by dogs. And on December 23, after an often bumpy ride, **Dick Rutan** and **Jeana Yeager** landed their experimental plane *Voyager* at Edwards Air Force Base in California, having circled the globe in the longest flight ever made without refueling. They had taken off from the same airfield 9 days, 3 minutes, and 44 seconds before.

Among the year's more unlikely winners were **Evelyn Marie Adams,** who beat odds of more than 17 trillion to 1 by winning the top prize in the New Jersey lottery twice within a six-month span, for a total of $5.4 million; the

Carried into the Philippines' presidency by a wave of popular support that drove longtime dictator Ferdinand Marcos from the country, Corazon Aquino has impressed a watching world with her courage and determination, as she steers the nation back toward democracy.

Amazing (James) Randi, a magician and debunker of psychics who, amid a flock of tonier types, won a MacArthur Foundation "genius" grant worth $272,000; and Texas gem dealer **Roy Whetstine,** who purchased for $10 from an amateur rock collector a star sapphire worth more than $2 million. Former chambermaid **Barbara Piasecka Johnson** emerged from a bitter court battle with a $340 million share of the Johnson & Johnson pharmaceutical fortune, and singer **Wayne Newton** was awarded $19.2 million (pending appeal) in a libel case against NBC, which had linked him to organized crime in a series of broadcasts. Entrepreneur **H. Ross Perot,** already worth more than $2 billion, so badgered fellow General Motors board members that they insisted on buying his GM stock for $700 million, twice its value when he acquired it.

As for the year's biggest loser, that probably was **Ivan Boesky,** a Wall Street speculator fined $100 million by the Securities and Exchange Commission for illegal insider trading. However, even in disgrace, Boesky was able to retreat to his comfortable Westchester County compound with a huge salvaged fortune.

G.M.H.

AQUINO, CORAZON (COJUANGCO)

President of the Philippines, born January 25 1933, in Tarlac province, the Philippines Carrying on the work of her martyred husband, Corazon Aquino rode to victory as spiritual head of the "people power" revolution that drove President Ferdinand Marcos from the country. Her administration was beset with problems, including a huge foreign debt, a growing Communist insurgency, and restiveness on the right, but she appeared to retain high support as she sought to solve these problems and promote national reconciliation.

Corazon "Cory" Aquino did not start out in life as a likely future president. Reared in a society where women stayed in the background, she attended elite convent schools in Manila and in New York, where in 1953 she graduated from the College of Mount St. Vincent with a degree in French. Even after having married Benigno ("Ninoy") Aquino, Jr., a rising politician, she rarely attended political functions, preferring to devote her time to the couple's five children.

That all changed in 1972, when Ninoy was arrested and sentenced to 7½ years in prison for his activism against the Marcos regime, and Cory became his link with the outside world. Later, the couple spent 3½ relatively quiet years in the United States, after Benigno Aquino was allowed to go there for heart surgery. Then, on August 21, 1983, as he was stepping off a plane bringing him back to the Philippines, Aquino was assassinated, allegedly by the military. His widow suddenly found herself thrust into the role of head of the opposition, which turned to her as its standard-bearer in the presidential election of February 7, 1986. Although she "lost" the election to Marcos according to official results, she won power after Defense Minister Juan Ponce Enrile and deputy Army chief of staff Fidel Ramos rallied to her side, along with large numbers of Filipino soldiers and civilians, forcing Marcos to flee.

Critics assailed many of the changes she made upon assuming office. Perhaps the most controversial was her release of leftist political prisoners, in the hope of quieting the Communist insurgency in the countryside, and her willingness to negotiate with Communists (which led to a 60-day cease-fire, beginning in early December). But few questioned her intentions or her courage. In September when she visited the United States, she met with President Ronald Reagan, addressed the UN General Assembly, and gave a speech before a joint session of Congress which House Speaker Tip O'Neill called the "finest I've heard in my 34 years in Congress." A.L.N.

BHUTTO, BENAZIR

Pakistani opposition leader, born June 21, 1953, in Karachi. The daughter of Zulfikar Ali Bhutto, former president of Pakistan, Benazir Bhutto became a major political figure in her own right, returning from voluntary exile in London during April 1986 to be greeted by hundreds of thousands of fervent Pakistanis. Her ambitions included nothing less than becoming the first woman to lead the government of an Islamic state.

Bhutto's father, member of a wealthy landowning family, held high government posts while she was growing up and eventually became president (1971) and then prime minister (1973). Benazir Bhutto graduated from

Since her return to Pakistan in April, Benazir Bhutto, daughter of former Pakistani leader Zulfikar Ali Bhutto, has become an influential force in politics, campaigning openly for the overthrow of the repressive regime that ousted, and later executed, her father.

Radcliffe College and took another degree at Oxford University. Bhutto's enthusiasm for politics began early—she was among the first to join her father's new Pakistan People's Party (PPP) in 1967. Ten years later, her father was deposed in a military coup and her political life began in earnest with her efforts to save him from being executed. Despite her efforts, he was hanged in 1979. Subsequently, as acting head of the PPP, she campaigned against the military government of President Muhammad Zia ul-Haq, spending much of her time in detention until she left for London in 1984.

When Bhutto returned to Pakistan, she appeared at first to receive overwhelming support in her crusade against Zia's regime. But her father's regime had itself engaged in repression, and, while she was popular among poor Pakistanis and the left, she lacked a solid base of support in the middle class and the military.

309

Vice President George Bush, long the unofficial front-runner for the 1988 Republican presidential nomination, saw his popularity endangered by the Iranian arms disclosures.

Also, for many Pakistanis, the idea of a Muslim woman participating in politics was unacceptable.

Bhutto's strategy was apparently to provoke the government to repressive action by means of mass demonstrations and thus discredit its claims to be moving toward democracy. The number who turned out for the Independence Day demonstrations in August, when Bhutto was arrested and jailed for several weeks, did not approach that needed to bring down the government. Nevertheless, she remained a strong rallying point for opposition, possibly with a key role to play in shaping her country's future.

BUSH, GEORGE H(ERBERT) W(ALKER)

U.S. vice president, born June 12, 1924, in Milton, Mass. As front-runner in the 1988 Republican presidential sweepstakes, George Bush sought to consolidate support within his party and woo conservatives, many of whom regarded him as too liberal. His tactics did not always succeed. An attack on New York's Democratic Governor Mario Cuomo for alleg-

edly having fostered divisiveness drew bitter criticism from a prominent conservative commentator, George Will. Bush was also widely denounced as favoring the special interests of the oil industry when, on a visit to Saudi Arabia, he called for "stability" in the oil markets, saying petroleum prices were dropping too fast. But such problems were overshadowed late in the year when news of the Iranian arms scandal leaked out. Bush was severely damaged, though he appeared to retain his position as GOP presidential front-runner.

After keeping a low profile for a time, he delivered a public statement in early December. While generally supportive of the president, he acknowledged that "mistakes were made" in the Iranian affair and that the administration's "credibility" had been damaged. He said he had known of and supported the decision to sell arms to Iran but denied any knowledge of the diversion of arms-sale profits to the rebels, or contras, fighting Nicaragua's Sandinista regime. Although Bush had met a few times with a former CIA agent involved in a clandestine network supplying arms to the contra rebels, and Bush staff members had communications with the operative—Felix Rodriguez, who used the nom de guerre of Max Gomez—Bush said he was unaware of any connection between Rodriguez and the resupply effort.

Aside from the Iranian affair, Bush's record of government service, his visibility as vice president, and his generally efficient political organization had given him formidable advantages over other GOP contenders, helping him to win the first tentative test of the presidential race—the election of precinct delegates in Michigan, in August. Bush also gained favorable publicity in meetings with world leaders during various trips abroad. Still, the vice presidency has its disadvantages as a stepping stone to the White House. As Bush awkwardly sought to deal with the Iran/contra scandal, his key GOP rival, Senator Bob Dole of Kansas, was taking the initiative in calling for investigation and full disclosures. And as the Bush forces geared up for the campaign, they bore in mind that the last sitting vice president ever to win a presidential election was Martin Van Buren, in 1836.   G.M.H.

CLEMENS, (WILLIAM) ROGER

Baseball player, born August 4, 1962, in Dayton, Ohio. On April 29, Roger Clemens of the Boston Red Sox pitched himself into baseball's record books. The 6'4" right-handed fireballer struck out 20 Seattle Mariners on his way to a three-hit, 3-1 victory, surpassing the record of 19 strikeouts for a nine-inning game set by such certain Hall-of-Famers as Tom Seaver, Nolan Ryan, and Steve Carlton. But Clemens's accomplishments for 1986 did not stop there. With his 24-4 record, Clemens led the major leagues in both wins and winning percentage. He led the American League with a 2.48 earned run average and was second in strikeouts with 238. So overpowering was he that he won the American League Cy Young Award and the league's Most Valuable Player honors as well.

What made these achievements even more remarkable was that, in 1985, Clemens underwent arthroscopic surgery on his right shoulder, and it wasn't clear that he would ever pitch again. He did—and more, leading Boston to the 1986 Eastern Division title. He also won the seventh and deciding game of the league playoff series against the California Angels, to put Boston in its first World Series since 1975.

Clemens spent much of his youth in Houston, where he adopted as his idol another flame-throwing right-hander—Nolan Ryan. In college, he led the University of Texas to the 1983 College World Series championship. Selected by the Red Sox in the first round of the 1983 baseball draft, he was called up to the majors in May 1984.

Clemens posted good numbers in that short season, but in 1985 he was plagued by pain and weakness in his right shoulder. In August

Boston Red Sox pitcher Roger Clemens battled back from an injury-plagued 1985 season to dominate the major leagues in 1986, compiling a 24-4 record, winning the Cy Young Award, and leading his team to their first World Series since 1975.

Former White House deputy chief of staff Michael Deaver, a Washington lobbyist, was the subject of a federal investigation into charges that he broke conflict-of-interest laws.

he had some cartilage removed from around the rotator cuff, and his return to action couldn't have been more dramatic—he opened the 1986 regular season with 14 straight victories, just one short of the American League record and five short of the major league record.

Clemens lives with his wife, Debbie, in Katy, Texas.

DEAVER, MICHAEL (KEITH)

Lobbyist and former presidential aide, born April 11, 1938, in Bakersfield, Calif. Deaver had been a highly trusted aide and close friend of Ronald Reagan before leaving his post in 1985 to start a lobbying and public relations firm. He fell into some disrepute in 1986, because of his blatant and possibly illegal use of federal government contacts.

Michael Deaver had jumped into politics as a Republican organizer in Santa Clara County, Calif. As director of administration under Reagan when the latter was governor of California, he won credit for his astute management of Reagan's schedule and personal appearances.

Meanwhile, he and his wife Carolyn became close friends of the Reagans. Deaver held a similar position at the White House during Reagan's first term as president; when he left, he was rewarded with a White House pass and copies of the president's daily schedule. By early 1986, his clients included Rockwell International, CBS, Trans World Airlines, and the governments of Saudi Arabia, South Korea, Singapore, Puerto Rico, Mexico, and Canada. Deaver put his federal contacts to quick use. He met with the director of the Office of Management and Budget to promote Rockwell International's desire to build more bombers, and investigators were probing his possible role in influencing Reagan to cooperate with Canada on the acid rain problem.

Accused of violating a federal law limiting lobbying by ex-government officials, Deaver surrendered his White House pass and called for the appointment of a special prosecutor to clear his name. U.S. Attorney Whitney North Seymour, Jr., was subsequently named to head a federal inquiry. After a House subcommittee concluded Deaver had lied in sworn testimony before it, Seymour convened a federal grand jury to look into the conflict of interest and perjury allegations. Meanwhile, Deaver's firm had reportedly lost over $1 billion in billings. Despite these problems, Deaver reemerged late in the year as an informal adviser to President Reagan and first lady Nancy Reagan, reportedly playing a role in efforts to engineer the departure of chief of staff Donald Regan in the wake of the Iranian arms scandal.   G.M.H.

GORBACHEV, MIKHAIL S(ERGEEVICH)

General secretary of the Soviet Communist Party, born March 2, 1931, in Privolnoe in southern Russia. By the end of his first year as Soviet leader in March, the relatively youthful Gorbachev (who was just turning 55) had renewed the party leadership, inaugurated massive campaigns against corruption, alcoholism, and workplace indiscipline, and forcefully urged "radical reforms" in the economy. Throughout 1986, he continued to stress these themes. By late summer, his campaign against alcoholism had reportedly produced a 38 percent reduction in vodka sales, compared with a year earlier.

Gorbachev's stress on "openness" in government contrasted with his predecessors' style. He traveled extensively throughout the Soviet Union and, in impromptu sessions, frequently urged people to speak more openly about their problems. "Trying to cover up shortcomings or to put on rose-colored glasses is no good for us," he told one group of farmers. Gorbachev personally telephoned physicist and human rights advocate Andrei Sakharov to tell him he was released from banishment in Gorky. Gorbachev also was associated with a new style in foreign policy and diplomacy. In 1986 the Soviet diplomatic corps was reorganized, new arms reduction proposals were made, and overtures were made for rapprochement with China.

Nevertheless, Gorbachev remained within the mainstream of Soviet political traditions. Aside from a few prominent cases, the handling of dissent remained harsh and repressive, and there were limits to the new openness. After the April 26 nuclear reactor disaster at Chernobyl, for example, the Soviet government was slow to reveal details to the Soviet people or the outside world.

In October, Gorbachev met with President Ronald Reagan in Iceland. The talks, on a broad array of arms control issues, ended without an accord, as Reagan refused to accept stringent limits on the U.S. Strategic Defense Initiative. A somber Gorbachev subsequently charged that Reagan lacked the courage to make a "turn in world history."　　M.R.B.

HOUSTON, WHITNEY

Singer, born August 18, 1963, in Newark, N.J. Whitney Houston has enjoyed a spectacular rise to stardom since the release of her pop-soul debut album *Whitney Houston* in early 1985. By late in 1986, the album was the best-selling album by a black female vocalist in pop music history, as well as the top-selling album of the year. The singer also had four top-ten singles to her credit, she had won rave reviews for a summer concert tour, and a *People* magazine poll had rated her as the year's top new star.

Houston is no overnight sensation, however. She comes from a musical family that gave her top-notch coaching as well as a love for music. Her mother is the gospel and soul singer Cissy Houston, and singer Dionne Warwick is a first

cousin. Houston started singing gospel music in the New Hope Baptist Church in Newark at the age of seven and used to accompany her mother to recording sessions where Cissy and her group sang backup vocals for stars like Aretha Franklin and Wilson Pickett. She sang her first church solo at age 12, and, while still in her early teens, began singing backup with her mother in recording sessions for Chaka Khan, Lou Rawls, and the Neville Brothers. After she joined her mother's nightclub act, at 15, critics were calling her "star material."

At 17, Houston was spotted by a modeling agency scout, and her pictures started appearing in *Seventeen, Glamour,* and *Cosmo-*

In contrast to Soviet leaders of the past, Mikhail Gorbachev is credited with seeking to modernize Soviet society through widespread economic and social reforms and has expressed a strong desire for improved East-West relations.

Talented Whitney Houston took the music world by storm when she released her first solo album in early 1985; by late 1986 it had become the best-selling pop album ever by a black female singer and helped earn her the Grammy award for top female pop vocalist.

politan. After finishing high school, she signed with Arista Records, where her career was supervised by company president Clive Davis.

Houston sings in a clear soprano that doesn't have the rough edges of classic soul singing, but her sure control, strong voice, and directness give her songs emotional depth. Although she keeps some of her voice in reserve on records, when she releases it fully in concert, she brings people to their feet cheering.

In 1986, Houston won two American Music Awards, for best soul single and best soul music video, and received the Grammy award for top female pop vocalist.

MANDELA, WINNIE (NOMZANO WINIFRED MADIKIZELA)

South African activist, born 1934 or 1936 (sources vary) in the rural district of Pondoland in the Transkei. After completing high school, she moved to Johannesburg, where she studied social work. While still a student, she came into contact with the African National Congress (ANC), and in 1956 she met Nelson Mandela, a top ANC leader, who was standing trial for treason; two years later they were married. The treason trial ended in 1961 with Nelson Mandela's acquittal (by then they had two children), but Nelson went underground to launch the military wing of the ANC, outlawed by the government in 1960. He was arrested in 1962 and eventually sentenced to life in prison.

Over the next 20 years, Winnie Mandela was repeatedly placed under government restrictions and often jailed. In August 1985, her home in a remote village in the Orange Free State, where she had been ordered by the government, was destroyed in a bomb attack. The event was a turning point. Mandela salvaged the few possessions that survived and, defying her banishment order, moved back into the Soweto home she had once shared with her husband.

She began to assume an increasingly high profile, becoming one of South Africa's leading black activists in her own right. After she addressed a funeral rally in 1985, she was arrested, jailed, and released three times in two weeks for defying the order forbidding her to live in Soweto. In July 1986, however, the restrictions were formally lifted.

Mandela spoke out repeatedly during 1986.

She criticized the policies of U.S. President Ronald Reagan and British Prime Minister Margaret Thatcher, both of whom opposed stringent economic sanctions against South Africa, and at various public meetings, she called for increased defiance of the Pretoria government.

Mandela's autobiography (based on taped interviews) was published in the United States in late 1985 (it was banned in South Africa). The following August, Camille Cosby, television star Bill Cosby's wife, announced plans to produce a film on her life.   J.F.

MULRONEY, (MARTIN) BRIAN

Prime minister of Canada, born March 20, 1939, in Baie-Comeau, Québec. It was not an easy year for Brian Mulroney. Fewer than 24 months after his Progressive Conservatives had won a historic electoral victory, the Mulroney government had fallen well behind the opposition Liberals in the opinion polls, and the prime minister himself was being accused of indecision and worse.

Part of the problem was a series of scandals of varying dimensions. One senior minister resigned as a judicial inquiry began hearing conflict-of-interest allegations against him. A Tory member of Parliament faced prosecution for corruption. Michael Deaver, a former high-level Reagan aide hired by Ottawa to represent its views on the acid rain controversy, came under investigation for violation of U.S. lobbying laws.

Mulroney argued that appearances were deceiving. "We have media who are captivated

Canadian Prime Minister Brian Mulroney weathered a series of minor scandals and faced controversy over his decision to launch free-trade negotiations with the United States.

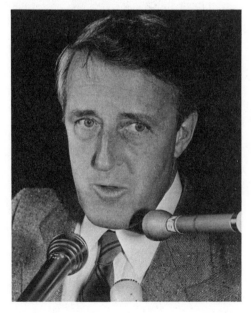

315

Libyan leader Muammar al-Qaddafi's apparent sponsorship of international terrorism sparked a retaliatory air raid by U.S. bombers in April.

QADDAFI, MUAMMAR AL-

Libyan head of state and "revolutionary leader," born in 1942 in the Libyan desert near Surt. The Qaddafi regime has been linked to a number of terrorist incidents, and Reagan administration officials blamed Libya particularly for the April 5 bombing of a West Berlin discotheque frequented by off-duty U.S. soldiers; in response, U.S. jets struck at targets in Libya, including Qaddafi's headquarters, early on April 15. A 15-month-old adopted daughter of Qaddafi was said to have been among those killed in the raid, and two of his six sons were apparently wounded. Afterward, Qaddafi was reported to be despondent and exhausted, and for some time he kept a low profile.

In August some U.S. officials reported that Qaddafi was hatching new plots and that both U.S. armed forces and his domestic opponents were preparing to move against him. Subsequently, however, a White House memorandum was leaked, suggesting that these reports were fabrications and that the Reagan administration had been engaging in a disinformation campaign designed to keep Qaddafi off balance.

Meanwhile, Qaddafi had been taking a more visible role in public affairs. He led a large rally on August 30 and, two days later, reviewed a military parade celebrating his regime's 17th anniversary. At a summit conference of nonaligned nations in September, he denounced fellow heads of state for not coming to his aid after the U.S. attack.

Qaddafi's father was said to have been a nomadic farmer or shepherd of humble birth. The young Qaddafi idolized the charismatic Egyptian leader Gamal Abdel Nasser, who seized power in 1952, preaching social revolution and Arab nationalism. In 1969, Qaddafi, along with other young army officers, deposed Libya's King Idris. As Libyan leader he crusaded for Arab unity and proclaimed a "cultural revolution" at home. Qaddafi's *Green Book,* published in the 1970's, set forth his philosophy, an idiosyncratic combination of Islam and socialism.

Qaddafi lives under heavy security. Fond of mirrored sunglasses, he frequently carries a green swagger stick. He has been married to his second wife, Safia, since 1970.   G.M.H.

by trivia and, as a result, are not giving the government full marks," he told one interviewer. "I think we do the big things well and the small things poorly." Among the "big things" he cited were lower interest rates, lower (but still high) unemployment, strong economic growth, smoother federal-provincial relations, and the launching of free-trade negotiations with the United States (which, however, were controversial). Farther afield, Mulroney made a 12-day Asian tour to attract new trade and investment to Canada.

Still, a Gallup Poll in October found only 31 percent of decided voters favoring the Conservative government. Mulroney was taking what he hoped was corrective action. He radically rearranged his cabinet and reorganized the senior bureaucracy. On October 1 he convened a new session of Parliament to unveil his upcoming legislative agenda, which combined regional developmental and social programs with a call for fiscal restraint.   J.H.

REHNQUIST, WILLIAM (HUBBS)

Chief justice of the U.S. Supreme Court, born October 1, 1924, in Milwaukee. Appointed to the Court as an associate justice in 1971 by President Richard Nixon, William H. Rehnquist has a political philosophy close to that of President Ronald Reagan, who named him in 1986 to replace retiring Chief Justice Warren Burger. In 15 years as an associate justice, Rehnquist voted consistently to the right of center on issues ranging from affirmative action to criminal rights. His views were controversial, but his legal expertise was considered beyond question.

While he was an advocate of judicial restraint, Rehnquist nevertheless played an active role in pruning back liberal rulings made by the Court in the 1950's and 1960's under Chief Justice Earl Warren. For example, he voted to narrow the so-called Miranda warnings, ad-

Associate Justice William Rehnquist was sworn in as chief justice of the U.S. Supreme Court in September to replace retiring Chief Justice Warren Burger; a staunch conservative, Rehnquist was expected to steer the Court to the right.

vising criminal suspects of their rights. He was one of two dissenters from the Court's landmark 1973 decision creating a constitutional right to abortion.

Confirmation hearings in the Senate were contentious, with anti-Rehnquist senators focusing on civil-rights-related issues and on specific charges that, as a young Republican activist, he had harassed black and Hispanic voters at polling places. His nomination was approved in September, but the 33 negative votes were the most ever received by a justice who won confirmation.

Raised in Milwaukee, Rehnquist attended Stanford Law School, clerked for Associate Justice Robert H. Jackson, practiced law in Arizona, and worked for the Justice Department, before President Nixon named him to the Court in 1971. On September 26, 1986, Rehnquist was sworn in as chief justice, becoming the fourth associate justice to reach that post. He and newly appointed Associate Justice Antonin Scalia were expected to form the hub of a formidable conservative coalition. 								C.J.S.

SHEPARD, SAM(UEL)

Playwright, director, and actor, born November 5, 1943, in Fort Sheridan, Ill. As the year began, Sam Shepard's new play *A Lie of the Mind,* which he was also directing, was being hailed as the most mature and powerful work in an already distinguished career, and his performance in the film version of his play *Fool for Love,* for which he wrote the screenplay, was evoking comparisons with Gary Cooper and enhancing his already potent box-office appeal.

Shepard's father was a moody, alcoholic man who quarreled constantly with his son, and at age 19, the young Shepard left home to pursue a career in the theater. He supported himself as a waiter and began writing bizarre avant-garde plays; in 1970 he collaborated on his first screenplay, for *Zabriskie Point.* A few years later, Shepard turned to a more naturalistic style that brought him to the attention of a wider public and the critical establishment.

The playwright's "family trilogy" of *Curse of the Starving Class, Buried Child,* and *True West* began an exploration of the dark underside of American family life that he continued in *Fool*

Writer, actor, and director Sam Shepard enjoyed continued successes in 1986, winning the New York Drama Critics Circle Best Play Award for his Lie of the Mind *and garnering praise for his role in the film* Fool for Love.

for Love and *A Lie of the Mind*. Although *Buried Child* won the 1979 Pulitzer Prize for drama, Shepard remained outside the commercial mainstream of American theater. His dramatic world is populated by rootless, shiftless Westerners on the social and financial edge and by disintegrating families whose members savage one another in body and spirit even as they cling together.

Shepard's career took a new turn when he was cast in a leading role in the 1978 film *Days of Heaven*. His portrayal of a Texas farmer who becomes involved in a fatal love triangle was widely praised and was followed by half a dozen other movie roles, including that of a homicidal motorcyclist in *Resurrection* and that of test pilot Chuck Yeager in *The Right Stuff*.

Shepard lives with actress Jessica Lange, with whom he had a daughter in January.

SHULTZ, GEORGE (PRATT)

U.S. secretary of state, born December 13, 1920, in New York City. During the year, Shultz seemed to be plunged into one controversy after another, with the Iranian arms scandal as the climax. Often he was also placed in the role of selling some of Reagan's less popular policies to unsympathetic audiences. On May 29, for example, the secretary defended President Ronald Reagan's decision to stop adhering to the unratified SALT II strategic arms treaty—at a meeting of NATO foreign ministers whose countries had all pressed the administration to work harder for arms control. In July, after a presidential speech on South Africa that essentially restated the administration's widely criticized "constructive engagement" policy, Shultz was on the hot seat again. Testifying before the Senate Foreign Relations Committee, he was subjected to harsh words from Senator Joseph Biden, who angrily accused the administration of "refusing to act on a morally abhorrent point." Shultz, in return, suggested that supporters of tough sanctions against South Africa were encouraging violence. "Just because I'm secretary of state," he added, "you can't kick me around. I'm a taxpayer."

Some observers questioned the extent of the secretary's influence. On August 1, for example, Reagan announced that the United States was willing to subsidize the sale of grain to the Soviet Union. The decision violated an agreement negotiated by Shultz between the United States and its European allies, and only days before, Shultz had publicly called the idea "ridiculous."

Shultz's influence was more seriously called into question in November, after it was revealed that the White House had negotiated with Iran and secretly sold that country military equipment (apparently, at least in part, to help gain the release of American hostages being held by a pro-Iranian group in Lebanon). The secretary, who had consistently spoken out against concessions to terrorists, said he opposed the shipments of military equipment, about which he had not been fully informed. Speaking before the House Foreign Affairs Committee in December, he also expressed "shock" that administration officials had established—without his knowledge—back-door communications with the U.S. ambassador to Lebanon on negotiations for the release of hostages. As to the diversion of arms-sale profits to anti-Sandinista rebels in Nicaragua, Shultz said he had "zero" knowledge of the transactions, which he criticized as ill-advised and illegal.

On November 16, appearing on the CBS News program *Face the Nation,* Shultz admitted that he had considered resigning over the Iran affair. President Reagan later indicated that he wanted Shultz to remain and said he had ordered all arms sales to Iran stopped (as Shultz wanted). A.T.

THATCHER, MARGARET (HILDA ROBERTS)
Prime minister of Great Britain, born October 13, 1925, in Grantham, England. Margaret Thatcher, visiting a NATO training ground in West Germany, was dressed for the occasion in scarf and goggles. Seated in the gunner's perch of a Challenger tank and locking on her target with a laser beam, she scored a direct hit with a practice shell at a distance of 1,000 yards. "I loved it!" said the British prime minister, giving one more indication of why she is known as the Iron Lady.

Margaret Thatcher has long been Ronald Reagan's staunchest foreign ally, and when the United States launched its April attack on Libya, she was the only European leader to express wholehearted support. But her decision to let U.S. F-111 fighter-bombers take off from British bases was not popular in her own Parliament. "When Mr. Reagan tells Mrs. Thatcher to jump," complained Labor foreign policy spokesman Denis Healey, "her reply is 'How high?' "

For Secretary of State George Shultz, 1986 was a trying year. Called upon to defend controversial White House stands on such issues as SALT II and South African sanctions, Shultz seldom left the hot seat. Furthermore, news late in the year that U.S. arms had been sold to Iran over his opposition, and the profits diverted to the contras without his knowledge, raised serious questions about his influence within the administration.

Plagued by a weak economy, a divided cabinet, and controversy over South Africa and other foreign policy issues, British Prime Minister Margaret Thatcher had a difficult year.

Thatcher also faced problems on other fronts. In January, with the pound weak, the economy sluggish, and unemployment still high, she endured her gravest cabinet crisis since taking office in 1979. Sharp differences and infighting within the cabinet led to the resignation of Defense Secretary Michael Heseltine and Trade and Industry Secretary Leon Brittan. Thatcher was also embarrassed in October by the resignation of Jeffrey Archer, the Conservative Party vice chairman (and best-selling novelist), after a tabloid newspaper revealed he had made a payoff to a prostitute. And in July a story appeared in the *Sunday Times* of London that Queen Elizabeth felt reservations about Thatcher's policies. Though denied by Buckingham Palace, the story was damaging.

Meetings abroad offered some respite. In May, enroute to the Tokyo summit meeting of the seven leading industrial democracies, Thatcher made the first visit by a British prime minister to South Korea. At the summit, she played a key role in the adoption of a strongly worded declaration against terrorism. Late the same month, Thatcher became the first British prime minister to visit Israel. In July she made a trip to Canada, where she visited Expo 86 and met with Prime Minister Brian Mulroney. Later, she traveled to Norway and had a cordial meeting with Premier Gro Harlem Brundtland, Europe's only other female head of government—though the visit provoked several demonstrations against her policies on South Africa and Northern Ireland.

In November, Thatcher met with Reagan in the United States; their talks were said to have produced agreement on "priorities" in arms control negotiations along the lines Thatcher had been seeking. Meanwhile, late in the year, as Thatcher looked forward to elections in 1987, she could take comfort in an opinion poll that still gave the Conservatives 40 percent support, as against 36 percent for Labor and 21 percent for the Liberal/Social Democratic Alliance.   G.M.H.

WALDHEIM, KURT

Austrian president, born December 21, 1918, near Vienna. The 1986 presidential election in Austria set Kurt Waldheim, the candidate of the conservative People's Party, against Socialist nominee Kurt Steyrer, a former health minister. For more than 40 years, Waldheim had compiled a distinguished record in the Austrian diplomatic service and as secretary-general of the UN (1972–1982). He began his campaign for the largely ceremonial post of president with the slogan "the candidate the world trusts." That image was shattered, however, when documents uncovered by the World Jewish Congress and other investigators revealed extensive evidence of Waldheim's involvement with the Nazi movement.

The materials showed that Waldheim had enrolled first in a Nazi student union and then in the notorious paramilitary SA (storm troopers) after Hitler annexed Austria. He was posted as a first lieutenant to the Balkans from 1942 until the end of the war, where he served as an interpreter and intelligence officer with Army Group E, which conducted operations against Yugoslav partisans (guerrillas) and civilians and supervised the mass deportation of Greek Jews to German death camps. The commanding officer of Army Group E was executed as a war criminal in 1947, and Yugoslav documents show that Waldheim was wanted in connection with "murder, slaughter, shooting of hostages, and ravaging of property by burning of settlements." The UN War Crimes Commission accused Waldheim of similar offenses, but for reasons that remain unclear, he was never brought to trial. Waldheim denied he was ever a Nazi or had collaborated in war crimes, and no evidence emerged that he personally had committed any atrocities.

Portraying himself in the campaign as a "decent soldier" who had done his wartime duty, Waldheim may have benefited from a backlash against criticism by outsiders as well as, possibly, from anti-Semitism among some Austrians and defensiveness about the Nazi era. In any case, he won the runoff election on June 8 with 54 percent of the vote. Sworn in to a six-year term a month later, the new president recalled "the horror of the Holocaust" and pledged himself to oppose ethnic and religious bigotry. There were few protests within Austria over his inauguration, but groups in several other countries organized support to bar Waldheim from official visits. Waldheim announced that he planned no such trips during his first year in office.   G.M.H.

PERSIAN GULF STATES. The tumbling price of oil and fall in the value of the U.S. dollar were serious blows to the economy of the small Persian Gulf states (Bahrain, Oman, Qatar, and United Arab Emirates). In Oman, where oil accounts for 90 percent of all revenues, the government devalued the rial by 10 percent against the U.S. dollar in February. Oman, not an OPEC member, also agreed to cooperate with Qatar, the UAE, and other OPEC states in cutting oil production to bolster prices.

A dispute between Bahrain and Qatar over ownership of Fasht Al-Dibil island reached a climax in April, when Qatari forces seized foreign workers on the island after Bahrain built a coast guard station there for the Gulf Cooperation Council. Qatari forces continued to occupy the island after unsuccessful mediation efforts by the GCC.

The UAE excluded Israel from an international chess olympics being held in 1986 in Dubai; the U.S. chess champion boycotted the event in protest.

See STATISTICS OF THE WORLD.   L.A.K.

PERU. Peru's dynamic president, Alan García Pérez, celebrated completion of his first year in office in July 1986 having had some success in grappling with the country's perennial problems. His popularity remained high, and he bolstered his image further with his party's good showing in November municipal elections.

The government's achievements included slashing the budget deficit and bringing inflation down to about 60 percent, less than half the 1985 rate. The economic growth rate for 1986 was forecast at about 6.5 percent. However, mining was depressed, with some mines closed because of low world prices. García

Miners and their families rally outside the Ministry of Economy in Lima to protest the closing of Andean gold and silver mines.

grappled with Peru's overseas creditors—nearly 300 banks, international agencies, and foreign governments—to whom the country owed more than $14 billion. In an effort to extract more favorable terms of repayment, the president continued to assert that Peru would limit its remittances to 10 percent of export earnings. He also refused an International Monetary Fund austerity program.

The Reagan administration was unhappy with García's limitation on payments and angered by his sharp criticisms of U.S. foreign policy. Nevertheless, García won praise for his drug eradication program, which destroyed coca fields and processing plants that were a major source of cocaine entering the United States. García also fired many police officers linked to the drug trade.

In November municipal elections the president's party captured nearly all the big-city

mayoral posts, with his handpicked candidate winning election as mayor of Lima. The vote was considered a personal victory for García, who had campaigned actively for his party. In December the government replaced price freezes with a system of price controls, announced new wage increases, and allowed the currency to be devalued.

Warfare by the Maoist Sendero Luminoso (Shining Path) guerrillas showed no signs of abating. The group was highly active in the Lima area, where bombings and murders took 150 lives in one six-week period and a state of emergency was declared. Meanwhile, uprisings at three prisons in June led to clashes in which government forces killed at least 260 inmates.

See STATISTICS OF THE WORLD.   D.P.W.

PETROLEUM AND NATURAL GAS. See ENERGY; ORGANIZATION OF PETROLEUM EXPORTING COUNTRIES.

PETS. While the demand for both wild-caught and artificially cultured small mammals, birds, and ornamental fishes continued to rise in 1986, governmental regulations were increasingly determining just what could legally be brought in and sold to U.S. hobbyists and pet owners. With the primary aim of controlling illegal trade in endangered or threatened species, the U.S. Fish and Wildlife Service had already imposed bans in 1985 on live animal imports from Bolivia and, for a brief period, from the Philippines. In September 1986 the federal government imposed a total wildlife ban against live animal imports from Singapore, the largest single supplier to the Western world of exotic birds, "herptiles" (reptiles and amphibians), and ornamental fishes. Singapore exports account for more than 40 percent of all live animals imported into the United States yearly. The ban on ornamental and tropical fishes was lifted the following month, but the ban against exotic birds, reptiles, and mammals remained in effect.

The overall theme in canine ownership continued to be that of security. Among the fastest-growing breeds in popularity were the rottweiler, the German shepherd, the Doberman pinscher, and a newcomer, the akita. All are large, powerful dogs, and many were purchased as guard dogs.

Andre the Seal, who was known and loved by the national news media as well as by his native Rockport, Me., where he served as honorary harbormaster and main tourist attraction for 25 years, was found dead on July 19 after a fight with another seal.

A source of controversy in the dog world was the rapidly growing popularity of pit bulls, who reportedly have been attacking humans. The term "pit bull" actually covers three breeds—the American Staffordshire terrier, the Staffordshire bull terrier, and the American pit bull terrier. All three are rather placid and amiable, unless bred and trained specifically to be fighters, but reports of pit bull attacks have sparked lawsuits and moves to have ownership of the dogs controlled or banned.

Among pet birds, the cockatiel accounted for more than 30 percent of overall bird sales in the United States, outstripping the budgerigar and the canary among small birds. Despite growing import and export restrictions, the larger psittacine birds (such as macaws, amazons, and cockatoos) continued to be in high demand, with the market increasingly supplied by captive-bred stock.

The gerbil was the front-runner in small animal sales, with the hamster second. About 20 percent of small animal sales in pet shops in the United States were those of herptiles, primarily snakes and lizards; the best-sellers were smaller pythons and boas, king snakes, iguanas, and several species of desert-dwelling lizards. J.Q.

PHILIPPINES. In 1986 a demure former housewife, Corazon (Cory) Aquino (see biography in PEOPLE IN THE NEWS), led a peaceful "people power" revolution that overthrew the entrenched regime of Philippines President Ferdinand E. Marcos. Marcos's ouster, after 20 years of nearly absolute power, brought relief and excitement to many but left the new government with monumental problems.

Peaceful Revolution. Long-standing popular discontent with the Marcos regime, which became increasingly widespread after the 1983 assassination of opposition leader Benigno S. Aquino, continued to grow during the two-month campaign leading up to the February 7, 1986, presidential eiection between Marcos and Corazon Aquino, Aquino's widow and political heir. During the campaign, despite Marcos's control of the mass media, Aquino emerged as a political phenomenon in her own right; shouts of "Cory! Cory! Cory!" followed her everywhere. Her cause was aided by active support of the hierarchy of the Roman Catholic

A dignified Ch. Marjetta National Acclaim poses with his proud owners, Michael Volla and Mrs. Alan Robson, after the pointer won Best of Show in the 110th Westminster Kennel Club Dog Show.

Church. In addition, the U.S. government, unsuccessful in persuading Marcos to make major reforms, had grown unsympathetic to the regime.

On election day itself, Marcos operatives reportedly stole ballot boxes, rigged vote counts, and even shot Aquino supporters. By the official count, which he controlled, Marcos won. But a citizens' group acting as poll-watchers concluded differently, and the Aquino camp declared a campaign of nonviolent protests.

The turning point came later in February, when Defense Minister Juan Ponce Enrile barricaded himself in his military headquarters and the surrounding installation and an-

Crowds in Angeles City show their support for Corazon ("Cory") Aquino during the postelection period of political unrest in the Philippines, early in the year.

nounced that he supported Aquino. He was joined at first only by General Fidel Ramos, the deputy chief of staff, and a few hundred soldiers and reform-minded officers. But by nightfall on February 22, thousands of Filipinos had surrounded the Defense Ministry, protecting the rebels from tanks and troops sent to attack them. With military leaders opposing him and his troops divided, Marcos had little hope of retaining power. Both he and Aquino took the oath of office in separate ceremonies on February 25. But just before midnight, Marcos and his entourage fled aboard a U.S. aircraft to Hawaii, leaving Aquino as the president.

Communist Insurgency. The new administration inherited challenges on both sides of the political spectrum. On the right, there was the restive Enrile and an army teeming with Marcos loyalists. On the left, there was a growing, ten-year-old Communist insurgency in the countryside, carried on by the New People's Army, which controlled about one-fifth of the towns and villages.

Moving to deal with the latter challenge first, Aquino, over the objections of her military aides, released many political prisoners, including Jose Maria Sison, founder of the Philippine Communist Party. She also began negotiations with the New People's Army, even while the NPA kept up its attacks. Aquino's rightist critics doubted whether this conciliatory approach would work.

In October, after government soldiers captured Philippine Communist leader Rodolfo Salas, the Communists, who had appeared ready to accept a 30-day cease-fire, claimed bad faith, broke off talks with the government, and demanded Salas's release. The government refused. Talks resumed, however, and Aquino declared a deadline for the insurgents to accept a cease-fire or face a "declaration of war." Talks again broke down temporarily when a leftist political leader was slain; his associates blamed the military. Finally, on November 27, the government and the insurgents agreed on a 60-day cease-fire pact, which went into effect on December 10. The pact allowed the left to set up headquarters in Manila and granted immunity from search, arrest, and prosecution to Communists involved in the continuing peace talks. The military was given the right to respond to certain "hostile acts."

Cabinet Changes. On November 23, Aquino took up the offensive against opposition within her own government and a threatened rightist coup. The night before, General Ramos, the armed forces chief of staff, had blocked a burgeoning plan by armed forces loyal to Defense Minister Enrile, together with groups loyal to Marcos, to declare a rebel government. Aquino asked for resignations from all cabinet members and immediately accepted the resignation of Enrile; he was replaced by Rafael M. Ileto. On November 28 she accepted the resignation of two cabinet ministers who had been accused of corruption.

New Constitution. Earlier, in March, Aquino had abolished the 1973 constitution imposed by Marcos and dissolved Parliament. In another controversial move, she also replaced hundreds of local officials with her own followers and appointed a constitutional commission; its new draft constitution called for a six-year presi-

dency, a bicameral legislature, and an independent judiciary, and for making the Philippines a nuclear-free zone. It also gave the legislature a voice in the future of U.S. military bases. If the constitution should be approved, in a plebiscite scheduled for January 1987, elections for the national legislature were to be held in May 1987.

Economy. The economy inherited by Aquino was a shambles, with 70 percent of the population below the poverty line, the highest rate of malnutrition in Asia, and a per capita income that had been declining for five years. Continued low prices for the Philippines' main exports made progress difficult. Her government did, however, manage to cut inflation sharply.

U.S. Relations. Aquino's stature in both the Philippines and the United States was bolstered by a nine-day visit to the United States in September. After her well-received speech to a joint session of Congress, both houses voted to give the Philippines an additional $200 million in economic aid, bringing the total U.S. aid to the Philippines to $500 million for fiscal 1987. During her visit, Aquino also met with leaders representing 483 foreign banks,

After the Philippine presidential elections in February, in which both Ferdinand Marcos and Corazon Aquino claimed victory, two of Marcos's key military leaders, Juan Ponce Enrile (left) and Fidel Ramos (right), pictured here among soldiers and supporters, abandoned him to shift support to Aquino.

to whom the Philippines owed $14 billion of its $26 billion foreign debt. (The rest was owed to international agencies such as the International Monetary Fund.) Later in the year, the IMF approved a $500 million loan, and the foreign banks granted an extension on debt repayment.

The debt was largely compiled during the Marcos era, as a result of expensive projects from which the Marcoses and their friends allegedly embezzled billions of dollars. A commission established by the Aquino government to recover assets acquired by the Marcoses estimated they had left the country with up to $10 billion, invested in everything from New York City office buildings and secret Swiss bank accounts to Australian resort properties. Part of Malacañang Palace, where Imelda Marcos kept thousands of pairs of shoes and hundreds of gowns, was turned into a museum to remind Filipinos of the Marcoses' opulent life-style. In September the search for assets began to pay off, when a New Jersey judge ordered that a $1 million estate near Princeton be turned over to Philippine government ownership.

Aquino had at first favored removal of Clark Air Base and Subic Bay Naval Station, U.S. bases that were the two largest military installations in the Western Pacific. She later indicated she would respect the current base arrangement until its expiration in 1991.

See STATISTICS OF THE WORLD. F.B.

PHOTOGRAPHY. In 1986 there were retrospectives of such photographic artists as Robert Frank, Laura Gilpin, and Edward Weston.

Major Exhibitions. "Robert Frank: New York to Nova Scotia," the first major retrospective of this seminal artist in 20 years, presented four decades of work, much of which had rarely been seen before. Organized by the Museum of Fine Arts in Houston, the show included not only Frank's photographs but also his work in other media, including film, video, and one-of-a-kind books.

"L'Amour fou: Photography and Surrealism" presented the first comprehensive examination of surrealist photography in Europe between the two world wars. The most important exhibition of fall 1985, the show traveled in 1986 to San Francisco, Paris, and London. Works

by such prominent artists as Man Ray, Hans Bellmer, and Georges Hugnet dominated, but the remarkable work of lesser-known figures like Claude Cahun and Jacques-André Boiffard were also represented.

This year marked the centennial of the birth of Edward Weston, the great formalist photographer whose exquisite images of shells, peppers, sand dunes, nudes, even toilets, represented an apex of abstract photographic beauty. The Center for Creative Photography in Tucson, Ariz., organized a 250-print retrospective, "Supreme Instants," which included Weston's seldom-seen color work. The show opened at the San Francisco Museum of Modern Art in November, at the beginning of a two-year U.S. tour.

Major History Shows. Although John Thomson is well-known for his documentary book *Street Life in London* (1878), his earlier work had been dispersed and all but lost to history. "A Window to the Orient," organized by the George Eastman House in Rochester, N.Y., brought to light the full range of his Asian photographs. The history of photography in Spain was detailed in two New York shows: "Idas y Caos: Trends in Spanish Photography, 1920–45" and "Arcadian Images: The Spanish Landscape Through Pictorial Photography."

Other Retrospectives. Laura Gilpin, a Southwestern photographer of the 1920's and 1930's, was the subject of a huge retrospective organized by the Amon Carter Museum in Fort Worth, Texas. "Ilse Bing: Three Decades of Photography," organized by the New Orleans Museum of Art, was the first full retrospective of this German photographer of the 1930's. A survey of Ralph Steiner's work appeared at the midtown branch of New York's International Center of Photography (ICP).

Contemporary Photography. Museums and prestigious art galleries, as well as photography galleries, featured innovative works by young photographers. Receiving the most attention were those whose work was more allied with trends in contemporary art than with the traditions of photography. New York's Museum of Modern Art reorganized its gallery and for the first time displayed contemporary works by John Divola, Wendy Snyder MacNeil, and Tina Barney.

The New Museum of Contemporary Art in New York featured photography as a major expressive medium of the 1980's in "The Art of Memory, The Loss of History." Central to the show was the work of photographers like Richard Prince, Sarah Charlesworth, and Christopher Williams, who appropriate the imagery and techniques of advertising and the mass media to comment on contemporary culture. Related to this art of appropriation were the photographs of Frank Majore, shown simultaneously in three New York settings—the ICP, Nature Morte, and 303 Gallery.

News and Events. Foto Fest, the first international photography festival on U.S. soil, proved to be the event of the year in the photography art world. Organized in Houston by gallery owner Petra Benteler and photographer Fred Baldwin, it was a month-long Texas-size extravaganza that attracted dealers, curators, photographers, and critics from the United States, Europe, and Japan.

New Technology. With its RC701, an electronic camera that records images on magnetic disks rather than on conventional film, Canon introduced the first electronic still-photography (ESP) camera to be made available commercially. It can store as many as 50 still pictures on a 47-millimeter floppy disk, and these can be erased or transferred to other disks. Disks can be inserted into a player for viewing on a TV screen, put into a printer to make hard copies, and even transmitted over telephone lines. The system is intended for commercial users who need instantly transferable images.

The sophistication of fully automated single-lens reflex (SLR) cameras continued to grow. Nikon produced the N2020, an autofocusing SLR that retained the Nikon bayonet mount, thereby enabling nearly all Nikon lenses, manual or automatic, to be used. Olympus had an autofocusing SLR on the market—the OM-77AF—with four interchangeable lenses. Minolta introduced the Maxxum 5000, a simplified version of last year's breakthrough Maxxum 7000.

Art Market. Records were set at Sotheby's in May, when Edward Steichen's great 1908 pigment print of *Balzac, Open Sky, 11 p.m.* sold for $49,000 and a print of Paul Strand's *Young Boy* soared to $38,500.   B.B.S.

A major retrospective of Laura Gilpin's work organized by the Amon Carter Museum in Texas featured powerful photographs of the American Southwest such as Navaho Woman, Child, and Lambs (above), as well as more delicate themes (below, Narcissus).

PHYSICS. In 1986 suspense continued over whether the U.S. government would fund the Superconducting Super Collider (SSC). The National Academy of Sciences released a report on progress in physics.

Particle Accelerators. Particle accelerators—popularly but misleadingly called atom-smashers—are designed to produce collisions between elementary particles. Physicists hoped that collisions between the protons in the proposed SSC would generate new elementary particles and the answers to questions about the ultimate structure of matter. With a planned circumference of 52 miles and a cost estimated at $4 billion, the SSC, if approved by the White House and Congress, would be the biggest particle accelerator ever made. It would have two beams of protons that circulate in opposite directions at an energy of 20 trillion electron volts, 20 times greater than the highest energy available at present.

One of the most contentious technical aspects of the SSC—what kind of magnet to adopt—was settled by scientists. Magnets serve two functions: they guide the particle beam around the circular course of the accelerator, which would be entirely underground, and they keep the beam tightly focused. In May a panel of physicists opted for high-strength magnets that could confine the beam to a 52-mile circumference, rather than weaker, less expensive magnets.

In December, researchers at AT&T Bell Laboratories reported the production of an alloy—lanthanum-barium-copper oxide—that at normal pressure enabled materials to begin be-

The world's most powerful particle accelerator, a research device used to split atoms into their constituent parts, was being constructed 200 feet below ground in a 13-mile-long circular tunnel near Moscow in the Soviet Union. Scheduled for completion in 1993, the accelerator was expected to propel the Soviet Union into the forefront of particle physics.

coming superconductive at 40 degrees Kelvin. The ability to produce superconductivity at such a relatively high temperature would have many important applications and, in particular, could reduce the cost of the SSC.

Meanwhile, the Soviet Union continued construction of its own particle accelerator outside Moscow. It was the largest such device yet undertaken, though smaller than the proposed U.S. accelerator.

Physics Survey. In April the National Academy of Sciences released a report entitled *Physics Through the 1990's,* in which American physicists discussed where they had been during recent years and where they would like to go in the next decade. The report detailed the accomplishments in a field that has blossomed to encompass an enormous breadth and that has made numerous practical contributions. It argued that continued progress depends on a revitalization of research universities, the homes of many past triumphs. For some time, the universities have been plagued by a significant disparity between the size of research grants from federal agencies and the actual costs of equipping and maintaining a laboratory.

Solar Puzzle. Ever since the 1938 explanation for which Hans Bethe of Cornell University later won a Nobel Prize, physicists have been confident that they understand the nuclear reactions by which the sun and other stars generate their energy. Nonetheless, a serious contradiction between theory and experiment has remained unresolved. In a long-running, deep underground experiment that measures the number of neutrinos coming from the sun, Raymond Davis of Brookhaven National Laboratory and numerous coworkers have consistently found only one-third the theoretically predicted number.

In 1985, two Soviet physicists proposed a resolution for the discrepancy. In March 1986, Bethe published an analysis that reached the same conclusion, though by a different method. Nuclear physicists regard the proposed solution as highly plausible, but difficult to verify by experiment.

The solution stems from the fact that there are three types of neutrinos. Nuclear reactions in the sun generate only one of the three—so-called electron neutrinos—and Davis's under-ground detector is sensitive only to this type. Physicists have realized for some time that, if the three types of neutrinos actually had small but different masses, an electron neutrino might turn into one of the other types while traveling from the sun to the earth, so that it could not be detected in Davis's experiment. Such a change is highly improbable. However, the Soviet physicists and Bethe showed that such a transmutation is considerably more probable in the sun itself, because the sun is such a massive body. The most direct verification of the theory would be a measurement of the electron neutrino mass, but the mass required to explain Davis's experimental results is too small to measure. Indirect tests are possible, however, and at least two were planned.

Quantum Optics. All electrical and optical signals consist of two elements. One is the information being transmitted,while the other consists of random fluctuations, or noise. The presence of noise limits the performance of an electrical or optical device. Researchers have now demonstrated that, under certain circumstances, it is possible to effectively reduce the noise in optical signals by "squeezing" the light. Squeezing means the signal is divided into two components, manipulated in such a way that the noise associated with one component is reduced (squeezed) while that associated with the other is enhanced. The overall noise is no different from that prescribed by the quantum theory, but researchers can make measurements using only the low-noise component of the signal, thereby circumventing the limit. Possible beneficiaries of squeezed light include the interferometer, optical data storage, optical communications systems, and high-resolution optical spectroscopy.

The first measurable squeezing was reported in October 1985 by Richart Slusher and several colleagues at AT&T Bell Laboratories, who achieved a 7 percent noise reduction. By June 1986, the group had increased the squeezing to 17 percent, but most optical physicists think that a figure near 90 percent must be attained before practical applications become possible. Meanwhile, also in June, a group at the University of Texas at Austin, led by H. Jeffrey Kimble, came closer, reportedly achieving a 42 percent squeezing.　　　　　A.L.R.

POLAND. During 1986 the regime headed by General Wojciech Jaruzelski in the dual roles of party head and chief of state remained unable to generate support among the majority of the Polish population. In September the government released virtually all its political prisoners, as a conciliatory gesture.

Party Congress. At the Tenth Congress of the Polish United Workers' (Communist) Party, held from June 29 to July 3, Jaruzelski continued the internal transformation of the party, begun in 1981, with the appointment of three more generals to the Politburo; Soviet leader Mikhail Gorbachev praised Jaruzelski and the party leadership for their victory in what he termed "the struggle for the very existence of socialism in Poland."

Solidarity. The government kept up its efforts to eliminate the vestiges of the outlawed Solidarity labor movement, and several underground Solidarity activists were arrested in the spring, including Zbigniew Bujak, the last major underground Solidarity leader. In September, however, the government surprised everyone by releasing more than 200 political prisoners, including Bujak and other prominent Solidarity figures. Their release had been a condition set by the Catholic Church for any fruitful dialogue with the Jaruzelski government; moreover, because of the continued detention of political prisoners the United States had refused to consider lifting its remaining economic sanctions against Poland. In October, Solidarity chairman Lech Walesa and nine other government critics asked President Ronald Reagan to lift all sanctions.

The Solidarity leadership responded to the government's amnesty with an intensification of open activism. At the end of September, Walesa named seven former fugitive leaders, including Bujak, to a new council that would openly seek the restoration of the Solidarity labor union. The government declared the council illegal.

Consultative Council. In December the government announced the creation of a new consultative council, composed of both Communists and non-Communists, which would advise the Council of State on social policy. Some prominent Catholic laymen and three former Solidarity members who had disavowed that organization were named to the body. Reaction was mixed, with many Solidarity leaders describing it as a purely cosmetic reform.

Economic Downturn. A wide range of evidence indicated that the quality of life for the country's more than 37 million people was still deteriorating. Lagging investments in industry, agriculture, and basic services were undermining the ability of Poland to emerge from its decade-long economic crisis. Modest economic reforms had practically no impact on vital areas of the country's economy and did not reduce the excessive use of energy or the waste of raw materials and investments or lessen the Poles' overdependence on imports. Foreign debt and lagging exports continued to plague the nation's economy.

Poland was readmitted to membership in the International Monetary Fund in June, after an absence of 36 years. Although the readmission signified a measure of normalization in Warsaw's economic relations with the West and promised to give access to additional credits, the major Western European trading partners of Poland still expected it to meet interest payments on past debt.

Foreign Relations. Official ties between the Soviet Union and Poland remained close, as the Warsaw leadership continued to rely heavily on Moscow for economic and political support. With Sino-Soviet relations improving, Jaruzelski in September traveled to China for an official visit, the first by a Polish head of state in over 25 years.

Relations with the United States remained strained, though high-level talks were resumed in November. Although the Reagan administration agreed to Poland's readmission to membership in the IMF, it appeared still unwilling to grant most-favored-nation status to Polish exports.

Soviet Nuclear Disaster. Northeastern Poland was particularly seriously affected by the radioactivity released by the explosion of a nuclear reactor at Chernobyl in the Soviet Union in late April. At Mikolajki, about 400 miles from Chernobyl, the amount of radiation briefly reached 500 times the normal background level.

See Statistics of the World. R.E.K.

PORTUGAL. In 1986 former Premier Mário Soares was elected president, and Portugal officially entered the European Community.

A Socialist, Soares came to the largely ceremonial office as the country was still marked by deep political divisions. His accession to the presidency, after a two-round ballot, confounded prognosticators. In the first round, on January 26, the political left wing had splintered, and Soares had lost by a 47 to 25 percentage margin to conservative Diogo Freigas do Amaral. However in the second round, on February 16, leftists united, enabling Soares to squeeze in by several percentage points. He was inaugurated on March 9, succeeding the popular António Ramalho Eanes.

In his inaugural address Soares struck a conciliatory note; nevertheless, many wondered how well he would get on with Prime Minister Anibal Cavaco Silva, the Social Democratic Party leader, who in 1985 had toppled then-Premier Soares's government by pulling his party out of the ruling coalition and forming a minority government. Soares and Cavaco Silva sought to downplay any problem. In fact, the minority government ran into considerable difficulty in getting its legislation through the 250-member Parliament. But in late June it won a vote of confidence when the Christian Democrats joined the Social Democrats to give it 108 votes—enough to remain in power.

After a period of deep recession, Portugal faced brighter prospects, enhanced by its accession on January 1 to the European Community. The 1986 budget, approved by Parliament in April, provided for large investments in industry, agriculture, education, and roads and water supplies, with matching funds to come from the EC.

Although Portugal's entry into the EC posed problems for the United States—which feared the loss of millions of dollars in agricultural exports because of changes in Portuguese tariff and quota structures—overall relations between Lisbon and Washington remained warm. The Reagan administration was heartened by Soares's outspoken support for NATO.

On February 15, Gaspar Castelo Branco, the head of prison services, was gunned down in Lisbon. Three days later, a car bomb exploded outside the U.S. embassy; no one was hurt.

Mário Soares was elected president of Portugal in February, becoming the country's first civilian president in nearly 60 years. The former Socialist prime minister was backed by a briefly united left in the second round of the election.

An extreme left-wing group called Popular Forces of the 25th of April claimed responsibility for both acts.

See Statistics of the World. J.O.S.

PRESIDENT OF THE UNITED STATES. See United States of America: *The Presidency.*

PRINCE EDWARD ISLAND. See Statistics of the World.

PRIZES AND AWARDS. The following is a selected listing of prizes awarded during 1986 and the names of the persons who received them. For some awards given in specific fields, see the appropriate subject entry, such as Motion Pictures.

NOBEL PRIZES

Although Americans accounted for the greatest number of 1986 Nobel laureates, three Europeans shared the physics prize. The awards, presented on December 10, carried with them approximately $290,000 in prize money for each category.

The first African recipient of the Nobel Prize in literature, Nigerian Wole Soyinka, is a novelist, poet, and playwright who uses Western forms and generally writes in English but draws heavily on the mythology of the Yoruba tribe.

Chemistry. For their development of powerful new tools that help scientists study in detail what happens when chemicals react:

Dudley R. Herschbach (1932–   ), professor at Harvard University. Born in San Jose, Calif., he attended Stanford University, where he received a B.S. in mathematics and an M.S. in chemistry. He earned his Ph.D. at Harvard in 1958 in chemical physics and was appointed to the Harvard faculty in 1963.

Yuan Tseh Lee (1936–   ), professor at the University of California at Berkeley. Born in Hsinchu, Taiwan, he received degrees from several Taiwanese universities. He moved to Berkeley in 1962, where he earned his Ph.D. in chemistry from the University of California. After postdoctoral studies at Berkeley and Harvard—where he worked with Herschbach—and a teaching stint at the University of Chicago, he returned to Berkeley in 1974; that year he also became an American citizen.

John C. Polanyi (1929–   ), professor at the University of Toronto. Born in Berlin, he moved to Great Britain while he was still a child. After receiving his Ph.D. in 1952 from England's Manchester University, he took a research post in Canada. He moved to the University of Toronto in 1956.

Economics. For his development of the "public choice" theory, which focuses the analytical methods of economics on political decision making:

James M. Buchanan (1919–   ), professor at George Mason University in Virginia. Born in Murfreesboro, Tenn., he graduated from the University of Tennessee and served in the Navy, before earning his doctorate at the University of Chicago in 1948. He taught at various universities before taking a position in 1969 at the Virginia Polytechnic Institute, where he helped found the Center for the Study of Public Choice. The center moved to George Mason University in 1982.

Literature. For using a "wide cultural perspective" and "poetical overtones" to fashion the "drama of existence":

Akinwande Oluwole Soyinka (1934–   ), Nigerian playwright, poet, and novelist. Born in Nigeria, Soyinka was educated at the University of Ibadan and at the University of Leeds in Great Britain. He worked with the Royal Court Theatre in England and on returning to Nigeria in 1960 founded the Masks drama company. He was visiting professor of theater at Cornell University when the Nobel Prize was awarded. Soyinka regards himself politically as a man of the left. After civil war broke out in 1967, he was arrested and spent 22 months in prison, where he did a great deal of writing, mainly on sheets of toilet paper. His works include *A Dance of the Forests,* a satiric verse play written for the 1960 Nigerian independence celebrations, the plays *Kongi's Harvest* (1965) and *Death and the King's Horsemen* (1975), and the novels *The Interpreters* (1965) and *Season of Anomy* (1973). Poems written during his imprisonment were collected in *Poems From Prison* (1969), republished as *A Shuttle in the Crypt* (1973).

Peace. For "bearing witness" in his writings to what he saw during the Holocaust:

Elie Wiesel (1928–   ), author and professor of

humanities at Boston University. Born in the Romanian town of Sighet, Eliezer Wiesel was raised in an Orthodox Jewish home. In 1944, he and his family were deported to German concentration camps, where he lost his parents and youngest sister. Liberated by American troops in 1945, he settled in France, where he wrote *Night* (the first of 26 books) depicting his wartime ordeal. Wiesel moved to the United States in the 1950's and became a citizen in 1963. In 1976, he was named Andrew W. Mellon professor in the humanities at Boston University.

Physics. For creating such tools as the electron microscope, "one of the most important inventions of this century," and the even more powerful scanning tunneling microscope, which creates an atomic-scale contour map of specimens:

Gerd Binnig (1947–), physicist. Born in Frankfurt, West Germany, he studied at the Johann Wolfgang Goethe University, taking his doctorate in physics and superconductivity in 1978. He then went to work at International Business Machines Research Laboratory in Zurich, Switzerland, where he collaborated with Heinrich Rohrer on the research that produced the scanning tunneling microscope.

Heinrich Rohrer (1933–), physicist. Born in Switzerland, he studied at the Federal Institute of Technology at Zurich and in 1960 earned his doctorate researching the pressure and volume effects of superconductivity. He works at the IBM laboratory where he and Binnig invented the scanning tunneling microscope in 1981.

Ernst Ruska (1906–), inventor of the electron microscope. Born in Heidelberg, West Germany, he studied at the Technical University of Munich and the Technical University of Berlin. From the late 1930's to the mid-1950's, he was a researcher with the Siemens and Halske Company. He was also a professor for many years in West Berlin at the Free University and the Technical University and in 1954 joined the Fritz Haber Institute of the Max Planck Society. He retired from active research in 1972.

Physiology or Medicine. For the discovery of two proteins, called growth factors, that promote and help regulate cell growth:

Stanley Cohen (1922–), biochemistry professor at Vanderbilt University School of Medicine in Nashville, Tenn. Born in Brooklyn, N.Y., he received his doctorate in biochemistry from the University of Michigan in 1948. Following stints at the University of Colorado and Washington University, where he collaborated with Levi-Montalcini on the work that won the Nobel Prize, he moved to Vanderbilt in 1959.

Rita Levi-Montalcini (1909–), developmental biologist at the Institute of Cell Biology in Rome. Born in Turin, Italy, she graduated

Elie Wiesel, a leading spokesman for survivors of the Nazi Holocaust and an indefatigable opponent of anti-Semitism and racism, was awarded the Nobel Peace Prize as a "messenger to mankind."

from the University of Turin's medical school. Forced in the late 1930's to give up her research position at the university because of Italy's anti-Semitic laws, she continued her work in a makeshift bedroom laboratory. In 1947 she went to Washington University, where she worked with Cohen; she became an American citizen in 1956. She retired in 1977 and moved back to Rome, where she joined the staff of the Institute of Cell Biology.

PULITZER PRIZES

The winners of the 1986 Pulitzer Prizes were announced on April 17. Larry McMurtry received the fiction award for his novel *Lonesome Dove*. George Perle won the music prize for *Wind Quintet IV*. The general nonfiction award was shared by J. Anthony Lukas, who wrote *Common Ground: A Turbulent Decade in the Lives of Three American Families,* and Joseph Lelyveld, author of *Move Your Shadow: South Africa, Black and White.* Henry Taylor won the poetry prize for his collection *The Flying Change.* The history award went to Walter A. McDougall for *. . . the Heavens and the Earth: A Political History of the Space Age.*

Other Pulitzer Prizes in letters and journalism were:

Biography. Elizabeth Frank, for *Louise Bogan: A Portrait.*

Commentary. Jimmy Breslin, New York *Daily News.*

Criticism. Donal Henahan, New York *Times.*

Editorial Cartooning. Jules Feiffer, *Village Voice* (New York City).

Editorial Writing. Jack Fuller, Chicago *Tribune.*

Feature Writing. John Camp, St. Paul (Minn.) *Pioneer Press and Dispatch.*

Photography, Feature. Tom Gralish, Philadelphia *Inquirer.*

Photography, Spot News. Michel duCille and Carol Guzy, Miami *Herald.*

Reporting, General News. Edna Buchanan, Miami *Herald.*

Reporting, International. Pete Carey, Katherine Ellison, and Lewis M. Simons, San Jose (Calif.) *Mercury News.*

Reporting, Investigative. Jeffrey A. Marx and Michael M. York, Lexington (Ky.) *Herald-Leader.*

Reporting, National. Craig Flournoy and George Rodrigue, Dallas *Morning News;* Arthur Howe, Philadelphia *Inquirer.*

Reporting, Specialized. Andrew Schneider and Mary Pat Flaherty, Pittsburgh *Press.*

OTHER PRIZES AND AWARDS

Among other awards made during 1986 were the following:

Academy of American Poets. Fellowships to Irving Feldman and Maxine Kumin; Walt Whitman Award to Chris Llewellyn for *Fragments From the Fire.*

Albert and Mary Lasker Foundation. $15,000 shared by Dr. Robert C. Gallo, Dr. Myron Essex, and Dr. Luc Montagnier for clinical research. $15,000 shared by Dr. Stanley Cohen and Dr. Rita Levi-Montalcini for the discovery of two cell growth factors. $15,000 to Ma Haide, for public service.

American Academy and Institute of Arts and Letters. Gold medals to Jasper Johns (graphic art) and Sidney Kingsley (drama). Award for Distinguished Service to the Arts to Brooke Astor. Arnold W. Brunner Memorial Prize to John Hejduk (architecture). Charles Ives Fellowship in music ($10,000) to Eric David Chasalow. Goddard Lieberson Fellowships in music ($10,000 each) to Susan Blaustein and Andrew Mead.

American Film Institute. Life Achievement Award to Billy Wilder.

Association of American Publishers, American Book Awards. Awards of $10,000 each to E. L. Doctorow for *World's Fair* (fiction) and to Barry Lopez for *Arctic Dreams* (nonfiction).

Bristol-Myers Award. $50,000 award for cancer research to Dr. Susumu Tonegawa, of the Massachusetts Institute of Technology Center for Cancer Research.

Kennedy Center Honors. For outstanding achievement in the performing arts, awarded to Ray Charles, Lucille Ball, Hume Cronyn, Jessica Tandy, Yehudi Menuhin, and Antony Tudor.

Medal of Freedom. Highest U.S. civilian honor, awarded to Dr. Albert B. Sabin, developer of the oral polio vaccine, Senator Barry Goldwater, actress Helen Hayes, World War II General Matthew B. Ridgway, former West Point football coach Earl (Red) Blaik, journalist Vermont Royster, and former ambassador and publisher Walter H. Annenberg.

Medal of Liberty. Awarded to naturalized citizens who have become leaders in their fields.

First recipients of this award (presented by President Ronald Reagan on July 3, 1986) were: composer Irving Berlin, astronaut Franklin Chang-Diaz, psychologist Kenneth Clark, university professor Hannah Gray, entertainer Bob Hope, former Secretary of State Henry Kissinger, architect I. M. Pei, violinist Itzhak Perlman, journalist James Reston, physician Albert B. Sabin, businessman An Wang, and author Elie Wiesel.

National Medal of Arts. Award given to artists and patrons for contributions to American culture. Artists receiving metals were singer Marian Anderson, film director Frank Capra, composer Aaron Copland, artist Willem de Kooning, choreographer Agnes de Mille, actress Eva Le Gallienne, folklorist Alan Lomax, critic Lewis Mumford, and writer Eudora Welty.

Onassis Foundation. $100,000 awards to Helmut Schmidt, former chancellor of West Germany; to the Salzburg Festival and the European Community's Youth Orchestra; to Agence France Presse and the Copenhagen-based International Center for Research and the Rehabilitation of Torture Victims.

Samuel H. Scripps-American Dance Festival Award. $25,000 award to Katherine Dunham.

Templeton Foundation. $250,000 Templeton Prize for Progress in Religion to Dr. James I. McCord, founder of the Center for Theological Inquiry at Princeton University.

Wolf Foundation. $100,000 each to Dr. Osamu Hayaishi (medicine), Ernest R. Sears and Sir Ralph Riley (agriculture; shared), James Corey and Albert Eschenmoser (chemistry; shared), Mitchell Jay Feigenbaum and Albert Joseph Libchaber (physics; shared), and artist Jasper Johns (arts).

PUBLISHING. Among the top-selling titles in 1986 were books by and about famous people and books in such popular categories as romance and espionage. The buying and selling of newspaper properties continued at a brisk pace.

Books. According to figures from the Association of American Publishers for the first nine months of the year, sales of children's paperbacks rose 24 percent over the same period in 1985, and hardcover adult sales rose 13 percent. Other healthy increases were experienced by university press and science and technology titles. College texts and trade and mass-market paperbacks held steady.

One of the hottest books published during the year was comedian and TV star Bill Cosby's *Fatherhood,* which appeared on the hardcover best-seller lists as soon as it was published and promised to become the most successful hardcover general-interest best-seller of the decade. *His Way,* the controversial unauthorized biography of show biz giant Frank Sinatra, by Kitty Kelley, shot to the No. 1 spot virtually upon publication in the autumn. *Rock Hudson: His Story,* which the late actor wrote with Sara Davidson during his much-publicized battle with AIDS, was a strong seller. Memoirs by Carol Burnett, Gelsey Kirkland, Sir Alec Guinness, Linda Ellerbee, and Chicago Bears quarterback Jim McMahon also did well. Among other entries on the best-seller lists were the biography *Bess W. Truman,* by her daughter, Margaret Truman; a biography of first lady Pat Nixon by her daughter Julie Nixon Eisenhower; and *You're Only Old Once,* in which Dr. Seuss checked up on graying America. Julie Eisenhower's husband, David, also made the best-seller lists during the year with the first of three volumes of his biography of his grandfather,

---

Children of Invention

When *Weekly Reader,* a national newspaper for schoolchildren, challenged students to an invention contest, the response took the paper somewhat by surprise. Thousands of future Edisons answered *Weekly Reader's* call, with ideas ranging from the delightfully fanciful (featherless turkeys for more efficient Thanksgivings, elastic shoelaces that never need tying) to the downright practical (travel bags with zippers on the bottom for retrieving buried clothes, combination flashlight/umbrellas for avoiding nighttime puddles, peanut butter jars with lids on both ends for easier scooping). Grand prizes went to a long "safety leash" with multiple handles, for class trips (it beeps if a child lets go), and to a sophisticated hydraulic log lifter. The purpose of the contest? To teach children to think creatively. Considering the products of their efforts, maybe it is the children who should be doing the teaching.

The 50th anniversary of Margaret Mitchell's novel Gone With the Wind *was feted with a Tara Ball and Bazaar in Georgia; above, guests costumed as Scarlett and Rhett pose before a model of the famous plantation. Inset: author Margaret Mitchell, who won a Pulitzer Prize for her only book.*

former President Dwight D. Eisenhower.

Danielle Steel returned to the lists with *Wanderlust* and *Secrets.* Judith Krantz portrayed glamorous living in *I'll Take Manhattan.* Jean M. Auel again delved into the prehistoric past in *The Mammoth Hunters,* and Western writer Louis L'Amour rounded up more sales with *Last of the Breed.* Big thrillers were Robert Ludlum's *The Bourne Supremacy* and Ken Follett's *Lie Down With Lions.* Espionage master John le Carré had the No. 1 spot for much of the year with *A Perfect Spy.* Tom Clancy scored again with *Red Storm Rising,* about a nuclear-free World War III between NATO and the Warsaw Pact.

Inspirational and self-help books did well, among them Leo Buscaglia's *Bus 9 to Paradise,* Harold S. Kushner's *When All You've Ever*

Wanted Isn't Enough, and Robert Schuller's *The Be-Happy Attitudes.* A popular health title was *The Rotation Diet* by Martin Katahn.

Even two late authors, Margaret Mitchell and Ernest Hemingway, enjoyed success. Macmillan celebrated the 50th anniversary of *Gone With the Wind,* Mitchell's epic Civil War novel, with the publication of a special facsimile first edition. In May, 25 years after Hemingway's death, Charles Scribner's Sons issued his "last unpublished major work," *The Garden of Eden,* about a honeymooning young American writer and his wife who are attracted to the same young woman.

Sales within the industry continued active. Gulf + Western bought Silver Burdett, primarily an elementary school textbook publisher, from SFN Companies for an estimated

$125 million. SFN also agreed to sell its Scott, Foresman division to Time, Inc., for $520 million and to accept $270 million in cash from the Toronto-based International Thompson Organization for South-Western Publishing Company. Within a single week, the West German publishing group Bertelsmann A.G. agreed to buy Doubleday's publishing units for $475 million in cash, and Britain's Penguin Publishing Company agreed to buy New American Library and its hardcover affiliate, E. P. Dutton.

Religious publisher Thomas Nelson sold Dodd, Mead to the company's senior management. Mortimer Zuckerman, owner of the *Atlantic* and *U.S. News & World Report*, sold the Atlantic Monthly Press to Tennessee businessman Carl Navarre, Jr. Media king Rupert Murdoch bought Salem House Publishers and the Merrimack Publishers' Circle. Forbes, Inc., acquired the American Heritage Publishing Company. Harper & Row bought Winston-Seabury Press.

Successful, established authors and several public figures signed large contracts to write books. Random House paid approximately $4.3 million for John Jakes's unwritten novel *California Gold*. William Morrow acquired James Clavell's new novel, *Whirlwind,* for over $5 million. Random House bought rights to a personal memoir by Nancy Reagan.

In February the U.S. Supreme Court upheld two lower court decisions that declared Indianapolis's antipornography ordinance unconstitutional. The law was supported by some feminists and opposed by publishers and others on the grounds that it defined pornography too broadly.

Newspapers. When 79-year-old Barry Bingham, Sr., was unable to resolve a dispute among his heirs, he announced plans to liquidate the family's Louisville, Ky., communications empire. The Gannett Company, having outbid other media groups, completed the purchase of the Louisville (Ky.) *Times* and *Courier-Journal* in July for $306.9 million. The papers had a combined daily circulation of some 300,000 and had been owned by the family for nearly seven decades; the price was said to be the largest ever paid for a newspaper property alone.

In June the Los Angeles-based Times Mirror Company purchased the prestigious Baltimore *Sun* and *Evening Sun* and two television stations from the family-owned A. S. Abell Company for $600 million. It then sold the two stations. By acquiring the papers, the company gained a monopoly in the growing Baltimore market. Only two weeks earlier, the Hearst Corporation had closed the rival, 213-year-old Baltimore *News American,* after failing to find a suitable buyer for the faltering evening daily. The number of independent newspapers was reduced further by the sale of family-owned dailies in Washington state, Connecticut, and Virginia.

International tycoon Rupert Murdoch found a buyer in June for the Chicago *Sun-Times,* a 631,000-circulation morning tabloid. The paper, a respected but trailing rival of the Chicago *Tribune,* was sold for $145 million to a group headed by its president and publisher. The Gannett Company and the Times Mirror Com-

After 213 years of publication, faltering circulation and lack of a buyer closed the Baltimore News American; *here, an employee displays the final edition.*

337

pany each shed a newspaper during the year, the Knoxville (Tenn.) *Journal* and the Dallas *Times Herald*. In October, however, Gannett said it would buy the Arkansas *Gazette*.

Gannett, new owner of the 645,000-circulation Detroit *News,* and Knight-Ridder Newspapers Inc., owner of the 634,000-circulation Detroit *Free Press,* agreed in April to merge all operations of the two papers except news gathering and editing, ending a costly battle that had made both unprofitable.

Reorganization of United Press International (UPI), the nation's second-largest news agency, was approved by a U.S. bankruptcy court in June. UPI then became the first major U.S. news service controlled by a foreign national. The new head and 95 percent owner of UPI was Mario Vázquez-Raña, owner of a chain of Mexican newspapers.

The number of U.S. daily newspapers continued to dwindle, after dropping to 1,674 as the year began. Total circulation of daily papers remained sluggish, but Sunday newspapers continued to grow in number and circulation. It was estimated that ad revenues for the year would exceed $27 billion, a gain of 7 to 8 percent over 1985. Most publicly held newspaper companies reported moderate to substantial increases in profits, and the industry mood was optimistic.

For half a century, the unions in London's Fleet Street, the traditional center of British newspaper publishing, have maintained tight control over the papers' press rooms, blocking the introduction of new technology. In 1986, the unions were challenged by Rupert Murdoch, whose British newspapers include the prestigious London *Times*, the *Sunday Times,*

British print union workers march down Fleet Street in protest against newspaper tycoon Rupert Murdoch, whose latest printing plant relies heavily upon computer technology to replace human labor.

the racy, 4.1 million-circulation tabloid *Sun,* and the weekly *News of the World.* Murdoch had begun in 1980 to build a modern, $140 million plant in Wapping, an East London dock area. In February 1986, when long-running negotiations with the unions broke down, he abruptly fired nearly 6,000 striking printers and moved his newspapers from Fleet Street to the Wapping plant, which he had quietly equipped with U.S.-made computers. Nearly all of the papers' 700 journalists accepted Murdoch's offer of a pay increase of $2,800 a year and free private medical insurance. The bold maneuver, allowing Murdoch to operate the presses with a much smaller labor force, came as a severe blow to the British union movement.

Magazines. Many new magazines appeared during the year, almost all of them relatively small special-interest publications. Advertising revenues grew slightly, mostly because of higher rates. Circulation of consumer magazines showed little improvement on the whole. Most well-established magazines added subscribers, and many of them reported modest overall gains in circulation. But single-copy sales, which accounted for only a little over 30 percent of total circulation income, continued to decline.

After 15 months of development, Time, Inc., jettisoned its $30 million new mass-market magazine, *Picture Week,* announcing a decision to cater more to special-interest markets with such publications as *Home Office* and *Real Estate.* Later in the year, Time agreed to buy a 50 percent interest in *McCall's* and two other women's magazines, *Working Woman* and *Working Mother.*

The so-called adult magazines, including *Penthouse* and *Playboy,* suffered substantial losses in newsstand sales, partly because of the growing popularity of videocassettes that serve the same market. Then, in April, the nation's largest convenience store chain, Southland Corporation, announced it would no longer carry *Penthouse, Playboy,* and *Forum* magazines in its 4,500 company-owned 7-Eleven stores, citing testimony before the Attorney General's Commission on Pornography about alleged links between sexually explicit materials and violence. Publishers of the affected magazines filed suit and prevented the

commission from making public any list of alleged distributors of pornography. The final report of the commission, in July, called for strict law enforcement and citizen efforts against pornography, arousing concern in the publishing community.

Playboy also made news at the Library of Congress. When the library ceased to produce the Braille edition of the magazine after Congress withheld funds equal to the cost of producing it, the American Council of the Blind and other organizations sued in U.S. district court. In August a federal judge ruled for the plaintiffs, finding that the library had violated the First Amendment rights of blind people.   J.M. & J.L.

PUERTO RICO. The convoluted relations between Puerto Rico and the federal government dominated the political and economic scene in 1986. The Puerto Rican government attempted to reinforce the commonwealth's status as an "associated free state" by taking independent initiatives in foreign affairs, such as a proposal to offer tax breaks to Japanese manufacturers. U.S. Secretary of State George Shultz declared that Puerto Rico "does not have the authority on its own to sign international agreements," although federal officials were not averse to the possibility of a more significant role for Puerto Rico in the Caribbean.

Governor Rafael Hernández Colón of the pro-autonomy Popular Democratic Party (PDP) pledged to create new jobs. In addition to the tax incentives, industrial parks, and cheap labor used since the 1940's to attract foreign investors to Puerto Rico, the government proposed "twin plants"—companies with operations in both Puerto Rico and another Caribbean island.

Manufacturing output and exports were up slightly during the year, but employment and new investment were flat, and agriculture remained in a deep slump. The decline in U.S. tourism to Europe helped Puerto Rico. Increased tourism, however, also contributed to the island's becoming a major center for the transshipment of drugs to the United States. A raid by U.S. and Puerto Rican authorities in August broke up several drug-shipping rings with ties to Colombia.

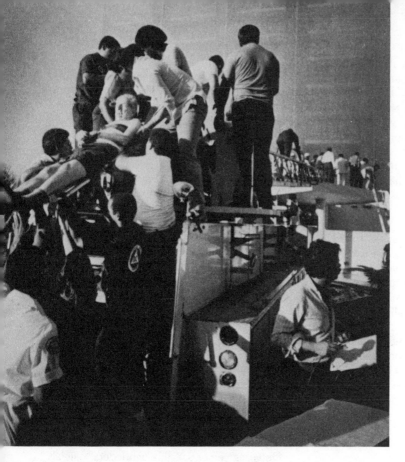

Rescue workers in San Juan, Puerto Rico, lower to safety a victim of one of the worst hotel fires in U.S. history. Believed to have been set deliberately, the fire raced through the Dupont Plaza Hotel on New Year's Eve, killing 96 people and injuring more than 100.

A New Year's Eve fire at the Dupont Plaza Hotel in San Juan killed 96 people, most of them holiday tourists who were gambling in the hotel casino, and injured many others. Federal and commonwealth investigators concluded that the blaze had been caused by arson, and suspects in the case were arrested in early 1987; the fashionable hotel had been the focus of a continuing labor-management dispute, and three small fires had been set there in the ten days preceding the disaster.

See STATISTICS OF THE WORLD.   A.S.

Q

QATAR. *See* STATISTICS OF THE WORLD. *See also* PERSIAN GULF STATES.

QUÉBEC. *See* STATISTICS OF THE WORLD. *See also* CANADA.

R

RADIO. *See* TELEVISION AND RADIO BROAD-CASTING.

RAILROADS. *See* TRANSPORTATION.

RECORDINGS. *See* MUSIC.

Religion

In 1986, as the pope spread the gospel message around the world, dissent was increasingly vocal among U.S. Catholics. Church workers were convicted for their role in the sanctuary movement. Protestant fundamentalists battled textbooks they considered anti-Christian. Jewish communities in Lebanon and Turkey suffered from terrorism. The Sikhs' Golden Temple in Punjab, India, was again a focus of conflict and violence.

In other developments, Soviet Jewish dissident Anatoly Shcharansky was allowed to emigrate, and television evangelist Pat Robertson tested the waters for a presidential bid. Three U.S. Lutheran groups moved toward a merger. At least one event united adherents of many faiths. On October 27, leaders of 12 religions joined in ceremonies at Assisi, Italy, to mark a day of world prayer for peace. The event, sponsored by Pope John Paul II, was attended by such disparate figures as Most Reverend Robert Runcie, archbishop of Canterbury, the Dalai Lama, the head of the Zoroastrian community in Bombay, and leaders of African animist cults.

ROMAN CATHOLIC CHURCH

The Vatican and the pope, John Paul II, were a focus of the year's Catholic news. In the United States, the cases of Father Charles Curran and Archbishop Raymond Hunthausen drew attention to the issue of dissent.

Assassination Plot Trial. The ten-month trial in an Italian court of alleged conspirators in the 1981 shooting of Pope John Paul II ended on March 29 with the discharging of three Bulgarians and three Turks "for lack of proof." The verdict stopped short of full acquittal and under Italian law implied that evidence existed to support both the guilt and the innocence of the defendants. Mehmet Ali Agca, the Turkish terrorist already serving a life sentence for the shooting, had been the state's key witness, but his credibility eroded, and with it the state's case, as he showed signs of religious deliriums. Several times he proclaimed himself to be Jesus Christ reincarnated. The Vatican made no formal comment on the verdict, although the influential Jesuit journal *La Civiltà Cattolica* termed it "disconcerting."

Papal Trips. In February, John Paul II made a ten-day pastoral visit to India, whose 13 million Catholics constitute only about 2 percent of the population. The visit was marked by enthusiasm in Madras and southern India but by relative indifference elsewhere. The pope laid a wreath at the Gandhi memorial in Delhi and lauded Indian spirituality. In July, John Paul made his seventh visit to Latin America, traveling to Colombia and the island country of St. Lucia. He crisscrossed western Colombia, preaching peace and social justice in a country beset by guerrilla warfare, indebtedness, and illegal drug trade. In early October, he made a four-day visit to southeastern France, where he called on combatants throughout the world to observe a one-day truce on October 27, which he had previously designated as a day of interfaith prayer for peace.

On December 1, John Paul returned to the Vatican after the longest trip of his pontificate. On the two-week trip he spent 6½ days in Australia, besides visiting Bangladesh, Singapore, Fiji, New Zealand, and the Seychelles.

Instances of Dissent. Father Charles E. Curran, a moral theologian at Catholic University of America in Washington, D.C., made public in March an ultimatum from the Vatican that he retract views on birth control, divorce, and other issues of sexuality or else lose authorization to teach Roman Catholic doctrine. The revelation sparked a strong protest from many Catholics, with more than 18,000 signing statements urging the Vatican not to impose pen-

341

alties. Curran formally refused to retract. After various compromises were rejected, the Vatican disciplined the priest, revoking his license to teach as a Catholic theologian. Curran vowed to fight the action through academic and, if necessary, legal channels.

The Vatican was said to have quietly resolved the cases of 22 of the 24 nuns who, in 1984, signed a newspaper advertisement contending that Roman Catholics hold a "diversity of opinions" on abortion. Authorities lifted a threat to expel them from religious life. Eleven of the nuns, however, challenged claims that they had retracted their views and charged the Vatican with an effort to "pressure and isolate" the two hold-out nuns. In June, superiors of the two nuns reprimanded them for "lack of respect" for the church's teaching authority but did not dismiss them.

In a third case of dissent, Seattle's Archbishop Raymond G. Hunthausen revealed in September that he had been stripped of decision-making power in several areas of authority, including liturgy, ministry to homosexuals, moral issues in church medical facilities, annulments, and training of priests. He was ordered to turn over this authority to Auxiliary Bishop Donald W. Wuerl.

In September, Archbishop Rembert G. Weakland of Milwaukee criticized the church's efforts to enforce orthodoxy by silencing dissent. Writing in the newspaper of his archdiocese, he said that the price of enforcing orthodoxy in the past had been cruelty, suppression of theological creativity, and lack of growth.

U.S. Bishops. The issue of dissent was a dominant one at the four-day annual meeting of the National Conference of Catholic Bishops, held in Washington, D.C., in November. The event began with a call for a meeting with the pope to discuss growing tensions between some U.S. Catholics and the Vatican. Two moderate prelates were elected to head the body for the next three years, defeating liberal and conservative candidates. Archbishop Hunthausen made an emotional appeal at the conference, asking fellow bishops to intervene with the

Pope John Paul traveled through India for ten days in February; here he joins Mother Teresa, founder of the Missionaries of Charity, outside her Calcutta hospital.

Vatican on his behalf. But, though the bishops issued a statement expressing sympathy for him, they supported the Vatican's authority to limit his powers.

The bishops' conference also adopted a 115-page pastoral letter, titled "Economic Justice for All," calling the levels of poverty in the United States "a social and moral scandal." The letter—the result of five years of work—asked for more economic planning, expansion of federal welfare programs, and reductions in military spending, among other things. A group of prominent lay Catholics issued a report that criticized the bishops, for allegedly failing to recognize the role of the free market in creating wealth and stimulating growth.

Around the World. Catholic bishops in the Philippines were deeply involved in events that led to the toppling of Ferdinand Marcos as president of that nation. The bishops labeled the presidential election, which had given Marcos an apparent victory over challenger Corazon Aquino, as "unparalleled" in fraud, and Cardinal Jaime Sin of Manila called on people to gather in the streets and block Marcos's tanks, a decisive factor in Marcos's eventual capitulation.

In Latin America, strains between the Brazilian hierarchy and the Vatican appeared to ease after a three-day meeting in March of 21 Brazilian bishops with the pope in Rome. At particular issue was liberation theology, an approach that emphasizes commitment to the poor, while sometimes borrowing ideas from Marxism. The pope told the bishops they should not try to "substitute for politicians" and said forms of liberation theology needed revision. Two weeks later, the Vatican lifted the "penitential silence" it had imposed on Father Leonardo Boff, a leading Brazilian exponent of liberation theology.

Meanwhile, the Vatican issued its long-awaited document updating Catholic social teaching as applied to liberation theology. Entitled "Christian Freedom and Liberation," the 59-page "instruction" cautioned against losing sight of the church's fundamentally spiritual mission but embraced the principle that the gospel justifies the struggles of the poor for political freedom.

Tensions between Nicaragua's bishops and

Reverend Charles Curran, a professor of moral theology at the Catholic University of America, lost his license to teach Roman Catholic doctrine because he refused to retract his unorthodox positions on issues of sexual morality.

the Sandinista government heightened in July with the expulsion from the country of Bishop Pablo Antonio Vega Mantilla, vice president of the Nicaraguan Catholic Bishops' Conference. Pope John Paul II, visiting Colombia at the time, termed the action a "nearly incredible event" evoking memories of the "dark ages."

Five French bishops broke with their national hierarchy in April on the issue of nuclear deterrence. The French Bishops' Conference in 1983 had termed nuclear deterrence a legitimate tactic of defense. The dissenters contended that a nation "does not have the right to possess arms which it will never have the right to use."

Ecumenism. The first recorded visit of a pope to a Jewish house of worship took place on April 13, when John Paul visited Rome's central synagogue, spiritual center of what was believed to be the oldest Jewish group in the Diaspora. In an important ecumenical step in

Brazil, Roman Catholic bishops, collaborating with Jewish religious leaders, published a detailed manual intended to promote mutual dialogue and understanding.

On June 30 the Vatican made public an exchange of letters between the pope and the archbishop of Canterbury, in which the pope declared that the ordination of women as priests by some Anglican churches presented an "increasingly serious obstacle" to Anglican-Roman Catholic reunion. Archbishop Runcie had suggested that since the humanity of Christ includes male and female, the priesthood should now be opened to women.   J.G.D.

PROTESTANT AND ORTHODOX CHURCHES

Eight church workers were tried and convicted of smuggling illegal Central American refugees into the United States, as part of the church-led sanctuary movement. Other major news of 1986 included the launching of a presidential campaign by a television evangelist, a visit to the United States by top church leaders from the Soviet Union, and progress toward a possible merger of three Lutheran denominations into a single group with more than 5 million adherents.

Sanctuary Movement Trial. In May, six members of the sanctuary movement, including Presbyterian minister John Fife, one of its founders, were found guilty of conspiring to smuggle Salvadorans and Guatemalans into the United States in violation of U.S. immigration laws. Two others were convicted of lesser offenses. All eight were put on probation. Three other defendants were cleared in the highly publicized federal trial in Tucson, Ariz., which had begun in October 1985.

Evangelist's White House Plans. On September 17 the Reverend M. G. "Pat" Robertson, founder and president of the Christian Broadcasting Network and a popular television evangelist, announced tentative plans to seek the Republican nomination for president in 1988. Robertson said that he was certain God wanted him to run but that his decision would not be final unless 3 million people signed petitions in his support within a year.

Robertson's White House bid continued a decade-long trend of political activism by conservative Protestants. Critics of his candidacy, led by the organization People for the American

Way, maintained that, if elected, he would try to foist his own code of behavior on society at the expense of individual freedom. He was endorsed by two other leading television evangelists, Oral Roberts and Jimmy Swaggart, but Jerry Falwell, U.S. fundamentalism's most widely known spokesman, endorsed Vice President George Bush. Late in the year, former Congressman Paul N. McCloskey, Jr., who had served with Robertson in the U.S. Marines, claimed Robertson had used the political influence of his father, then a Democratic U.S. senator from Virginia, to avoid combat duty in the Korean war. Robertson, whose autobiography speaks of his having served in combat duty in Korea, denied the charge and filed a libel suit against McCloskey.

Soviet Visit. In April the National Council of Churches hosted a 17-member delegation of church leaders from the Soviet Union, most of them from the Russian Orthodox Church. Religious leaders from the two superpowers stressed a need for Christians to display their unity in the pursuit of peace. At several points, the Soviets encountered groups of Ukrainian Catholics and Soviet Jews protesting religious persecution in the Soviet Union.

Denominational News. *Lutheran Merger.* On August 29, concurrent conventions of three U.S. Lutheran denominations voted overwhelmingly to merge into a 5.3-million-member Evangelical Lutheran Church in America, which would be the nation's fourth-largest Protestant denomination, effective January 1, 1988. The 110,000-member Association of Evangelical Lutheran Churches gave final approval to the merger; similar action by the American Lutheran Church and the Lutheran Church in America was needed for the change to go into effect.

Methodists and Militarism. In April the Council of Bishops of the United Methodist Church adopted a statement condemning all forms of nuclear weaponry and nuclear war. The pastoral letter, which criticized the concept of deterrence and declared that the nuclear arms race increased social injustice, was said to be intended as a guide for discussion of nuclear arms rather than as a statement of official church policy. After narrowly voting in May to delete "Onward Christian Soldiers" and

"The Battle Hymn of the Republic" from a new United Methodist hymnal, because of the hymns' "unrelenting militaristic images," the church's hymnal revision committee reversed itself in July in the face of more than 8,000 letters and other expressions of protest.

Southern Baptist Election. Delegates to the Southern Baptist Convention elected Adrian Rogers as SBC president, marking the eighth consecutive year that a conservative was chosen to lead the 14.5-million-member denomination. Moderates resisting the growing power of fundamentalist conservatives had supported Texas pastor Winfred Moore for president, in his second consecutive attempt to win the office.

Textbook Lawsuits. In two lawsuits heard in Tennessee and Alabama, fundamentalist Protestants charged that textbooks used in public schools advanced anti-Christian and "secular humanist" views, promoting such concepts as evolution, feminism, pacifism, and world government. Both cases involved the widely used Holt Basic Reading Series for grades one through eight, published by Holt, Rinehart and Winston. In October a federal judge in the Tennessee case ruled that the plaintiffs' children should be excused from classes in which the books were used; he also later awarded their parents reimbursement for sending their children to other schools. The ruling was appealed.

Billy Graham. Evangelist Billy Graham led a major crusade in Washington, D.C., where he had not preached since 1960. The large-scale participation of black church members was noted. Graham also held a conference in Amsterdam for evangelists from 173 nations, which was a larger version of his 1983 International Conference for Itinerant Evangelists.

Martin Luther King Holiday. On January 20, the late Reverend Martin Luther King, Jr., became the first black person and the first clergyman to be honored with a federal holiday. Black religious leaders used the event to address racial issues. On January 15, King's birthday, the Reverend Jesse Jackson led a demonstration at the U.S. Department of Justice in Washington, where he said that the Reagan administration, which had initially opposed the holiday, stood against the principles King had represented. At a January 20 ceremony in

Atlanta, South African Anglican Bishop Desmond Tutu charged that Western leaders had abandoned the cause of apartheid's victims in South Africa.

Tutu Named to Post. In September, Bishop Tutu was installed as archbishop of Cape Town and leader of the Anglican Church in southern Africa, the first black ever to serve in that position. In his sermon, Tutu, the 1984 Nobel Peace Prize laureate, reiterated his belief in nonviolence but stated that "the primary violence in this country is the violence of apartheid."

Pro-life PAC. A coalition of U.S. Protestants and Catholics formed a political action committee with a platform linking opposition to poverty, the arms race, and abortion. The group described its philosophy as a "consistent pro-life ethic." Most of the PAC's leadership consisted of Protestant evangelicals.

"Televangelist" Pat Robertson, founder and head of the Christian Broadcasting Network, announced tentative plans to seek the Republican nomination for president in 1988.

Named as the first black archbishop of Cape Town and head of the Anglican Church in South Africa, Desmond M. Tutu, Nobel Peace Prize winner and outspoken opponent of apartheid, was officially installed in his new post on September 7.

Jerry Falwell. Fundamentalist leader Jerry Falwell announced in January the formation of Liberty Federation, which would expand his Moral Majority organization to focus on political issues; Moral Majority was to be a subsidiary of Liberty Federation. Late in the year, Falwell indicated, however, that he was backing away from politics. In August, a federal appeals court upheld a $200,000 award that Falwell had won in 1984 for "emotional distress" he had experienced as a result of a parody published in *Hustler* magazine.

Leadership Changes. Eva Burrows became only the second woman to be elected general of the worldwide Salvation Army in its 121-year

history. Former Beirut hostage Benjamin Weir was named moderator of the Presbyterian Church (U.S.A.).

Deaths. Religious leaders who died during the year included L. Ron Hubbard, whose book *Dianetics: The Modern Science of Mental Health* became the basis for the Church of Scientology; pacifist Edwin T. Dahlberg, former president of the National Council of Churches; ecumenist Cynthia Wedel, who served as president of both the National and World Councils of Churches; Herbert W. Armstrong, founder and leader of the 80,000-member Worldwide Church of God; Canadian missionary Oswald Smith; and German Lutheran scholar Helmut Thielicke, who was dismissed from the University of Heidelberg in 1940 because of his repeated criticism of the Nazi government.   R.L.F.

JUDAISM

Events of interest in 1986 included the freeing of Soviet dissident Anatoly Shcharansky and the awarding of the Nobel Peace Prize to Holocaust "witness" Elie Wiesel. Anti-Semitism surfaced in acts of terrorism against Jews and in the campaign of Kurt Waldheim for the presidency of Austria.

World Jewry. Anatoly Shcharansky, the leading Soviet Jewish "refusenik"—a Soviet citizen denied permission to emigrate—was freed from a Soviet labor camp on February 11 and allowed to emigrate to Israel. Shcharansky had served in the 1970's as a spokesman for the Helsinki Watch Committee, formed to monitor Soviet observance of human rights. Convicted of espionage and treason, he was sentenced in 1978 to detention; his release became the object of a long and ultimately successful international campaign but did not herald a change in Soviet policy. Only 1,140 Soviet Jews were known to have emigrated in 1985 and only 735 during the first ten months of 1986. As many as 400,000 may have wanted to leave.

The tiny Jewish community in Lebanon was a target of violence, with several Jews kidnapped and killed by a Muslim group. In Turkey the main synagogue in Istanbul was attacked by terrorists in early September; 22 Jews were killed (including 7 rabbis). A number of Arab terrorist groups claimed responsibility for the attack—the first ever in the history of Turkey's

Jewish community—which occurred on the Sabbath as worshippers gathered for the first services to be held in the newly renovated Neve Shalom Synagogue.

Nobel Prize. Elie Wiesel, world Jewry's most eloquent "witness" to the horrors of the Holocaust, received the Nobel Peace Prize at December ceremonies in Oslo. The 58-year-old author, who accepted the prize "as one who has emerged from that kingdom of night," was invited to bring his 14-year-old son with him to the podium, as a demonstration of the survival of Jewish generations.

Waldheim Scandal. Anti-Semitism surfaced when former UN Secretary-General Kurt Waldheim (see biography in PEOPLE IN THE NEWS) ran for the largely ceremonial post of president of Austria. In March, the World Jewish Congress charged Waldheim with knowledge of, and possible participation in, Nazi war crimes in Yugoslavia and Greece during World War II. Waldheim initially denied the charges, then said that he knew of but was uninvolved in

atrocities; no evidence emerged that he personally committed any atrocities. Many of his supporters and much of the Austrian press cast anti-Semitic slurs on Waldheim's opponents and on the Austrian Jewish community. Waldheim was elected president in June. In September the American Jewish Committee announced plans to launch, with Austrian government backing, an educational and research program in Austria that would examine Austria's anti-Semitic record and highlight the contributions of the country's Jewish community to Austrian society.

U.S. Jewry. In March the Georgia Board of Pardons and Paroles granted a posthumous pardon to Leo Frank, an Atlanta Jew lynched in 1915 after being convicted of murdering a 13-year-old girl. The case had been reopened in 1983 after one of Frank's coworkers said he had seen someone else commit the crime.

In September several thousand Holocaust survivors gathered on Liberty Island in New York Harbor to commemorate the 40th anni-

A synagogue in Istanbul, Turkey, was the target of an Arab terrorist attack when gunmen opened fire on the congregation at the start of Sabbath services; 22 worshippers were killed. Below, the aftermath of the attack.

Free at Last

In February, Anatoly Shcharansky was freed from a Soviet labor camp and allowed to emigrate to Israel, where his arrival was treated as a national celebration. His release climaxed eight years of public pressure and private diplomacy, spurred on by the tireless efforts of his wife, Avital, to see that his name was not forgotten. A mathematician and computer specialist, Shcharansky was sentenced in 1978 to three years in prison and ten years in a labor camp, after being convicted of espionage and treason. He had been prominent as an activist monitoring Soviet compliance with the human rights provisions of the 1975 Helsinki accords. In prison, Shcharansky spent long periods in solitary confinement and undertook hunger strikes when denied contact with his family. In May 1986, Shcharansky visited the United States as a free man, met with President Ronald Reagan and others, and spoke at the annual rally in New York City for Soviet Jewry, where over 300,000 people turned out to see him. In August, his mother, his brother, and other family members were allowed to join Shcharansky and his wife in Israel, and in November, Avital gave birth to their 5½-pound daughter.

Anatoly Shcharansky

versary of the first arrival of a group of survivors in the United States.

The North American Jewish Data Bank was established in July to pool and computerize population survey information on the hundreds of Jewish communities across North America.

Religious Life. The first new synagogue to be built in Eastern Europe since World War II was inaugurated in Hungary, in ceremonies attended by high-ranking government officials and representatives of the Budapest Jewish community.

Rabbi Moshe Feinstein, regarded as perhaps the world's leading Jewish Talmudist, died in New York City on March 23. He was 91.

L.G.

MORMON CHURCH

In May, Mark W. Hofmann was bound over for trial in state district court on charges of first-degree murder, fraud, theft, and bomb-making. The charges stemmed from the 1985 bombing deaths of Steven Christensen and Kathy Sheets in Salt Lake City and involved a bizarre alleged scheme of forged documents pertaining to the Mormon Church. Prosecutors claimed Hofmann had borrowed thousands of dollars from investors, ostensibly to purchase historical papers whose contents apparently conflicted with accepted Mormon accounts of their church's founding. Actually, prosecutors said, Hofmann intended to give the investors forged documents, and killed his associate Christensen with a shrapnel bomb to prevent him from disclosing the scheme. Sheets was killed the same day by a similar bomb, allegedly in an attempt to divert investigators to a financially troubled business that was operated by Sheets's husband and that formerly employed Christensen. Hofmann was arrested the next day, after being injured by a bomb that investigators said he had accidentally detonated in his car. He pleaded not guilty to all counts.

HARE KRISHNA

Kirtanananda Swami Bhaktipada, head of the New Vrindaban Hare Krishna community near Moundsville, W. Va., was the center of controversies that have divided the Hare Krishna movement in the United States. In a federal suit filed by a Krishna temple in Berkeley, Calif., Bhaktipada was accused of sending 15 followers to Berkeley in June in an unsuccessful attempt to seize control of that temple. Followers of Bhaktipada were also charged in the murders of Steven Bryant, a Krishna dissident, and of Charles Saint-Denis, a Krishna devotee. Bryant, an excommunicated member of the Krishna movement, had made allegations of illegal activities at New Vrindaban, including drug dealing, to finance temples and other projects, such as the Palace of Gold, a tourist attraction in West Virginia. A former New Vrindaban resident, Thomas Drescher, was charged with his murder; sources close to the investigation said he may have been paid to kill Bryant. In December, Drescher was convicted of murder in the presumed death of Saint-Denis; in January 1987 an accomplice who pleaded guilty to manslaughter in this crime led police to what was identified as Saint-Denis's body, in a muddy creekbed on the New Vrindaban property.

SIKHISM
The Golden Temple in Amritsar, the holiest Sikh shrine, again became the focal point of tensions in Punjab, India, as Sikh extremists seized control of it in January and government troops recaptured it in April. In 1984 the temple had been occupied by militant Sikhs and then captured by government troops in a bloody assault that left hundreds of Sikh defenders dead and provoked a wave of terrorist attacks against Hindus, including the assassination of Indian Prime Minister Indira Gandhi. The temple, largely destroyed in 1984, had been restored by the moderate Sikh party that governed Punjab, but in January the extremist All-India Sikh Students Federation took it over and began dismantling the Akal Takht, the holy seat of authority at the temple, because they believed that the moderate Sikhs had compromised themselves by cooperating with the central government and that their reconstruction of the temple was therefore sacrilegious. They also expelled the five official high priests of Sikhism from the temple, substituting a new five-member committee, and excommunicated the Sikh president of India, Zail Singh.

Sikh violence against the Hindu minority in Punjab was believed to be aimed at driving out the Hindus from Punjab to facilitate Sikh autonomy. Some extremists occupying the temple urged Sikhs to take up arms and fight for independence, and on April 29 several factions in the temple proclaimed an independent Sikh state, which they called Khalistan. It was this that apparently moved the moderate Sikh government of Punjab to order an assault on the temple, though some observers said that it had been under pressure to do so from the central government. On April 30, commandos from the central government and paramilitary police stormed the temple. This time, there was little resistance; only two people were believed to have died in the raid. But terrorist attacks against Hindus in Punjab continued to increase in the following months. Elsewhere in India and in Sri Lanka, other ethnic-religious conflicts also bred violence. (See INDIA; SRI LANKA.)
ISLAM
The Muslim community in India was disturbed by the Indian Supreme Court's decision to grant alimony to an elderly divorced Muslim woman. Alimony, as opposed to other provisions for the care of a divorced wife, is not permitted in Islamic law. To appease his Muslim constituents, Prime Minister Rajiv Gandhi successfully introduced a bill in Parliament to rescind the court's decision.

The new Sudanese prime minister, Sadiq al-Mahdi, pledged to end Sharia, the strict Islamic legal code imposed on Sudan by President Jaafar al-Nimeiry in 1983. The abolition of the code has been a major demand of the non-Muslim rebels in southern Sudan, and Mahdi, though a devout Muslim, agreed to a less severe code as part of his attempt to end the insurrection.

Reports from Iran indicated that the government was deliberately invoking Shiite Muslim devotion to the holy places in Iraq to spur on the soldiers at the war front. Iranian tanks, for instance, were painted with signs saying, "To Karbala." Karbala is the place in Iraq where Hussein, the grandson of the Prophet Muhammad, together with his infant son and others, were martyred in the year 680 A.D. Their martyrdom is a principal focus of Shiite Muslim fervor.   C.S.J.W.

REPUBLICAN PARTY. See United States of America: *Political Parties*.

RHODE ISLAND. See Statistics of the World.

RHODESIA. See Zimbabwe.

ROMANIA. Party and state chief Nicolae Ceauşescu's 68th birthday on January 26, 1986, was marked by the usual outpouring of laudatory books, films and broadcasts, and extravagant praise. This time, however, perhaps reflecting awareness of Ceauşescu's apparently poor state of health, the adulation dwelt less on current triumphs and more on achievements he would leave to posterity.

The exceptionally tight state budget for 1986 reflected the strain of repaying a major part of Romania's foreign debt and, at the same time, the poor performance of the economy. There were losses especially in agriculture and the mining and chemical industries. On November 23, according to the government, 17,650,974 voters approved a referendum backing Ceauşescu's decision to cut military spending, arms, and personnel by 5 percent. Reportedly, no negative votes were cast.

Continuing its campaign to raise the birthrate from 15 per 1,000 citizens to 20 or more, the Romanian government made its demographic policy into a matter of national and patriotic duty. Using the mass media and various public organizations, the authorities appealed for birthrate competitions between the counties and for literary and historical recollections extolling the old days of large families, in addition to offering financial inducements for larger families.

In contrast to a few years before, when Romania appeared to be striving for greater independence from the Soviet bloc, significant expansion of Romanian-Soviet industrial cooperation and trade was underway. This reflected Romania's increasingly heavy need for Soviet technology and Soviet industrial orders to keep its production capacities filled and its work force occupied.

See Statistics of the World.   R.A.P.

RUSSIA. See Union of Soviet Socialist Republics.

RWANDA. See Statistics of the World.

S

SAHARA, WESTERN. See Africa; Morocco.

ST. KITTS-NEVIS (ST. CHRISTOPHER AND NEVIS). See Statistics of the World.

ST. LUCIA. See Statistics of the World.

ST. VINCENT AND THE GRENADINES. See Statistics of the World.

SAMOA, AMERICAN. See Statistics of the World: *American Samoa*.

SAMOA, WESTERN. See Statistics of the World: *Western Samoa*.

SAN MARINO. See Statistics of the World.

SÃO TOMÉ and PRÍNCIPE. See Statistics of the World.

SASKATCHEWAN. See Statistics of the World.

SAUDI ARABIA. Petroleum dominated the news of 1986 in Saudi Arabia. Domestic finances were hurt by low oil prices, and the kingdom finished the 1985–1986 fiscal year in the red for the third year in a row.

Petroleum. For most of the year, the Saudis acted on their new policy of boosting oil production, so as to maintain their market share and thus put pressure on other oil producers to cut world oil production in order to stabilize prices. The results were predictable: Spot market prices for Saudi crude fell to $12.50 per barrel by late February; they rebounded to $14 in April, then headed downward again. After a June OPEC meeting failed to produce new production quotas, the kingdom again used its production capability as a lever, raising its output to 6 million b/d and forcing prices still lower, to the $10-per-barrel range. The OPEC oil ministers reconvened in Geneva on July 28 and finally accepted an Iranian proposal whereby OPEC production would be cut in September and October to roughly the level established in 1984, in an effort to stabilize the price of crude oil at $14. Under this agreement, Saudi Arabia reduced its production to 4.35 million b/d.

An OPEC meeting in October resulted in the Saudi production quota being kept at the same level. A week later, however, King Fahd removed Ahmed Zaki Yamani, Saudi oil minister for 24 years, and replaced him with Hisham Nazer, the planning minister. With the support of the king, who publicly indicated a desire to change strategy and push oil prices up toward $18 a barrel, Nazer, at a December OPEC meeting, urged colleagues to agree to across-the-board production cuts, as Iran sought. Iraq refused to go along, but the other OPEC nations finally agreed to an output-cutting plan without Iraq's participation. Saudi Arabia's quota was cut down to 4.1 million b/d.

Finance and Trade. Citing the inability to plan for the 1986–1987 fiscal year because of uncertain oil prices, King Fahd announced in March that the 1985–1986 budget would be extended for at least five months. Then the government announced a freeze on all new development projects. In December the long-awaited budget was introduced; it cut spending by about 6 percent and projected a $14 billion deficit, to be funded out of reserves.

In January the European Economic Community imposed punitive duties of 12.5 percent on polyethylene products, 13 percent on methanol, and 11 percent on urea fertilizers on the grounds that Saudi imports had exceeded annual limits set by the EEC. The kingdom has been seeking trade agreements with the EEC that would abolish these limits.

Trade with the United States increased during 1986, with oil exports rising to almost 600,000 b/d. Saudi Arabia thus became the second-largest U.S. supplier, after Mexico. The United States also agreed to reduce its tariff on steel imported from Saudi Arabia to 5.5 percent.

Military Purchases. On April 8 the Reagan administration formally notified Congress of a proposed $354 million sale of 1,700 side-winder air-to-air missiles, 800 Stinger shoulder-launched antiaircraft missiles, and 100 harpoon antiship missiles to the Saudi Ministry of Defense, for 1989 delivery. Congressional opposition to the sale was overwhelming; opponents claimed that the Saudis had not done

enough to help resolve the Arab-Israeli dispute and that the arms might fall into terrorist hands. In May both houses of Congress voted against the sale. But Saudi agreement to drop the Stingers from the deal, combined with the administration's lobbying efforts, proved successful when on June 5 the Senate fell one vote short of overriding Reagan's May 21 veto.

Also in June, President Reagan notified Congress that the Saudis had satisfied U.S. conditions for delivery of the first of five Awacs planes originally contracted for in 1981 and due to be delivered in 1985. The first plane was turned over to the Saudis on June 30. Congressional opposition was muted by the $3 billion advance payment made by the Saudis.

In November it was revealed that Saudi businessman and arms dealer Adnan M. Khashoggi had played a significant role in the arrangement of secret arms sales by the United States to Iran. He reportedly might have acted in concert with some Saudi officials, who saw an opportunity thus to promote good relations with the United States and create an opening for dialogue with Iran.

See STATISTICS OF THE WORLD.   C.H.S.

SENEGAL. See STATISTICS OF THE WORLD.

SEYCHELLES. See STATISTICS OF THE WORLD.

SIERRA LEONE. See STATISTICS OF THE WORLD.

SINGAPORE. Singapore's economic slump, which brought the growth rate from 10 percent down to negative figures, showed signs of abating in the second half of 1986. To spur the economy, the government announced a two-year wage freeze and a series of tax breaks, as well as reduced employer contributions to the national retirement fund. The economic problems led Prime Minister Lee Kuan Yew to indicate that he might delay his retirement for one or two years. He had unofficially announced that he would retire in 1988, when he would be 65.

Lee's son, Lee Hsien Loong, continued his meteoric political rise. As acting minister of trade and industry, he chaired a key economic committee whose recommendations for economic recovery and future growth became government policy. In November he was named to the ruling party's executive committee.

The government passed a law permitting it to limit the sale of foreign publications with

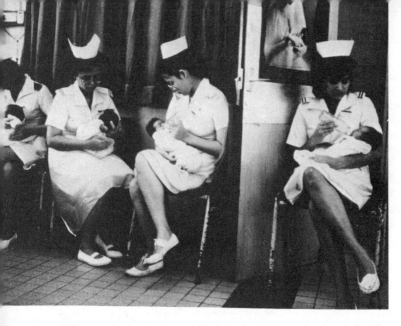

Singapore has a new slogan for its family planning program in light of the success of its old motto ("Two Is Enough"). The population decline has led to the adoption of "At Least Two. Better Three. Four If You Can Afford It." Here, nurses care for a few happy results of the new campaign.

which it disagrees. A law was also enacted allowing the eviction of residents of high-rise government housing if they throw furniture out of their windows. The overwhelming success of the nation's family planning program has resulted in an average family size of 1.5 children, which has led to projections of an aging and dwindling labor force and population. Reversing previous policies that penalized families with more than two children, the government began to urge couples to have at least two and preferably three or four children.

In November opposition leader J. B. Jeyaretnam was convicted of fraud and related charges; he was sentenced to a month in prison and expelled from Parliament, leaving only 1 of the 79 parliamentary seats in opposition hands.

See STATISTICS OF THE WORLD. K.M.

SOCIAL SECURITY. *See* ECONOMY AND BUSINESS.

SOLOMON ISLANDS. *See* STATISTICS OF THE WORLD.

SOMALIA. The usual uncertainty about the political and economic future of Somalia was heightened in May 1986 by the automobile accident in which the president, Muhammad Siad Barre, was seriously injured. Although Siad Barre, who was hospitalized for a while in Saudi Arabia, had exercised personal control over all decisions in the Somali government, it continued to function in his absence as it

always had. At the same time, great attention was focused on the long-term succession. Dissident groups in the north stepped up their military attacks in hopes of forcing political changes that would be to their liking. By late in the year, Siad Barre remained nominally in charge, but he was no longer the central figure he had been since becoming president in 1969.

In January, at the East African drought and development summit meeting in Djibouti, Siad Barre held what amounted to his most cordial talks in years with the Ethiopian leader, Mengistu Haile Mariam. The two countries agreed to form a joint committee to work out disputes as they arose over their undefined border and refugee movements in both directions. In March, President Li Xiannian of China visited Somalia for several days, marking several decades of Chinese assistance to Somalia.

The rule of Siad Barre had been marked for years by the pursuit of "scientific socialism," but in the early 1980's the government decided to reform the economy. By 1985 the government had legalized a freely floating currency exchange rate, and additional key measures were undertaken in 1986: much of the agricultural trade was transferred to the private sector, as was most banking activity, and prices for agricultural goods were allowed to rise in order to encourage farmers to grow more food. The civil service was cut back.

The United States strongly supported Somali

efforts at economic reform and provided about $42 million in direct economic assistance. Italy and West Germany also provided substantial aid.

See STATISTICS OF THE WORLD.   R.E.B.

SOUTH AFRICA. In 1986 the South African government greatly tightened security provisions and restrictions on media coverage of events. Other nations increasingly imposed sanctions.

Government Restrictions. On June 12 the white minority regime imposed a nationwide state of emergency, three months after lifting a previous order imposed on parts of the country. All South African security forces were given broad powers to arrest and interrogate persons, curb political activity, and conduct searches without a warrant. Television and radio coverage of most public disturbances was prohibited, as was publishing information deemed subversive. Pictures of such events could not be taken without permission. President Pieter W. Botha said the measures were imposed to curb growing violence by the outlawed African National Congress (ANC), which was seeking to overthrow the government. The action came four days before the tenth anniversary of the Soweto riots, in which 176 people, mostly blacks, were killed.

Six months later, on December 11, tightened regulations were issued. The new regulations, covering 24 pages of print, prohibited, among other things, taking part in boycotts or resisting or opposing enforcement of the emergency decree. Reporters were forbidden to publish unauthorized accounts of violence, boycotts, deployments of security forces, or speeches by persons said to be hostile to the government. On December 12, police executed what they called a "swoop" against possible internal foes, and made arrests. Details of the action could not be fully learned because of censorship.

The ANC. In January, exiled ANC leader Oliver Tambo had called for "rapid, extensive escalation" of action against white rule. During the same month, land mines exploded along the Botswana border. After pressure from South Africa, ANC personnel left Botswana in March. Meanwhile, ANC members were ordered to leave Lesotho after a new government took power there in the wake of a three-week South

African blockade of the small country, which is surrounded by South Africa.

In May, Pretoria simultaneously raided what it said were ANC facilities in Zambia, Zimbabwe, and Botswana. A land mine that claimed five lives in South Africa near the Swaziland border in August prompted a series of govern-

The International Business Machines Corporation (IBM), in what was largely a symbolic move, announced on October 21 that it would pull out of South Africa by selling its South African-based subsidiaries to local managers. Below, IBM offices in a Johannesburg suburb.

ment raids against Swaziland. Another raid was launched against Swaziland in December, in conjunction with the "swoop" against possible sources of internal opposition.

Winnie Mandela (*see biography in* PEOPLE IN THE NEWS), the wife of imprisoned ANC leader Nelson Mandela and herself a leading anti-apartheid activist, refused to leave her home in Soweto, to which she had returned despite a 1985 order forbidding her to leave her "exile home" in the Orange Free State. The banning order was formally lifted in July.

Domestic Events. In a January 31 speech, President Botha proposed the establishment of a multiracial national statutory council that would include black members, but no major black leader publicly declared willingness to serve on the proposed council. In March, black parents, students, and teachers decided to call off a longstanding school boycott and instead begin a three-day general strike on the June 16 Soweto anniversary. The planned protest was prevented by the declaration of the state of emergency, though many people stayed away from school and work on June 16. The new Cosatu labor union coalition, representing 500,000 workers, mostly blacks, joined with political and student groups in endorsing a general strike on May 1; some 1.5 million blacks participated in the action, to protest apartheid and to support making the day a public holiday.

On July 1, the laws requiring blacks to carry passbooks indicating their birthplace and ethnic group, as well as whether they could live in a black township near a white city, were abolished, and uniform identity cards were issued for all South Africans. All those arrested for violating the pass laws were to be freed. However, later in July the government announced that blacks in the four independent homelands of Transkei, Bophuthatswana, Venda, and Ciskei, who are not South African citizens, would have to obtain permits to work in South Africa. (The homeland concept was dealt a blow in August, when the legislative assembly of the homeland of KwaNdebele rejected plans for independence.)

Violence. The United Democratic Front, a multiracial alliance of trade unions with community, religious, and student groups, said in April that it was under increasing pressure to review its commitment to nonviolence, after the death in detention of the UDF's Northern Transvaal province president, Peter Nchabeleng, and two bomb attacks on UDF leaders.

Violence and unrest in black areas had led to more than 2,300 deaths since September 1984. Some deaths resulted from attacks by black vigilante forces against other blacks;

At the Crossroads squatter camp near Cape Town, vigilantes, reportedly supported by the South African police, clashed with black residents resisting government relocation.

others from clashes with security forces. One of the most publicized incidents occurred at the Crossroads squatter settlement outside Cape Town in May and June; at least 50 people were killed and tens of thousands left homeless in clashes, as residents sought to avoid eviction. Rent strikes took place in black townships throughout South Africa. In August security forces opened fire on Soweto residents who, fearing eviction, had barricaded the streets with burning cars and other debris; more than 20 residents were killed. At least eight people were shot dead during funerals for the victims (funeral gatherings were prohibited under the state of emergency).

Foreign Relations. The Eminent Persons Group created at a 1985 Commonwealth summit meeting visited South Africa twice in 1986, meeting with government leaders, Nelson Mandela, and others. The seven members suggested that the government release Mandela and lift its ban on the ANC and other groups. The leaders of seven Commonwealth nations, meeting in London in August, called for strong economic sanctions, including bans on new bank loans, agricultural and uranium imports, contracts with South African companies, and air links. Britain refused to go along, agreeing only to weaker measures. In September the foreign ministers of the European Community agreed on limited sanctions, banning imports of South African gold, steel, and gold coins and prohibiting new investment in the country by European firms (which had already slowed to a trickle). In October the U.S. Congress enacted, over President Ronald Reagan's veto, a law imposing tough economic sanctions against Pretoria. Meanwhile, many U.S. institutions sold investments in companies with ties to South Africa, and some U.S. companies, including General Motors and IBM, decided to sell off their South African operations.

Archbishop Tutu. Desmond Tutu, Johannesburg's bishop, was elected archbishop of Cape Town and head of the Anglican Church in Southern Africa on April 14. Tutu, winner of the 1984 Nobel Peace Prize, spoke out for international sanctions against the Pretoria government several times during the year.   J.F.

SOUTH CAROLINA. See STATISTICS OF THE WORLD.

SOUTH DAKOTA. See STATISTICS OF THE WORLD.

SOUTH WEST AFRICA, or NAMIBIA. In a March 1986 speech to Parliament, South African President Pieter W. Botha announced that South Africa was prepared to begin implementing, on August 1, United Nations Resolution 435, which provides for independence for Namibia (now administered by South Africa) and for UN-sponsored general elections. He made this conditional, however, on "a firm and satisfactory agreement" that Cuba would withdraw its troops from Angola, Namibia's northern neighbor. The August date came and went with no change in status.

A UN conference on Namibia, held in Vienna in July, ended with the delegates appealing to the Security Council to impose mandatory comprehensive sanctions against South Africa. The delegates said that Pretoria's linkage of Namibian independence to a Cuban withdrawal from Angola—a policy supported by the United States—introduced an "irrelevant and extraneous" condition. The UN General Assembly, meeting in special session in September, also asked the Security Council to adopt comprehensive sanctions.

The South West Africa People's Organization (Swapo), a guerrilla organization fighting for Namibian independence from South Africa, claimed to have killed at least 132 South African soldiers during actions in April and May. On May 7, seven members of Swapo were sentenced to prison terms ranging from 5 years to 16 years, after having been convicted under South Africa's Terrorism Act. In November—in the first such act in more than a year—South African military forces attacked a Swapo camp in Angola.   J.F.

SOVIET UNION. See UNION OF SOVIET SOCIALIST REPUBLICS.

SPACE EXPLORATION. The loss of the space shuttle *Challenger* and its seven astronauts in a fiery explosion January 28, 1986, threw the U.S. space program into turmoil. Several rocket failures also contributed to a drastic reduction in space flight activity during the year. However, NASA's Voyager 2 spacecraft flew by Uranus, transmitting pictures; and the European Space Agency's Giotto spacecraft, the Soviet Union's Vega 1 and Vega 2 vehicles, and Japan's Suisei all intercepted Halley's comet.

Two Soviet cosmonauts, Vladimir Solovyov (below, left) and Leonid Kizim, returned happily to earth on July 16, after spending 125 days in space, inhabiting two space stations. On March 13 they had been sent in a Soyuz spacecraft to Mir, a recently launched modular space station (shown above during its earth-based preparations). Mir (which means peace) has six landing docks and almost luxurious living space; it is designed to be the hub of a permanently manned space research complex. On May 5 the cosmonauts left Mir for the Salyut 7 space station, in the first-ever transfer between orbiting stations.

(*See also* ASTRONOMY.) The Soviets also launched a new space station.

***Columbia* Launch.** On January 12, after several weather delays, *Columbia,* on the year's first shuttle mission, achieved a spectacular dawn launch. The crew, commanded by astronaut Robert L. Gibson, deployed a large RCA communications satellite, but materials processing tests planned for the mission were less suc-

cessful. Representative Bill Nelson (D, Fla.), chairman of the House Science and Technology subcommittee, was aboard as a guest. *Columbia* landed before dawn on January 18 at Edwards Air Force Base, Calif., after bad weather prevented landing at the Kennedy Space Center in Florida.

***Challenger* Disaster.** The space shuttle *Challenger* took off from Kennedy Space Center with a crew consisting of Francis R. (Dick) Scobee, commander; Michael J. Smith, pilot; Ellison S. Onizuka; Ronald E. McNair; Judith A. Resnik; Hughes Aircraft Company engineer Gregory B. Jarvis; and New Hampshire schoolteacher S. Christa McAuliffe. They became the first U.S. space crew to die in flight when *Challenger* exploded 73 seconds after lift-off. A commission headed by Secretary of State William P. Rogers was appointed by President Ronald Reagan to investigate the accident. The commission found that the joints on the shuttle's booster rockets—and especially their rubber seals, or O-rings—had been poorly designed and that the disaster began with the failure of the lowest joint on the right booster rocket. It was learned that boosters on previous shuttle flights had given indications of problems but that NASA had nonetheless allowed the shuttles to fly. The Rogers commission also found that, on the night before *Challenger*'s launch, engineers at Morton Thiokol (the company that made the booster rockets) had argued both with their own managers and with those at NASA's Marshall Space Flight Center in Huntsville, Ala., contending that cold temperatures at the time could cause the booster seals to fail. The engineers' objections to launching were overruled. Late in the year, an independent analysis found that high stresses on a strut linking the external fuel tank to the right booster might also have played a role in the disaster. In another investigation, the U.S. House Science and Technology Committee concluded that NASA had suffered from poor technical decision-making over a period of years.

Plans for Recovery. NASA grounded the remaining shuttles and eventually indicated it was planning a number of design changes in the shuttle. Besides a redesign of the booster rockets, these would probably include some sort of emergency escape system for astronauts. Some of the less pressing safety changes would not be complete until the mid-1990's, but it was hoped that adequately modified shuttles could be put into service by 1988. In addition to the existing shuttles, a new shuttle was to be built to replace *Challenger*—at a cost of close to $3 billion—but the replacement was not slated to be ready until 1991. Once the shuttles start flying again, there will be two

years of payloads backed up, and the number of shuttle flights made will be reduced significantly from what had been planned earlier.

The most serious long-term effects of such delays and cutbacks will be on the scientific community, because it had tied most of its future programs to the shuttle and had little money left to reorient its plans. For instance, the Spacelab program, which allows the shuttle to function as an orbiting laboratory, was severely cut back. Other high-priority scientific payloads, such as the Hubble Space Telescope (which can be launched only by the shuttle), previously scheduled for a late 1986 launch, faced delays of two years or more. The *Galileo* spacecraft to orbit Jupiter and send a probe into its cloud tops was to have been launched from the shuttle in May but was delayed until about 1991.

Many of the backlogged payloads were commercial communications satellites. After the accident more than a dozen companies switched their payloads from a planned shuttle launch to one from the unmanned, expendable Ariane rocket of the ESA. In a move to broaden the U.S. launch base by fostering a private U.S. satellite-launching industry (that would use unmanned rockets), President Ronald Reagan in August directed that the shuttle eventually stop handling commercial payloads. This ban would not take effect until about 1995, however, because the administration did not wish to cancel existing contracts. Several companies that were developing the capability to launch payloads on unmanned rockets were vying for the commercial satellites that would not be able to find room on either the shuttle or the Ariane.

The Defense Department's plans in space were also stymied by the shuttle accident. By mid-1987 about ten large military satellites that were to have been carried into space by the shuttle will be backlogged on the ground; by 1992 the number will grow to 30.

The U.S. Air Force realized even before the *Challenger* accident that it could not rely solely on the shuttle to launch its satellites, and hence was having ten large Titan 4 rockets built. Following the shuttle accident the Air Force purchased 13 more of the large unmanned rockets. The new purchase provided a strong production base for the Titans, which could also be used for commercial satellite launches. In addition, the Air Force was procuring a smaller rocket than the Titan, so that at least two types of U.S. expendable rockets would be available to compete with the ESA's Ariane for launches of commercial payloads.

Other Launch Problems. The enthusiasm for unmanned expendable rockets was tempered by a series of unmanned rocket accidents after the *Challenger* disaster. A military payload was successfully launched in an Atlas rocket on February 9. However, when the Air Force tried to launch another military payload, believed to be a reconnaissance satellite, on a Titan 34D on April 18, the vehicle rose to about 800 feet and then one of its solid-fuel boosters exploded, destroying the craft. The next U.S. launch attempt, of an unmanned Delta rocket carrying a National Oceanic and Atmospheric Administration weather satellite, ended in failure because of an electrical short. That accident, on May 3, not only grounded Delta rockets but also forced grounding of the Atlas rockets, which have similar main electrical systems.

On May 9, NASA announced that a Nike-Orion research rocket had failed in late April over New Mexico. On May 30 an ESA Ariane rocket carrying an Intelsat-5 satellite had to be destroyed when its third-stage engine failed to ignite. That temporarily grounded the West's only remaining large rocket, which was to be redesigned. In August a NASA Aries rocket carrying a research telescope had to be destroyed after going off course. Days later the Air Force blew up an unarmed intercontinental missile when a problem developed during its flight over the Pacific.

Finally, on September 5, a Delta rocket was launched successfully from Cape Canaveral carrying two Strategic Defense Initiative spacecraft. It was the first large space mission conducted by the SDI missile defense program. Subsequently, an Atlas successfully launched a weather satellite, a Scout booster launched a scientific payload, and an Atlas-Centaur rocket launched a $125 million military communications satellite.

U.S. Space Station. NASA's next big project, the space station planned for the early 1990's,

also got into trouble. The publication *Aviation Week & Space Technology* obtained a memo by senior astronaut C. Gordon Fullerton charging that the station was being designed improperly. Fullerton's memo said that the shuttle could not build and support the space station as envisioned and that NASA might be making the same mistakes with the station that led to its shuttle problems. NASA drafted a revision of its plans for the space station that increased the size of some of its components and changed their configuration so that fewer shuttle flights would be needed to construct it.

Soviet Flights. The Soviet Union made progress in its manned space program by launching the new Mir space station on February 20. Mir is essentially a modernized version of the Salyut space station design used by the Soviets for over ten years. Its importance lies in its new docking hub, capable of holding five additional space station modules. Mir is the first station capable of being enlarged to any number of size options—depending upon whether the modules themselves have docking hubs.

On March 13 the Soviets launched cosmonauts Leonid Kizim and Vladimir Solovyov in the Soyuz T-15 to the new station, which they activated and lived aboard for almost two months. On May 5 the two undocked their Soyuz and flew across 1,860 miles of space to the unmanned orbiting Salyut 7 space station, where they completed the first crew transfer in history between two orbiting stations. They returned to earth on July 16 after a 125-day mission. The Salyut was then maneuvered to a high "storage orbit," where the Soviets will allow it to drift for several years while they study the performance of its aging systems.

Japan and China. During 1986, China launched its second geosynchronous-orbit communications satellite and two low-altitude reconnaissance spacecraft. The Japanese made major progress in their space program with the first launch of their new, advanced H-1 rocket—capable of placing 1,200 pounds in geosynchronous orbit.

See also the feature article SPACE: REBOUNDING FROM DISASTER? C.C.

SPAIN. Prime Minister Felipe González Márquez demonstrated his acuity and clout in 1986, winning a carefully worded referendum

Spain's Prime Minister Felipe González Márquez demonstrated his political clout with his successful campaign for Spain's continued participation in NATO; in a referendum on March 12, voters chose to remain in the alliance.

November 30 the coalition lost 5 of 7 seats there. In December the coalition's respected and popular leader, Manuel Fraga Iribarne, resigned because of poor election results, after a long and influential career in Spanish politics.

González had called for parliamentary elections in April, following his victory in the NATO vote. While some grumbled at his austerity program, with its accompanying high unemployment, others seemed to accept the program as necessary for economic growth. González promised to govern "with a spirit of dialogue."

NATO Referendum. Spain joined NATO in 1982—the same year González took office with a promise to pull the country out of the treaty alliance. Underlying opposition to NATO had been an undercurrent of anti-Americanism, made more acute by objections to the presence of three American bases on Spanish soil. However, before the March 12 vote, González came to favor NATO membership as an indication that Spain was a participating member of the democratic West, and as a possible counter to right-wing Spanish militarism. Tying Spanish membership in NATO to Spain's membership in the EC (rather than to friendship with the United States), the referendum he presented asked voters to judge the "suitability" of remaining in NATO "under conditions already agreed upon by the government of the nation," including reduction of U.S. troop strength, prohibition of nuclear weapons on Spanish soil, and an independent military status analogous to that of France. Given such conditions, 53 percent opted for continuing—and González had won a major political victory.

Terrorism Campaign. Political violence, particularly from the terrorist wing of the Basque separatist ETA movement, continued to plague the Madrid government—and Madrid itself. Major incidents in the capital included the assassination of a Spanish vice admiral (and a direct descendant of Christopher Columbus), two car bombings which killed 15 members of the Guardia Civil, and a rocket attack on the Ministry of Defense. Spanish and French police recorded a few counterterrorist victories, including a successful police raid in northern Spain, which freed an abducted industrialist and netted three of his abductors.

See STATISTICS OF THE WORLD.   J.O.S.

on Spanish membership in the North Atlantic Treaty Organization in March, then calling for parliamentary elections and winning his second four-year term at the polls on June 22. On January 1, Spain entered the European Community (*see* EUROPEAN COMMUNITIES).

Elections. In the June parliamentary elections González's Spanish Socialist Workers' Party won 184 seats in the 350-seat lower chamber of the Cortes, or Parliament, a decline of 18. However, the conservative Popular Coalition, in coalition with two smaller parties, was unable to profit, losing 1 seat, for a total of 105. Various smaller centrist, leftist, and regionally based parties made gains. In July, one party defected from coalition with the Popular Coalition, and in Basque regional elections on

Sports

During 1986, Argentina won the battle for soccer's World Cup, and the New York Mets beat the Boston Red Sox in the World Series. Among other big winners, the Montréal Canadiens took their 23rd Stanley Cup and the Boston Celtics their 16th NBA title.

Fans thrilled to the performances of such stars as Bobby Rahal, Roger Clemens, Larry Bird, Vinny Testaverde, Debi Thomas, Diego Maradona, Martina Navratilova, and Ivan Lendl. Off the field, the problem of drugs in sports and the antitrust suit by the United States Football League attracted wide attention.

AUTOMOBILE RACING

Bobby Rahal slipped past Kevin Cogan with two laps remaining to capture his first Indianapolis 500, the premier race in the United States. Driving a British-built March-Cosworth racing car, Rahal turned the fastest lap in race history—209.152 miles per hour (mph) on the final lap—to stave off Cogan, who finished only 1.441 seconds behind in second place, and Rick Mears, who was only .440 seconds back of Cogan. Rahal went on to win five more races in the season and subsequently nailed down the Championship Auto Racing Teams (CART) title, along with the $300,000 prize.

Dale Earnhardt, driving home five wins during the National Association for Stock Car Auto Racing (Nascar) season, clinched the overall points championship two weeks before the end of the season with a victory in the Atlanta Journal 500 on November 2.

Alain Prost of France, driving a McLaren-TAG Porsche, became the first driver since 1960 to win consecutive world Grand Prix championships when he won the final race of the season, the Australian Grand Prix in Adelaide, to overtake Nigel Mansell of Great Britain. Mansell won four out of five races in midseason and would have won his first championship had he finished third or better in Australia, but he was forced out of the race when a rear tire shredded. Mansell and former world champion Nelson Piquet of Brazil enabled the Williams team, headed by Frank Williams of England, to win its third consecutive World Constructors' championship.

American Al Holbert, Derek Bell of Britain, and Hans Stuck of West Germany drove a factory-prepared Rothmans Porsche 962C to victory in the 54th annual 24 Hours of LeMans race in May. It was Holbert's second and Bell's fourth LeMans win. The race was marred by the death of Jo Gartner, a veteran Austrian driver, who crashed at high speed.   S.G.

BASEBALL

Major league baseball proudly proclaimed 1986 as its most successful season ever: for the first time, all 26 teams drew more than 1 million fans. After winning gripping playoffs to take the two league titles, the New York Mets and the Boston Red Sox met in the World Series, where New York staged a string of comebacks to win, four games to three.

Season Highlights. Boston's Roger Clemens (see biography in PEOPLE IN THE NEWS) brought new meaning to the world of power pitching. He posted an American League 24-4 record, led the league with a 2.48 earned run average, and struck out 238 batters, second behind Seattle's Mark Langston, who notched 245 strikeouts. In addition, on April 29, Clemens set a major league record for a nine-inning game by striking out 20 Seattle Mariners. He was the unanimous choice for the American League's Cy Young Award and was named the league's Most Valuable Player.

Clemens's teammate, Wade Boggs, led the American League in hitting with a .357 batting average, edging out the New York Yankees' Don Mattingly (.352). But Mattingly hit for

360

power and production that Boggs couldn't match—31 home runs and 113 runs batted in—and finished second in MVP voting. Toronto's Jesse Barfield led the league with 37 home runs; Cleveland's Joe Carter had the most RBI's (121), and the Yankees' Dave Righetti set a major league record with 46 saves.

The Mets dominated the National League, winning 108 games—the most by any National League club since the 1975 Cincinnati Reds—and setting a major league record for their 21½-game margin of victory over second-place Philadelphia in the Eastern Division. The team led the league in hitting and received solid pitching from Dwight Gooden (who slipped to 17-6 from his 1985 mark of 24-4), Bob Ojeda (18-5), Ron Darling (15-6), Sid Fernandez (16-6), and Roger McDowell (14-9).

Curiously, the Mets didn't have an obvious candidate for the league's Most Valuable Player.

The Boston Red Sox were just one strike away from losing the American League playoffs when Dave Henderson cracked a dramatic two-run homer to lead his team to an exciting 11th-inning victory over the California Angels.

Those honors went to Philadelphia's Mike Schmidt, who hit .290 with a league-high 37 homers and 119 RBI's. Schmidt became only the seventh player to win the award three times. Houston's Mike Scott won the National League's Cy Young Award. The master of the split-fingered fastball, he became only the fourth pitcher to strike out 300 hitters (he finished with 306), led the league with a 2.22 ERA, and finished with an 18-10 record. He helped the Astros clinch the Western Division title with flair: on September 25 he threw a 13-strikeout no-hitter against San Francisco, walking only two batters and allowing only two balls to be hit out of the infield.

Montréal's Tim Raines won the batting title with a .334 average; Los Angeles's Fernando Valenzuela led the league with 21 wins; and rookie Todd Worrell of St. Louis posted a league-high 36 saves.

Playoffs. Boston staged a dramatic comeback against California to win the American League

NATIONAL LEAGUE

Eastern Division	W	L	Pct.	GB
New York Mets	108	54	.667	—
Philadelphia Phillies	86	75	.534	21½
St. Louis Cardinals	79	82	.491	28½
Montréal Expos	78	83	.484	29½
Chicago Cubs	70	90	.438	37
Pittsburgh Pirates	64	98	.395	44

Western Division	W	L	Pct.	GB
Houston Astros	96	66	.593	—
Cincinnati Reds	86	76	.531	10
San Francisco Giants	83	79	.512	13
San Diego Padres	74	88	.457	22
Los Angeles Dodgers	73	89	.451	23
Atlanta Braves	72	89	.447	23½

AMERICAN LEAGUE

Eastern Division	W	L	Pct.	GB
Boston Red Sox	95	66	.590	—
New York Yankees	90	72	.556	5½
Detroit Tigers	87	75	.537	8½
Toronto Blue Jays	86	76	.531	9½
Cleveland Indians	84	78	.519	11½
Milwaukee Brewers	77	84	.478	18
Baltimore Orioles	73	89	.451	22½

Western Division	W	L	Pct.	GB
California Angels	92	70	.568	—
Texas Rangers	87	75	.537	5
Kansas City Royals	76	86	.469	16
Oakland Athletics	76	86	.469	16
Chicago White Sox	72	90	.444	20
Minnesota Twins	71	91	.438	21
Seattle Mariners	67	95	.414	25

PENNANT PLAYOFFS
National League—New York defeated Houston, 4 games to 2.
American League—Boston defeated California, 4 games to 3.

WORLD SERIES—New York defeated Boston, 4 games to 3.

pennant. Behind three games to one and down to their last strike in Game 5, Boston rallied on homers by Don Baylor and Dave Henderson to tie and eventually win the game; the Red Sox went on to take the next two games convincingly. Meanwhile, the Mets were leading the Astros three games to two and were hoping to end the playoffs in six games and thus avoid facing Mike Scott in Game 7. Scott had already beaten the Mets twice in less than a week, allowing just one earned run while striking out 19 in 18 innings. Down 3-0 going into the ninth inning, the Mets rallied to tie the game and went on to win a 16-inning thriller, 7-6, when reliever Jesse Orosco struck out Kevin Bass with the potential tying and winning runs on base.

World Series. Pitching dominated the first game, which the Red Sox won, 1-0, on an unearned run that scored when a ground ball rolled under infielder Tim Teufel's glove, al-

lowing Jim Rice to come home from second. The Red Sox unleashed an 18-hit attack to win the second game, 9-3, but the Mets replied with a barrage of their own in the third game, roughing up Dennis "Oil Can" Boyd for four first-inning runs on their way to a 7-1 victory. The Mets evened the Series in the fourth game, winning 6-2 behind the strong pitching of Ron Darling. The Red Sox took the fifth game, 4-2, as lefthander Bruce Hurst, who shut out the Mets in the first game, mastered them again. The sixth game will be remembered for the Mets' remarkable 10th-inning comeback. Trailing 5-3 and with the Red Sox one out away from their first World Series title since 1918, the Mets tied the game on three consecutive singles and a wild pitch, then won the game when first baseman Bill Buckner allowed a soft grounder to go through his legs, permitting Ray Knight to scamper home with the winning run. The Mets came from behind to win the deciding

In Game 6 of the World Series, the New York Mets—after twice being down to their last strike—staged a spectacular three-run rally against the Boston Red Sox in the bottom of the 10th to keep their championship hopes alive. Here, Series MVP Ray Knight brings home the winning run.

seventh game, 8-5, taking the lead on a homer by series MVP Knight in the seventh inning and adding to it with a homer by Darryl Strawberry in the eighth.

Drug Scandal. In February, Commissioner Peter Ueberroth disciplined the 21 players implicated in 1985 during trials of Pennsylvania men involved in selling cocaine to professional baseball players. Several star players—granted immunity—had testified about their own and other players' drug use. Seven players (Joaquin Andujar, Dale Berra, Enos Cabell, Keith Hernandez, Jeff Leonard, Dave Parker, and Lonnie Smith) had the choice of taking a one-year suspension without pay or paying a fine equal to 10 percent of their base salaries, donating 100 hours of community service in each of the next two years, and submitting to random drug testing for the rest of their careers. The others were given lesser variations on this theme. All players involved complied with the penalties. In April the Major League Players Association filed a grievance on behalf of the players.

All-Star Game. The American League won the All-Star game for the second time in 4 years but for only the third time in 15 seasons, beating the National League by a score of 3-2 in a game highlighted by the pitching of Clemens (three perfect innings) and Valenzuela (six consecutive strikeouts).   B.K.

BASKETBALL

Louisville became the only school since 1973 to have won two National Collegiate Athletic Association championships. The Boston Celtics took their 16th National Basketball Association title. The sport was shaken when University of Maryland forward Len Bias died June 19 of cocaine intoxication, two days after being picked second overall (by the Celtics) in the NBA draft. (See also EDUCATION.)

College. The NCAA championship game between Duke and Louisville on March 31 in Dallas was to have belonged to a few heralded seniors—Duke's Johnny Dawkins and Louisville's Billy Thompson and Milt Wagner. Instead, freshman Pervis Ellison surfaced as the hero. The 6'9" center scored 25 points, grabbed 11 rebounds, blocked 2 shots, make a key steal, and did not commit a turnover in leading the way to Louisville's 72-69 victory. It was

"Never Nervous Pervis" (number 43) made the Blue Devils more than nervous in the NCAA championship game between Duke and Louisville. Pervis Ellison led the Louisville Cardinals to a 72-69 victory and became the first freshman in 42 years to be named the Final Four's Most Valuable Player.

the Cardinals' second national title in seven years.

Louisville had reeled off 16 straight victories—including wins over Drexel, Bradley, North Carolina, Auburn, and Louisiana State in postseason play—to earn the berth against Duke. Duke entered the championship game having won an NCAA record 37 games. The Blue Devils had defeated Mississippi Valley State, Old Dominion, DePaul, Navy, and Kansas before meeting Louisville.

363

A Living Legend

As Larry Bird led the Boston Celtics to their third NBA title in his seven-year career, the 6'9" forward's performance sparkled in all facets of the game. He won MVP honors for the third consecutive time during regular season and for the second time in the championship series. He also finished among the top ten in five of the NBA's eight statistical categories, and some fans called him the best team player in sports. Indiana-born Larry Joe Bird arrived in Boston in 1979 after having been College Player of the Year at Indiana State. With Bird as a catalyst, the Celtics emerged from two dark years to new prosperity, and he emerged as a star to be compared with the legendary Bill Russell. Other players have scored more points than Bird and been better passers and rebounders. But rarely has anyone wrapped it all up in a package as he has. With his alert eyes, craning neck, and large hands, Bird has the knack to see the whole game even as he fights for a rebound, drives to the basket, or launches a shot from deep in the corner. With his skills and innate understanding of the game, Bird knows how to create magic on the court.

Larry Bird

Ellison's performance made him the first freshman in 42 years to be chosen as the Final Four's Most Valuable Player. His play and coolness under pressure were so impressive that some saw the start of "the Ellison era."

In women's play, another freshman stole the thunder in the title game played March 30 at Lexington, Ky. Clarissa Davis came off the bench to score 24 points and collect 14 rebounds, leading Texas to a 97-81 victory over the University of Southern California and its first national title. The Lady Longhorns finished 34-0, the first team in the five-year history of NCAA Division I women's play to go undefeated. USC's Cheryl Miller, the dominant player of the past four years, finished the title game with 16 points. Texas's Kamie Ethridge was later named the woman player of the year.

In other news, John (Hot Rod) Williams was acquitted on June 16 of having taken part in a bribery scheme while at Tulane; the decision cleared the way for Williams to report to the Cleveland Cavaliers' training camp for the 1986–1987 season. Alfredo William (Tito)

Horford, the 7'1" Dominican player who had bounced between several colleges because of recruiting violations and other problems, found a home at Miami, where he was eligible to play in 1986–1987 providing his grades were satisfactory. Charges of rape leveled in January against three players caused Minnesota coach Jim Dutcher to resign, and his team finished the season with a patchwork lineup. The three players were later acquitted.

Memphis State University was subjected to fines and other penalties for making illegal payments to players. The Memphis State program was further rocked by the firing of head coach Dana Kirk, whose personal finances were under investigation as part of a federal sports gambling probe. Northeast Louisiana University became the first school to be placed on probation for a women's basketball recruiting violation.

Professional. With their victory over the Houston Rockets in the championship series, the Boston Celtics earned consideration as one of the greatest teams in NBA history. The key to

NATIONAL BASKETBALL ASSOCIATION
1985–1986 Regular Season

EASTERN CONFERENCE

Atlantic Division	W	L	Pct.	GB
Boston Celtics	67	15	.817	—
Philadelphia 76ers	54	28	.659	13
Washington Bullets	39	43	.476	28
New Jersey Nets	39	43	.476	28
New York Knicks	23	59	.280	44

Central Division	W	L	Pct.	GB
Milwaukee Bucks	57	25	.695	—
Atlanta Hawks	50	32	.610	7
Detroit Pistons	46	36	.561	11
Chicago Bulls	30	52	.366	27
Cleveland Cavaliers	29	53	.354	28
Indiana Pacers	26	56	.317	31

WESTERN CONFERENCE

Midwest Division	W	L	Pct.	GB
Houston Rockets	51	31	.622	—
Denver Nuggets	47	35	.573	4
Dallas Mavericks	44	38	.537	7
Utah Jazz	42	40	.512	9
Sacramento Kings	37	45	.451	14
San Antonio Spurs	35	47	.427	16

Pacific Division	W	L	Pct.	GB
Los Angeles Lakers	62	20	.756	—
Portland Trail Blazers	40	42	.488	22
Los Angeles Clippers	32	50	.390	30
Phoenix Suns	32	50	.390	30
Seattle SuperSonics	31	51	.378	31
Golden State Warriors	30	52	.366	32

PLAYOFFS

First Round
Boston defeated Chicago, 3 games to 0
Philadelphia defeated Washington, 3 games to 2
Milwaukee defeated New York, 3 games to 0
Atlanta defeated Detroit, 3 games to 1
Los Angeles defeated San Antonio, 3 games to 0
Houston defeated Sacramento, 3 games to 0
Denver defeated Portland, 3 games to 1
Dallas defeated Utah, 3 games to 1

Second Round
Boston defeated Atlanta, 4 games to 1
Milwaukee defeated Philadelphia, 4 games to 3
Los Angeles defeated Dallas, 4 games to 2
Houston defeated Denver, 4 games to 2

Conference Finals
Boston defeated Milwaukee, 4 games to 0
Houston defeated Los Angeles, 4 games to 1

Championship Finals
Boston defeated Houston, 4 games to 2

While Boston swept through the Eastern Conference playoffs, the Rockets, led by their "twin towers," 7'0" Akeem Olajuwon and 7'4" Ralph Sampson, stunned the favored Los Angeles Lakers in the Western Conference final. In the championship series, the Celtics won easily in the first two games, in Boston; the scene then shifted to Houston, where the teams split two close games and the Rockets won the fifth game handily. On June 8, back in Boston, the Celtics finished the Rockets, 114–97. The Boston defense forced 11 first-quarter Houston turnovers, and Larry Bird, who was later named the Most Valuable Player of the championship series, scored 29 points, also collecting 11 rebounds, 12 assists, and 3 steals.

The Boston Celtics' Bill Walton, perhaps the best passing center in the NBA, shows his form during the championship series against the Houston Rockets.

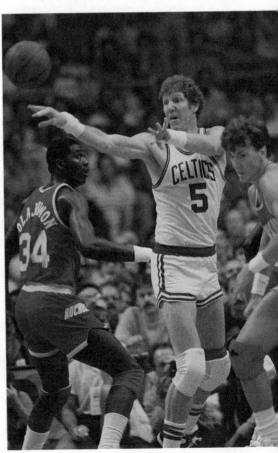

the season that produced 67 victories (and 15 more in the playoffs) was depth, achieved mainly through trades for Jerry Sichting and Bill Walton. Sichting's excellent outside shooting helped to counter the double-teaming routinely used against the Celtics' big front line. Walton gave Boston another shot blocker, more rebounding and defense, and probably the best passing from center in the league. The Celtics posted a league record of 40-1 at home.

Atlanta forward Dominique Wilkins won the scoring title, averaging 30.3 points a game, while Detroit center Bill Laimbeer was the league's top rebounder, averaging 13.1 a game. Earvin ("Magic") Johnson led in assists, with a 12.6 average. Alvin Robertson of the Spurs set a season record for steals (301), and Craig Hodges of the Bucks set another, for three-point field-goal accuracy (.451). Bird, who led in free throw percentage (.8963), was named Most Valuable Player for the third straight season, and the Knicks' Patrick Ewing, despite knee problems that caused him to miss 32 games, was Rookie of the Year.

In addition to the shock of Bias's death, the NBA saw its Comeback Player of the Year for 1984–1985, the Nets' Micheal Ray Richardson, banned after testing positive a third time for cocaine use. S.M.G.

BOWLING

After the winter and summer tours Walter Ray Williams, Jr., of Stockton, Calif., a four-time world champion horseshoe pitcher, had won 4 of the 28 major tournaments on the Professional Bowlers Association tour, for a total of $122,360. Steve Cook of Roseville, Calif., a noted archer, had won 3 matches and $110,260.

In the biggest PBA events, Cook won the U.S. Open, defeating Frank Ellensburg of Mesa, Ariz., 245-211; Tom Crites of Tampa, Fla., took the PBA national championship, beating defending champion Mike Aulby of Indianapolis, 190-184; and Marshall Holman of Medford, Ore., won the Firestone Tournament of Champions with a 233-211 victory over Mark Baker of Garden Grove, Calif.

Women. On the Ladies Professional Bowlers Tour, Lisa Wagner of Palmetto, Fla., led in earnings ($21,230) and average (213.04), and Jeanne Maiden of Solon, Ohio, in victories (three) after summer competition. Patty Costello became the first woman to win 25 career victories. F.L.

BOXING

Since 1978, when Muhammad Ali lost his position as unchallenged world heavyweight champion, various governing bodies have recognized different champions at the same time. In 1986 a series of bouts began, with the intention of ultimately unifying the title in 1987.

Larry Holmes, who was a heavyweight champion from 1978 to 1985, came out of retirement to fight unbeaten Michael Spinks, recognized as champion by the International

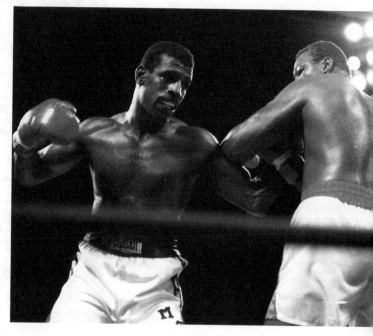

International Boxing Federation champion Michael Spinks aims a punch at Larry Holmes during their April 19 match in Las Vegas. Holmes, who came out of a brief retirement for another crack at the IBF title, was favored 8-5, but Spinks won the bout in a hotly debated split decision.

Boxing Federation. Spinks, the underdog, won an unpopular split decision in Las Vegas on April 19. He successfully defended his title against Steffen Tangstad of Norway, on September 6 in Las Vegas; the victory put Spinks into the final for the unified title in 1987.

Meanwhile, Tim Witherspoon, who successfully defended his World Boxing Association title against Frank Bruno of England, in Wembley on July 19, was dethroned in December in New York's Madison Square Garden by James "Bonecrusher" Smith. Smith was thus slated to play against Mike Tyson, the World Boxing Council champion, who won that title on November 22 in Las Vegas by stopping Trevor Berbick in the second round. (Berbick had captured the WBC title by beating the favored Pinklon Thomas in a unanimous decision on March 22 in Las Vegas.)

Marvelous Marvin Hagler, the undisputed middleweight champion, had a difficult fight March 10 in Las Vegas. In his 12th title defense, he knocked out John ("the Beast") Mugabi of Uganda in 11 rounds, after Mugabi had almost closed Hagler's right eye. In November, Hagler and Sugar Ray Leonard, a former welterweight champion who had retired, agreed to fight for the middleweight title in 1987.

Donald Curry of Fort Worth, Texas, was universally recognized as the welterweight champion and was projected to be Hagler's challenger after Leonard, assuming Hagler won. But in a stunning upset September 27 in Atlantic City, N.J., Lloyd Honeyghan of Jamaica, an 8-1 underdog, captured Curry's title. On the advice of the ringside physicians, referee Octavio Meyran had stopped the fight after six rounds because of a deep cut over Curry's left eye.   F.L.

FOOTBALL

Penn State, the only major-college team to finish the regular season and bowl season undefeated, won the unofficial 1986 national championship. In the National Football League, the New York Giants beat the Denver Broncos in Super Bowl XXI, on January 25, 1987.

The newer United States Football League (USFL), which had started play in 1983, won an antitrust suit against the NFL but was awarded only a token $1 of the $1.69 billion it had sought in damages.

A pleased Pete Rozelle, commissioner of the National Football League, speaks to the press after a U.S. district court found the NFL guilty on one count of violating antitrust laws but awarded the rival United States Football League, which had brought the suit, only $1 in damages.

College. After the regular season, Miami of Florida and Penn State, both with 11 victories in 11 games, were the only major colleges with undefeated records. The wire-service polls ranked Miami first in the nation, Penn State second, and Oklahoma third. But Penn State upset Miami, 14-10, in the Fiesta Bowl on January 2, 1987, in Tempe, Ariz., and the final wire-service polls put Penn State first, with Miami second and Oklahoma third. (Separate computer rankings by the New York *Times* and *USA Today* placed Oklahoma first, Penn State second, and Miami third.)

Oklahoma went to the Orange Bowl without star linebacker Brian Bosworth, when a mandatory NCAA drug test revealed traces of anabolic steroids in his system. The Sooners defeated Arkansas anyway, 42-8, while Bosworth walked the sidelines in a shirt reading "National Communists Against Athletes." Arizona State, playing in its first Rose Bowl, defeated Michigan, 22-15. Ohio State, in the

Penn State running back D. J. Dozier (number 42, at center, in blue jersey) goes 6 yards for the dramatic touchdown that clinched his team's Fiesta Bowl victory over the favored University of Miami Hurricanes.

first Cotton Bowl appearance by a Big Ten team, trounced Texas A&M, 28-12.

Vinny Testaverde, Miami's senior quarterback, was voted the Heisman Trophy in December 1986 as the outstanding U.S. college player. However, after he had thrown only nine intercepted passes in the regular season, he threw five in the Fiesta Bowl. Other players of note included Temple running back Paul Palmer, two-way player Gordon Lockbaum of Division I-AA Holy Cross, and Penn State running back D. J. Dozier.

Professional. The NFL's average attendance of 60,635 was its second highest ever. The best regular-season records were achieved by the Giants (14-2), the Chicago Bears (14-2), the Cleveland Browns (12-4), the Washington Redskins (12-4), the Broncos (11-5), and the New England Patriots (11-5). They were among the ten teams that advanced to the conference playoffs leading to the Super Bowl. In the conference championship games on January 11, the Giants shut out the Redskins, 17-0, and the Broncos beat the Browns in overtime,

23-20. Two weeks later, the Giants trounced the Broncos in Pasadena, Calif., 39-20.

The defending champion Bears, despite their regular-season success, were eliminated in their first playoff game by the Redskins, 27-13. Doug Flutie, the former USFL quarterback signed by the Bears in midseason, started for them because Jim McMahon had undergone shoulder surgery. McMahon, who had led Chicago to victory in Super Bowl XX, was limited to six games in the 1986 season because of injuries. The Associated Press chose Lawrence Taylor, the Giants' outside linebacker, as the league's most valuable player and Bill Parcells of the Giants as coach of the year.

This was the last year of the NFL's television contracts with CBS, NBC, and ABC and the final year of the NFL's collective bargaining agreement with its players. Richard Kasher, an arbitrator, ruled that the NFL could not unilaterally impose a new drug-testing plan on the players; the subject was expected to be discussed in negotiations for a new agreement.

Despite the importance of the looming television and labor relations negotiations, the NFL's major concern was the suit by the USFL. The new league had started in 1983, playing in the spring. When it voted in 1985 to switch to a fall schedule for 1986, none of the three major TV networks would agree to broadcast its fall games. The USFL, which could not continue without television income, sued the NFL. It said the NFL had monopolized pro football, had conspired to put the USFL out of business, and had put pressure on the three major networks not to televise USFL games. The NFL responded that if it was a monopoly, it had not tried to become one, and contended that the USFL's four-year losses of $163 million had resulted from poor business decisions.

The trial began in New York on May 12. On July 29 the jury found the NFL guilty of violating one antitrust law. However, it awarded the USFL only $1 (which, under the triple-damages provision of federal law, became $3). Both

sides considered the outcome a victory for the NFL. The USFL promptly called off its 1986 fall season, and an appeal of the verdict failed in October. Despite the result of the suit, three of the USFL's eight remaining teams wanted to play in 1986, but they were outvoted. Though the USFL said it planned a 1987 season, it released all its players from their contracts, and many, such as Herschel Walker and Jim Kelly, both of the New Jersey Generals, signed with NFL teams.

Five retired players—Paul Hornung, Fran Tarkenton, Willie Lanier, Ken Houston, and Doak Walker—were voted into the Pro Football Hall of Fame. In Canada, the Hamilton Tiger-Cats won the Grey Cup, becoming Canadian Football League champions by defeating the Edmonton Eskimos, 39-15, November 30 in Vancouver, British Columbia.   F.L.

GOLF

A couple of old-timers, Jack Nicklaus and Raymond Floyd, showed the younger players of the Professional Golfers' Association (PGA) tour that they were not worn out, by winning the Masters and the U.S. Open, respectively. Nicklaus at 46 was the oldest winner in the tournament's history; still four behind at the end of the third round, he recovered to win his sixth Masters and defy pundits' predictions. Floyd, at 43, won the first open of his career.

The four major men's championships had dramatic finishes; Greg Norman was involved in all, winning one—the British Open—but narrowly losing the PGA Championship to Bob Tway. He did go on to win the European Open in sudden death over England's Ken Brown, becoming the first player to take both the British and the European opens the same year. For the first time, 2 golfers on the men's tour exceeded $600,000 in PGA earnings, while 12 more amassed over $300,000.

PGA Tour Commissioner Deane Beman suspended Spain's Severiano Ballesteros for all but one of the tour events because he had failed to play in the required number of tournaments in 1985.

The Ladies Professional Golf Association tour was dominated by Pat Bradley, who won the LPGA Championship, the Nabisco Dinah Shore, and the du Maurier Classic, three of the four major championships, becoming the first woman

---

The UK Tackles Football

That "subtle blend of chess, ballet, and grievous bodily harm" known in the United States as football, and elsewhere as gridiron or American football, is catching on across the Atlantic. Over a hundred teams playing football American-style have sprung up in England, with names like the Heathrow Jets and the Streatham All Powerful Olympians. Millions of Britishers stay up late to watch the Super Bowl on live TV and enjoy *American Football*, a program of recorded highlights from the week's National Football League games. Why should American football hold interest for Britons brought up on cricket, soccer, and rugby? They seem fascinated by the strategy, the physical contact, the sheer bulk of the players, and the glamour of celebrities like Jim McMahon and William "The Refrigerator" Perry. Also, the British teams have not achieved a level of play to match their American counterparts (a visiting City College of San Francisco team once beat the Brighton B-52's by a score of 76-0). But observers say the home-grown squads are improving, and Anheuser-Busch has stepped in to sponsor a "Budweiser League," giving a boost to Britain's newest spectator sport.

Jack Nicklaus birdies the 17th hole on the road to winning his sixth Masters. At age 46, he was the oldest winner in the tournament's history.

24-year-old Yuri Korolev of the Soviet Union, the world champion, and 22-year-old Li Ning of China, the winner in the last World Cup in 1982. In the women's all-around, 17-year-old Elena Shoushounova of the Soviet Union, the world champion, held off 16-year-old Daniela Silivas of Romania, 39.825 to 39.70, out of a possible 40.

From 1983 through 1985, Mary Lou Retton of the United States won the American Cup women's competition. She did not enter the competition in 1986 and announced in late September that she was retiring, at age 18, from gymnastics competition. The new winner was 13-year-old Kristie Phillips of Baton Rouge, La., the youngest gymnast ever to compete for the trophy. Aleksei Tikhonkin of the Soviet Union was the men's winner, with Brian Ginsberg of Los Angeles second.   F.L.

HARNESS RACING

At the Hambletonian in East Rutherford, N.J., on August 2, Ulf Thoresen of Norway guided Nuclear Kosmos to straight-heat victories and a purse of $586,041. Riding Habib, he went on to win the prestigious Roosevelt International Trot at Roosevelt Raceway on August 23, becoming the first driver to win both those events the same year. Gunslinger Spur won the Yonkers Trot but was declared ineligible for the Kentucky Futurity, taken by Sugarcane Hanover. Barberry Spur won the first two legs of pacing's triple crown, but failed to take the Messenger at Roosevelt Raceway, won by Amity Chief.

On July 5, Billy Haughton, the Babe Ruth of standardbred racing, suffered fatal injuries when a horse in front of him stumbled and he was catapulted from his sulky.   W.L.

HORSE RACING

Charlie Whittingham is regarded as the dean of American horse trainers, but until May 3, 1986, he had never won the country's premier race, the Kentucky Derby. It had been his long-held belief that the 1¼-mile race for three-year-olds demanded too much of a horse so early in its career. Whittingham, 73, had had only two previous Derby starters before he entered Ferdinand for the 112th running of the race, which carried a purse of $784,600. He chose 54-year-old Bill Shoemaker as Ferdinand's jockey.

to achieve a career Grand Slam. Jane Geddes won the other major championship, the U.S. Open, in her first victory of any kind on the LPGA tour. Bradley was the year's top female money-earner, taking in more than $400,000 and becoming the first woman to surpass $2 million in career winnings.   T.McC.

GYMNASTICS

The Soviet Union continued its domination of gymnastics in 1986. In the year's most important competition, the World Cup, held August 30 to September 1 in Peking, the Soviets won 11 gold, 4 silver, and 5 bronze medals, far more than any other nation. China was next with 4 gold and 3 bronze. The United States did not come close to winning a medal.

The men's all-around ended in a tie between

The crowd of 123,189 had dismissed Ferdinand at odds of almost 18-1 in the field of 16 starters. After the first half-mile, Ferdinand was the caboose on the train, but by three-quarters of a mile he had passed five opponents; he then went by six others to reach the fifth position at the end of a mile. Approaching the top of the stretch, Ferdinand ran between horses until Shoemaker sent his mount through to win by 2¼ lengths over Bold Arrangement. Broad Brush was third and the 2-1 betting favorite, Snow Chief, 11th. The moderate running time of 2:02⅘ was good enough to earn Ferdinand a winner's share of $609,400.

Later, Whittingham won the Budweiser-Arlington Park Million in Chicago with Estrapade, a six-year-old mare who became the first female winner of the Million when she galloped away from the field to win by five lengths under jockey Fernando Toro in 2:00⅘.

The mystery of the Derby was Snow Chief, who between December 15, 1985, and April 6 had won five consecutive stakes and stuffed his saddlebags with $1,719,040 in earnings. On May 17, he tried Ferdinand and six other starters in the $534,400 Preakness Stakes, the second leg of the Triple Crown. He atoned for his Derby loss by beating Ferdinand by four lengths in 1:54⅘ under rider Alex Solis. Later, Snow Chief won the $1 million Jersey Derby at Garden State Park in Cherry Hill, N.J., by two lengths.

Although Snow Chief did not compete in the Belmont, the event had its share of drama, as Woodford Cefis (Woody) Stephens, the 72-year-old trainer who had won four consecutive Belmonts, provided another winner. Stephens's Danzig Connection, who had raced only three times in 1986, winning only the Peter Pan at Belmont Park, was an 8-1 proposition in the betting. He fought off several challenges before getting clear to win by 1¼ lengths in 2:29⅘. John's Treasure finished second, a neck in front of Ferdinand, who was the only three-year-old to try all the Triple Crown races.

The two leading entries in the 1¼-mile

Moving from dead last to head of the pack, Ferdinand was given a classic ride by veteran jockey Bill Shoemaker to win the 112th Kentucky Derby by 2¼ lengths; it was trainer Charlie Wittingham's first Derby triumph.

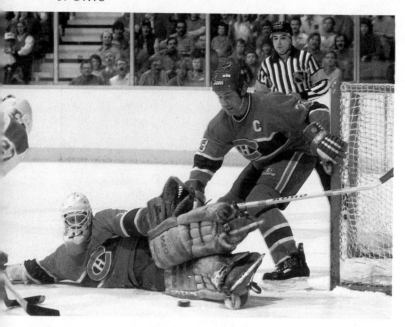

Twenty-year-old rookie goal-tender Patrick Roy stops the puck, as the Montréal Canadiens beat the Calgary Flames in the NHL championship final for their 23rd Stanley Cup. Roy was the youngest player ever to receive the Conn Smythe trophy for most valuable player in the postseason.

Marlboro Cup Handicap at Belmont were Precisionist, the favorite, and Turkoman. Approaching the top of the stretch, the two ran briefly in tandem before Turkoman pulled away to win by 1½ lengths. In the Jockey Club Gold Cup, Creme Fraiche, benefiting from a slow early pace, took the lead with ⅛ mile remaining in the 1½-mile race and held on to win by a desperate head from Turkoman.   W.L.

ICE HOCKEY

The Montréal Canadiens magnificently finished the 1985–1986 National Hockey League season by capturing their 23rd Stanley Cup. The victory made them North America's most successful professional sports team in history. The Canadiens used a defense-oriented strategy centered on rookie goalkeeper Patrick Roy, who was voted most valuable player in postseason competition; at 20, he was the youngest player ever to receive this award. On May 16 the Canadiens lost the first game of the best-of-seven finals to the Calgary Flames, 5-2; Montréal then roared back to gain four consecutive triumphs, during which they yielded only eight goals. In game four, Roy became the first rookie goalkeeper to post a shutout in the Stanley Cup finals since 1955. Unfortunately, the contest was marred by a lengthy

postgame brawl that resulted in fines to both teams totaling $42,000. (In October, NHL team owners adopted a rule calling for two extra penalty minutes for any player who starts a fight during a game.)

During the 80-game regular season, Montréal achieved a total of 40 victories, 33 defeats, and 7 ties for 87 points (two points for each victory, one for each tie). That was 32 points behind the Edmonton Oilers, the leader in points. However, the Canadiens won 15 of 20 postseason games, yielding only 41 goals. The Flames, meanwhile, created shock waves by upsetting the Edmonton Oilers, who were heavily favored to retain the Stanley Cup for the third year. All four teams leading their division at the end of the regular season were eliminated during the playoffs. The Québec Nordiques, ahead in the Adams Division, were stunned by fourth-place Hartford. The Chicago Black Hawks, leaders in the Norris Division, were eliminated by the Toronto Maple Leafs. The Philadelphia Flyers, who won the strong Patrick Division, were felled by the fourth-place New York Rangers.

Awards. Wayne Gretzky, center for the Oilers, amassed 52 goals and 163 assists for 215 points, capturing a record sixth consecutive scoring

NATIONAL HOCKEY LEAGUE
1985–1986 Regular Season

PRINCE OF WALES CONFERENCE

Patrick Division	W	L	T	Pts.
Philadelphia Flyers	53	23	4	110
Washington Capitals	50	23	7	107
New York Islanders	39	29	12	90
New York Rangers	36	38	6	78
Pittsburgh Penguins	34	38	8	76
New Jersey Devils	28	49	3	59

Adams Division	W	L	T	Pts.
Québec Nordiques	43	31	6	92
Montréal Canadiens	40	33	7	87
Boston Bruins	37	31	12	86
Hartford Whalers	40	36	4	84
Buffalo Sabres	37	37	6	80

CAMPBELL CONFERENCE

Norris Division	W	L	T	Pts.
Chicago Black Hawks	39	33	8	86
Minnesota North Stars	38	33	9	85
St. Louis Blues	37	34	9	83
Toronto Maple Leafs	25	48	7	57
Detroit Red Wings	17	57	6	40

Smythe Division	W	L	T	Pts.
Edmonton Oilers	56	17	7	119
Calgary Flames	40	31	9	89
Winnipeg Jets	26	47	7	59
Vancouver Canucks	23	44	13	59
Los Angeles Kings	23	49	8	54

STANLEY CUP PLAYOFFS

Division Semifinals
Hartford defeated Québec, 3 games to 0.
Toronto defeated Chicago, 3 games to 0.
Washington defeated N.Y. Islanders, 3 games to 0.
N.Y. Rangers defeated Philadelphia, 3 games to 2.
Edmonton defeated Winnipeg, 3 games to 0.
Montréal defeated Boston, 3 games to 0.
St. Louis defeated Minnesota, 3 games to 2.
Calgary defeated Vancouver, 3 games to 0.

Division Finals
N.Y. Rangers defeated Washington, 4 games to 2.
Calgary defeated Edmonton, 4 games to 3.
St. Louis defeated Toronto, 4 games to 3.
Montréal defeated Hartford, 4 games to 3.

Conference Finals
Montréal defeated N.Y. Rangers, 4 games to 1.
Calgary defeated St. Louis, 4 games to 3.

Championship Finals
Montréal defeated Calgary, 4 games to 1.

Eighteen-year-old Debi Thomas dominated women's figure skating during 1986, winning both the U.S. and World Championships. A pre-med student at Stanford University, Thomas became the first black skater to hold either title.

title and being named the regular season's most valuable player for an unprecedented seventh time in a row. B.V.

ICE SKATING

The 1986 figure skating season was filled with surprises, as several new champions emerged. Brian Boitano retained the U.S. senior men's figure skating title; fellow Californian Debi Thomas, the 1985 women's runner-up, became the first black senior women's champion, dethroning 1985 champion Tiffany Chen, who was sidelined for much of the season. In a major upset, Gillian Wachsman and Todd Waggoner of Delaware defeated the 1985 champions, Jill Watson and Peter Oppegard, for the pairs title. Renee Roca and Donald Adair of Michigan edged out favorites Suzanne Semanick and Scott Gregory for the ice dancing title. During the 76th World Figure Skating Championships, three reigning titlists were upset. Boitano won the long program and took the gold medal as world champion. Thomas gained the women's world championship. In a stunning upset, 14-year-old Ekatarina Gordeeva and 19-year-old Sergei Grinkov won both the short and long programs to defeat fellow Soviets Elena Valova and Oleg Vasiliev in the pairs competition.

At the World Speed Skating Championship, Hein Vergeer of the Netherlands successfully defended his title. East Germans took the three top spots in the women's competition, with Karin Kania taking three of the four races for first place. Just two weeks later, she won the women's sprint championship with a dazzling display. Igor Zhelezovski of the Soviet Union again won the men's sprint title.   D.M.

SKIING

The question of how much control skiers should be allowed to exert over the sport spilled into the open in March, when World Cup racers, protesting the supposedly advantageous weather conditions for the first skiers on the course, blocked an Aspen, Colo., racecourse, preventing a giant slalom event from being held. Although skiing's amateur format seemed safe for the time being, many felt that growing discontent could lead to a new era of "open" competition in the sport, with the athletes deciding when and where to compete and receiving prize money, as in tennis and golf.

In World Cup play, the renewed battle between the men's circuit's only triple (downhill, slalom, giant slalom) threats—Switzerland's Pirmin Zurbriggen and Austrian-turned-Luxembourger Marc Girardelli—came down to the final slalom, at Bromont, Québec. Girardelli skied off course, but Zurbriggen was unable to come away with the necessary win for the overall title. Peter Wirnsberger locked up the downhill title, winning four consecutive victories by the end of January. Roc Petrovic of Yugoslavia took the slalom title, and Switzerland's Joel Gaspoz the giant slalom. West Germany's Markus Wasmaier won the super giant slalom and combined crowns. In a memorable comeback, Sweden's Ingemar Stenmark ended up second in the slalom and giant slalom standings. Switzerland's Maria Walliser was overall women's champion.

Sweden's Gunde Svan again left the field behind in the Nordic World Cup, capturing five of nine races. Marjo Matikänen of Finland edged out her competitors for the women's title. The ski-alike Halsnes brothers, Jarle and Edvin, dominated the Peugeot Grand Prix Alpine pro circuit for the third year.   S.C.

SOCCER

World Soccer. Argentina won the 13th edition of the World Cup, hosted by Mexico in June, for its second championship in the last three World Cups. The team's captain, Diego Maradona, performed brilliantly and confirmed his right to the title of the world's best soccer player.

Morocco became the first African country ever to advance beyond the first round in World Cup play (it was then narrowly defeated by West Germany). In the quarterfinals, England met Argentina in the first soccer match between the national teams since the 1982 Falkland Islands war. Criticism of the refereeing reached a climax during this game, when the Tunisian referee allowed a goal by Maradona, even though he had punched the ball home with his fist. This illegal goal was overshadowed when, four minutes later, Maradona set off on a spectacular 60-yard run on which he beat five English defenders before faking out goalkeeper Peter Shilton to score a spectacular goal.

In the other quarterfinals, Brazil was bested by France, West Germany overcame Mexico, and the surprising Belgians beat Spain. The West Germans took their semifinal match with France, 2-0, and Argentina beat Belgium, 2-0, on two more superb goals from Maradona. France beat Belgium, 4-2, for third place. In the final, after Germany tied the score at 2-2 with ten minutes left, Maradona sent Jorge Burruchaga away with an exquisitely timed pass. Burruchaga drew out goalkeeper Harald (Toni) Schumacher and calmly slipped the ball past him for the winning goal. Maradona was viewed as the tournament's all-around most valuable player; England's Gary Lineker was the top scorer, with six goals. The final game was seen on television by nearly 600 million people in 160 nations.

South America. The 1985 South American club championship (the Libertadores Cup) was won by Argentinos Juniors of Buenos Aires. The South American Player of the Year award went to Julio César Romero of the Brazilian club Fluminense.

Europe. The ban on English clubs playing in Europe was continued. When Manchester United and West Ham United were allowed to play preseason exhibition games on the continent, fans of the two clubs got into a vicious fight on a ferryboat crossing the English Channel. The vessel had to return to England.

In European club competition, Eastern European teams took two trophies, for the first time. In the European Cup final, Steaua of Bucharest, Romania, beat Barcelona on penalty kicks after a 0-0 tie, while Dynamo Kiev (Soviet Union) took the Cup Winners' Cup with a 3-0 victory over Atlético Madrid. Italy's Juventus, the 1985 European champions, beat Argentinos Juniors of Buenos Aires, taking the Toyota Cup and the unofficial title of world club champions.

Liverpool won the English First Division for a record 16th time and took the English Football Association Cup as well. France's Michel Platini was again named European Player of the Year.

United States. The absence of a national pro league continued to prove a major obstacle to forming a national team that would be competitive at the world level. The championship of the Major Indoor Soccer League (MISL) was again won by the San Diego Sockers. Bill Kentling was named MISL commissioner.

The U.S. women's team was impressive in an international tournament in Italy, beating China, Brazil, and Japan before losing, 1-0, to Italy in the final.   P.G.

SWIMMING

U.S. dominance in swimming was shaken in 1986. While several Americans, notably Matt Biondi, did well at the fifth World Aquatics Championships held at Madrid in August, the overall performance was the poorest ever by U.S. swimmers at a major international meet. Americans won only 9 gold medals, compared with East Germany's high of 14—although the United States still had the highest total, 32. An intestinal disorder affecting several American swimmers (among others) may have been a factor.

But hardly anything stopped Biondi, who won 3 gold, 1 silver, and 3 bronze medals. Though his only individual victory came in the 100-meter freestyle (in 48.94 seconds), as the anchor leg he helped notch American triumphs in the 400-m freestyle relay (3 minutes, 19.89 seconds) and the 400-m medley relay (3:41.25).

Another outstanding male performer was West German Michael Gross, who won the 200-m freestyle (1:47.92) and the 200-m butterfly (1:56.53) plus two bronze medals. The major winners among the women were East Germans Kristin Otto and Heike Friedrich, who took 10 medals (including 8 gold) between them. Otto won the 100-m freestyle (55.05 seconds) and the 200-m individual medley (2:15.56) and set a 100-m world record of 54.73 seconds on the opening leg of the 400-m freestyle relay. Friedrich won the 200-m (1:58.26) and 400-m (4:07.45) freestyle.

The United States shone at the Goodwill Games at Moscow in July, besting the host in total medals (39 to 29) and gold medals.

One notable men's record set during the year was by Vladimir Salnikov of the Soviet Union in 800-m freestyle (7:50.64).   F.L.

Diego Maradona (at right), acclaimed as probably the world's best soccer player, led the Argentine team to victory in the 13th World Cup competition, hosted by Mexico in June.

"Beckermania"

A redheaded West German youth named Boris Becker defied the myth that lightning never strikes in the same place twice, when he won the Wimbledon men's singles title in summer 1986 for the second year in a row. In the 12 months following his 1985 win (when he was the youngest—and only unseeded—player ever to triumph at Wimbledon), Becker's record had been spotty; in 18 competitions, he had won only twice. But at Wimbledon in 1986 his serves were lethal and his volleys masterful, as he moved up to the final and then beat number-one-ranked Ivan Lendl in straight sets. A millionaire at 18, Becker continued to be followed, off court as well as on, by reporters, TV crews, gossip columnists, and fans. His easygoing personality, boyish smile, and sense of humor added to the "Beckermania." By the end of November, he had won six Grand Prix events for the year and established himself as the world's number-two player. Defeated by Lendl in December's Nabisco Masters, he hoped to come back in 1987 and advance to number one.

Boris Becker

TENNIS

In 1986, Czechoslovakia's Ivan Lendl was the dominant male tennis player, with West Germany's Boris Becker struggling to challenge his position and American superstar John McEnroe on leave of absence for much of the year. Czech-born Martina Navratilova (now a U.S. citizen) and American Chris Evert Lloyd once again dominated women's tennis.

Women's Tour. Both Navratilova and Evert Lloyd did well in tournaments early in the year. After a six-week break, Evert Lloyd gained her 143rd career title, besting West German teenager Steffi Graf at the Virginia Slims of Florida event, 6-3, 6-1. In mid-March, Navratilova won the Virginia Slims Championships in New York, becoming overall 1985 women's tour winner, in her third such victory in a row. She defeated Czechoslovakia's Hana Mandlikova, 6-2, 6-0, 3-6, 6-1, in a final touted as a milestone for women's tennis because the two women played a best-of-five match and went four sets.

Graf had her own winning streak in mid-April. In the Family Circle Magazine Cup at Hilton Head Island, S.C., she upset Evert Lloyd in the final, 6-4, 7-5, for her first pro title. Then, in successive tournaments, Graf won three more titles, one of them by stunning Navratilova, 6-2, 6-3, in the final of the German Open.

In the French Open, Navratilova and defending champion Evert Lloyd went head to head in the final round. Evert Lloyd's win gave her at least one Grand Slam singles title in each of the last 13 years, a record many experts predicted would never be broken.

Men's Tour. The early part of the 1986 season unquestionably belonged to the already dominant Lendl, who won the first four tournaments he entered. His 29-match winning streak was finally stopped by Becker in the final of the Volvo-Chicago event, 7-6, 6-3. At the French Open, Lendl captured his third Grand Slam title, beating Mikael Pernfors, a Swede, in the final. Lendl ended 1986 still number one, despite a major setback at Wimbledon.

Wimbledon. At the 1986 All-England Lawn Tennis Championships, Navratilova won her fifth consecutive singles title and her seventh overall, knocking out Mandlikova after the latter had upset Evert Lloyd in the semifinals. In men's play, Becker had been considered a long shot to defend his singles title, but he reached the finals and then defeated Lendl in straight sets, 6-4, 6-3, 7-5. Lendl had barely managed to beat American Tim Mayotte in a grueling quarter-final and then had narrowly survived a semifinal marathon against unseeded Yugoslav Slobodan Zivojinovic. In men's doubles, the Swedish team of Mats Wilander and Joakim Nystrom defeated the U.S. pair of Gary Donnelly and Peter Fleming. Navratilova teamed with Pam Shriver to beat Mandlikova and Wendy Turnbull in the women's doubles final. In mixed-doubles play, Kathy Jordan and Ken Flach of the United States stopped Navratilova's quest for a sweep of the Wimbledon titles by downing Navratilova and her partner, Heinz Gunthardt of Switzerland, 6-3, 7-6.

U.S. Open. Lendl won his second consecutive U.S. Open singles title, beating fellow Czech Miloslav Mecir, 6-4, 6-2, 6-0, in the final. The most interesting match of the women's competition was a semifinal encounter between Navratilova and Graf that was interrupted for 22 hours by rain. Navratilova finally won the tense match, then quickly disposed of Czech Helena Sukova in the final to win her third U.S. Open singles title.

Team Competition. At the women's Federation Cup, held in Prague, Navratilova went unde-feated to help gain victory over the host team of Czechoslovakia, 3-0, in her first visit to her native country in 11 years. In men's Davis Cup play, the U.S. team lost to Australia, and the Czechoslovakian team to Sweden, in the semifinals. Pat Cash defeated Pernfors in the finals, to clinch the title for Australia, for the 26th time.   R.J.L.

TRACK AND FIELD

In a sport traditionally dominated by men, women made a strong impact in 1986. The outstanding women included Jackie Joyner of Los Angeles, Heike Drechsler of East Germany, Ingrid Kristiansen of Norway, and Yordanka Donkova of Bulgaria.

No athlete was more impressive than the 24-year-old Joyner, a native of East St. Louis, Ill. In 1986, she broke the world record for the heptathlon twice in 27 days and became the first to surpass 7,000 points in this two-day, seven-event test for women.

Although the East German women remained the best in the world, their only record-breaker was Drechsler. She raised her world record in the long jump to 24'5½" on June 21 in Moscow and equaled the record on July 3 in Dresden, East Germany. She also became a world-record holder in the sprints, equaling the 200-meter record of 21.71 seconds on June 29 in Jena, East Germany, and again on August 29 in the European championships in Stuttgart, West Germany.

Jackie Joyner of Los Angeles, considered the world's best all-around female athlete, set a new world record of 7,161 points in the heptathlon, a seven-event test for women, at the U.S. Olympic Festival in Houston. Here she runs the 100-meter hurdles.

The 30-year-old Kristiansen decimated the world records for 5,000 and 10,000 m and became the first runner, male or female, to hold simultaneous world records in those events and the marathon. The 24-year-old Donkova bettered the world record for the 100-m hurdles four times in 26 days.

In 1985, Sergei Bubka of the Soviet Union became the first person to pole-vault 6 meters, or 19'8¼". On July 8, 1986, before an adoring Moscow crowd at the Goodwill Games, the Soviet athlete raised the record to 19'8¾", clearing the bar by at least 8 inches.

World records were set by Udo Beyer of East Germany in the shot-put (74'3½", August 20, in East Berlin), Jurgen Schult of East Germany in the discus throw (243', June 6, in Neubrandenburg, East Germany), and Yury Sedykh of the Soviet Union in the hammer throw (284'4", June 22, in Tallinn, Soviet Union, and 284'7", August 30, in Stuttgart).   F.L.

YACHTING

From October 1986 through January 1987, elimination races took place in the waters off Fremantle, Western Australia, to select an Australian defender and a foreign challenger for the America's Cup, the coveted trophy wrested from the United States in 1983. The final Australian contenders to defend the Cup were the *Australia IV*, a descendant of *Australia II*, the 1983 Cup winner; *Kookaburra III*, in the lead late in 1986; and *Steak 'n' Kidney.* Four challengers survived to compete in the semifinals starting December 28: *New Zealand,* the leader; *Stars & Stripes,* in second place, skippered by Dennis Connor, who lost the Cup in 1983; *USA*; and *French Kiss.* The two winners in the semifinals were *Stars & Stripes* and *Kookaburra III*; they competed in the final series beginning January 31, 1987.

Arriving in Bermuda on April 11 aboard his 60-foot sloop *American Promise,* 54-year-old Dodge Morgan of Cape Elizabeth, Me., became the first American to sail alone around the world nonstop, and in a record 150 days.

French sailor Loic Caradec teamed with Olivier Despaigne to win the Carlsberg Transatlantic doublehanded race with the catamaran *Royale.* France also cheered the victory of Lionel Pean's *L'Esprit d'Equipe* in the Whitbread Round-the-World race.   D.M.P.

New Zealand (below), the first fiberglass boat in America's Cup history, sailed to a 44-point year-end lead in elimination trials begun off the coast of Fremantle, Western Australia, in October. But New Zealand's hopes of capturing the prestigious trophy sank when United States entry Stars & Stripes (above) came back to win the elimination finals in January 1987, earning the right to challenge Australian defender Kookaburra III in the championship round.

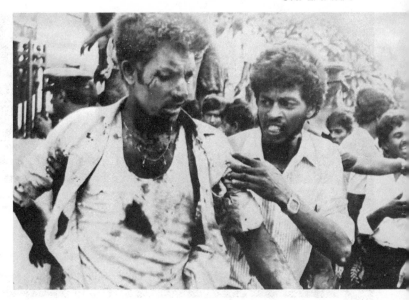

Bloodshed continued between minority Tamils and the Sinhalese majority in Sri Lanka. Here, an injured man is helped from the scene following a bomb explosion at Colombo's Central Telegraph Office on May 7.

SRI LANKA. Clashes between the Buddhist Sinhalese majority and the Hindu Tamil minority dominated events in Sri Lanka during 1986. Frequent warfare and casualties marked the conflict between Tamil separatist guerrillas and the government, but attempts to negotiate a peaceful solution offered some promise.

Negotiations between the government and the Tamil United Liberation Front (TULF) continued, with the Indian government acting as intermediary. In June the Sri Lankan government offered to give the Eastern and Northern provinces a special status, with their own assemblies and police forces. India later endorsed the proposal. The TULF, however, insisted on one unified Tamil province.

Haunting the negotiations was uncertainty over acceptance by Tamil guerrilla groups, known as the Tigers, of any agreement that might result. Heavy fighting between several Tiger groups erupted in April and May; the Liberation Tigers of Tamil Eelam (LTTE) emerged victorious and in October announced they would declare an independent Tamil state in northern Sri Lanka in January 1987. In November, India rounded up hundreds of Tamil guerrillas and placed several guerrilla leaders under house arrest at their base in Madras, marking an unexpected shift in India's willingness to help put an end to Sri Lankan fighting.

Bloodshed between Tamils and Sinhalese was continuing at an alarming rate. A rash of bombings in May and June caused 70 deaths; 16 of these resulted from the May 3 bombing of an Air Lanka plane loaded with tourists.

On January 1 the government restored the civil rights of former Prime Minister Sirimavo Bandaranaike, allowing her to resume leadership of the opposition Sri Lanka Freedom Party. Her return invigorated the party.

The economy suffered from budget problems brought on by the declining tourism, low world prices for tea and coconuts, and lagging foreign investment. Sri Lanka's main development project, the Mahaweli irrigation scheme, was plagued by guerrilla attacks that hampered construction, by an outbreak of encephalitis in newly opened irrigated lands, and by the April 20 collapse of the Kantalai dam, which inundated villages and left over 100 people dead and some 2,000 homeless.

The government was embarrassed by publicity given to Tamil refugees fleeing the ethnic conflict. Several European countries tightened visa requirements in response. In August, 155 Tamils were discovered in small boats off the Canadian coast, where they had been left by a German ship captain whom they had paid to take them to Canada.

See STATISTICS OF THE WORLD.   R.C.O.

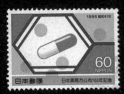

STAMPS, POSTAGE. The Statue of Liberty centennial, the AMERIPEX stamp show, national heritages, and various anniversaries were among themes noted on postage stamps issued during 1986.

United States Issues. An impressive total of 67 U.S. commemorative and special stamps were released during the year. Among those honored were black abolitionist Sojourner Truth, poet T. S. Eliot, and musician Duke Ellington. A special block of four se-tenant commemoratives (stamps attached together, each with a different design) honored polar explorers; two other blocks featured Navajo art and early American carved wooden figures. Other themes featured on U.S. stamps included the Statue of Liberty centennial (a joint issue with France), the 150th anniversaries of Arkansas and Texas, and the role of public hospitals.

A unique group of four miniature sheets with nine different stamps each was released on May 22 when AMERIPEX '86 opened; the international stamp show, held in Chicago, attracted 160,000 people, a record for a stamp show. The special stamps honored the 35 deceased U.S. presidents, with one stamp picturing the White House. A commemorative stamp booklet on stamp collecting contained two panes of four different designs (*see color plate*). Another such booklet featured U.S. fish, with two panels of five different designs.

Three special annual stamps were issued. One featured the "love" theme; the other two were contemporary and traditional Christmas designs. New definitive stamps were released with values of 1¢, 3¢, 4¢, 5¢, 5.5¢, 17¢, 25¢, 56¢, $1.00, and $2.00.

Worldwide Issues. Two new stamp-issuing entities were recognized by the Universal Postal Union: the Caribbean island of Aruba, in the Netherlands Antilles, and the former French colony of St. Pierre and Miquelon, near Newfoundland. Many special stamps recognized 1986 as International Peace Year. Also commemorated were the centennial of the Statue of Liberty, the passage of Halley's comet, the World Cup soccer matches held in Mexico City, and AMERIPEX. Members of the European Communities issued their annual Europa stamps, with the theme of environmental conservation. British Commonwealth members produced special stamps to commemorate the 13th Commonwealth Games, held in Edinburgh, Scotland, as well as the royal wedding of Prince Andrew and Sarah Ferguson, Queen Elizabeth's 60th birthday, and the 86th birthday of the queen mother.

United Nations Issues. The United Nations Postal Administration released five special issues, on Africa in Crisis, the United Nations Development Program, Philately—The International Hobby, the International Year of Peace, and the 40th Anniversary of the World Federation of UN Associations. On September 19 the UNPA released the seventh group of 16 stamps in its continuing flag series. The countries represented were: New Zealand, Laos, Upper Volta (Burkina Faso), the Gambia, Maldives, Ethiopia, Jordan, Zambia, Iceland, Antigua and Barbuda, Angola, Botswana, Romania, Togo, Mauritania, and Colombia.

J.W.K.

Opposite page: Some outstanding stamp issues of 1986. Top row (left to right): The Channel Island of Jersey commemorates a royal wedding; the United States and France release a joint issue for the centennial of the Statue of Liberty; Ireland observes the International Year of Peace. Second row: Hong Kong hails the arrival of Halley's comet; Japan stresses drug awareness; the Isle of Man publicizes the 1986 Commonwealth Games. Third row: a pane from the first commemorative stamp booklet issued by the United States. Fourth row: Iceland pays tribute to the Nordic Council; Chile takes note of the World Cup soccer matches, held in Mexico City; Barbados recognizes AMERIPEX '86. Fifth row: Faroe Islands honors Amnesty International; Great Britain celebrates Queen Elizabeth's 60th birthday; Canada looks forward to the 1988 winter Olympics, to be held in Calgary, Alberta.

STATE GOVERNMENT REVIEW. For state governments, whether 1986 was a good or a bad year depended very much on location. The New England and Middle-Atlantic states generally were well off, while Midwestern farm states suffered, along with Southern and Western oil- and timber-dependent states. There was a resurgence of budget-cutting, with at least 18 states reducing their spending from planned levels. Only a few made cutbacks that required layoffs of government workers.

After the November elections, Democrats were set to hold 26 governorships in 1987,

The skyrocketing cost—and increasing scarcity—of liability insurance is hitting Americans where they live—and play. Workers here are pictured dismantling an uninsured playground in the city of Chicago.

with Republicans controlling 24 statehouses. This was a sizable shift from the 34-16 margin the Democrats had held prior to the elections. Democrats did well in state legislatures, however, scoring a net gain of about 180 seats out of the 6,000 contested in the 50 states. (See ELECTIONS IN THE UNITED STATES.)

Liability Insurance Crisis. More than 1,000 bills dealing with the liability insurance crisis were considered by legislatures during the year. At least 40 states passed measures to deal with the crisis and make liability insurance affordable and obtainable by cities, schools, physicians, and companies, whose premiums have skyrocketed in recent years. Many of the laws enacted were aimed at reforming court procedures and lawyers' practices, which insurers blamed for escalating jury awards in personal injury suits. With doctors marching on some state capitols and abandoning some medical specialties because of high malpractice insurance premiums, several states responded by limiting "pain and suffering" awards and/or placing ceilings on lawyers' fees. Florida and Hawaii were among the states that both rolled back commercial liability insurance rates and limited amounts that juries could award for noneconomic damages.

California voters in June approved limits on victims' right to collect all damages from a single defendant in so-called deep-pocket cases, where a city, a state, or a hospital is required to pay for harm chiefly caused by another defendant who is unable to pay. About ten states passed legislation making it easier for municipalities to adopt self-insurance plans. Measures were also adopted to increase reporting requirements by insurers so that more information could be gained about the costs of settlements. Although the crisis appeared to have eased toward year's end, some observers believed the problem was deep-seated and would resurface in years to come.

Farm Crisis. Low agricultural prices, falling land values, and high interest payments on huge farm loans all combined to stagger farmers in the Midwest, as well as in parts of the South, which was hit by a severe drought. With farm auctions and foreclosures becoming increasingly common, more than 20 states acted to aid affected farmers and their families, as well as small towns dependent on a healthy agricultural economy. States offered emergency aid to affected farmers, set up hotlines that farmers could call for psychological or financial counseling, provided job training to those who had lost their land, limited foreclosures, and promoted economic development measures.

Economic Development. Economic development was a major concern of states, regardless of their financial condition. In the middle of its oil bust, Oklahoma appropriated money for promoting international trade. West Virginia, with its still-high jobless rates, offered tax credits to firms from out of state that would relocate there. Meanwhile, Pennsylvania, which was economically well off by comparison, expanded programs to generate public and private funds for new business. The Kentucky legislature, by approving tax and other incentives, cleared the way for building Toyota's first U.S. plant. (At the same time, Tennessee, which had landed General Motors' revolutionary Saturn plant in 1985 without concessions, learned that the plant might not be as innovative as first believed and might employ fewer workers than first expected, as a result of GM's economic woes.)

Four states, of which the largest was California, modified their tax laws affecting multinational corporations, so as to stimulate investment within their boundaries.

Meanwhile, many states sought to reduce foreign investment in South Africa by calling for U.S. businesses to pull out unless racial policies in the white-ruled country changed. Before Congress enacted U.S. economic sanctions, some 20 states, including California, acted to cease investing their own assets in corporations doing business in South Africa.

Environment. Disposing of toxins and hazardous waste continued to be prime concerns. In a move to better protect underground water supplies, states regulated underground tanks for storage of gasoline and petroleum products. In California, voters on November 4 approved a $1.2 billion toxic cleanup bond put on the ballot by citizen petitions (the legislature had also passed hazardous-waste cleanup measures), and in New Jersey voters approved a $200 million toxic-waste cleanup bond.

Education. More states focused on testing teacher competency in 1986. A few showed concern over teacher shortages and responded with programs designed to lure graduates majoring in other fields of study into teaching. Delaware,

for instance, offered a cost-free means for college graduates to become certified to teach. On another issue, following the lead of Texas and West Virginia, California enacted a "no pass, no play" law to limit participation in sports and other extracurricular activities for students who do not keep their grades up.

Most states increased their spending on public colleges and universities. Some also sought ways to ease the financial burden of obtaining a college education. Michigan became the first state to adopt for public colleges and universities a concept private colleges had begun to use; a law enacted in December provided guaranteed free tuition at any state college or university for students whose parents prepay a certain amount of money into a special trust fund. For some years, until the capital has grown sufficiently, participation in the fund would be limited, with the participants chosen by lottery.

On the Road. Eight states and the District of Columbia continued to allow 18- to 20-year-olds to buy alcoholic beverages after September 30, 1986, despite the prospect of losing a portion of federal highway aid. The U.S. Supreme Court agreed to decide on whether the funds could be withheld as provided by federal law. Also in defiance of federal sanctions, the Nebraska and Nevada legislatures enacted speed limits higher than the federal limit of 55 miles per hour. Arizona and Vermont were notified that up to 10 percent of their share of federal highway funds could be withheld because they had been found remiss in enforcing the 55-mph speed limit. A federal bill to raise the nationwide speed limit got caught in Congress's fever to adjourn for midterm elections.

Seat belts were required to be used in cars in about ten more states in 1986, but voters in Massachusetts and Nebraska repealed existing laws that had required riders in the front seat to wear seat belts. A few states mandated safety belts in school buses; particular attention was focused on school bus safety when accidents in several Southern states were publicized involving drivers under age 21.

Dealing With AIDS. By year's end, about 20 states had acted in some manner to combat the spread of the virus associated with acquired immune deficiency syndrome (AIDS). States provided for public education programs on AIDS and for measures to better protect blood supplies. Seeking to uphold the rights of AIDS victims, California banned employers and landlords from turning away AIDS-infected workers and renters, and California voters defeated a citizen initiative that could have led to quarantining AIDS victims.

Prisons. Tennessee approved a pilot test of a privately operated prison, after Kentucky instituted a similar program. Pennsylvania, alarmed by the possibility that a prison operator might bring prisoners from other states into Pennsylvania without state permission, put a moratorium on the establishment of privately run prisons in the state until mid-1987. Other states continued to study the possibility of handing over prison management to private contractors.

Politics. Looking ahead to 1988, more Southern states chose to participate in a regional Southern primary election during the week of March 8, 1988, for selecting Democratic and Republican presidential nominees. Texas became the latest of 13 Southern states to act, bringing with it the biggest bloc of votes.

In Louisiana, Governor Edwin W. Edwards was acquitted on all counts, in his retrial on 1985 charges related to alleged improper manipulation in the awarding of state permits for hospital construction. In Alabama, George Wallace retired as governor, after having dominated state politics since 1962.   E.S.K.

SUDAN. In 1986, Sudan held its first multiparty elections in almost 20 years, and a civilian government took over from the military regime that had overthrown President Jaafar al-Nimeiry in April 1985. Thirty political parties competed for 301 National Assembly seats when long-promised elections were held in early April. The centrist Umma Party, led by Sadiq al-Mahdi, won a majority of seats in the new National Assembly, which took over the government from the Transitional Military Council. Mahdi became prime minister.

The civil war continued its course, with the Sudanese People's Liberation Army (SPLA), led by the American-educated John Garang, taking additional towns and territory in the south, including the key town of Rumbek in the Lake Province. After several abortive attempts, peace

Departing Legend

A political era came to an end in Alabama when George Corley Wallace, 67, completed his fourth term as governor, having declined to seek reelection. "I have climbed my last political mountain," said the governor with apparent regret, citing ill health as his major reason. Wallace had come a long way since 1963, when he was inaugurated on the steps of the Alabama capitol proclaiming "Segregation now, segregation tomorrow." The onetime ardent segregationist who stood in the schoolhouse door at the University of Alabama to keep blacks from attending classes eventually adapted to a new era of biracial politics and brought blacks into his political coalition. Both in and out of office, Wallace had dominated Alabama politics for 25 years and also became a major national figure, running for president on a third-party ticket in 1968 and seeking the Democratic presidential nomination in 1972. During the latter campaign, he was shot five times in an assassination attempt which left him wheelchair-bound and required him to receive frequent medical treatments.

George Wallace

talks were held in Ethiopia in July, but no concrete results were announced.

In August a Sudanese civilian airliner was shot down over rebel territory, killing 61 people; the SPLA claimed responsibility. As a result, the Red Cross and other agencies halted emergency relief operations for a period of time in the fall. International relief agencies said the deteriorating situation in the war-torn south could touch off a famine on a scale of the Ethiopian famine of 1985. Sudan already had the largest refugee population in Africa, with about 1 million displaced persons.

Sudan imposed austerity measures and devalued its currency early in the year, as the government fell into arrears on virtually all its international debt. After the International Monetary Fund declared Sudan ineligible for further loans in February, the nation was forced to barter for critical supplies. However, loans and foreign aid were received during the year, and in November the IMF endorsed a government reform plan, with reservations; talks with the IMF were to continue in early 1987. On a more positive note, Saudi Arabia provided Sudan with oil, and Chevron Oil resumed prospecting operations in southern Sudan.

Both the Transitional Military Council and the Mahdi government attempted to steer a new course in international relations. The former Nimeiry government had been closely identified with the United States and Egypt, but the new regime preferred to maintain a close relationship with Libya, which eagerly complied with a Sudanese request for military assistance, supplying war materièl and, reportedly, 1,000 Libyan troops and advisers.

The United States watched with concern, particularly following the U.S. bombing of Libya in April. Within hours after that attack, an American diplomatic official in Khartoum was shot and gravely injured. A mob of 10,000 Sudanese chanting anti-American slogans took to the streets, and 300 Americans were evacuated from the country. In June, apparently in an effort to maintain some influence, the United States agreed to provide $30 million in aid. Meanwhile, relations with Egypt, which had cooled, improved with the arrival of Egyptian military equipment.

See STATISTICS OF THE WORLD.   R.E.B.

SUPREME COURT OF THE UNITED STATES. *See* UNITED STATES OF AMERICA: *Supreme Court.*

SURINAME. *See* STATISTICS OF THE WORLD.

SWAZILAND. *See* STATISTICS OF THE WORLD.

SWEDEN. The assassination of Prime Minister Olof Palme overshadowed all other events in Sweden in 1986. A fixture of Swedish—and world—politics for many years, Palme, 59, was shot in the back on the evening of February 28 by an unknown assailant, as he and his wife Lisbeth walked home from a Stockholm movie. The Social Democratic leader was pronounced dead on arrival at the hospital; his wife survived with a slight bullet graze. Deputy Prime Minister Ingvar Carlsson was immediately named acting prime minister. He was also elected as chairman of the Social Democrats and, on March 12, was approved as prime minister.

The mysterious assassination shocked a nation accustomed to more than 170 years of external peace and internal tranquility. Typical of Swedish leaders, Palme frequently mingled among citizens after work and on the weekends; on the day of the shooting, he had released his personal bodyguards. Despite an international investigation led by Stockholm's police commissioner, and evidence from nearly 40 witnesses, clues to the identity and motivation of the assassin remained elusive.

The articulate, if acerbic, son of aristocratic parents, Palme had dedicated his adult life to the cause of economic justice and world peace. He joined the Social Democratic Party after finishing his studies at Ohio's Kenyon College and the University of Stockholm, entering the Riksdag (Parliament) in 1956. By 1969 he had risen to prime minister and party chairman. During the next 16 years, he led his party to electoral victory three times, while also presiding over embarrassing defeats in two elections. Palme had also been a prominent figure on the world scene, speaking out against U.S. involvement in Vietnam during the 1960's and 1970's and in favor of international peacekeeping and disarmament. His funeral, on March 15, was attended by dignitaries from more than 130 countries, including U.S. Secretary of State George Shultz and Soviet Premier Nikolai Ryzhkov.

Ingvar Carlsson was confirmed as prime

Swedish Prime Minister Olof Palme was assassinated in Stockholm on February 28. Known for his tireless efforts to promote peace and international cooperation, the Socialist leader was deeply mourned by his country (above, a crowd gathers around the flower-strewn site of his death).

minister by the Riksdag without opposition. Under Palme he had held the portfolios of education, housing, the environment, and the future, before becoming deputy prime minister. On the other side of the aisle, 37-year-old Carl Bildt replaced Ulf Adelsohn as leader of the Moderates, the largest opposition party.

In other developments, a last-minute compromise wage agreement averted a threatened strike by 300,000 public sector workers in April. The next round of wage negotiations, scheduled for spring 1987, was expected to be a crucial test of the famed Swedish model of labor peace which has helped the country maintain a high living standard and low unemployment levels. Also, the government joined Norway and Denmark in proclaiming a more restrictive Scandinavian policy toward Third World refugees and pressuring East Germany, a frequent transit stop to the region, into denying transit rights to Nordic-bound refugees from the Middle East and Asia who use the East Berlin airport.

Another notable Swede, diplomat and disarmament expert Alva Myrdal, died on February 1 at the age of 84. She was corecipient of the 1982 Nobel Peace Prize.

See STATISTICS OF THE WORLD.   M.D.H.

SWITZERLAND. Various events of international interest put Swiss banking in the spotlight in 1986. There was also a major toxic chemical spill in the Rhine River, originating from a plant in Basel (*see* ENVIRONMENT). And Swiss voters rejected a proposal for Swiss membership in the United Nations.

Perhaps the major banking story involved the disclosure late in the year that profits from secret U.S. arms sales to Iran were being diverted to antigovernment guerrillas in Nicaragua, through accounts in at least two Swiss institutions—a large bank (Crédit Suisse) and a small Geneva trust company (Compagnie de Services Fiduciaires S.A.). Banking officials said they had done nothing illegal. In December, Crédit Suisse placed various accounts at its Geneva branch under "heightened surveillance" in response to a U.S. Justice Department request relating to a pending criminal investigation. The U.S. investigation was said to involve Lieutenant Colonel Oliver North, formerly of the U.S. National Security Council staff, and others. Steps toward freezing such accounts and lifting bank secrecy regulations were expected in the new year.

Earlier in the year, Zurich's Bank Leu Ltd. agreed to help the U.S. Securities and Exchange Commission (SEC) investigate a major insider trading scandal, involving Dennis Levine, a former Wall Street investment banker, and Bernhard Meier, a Zurich bank employee in the Bahamas. The two had bought and sold stock using inside information and hidden the profits in Swiss accounts registered to two dummy Panamanian corporations. Levine pleaded guilty to the U.S. charges against him; Meier, his agent, was ordered to pay more than $470,000 into a fund to recompense defrauded investors.

Six Swiss banks were ordered in March to freeze the assets of former Philippine President Ferdinand Marcos. To get money from the accounts, Manila still had to prove that Marcos had acquired it illegally. The Swiss government also froze assets of deposed Haitian President Jean-Claude Duvalier. In May, three Swiss and an Italian were put on trial in Ticino for their parts in a Mafia-run drug money-laundering operation involving Traex S.A., a Lugano-based finance company. The only defendant to receive a significant sentence (13 years) was the Swiss drug dealer, Paul Wandel.

In a referendum on March 16, voters defeated a proposal calling for Switzerland to join the United Nations. The measure was defeated by a three-to-one margin, failing to obtain a majority in any of the 26 Swiss cantons and half-cantons. Opponents had argued that UN membership would threaten the country's long-standing neutrality.

See STATISTICS OF THE WORLD. J.F.S.

SYRIA. Charges that Syria had played a role in terrorist attacks in Western Europe—which were denied by President Hafez al-Assad—caused concern in 1986. Syria's efforts to impose order in Lebanon appeared to unravel.

Possible Terrorist Role. The bombing on April 5 of a West Berlin discotheque frequented by American troops, which killed 3 people, and an unsuccessful attempt on April 17 to place a bomb aboard an El Al airliner embarking from London for Israel raised questions about Syria's role in sponsoring terrorism. President Ronald Reagan said in late April, following the U.S. bombing of Libya for that country's alleged support of terrorist activities, that the United States would take military action if terrorism could be traced to Syria or Iran.

On May 6 a Jordanian arrested in West Germany in connection with the discotheque bombing confessed to the March 29 bombing of the German-Arab Friendship Society, in West Berlin, and claimed the attack had been organized by the Syrian embassy in East Berlin. Subsequently, Israeli Defense Minister Yitzhak Rabin accused Syria of responsibility for the attempted bombing of the El Al airliner, and Britain expelled three Syrian diplomats it strongly suspected of involvement in that incident; Syria responded by expelling three British diplomats.

The first public airing of evidence linking Syria to West European terrorism occurred at the trial of the man charged with the attempted El Al bombing. According to the prosecutor, the defendant, a Jordanian named Nezar Hindawi—the brother of the man arrested for alleged terrorist activities in West Berlin—told investigators that Syrian military intelligence officials had provided him with a Syrian passport, $12,000, deadly explosives, and training in their use. The bomb intended for the El Al flight was hidden in luggage Hindawi had given to an unwitting Irish woman who was pregnant with his child and whom he had assured he would meet later in Israel so they could be married.

On October 24, Hindawi was convicted and sentenced to 45 years in prison; Britain broke off diplomatic relations with Damascus the same day. The United States and Canada withdrew their ambassadors from Syria as a sign of support. Syria responded by breaking its ties with London. Shortly thereafter, Britain and most of its partners in the European Community agreed to ban new arms sales and take other limited steps against Syria.

In November, Hindawi's brother and another Palestinian were convicted in West Berlin for their roles in the March 29 bombing there.

Bonn subsequently expelled three Syrian diplomats, downgraded its ties with Syria, and announced other sanctions.

Involvement in Lebanon. A Syrian-mediated peace pact signed in December 1985 collapsed in January 1986 when many Christian leaders, including Lebanese President Amin Gemayel, rejected the accord. The failure sparked intra-Christian fighting and an attack on Christians by Syrian-backed Muslim militias and was considered an embarrassment to Assad. In July, Syrian attempts to restore law and order in the Lebanese capital also broke down when a huge car bomb killed 33 people in East Beirut, beginning a bloody series of reprisal car bombings. Reported Syrian involvement in an attempted military thrust into East Beirut in September further splintered an already-torn country.

Attacks in Syria. A truck rigged with explosives was detonated in central Damascus on March 13, killing some 50 people. A Lebanese man confessed on Syrian television that he had obtained the vehicle in Baghdad; he was subsequently hanged in public. On April 16, bombs exploded on nine intercity buses and on a train, killing at least 140 people. Three Syrians and two Turks accused of the attacks said they had received money and explosives from Iraq.

See STATISTICS OF THE WORLD.   A.D.

T

TAIWAN. In 1986 it was announced that martial law would be lifted in the future, and an opposition party was permitted to run for seats in a general election, for the first time. However, the ruling Kuomintang (KMT) and President Chiang Ching-kuo retained strong power.

On October 15, the KMT announced that martial law would be replaced with less restrictive security rules, after an unspecified time was allowed to "legislate and review the regulations." The KMT also said that political parties would be allowed, so long as they opposed Communism, renounced violence, and supported the long-range KMT goal of reunification with mainland China. In limited national elections on December 6, the new opposition Democratic Progressive Party won an unexpectedly large 23 percent share of the vote, to receive 12 parliamentary seats. (The body has limited powers, however, and most of its seats were held by KMT members and were not up for election.) Prior to the election, an airport opposition rally had led to violent clashes with police and to a canceling of other demonstrations by opposition leaders, who said the rallies might be used by others to incite violence and possibly discredit the opposition. On December 2, a prominent dissident, who

had wanted to return and participate in the campaign, was refused admittance to Taiwan.

Earlier in the year, following a March meeting of the KMT Central Committee, President Chiang appointed a committee of KMT officials to study and recommend political reform measures for the future. He also approved a "dialogue" between KMT officials and Taiwanese opposition leaders.

In May the pilot of a Taiwanese China Airlines cargo plane flew to Canton and defected. In a new departure, airline representatives in Hong Kong, reportedly acting on President Chiang's initiative, negotiated directly with mainland Chinese officials to win return of the plane and of two other crew members aboard.

Taiwan's gross national product was expected to increase 8 percent in 1986. Among factors contributing to recovery was the rebounding of the U.S. economy, which boosted Taiwan's exports to the United States. Meanwhile, Taiwanese officials agreed on reduced tariffs and other concessions to open up Taiwan to increased sales of U.S. products.

See STATISTICS OF THE WORLD.   P.H.C.

TANZANIA. In 1986 newly-elected President Ali Hassan Mwinyi visited many countries, including several other "frontline" states bordering or near South Africa. At the same time, former President Julius Nyerere, still chairman of the ruling Chama Cha Mapinduzi Party, still enjoyed considerable power and prestige, both at home and abroad.

Nyerere, who said he would step down as CCM chairman in 1987, travelled throughout the country in a personal drive to rejuvenate the party. In August he reshuffled regional secretaries. The next month, he ousted 30 party officials, mostly for alleged corruption. Meanwhile, the elder statesman of Tanzanian politics was asked by the Organization of African States to join a "council of wise men" to help mediate in inter-African disputes. In September he was named head of an independent commission of the nonaligned nations movement to design a Third World economic strategy.

After nearly a decade of resistance, Tanzania, still in dire economic straits, "bit the IMF [International Monetary Fund] bullet," as the media put it, and basically accepted the organization's terms for emergency assistance. The shilling was devalued by nearly 60 percent and producer prices were raised by 30-80 percent. The IMF subsequently approved a $78 million 18-month aid package, and various Western donors pledged close to $1 billion of the $3.7 billion which Finance Minister Cleopa David Msuya said he needed to import goods essential for economic recovery. The 1986–1987 budget, announced in June, called for spending of $1.4 billion, compared with $1.9 billion in 1985–1986. The largest single expenditure was for servicing the $3.5 billion foreign debt.

In July the president's pay, which had remained unchanged since independence in 1961, was increased substantially, and government employees received pay raises.

See STATISTICS OF THE WORLD. S.K.

TECHNOLOGY. *See* COMPUTERS; ELECTRONICS; ENVIRONMENT; HEALTH AND MEDICINE; LIFE SCIENCES; SPACE EXPLORATION.

TELEVISION AND RADIO BROADCASTING. The three major U.S. networks fought out their perennial ratings war, stressing comedy on the fall schedule for 1986. Behind the scenes, there were major personnel changes, especially at CBS. In Canada, the government-

After a summer of public speculation as to how Bobby Ewing (played by Patrick Duffy) would be returned to Dallas, the first show of the tenth season revealed that his "death," and the entire ninth season, had only been a dream.

owned Canadian Broadcasting Company suffered from tight revenues but launched interesting new programs.

Turmoil at CBS. A bitter boardroom struggle for power at CBS dominated the year's television news. The loser was Thomas Wyman, whose stormy six-year tenure as the network's chief executive ended when he was asked to tender his resignation in September. The winners were Laurence Tisch, chairman of the Loews Corporation, the New York-based conglomerate that owns 25 percent of CBS, and William Paley, at 84 a legend at the network he founded and ran for 55 years.

The immediate cause of Wyman's downfall was what financial observers called his "critical blunder" of attempting to persuade the CBS board of directors that the Coca-Cola Company should be permitted to take over the financially troubled network. Wyman said the sale would be a way "to get more money for the shareholders." Not long after he made the Coca-Cola proposal, the board unanimously agreed to ask Wyman to resign.

Wyman had been locked in a bitter power struggle with Tisch and was under tremendous pressure to turn CBS around. Profits were declining, as they were elsewhere in the network television industry, with advertisers spurning the high costs of TV programming and with competition increasing from cable and the independent stations. Morale in the CBS News division had dropped sharply as cost-cutting layoffs were imposed. The news department was criticized for putting profits ahead of quality programming.

After Wyman's resignation, Paley became acting chairman of the CBS board and Tisch became acting chief executive officer. The network's news chief, Van Gordon Sauter, was also asked to resign. Among other things, he was faulted for an upheaval at the *CBS Morning News* (coanchors Forrest Sawyer and Maria Shriver left the show after CBS announced that it would be cancelled at the end of the year) and for squandering the huge lead *CBS Evening News* had once enjoyed over its rivals. In late October, Howard Stringer, acting head of CBS News, was appointed president of the division. Meanwhile, Tisch instituted layoffs and sold off various company businesses, in a stringent austerity program.

Other Executive Changes. Two other highly significant changes occurred in the upper echelons of broadcasting. At ABC, which completed its friendly merger with Capital Cities Communications Inc., in January, Frederick S. Pierce resigned as chairman and chief executive officer of ABC and vice chairman of Capital Cities/ABC Inc. He was replaced by John B. Sias.

At NBC, Grant Tinker, chief executive officer and chairman of the board since 1981, announced his resignation after accomplishing his goal of bringing NBC to the top of the ratings. He was succeeded by Robert C. Wright, head of the General Electric Company's financial services division and a newcomer to broadcasting. Tinker was that rarity among the executive ranks of television—a man who was virtually never criticized and whose work was characterized by taste, talent, and integrity. In 1970, Tinker's MTM Enterprises had introduced the *Mary Tyler Moore Show*, an award-winning comedy series immediately recognized for its high quality. The Tinker philosophy essentially involved hiring talented people and giving a series reasonable time to develop.

Ratings Game. When Tinker assumed the reins, NBC had languished in third place in the

Television news was an arena of intense rivalry for top ratings among the three major networks; shown here is Tom Brokaw of NBC Nightly News, a major contender.

ratings. Under his guidance, the network won the 1985–1986 prime-time A. C. Nielsen ratings race—the first time the network held sole possession of the title since the current ratings system went into effect in 1960. NBC's *The Cosby Show,* starring Bill Cosby, was the most popular series of the season by a wide margin. NBC also boasted the season's top-rated new series, *The Golden Girls,* a comedy about four older women living together in Florida, as well as the highest-rated television movie of the season, *Return to Mayberry,* which starred Andy Griffith and Don Knotts in a nostalgic reunion of the characters from the old *Andy Griffith Show.* The top-rated miniseries of the 1985–1986 season was ABC's *North and South,* produced by David Wolper.

As of the end of 1986, NBC was also well ahead in ratings to date for the new season, with CBS ranked second. In news, *The CBS Evening News With Dan Rather,* long the top evening news show, sometimes lagged behind *The NBC Nightly News With Tom Brokaw.*

The top ten regularly scheduled network programs for the 1985–1986 season were *The Cosby Show,* NBC; *Family Ties,* NBC; *Murder, She Wrote,* CBS; *60 Minutes,* CBS; *Cheers,* NBC; a three-way tie for sixth place among NBC's *The Golden Girls,* CBS's *Dallas,* and ABC's *Dynasty; Miami Vice,* NBC; and *Who's the Boss?,* ABC.

Fall Season. In a bow to nostalgia, a number of veteran performers returned to the networks in new series during the fall season. In ABC's comedy *Life With Lucy,* Lucille Ball starred as a recently widowed grandmother who moves in with her daughter's family—but ratings were low and the show was taken off the air. Andy Griffith—once Andy Taylor, the sheriff of Mayberry—played a wily country lawyer in NBC's *Matlock.* Raymond Burr returned in his old role as lawyer Perry Mason for a TV movie.

Many comedies were featured in the fall season, with more than two dozen on network television alone, plus a dozen or more on independent stations. Among the few new entries of more than passing interest were ABC's *Perfect Strangers,* with Bronson Pinchot and Mark Linn-Baker; ABC's *Head of the Class,* starring Howard Hesseman; and CBS's *The Cavanaughs,* with Barnard Hughes and Chris-

Among several television veterans who returned to prime time were Raymond Burr and Barbara Hale, stars of the old Perry Mason Show. *In November they appeared in the NBC movie* Perry Mason: The Case of the Shooting Star.

tine Ebersol. The most successful new shows were *L.A. Law* (NBC), a drama about the doings of a high-powered Los Angeles law firm, and *Amen* (also NBC), starring Sherman Hemsley as a church deacon.

Dallas fans breathed a sigh of relief in September when Patrick Duffy returned to the show as Bobby Ewing, younger brother of the evil J. R. Ewing. In May 1985 viewers saw Bobby supposedly die, but the last episode of the 1985–1986 season closed on a shot of Bobby's ex-wife finding him in her shower. For four months speculation mounted as to how

Dazzling TV Sleuth

As beautiful blond detective Maddie Hayes, Cybill Shepherd carries on a snappy verbal battle of the sexes with costar Bruce Willis, in one of the brighter recent TV hits, ABC's *Moonlighting*. The show won 16 Emmy nominations in 1986, including one for Shepherd as best actress, though it got only one award (in editing), to the disappointment of its fans. Shepherd, 36, was a natural for the Maddie Hayes role. She had the smile that won her the Miss Congeniality award at a 1967 Miss Teenage America pageant, plus the looks that made her a famous cover girl. She had launched her acting career as a provocative teen beauty in *The Last Picture Show* (1971), directed by Peter Bogdanovich, with whom she lived for several years. But, after teaming up with him on two flops, Shepherd eventually left Hollywood and Bogdanovich to become married and later divorced in her hometown of Memphis. She subsequently hit her stride in regional theater and returned to Hollywood, where she achieved her big success in *Moonlighting*.

Cybill Shepherd

Bobby would be resurrected. On the opening night of the show's tenth season, the truth was revealed; his former wife had only dreamed of his death—and of the show's entire 1985–1986 season.

Talk Shows. An era ended in September when Merv Griffin elected to conclude his run as a talk show host after 23 years. Griffin's syndicated show had faltered in the ratings in recent years. However, in the same month Johnny Carson hosted an NBC special celebrating his 24th year as host of the late-night *Tonight Show*. And David Letterman's *Late Night With David Letterman*, airing after the *Tonight Show* on NBC, had a strong following among viewers attracted by his offbeat humor. Carson faced new competition for late-night viewers, though. Comedians David Brenner and Joan Rivers—who had both furthered their careers by appearing frequently on Carson's show—launched their own talk shows in the fall. Brenner's show was syndicated by King World, and Rivers's entry was broadcast on the Fox network. Dick Cavett, who had hosted an ABC talk show from 1969 to 1972, returned to the network with a show that had run on the USA cable network

in the last few years, but it was canceled by ABC in November, along with *Jimmy Breslin's People*, another late-night entry. (Prior to the public announcement, Breslin himself had announced that he was canceling the program on his own.)

An intense daytime talk-show rivalry developed between the widely syndicated shows of Phil Donahue and Oprah Winfrey. *Donahue!* has been on television for the last 17 years; *Oprah Winfrey* is a newcomer, hosted by a black woman, known for her candor and irreverence, who received national attention for her acclaimed performance in the movie *The Color Purple*. Both shows are aimed primarily at women at home during the day, and their topics and formats are similar.

Awards. The 38th annual Emmy awards were presented in September by the Academy of Television Arts and Sciences. NBC took 19 of the 31 Emmys awarded (outside of the crafts categories); CBS won 10, and ABC and PBS were awarded just one each. The prestigious Governors Award was presented to 73-year-old comedian Red Skelton, who was introduced by Lucille Ball. Skelton told reporters backstage, "When I was a young man I used to perform in medicine shows. They would have an act and then they'd sell a product—now they call that TV." Skelton had his own show on CBS for nearly 20 years, until 1970.

NBC's hospital drama series *St. Elsewhere* was the biggest single winner with six awards, although the Emmy for best dramatic series went to *Cagney and Lacey*, the CBS program about two female police officers. *Cagney and Lacey* won a total of four awards. The best comedy series was *The Golden Girls*, which won five Emmys overall. NBC's *Peter the Great*, about the powerful Russian czar, won two awards, including best miniseries, and the award for outstanding special went to NBC's *Love Is Never Silent*, about a young woman with deaf parents. The NBC dramatic special *An Early Frost*, about a family torn apart when their son develops AIDS, picked up four awards. The big loser in the Emmy awards was *Moonlighting*, the critically praised ABC detective series, starring Cybill Shepherd, that was nominated for 16 awards, but won only 1.

In May the winners of the prestigious George Foster Peabody Awards were announced. Among them was Johnny Carson, host of the *Tonight Show*, which the Peabody judges said had "entertained and amused American television viewers as no other program has" for nearly 25 years. Also honored was Irish rock musician Bob Geldof, who organized the Live Aid concert broadcast from Philadelphia and London in 1985 to fund hunger relief.

Specials and Spectacles. One of the year's more bizarre offerings was a live television special that centered around the opening of a mysterious sealed vault in Chicago's Lexington Hotel, where gangster Al Capone lived from 1928 until 1931. Some believed he had hidden cash in the vault. With Geraldo Rivera as on-camera reporter, the program showed workers digging into the chamber, but they found only a few dusty bottles that once may have held bathtub gin. The two-hour syndicated program nevertheless won high ratings. So did *American Vice: The Doping of a Nation*, another syndicated special hosted by Rivera, featuring on-the-spot coverage of police drug raids, among other sensational material.

More sophisticated was the syndicated *All-*

Star Tribute to General Jimmy Doolittle, celebrating the 90th birthday of the World War II hero who led the first U.S. bombing raid over the Japanese mainland in 1942. Bob Hope's production company presented the show, which followed the pattern of Hope's World War II USO shows. Among the stars was actor James Stewart, a World War II bomber pilot who flew under Doolittle's command in Europe.

Among network dramatic offerings of interest were "Nobody's Child," starring Marlo Thomas as a woman confined to mental institutions because of misdiagnosis; "Promise," with James Garner as a bachelor coping with a schizophrenic brother; "Second Serve," starring Vanessa Redgrave as transsexual tennis star Renee Richards; and "Unnatural Causes," with John Ritter—a sympathetic treatment of charges by Vietnam veterans that exposure to Agent Orange had led to disastrous health problems. NBC's lavish miniseries *Peter the Great* was of interest early in the year, but generally speaking there were few quality miniseries on the networks. On public television, highlights included the miniseries *Roanoke*, on *American*

A small-town Québec youth, portrayed by Toronto actor Carl Marotte, rises to hockey stardom in the Canadian series He Shoots, He Scores, *produced by the same cast in French and English.*

Playhouse; the frothy British miniseries *Mapp & Lucia*; and "Shadowland," a British drama based on events from the life of the writer C. S. Lewis, starring Claire Bloom and Joss Ackland.

The CBS broadcast of Vladimir Horowitz's piano concert in Moscow was a major television event. As a result of a U.S.-Soviet cultural agreement, Horowitz, one of the most extraordinary piano virtuosos of all time, returned to his homeland after an absence of 61 years. He played before 1,800 applauding, shouting, flower-offering concertgoers in the Great Hall of the Moscow Conservatory. Millions more shared the emotional event because his performance was widely televised in the West.

Star Trek. To the delight of *Star Trek* fans, Paramount Television Group announced in October that the legendary series would return in the fall of 1987, nearly 20 years after its cancellation, with an all-new cast.

Radio. During the year the Federal Communications Commission recommended rule changes to increase the listenership of AM radio, which has dropped by half in the past decade. Earlier FCC efforts to bolster FM radio inadvertently damaged AM: overall listenership did not increase, as radio audiences merely shifted their listening choices. The new FCC recommendations would relax restrictions on multiple ownership, among other steps.

Radio stations reported a trend to substitute "classic rock" for current popular music. Some stations were appealing to audiences over 25—and the advertisers who sell to them—by playing older material as much as 80 percent of the time.

Canadian Broadcasting. The government-owned Canadian Broadcasting Company (CBC) faced severe federal budget cuts for the 1986 fiscal year. Although the network marked its 50th anniversary in 1986, it lacked the resources to stage a proper on-the-air celebration. Despite the budget crunch, CBC did manage to launch an ambitious $8 million series in the fall. *He Shoots, He Scores* was a soap-opera-style drama following a small-town Québec boy as he rises to stardom in the National Hockey League. The network also filmed a sequel to its highly successful miniseries *Anne of Green Gables*.

In September a report was released by the federal government's task force on broadcasting that suggested increasing CBC's budget, raising its prime-time minimum for Canadian content from 80 to 95 percent, and creating a separate news channel at the network, as well as establishing a new, commercial-free network that would be independent from CBC.

B.D.J. (Canadian Broadcasting) & D.F.

TENNESSEE. See STATISTICS OF THE WORLD.

TEXAS. See STATISTICS OF THE WORLD.

THAILAND. General Arthit Kamlang-ek, once thought of as a possible successor to Prime Minister Prem Tinsulanonda, was dismissed as army commander in chief in May 1986. Prem contended that General Arthit had been working to undermine his civilian government. Arthit was replaced by General Chaovalit Yongchaiyut, a strong Prem supporter.

Parliament was dissolved in May and an election was scheduled for July 27, after several members from the Social Action Party, the largest party in Prem's coalition government, rebelled over the government's unpopular austerity measures. Prem—appointed once again by King Adulyadej—chose not to run, taking advantage of a constitutional provision allowing a nonelected person to serve as prime minister; the decision drew criticism from student and political leaders. The Democrat Party, led by Bhichai Rattakul, was the biggest winner, taking 100 out of 347 seats. The other three members of the new coalition were the Social Action Party, the Thai Nation, and the new Rassadorn, or People's Party.

Fears of a renewal—and perhaps an intensification—of recent border conflict between Thai forces and Vietnamese troops based in neighboring Cambodia subsided as the Vietnamese appeared to concentrate on strengthening their defenses. Instead, the main focus of Thai foreign policy shifted to economic issues, particularly those affecting U.S.-Thai relations. President Ronald Reagan vetoed a U.S. bill which would have restricted textile imports from Thailand and other Asian countries. However, a 1985 U.S. law providing subsidies for American rice growers went into effect in April, causing resentment and fears of hardship among Thai rice farmers.

The government reported progress in keeping inflation low and reducing the deficit, but the economy remained sluggish. Steps were taken toward triggering growth, including reductions in personal and corporate income taxes, retail oil prices, and interest rates.

In late December, Thailand announced it was closing its principal refugee camp, Khao I Dang, which meant that the camp's 26,000 Cambodian residents would lose refugee status and become displaced persons, subject to being returned to war-torn Cambodia when possible. The Thai government also indicated plans to phase out all remaining refugee camps. It said Western governments had not cooperated in processing Cambodian and other refugees in Thailand for resettlement abroad.

See STATISTICS OF THE WORLD. A.R.

THEATER. The uncertain state of the American theater manifested itself in various ways in 1986. The midyear report issued by the League of American Theaters and Producers for the 1985–1986 season showed that Broadway ticket sales had declined to 6.6 million from the 7.4 million of the previous season, while gross box-office receipts had dropped from $213 million to $191 million. However, Broadway touring companies had an increase in gross receipts.

Broadway. Among straight plays, there was nothing truly outstanding in early 1986. The murders of San Francisco Mayor George Moscone and Supervisor Harvey Milk inspired Emily Mann's *Execution of Justice*, which fared far less well in New York than in regional productions. Hume Cronyn and Jessica Tandy conducted a witty debate over marital and nuclear issues in Brian Clark's *The Petition*, but the British import did not last long. Although John Cullum and George C. Scott enlivened Bernard Sabath's *The Boys in Autumn*, they couldn't transform the sketchy play into a satisfying theater experience. *Social Security*, with Marlo Thomas and Ron Silver and directed by Mike Nichols, was received more favorably by audiences than by critics.

Documenting the toll idealism takes on relationships, Benefactors, by British playwright Michael Frayn, proved to be both a critical and financial success on Broadway. Its four-member cast featured (from left) American actors Glenn Close, Mary Beth Hurt, and Sam Waterston and the British actor Simon Jones.

A revival of The Front Page, *the classic 1928 drama about tabloid journalism, opened at New York City's Lincoln Center in December. Here, editor Walter Burns (John Lithgow) evokes visions of power and glory in an effort to keep disillusioned reporter Hildy Johnson (Richard Thomas) from quitting the seedy business.*

Among the year's major events were the London hit *Wild Honey*, Michael Frayn's adaptation of an early Chekhov play, and *Broadway Bound*, the final installment of Neil Simon's trilogy about his alter ego Eugene Morris Jerome, played by Jonathan Silverman, with Linda Lavin as the mother. The British drama *Benefactors*, by Michael Frayn, which opened on Broadway in late 1985, was a big critical and popular success.

Broadway revivals covered a wide range of emotional territory. Director Jonathan Miller's controversially tightened version of Eugene O'Neill's *Long Day's Journey into Night* starred Jack Lemmon. The Steppenwolf Theatre Company of Chicago brought its version of Harold Pinter's *The Caretaker* to New York. Jean Stapleton and Polly Holliday appeared as the lethal Brewster sisters in the thriller spoof *Arsenic and Old Lace*. The Circle in the Square launched its season by reviving George Bernard Shaw's *You Never Can Tell*. The Royal Shakespeare Company brought back *The Life and Adventures of Nicholas Nickleby* for a limited engagement. The recently reestablished Lincoln Center Theater Company leapt into the limelight with John Guare's *The House of Blue Leaves*. Opening at the small Mitzi E. Newhouse Theater, the far-out 1971 comedy moved to the larger Vivian Beaumont before transfer-

ring to Broadway. It was followed at the Beaumont by *The Front Page*, the 1928 comedy melodrama by Ben Hecht and Charles MacArthur. The company also presented *Woza Afrika!*, a festival of South African plays.

Broadway relied on revivals and/or the British for its principal musical comedy treats. Debbie Allen was irresistible in the revival of *Sweet Charity* (1966), and Bob Fosse again provided superb direction and choreography. Robert Lindsay delighted audiences with his dazzling performance as the suddenly titled cockney in *Me and My Girl*, the revival of a 1937 British hit.

Two ambitious but unsuccessful musical efforts were Bob Fosse's *Big Deal*, based on the 1958 Italian film *Big Deal on Madonna Street*, and *Rags*, a sequel to *Fiddler on the Roof*, with opera star Teresa Stratas. When a cast member announced at the end of a matinee that the show was scheduled to close that night, the audience marched down Broadway in support of the show, which then sold out for the evening performance. Producers briefly considered reopening it. In the wake of the successful *Tango Argentino* came *Flamenco Puro*, a sampling of Spanish gypsy styles and rhythms.

Off Broadway. The year Off Broadway started with *Today I Am a Fountain Pen*, the first part of Israel Horowitz's trilogy of family comedies based on *A Good Place to Come From,* Morley Torlog's memories of a Jewish-Canadian youth. After the conclusion of the trilogy with *The Chopin Playoffs, Today I Am a Fountain Pen* resumed performances for an extended run. A. R. Gurney, Jr., pleased audiences with *The Perfect Party,* his most antic comedy to date. Twenty-six-year-old Reinaldo Povod made an impressive debut with *Cuba and His Teddy Bear,* starring Robert DeNiro, which began at the Public Theater and subsequently moved to Broadway. Tina Howe's *Coastal Disturbances* drew acclaim.

Off Broadway received two Samuel Beckett works: the world premiere of *Worstward Ho,* Frederick Neumann's dramatization of a 1983 Beckett text; and *Krapp's Last Tape,* with Rick Cluchey (a former San Quentin Prison inmate) in a performance directed by Beckett. British dramatist Simon Gray staged the Off Broadway production of his *The Common Pursuit,* which recounts the 1960's attempts of six Cambridge University graduates to start a literary magazine.

The New York Shakespeare Festival presented a lively agenda that included Czech dissident Vaclav Pavel's mordant *Largo Desolato* and a *Hamlet* in which Kevin Kline managed to rise above an uneven production. In Central Park's Delacorte Theater, the NYSF staged a clumsily slapstick *Twelfth Night* and a striking version of Euripides' *Medea* by a Japanese company employing Nō, Kabuki, and Western techniques. Martha Clarke's dance-drama *Vienna: Lusthaus,* a powerful portrait of pre-World War I Vienna, which originated at the Music-Theater Group/Lenox Arts Center, played to sold-out crowds at St. Clement's and then at the Public Theater. Another success at the Public was George C. Wolfe's satirical sketches, *The Colored Museum.*

A variety of musicals, vaudevilles, and solo performances enlivened the Off Broadway scene. In Vincent D. Smith's *Williams and Walker,* black entertainers Bert Williams and George Walker were richly portrayed by Ben Harney and Vondie Curtis-Hall. Lonette McKee evoked the life and world of jazz singer Billie Holiday in Lanie Robertson's enthusiastically received *Lady Day at Emerson's Bar & Grill.*

Olympus on My Mind spoofed simultaneously the Amphitryon legend and bygone Broadway musicals. *Groucho: A Life in Revue* traced the life of the mustached Marx.

Calling their show *The Alchemedians,* jugglers Bob Berky and Michael Moschen joined the growing company of "new vaudevillians" to display their prowess Off Broadway. *Sills & Company* came to New York from California with its latest theatrical fun-and-games and improvisations. Comedian Eric Bogosian drew

A shining star of the 1985–1986 Broadway season was the warm-hearted British musical Me and My Girl. This loving revival of a 1930's hit remained true to music-hall tradition, with inspired cavorting by comedian Robert Lindsay (shown here with female lead Maryann Plunkett).

raves for his satirical one-man show, *Drinking in America*.

Regional Theater. Regional theater could point to encouraging advances and solid achievements in 1986. The Alabama Shakespeare Festival opened its $21.5 million complex with a sold-out production of *A Midsummer Night's Dream*. After a 20-year intermission, the storied Pasadena Playhouse launched a three-play season led off by Shaw's *Arms and the Man*. The South Coast Repertory Theater at Costa Mesa, Calif., announced that its 1986–1987 season of 11 plays would include 5 world premieres. A distinctive dark comedy, *Progress*, by British playwright Doug Lucie, was presented at the Long Wharf in New Haven.

Baltimore became the first North American city to host the International Theater Institute's Theater of Nations Festival, although the occasion was marred by the ITI's announcement that it was withdrawing sponsorship of the British National Theater's adaptation of George Orwell's *Animal Farm* because of protests by representatives of the Soviet Union and other Communist regimes. *Animal Farm* became a nonfestival event; Baltimore saw it without the ITI imprimatur. Other international festivals were held in New York City and Purchase and Stony Brook, N.Y.

Awards and Honors. Since the previous New York productions of *The House of Blue Leaves* and Athol Fugard's *The Blood Knot* had been Off Broadway, the two works were finally ruled eligible for consideration as new Broadway plays for the 1986 Antoinette Perry (Tony) Awards. Later in the year, however, the Tony award committee issued new guidelines, under which any play produced on or off Broadway more than three years previously could only win an award as best revival.

The best play Tony went to Herb Gardner's *I'm Not Rappaport,* and Judd Hirsch was voted best actor in a play for his work in it. *The Mystery of Edwin Drood* was named best musical and also earned Tonys in musical categories for George Rose (best actor), Rupert Holmes (best book and best score), and Wilford Leach (best direction). The Tony for best actress in a musical went to Bernadette Peters, the star of Andrew Lloyd Webber's *Song & Dance*. Lily Tomlin received the Tony for best actress in a play for her bravura solo performance in *The*

Herb Gardner's Tony award-winning I'm Not Rappaport *starred Judd Hirsch (left) and Cleavon Little as two elderly gentlemen, both determined survivors, who meet on a park bench to trade tales and eventually become friends.*

Search for Signs of Intelligent Life in the Universe, by Jane Wagner. *The House of Blue Leaves* won Tonys for Jerry Zaks (director), John Mahoney and Swoosie Kurtz (actor and actress), and Tony Walton (scenic design). The American Repertory Theater of Cambridge, Mass., received a Tony for distinguished work in regional theater.

The Off-Broadway (Obie) award for best performance also went to Swoosie Kurtz for *The House of Blue Leaves*. Distinguished playwriting Obies went to Wallace Shawn for *Aunt Dan and Lemon*; Eric Bogosian, *Drinking in America*; Martha Clarke, *Vienna: Lusthaus*; John Jesurun, *Deep Sleep*; Tadeusz Kantor, *Let the Artist Die*; and Lee Nagrin, *Bird/Bear*. Edward Herrmann and Kevin Kline were given sustained performance awards, and Richard Foreman received the direction award for *Largo Desolato*. Among ten distinguished performance awards were those to Farley Granger for *Talley & Son* and Elisabeth Welch for her one-woman show *Time to Start Living*.

The New York Drama Critics Circle gave its best-play award to *A Lie of the Mind* by Sam Shepard (*see biography in* PEOPLE IN THE NEWS). *Benefactors* was chosen best foreign play, and Tomlin and Wagner were honored with a special citation for their *Search* work. For the second year in a row, the Critics Circle voted to omit an award for best musical. There was also no Pulitzer Prize for drama.

Canadian Theater. Both commercial and non-profit theater flourished in Toronto. The city's main road-show theater, the Royal Alexandra, became a producing house, starting with a Canadian production of Tom Stoppard's *The Real Thing*. Nationalist Bill Glasco took over Toronto's major municipal theater, Centre-Stage, and revived Canadian playwright David French's *Jitters*, setting box office records. Elsewhere, Winnipeg's Manitoba Theatre Centre did a mainstage production of Ted Galay's epic play about Ukrainian-Canadians, *Tsymbaly*. The Shaw Festival in Niagara-on-the-Lake, Ont., revived Noel Coward's *Cavalcade*.

In Montréal, Théâtre des Quat' Sous had a hit with *Being at Home With Claude*, Théâtre Repère's *Dragon Trilogy* was a hit at the new Harbourfront World Stage Festival in Toronto, and Michel Tremblay's *Albertine in Five Times*

won a Chalmers Award as the best new play produced in Toronto.

R.C. (Canadian Theater) & J.B.

TOGO. See STATISTICS OF THE WORLD.

TONGA. See STATISTICS OF THE WORLD.

TRANSPORTATION. Mergers and labor problems dominated U.S. transportation industry news in 1986. Business was sluggish for all carriers except airlines. The airline industry, amid a backdrop of frenzied merger activity, enjoyed good domestic passenger business, although fewer passengers traveled internationally because of fears of terrorism.

AVIATION

The Air Transport Association, which represents all major U.S. airlines, reported that, for the first nine months of 1986, total traffic on member airlines was 9 percent above the previous year. However, international business was down 3 percent, with the sharpest drop-off on North Atlantic routes to Europe. The increased availability of discounted air fares was a major factor behind the strength of U.S. airline traffic. Over 90 percent of all passengers flew with tickets priced more than 60 percent off standard coach fares. Attractions like the Statue of Liberty festivities in New York City were another factor, as was fear of terrorism abroad. However, there were predictions that the wide availability of low fares might be curtailed as the airline industry continued to consolidate.

Mergers. In February, troubled Eastern Air Lines accepted a merger offer of more than $600 million from Texas Air Corporation, headed by Frank Lorenzo. To overcome federal antitrust objections to the deal, Texas Air agreed to sell to Pan American some passenger gates and arrival and departure slots for shuttle service that would compete with those run by Eastern and New York Air (owned by Texas Air). Pan American began shuttle service in the fall, and the Eastern acquisition won federal approval on October 1. The merger, approved by Eastern stockholders in November, made Texas Air the largest U.S. airline operator under a single corporate entity.

After an initial success as a no-frills, low-fare airline, People Express had run into trouble through rapid expansion and because of increased fare competition from major carriers.

From Peanuts to Empire-Building

The moves by Texas Air to take over Eastern Air Lines and People Express were typical of the bold management style of Texas Air chairman Frank Lorenzo, who rose from small beginnings to control the largest airline system in the United States. The son of Spanish immigrants who operated a beauty parlor, Lorenzo put himself through college by driving a Coca-Cola truck. In 1972 a company he started with classmates from Harvard Business School bought the small Trans Texas Airlines; Lorenzo transformed troubled Trans Texas into Texas International, which achieved great success, partly by offering "peanuts" fares long before the practice became widespread. In 1982 Texas Air, the holding company for Texas International, merged with the much larger Continental Air Lines and Lorenzo put Continental into Chapter 11 bankruptcy in order to tear up its union contracts—a controversial cost-cutting move.

Frank Lorenzo

During summer 1986, People rejected a $236 million acquisition bid from Texas Air. United Airlines agreed to buy Frontier, which People had acquired in 1985, for $146 million, but difficulties over pilots' pay schedules held up negotiations. Late in August, Frontier suddenly filed a bankruptcy petition; thousands of Frontier ticket holders were stranded, and the United deal fell through. Texas Air then announced that it would buy both People and Frontier, in a complex transaction involving an exchange of stock. The acquisition was approved by the U.S. Department of Transportation in October and by People Express stockholders in late December.

Other mergers in 1986 included the $884 million purchase of Republic Airlines by Northwest, finalized in August; the purchase of Ozark Air Lines by TWA; and the merger of Delta and Western Air Lines, completed in December. In September, World Airways announced that it was giving up scheduled passenger service to concentrate on its charter and aircraft maintenance business.

RAILROADS

Freight traffic on U.S. railroads in 1985 totaled 884 billion ton-miles, a 4 percent decrease from 1984, according to the Association of American Railroads. Earnings for major carriers totaled $1.7 billion in 1985, a 22 percent decrease from 1984. Traffic and earnings were expected to remain about the same for 1986.

Conrail. The Senate in February approved the Department of Transportation's plan to sell the government's 85 percent share of Consolidated Railroad Corporation, or Conrail, stock to Norfolk Southern Corporation. However, the proposed deal failed to win the critical support of Representative John D. Dingell (D, Mich.), chairman of the House Energy and Commerce Committee, who said that the sale price was too low and that the merger would reduce competition. Norfolk eventually withdrew its offer, and Congress approved a plan to sell Conrail on the stock market.

Santa Fe-Southern Pacific Merger. The Interstate Commerce Commission surprised everyone by rejecting the merger of the Atchison, Topeka and Santa Fe Railway Company and Southern Pacific Transportation Company railroads. During the last 20 years, the ICC had approved most major railroad mergers. If the ICC's order stands, the Santa Fe Southern Pacific Corporation, the holding company that owns the Santa Fe, must divest the stock of Southern Pacific, which it had held in trust pending the merger. But SFSP appealed the order and, in an attempt to allay concern that the merger would be anticompetitive, agreed to give the Denver and Rio Grande Western Railroad Company access to some of its Western markets.

Union Pacific. In September, Union Pacific Corporation made a $1.2 billion tender offer for Overnite Transportation Company of Richmond, Va., the fifth largest U.S. trucking company. Union Pacific also agreed to purchase the Missouri-Kansas-Texas Railroad, a regional carrier that operates in those states and Nebraska and Oklahoma. Both purchases were subject to ICC approval.

Labor Problems. Guilford Transportation Industries was struck March 3 by members of the Brotherhood of Maintenance of Way Employees in a dispute over wages and personnel cuts. Guilford operates three small Northeastern railroads, the Maine Central, Delaware & Hudson, and Boston & Maine. The dispute threatened to escalate into a nationwide strike when BMWE picketing spread to major railroads in May, after the union learned they were giving financial assistance to Guilford. When picketing spread to Conrail, President Ronald Reagan ordered BMWE back to work. Congress in September imposed a contract settlement on Guilford and the union, which the president signed the following month.

ICC. Although new ICC chairman Heather J. Gradison was an advocate of deregulation, the commission began regulating railroads more strictly, after years of what critics saw as prorailroad bias following the deregulation law of 1980. In 1986 the ICC rescinded rail rate increases granted earlier to offset inflation and reimposed rate regulation on boxcar shipments by small railroads and leasing companies. However, the ICC assisted the growth of smaller railroads by making it easier for new operations to begin. Short lines, which preserve rail service that might otherwise be lost, blossomed across the nation in 1986, as major carriers shed unprofitable tracks. The small railroads are viable because they generally have lower labor costs and overhead than major carriers.

SHIPPING

The major shipping industry development of the year was the proposed purchase of Sea-

Land Corporation by CSX Corporation. CSX is owner of CSX Transportation, a major Eastern and Southern railroad, and American Commercial Lines, one of the biggest U.S. barge companies. Completion of the deal would represent the first railroad purchase of a major steamship line in American history.

Dockworkers' Strike. About 30,000 dockworkers in ports from Maine to Virginia walked off their jobs on October 1 after the International Longshoremen's Association's master contract with shipping management expired without a new contract having been reached. The strike, which halted international commerce on the East Coast and resulted in an estimated economic loss of tens of millions of dollars daily, ended October 3 when the ILA agreed to a temporary extension of the old contract. Negotiations continued for a time, but all major port locals eventually signed a new contract with management. The job action represented the first major dockworkers' strike since 1971.

MOTOR TRANSPORT

Final ICC statistics for 1985 showed that operating revenues for the 100 largest motor carriers totalled about $17.3 billion, up 2.3 percent from 1984. Traffic declined 3.1 percent, and net carrier income fell 28 percent.

Insurance Crisis. Like other U.S. industries, trucking was hit hard by skyrocketing insurance premiums and policy cancellations. The ICC offered some help by authorizing truckers and bus lines to set special insurance surcharges. The ICC and Federal Highway Administration also allowed truckers to set up self-insurance plans.

Bankruptcies. The fifth largest U.S. trucker, McLean Trucking Company of Winston-Salem, N.C., ceased operations in January after declaring bankruptcy. In March, another major trucker, Hall's Motor Transit Company of Mechanicsburg, Pa., filed for protection under Chapter 11 of the U.S. bankruptcy code while reorganizing.

Bus Industry. ICC statistics showed that the 20 largest bus companies in 1985 suffered declines of 4.5 percent from 1984 in operating revenues and 5.3 percent in revenue passengers carried. Net carrier operating income, however, rose to $55.8 million. In October, Greyhound Corporation announced that it would consider purchase offers for Greyhound Lines. The corporation was subsequently purchased by Dallas businessman Frederick G. Currey and two other investors.

New Standards for Drivers. In October, as part of an antidrug legislative package, Congress authorized the Transportation Department to set national standards for licenses for bus drivers and commercial truck drivers. The change was intended to prevent drivers from obtaining licenses in—and spreading violations over—several states, as they previously could. Under the legislation, bus and truck drivers could be licensed only in one state, under standards meeting minimum federal requirements.

MASS TRANSIT

In September, Portland, Ore., opened a 15-mile light rail system designed to relieve traffic on nearby Interstate 84. Also in September, ground was broken for Los Angeles's subway system. Federal assistance approved in August covered only a 4.4-mile downtown stretch of what planners envisioned as a 150-mile system covering all of Los Angeles County. In April, Miami opened a $148 million elevated electric "people mover," running in a nine-stop downtown loop.

AROUND THE WORLD

In July the government of Prime Minister Brian Mulroney proposed sweeping reforms of Canada's system of transportation regulation. The major changes would allow Canadian railroads to sign transportation contracts with customers, as U.S. railroads have been allowed to do since 1980, and would create a system of so-called joint-line rates, under which a shipper served by only one Canadian railroad could insist that a second be allowed to gain access to the shipper's plant or that the first railroad charge no more than the second railroad offered.

The governments of Britain and France agreed in January to build a rail tunnel beneath the English Channel between the Dover and Calais areas for $6.7 billion. The so-called Chunnel, to be started in 1987 and completed in 1993, would include twin 31-mile tunnels about 130 feet under the seabed through which 4,000 train cars per hour could move at peak hours. It would be the world's longest underwater tunnel.   R.E.B. (Aviation) & R.J.K.

Winding above the palm trees, the first "people mover" system to connect with a mass transit line was opened in Miami during April. Called the Metromover, the new system has automated electric cars that circle the downtown area between nine stations about 1,000 feet apart.

U.S. Secretary of State George P. Shultz and his wife enjoy a musical performance, during a visit to Turkey by the secretary. Later in the year, an agreement was finalized providing for continued U.S. military bases in Turkey.

TUNISIA. Habib Bourguiba, the frail, 83-year-old president of Tunisia, completed his third decade of rule in 1986. Bourguiba's actions—notably the firing of Premier Muhammad M'zali, his heir apparent—left little doubt as to his continuing political control.

M'zali's demise was augured in April, when he lost his post as interior minister and several of his associates were removed. Bourguiba did proclaim his confidence in M'zali "now and in the future" at the 12th congress of the ruling Destour Socialist Party (DSP) in June. However, the president assumed direct responsibility for selecting both the party's 90-member central committee and its 20-member political bureau. Many of M'zali's associates were ignored, and new recruits were tapped for the political bureau. After the congress closed, M'zali's wife lost her post as minister of family and women's affairs. On July 8, M'zali himself was dismissed.

M'zali was replaced by Rachid Sfar, a technocrat who had been serving as finance minister. Bourguiba also distanced himself from his own family, removing his son as presidential

adviser and divorcing his influential wife of many years, Wassila.

On January 1, Habib Achour, leader of the General Union of Tunisian Workers (UGTT), was sentenced to three years of detention, following his conviction on the dubious charge of having mismanaged UGTT funds. The continuing clash between the government and the UGTT spilled over onto campuses, leading to demonstrations and university closings. Prior to November parliamentary elections, authorities also moved against the previously tolerated Socialist Progressive Assembly, jailing its leader and 13 other members. The elections themselves were boycotted by the opposition, and the government party won all 126 seats.

In October, Palestine Liberation Organization leader Yasir Arafat announced that the PLO (whose headquarters in Tunisia had been bombed by Israel in 1985) was moving to Yemen and Iraq and that all its military forces had been removed from Tunisia.

See STATISTICS OF THE WORLD.   K.J.B.

TURKEY. In 1986, Prime Minister Turgut Özal's right-wing Motherland Party continued to govern Turkey with a strong parliamentary majority, increasing its seats in the 400-member Grand National Assembly to 237 after September by-elections.

The 1980 U.S.-Turkish Defense and Economic Cooperation Agreement, which had ended with 1985, was renegotiated late in 1986. Turkey, which had been letting the United States use at least 15 Turkish military installations in exchange for U.S. military and economic assistance, had wanted a pledge of about $1 billion in aid annually, for ten years. As part of a wide program of military aid cuts, the U.S. Congress voted only $590 million in military aid for Turkey for fiscal 1987—much less than the $824 million requested by the Reagan administration. Under the base agreement finally accepted by Turkey, the United States agreed only to make its "best efforts" to provide adequate levels of military aid in the future.

On September 6, at least 2 men, believed to be Arabs, killed 22 people and wounded several others when they gained entry during Sabbath services at Istanbul's newly refurbished main synagogue and launched an attack, firing machine guns and throwing grenades. Police were uncertain whether two assailants found dead amid the carnage had committed suicide or had accidentally killed themselves with the grenades. Several militant anti-Israel groups claimed responsibility; Turkish authorities blamed the Abu Nidal Palestinian group.

In February, 56 persons arrested in August 1984 after calling for democratic reforms and an end to prison torture were acquitted by a military court. The New York-based Helsinki Watch organization, meanwhile, charged that the torture of prisoners continued.

Massive Turkish forces attacked three suspected Kurdish bases in northern Iraq in August, in retaliation for an attack by Kurdish rebels on a Turkish Army truck in which 12 soldiers were killed. Turkey and Iraq had agreed in October 1984 to allow the armed forces of each country to pursue Kurdish rebels in a six-mile-deep zone along their common border.

In the economy, inflation was running at over 30 percent, and imports far exceeded exports. However, the harvest was excellent, and completion of the Atatürk Dam raised hopes that irrigation could create 4.4 million acres of arable land.

See STATISTICS OF THE WORLD. See also CYPRUS. P.J.M.

TUVALU. See STATISTICS OF THE WORLD.

U

UGANDA. Yoweri Museveni, leader of the National Resistance Movement, was sworn in on January 29, 1986, as Uganda's ninth head of state since independence. Three days earlier, the movement's military wing, the National Resistance Army (NRA), had ousted the ruling Military Council of General Tito Okello after winning a battle for control of the country's capital, Kampala. The overthrow of Okello's six-month-old regime shattered a shaky power-sharing agreement the two leaders had adopted in December 1985, following protracted negotiations. On February 12, Museveni named a cabinet under Prime Minister Samson Kisekka.

The following month, Museveni claimed that all towns were firmly under NRA control and that resisting troops had been pushed out of the country. However, the government charged in August that rebels loyal to Okello and to former Ugandan leaders Idi Amin and Milton Obote had formed a front to stop a rehabilitation program in the north, and the NRA said it had repulsed a major attack on the northern garrison town of Gulu. Museveni, in response, ordered the Sudanese border sealed, halting drought relief supplies for Sudan; he claimed its government had aided rebels in the Gulu assault. Following talks with Uganda, Sudan offered to settle Ugandan refugees farther away from the border. Rebels launched new attacks on the north in November and December.

In October, after continuing rumors of a coup attempt, at least 26 persons—including a former vice president, three cabinet ministers, a newspaper editor, and six senior army commanders—were charged with treason in connection with a coup attempt. A human rights organization accused Museveni of rights violations in the aftermath of the alleged plot. Museveni himself had earlier established a commission to investigate human rights violations by previous governments.

While attempting to restore internal order, the new head of state sought to promote regional cooperation with a series of summit meetings. Concluding one such meeting in Tanzania during July, Museveni met with the exiled Okello and said the latter was free to return to Uganda as an "elder statesman." Subsequently, at an Organization of African Unity meeting, Museveni criticized African leaders for keeping silent during the years of bloodshed in Uganda, which had claimed over 750,000 lives.

In the budget for fiscal 1987, government spending was set at $805 million, up 119 percent, but in view of the country's triple-digit inflation, planned spending actually decreased in real terms. The government hoped to plug a projected $250 million deficit with the sale of properties belonging to Asians expelled in 1973.

See STATISTICS OF THE WORLD.   S.K.

UNION OF SOVIET SOCIALIST REPUBLICS. Communist Party General Secretary Mikhail Gorbachev (see biography in PEOPLE IN THE NEWS) entered his second year in office in March 1986. Signs of change could be observed across the board in Soviet policies, although there still were limits to what the government would or could do. Probably the most memorable single event of the year was the tragic disaster at the Chernobyl nuclear power station.

Party Congress. By the end of the 27th Congress of the Communist Party of the Soviet Union, held from February 25 to March 6, the Soviet leadership had been significantly altered. Of the 319 full members of the party's Central Committee elected at the 26th congress in 1981, fewer than half remained in office—a break with the personnel stability that had

prevailed over the previous two decades. Three new members were added to the Politburo and five to the Central Committee Secretariat, the Politburo's administrative arm. Among the latter was former Soviet ambassador to the United States Anatoly Dobrynin, who was put in charge of foreign affairs.

The main order of business at the 27th congress was the approval of a new party program, the third since the Russian Revolution. Most Western observers found the plans ratified by the congress excessively ambitious in the light of Soviet capabilities. Plans for long-range economic development, for instance, called for nearly doubling national income and ending rampant food and consumer goods shortages by the year 2000. Both Gorbachev and Prime Minister Nikolai Ryzhkov issued calls for "radical reforms" in the economy. They spoke of "speeding up" technological innovation, shifting emphasis from quantity to quality and efficiency, and using prices and profits as economic incentives. Attention was called to the discovery of widespread corruption networks. Gorbachev also emphasized the need for greater "openness" in discussing Soviet problems and shortcomings.

Economic Reform. Two major economic themes in 1986 were discipline and reform. In May the Soviet leadership promulgated tough new measures against black-marketeering and bribe-taking. At the same time, the struggle continued against widespread alcoholism and worker absenteeism. Soviet economic performance during the first half of 1986 showed considerable improvement over the first six months of the previous year.

In March, agricultural reforms were announced, to take effect in 1987. Collective farms would be able to sell up to 30 percent of their produce (as well as their production above the planned targets) directly to local consumer cooperatives, to state stores, or at collective farmers' markets, and the prices of fruits and vegetables would be set locally. Such reforms were also slated for state farms. Gorbachev hinted at the need for an analogous decentralization in industry, but he eventually conceded that true reform would require a psychological "reorientation" of the entire bu-

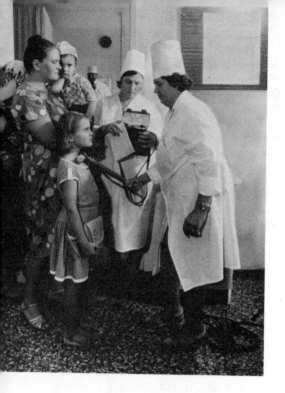

reaucracy, long accustomed to central planning.

Chernobyl. Early on April 26 an experiment at the Chernobyl nuclear power station, about 80 miles from Kiev, went awry. The resulting explosions and lingering fire spewed large amounts of radioactive material from a reactor into the atmosphere, where it was carried by winds to nearby regions and, eventually, in diluted form, over much of the world. The accident apparently occurred during an unauthorized experiment. Well over 100,000 residents of the area had to be evacuated, perhaps permanently, though the evacuation did not begin for 36 hours after the accident. Initial Western reports, in the absence for some time of information from the Soviet Union, greatly overestimated the death toll, but the accident did have tragic consequences—two workers killed in the initial explosion, about 30 other deaths in the short term; hundreds of people hospitalized, many suffering from se-

The world's worst nuclear accident occurred on April 26 at the Chernobyl nuclear power plant (below), when the No. 4 reactor (at center; see arrow) went out of control during an unauthorized experiment. Over 100,000 people were evacuated within an 18-mile radius of the plant, and thousands of others from Kiev and outlying areas, as airborne radiation spread. Above, a hospital near Kiev checks radiation levels in local residents.

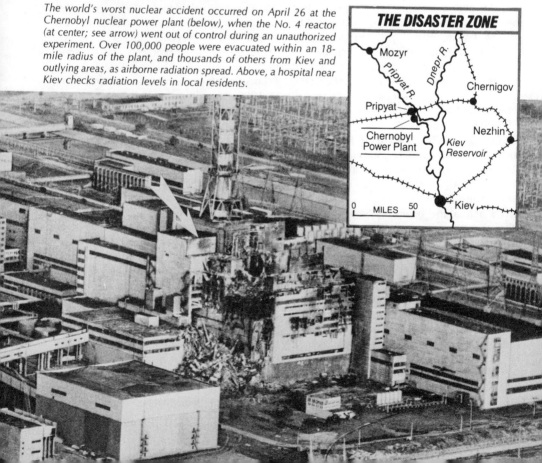

THE DISASTER ZONE

Mozyr

Pripyat R.

Dnepr R.

Chernigov

Pripyat

Nezhin

Chernobyl Power Plant

Kiev Reservoir

0   MILES   50

Kiev

rious radiation exposure; and increased long-term risks of cancer and genetic defects.

A July Politburo report estimated the direct economic damage at about $2.7 billion. In a 1,000-square mile area around the plant, topsoil had to be scraped away and handled as nuclear waste. Thousands of wells were sealed. A portion of the Ukrainian wheat harvest had to be discarded because of radiation exposure. The Soviet Union nevertheless expected to continue plans to double its nuclear power output by 1990.

Foreign Relations. After the 27th party congress, the Soviet foreign policy bureaucracy was thoroughly overhauled. Eight new deputy foreign ministers were named, and new ambassadors were appointed to important posts. New departments were created to handle arms control, international trade, and cultural exchanges.

The Soviet Union stepped up efforts to improve relations with China, which sought Soviet concessions on Afghanistan, the Soviet-backed Vietnamese occupation of Cambodia, and troop concentrations on the Sino-Soviet frontier. In July in Vladivostok, Gorbachev announced that six Soviet regiments (about 8,000 troops) would be withdrawn from Afghanistan (the withdrawal was implemented in October). He also said the Soviet Union was considering withdrawing a "substantial part" of its forces stationed in Mongolia, which lies on the Chinese border. China welcomed the proposals, but said they fell short of removing the obstacles to improved relations. Meanwhile, guerrillas continued to offer resistance against Soviet and Afghan troops backing the Soviet-installed regime in Afghanistan.

In August, in a major turnabout, Soviet and Israeli diplomats met in Helsinki for the first formal talks between their two nations in 19 years. The brief session ended abruptly in discord, but at a top-level United Nations meeting, it was agreed that the two countries would consider normalizing relations. Also in August an agreement was reached to resume Iranian gas exports to the Soviet Union; in exchange the Soviets promised to cut oil exports to help stabilize world oil prices. In December, Gorbachev and his wife paid a four-day visit to India; the visit reportedly

American reporter Nicholas Daniloff (shown here with his wife Ruth), was arrested in Moscow by Soviet authorities; he was later freed in an apparent exchange for Gennadi Zakharov, a Soviet UN employee who had been arrested by FBI agents in New York on espionage charges.

helped cement friendly relations but broke no new ground.

Espionage. In March the United States ordered the Soviet, Ukrainian, and Byelorussian missions at the United Nations, alleged by U.S. officials to be hotbeds of espionage, to reduce their personnel by more than one-third over two years, beginning October 1. Moscow protested the order. On August 23 a Soviet physicist employed by the UN, Gennadi Zakharov, was arrested by FBI agents in New York while allegedly buying classified defense documents. A week later, Nicholas Daniloff, Moscow correspondent for the magazine *U.S. News &*

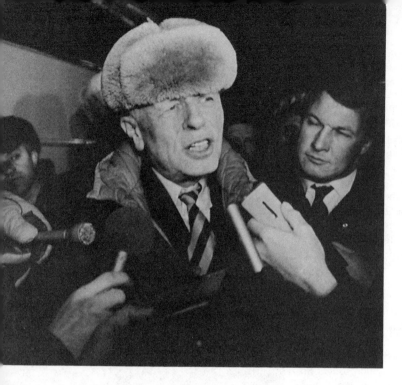

Soviet physicist and Nobel Prize winner Andrei Sakharov's seven years of exile in Gorky was brought to an end in late December; he is seen here upon his arrival in Moscow, surrounded by reporters.

World Report, was arrested in the Soviet capital and accused of espionage, after a Soviet acquaintance handed him a sealed package containing secret maps and photos. U.S. officials said Daniloff had been framed; the Soviets threatened to put him on trial. On September 12, Daniloff and Zakharov were released into the custody of their respective ambassadors.

Soviet Foreign Minister Eduard Shevardnadze arrived in Washington on September 18, just after the United States had ordered the expulsion of 25 specific members of the Soviet UN mission. U.S. officials said the 25 were spies; the Soviets again protested. After Shevardnadze met several times with Secretary of State George Shultz and once with President Ronald Reagan, Daniloff was permitted to leave the Soviet Union on September 29. The next day Zakharov was freed to return to Moscow, after pleading "no contest" to the charges against him and being given a suspended sentence; at the same time, scheduling of a Reagan-Gorbachev summit meeting in Iceland was announced in both countries' capitals, and the Soviets agreed to allow dissident Yuri Orlov and his wife, to emigrate. The 25 Soviets at the UN were given a grace period but eventually had to leave.

Arms Control. Earlier, U.S. officials had expressed impatience over the Soviet refusal to set a date for a promised Gorbachev visit to Washington. The Soviets had complained of a lack of progress in arms negotiations and wanted a Washington summit only if a concrete agreement would result. After the U.S. bombing attack on Libya in April, the Soviets canceled a preparatory meeting between Secretary of State Shultz and Foreign Minister Shevardnadze, but it took place later, in September. Following intensive negotiations and a resolution of the Daniloff case, the two sides agreed to the preliminary summit.

Meanwhile, on January 15, Gorbachev outlined an ambitious timetable for eliminating all nuclear weapons by the year 2000. The Reagan administration had made a counterproposal, for eliminating medium-range missiles in Europe and Asia. The Soviets at first insisted that the Reagan administration abandon the Strategic Defense Initiative (the "Star Wars" plan for a defensive shield against Soviet nuclear missiles) but later fielded a new proposal which raised the possibility that some research would be allowed if deployment or testing outside the laboratory was delayed. The Soviets also criticized the Reagan administration's decision (carried out in November) to cease abiding by the unratified 1979 Strategic Arms Limitation Treaty (SALT II).

In September, at a Stockholm conference, a major accord aimed at reducing the risk of war was reached. The signatories, including the United States, Canada, the Soviet Union, and all European countries except Albania, agreed to give advance notice of certain military maneuvers, among other things. Late in the year, the Soviet government announced it would end its unilateral moratorium on underground nuclear tests in 1987, as soon as the United States made its first nuclear test of the year. The United States, citing security reasons, had refused to join the Soviet moratorium, declared in August 1985.

Iceland Meeting. The Iceland summit took place on October 11–12 at Reykjavík. Gorbachev presented a package of major proposals, including complete elimination of Soviet and U.S. medium-range missiles in Europe, a 50 percent cut in strategic nuclear weapons over five years, and a ten-year ban on deployment and testing (except laboratory research) of antimissile systems like those in the Star Wars plan. Preliminary understandings were reached on some arms cuts that went further than the Soviet proposal. However, the talks collapsed when Reagan declined to accept Gorbachev's restrictions on Star Wars.

Diplomatic Cuts. The Soviets expelled 5 U.S. diplomats on October 19; the United States then ordered 55 Soviet diplomats to leave the country. On October 22, the Soviet Union expelled 5 more U.S. diplomats and withdrew all 260 Soviet employees of the U.S. embassy in Moscow and the consulate in Leningrad.

Foreign Trade. The world oil glut of 1986 threatened to cut deeply into Soviet hard-currency earnings, 75 percent of which come from sales of oil and natural gas. Imports were scaled back in response. In August the Soviets indicated that they were considering joint ventures with Western companies; it was later announced that more than 20 ministries and nearly 70 major enterprises would be authorized to deal directly with foreign companies.

Riots. In mid-December an outbreak of rioting was reported in the Central Asian republic of Kazakhstan. The official press agency Tass said that students had burned cars and set fire to a food store, but it did not report any deaths or injuries. The riots followed the ouster of the republic's longtime party leader, Akhmedovich Kunayev, a Kazakh (and Brezhnev loyalist), and his replacement with an ethnic Russian.

Emigration and Human Rights. In February, Anatoly Shcharansky, a leading Jewish dissident who had been imprisoned for eight years, was released and allowed to emigrate to Israel. (*See also* RELIGION.) As a whole, however, Jewish emigration from the Soviet Union remained at low levels and arrests of dissidents continued.

In December, Soviet dissident Anatoly Marchenko died in prison, after a long hunger strike. Later the same month, however, Andrei Sakharov, the physicist who won the 1975 Nobel Peace Prize for activity on behalf of human rights, was allowed to return to Moscow from exile in Gorky, where he had been confined without trial in 1980. His wife, Yelena Bonner, convicted of anti-Soviet activity and also restricted to Gorky, was pardoned.

See STATISTICS OF THE WORLD.   M.R.B.

UNITED ARAB EMIRATES. *See* STATISTICS OF THE WORLD.

UNITED NATIONS. The United Nations was threatened with bankruptcy in 1986, as major donors, criticizing the organization's financial management and budget-making procedures, withheld funds from programs or were overdue in paying assessments. Secretary-General Javier Pérez de Cuéllar linked his willingness to seek a second term to assurances of support from major donor nations; he did seek and win reelection, though reportedly receiving no firm commitments. Terrorism and Middle East conflict engaged the UN anew. The problem of South West Africa (Namibia) prompted a special session of the General Assembly.

Financial Crisis. At the beginning of the year, the UN found its reserves exhausted. Then the first U.S. funding installment for the year was reduced to $36 million from the $70 million expected, because of congressionally mandated cuts and executive withholdings. Both the United States and the Soviet Union were substantially in arrears. The so-called Kassebaum amendment, passed by Congress in 1985, mandated further reductions in the U.S. contribution unless a system of weighted voting on budgetary items was adopted.

In response, the secretary-general achieved $30 million in cutbacks and proposed other economy measures to yield another $30 million. The 40th General Assembly, meeting in a special spring session on finances, adopted the bulk of the secretary's suggestions. At the 41st UN session, which opened on September 16, the General Assembly approved the report of an 18-member high-level group, which proposed extensive staff layoffs and alterations in the budget process but recommended no changes in voting rules. Ultimately, after additional debate in closed-door sessions, the General Assembly was presented with, and unanimously adopted, a compromise economy plan carrying out many of the revisions proposed by the high-level group. Under the plan, the 21-country Committee for Program and Coordination was to approve a budget and set a limit on spending that could be allocated outside the budget; the committee vote was to be by consensus, with each member (including the United States and the Soviet Union) having a veto. Final approval of the budget was still at the discretion of the General Assembly, however, which could theoretically vote down a budget passed by the committee.

The chief U.S. delegate to the UN, Vernon Walters, praised the plan as an acceptable compromise and said he would urge Congress to restore cuts made in the U.S. contribution to the UN. Some Third World countries criticized the compromise as giving too much leverage to individual major donors.

Soviets at the UN. On March 7 the United States ordered the Soviet, Ukrainian, and Byelorussian missions to the United Nations to cut their combined personnel in phases, reducing the total from 275 to 170 by April 1, 1988. The size of the missions was said to pose a threat to U.S. national security. The Soviet Union challenged the order as illegal; the United States insisted its action was both legal and nonnegotiable.

On September 17 the United States presented the Soviet mission with a list of 25 specific personnel ordered to leave by October 1 because of alleged involvement in espionage; by the end of October, after a deadline extension, all 25 had departed. The U.S. order was seen as linked to the superpowers' confrontation over the case of Nicholas Daniloff, Moscow correspondent for the magazine *U.S. News & World Report,* who had been seized in the Soviet capital on apparently trumped-up espionage charges, a week after U.S. authorities in New York arrested Gennadi Zakharov, a scientist employed by the UN, as an alleged Soviet spy. (Daniloff was permitted to leave the Soviet Union, and Zakharov, after pleading "no contest" to charges against him, was allowed to depart for Moscow.) The secretary-general criticized the U.S. demand as illegal; he also disputed a U.S. Senate report describing one of his special assistants at the UN, Soviet appointee Vladimir Kolesnikov, as a KGB agent.

Southern Africa. Prospects for implementing the UN plan for Namibian independence continued to hinge on the removal of Cuban troops from neighboring Angola. South Africa's insistence on this point was bolstered in January by a U.S. decision to supply military aid to Jonas Savimbi's insurgent forces opposing the Angolan government. The aid was delayed during March pending Angola's response to a South African proposal to initiate the UN plan on August 1, conditional on Cuban withdrawal from Angola. Angola again rejected this condition. South African forays in support of Savimbi continued, and on June 18 the Security Council condemned the South African attacks. However, a call for limited economic sanctions against South Africa was vetoed in the Security Council by Britain and the United States.

A UN Conference for the Immediate Independence of Namibia was held in Vienna in July. Later, at a special session of the General Assembly, comprehensive mandatory sanctions against South Africa were again urged, by a vote of 126-0, with 24 abstentions.

Terrorism and Libya. On February 4, a Libyan passenger aircraft was intercepted and forced to land at an Israeli military airfield, but no terrorists were found on board. The United States vetoed a Security Council resolution condemning the Israeli action. The vote was 10-1, with 4 abstentions. The Council of the International Civil Aviation Organization (ICAO) condemned the Israeli action as a threat to air traffic safety.

The Orderly Departure Program run by the United Nations reached a milestone in January when Vo Thi Hau became the 100,000th person to legally leave Vietnam; she and her two children joined her husband, Hoang Ngoc Minh, in Amsterdam. The program was subsequently suspended by Hanoi because of the slow processing of visas by the United States.

Tension between the United States and Libya flared in March, when Libyan missile attacks on carrier-based planes of the U.S. Sixth Fleet in the Gulf of Sidra were met with air strikes against Libyan installations and patrol boats. A proposed Security Council resolution condemning the U.S. actions failed to command support. After the United States bombed what it termed terrorist-related targets in the Libyan cities of Tripoli and Benghazi on April 15, a Security Council vote to condemn the U.S. action was vetoed by the United States, Britain, and France.

Lebanon. The future of Unifil, the nine-nation UN peacekeeping force in Lebanon, became increasingly precarious. Unifil's deficit was already in excess of $230 million, and the U.S. Congress had voted to cut the U.S. share by nearly 60 percent. The Soviet Union, however, after refusing its support in previous years, agreed to share in the budget. On January 17 the United States vetoed a Security Council resolution calling for Israeli withdrawal from a 6-mile-wide "security zone" and deploring Israeli acts of violence in southern Lebanon. Continued harassment of the UN peacekeeping force by the Israeli-supplied South Lebanon Army was another cause for concern. But in view of the likelihood that cross-border violence would escalate if Unifil were withdrawn, the Security Council voted to extend the force for three months, and in July for six more months. The decision resulted in an unprecedented series of Lebanese attacks, mostly against the French contingent. In August battles between the Shiite Muslim Amal militias and UN troops left 17 French soldiers wounded. In August and September, an Irish soldier and three French soldiers were killed by bombs. In response to French requests, the Security Council asked the secretary-general to pursue "effective reinforcement of the security of members of the force." In September, a Security Council resolution in support of Unifil, calling for deployment of the force to the southern border of Lebanon, was adopted without objection; the United States abstained.

Central America. In June the World Court ruled that the United States had violated Nicaraguan sovereignty and international law by aiding the counterrevolutionaries, or contras, seeking to overthrow the Sandinista government. The United States, which had denied the court's jurisdiction, was ordered to cease supplying arms and training to the rebels and to compensate Nicaragua for damage inflicted. At Nicaragua's request, the Security Council met in July to discuss how to bring about U.S. compliance with the ruling. A resolution calling on all countries to refrain from supporting actions of any kind against any state in the region was vetoed by the United States.

Iran-Iraq War. In February the Security Council, in a unanimous resolution, deplored, for the first time, the "initial acts" that gave rise to the Iran-Iraq war, as well as territorial violations and the use of chemical weapons. After investigation, a UN medical team concluded that Iraq had used chemical weapons on many occasions.

Cyprus. In March the secretary-general presented to the Greek and Turkish Cypriots a revised draft agreement proposing a federated republic comprising two semiautonomous states. However, Cypriot President Spyros Kyprianou said the draft had failed to deal with the major issues: withdrawal of Turkish troops, guarantees against future Turkish invasions, and freedom of movement and property ownership in a united island. The Turkish Cypriot leader, Rauf Denktash, regarded the Greek Cypriot response as a rejection of the UN plan. In response to the protests over a July visit to northern Cyprus by the Turkish prime minister, the Turkish Cypriot leader closed for a week all crossing points between the two communities, separating units of the UN peacekeeping force, whose mandate had been renewed in June for another six months.

African Development. From May 27 to June 1 the General Assembly devoted a special session to Africa, stressing a need to restore the economies of some 50 African countries. The Organization of African Unity presented a priority program stressing the importance of agricultural growth, economic incentives, and better economic management. While the African states proposed to meet much of the cost of the program themselves, they also sought international aid. In July the United States pledged $2.85 billion over three years to the International Development Association (IDA), the primary UN agency through which interest-free loans are provided to the poorest countries.

Nuclear Safety. The release of radioactive elements into the atmosphere after the April explosion at the Chernobyl nuclear power plant in the Soviet Union's Ukraine region put at risk not only those in the immediate area but also large numbers of people in neighboring countries. The International Atomic Energy Agency (IAEA), a UN agency, served as host for a five-day gathering of experts who evaluated safety procedures and health effects in the light of a detailed Soviet report on the Chernobyl accident. IAEA members also agreed on language for two draft conventions covering nuclear accidents—one providing for early notification of possible transboundary effects and the other committing outside parties to offer assistance when such an accident occurs. Both were adopted by a special session of the IAEA general conference on September 26 and came into force the next day.

Human Rights. In November, Iran and Chile were named in General Assembly resolutions as guilty of human rights violations; government and Soviet forces in Afghanistan were cited for civilian atrocities. The General Assembly, by varying margins, adopted resolutions endorsing each of these charges.

Election for Secretary-General. In October the General Assembly and the Security Council both unanimously elected Pérez de Cuéllar to a second five-year term as UN secretary-general. His decision to run circumvented possible wrangling over a successor to the post, in the aftermath of embarrassing disclosures involving former Secretary-General Kurt Waldheim (*see biography in* PEOPLE IN THE NEWS).   I.C.B.

United States of America

During 1986 a sweeping tax reform measure was enacted, President Ronald Reagan met with Soviet leader Mikhail Gorbachev in an Iceland summit that reached an impasse over "Star Wars," and the United States had major confrontations with Libya. Late in the year a major scandal erupted over U.S. arms sales to Iran and the diversion of profits to rebels in Nicaragua.

These and other developments are examined in the sections which follow, covering the Presidency, Congress, Political Parties, the Supreme Court, and Foreign Affairs. Relevant articles elsewhere in the book include ECONOMY AND BUSINESS, ELECTIONS IN THE UNITED STATES, MILITARY AND NAVAL AFFAIRS, and SPACE EXPLORATION.

THE PRESIDENCY

President Ronald Reagan's immense personal popularity persisted through most of the year, despite clashes with Congress, but late in the year, he was damaged by a major scandal. The president won some victories—notably when his tax reform proposal was enacted (albeit in modified form). But a summit meeting with Soviet leader Mikhail Gorbachev in October collapsed without an arms reduction agreement, and in November, despite energetic campaigning, the president failed to preserve Republican control of the Senate. Subsequently, it was revealed that he had approved

President Ronald Reagan signs the Tax Reform Act of 1986, underscoring what some predicted would be considered the biggest victory of his second term.

Following disclosures of U.S. arms sales to Iran, President Reagan (top) announced that he had accepted the resignation of his national security adviser, Vice Admiral John Poindexter, and that Lieutenant Colonel Oliver North, one of Poindexter's key assistants, had been fired. Poindexter (center) and North (bottom) both took the Fifth Amendment at hearings before a House committee and declined to answer questions about the arms sales.

secret military sales to Iran and, further, that profits from the arms sales had gone, apparently without his knowledge, to the so-called contra guerrillas fighting the Sandinista regime in Nicaragua.

U.S.-Soviet Relations. The year began on a positive note, with Reagan and Gorbachev extending televised greetings to each other's nations. But there was little discernible movement in the Geneva arms talks, and in May the president, citing Soviet violations, said the United States would no longer adhere to the unratified 1979 Strategic Arms Limitation Treaty (SALT II); the first actual U.S. violation came when the United States exceeded a key SALT II weapons ceiling in November.

Efforts toward a 1986 summit, and perhaps an arms agreement, hit an apparent snag in August, when the Soviets arrested American journalist Nicholas Daniloff on espionage charges, seemingly in retaliation for the U.S. arrest of Soviet UN employee Gennadi Zakharov, accused of spying. In late September, after intensive negotiations, both men were permitted to return home. The president denied that a "trade" had occurred, despite appearances to the contrary.

On the day Zakharov was released, it was announced unexpectedly that Gorbachev and Reagan would meet shortly in Reykjavík, Iceland. In two days of talks there, sweeping tentative agreements were reached in major arms control areas; but the talks collapsed after Reagan rejected Gorbachev's demands for limits on the Strategic Defense Initiative ("Star Wars"). Besides receiving criticism for this outcome, Reagan found himself in a new controversy when the Kremlin said he had tentatively agreed to a complete elimination of all nuclear forces in ten years. The White House replied that he had talked only of scrapping all ballistic missiles. Even that seriously concerned Reagan's European allies, and after he met with British Prime Minister Margaret Thatcher in November, the administration said any such sweeping action would be deemphasized in future U.S.-Soviet talks.

Libya. Early in the year, accusing Libyan leader Muammar al-Qaddafi of complicity in terrorism, Reagan ordered Americans to leave Libya and imposed economic sanctions on that country. In March, U.S. ships and planes clashed with Libyan forces in the Gulf of Sidra, off the Libyan coast; officials denied, however, that U.S. maneuvers in the area had been designed to goad Qaddafi into a military confrontation. The following month, after the terrorist bombing of a West Berlin nightclub frequented by U.S. servicemen, American warplanes attacked targets in the Libyan cities of Tripoli and Benghazi. In a television address, Reagan asserted that the evidence was "conclusive" connecting Libya with the Berlin bombing.

Iran/Contra Scandal. Partly because of his announced policy of toughness toward terrorism, Reagan was seriously embarrassed in early November by disclosures that U.S. arms had been secretly sold to Iran—apparently at least in part in the hope of gaining the release of U.S. hostages held by pro-Iranian Lebanese groups. (Three such U.S. hostages were released in 1985 and 1986.) The operation, carried out with Israeli assistance, had been directed by White House officials and approved by Reagan, over the opposition of Secretary of Defense Caspar Weinberger and Secretary of State George Shultz. After maintaining a low profile on the issue for a time, Reagan admitted, in a speech from the Oval Office on November 13, that he had authorized shipping "small amounts of defensive weapons and spare parts" to Iran, but said that the purpose had been to improve relations, not to "ransom" hostages. These characterizations were later questioned. Reagan formally approved the arms shipments in a January 1986 executive order. Israel had shipped U.S.-made arms to Iran prior to that time, in 1985, with U.S. agreement that it would replace them. There were conflicting accounts as to whether Reagan gave advance oral approval to the first such Israeli shipment or merely acquiesced in it after the fact.

On November 25, the president announced that he had not been "fully informed" as to a key aspect of the arms transactions; Attorney General Edwin Meese, who had been ordered to conduct an investigation, said he had learned that some $10 million to $30 million in profits from the arms transactions had been channeled through secret bank accounts to the Nicaraguan contras—during a time when Congress had sharply restricted contra aid. (Later, it became less clear how much arms profit was received and how much actually reached the contras.) Reagan also announced that the White House national security adviser, Vice Admiral John Poindexter, had resigned and that his aide, Lieutenant-Colonel Oliver North, had been dismissed. (Both invoked the Fifth Amendment in testifying before congressional committees later in the year.) High officials in the administration, including Shultz, Weinberger, Vice President George Bush, and Chief of Staff Donald Regan, denied knowledge of the contra link. On November 26, Reagan appointed a three-member panel, headed by former Senator John Tower, to investigate the role of the National Security Council staff in the affair.

In early December, Reagan named Frank Carlucci, former deputy CIA director, as his new national security adviser. (It was later announced that the council would be restructured to give it a clear role in coordinating government policy while removing it from any involvement in covert operations.) Reagan also agreed to the appointment of a special prosecutor to investigate the scandal; a panel of three federal judges named Lawrence Walsh, a former federal prosecutor and judge, to the post and gave him a broader mandate than the administration had sought. On December 26, the White House announced that a special crisis team would be formed, headed by departing U.S. NATO delegate David Abshire, to coordinate administration responses in ongoing investigations of the scandal.

New York Times/CBS News polls taken in late November and early December indicated that the president's approval rating had dropped from 67 percent prior to the scandal to 46–47 percent; around the same proportion of the public believed Reagan had been lying when he denied knowledge of the diversion of funds to the contras, although half or more still believed the president had "more honesty and integrity than most people in public life."

Successes and Failures. The president was a strong ideological supporter of the contras and during the year had pushed through Congress a measure legally providing them "humanitarian" and military aid. He did not, however, succeed in getting Congress to go along with

Cabinet of the United States

Vice-President   George Bush

Secretary of State   George Shultz
Secretary of the Treasury   James Baker
Secretary of Defense   Caspar Weinberger
Attorney General   Edwin Meese III
Secretary of the Interior   Donald Hodel
Secretary of Agriculture   Richard Lyng
Secretary of Commerce   Malcolm Baldrige
Secretary of Labor   William Brock
**Secretary of Health and Human
Services**   Otis Bowen
**Secretary of Housing and Urban
Development**   Samuel Pierce, Jr.
Secretary of Transportation   Elizabeth
Dole
Secretary of Energy   John Herrington
Secretary of Education   William Bennett

**Director of the Office of Management and
Budget**   James Miller III
**Director of the Central Intelligence
Agency**   William Casey
**U.S. Representative to the United
Nations**   Vernon Walters
U.S. Trade Representative   Clayton K.
Yeutter

his policy toward South Africa. In October, Congress overrode his veto of a tough South Africa sanctions bill. Even many loyal Republican allies split with him on this issue. Reagan also suffered a significant defeat when the Democrats won control of the Senate in November elections, but he won passage of major tax reform legislation in what some predicted would be considered the greatest accomplishment of his second term. The final tax bill approved by Congress, and signed by the president in October, shifted a portion of the tax burden from individuals to business and simplified tax brackets while eliminating many individual deductions.

Cabinet. The only cabinet change during the year involved the resignation of Agriculture Secretary John Block and his replacement in March by Richard Lyng. CIA Director William Casey was hospitalized in December, following a cerebral seizure, and was operated on for a

brain tumor; at year's end it was unknown whether he would be able to return to the job.

President's Health. During 1986 and early 1987, Reagan underwent a number of medical examinations and procedures, none of which turned up evidence that the colon cancer for which he had been operated on in July 1985 had returned or spread. In January, in June, and again at the beginning of 1987, he had benign intestinal polyps removed, and on the last occasion he also had minor prostate surgery, but he was reported to be in sound basic health.   R.T.

CONGRESS

By the close of the 99th Congress, two of President Ronald Reagan's main legislative initiatives—an overhaul of the federal tax system and aid to antigovernment rebels in Nicaragua—had received congressional backing, but neither victory had come easily. Meanwhile, Congress handed Reagan a major defeat by overriding his veto of a bill imposing sanctions against South Africa (see UNITED STATES: Foreign Affairs.) Dominating much of the session's debate was continued concern about the huge federal deficit. The midterm elections were awaited with great interest, especially in the Senate, where the Democrats, who already controlled the House, could gain a majority. In fact, they did so (see ELECTIONS IN THE UNITED STATES). In the weeks before adjournment, aroused by national concern over drug abuse, Congress passed a $1.7 billion antidrug bill (see CRIME AND LAW ENFORCEMENT). After the November elections, Congress became involved in investigating the emerging Iran/contra scandal.

Budget. When Congress passed the so-called Gramm-Rudman bill in 1985, legislators thought they finally had devised a way to bring the federal deficit under control. The law established progressively lower federal deficit ceiling targets year by year through fiscal 1991, by which time the budget was to be balanced. If Congress failed to cut enough spending to meet each year's targeted level, the measure required the comptroller general (who is subject to removal only by Congress) to impose automatic spending reductions that would fall equally on military and nonmilitary programs, with certain exceptions. Fearing that parts of the new procedure would be ruled unconstitutional, legislators included a "fallback" provision that required Congress to use its normal legislative process to enact the spending reductions. For fiscal 1986, a cut of $11.7 billion was mandated; for each of the next five years a reduction of $36 billion was seen as needed to meet required targets.

On February 5, President Reagan submitted his fiscal 1987 budget request, which he claimed met the Gramm-Rudman requirement for a $144 billion deficit in the upcoming fiscal year. The president's budget called for $994 billion in outlays and $850.4 billion in revenues, for a deficit of $143.6 billion. Members of both parties balked at the president's proposal to raise overall defense spending authority to $320.3 billion, a 12 percent increase over the previous year, while dramatically cutting back domestic programs. In June both houses approved a fiscal 1987 budget resolution that would hold overall defense spending authority to some $292 billion.

Over the following months, Congress struggled with little success to achieve the savings called for in its nonbinding budget blueprint and to meet the requirements of Gramm-Rudman. In early July those efforts were made more complicated when the Supreme Court ruled that a key provision of the budget law, giving budget-cutting powers to the comptroller general, violated the Constitution's doctrine of separation of powers. The Court left intact the fallback position, however. Later in the month, Congress ratified the $11.7 billion in fiscal 1986 reductions it had already made under the now-unconstitutional spending-cut mechanism.

On July 30 the Senate voted to revise Gramm-Rudman so as to meet the objections of the Supreme Court. They proposed allowing the Office of Management and Budget (which is part of the executive branch), instead of the General Accounting Office (headed by the comptroller general), to determine how across-the-board cuts should be made. The proposal was attached in August to a bill to raise the public debt limit from $2.079 trillion to $2.323 trillion, enough to carry the government through September 1987. But the House, led by Democrats, steadfastly opposed the Gramm-Rud-

man revision. Their opposition also stalled the debt ceiling bill, and thus Congress was forced to pass a stopgap measure to tide the government over through mid-October. Finally, on October 17, Congress passed legislation raising the debt limit—but only until May 15, 1987. Congress did agree on a deficit-reduction package that was needed as part of overall efforts to stay within the ceiling set by the budget law for fiscal 1987. Some of the "savings"—including moving certain expenses to be charged against the previous year—were widely conceded to be questionable.

Meanwhile, legislators and the White House haggled over an omnibus spending bill, which was needed because Congress had failed to approve any of the 13 regular appropriations bills before the start of the 1987 fiscal year on October 1. On October 17, Congress ratified a $576 billion spending bill, which the president signed the next day; it provided a deficit of $154 billion.

Tax Reform. One of the biggest legislative successes of the year was congressional passage of a bill to revamp the federal tax system. The House had passed its version of the tax

---

Picking Roses on the Hill

When the House of Representatives abandoned flowery speeches in September for speeches on flowers, it was all in the line of duty. Calling the rose a symbol of "love, peace, friendship, courage, loyalty, and devotion," members ended nearly a century of debate by joining the Senate to proclaim the rose America's "national floral emblem." The rose has had a "long and proud American history," explained one of the bill's sponsors, Representative Lindy Boggs (D, La.). Dissenters argued that a national flower should not be an import, like most varieties of roses, but an exclusively native species—such as the marigold (long championed by the late Senator Everett Dirksen). Others felt the rose was too delicate to symbolize the rugged, pioneering spirit of America. But any hope that a veto would nip the rose bill in the bud was short-lived. Ronald Reagan, who's been known to enjoy the White House's Rose Garden, gladly signed the bill into law.

Among the best-known figures retiring from Congress were veteran Louisiana Senator Russell Long (shown above with Majority leader Bob Dole and Finance Committee chairman Robert Packwood), Arizona Senator Barry Goldwater (above right), and Speaker of the House Thomas P. "Tip" O'Neill, Jr. (far right).

reform bill in December 1985. The Senate Finance Committee began to work on its version in the spring of 1986, encountering strong resistance from a variety of interest groups. In a last-ditch effort to keep tax reform alive, committee chairman Bob Packwood (R, Ore.) proposed a measure that included a dramatic cut in tax rates along with limits on many deductions; the committee went along, and the full Senate passed the measure in June, by a vote of 97-3. Over the next two months, House-Senate conferees hashed out a compromise measure that reduced the previous 15 tax brackets to 2, lowered the top individual income tax rate from 50 percent to 28 percent, and increased the personal exemption, to $2,000 by 1989. (For a transitional period in 1987, there were five brackets, ranging from 11 percent to 38.5 percent.) The standard deduction was also increased. The top corporate rate was reduced from 46 percent to 34 percent by 1988.

To make up for these benefits, the new law did away with the special low tax rate for both individual and corporate capital gains. Business lost the 10 percent investment tax credit,

and depreciation allowances for real estate, business equipment, plants, and machinery were tightened. The new law also eliminated or limited dozens of personal deductions, including those for state and local sales tax and consumer-loan interest. Mortgage interest remained deductible for first and second homes, but not for additional homes. Allowances for tax-deferred contribution to Individual Retirement Accounts were tightened. The use of tax-shelter paper losses to offset income from wages and other sources was phased out.

The Tax Reform Act of 1986 passed overwhelmingly in both houses, and President Reagan signed it at a well-publicized White House ceremony in October.

Environment. House-Senate conferees worked through most of the year to resolve differences over the so-called Superfund hazardous waste cleanup legislation. One of the most contentious issues was how to fund the five-year, $9 billion program. After months of negotiation, agreement was reached on a mixture of funding methods, including taxes on crude oil and a new across-the-board tax on large corporations. Despite reservations, the president signed

418

sell firearms. President Reagan signed the bill. In October, Congress ratified legislation that made it illegal for employers, in most cases, to require workers to retire when they reach a certain age.

Judicial Affairs. After often acrimonious hearings before the Senate Judiciary Committee, Supreme Court Justice William H. Rehnquist was confirmed by the Senate to succeed the retiring Warren Burger as the Court's chief justice. The vote was 65-33, the "nay" votes representing the most ever cast against a successful nominee for the post. The Senate also confirmed, 98-0, conservative Appeals Court Judge Antonin Scalia to take Rehnquist's place as an associate justice. (See also UNITED STATES: Supreme Court.)

In October the Senate removed a federal judge from office for the first time in 50 years, convicting Judge Harry Claiborne on three of four articles of impeachment voted by the House in July.

Congressional Affairs. House Speaker Thomas P. ("Tip") O'Neill, Jr. (D, Mass.), bade farewell in October after 10 years as speaker, the longest continuous tenure of any speaker in congressional history. Other well-known veterans to retire included Senators Barry Goldwater (R, Ariz.), Charles McC. Mathias (R, Md.), and Russell B. Long (D, La.). On December 8, House Democrats chose Texas Representative Jim Wright as the new speaker; Thomas Foley (Wash.) rose to majority leader, and Tony Coelho (Calif.) was named majority whip. On the Republican side, Robert H. Michel (Ill.) and Trent Lott (Miss.) were reelected minority leader and whip, respectively. In the new Senate, now under Democratic control, Robert Byrd (W. Va.) was slated to become majority leader, while the erstwhile majority leader, Robert Dole (Kan.), was relegated to minority leader.

Earlier in the year the Senate instituted rules allowing television and radio coverage of its floor debate; the House already had such coverage.

Iran/Contra Affair. Late in the year, regular committees in both the Senate and the House held hearings on the Iran/contra affair, and special committees were formed to investigate the affair. The 15-member House committee

the bill into law on October 17. House and Senate negotiators also agreed after a year of talks on an $18 billion, eight-year reauthorization of the Clean Water Act. The bill was killed by President Reagan's pocket veto, but supporters reintroduced it in early 1987.

Immigration. On October 9, after a five-year effort, legislators passed a bill revising the nation's immigration laws. The measure called for penalties against employers who knowingly hired illegal aliens and provided legal status for some of the millions of illegal aliens already living in the United States. The bill also included a plan to allow illegal aliens who had done some farm work to become temporary residents and to achieve permanent resident status and possible citizenship later on. President Reagan signed the legislation.

Other Legislation. In May, Congress enacted a law ending the federal ban on the interstate sale and transport of rifles and shotguns and easing licensing requirements for those who

419

was to be chaired, starting in January 1987, by Representative Lee Hamilton (D, Ind.). The 11-member Senate panel was to be headed by Senator Daniel Inouye (D, Hawaii).   P.F.

POLITICAL PARTIES

Beset by a shortage of cash and an excess of ideological confusion, the Democratic Party nevertheless managed to recapture control of the Senate in the November 1986 elections. Both financially and ideologically the Republicans found themselves more comfortably settled, but the GOP faced serious problems as the Reagan presidency entered its twilight era with a Democratic-controlled Congress and a scandal that was to be the subject of lengthy investigation.

Vice President George Bush, shown here campaigning in Guilford, N.H., was an early unofficial candidate for the 1988 Republican presidential nomination.

Democratic Party. Democratic leaders had much to be worried about. Several major urban areas, notably New York City and Washington, D.C., were wracked by local scandals that brought little credit to the cities' Democratic mayors. The March 18 victory in the Illinois Democratic Party primary of two followers of the right-wing extremist Lyndon LaRouche was a rude shock to the party. It was also a personal embarrassment to Democratic gubernatorial candidate Adlai E. Stevenson III, whose hand-picked running mates for the offices of lieutenant governor and secretary of state were defeated by the LaRouchians. In subsequent months, national party leaders moved to counter the LaRouchians' growing influence at the precinct level.

Reports in April revealed that the 1984 Democratic presidential candidates were still more than $6 million in debt. The leading debtor was Senator Gary Hart (Colo.), who declined to stand for reelection in 1986 and was widely regarded as the front-runner for the presidential nomination in 1988.

The Democratic National Committee (DNC), headed by Paul G. Kirk, Jr., approved a series of changes in the rules for the 1988 presidential nomination. The number of officially unpledged delegates was increased and seats at the convention were reserved for all 378 members of the DNC, 80 percent of Democratic members of the House of Representatives and Senate, and all Democratic governors. The committee also lowered the threshold for winning a proportional share of a state's convention delegates from 20 percent for states with caucuses and 25 percent for states with primaries to 15 percent.

Republican Party. The first Republican officially to declare candidacy for the 1988 presidential nomination was Pierre S. du Pont IV, who made his announcement on September 16. However, the former Delaware governor was not only a dark horse but a latecomer. Vice President George Bush (*see biography in* PEOPLE IN THE NEWS), Senate Majority Leader Robert Dole (Kan.), Representative Jack F. Kemp (N.Y.), and former Senator Howard H. Baker, Jr. (Tenn.), had all been unofficially off and running for more than a year. Bush was the apparent front-runner, although the out-

Extremist

Lyndon LaRouche stunned political observers in March when two of his followers were nominated lieutenant governor and secretary of state in the Illinois Democratic primary, defeating the handpicked running mates of former U.S. Senator Adlai Stevenson III, who won the gubernatorial nomination. Although the LaRouchians lost in November, the incident brought new attention to LaRouche, whose right-wing platform includes a dire warning of an impending financial crash and calls for the quarantining of all AIDS victims. A former leftist whose views changed in the 1970's, LaRouche has charged Queen Elizabeth II with drug trafficking and claims that the CIA, the Soviet secret police, and Colombian drug dealers all seek to assassinate him. He campaigned for president in the last three elections, attracting little attention. As his views became more widely known, his finances also came under closer scrutiny. Federal agencies began probing his fund-raising techniques, and late in the year, 13 of his associates were indicted on federal fraud and conspiracy charges.

Lyndon LaRouche

break of the Iran/contra scandal late in the year somewhat damaged his prospects.

Michigan, site of the first face-off among the major contenders, produced the first big surprise of the 1988 campaign. Signing up people willing to run for precinct delegate was the initial step in the state's cumbersome national convention delegate selection process. Predictably, Bush and Kemp finished among the leaders in the delegate sign-up race, but so did the Reverend Marion G. "Pat" Robertson, the millionaire founder of the Christian Broadcasting Network and host (until late 1986) of its popular *700 Club* program.

Court Decision. In December the U.S. Supreme Court, voting 5-3, struck down a Connecticut provision limiting voting in primaries to persons previously enrolled in a political party. The ruling came in a suit by Connecticut Republicans seeking open primaries to attract independents; it appeared to clear the way for open primaries in 20 other states with laws similar to Connecticut's, if parties in those states so desired.

See also ELECTIONS IN THE UNITED STATES.

G.M.H.

SUPREME COURT

The announcement in June by Chief Justice Warren E. Burger that he was retiring at the end of the 1985–1986 term, and the subsequent elevation of William H. Rehnquist (*see biography in* PEOPLE IN THE NEWS) to chief justice, along with the appointment of Antonin Scalia as an associate justice, marked the beginning of a new era on the nation's highest judicial tribunal. Meanwhile, in 1986 the Court decided various cases involving social issues, civil rights, mergers, and other issues. (See also BLACKS IN THE UNITED STATES; CIVIL LIBERTIES AND CIVIL RIGHTS; WOMEN.)

Court Changes. The nominations of Rehnquist and Scalia, both ideological conservatives, were approved by the Senate in September, Scalia's by a vote of 98-0 and Rehnquist's by a vote of 65-33—the most negative votes ever for a justice confirmed to the Court. Opposition to Rehnquist's elevation had been vociferous, as critics questioned his commitment to civil rights and civil liberties.

Rehnquist's elevation sparked discussion about the influence a chief justice could have in swaying other members of the Court. Chief

Members of the U.S. Supreme Court pose for a formal portrait in November. Seated from left to right are Thurgood Marshall, William J. Brennan, Jr., Chief Justice William H. Rehnquist, Byron R. White, and Harry A. Blackmun. Standing from left to right are Sandra Day O'Connor, Lewis F. Powell, Jr., John Paul Stevens, and Antonin Scalia.

Justice Earl Warren, who was appointed by President Dwight Eisenhower in 1953 and served through 1969, was an extremely strong chief justice and a key designer of many landmark liberal decisions. Burger was seen more as an effective administrator than as a shaper of jurisprudence; he also spoke out on law-related matters, such as a prison reform, judicial work load, and advertising by lawyers. Rehnquist, though generally a proponent of judicial restraint, was expected to be an activist leader.

Homosexual Rights. In a highly publicized and controversial privacy case, *Bowers* v. *Hardwick*, the Court decided by a 5-4 majority that there is no constitutional right to engage in private homosexual relations. The ruling upheld a Georgia sodomy law, at least when used to prosecute homosexuals. Critics of the ruling decried the Court's apparent retreat on the extension of privacy rights.

Freedom of Speech and Press. The press fared well in two important libel cases. In *Philadelphia Newspapers Inc.* v. *Hepps*, the Supreme Court held that a private person involved in a matter of public concern has, like a public figure under earlier rulings, the burden of proving the falsity of a report in order to establish that libel has occurred. And in *Anderson* v. *Liberty Lobby*, the Court held that judges should summarily dismiss libel suits brought by public figures and officials unless evidence of actual malice by the press is "clear and convincing."

In *Bethel School District No. 403* v. *Fraser*, the Court upheld the authority of school officials to discipline a student whose speech at a school assembly was filled with sexual innuendos. The Court held in *Posados de Puerto Rico Associates* v. *Tourism Company of Puerto Rico* that the government can ban advertising for products and services that are legal to sell (in this case, casino gambling).

Voting Rights. The Supreme Court held in *Davis* v. *Bandemer* that partisan political gerrymandering (the drawing of electoral district lines to create legislative representation to benefit one political party) could be subject to constitutional challenge. Such a challenge may stand, said the Court, if the redrawing of lines leads to continual frustration of the majority will or to the effective denial of influence to a majority. However, ruling on the case before it, the Court upheld a 1981 plan for legislative redistricting in Indiana, finding that the gerrymandering was not so severe as to violate the Constitution. The case arose following elections for the lower house of the legislature in which Democrats received 52 percent of the vote but won only 43 percent of the seats.

Church-State Issues. In *Witters* v. *Washington Department of Services for the Blind*, the Court said that a state award of financial aid to a blind student attending a private Christian college to prepare for a career as a pastor or missionary did not constitute a violation of the First Amendment's establishment clause. The Court, in reversing a state Supreme Court ruling, viewed this use of public funds as rehabilitation assistance rather than impermissible state support of religion.

In *Bowen* v. *Roy*, the Court found against an American Indian family who refused on religious grounds to obtain a social security number for its infant daughter. At issue was government issuance of food stamps, which were withheld because the family failed to produce social security identification. In *Goldman* v. *Weinberger*, a divided Court sanctioned the application of Air Force regulations banning the wearing of religious headgear indoors. An orthodox Jewish officer had sought to wear his yarmulka while on duty, saying this was required by his religious beliefs.

Death Penalty. In *Ford* v. *Wainwright*, the Court declared for the first time that a condemned prisoner who becomes insane awaiting execution can not be put to death unless and until the individual regains sanity.

Deficit Reduction Law. The key provision of a law passed by Congress in 1985 to control federal deficits was struck down by a 7-2 Court decision in *Bowsher* v. *Synar*. The Court found that the so-called Gramm-Rudman-Hollings Act violated the Constitution's separation of powers doctrine because it assigned executive powers to make budget reductions to the comptroller general, who, by law, is subject to removal only by Congress. A "fallback" provision was left intact by the Court; it called for using the normal legislative process to arrive at the goals delineated by the law.

Abortion. In *Thornburgh* v. *American College of Obstetricians and Gynecologists*, the Court

New Associate Justice
After President Ronald Reagan decided on William Rehnquist as his nominee for chief justice of the Supreme Court, the next step was to find a replacement for Rehnquist who might join him in building a strong conservative coalition on the Court. Reagan's choice, Antonin Scalia, a well-respected judge on the U.S. Court of Appeals for the District of Columbia Circuit, fit the bill perfectly; Scalia's record suggested he would often agree with administration positions on political and social issues, and he was regarded as an advocate of judicial restraint. At 50, he also had prospects of a long future on the Court. The affable Scalia (pronounced Skul-*lee*-uh) graduated first in his class from Georgetown University, completed Harvard Law School, and served in several federal posts, besides teaching at the University of Chicago Law School. He had no trouble gaining Senate confirmation to become the youngest member of the current Court and the first Italian-American member ever.

Antonin Scalia

struck down a Pennsylvania law as being too restrictive of a woman's constitutional right to an abortion. The statute required physicians to file detailed reports with the state on cases where abortions are performed and mandated that women seeking abortions be informed in detail of potential medical and psychological dangers of the operation and advised of alternatives. Antiabortionists, although disappointed by the decision, were heartened by the 5-4 margin of the vote, which was much narrower than the 7-2 vote in *Roe* v. *Wade*, the Court's landmark 1973 ruling on abortion.

Mergers. In *Cargill Inc.* v. *Monfort of Colorado* on December 9, the new Court ruled, 6-2, that a company could not legally challenge a merger merely on the basis that the company would be hurt by the increased competition or that such a merger could damage small businesses in the industry. Justices Rehnquist and Scalia voted with the majority. The decision, overturning two rulings by lower federal courts, found that it was "in the interest of competition to allow dominant firms to engage in competition, including price competition." The ruling appeared to clear the way for implementation of a 1983 merger agreement between the second- and third-largest U.S. meat packers.

FOREIGN AFFAIRS

In 1986, American attention focused on international terrorism and relations with Libya, on the contra war in Nicaragua, and on the ups and downs of U.S.-Soviet relations. The United States supported "peaceful transition" in the Philippines (*see* PHILIPPINES). In late 1986, the complicated story of U.S. arms sales to Iran—and diversion of some of the proceeds to the contras—came to occupy center stage.

Terrorism and Response. On January 7, President Reagan announced economic sanctions against Libya and ordered Americans in Libya to leave, except for journalists. Washington won little European backing for the sanctions, despite claiming evidence of Libyan support for terrorist attacks at the Rome and Vienna airports in late 1985. Meanwhile, U.S. naval maneuvers were held in the Gulf of Sidra, off Libya's coast. On March 24, Libyan missiles were fired at U.S. aircraft in the area; the Navy replied with two days of attacks on Libyan vessels and shore installations.

In April a bomb on an Athens-bound TWA jet and another in a West Berlin discotheque popular with GI's killed Americans. Washington again linked Libya to the attacks. On April 15, U.S. warplanes from carriers in the Mediterranean and bases in Britain raided what Washington called terrorist-related targets in Tripoli and Benghazi. The "surgical strike" killed some civilians and damaged the French embassy in Tripoli. Planes based in Britain had to fly thousands of miles around Europe to take part, since France had denied overflight permission. Western European countries, except for Britain, joined many other countries in condemning the raid. Later press reports of strong internal opposition to Libyan leader Muammar al-Qaddafi and an imminent confrontation with the United States became suspect when it was reported that the Reagan administration had undertaken a "disinformation" program against him. State Department spokesman Bernard Kalb resigned in protest over the program.

Iranian Operation. In November, after numerous press reports, Reagan admitted that a secret U.S. operation to establish contacts with moderate elements in Iran had been going on for 18 months. As part of the initiative, a U.S. delegation headed by former National Security Adviser Robert McFarlane had visited Iran, and Reagan had approved shipments to Tehran of military equipment. The arms sales caused a major split within the administration and harmed U.S. credibility with many of its allies.

Word of the Iranian operation came shortly after David Jacobsen, one of the Americans being held hostage in Lebanon, was released by his Iranian-supported captors on November 2. (Another American, Father Lawrence Jenco, had been freed in July, and a third, the Reverend Benjamin Weir, in September 1985.) Reagan eventually acknowledged the operation, contending that its purpose had been to improve overall relations. He did state that he had hoped the release of hostages would follow, and he acknowledged that the three hostage releases each followed closely on the heels of an arms transfer. The United States had barred arms exports to Tehran in 1979, at the time of the American hostage crisis in Iran; Reagan had secretly signed an executive order in

Reports that the Reagan administration deliberately misled the press in a "disinformation" campaign aimed at unsettling Libya's Colonel Muammar al-Qaddafi caused a growing sense of outrage in the journalistic community. The campaign supposedly began with a planted story that appeared in the Wall Street Journal; it reported that the United States was ready to take military action against renewed Libyan terrorism. The American Society of Newspaper Editors protested any dissemination of false information. State Department spokesman Bernard Kalb resigned, citing the "reported disinformation campaign."

Collision Course

New Signs That Libya Is Plotting Terrorism Bring Quick Response

U.S. Readies Air-Raid Plan, Three-Pronged Program; Naval Maneuvers Begin

Looking for a Smoking Gun

By JOHN WALCOTT
And GERALD F. SEIB
Staff Reporters of THE WALL STREET JOURNAL

The U.S. and Libya are on a collision course again.

Although the U.S. air raid on his country last April drove Moammar Gadhafi into the desert for the summer, growing evidence suggests that the bombing hasn't ended Libyan-sponsored terrorism. After a lull, Col. Gadhafi has begun plotting new terrorist attacks, U.S. and West European intelligence officials say. And the Reagan administration is preparing to teach the mercurial Libyan leader another lesson. Right now, the Pentagon is completing plans for new and larger bombing of Libya...

January 1986 allowing the sale of military supplies as part of a waiver of the arms embargo. (Prior to January 1986, U.S.-made arms were reportedly sold to Iran by Israel, with the understanding that the United States would then send new arms to Israel as replacements.) The administration, however, had long sought to persuade other countries not to ship arms to Iran, which was at war with Iraq and remained on the State Department's list of nations supporting terrorism. The U.S. arms sales hurt American relations with the moderate Arab states supporting Iraq in the war. Moreover, the administration's high-profile antiterrorism campaign had sought to discourage other countries from negotiating with terrorist groups or their state sponsors.

Secretary of State George Shultz (*see biography in* PEOPLE IN THE NEWS) said he opposed the arms shipments, about which he had not been kept fully informed, and he reportedly insisted that he could not remain as secretary of state unless all arms shipments to Iran stopped. Reagan did say there would be no further arms shipments to Iran, but he continued to defend the basic policy.

In late November, the administration announced that millions of dollars in profits from the Iranian arms sales had been diverted to the Nicaraguan contras through secret bank accounts, at a time when Congress had refused to authorize military aid. The president, who said he was not aware of the transfer of funds, stated that John Poindexter, his national security adviser, had resigned and that one of Poindexter's top aides, Oliver North—said to be channeling the money to the contras—had been dismissed. It was also reported that the State Department had persuaded the sultan of Brunei to contribute $10 million to the contras through a Swiss bank account; Shultz confirmed this report but said such assistance by a third nation did not violate congressional restrictions. (It was unclear whether the money from Brunei ever reached the contras or, if all or some did not, what happened to it.)

Middle East. The United States sought unsuccessfully to promote direct talks between Israel and a joint Jordanian-Palestinian delegation and later between Israel and Jordan. Prior to the Iranian arms scandal, ties with moderate Arab states were frayed by battles over proposed arms sales. Congressional opposition forced indefinite postponement of a weapons sale to

425

A hastily convened summit meeting held during October in Reykjavík, Iceland, ended in disappointment; while President Ronald Reagan and Soviet leader Mikhail Gorbachev came close to agreeing on major arms reductions, the Star Wars issue ultimately brought the talks to a standstill. Here the two leaders are shown at the end of the conference.

Jordan, but the White House did narrowly succeed in sustaining a veto of a congressional resolution that would have blocked a missile sale to Saudi Arabia.

Central America. In October, President Reagan won final congressional approval of renewed military aid to the contra rebels fighting the leftist Sandinista regime in Nicaragua. A unity agreement and reform effort adopted by the three principal contra leaders helped sway Congress, as did Sandinista human rights abuses and raids on contra base camps in Honduras.

Meanwhile, questions were raised about U.S. involvement in Central America, when Nicaragua in early October shot down a privately owned American cargo plane carrying arms to the contras. The one surviving crew member, American Eugene Hasenfus, initially claimed his supervisors in El Salvador were CIA agents, though he subsequently said he was unsure. (CIA involvement would have violated congressional restrictions in effect at the time.) It was later speculated that profits from Iranian arms sales had been used to finance the Hasenfus operation. Hasenfus was tried by a "people's tribunal" and sentenced to 30 years in prison, but he was pardoned and released in December.

Soviet Union and Arms Control. In January, Soviet leader Mikhail Gorbachev unveiled a plan to eliminate all nuclear weapons by the year 2000. But his proposal required an end to U.S. development of "space-strike" weapons (and thus of the Strategic Defense Initiative). In response, Reagan proposed phasing out all U.S. and Soviet medium-range nuclear missiles—including Soviet missiles in Asia—over three years. He brushed aside Gorbachev's total nuclear weapons ban and chided the Soviets for incomplete compliance with existing arms treaties. A few months later, the president announced an end to voluntary U.S. adherence to the unratified 1979 Strategic Arms Limitation Treaty (SALT II) and said that only "constructive" Soviet steps to comply with treaties could alter his decision. (In November the United States did exceed a SALT II weapons ceiling.) The Soviets also proposed to reduce offensive strategic weapons in return for U.S. adherence for 15–20 more years to the 1972 antiballistic missile (ABM) treaty—which would limit U.S. development of SDI and prevent deployment. The president reportedly offered not to deploy SDI for seven years, in return for deep cuts in Soviet offensive weapons.

In late August the Soviets arrested an American journalist on espionage charges, apparently to set up a trade for a Soviet UN official previously arrested in New York and accused of spying. At the end of September both men were returned home, and a preliminary Reagan-Gorbachev summit in Reykjavík, Iceland, was unexpectedly announced for October 11–12.

In Iceland the two leaders tentatively agreed to bar medium-range missiles from Europe, to limit and eventually end nuclear testing, and to reduce numbers of long-range missiles and bombers, with ballistic missiles, and perhaps all other nuclear weapons, to be eventually eliminated. But Gorbachev insisted that SDI be limited to laboratory research for ten years and deployed only with Moscow's approval; Reagan contended such a limitation would kill SDI. Afterwards, the two sides differed publicly on what had been tentatively agreed to. In November the Soviets said they would agree to U.S. development of prototype SDI weapons if they were not tested in space. Meanwhile, under pressure from European allies fearful that a ban on ballistic missiles would magnify Soviet conventional superiority, the administration said it would deemphasize seeking such a ban.

Southern Africa. The Reagan administration's policy of "constructive engagement" with South Africa—maintaining friendly relations while urging an end to apartheid—drew sharp criticism abroad and bipartisan opposition at home. Early in the year, Pretoria seemed to be pursuing modest reforms, but in May, South African forces raided alleged African National Congress strongholds in neighboring countries, and in June, President P. W. Botha declared a state of emergency. Soon after, the U.S. House passed a sweeping economic sanctions bill. Reagan called the measure "a historic act of folly" and praised Botha's reform program, but Congress approved a sanctions package and overrode its veto by Reagan. Apparently seeking to deflect criticism of its South Africa policy, the administration sought to name a black U.S. ambassador to that country; Edward Perkins, a veteran black diplomat, was appointed after two other potential candidates bowed out for various reasons.

Jonas Savimbi, head of the Pretoria-backed Unita rebels fighting the Marxist Angolan government, toured the United States early in the year seeking government support. The administration later told Congress it had decided to provide Unita with aid, thought to consist of $15 million in CIA funds, which did not require congressional approval. A.T.

UPPER VOLTA. *See* STATISTICS OF THE WORLD.

URUGUAY. In 1986, Uruguay's second year of democracy after 12 years of military rule, the country faced a growing set of unresolved political and economic problems. All-party talks in March and April involving the centrist Colorado Party of President Julio María Sanguinetti Cairolo, the National Party (Blancos), the Broad Front, and the Civic Union led to general agreement on a large number of legislative measures to be enacted as laws. However, the left-wing Broad Front coalition of 12 parties dissented on some legislation, as did the Blancos, and a new cabinet appointed in April contained no Broad Front members. In the Broad Front, the Communists were challenged by the "99" group of Hugo Batalla, the coalition's largest vote-getter in the 1984 elections. Ultimately, Batalla's group established itself as the new Socialist and Democratic Party and remained in the coalition.

There were several brief general strikes, including three in 19 days: on May 30, June 13, and June 17. Strikers demanded wage increases of 34 percent rather than the government's proposed 15 percent. A 26-day hospital strike took place in August and September.

Despite public opinion polls favoring trials for Uruguayan military figures, officials were slow to act on charges of military involvement in some 80 cases of death by torture and 160 disappearances in the 1970's. In December, after contentious debate, the House of Deputies, voting 60-37, approved an amnesty law covering members of the military accused of human-rights violations. Those accused of seeking financial gain or exceeding orders were not included.

Unemployment, inflation, and foreign debt remained problems. Sanguinetti put stress on efforts to increase exports. Interest due on the $5.5 billion foreign debt in 1986 was $450 million—50 percent of total export value.

Uruguay rejoined the nonaligned movement, the World Health Organization, and the International Labor Organization, and supported Contadora Group peace initiatives.

See STATISTICS OF THE WORLD.   J.F., Jr.

UTAH. *See* STATISTICS OF THE WORLD.

V

VANUATU. *See* Statistics of the World.

VENEZUELA. In 1986 the government of President Jaime Lusinchi had to deal with corruption and declining oil revenues.

In June the government's Acción Democratica (AD) party passed a motion in the National Congress to censure an opposition deputy who had exposed corruption in a government milk distribution program. Members of the deputy's Christian Democratic Party (COPEI) staged a walkout in response. Two former defense ministers had been convicted on charges of illegal arms transactions earlier in the year. Charges of police corruption were also being probed.

In February the government renegotiated terms on $21 billion in debt due to a consortium of 400 banks—but later invoked a clause in the agreement allowing a renegotiation of terms if income from oil fell. Resolution of the terms was still pending at year's end. Oil revenues were projected to decline substantially in 1986. To conserve foreign exchange reserves, President Lusinchi announced a partial devaluation of the bolívar, new import restrictions, and a drive to develop nontraditional exports. In the search for an alternative to oil, which had been providing 90 percent of export income, Caracas turned to bauxite; a loan for developing bauxite deposits was obtained from the Inter-American Development Bank.

Lusinchi visited Brazil, Argentina, and Uruguay in April, praising all three countries for their return to democratic rule. In June he addressed the sensitive question of the Los Monjes, a group of Caribbean islands facing the Gulf of Venezuela, reiterating Venezuelan sovereignty over these; although neighboring Colombia had conceded Venezuelan sovereignty, a constitutional amendment under consideration in Bogotá included the archipelago within Colombian borders. In August the Venezuelan president joined his Mexican counterpart, Miguel de la Madrid Hurtado, in extending the 1980 pact offering Mexican and Venezuelan oil on favorable terms to the two countries' poorer neighbors.

See Statistics of the World.   L.L.P.

VERMONT. *See* Statistics of the World.

VICE PRESIDENT OF THE UNITED STATES. *See* People in the News: *George Bush.*

VIETNAM. In 1986, Vietnam experienced a year of political turmoil. In June, eight government ministers, including Deputy Prime Minister To Huu, were dismissed for bureaucratic incompetence or opposing economic reforms. In July, Communist Party chief Le Duan died; he was replaced by 79-year-old Truong Chinh. Subsequently, Hanoi launched a broad "self-criticism" campaign, stressing instances of corruption or mismanagement, and many party members were disciplined by their local party organizations. Finally, at the sixth Communist Party congress, which opened on December 15, sweeping changes were announced. Chinh resigned as party general secretary and member of the Politburo; four other Politburo members also resigned or were dropped, including Prime Minister Pham Van Dong and Le Duc Tho, chief North Vietnamese negotiator in the Paris peace talks which led to the U.S. withdrawal from Vietnam.

Chinh was replaced as party chief by Nguyen Van Linh, 73, a political administrator who had been Hanoi's representative in the south. He was considered an economic pragmatist, and his ties to the strongly disaffected south were regarded as important. Subsequently, at a six-day session of the National Assembly in late December, no new names were announced for top government posts; the body did adopt budget and development plans for 1987, which called for a 7 percent economic growth rate.

Reforms introduced five years earlier continued to spark growth in food production. The overall economy had serious problems, however. The 1985 currency devaluation, coupled with an increased money supply caused by wage increases and with a greater demand from the free market after the country's ration system was abandoned, sent inflation spiraling to 700 percent by September 1986. Rationing was reintroduced for basic commodities such as rice and salt.

Production quotas for individual farmers are posted at the Lai Cach agricultural cooperative southeast of Hanoi; the government, which has been campaigning to promote food production, sought a 10 percent increase in staple crops for 1986.

Eight years after Vietnam invaded Cambodia, Hanoi maintained some 120,000 troops in the country, particularly to seal the border region and try to stop the frequent guerrilla attacks in the countryside. Vietnam rejected a peace proposal by the anti-Vietnamese Cambodian resistance, calling for withdrawal of Vietnamese troops and for a coalition government.

The highest level U.S. delegation to visit Vietnam since 1975 went to Hanoi in January to discuss the fate of 1,792 American servicemen missing since the war; it was quickly followed by two congressional delegations. In April, Vietnam turned over 21 sets of remains to the United States. In July the United States promised to reimburse Hanoi for the cost of looking for MIA remains and offered logistical

support; Vietnam agreed to inform Washington about American live-sighting reports and to allow U.S. experts to accompany the Vietnamese on some investigations. In November, Vietnamese officials turned over the remains of three more missing servicemen.

In January, Hanoi suspended the issuing of new exit visas under its Orderly Departure Program, in protest against the slow processing by the United States of those already given visas. The number of people leaving Vietnam in 1986 under the backlogged program was expected to be about 20,000. The number of boat refugees was projected at 25,000.

See STATISTICS OF THE WORLD.   L.G.H.

VIRGINIA. *See* STATISTICS OF THE WORLD.

VIRGIN ISLANDS. *See* STATISTICS OF THE WORLD.

WARSAW TREATY ORGANIZATION. *See* COMMUNIST WORLD.

WASHINGTON. *See* STATISTICS OF THE WORLD.

WESTERN SAHARA. *See* AFRICA. *See also* MOROCCO.

WESTERN SAMOA. *See* STATISTICS OF THE WORLD.

WEST VIRGINIA. *See* STATISTICS OF THE WORLD.

WISCONSIN. *See* STATISTICS OF THE WORLD.

WOMEN. Mixed results in the November elections and important decisions from the U.S. Supreme Court were among the highlights of 1986 for women in the United States. The National Organization for Women celebrated its 20th anniversary.

Elections. The 1986 elections featured an unprecedented number of women seeking office at all levels of government. In the nation's first gubernatorial race between two women, Nebraska's state treasurer, Kay Orr (R), defeated former Lincoln Mayor Helen Boosalis (D). Orr became the first woman Republican governor. In the Maryland U.S. Senate race—the first U.S. Senate race between two women since 1960—five-term U.S. Representative Barbara Mikulski (D) became the first woman Democrat elected to the Senate since that 1960 race, winning in a landslide over Linda Chavez (R), a former White House aide. Another victor was incumbent Vermont Governor Madeleine Kunin (D), who won a plurality in a three-candidate race; since she fell short of a majority she had to be confirmed for a second term by the state legislature in January.

However, other women did not succeed at the polls. Harriett Woods, Missouri's Democratic lieutenant governor, fought a tough battle against former Republican Governor Christo-

Nebraska Governor Kay Orr (shown here with her daughter during the Republican primary campaign) won the nation's first gubernatorial race between two women candidates.

pher Bond for the seat of retiring Senator Thomas F. Eagleton (D) but came up short. And despite major assistance from President Ronald Reagan, Florida Senator Paula Hawkins (R) could not hold her seat against Governor Bob Graham (D). For all the high hopes of major gains for women, the final result at the federal level was a continuation of the status quo. Mikulski replaced Hawkins as one of only two women in the Senate. (The other is Republican Nancy Kassebaum of Kansas.) In the House, the net total stayed at 23. Of seven women running against men for governorships, the only winner was Kunin, the sole incumbent. (The only other woman governor, besides Kunin and Orr, is Democrat Martha Layne Collins of Kentucky.)

Sexual Harassment. In the first sexual harassment case heard by the Supreme Court, *Meritor Savings* v. *Vinson*, the justices ruled that Title VII of the Civil Rights Act of 1964, which bars sex discrimination in the workplace, protects against sexual harassment even if the victim did not suffer the loss of a specific job benefit such as a raise or a promotion. The Court said employees have a right to be free of an offensive or hostile work environment involving intimidation, ridicule, and insult. The Court held that, in cases involving sexual advances, the key element to be determined is whether the advances were "unwelcome" and not whether the response was "voluntary."

Pornography. The Supreme Court dealt a setback to efforts by some women's groups to have pornography treated legally as discrimination against women. Affirming a lower court ruling in *Hudnut* v. *American Booksellers Association*, it voided an Indianapolis ordinance authorizing lawsuits against sellers of adult materials on the grounds of sex discrimination.

NOW Anniversary. The National Organization for Women celebrated its 20th anniversary in 1986. At a fund-raising event marking the occasion, held in Los Angeles in December, NOW President Eleanor Smeal announced that the group would renew its drive to gain passage of the equal rights amendment to the U.S. Constitution. The amendment was passed by Congress in 1972, but ratification by the states failed, even after the deadline was extended by three years to June 30, 1982. The ERA,

National Organization for Women president Eleanor Smeal (left) is joined by former First Lady Betty Ford (center) and actress Marlo Thomas as NOW celebrated its 20th anniversary at a Los Angeles gala in December.

abortion rights, and job and pay equity have been the main focuses of the organization since it was founded. Among the problems faced by NOW as it tried to define a course for the future were declining membership, financial debt, and an unclear agenda. Some observers said NOW should pay more attention to such issues as child care, pregnancy benefits, and concerns of minority women. Others argued that NOW's very success had created some of the current difficulties, in that many women took for granted things that had to be fought for years ago.

Woman Boy Scout Leader Denied. A Connecticut woman lost her bid to become the first female leader of a Boy Scout troop. Saying that boys aged 10 to 14 "need male role models," a superior court judge overturned a 1984 ruling by the state human rights panel that the Boy Scouts of America, in denying Catherine Pollard's scoutmaster application, had violated sex discrimination laws. Pollard, 67, who has been involved with the Boy Scouts since the 1940's, appealed the decision, which she called "the same old discriminatory baloney." Other types of troops sponsored by the Boy Scouts of America, such as Explorers (for older boys), are allowed to have women as leaders.

See also CIVIL LIBERTIES AND CIVIL RIGHTS.

R.T. (Elections), M.Gr., & R.A.

WYOMING. See STATISTICS OF THE WORLD.

Y

YEMEN, PEOPLE'S DEMOCRATIC REPUBLIC OF. An attempt by President Ali Nasser Muhammàd al-Hassani to strike against former President Abdel Fatah Ismail and members of his hard-line faction led instead to Muhammad's overthrow, in a bloody 12-day civil war in early 1986.

The violence in the People's Democratic Republic of Yemen (South Yemen) began on January 13, when Muhammad's bodyguards walked into a room where some of his opponents were assembled for a meeting and started shooting, killing Vice President Ali Ahmad Antar and Defense Minister Salih Muslih Qasim, among others. In the factional fighting that followed, more than 4,200 party members alone lost their lives, according to later official figures. Damage to public property was esti-

431

South Yemen's capital (seen here from the Gulf of Aden) was the site of a fierce, bloody civil war between rival Marxist factions battling for control of the country.

mated at $115 million. Ismail was reportedly killed in the fighting; Muhammad fled to Ethiopia.

The subsequent, somewhat more pro-Soviet regime was headed by President Haidar Abu Bakr al-Attas, with Yasin Said Numan as prime minister and Ali Salim al-Baith as secretary-general of the ruling party. Its priorities were to restore order and prevent a countercoup. Supporters of the deposed president were granted amnesty, and 1,500 political prisoners were released. In August, South Yemeni Air Force fighters intercepted an Air Djibouti jet over the Red Sea and forced it to land in Aden, where security men searched for Muhammad supporters among the plane's 59 passengers. In protest, Djibouti suspended air and sea links with South Yemen for 11 weeks.

The new president made friendly visits to other Arab countries, emphasizing a stated desire for good relations with moderate regimes. In July he met with Ali Abdullah Saleh, president of the Yemen Arab Republic (North Yemen), to discuss security matters and unification. South Yemeni-Soviet relations were bolstered by a new trade agreement. Despite

criticism of Muhammad's tendency to favor private enterprise over "scientific socialism," there was no apparent upheaval in economic policy. Foreign workers who had fled the civil war were invited back, and major projects begun under Muhammad were continued.

See STATISTICS OF THE WORLD.   C.H.A.

YEMEN ARAB REPUBLIC. For the Yemen Arab Republic (North Yemen), 1986 brought the beginning of oil production and hopes of greater prosperity.

Production of petroleum from Yemen Hunt Oil Company's Alif 1 well in the Marib concession began in April with the opening of the $18 million, 12,500-barrel-per-day refinery, providing about two-thirds of the country's domestic consumption. The government awarded an offshore concession to the French company Total. Exxon Corporation, already holding a concession in the central highlands, bought a 49 percent share of the Hunt concession in Marib, and the two companies established a joint venture called Yemen Exploration and Production Company.

In addition, the regime of Ali Abdullah Saleh made several moves to improve the balance-of-payments deficit. In February the riyal was devalued by 20 percent in an effort to control imports and help exports. In July, Muhammad Khadem al-Wajih, a British-educated former finance minister, assumed control of the new Ministry of the Economy, formed with the merger of the Ministry of Economy and Industry and the Ministry of Supply and Commerce. The new ministry issued controls on money changers, required that all foreign visitors exchange $150 at the official rate upon entry to the country, and mandated that a percentage of all government contracts go to local companies.

See STATISTICS OF THE WORLD.   C.H.A.

YUGOSLAVIA. Yugoslavia remained beset by chronic political and economic problems in 1986, including a weak, fragmented government, ethnic conflict, and high inflation and foreign debt.

In May the newly-elected National Assembly confirmed Sinan Hasani, an ethnic Albanian from the Serbian province of Kosovo, as president of the nine-member collective leadership. Branko Mikulic, a Croatian from Sarajevo who won plaudits for his organization of the 1984 winter Olympics there, and a known advocate of strong central government, was named as prime minister.

There was increasing official concern over nationalistic agitation by Kosovo Albanians, who comprise 80 percent of that province's population, and friction between the Albanians and the Serb and Montenegrin minorities there. In May, 46 Kosovo Albanians convicted of undermining the social order and of other offenses received prison terms ranging from 3 months to 13 years.

In July, after a petition and a march by Serbs and Montenegrins, protesting alleged Albanian crimes against minorities, official investigations were initiated. Kosovo Albanians were barred from acquiring Serb and Montenegrin property, while affected Serbs and Montenegrins were forbidden to leave the province until adjudication of their cases. Those who had left—or had been pushed out—were promised jobs and property if they returned.

In foreign affairs, Yugoslav officials were pleased by the completion of the 120-mile Shkodër-Titograd rail line with Albania. Begun in 1948, discontinued after Tito's break with Stalin, and recommenced in 1982, the line linked Albania with Europe for the first time since World War II. Nevertheless, Tiranë's media continued their relentless campaign against Yugoslav values and society.

The economic picture remained grim. Yugoslavs endured an inflation rate of 85–100 percent, a foreign debt of $20 billion, unemployment of 15 percent, and declining living standards. Agriculture suffered significant losses as a result of the Chernobyl nuclear accident. In July, soon after the 13th Congress of the Yugoslav League of Communists, tough economic measures were introduced, including a 60 percent rise in the price of bread. However, the price rise for bread was rescinded after two days.

See STATISTICS OF THE WORLD.   R.A.P.

YUKON TERRITORY. See STATISTICS OF THE WORLD.

Z

ZAIRE. Zaire continued to experience political tensions in 1986, as President Mobutu Sese Seko consolidated the powers of his centralized, authoritarian government. The nation continued to suffer from the heavy burden of a large foreign debt and a stringent austerity program.

The political rights of Zairians remained tenuous, as Mobutu's single-party state continued to prosecute organizers of a possible second party. A decentralization program instituted at the behest of international advisers actually resulted in further concentration of power in the Mobutu-appointed Executive

Council. Power struggles within the ruling group were contained by skillful political maneuvering, including cabinet shuffles in April and October.

In May, Zaire signed a 22-month, $225 million loan agreement with the International Monetary Fund. Meanwhile, Zaire's grave economic crisis continued unabated, as earnings from such Zairian exports as copper, diamonds, and tin remained low. Hopes for garnering foreign exchange centered on oil production, albeit in a sluggish oil market, and high coffee prices resulting from the drought in Brazil.

The government continued generally to follow austerity policies set down by the IMF in order to obtain new loans. However, wage increases, some of which exceeded IMF guidelines, were allowed. Late in the year, Mobutu announced that, if he did not get an accommodation from Zaire's creditors, Zaire would restrict interest payments on its $5 billion foreign debt to 10 percent of export earnings and 20 percent of the ordinary budget. He stressed Zaire's economic difficulties on a visit to the United States in December. President Ronald Reagan responded with a U.S. promise to "do our best" to help Zaire, which currently was receiving about $70 million in annual U.S. aid. Meanwhile, a coalition of civil rights, human rights, and congressional leaders urged the Reagan administration to cut its aid to Zaire because of human rights abuses there.

Relations with neighboring Angola appeared to be improved, following a series of state visits designed to counter charges that Zairian territory was being used as a staging area for supplying anti-Angolan insurgents led by Jonas Savimbi.

See STATISTICS OF THE WORLD.   B.S.

ZAMBIA. In 1986, President Kenneth Kaunda continued efforts to end minority white rule in South Africa and to deal with the deteriorating Zambian economy.

Kaunda devoted himself to strengthening the unity of the allied "front-line" states—Angola, Botswana, Mozambique, Tanzania, Zambia, and Zimbabwe—bordering or near South Africa. Meanwhile, Zambia and Zaire signed an agreement in April to end a frontier dispute that had crimped relations between the two

countries. Later, however, Kaunda accused Zaire of allowing its territory to be used by the United States to supply the Unita guerrilla forces seeking to overthrow the government of Angola.

South Africa made both its military and its economic power felt in Zambia. On May 19—the same day Zimbabwe and Botswana were attacked—South African bombers and commandos struck a refugee camp near Lusaka which South Africa claimed was an operational center of the insurgent African National Congress. In August, South Africa punished Zambia for declaring its intention to impose, along with Zimbabwe, severe economic sanctions on it, by temporarily delaying all truck traffic from Zambia and Zimbabwe.

The traffic blockade and other South African measures further set back Zambia's problematic economic recovery efforts. Copper exports, which earn most of the country's foreign exchange, were highly depressed. Maize, another major Zambian product, improved slightly in output, but in May, Kaunda banned all maize exports until the country should reach self-sufficiency in output and establish an emergency stockpile. Government measures to cut costs and bring economic accounts into line were unpopular and largely unsuccessful. Domestic prices had more than doubled in less than a year. In March, however, Zambia and the Paris Club of creditors reached an agreement on rescheduling Zambia's foreign debt to Western governments.

In April, Kaunda initiated a cabinet shuffle involving the team of financial specialists responsible for the latest economic programs. Finance Minister Luke Mwananshiku became foreign affairs minister; David Phiri, governor of the Bank of Zambia, was shifted to the price and incomes commission; and Dominic Mulaisho, who reportedly had drafted the new austerity policies, was demoted.

See STATISTICS OF THE WORLD.   K.W.G.

ZIMBABWE. Prime Minister Robert Mugabe's drive to create a one-party state, and alleged human rights violations by his ruling party, continued to dominate politics in 1986.

The principal area of contention between Mugabe's African National Union-Patriotic Front (Zanu-PF) and the opposition Zimbabwe African People's Union (Zapu) involved the Zapu stronghold of Matabeleland. The government made some conciliatory gestures toward Zapu—imposing a sentence of death on a Zanu-PF official convicted of murdering five opposition supporters and releasing a number of Zapu officials, including Stephen Nkomo, a former Zapu secretary-general and the brother of Zapu leader Joseph Nkomo. Nevertheless, the New York-based Lawyers Committee for Human Rights reported government abuses—including summary execution, torture, beating, and arbitrary arrest—against members of the Ndebele ethnic minority in Matabeleland. Although the government renewed its emergency powers, it continued to deny such allegations and spoke out against rights abuses. The prime minister intervened personally in June to order the release, soon after their arrest, of two human rights activists, Michael Auret and Nicholas Ndebele.

In June, Charles Duke, a member of Parliament, announced his resignation from former Prime Minister Ian Smith's Conservative Alliance to join the Zanu-PF "family," becoming the first white MP to do so. Smith, meanwhile, apologized to Parliament for having remarked on BBC-TV that majority rule in Zimbabwe was a "negation of democracy" and that most black Zimbabweans were "uneducated and uncivilized."

Zanu-PF was shaken by an internal dispute when a parliamentary committee accused Minister of Transport Herbert Ushewokunze of corrupt dealings in administering the railways. Ushewokunze charged that his Zanu opponents were fomenting tribal hatred. The party's Central Committee removed Ushewokunze from the Politburo and his chief accuser, Byron Hove, from Parliament.

South African force was felt in Zimbabwe during the year. In May, South African commandos blew up an unoccupied office of the African National Congress, a South African nationalist organization, in downtown Harare. In August, Zimbabwe, along with other Commonwealth nations, said it would impose stiff economic sanctions on South Africa. South Africa responded by delaying truck traffic from Zimbabwe and taking other temporary punitive measures.

The conference of nonaligned nations opened on September 1 in Harare with N. Krishnan of India presiding; C. B. Utete of Zimbabwe is at his left and Prakash Shah of India at right.

Relations with the United States deteriorated after a minor cabinet minister used the occasion of a July 4 reception in Harare to attack U.S. policies toward South Africa. Former U.S. President Jimmy Carter was present, along with the acting U.S. ambassador, and they walked out in protest. Mugabe later offered Carter an apology but did not extend regrets to the Reagan administration. In response, the United States cut $13.5 million from a planned 1986 fiscal-year aid package of $21 million and said it would provide no new aid. Mugabe, who began a three-year term as chairman of the nonaligned nations movement, again blasted the United States at the summit conference of the movement in Harare in September.

See STATISTICS OF THE WORLD.   K.W.G.

435

THE COUNTRIES OF THE WORLD

Nation Capital	Population	Area of Country (sq mi/ sq km)	Type of Government	Heads of State and Government	Currency: Value in U.S. Dollars	GNP (000,000): GNP Per Capita
AFGHANISTAN .... Kabul	15,400,000...... 2,000,000	250,000...... 647,497	People's republic	President: Haji Muhammad Chamkani Prime Minister: Sultan Ali Keshtmand	Afghani ....$ 0.02	NA NA
ALBANIA................. Tiranë	3,000,000...... 220,000	11,100...... 28,748	People's socialist republic	Chairman, Presidium of the People's Assembly: Ramiz Alia Chairman, Council of Ministers (Premier): Adil Çarçani	Lek 0.14	1,930[1] 645
ALGERIA................. Algiers	22,800,000...... 2,000,000	919,595...... 2,381,741	Republic...........	President:........... Col. Chadli Benjedid Premier: Abdelhamid Brahimi	Dinar............ 0.22	50,680 2,380
ANGOLA .... Luanda	8,200,000...... 1,200,000	481,354...... 1,246,700	People's republic	President:........... José Eduardo dos Santos	Kwanza........ 0.03	3,320 420
ANTIGUA AND .... BARBUDA St. Johns	100,000...... 25,000	171...... 443	Parliamentary state (C)	Governor-General: .... Sir Wilfred E. Jacobs Prime Minister: Vere C. Bird, Sr.	East .... Caribbean dollar 0.37	150 1,830
ARGENTINA .... Buenos Aires	31,200,000...... 2,908,000	1,068,302...... 2,766,889	Federal .... republic	President:............ Raúl Alfonsín	Austral........... 1.14	67,150 2,230
AUSTRALIA................ Canberra	15,800,000...... 273,600[5]	2,967,909...... 7,686,848	Federal parliamentary state (C)	Governor-General: .... Sir Ninian M. Stephen Prime Minister: Bob Hawke	Dollar 0.66	184,980 11,890
AUSTRIA.................. Vienna	7,600,000...... 1,531,300	32,374...... 83,849	Federal republic	President:...................................... Kurt Waldheim Chancellor: Franz Vranitzky	Schilling........ 0.07	68,800 9,140
BAHAMAS................. Nassau	228,000...... 135,400	5,380...... 13,935	Parliamentary state (C)	Governor-General: .... Sir Gerald C. Cash Prime Minister: Lynden O. Pindling	Dollar........... 1.005	960 4,260
BAHRAIN .... Manama	400,000...... 122,000	240...... 622	Emirate............	Emir: .... Isa bin Sulman al-Khalifah Prime Minister: Muhammad Khalifa bin Sulman al-Khalifa	Dinar............ 2.655	4,260 10,480
BANGLADESH........... Dacca	104,100,000...... 3,605,000	55,598...... 143,998	Republic........... (C)	President:................ H. M. Ershad Prime Minister: Atuar Rahman Khan	Taka............. 0.03	12,360 130
BARBADOS.............. Bridgetown	252,000...... 7,500	166...... 431	Parliamentary state (C)	Governor-General: .... Hugh Springer Prime Minister: Errol Barrow	Dollar 0.505	1,100 4,340
BELGIUM .... Brussels	9,900,000...... 982,400	11,781...... 30,513	Constitutional monarchy	King: .... Baudouin Prime Minister: Wilfried Martens	Franc............ 0.02	83,070 8,430

436

The section on countries presents the latest information available. All monetary figures are expressed in United States dollars. The symbol (C) signifies that the country belongs to the Commonwealth of Nations. NA means that the data were not available. * indicates that the category does not apply to the country under discussion. Footnotes at the end of the section contain more specialized information.

Imports Exports	Revenue Expenditure	Elementary Schools: Teachers Students	Secondary Schools: Teachers Students	Colleges and Universities: Teachers Students
$ 695,000,000 ....$ 708,000,000	675,600,000 988,800,000	15,008 449,948	6,170 124,488	1,212 13,611
246,000,000[2] .... 267,000,000[2]	1,134,100,000 1,127,100,000	27,100 531,520	5,500 95,380	1,360 19,670
10,289,000,000 11,886,000,000	13,897,000,000 13,897,000,000	109,173 3,336,536	46,196 1,136,848	11,601 95,867
636,000,000 3,029,000,000	2,467,000,000 2,723,000,000	32,004 1,178,430	NA .... NA	316 2,674
84,000,000 18,000,000	39,800,000 31,800,000	390 9,557	331 4,197	NA NA
4,583,000,000 8,107,000,000	8,276,600,000 11,190,000,000	212,932 4,315,752	193,551 1,466,424	33,450 416,571
23,424,000,000 23,998,000,000	46,343,900,000 43,043,900,000	NA 1,619,609	86,364 1,110,319	20,783 349,243
19,631,000,000 15,741,000,000	22,747,400,000 28,980,100,000	27,942 354,479	68,755 682,983	9,644 142,159
4,098,000,000 3,393,000,000	306,600,000 371,500,000	1,555 32,664	NA 17,255	NA NA
3,530,000,000 3,139,000,000	1,458,600,000 .... NA	2,774 46,364	1,196 29,602	148 835
2,042,000,000 934,000,000	1,261,300,000 962,200,000	189,884 8,915,442	115,751 3,083,643	2,626 40,527
659,000,000 391,000,000	324,900,000 324,300,000	1,317 30,907	1,368 27,715	200 1,664
55,303,000,000[3] .... 51,779,000,000[3]	26,226,900,000 34,949,300,000	40,894 758,663	NA 825,108	NA 100,362

Nation Capital	Population	Area of Country (sq mi/ sq km)	Type of Government	Heads of State and Government	Currency: Value in U.S. Dollars	GNP (000,000): GNP Per Capita
BELIZE Belmopan	160,000 2,900	8,867 22,965	Parliamentary state (C)	Governor-General: Minita Gordon Prime Minister: Manuel Esquivel	Dollar 0.50	$ 180 1,150
BENIN Porto-Novo	4,100,000 144,000	43,484 112,622	People's republic	President: Ahmed Kérékou	CFA franc[4] 0.003	1,060 270
BHUTAN Thimbu	1,400,000 20,000	18,147 47,000	Monarchy	King: Jigme Singye Wangchuk	Ngultrum 0.08	110 78
BOLIVIA Sucre La Paz	6,400,000 80,000 881,400	424,165 1,098,581	Republic	President: Víctor Paz Estenssoro	Peso 0.000001	2,560 410
BOTSWANA Gaborone	1,100,000 59,700	231,805 600,372	Republic (C)	President: Quett K. J. Masire	Pula 0.54	940 910
BRAZIL Brasília	143,300,000 411,000	3,286,488 8,511,965	Federal republic	President: José Sarney	Cruzado 0.07	227,280 1,710
BRUNEI Bandar Seri Begawan	220,000 49,900	2,226 5,765	Constitutional monarchy (C)	Sultan: Muda Hassanal Bolkiah	Dollar 0.46	4,270 20,520
BULGARIA Sofia	9,000,000 1,070,400	42,823 110,912	People's republic	Chairman, Council of State: Todor Zhivkov Chairman, Council of Ministers (Premier): Georgi Atanasov	Lev 1.09	37,390[1] 4,201
BURMA Rangoon	37,700,000 2,400,000	261,218 676,552	Socialist republic	President: U San Yu Prime Minister: U Maung Maung Kha	Kyat 0.14	6,620 180
BURUNDI Bujumbura	4,900,000 151,000	10,747 27,834	Republic	President: Col. Jean-Baptiste Bagaza	Franc 0.0099	1,010 220
CAMBODIA (PEOPLE'S REPUBLIC OF KAMPUCHEA) Phnom Penh	6,400,000 600,000	69,898 181,035	People's republic	President, Council of State: Heng Samrin Chairman, Council of Ministers (Premier): Hun Sen	New riel NA	NA NA
CAMEROON Yaoundé	10,000,000 485,200[5]	183,569 475,442	Republic	President: Paul Biya Prime Minister: Etecki Nbomou	CFA franc[4] 0.003	8,000 810
CANADA Ottawa	25,600,000 300,000	3,831,033 9,922,330	Federal parliamentary state (C)	Governor-General: Jeanne Sauvé Prime Minister: Brian Mulroney	Dollar 0.72	330,870 13,140
CAPE VERDE Praia	330,000 45,900	1,557 4,033	Republic	President: Aristides M. Pereira Premier: Pedro Rodrigues Pires	Escudo 0.011	100 320
CENTRAL AFRICAN REPUBLIC Bangui	2,700,000 400,000	240,535 622,984	Republic	Chairman, Military Committee for National Recovery (President): Gen. André Kolingba	CFA franc[4] 0.003	680 270
CHAD N'Djamena	5,200,000 303,000	495,755 1,284,000	Republic	President: Hissène Habré	CFA franc[4] 0.003	490 94
CHILE Santiago	12,300,000 4,132,000	292,258 756,945	Republic	President: Gen. Augusto Pinochet Ugarte	Peso 0.005	20,340 1,710
CHINA, PEOPLE'S REPUBLIC OF Peking	1,050,000,000 9,230,700[5]	3,691,515 9,560,980	People's republic	President: Li Xiannian Premier: Zhao Ziyang	Yuan 0.27	318,310 310
COLOMBIA Bogotá	30,000,000 4,584,000	439,737 1,138,914	Republic	President: Virgilio Barco Vargas	Peso 0.005	38,410 1,370
COMOROS Moroni	500,000 16,000	838 2,171	Federal Islamic republic	President: Ahmed Abdallah Abderemane	CFA franc[4] 0.003	110 220

Imports / Exports	Revenue / Expenditure	Elementary Schools: Teachers / Students	Secondary Schools: Teachers / Students	Colleges and Universities: Teachers / Students
$ 126,000,000	$ 53,000,000	1,463	474	NA
96,000,000	58,000,000	35,113	6,511	NA
464,000,000	170,400,000	11,399	1,816	NA
24,000,000	170,900,000	428,185	117,724	6,302
NA	21,300,000	1,149	581	NA
NA	69,600,000	44,275	5,872	564
631,000,000	NA	45,024	NA	3,480
773,000,000	NA	1,022,624	182,760	56,632
764,000,000	649,400,000	6,753	1,065	137
730,000,000	491,300,000	209,345	27,326	1,435
15,210,000,000	15,622,200,000	934,282	221,710	121,954
27,005,000,000	15,622,200,000	24,304,875	3,481,804	1,436,287
625,000,000	2,998,800,000	1,923	1.538	64
3,197,000,000	1,222,600,000	31,682	17,869	218
12,714,000,000	16,533,000,000	61,819	25,201	13,205
12,850,000,000	16,559,500,000	1,063,329	318,201	88,637
239,000,000	5,860,600,000	95,435	40,272	2,260
310,000,000	NA	4,541,900	1,195,400	27,830
186,000,000	128,600,000	6,135	1,543	NA
98,000,000	147,100,000	301,278	26,415	2,090
NA	NA	37,914	4,772	NA
NA	NA	1,540,335	153,064	NA
1,106,000,000	2,400,000,000	31,030	9,769	654
882,000,000	2,400,000,000	1,563,852	288,728	14,183
73,999,000,000	55,633,900,000	142,283	130,551	34,965
86,817,000,000	80,698,200,000	2,251,535	2,323,105	729,217
NA	181,100,000	1,436	103	NA
NA	237,100,000	57,587	3,192	NA
87,000,000	83,700,000	4,225	998	376
86,000,000	104,000,000	291,444	55,368	2,413
NA	39,600,000	4,494	NA	62
19,000,000	50,300,000	288,478	45,612	800
3,481,000,000	3,025,700,000	62,746	NA	10,097
3,657,000,000	3,485,300,000	2,092,597	608,327	127,353
26,130,000,000	50,000,000,000	5,369,600	2,821,400	302,919
24,871,000,000	49,300,000,000	135,571,000	48,618,800	1,237,394
4,052,000,000	488,700,000	132,675	93,121	34,876
3,462,000,000	541,000,000	4,054,891	1,889,023	331,477
NA	NA	1,292	NA	NA
NA	NA	59,709	NA	NA

Nation Capital	Population	Area of Country (sq mi/ sq km)	Type of Government	Heads of State and Government	Currency: Value in U.S. Dollars	GNP (000,000): GNP Per Capita
CONGO	1,800,000	132,047	People's	President:	CFA franc[4]	$ 2,060
Brazzaville	400,000	342,000	republic	Col. Denis Sassou-Nguesso Premier: Ange Edouard Poungui	0.003	1,120
COSTA RICA	2,700,000	19,575	Republic	President:	Colón	2,930
San José	265,400	50,700		Oscar Arias Sánchez	0.02	1,210
CUBA	10,200,000	44,218	Socialist	President of the	Peso	12,330
Havana	2,003,600	114,524	republic	Councils of State and Ministers: Fidel Castro Ruz	1.15	1,220
CYPRUS	652,000	3,572	Republic	President:[6]	Pound[6]	2,390[6]
Nicosia	161,000[6]	9,251	(C)	Spyros Kyprianou	1.96	3,590
CZECHOSLOVAKIA	15,500,000	49,370	Federal	President:	Koruna	89,260
Prague	1,185,900	127,869	socialist republic	Gustáv Husák Premier: Lubomir Štrougal	0.17	5,758
DENMARK[7]	5,100,000	16,629	Constitutional	Queen:	Krone	57,700
Copenhagen	638,200	43,069	monarchy	Margrethe II Prime Minister: Poul Schlüter	0.13	11,290
DJIBOUTI	300,000	8,495	Republic	President:	Djibouti	180
Djibouti	200,000	22,000		Hassan Gouled Aptidon Premier: Barkad Gourad Hamadou	franc 0.006	600
DOMINICA	100,000	290	Republic	President:	East	80
Roseau	20,000	751	(C)	Clarence A. Seignoret Prime Minister: (Mary) Eugenia Charles	Caribbean dollar 0.37	1,080
DOMINICAN REPUBLIC	6,400,000	18,816 48,734	Republic	President: Joaquin Balaguer	Peso 0.33	6,040 990
Santo Domingo	1,300,000					
ECUADOR	9,600,000	109,484	Republic	President:	Sucre	10,340
Quito	1,110,000	283,561		Léon Febrés Cordero Rivadeneira	0.007	1,220
EGYPT	50,500,000	386,660	Republic	President:	Pound	33,340
Cairo	12,000,000[5]	1,001,450		Hosni Mubarak Prime Minister: Atef Sedki	0.69	720
EL SALVADOR	5,100,000	8,124	Republic	President:	Colón	3,820
San Salvador	445,000	21,041		José Napoleón Duarte	0.40	710
EQUATORIAL GUINEA	400,000	10,831 28,051	Republic	President, Supreme Military Council: Lt. Col. Teodoro Obiang Nguema Mbasogo	CFA franc[4] 0.003	60 200
Malabo	37,200					
ETHIOPIA	43,900,000	471,778	Socialist	Head of State, Chairman,	Birr	4,780
Addis Ababa	1,277,200	1,221,900	state	Provisional Military Administrative Council and Council of Ministers: Mengistu Haile Mariam	0.49	110
FIJI	700,000	7,056	Parliamentary	Governor-General:	Dollar	1,250
Suva	71,300	18,274	state (C)	Penaia Ganilau Prime Minister: Kamisese Mara	0.87	1,840
FINLAND	4,900,000	130,129	Republic	President:	Markka	53,090
Helsinki	484,500	337,032		Mauno Koivisto Prime Minister: Kalevi Sorsa	0.21	10,830
FRANCE	55,400,000	211,208	Republic	President:	Franc	542,960
Paris	2,350,000	547,026		François Mitterrand Premier: Jacques Chirac	0.15	9,860
GABON	1,200,000	103,347	Republic	President:	CFA franc[4]	2,830
Libreville	250,000	267,667		Omar Bongo Premier: Léon Mébiame	0.003	3,480

Imports Exports	Revenue Expenditure	Elementary Schools: Teachers Students	Secondary Schools: Teachers Students	Colleges and Universities: Teachers Students
$ 618,000,000	$ NA	7,329	4,899	292
1,183,000,000	457,000,000	422,874	190,668	7,255
1,085,000,000	NA	10,784	6,540	4,343
978,000,000	NA	343,800	122,836	54,334
8,134,000,000	12,148,200,000	83,424	89,826	12,222
6,164,000,000	12,025,600,000	1,282,999	1,024,113	173,403
1,364,000,000[6]	593,900,000[6]	2,221[6]	3,137[6]	271[6]
575,000,000	601,400,000	46,653	49,274	2,201
17,078,000,000	46,344,900,000	92,435	32,386	20,574
17,153,000,000	46,321,800,000	1,992,400	372,503	181,524
16,585,000,000	19,928,200,000	NA	NA	NA
15,959,000,000	23,201,400,000	426,766	495,950	86,235
NA	NA	496	334	NA
NA	121,000,000	21,847	6,331	NA
58,000,000	24,800,000	665	145	59
25,000,000	22,700,000	13,283	3,234	284
1,257,000,000	NA	20,607	NA	NA
868,000,000	NA	980,808	353,729	42,412
1,716,000,000	1,522,500,000	50,437	39,909	11,679
2,581,000,000	1,470,000,000	1,677,364	650,278	258,064
10,766,000,000	17,695,100,000	158,636	149,437	26,631
3,140,000,000	20,788,800,000	5,349,579	3,201,703	589,899
1,314,000,000	629,600,000	17,633	3,390	2,202
607,000,000	728,200,000	851,895	81,318	46,941
58,000,000	23,400,000	NA	NA	68
26,000,000	24,800,000	NA	NA	1,140
942,000,000	1,161,800,000	42,347	12,570	1,446
417,000,000	1,095,900,000	2,511,050	535,152	16,030
450,000,000	319,900,000	4,150	2,749	NA
256,000,000	326,300,000	116,318	48,608	2,299
12,443,000,000	18,694,900,000	25,139	37,356	6,938
13,505,000,000	18,694,700,000	369,047	433,646	88,295
103,807,000,000	120,000,000,000	206,198	318,452	NA
93,276,000,000	127,000,000,000	4,387,003	5,124,403	951,042
888,000,000	1,700,000,000	3,781	1,743	594
2,018,000,000	1,138,000,000	165,559	32,692	2,992

441

STATISTICS OF THE WORLD

Nation Capital	Population	Area of Country (sq mi/ sq km)	Type of Government	Heads of State and Government	Currency: Value in U.S. Dollars	GNP (000,000): GNP Per Capita
GAMBIA, THE	800,000.....	4,361......Republic	President:	Dalasi..........$	180
Banjul	40,000	11,295	(C)	Sir Dawda K. Jawara	0.13	260
GERMAN..................	16,700,000.....	41,768......Socialist	Chairman, Council of State:	Mark............	120,940
DEMOCRATIC		108,178	republic	Erich Honecker	0.51	7,241
REPUBLIC				Chairman, Council of Ministers		
East Berlin	1,198,900			(Premier):		
				Willi Stoph		
GERMANY, FEDERAL	60,700,000......	95,976......Federal	President:	Deutsche.......	678,880
REPUBLIC OF		248,577	republic	Richard von Weizsäcker	mark	11,090
Bonn	291,700			Chancellor:	0.51	
				Helmut Kohl		
GHANA	13,600,000......	92,100......Republic	Chairman, Provisional	Cedi..............	4,730
Accra	840,000	238,537	(C)	National Defense Council	0.012	350
				(Head of State):		
				Jerry J. Rawlings		
GREAT BRITAIN[8]	56,600,000.....	94,227......Limited	Queen:	Pound...........	480,680
London	6,776,000	244,046	monarchy (C)	Elizabeth II	1.47	8,530
				Prime Minister:		
				Margaret Thatcher		
GREECE....................	10,000,000.....	50,944......Republic	President:	Drachma......	36,940
Athens	885,100	131,944		Christos Sartzetakis	0.007	3,740
				Prime Minister:		
				Andreas Papandreou		
GRENADA.................	90,000.....	120......Parliamentary	Governor-General:	East	80
St. George's	10,000	311	state (C)	Sir Paul Scoon	Caribbean	880
				Prime Minister:	dollar	
				Herbert A. Blaize	0.37	
GUATEMALA.............	8,600,000.....	42,042......Republic	President:	Quetzal.........	9,110
Guatemala City	754,200	108,889		Marco Vinicio Cerezo	1.00	1,120
				Arévalo		
GUINEA....................	6,200,000.....	94,926......Republic	President:	Franc............	1,810
Conakry	763,000	245,857		Lansana Conté	0.04	300
GUINEA-BISSAU	900,000.....	13,948......Republic	President, Council of ...	Peso	160
Bissau	109,200	36,125		the Revolution:	0.06	180
				Cmdr. João Bernardo Vieira		
GUYANA	800,000.....	83,000......Republic	President:	Dollar............	470
Georgetown	187,600[5]	214,969	(C)	Desmond Hoyte	0.24	580
				Prime Minister:		
				Hamilton Green		
HAITI	5,900,000.....	10,714......Republic	Head, military-civilian	Gourde	1,710
Port-au-Prince	719,700	27,750		council:	0.20	320
				Henri Namphy		
HONDURAS...............	4,600,000.....	43,277......Republic	President:	Lempira	2,980
Tegucigalpa	533,600	112,088		José Azcona del Hoya	0.50	700
HUNGARY	10,600,000.....	35,919......People's	Chairman, Presidential Council:	Forint............	21,950[1]
Budapest	2,064,000	93,030	republic	Pál Losonczi	0.02	2,050
				Chairman, Council of Ministers		
				(Premier):		
				György Lázár		
ICELAND....................	240,000.....	39,769......Republic	President:	New króna.....	2,250
Reykjavík	88,900	103,000		Vigdís Finnbogadóttir	0.02	9,380
				Prime Minister:		
				Steingrímur Hermannsson		
INDIA.......................	785,000,000.....	1,269,346......Federal	President:	Rupee	197,210
New Delhi	2,500,000	3,287,590	republic	Zail Singh	0.08	260
			(C)	Prime Minister:		
				Rajiv Gandhi		
INDONESIA...............	168,400,000.....	782,663......Republic	President:	Rupiah..........	85,400
Jakarta	6,503,400	2,027,087		Suharto	0.001	540
IRAN........................	46,600,000.....	636,296......Islamic	President:	Rial..............	69,170
Tehran	5,433,700	1,648,000	republic	Hojatolislam Sayed	0.01	1,533
				Ali Khamenei		
				Prime Minister:		
				Mir Hussein Moussavi		

442

Imports Exports	Revenue Expenditure	Elementary Schools: Teachers Students	Secondary Schools: Teachers Students	Colleges and Universities: Teachers Students
$ 98,000,000 47,000,000	$ 40,300,000 62,700,000	2,439 60,529	829 14,430	NA NA
22,940,000,000 24,836,000,000	68,967,500,000 68,400,000,000	171,381 2,024,220	NA 456,151	29,460 139,699
151,246,000,000 169,784,000,000	109,540,600,000 120,366,800,000	140,365 2,366,211	437,559 5,967,864	130,743 1,198,330
591,000,000 571,000,000	946,600,000 1,000,000,000	58,434 1,653,455	35,907 753,665	623 5,011
105,961,000,000 94,502,000,000	204,085,200,000 214,907,900,000	245,000 4,474,000	NA 5,296,000	NA 413,000
9,434,000,000 4,811,000,000	10,700,000,000 12,600,000,000	34,054 892,509	35,842 762,368	6,129 83,485
NA NA	87,500,000 87,500,000	764 17,704	NA NA	40 519
1,278,000,000 1,129,000,000	845,400,000 1,062,000,000	26,963 979,888	11,828 167,724	NA 47,433
351,000,000 428,000,000	NA NA	7,867 246,129	5,109 94,848	1,373 13,182
50,000,000 12,000,000	NA NA	3,363 74,359	465 6,294	NA NA
263,000,000 40,000,000	407,300,000 437,000,000	3,493 130,003	NA NA	447 1,580
472,000,000 179,000,000	NA NA	14,927 658,102	NA 101,519	559 4,099
823,000,000 670,000,000	1,351,700,000 1,369,400,000	18,966 703,608	5,342 156,665	1,940 30,119
8,091,000,000 8,563,000,000	12,156,000,000 12,206,000,000	83,496 1,296,899	NA 409,585	11,121 60,084
839,000,000 740,000,000	433,100,000 442,500,000	NA 25,280	NA 26,803	NA 5,212
13,953,000,000 8,793,000,000	18,056,000,000 20,032,000,000	1,389,356 77,038,922	1,849,504 34,032,130	277,648 5,345,580
13,882,000,000 21,888,000,000	19,203,000,000 19,203,000,000	10,564,470 29,108,580	403,422 6,320,013	NA 570,392
NA 13,979,000,000	36,826,500,000 41,000,800,000	297,298 5,994,403	196,541 2,832,841	7,214 113,993

STATISTICS OF THE WORLD

Nation Capital	Population	Area of Country (sq ml/ sq km)	Type of Government	Heads of State and Government	Currency: Value in U.S. Dollars	GNP (000,000): GNP Per Capita
IRAQ Baghdad	16,000,000 3,236,000	167,925 434,924	Republic	President and Chairman, Revolutionary Command Council: Saddam Hussein al-Takriti	Dinar 3.23	$ 39,500 2,548
IRELAND, REPUBLIC OF Dublin	3,600,000 526,000	27,136 70,283	Republic	President: Patrick J. Hillery Prime Minister: Garret FitzGerald	Punt 1.38	17,500 4,950
ISRAEL Jerusalem	4,200,000 420,000	7,992 20,700	Republic	President: Chaim Herzog Prime Minister: Yitzhak Shamir	Shekel 0.68	21,290 5,100
ITALY Rome	57,200,000 2,827,700	116,304 301,225	Republic	President: Francesco Cossiga Prime Minister: Bettino Craxi	Lira 0.0007	367,040 6,440
IVORY COAST Abidjan	10,500,000 1,800,000	124,503 322,462	Republic	President: Félix Houphouët-Boigny	CFA franc[4] 0.003	6,030 610
JAMAICA Kingston	2,300,000 565,500	4,244 10,991	Parliamentary state (C)	Governor-General: Florizel A. Glasspole Prime Minister: Edward P. G. Seaga	Dollar 0.18	2,480 1,080
JAPAN Tokyo	121,500,000 8,195,000	145,824 377,682	Constitutional monarchy	Emperor: Hirohito Prime Minister: Yasuhiro Nakasone	Yen 0.006	1,248,090 10,390
JORDAN Amman	3,700,000 1,300,000	37,738 97,740	Constitutional monarchy	King: Hussein I Prime Minister: Zaid al-Rifai	Dinar 2.89	4,340 1,710
KENYA Nairobi	21,000,000 906,400	224,961 582,646	Republic (C)	President: Daniel arap Moi	Shilling 0.07	5,950 300
KIRIBATI (GILBERT ISLANDS) Tarawa	60,000 21,000	342 886	Republic (C)	President: Ieremia T. Tabai	Dollar 0.66	30 460
KOREA, DEMOCRATIC PEOPLE'S REPUBLIC OF P'yŏngyang	20,500,000 1,800,000	46,540 120,538	People's republic	President: Marshal Kim Il Sung Premier: Li Gun Mo	Won 1.06	17,040 847
KOREA, REPUBLIC OF Seoul[5]	43,300,000 9,645,800	38,025 96,484	Republic	President: Chun Doo Hwan Prime Minister: Lho Shin Yong	Won 0.001	84,860 2,090
KUWAIT Kuwait	1,800,000 60,500	6,880 17,818	Constitutional emirate	Emir: Sheikh Jabir al-Ahmad al-Sabah Prime Minister: Sheikh Saad al-Abdullah al-Salem al-Sabah	Dinar 3.41	27,570 15,410
LAOS Vientiane	3,700,000 377,400	91,429 236,800	People's republic	President: Phoumi Vongvichit Premier: Kaysone Phomvihan	New kip 0.03	290 80
LEBANON Beirut	2,700,000 1,000,000	4,015 10,400	Republic	President: Amin Gemayel Prime Minister: Rashid Karami	Pound 0.014	NA NA
LESOTHO Maseru	1,600,000 45,000	11,720 30,355	Constitutional monarchy (C)	King: Moshoeshoe II Prime Minister: Justin Lekhanya	Loti 0.45	790 530
LIBERIA Monrovia	2,300,000 208,600	43,000 111,369	Republic	Head of State and Chairman, People's Redemption Council: Samuel K. Doe	Dollar 1.00	990 470

Imports Exports	Revenue Expenditure	Elementary Schools: Teachers Students	Secondary Schools: Teachers Students	Colleges and Universities: Teachers Students
$ NA 9,785,000,000	$ NA NA	112,428 2,698,542	42,374 1,068,224	4,907 84,751
9,663,000,000 9,629,000,000	9,383,100,000 11,110,000,000	14,829 420,871	20,402 309,600	2,897 33,982
8,411,000,000 5,804,000,000	NA NA	42,536 685,714	35,508 229,146	NA 60,610
84,215,000,000 73,303,000,000	160,673,000,000 210,830,000,000	276,716 4,204,272	532,264 5,319,934	48,590 1,112,487
1,511,000,000 2,698,000,000	1,300,000,000 1,400,000,000	31,297 1,134,915	NA 245,342	666 12,541
1,146,000,000 747,000,000	NA 1,040,000,000	10,374 341,748	NA NA	NA 4,884
136,522,000,000 170,107,000,000	349,000,000,000 349,000,000,000	476,991 11,665,452	589,577 10,244,607	181,286 1,935,033
2,784,000,000 752,000,000	2,200,000,000 2,600,000,000	15,179 487,890	14,443 311,402	1,011 22,305
1,574,000,000 1,083,000,000	1,525,200,000 2,372,600,000	117,705 4,323,822	20,381 517,033	1,183 9,223
36,000,000 3,000,000	10,900,000 10,900,000	471 13,194	130 1,901	NA NA
1,390,000,000 1,340,000,000	29,131,900,000 29,131,900,000	NA NA	NA NA	NA NA
30,631,000,000 29,245,000,000	15,500,000,000 15,500,000,000	126,233 5,040,958	134,509 4,718,225	24,835 933,032
7,699,000,000 10,751,000,000	10,377,200,000 11,531,700,000	8,968 165,696	16,965 220,981	848 13,233
NA NA	119,000,000 215,200,000	17,512 481,560	3,709 64,500	420 4,885
NA NA	690,900,000 747,700,000	22,810 398,977	NA NA	7,976 73,052
NA NA	156,100,000 118,000,000	5,295 277,945	1,495 28,717	212 1,350
363,000,000 452,000,000	375,400,000 428,000,000	9,099 227,431	NA NA	NA 3,702

Nation Capital	Population	Area of Country (sq mi/ sq km)	Type of Government	Heads of State and Government	Currency: Value in U.S. Dollars	GNP (000,000): GNP Per Capita
LIBYA Tripoli	3,900,000 990,700	679,362 1,759,540	Socialist republic	Head of State: Col. Muammar al-Qaddafi Secretary-General, General People's Congress: Mustafa Usta Omar	Dinar 3.14	$ 29,790 8,230
LIECHTENSTEIN Vaduz	26,700 4,900	61 157	Constitutional monarchy	Sovereign: Prince Francis Joseph II Chief of Government: Hans Brunhart	Swiss franc 0.61	NA NA
LUXEMBOURG Luxembourg	370,000 79,000	998 2,586	Constitutional monarchy	Grand Duke: Jean President: Jacques Santer	Franc 0.02	4,980 13,650
MADAGASCAR Antananarivo	10,300,000 773,000	226,658 587,041	Socialist republic	President: Cmdr. Didier Ratsiraka Prime Minister: Lt. Col. Désiré Rakotoarijaona	Franc 0.001	2,600 270
MALAWI Lilongwe	7,300,000 158,000	45,747 118,484	Republic (C)	President: Hastings Kamuzu Banda	Kwacha 0.51	1,430 210
MALAYSIA Kuala Lumpur	15,800,000 937,900	127,317 329,749	Federal constitutional monarchy (C)	Supreme Head of State: Sultan Mahmood Iskandar Prime Minister: Datuk Seri Mahathir bin Mohamad	Dollar 0.39	30,280 1,990
MALDIVES Male	200,000 29,500	115 298	Republic	President: Maumoon Abdul Gayoom	Rufiyaa 0.14	40 200
MALI Bamako	7,900,000 399,900	478,767 1,240,000	Republic	President: Moussa Traoré	Franc 0.003	1,060 140
MALTA Valletta	330,000 14,100	122 316	Republic (C)	President: Agatha Barbara Prime Minister: Carmelo Mifsud Bonnici	Pound 2.70	1,210 3,370
MAURITANIA Nouakchott	1,900,000 135,000	397,955 1,030,700	Islamic republic	President and Chairman, Military Committee for National Salvation: Maaouiya Ould Sidi Ahmed Taya	Ouguiya 0.01	750 450
MAURITIUS Port Louis	1,000,000 135,200	790 2,045	Parliamentary state (C)	Governor-General: Veerasamy Ringadoo Prime Minister: Aneerood Jugnauth	Rupee 0.07	1,100 1,100
MEXICO Mexico City	81,700,000 10,500,000	761,604 1,972,547	Federal republic	President: Miguel de la Madrid Hurtado	Peso 0.001	158,310 2,060
MONACO Monaco	27,000 4,000	0.58 1.49	Constitutional monarchy	Prince: Rainier III Minister of State: Jean Ausseil	French franc 0.15	NA NA
MONGOLIAN PEOPLE'S REPUBLIC Ulan Bator	1,900,000 488,000	604,250 1,565,000	People's republic	Presidium Chairman: Jambyn Batmönh Premier: Dumaagiyn Sodnom	Tugrik 0.30	1,100 578
MOROCCO Rabat	23,700,000 566,900	172,414 446,550	Constitutional monarchy	King: Hassan II Prime Minister: Muhammad Karim Lamrani	Dirham 0.11	14,340 670
MOZAMBIQUE Maputo	14,000,000 785,500	309,496 801,590	People's republic	President: Joaquim A. Chissano Prime Minister: Mário da Graça Machungo	Metical 0.02	2,800 201
NAURU Yaren	8,400 NA	8 21	Republic (C)	President: Hammer DeRoburt	Australian dollar 0.66	NA NA

446

Imports Exports	Revenue Expenditure	Elementary Schools: Teachers Students	Secondary Schools: Teachers Students	Colleges and Universities: Teachers Students
$ NA	$ NA	42,696	30,673	NA
11,136,000,000	4,800,400,000	721,710	340,703	27,535
NA	107,500,000	146	82	NA
NA	106,200,000	2,476	1,323	NA
NA	1,740,200,000	1,685	2,020	318
NA	1,739,100,000	22,826	24,341	982
370,000,000	452,200,000	23,937	NA	706
334,000,000	589,800,000	1,311,000	NA	32,599
269,000,000	300,000,000	13,476	1,135	NA
313,000,000	342,000,000	868,849	21,646	1,810
13,987,000,000	8,840,000,000	81,664[9]	54,787[9]	4,020
13,917,000,000	8,780,000,000	2,120,050[9]	1,173,202[9]	31,018
61,000,000	NA	NA	NA	NA
23,000,000	NA	34,090	3,800	NA
368,000,000	111,700,000	7,932	NA	499
181,000,000	119,400,000	296,301	69,754	5,792
717,000,000	490,600,000	1,656	2,253	146
394,000,000	502,800,000	33,208	27,257	1,010
246,000,000	192,400,000	2,401	921	NA
297,000,000	239,100,000	107,390	26,727	NA
472,000,000	332,000,000	6,572	NA	122
373,000,000	368,700,000	138,790	73,281	430
11,280,000,000	124,000,000,000	428,029	337,914	92,926
23,602,000,000	128,000,000,000	15,376,153	6,064,264	939,513
NA	214,300,000	NA	NA	NA
NA	169,800,000	1,354	2,274	NA
824,000,000	482,900,000	4,700	NA	1,300
541,000,000	482,000,000	150,100	256,700	18,700
3,907,000,000	2,652,000,000	71,731	53,457	3,901
2,172,000,000	3,464,000,000	2,467,611	1,046,136	82,944
487,000,000	476,200,000	20,769	3,519	327
86,000,000	654,800,000	1,162,617	121,033	1,110
NA	51,900,000	NA	NA	NA
NA	51,500,000	2,222	413	NA

Nation Capital	Population	Area of Country (sq mi/ sq km)	Type of Government	Heads of State and Government	Currency: Value in U.S. Dollars	GNP (000,000): GNP Per Capita
NEPAL Kathmandu	17,400,000 393,500	54,362 140,797	Constitutional monarchy	King: Birendra Bir Bikram Shah Deva Prime Minister: Marich Man Singh Shrestha	Rupee $ 0.05	2,630 160
NETHERLANDS, THE Amsterdam	14,500,000 675,600	15,770 40,844	Constitutional monarchy	Queen: Beatrix Prime Minister: Ruud Lubbers	Guilder 0.45	135,830 9,430
NEW ZEALAND Wellington	3,300,000 342,000	103,736 268,676	Parliamentary state (C)	Governor-General: Paul Reeves Prime Minister: David Lange	Dollar 0.53	23,530 7,240
NICARAGUA Managua	3,300,000 902,000	50,193 130,000	Republic	President: Daniel Ortega Saavedra	Córdoba 0.014	2,700 870
NIGER Niamey	6,700,000 360,000	489,191 1,267,000	Republic	President, Supreme Military Council: Col. Seyni Kountché Prime Minister: Hamid Algabid	CFA franc[4] 0.003	1,190 190
NIGERIA Lagos	105,400,000 4,200,000	356,669 923,768	Federal republic (C)	President: Ibrahim Babangida	Naira 0.43	74,120 770
NORWAY Oslo	4,200,000 487,300	125,182 324,219	Constitutional monarchy	King: Olav V Prime Minister: Gro Harlem Bruntland	Krone 0.13	57,080 13,750
OMAN Masqat	1,300,000 6,000	82,030 212,450	Sultanate	Sultan and Prime Minister: Qabus bin Sa'id	Rial 2.60	7,380 6,230
PAKISTAN Islamabad	101,900,000 388,000	310,404 803,943	Federal republic	President: Gen. Muhammad Zia ul-Haq Prime Minister: Muhammad Khan Junejo	Rupee 0.06	35,420 380
PANAMA Panamá	2,200,000 700,000	29,762 77,082	Republic	President: Eric Arturo Delvalle	Balboa 1.00	4,210 2,100
PAPUA NEW GUINEA Port Moresby	3,400,000 140,000	178,260 461,691	Parliamentary state (C)	Governor-General: Kingsford Dibela Prime Minister: Paias Wingti	Kina 1.05	2,480 760
PARAGUAY Asunción	4,100,000 474,100	157,048 406,752	Republic	President: Gen. Alfredo Stroessner	Guarani 0.004	4,120 1,250
PERU Lima	20,200,000 4,164,600	496,225 1,285,216	Republic	President: Alan García Pérez Prime Minister: Luís Alva Castro	Inti 0.07	17,960 980
PHILIPPINES Manila	58,100,000 1,630,500	115,830 300,000	Republic	President: Corazon C. Aquino Prime Minister: Salvador H. Laurel	Peso 0.05	35,040 660
POLAND Warsaw	37,500,000 1,625,000	120,725 312,677	People's republic	Head of State: Gen. Wojciech W. Jaruzelski Premier: Zbigniew Messner	Złoty 0.005	139,780 3,747
PORTUGAL Lisbon	10,100,000 812,400	35,553 92,082	Republic	President: Mário Soares Prime Minister: Anibal Cavaco Silva	Escudo 0.007	20,050 1,970
QATAR Doha	300,000 190,000	4,250 11,000	Constitutional emirate	Emir and Prime Minister: Sheikh Khalifa bin Hamad al-Thani	Riyal 0.28	6,020 20,600
ROMANIA Bucharest	22,800,000 1,861,000	91,699 237,500	Socialist republic	Head of State and President, State Council: Nicolae Ceauşescu Chairman, Council of Ministers (Premier): Constantin Dăscălescu	Leu 0.23	57,030 2,501

Imports Exports	Revenue Expenditure	Elementary Schools: Teachers Students	Secondary Schools: Teachers Students	Colleges and Universities: Teachers Students
$ 765,000,000	$ 405,000,000	38,016	15,910	NA
271,000,000	640,000,000	1,626,437	418,085	54,599
62,136,000,000	50,895,300,000	57,293	NA	NA
65,881,000,000	61,655,400,000	1,139,955	1,466,956	155,025
6,010,000,000	6,590,000,000	17,306	NA	4,699
5,358,000,000	7,919,600,000	359,011	360,411	46,470
826,000,000	1,584,700,000	17,969	6,014	1,423
385,000,000	2,674,100,000	534,317	161,745	31,537
442,000,000	186,400,000	5,475	NA	322
333,000,000	186,400,000	233,441	NA	2,450
9,392,000,000	10,964,400,000	NA	NA	7,759
14,124,000,000	10,939,400,000	13,787,736	NA	83,357
13,889,000,000	22,354,300,000	47,802	NA	NA
18,892,000,000	21,502,200,000	383,599	381,603	41,002
2,748,000,000	4,975,600,000	5,369	2,987	NA
4,422,000,000	5,551,700,000	155,389	39,892	NA
5,873,000,000	8,687,200,000	206,000	128,467	7,042
2,614,000,000	9,141,800,000	6,412,000	2,253,298	156,558
1,423,000,000	1,400,000,000	12,912	9,184	3,492
256,000,000	1,400,000,000	338,650	176,441	46,273
968,000,000	805,000,000	10,163	2,348	589
895,000,000	949,000,000	313,790	50,353	3,458
563,000,000	1,275,400,000	20,746	NA	1,945
386,000,000	1,275,400,000	539,889	164,464	20,496
1,870,000,000	2,658,000,000	89,370	55,959	16,913
3,131,000,000	3,604,000,000	3,343,631	1,429,219	305,390
6,051,000,000	3,445,000,000	272,134	90,266	NA
5,322,000,000	4,005,000,000	8,591,267	3,092,128	1,201,872
10,548,000,000	NA	279,013	142,696	58,750
11,649,000,000	NA	4,535,041	1,520,819	384,429
7,978,000,000	6,997,500,000	68,188	36,219	6,906
5,208,000,000	6,997,500,000	1,221,539	451,426	67,652
NA	2,678,600,000	2,789	2,210	235
4,513,000,000	4,689,900,000	35,920	19,607	4,627
9,959,000,000	75,555,000,000	150,539	49,208	13,344
13,241,000,000	53,280,000,000	3,067,446	1,272,245	174,042

Nation Capital	Population	Area of Country (sq mi/ sq km)	Type of Government	Heads of State and Government	Currency: Value in U.S. Dollars	GNP (000,000): GNP Per Capita
RWANDA Kigali	6,500,000 176,700	10,169 26,338	Republic	President: Juvénal Habyarimana	Franc 0.01	$ 1,610 270
SAINT KITTS– NEVIS Basseterre	40,000 14,700	65 105	Parliamentary state (C)	Governor-General: Sir Clement Arrindell Prime Minister: Kennedy Simmonds	East Caribbean dollar 0.37	60 1,390
SAINT LUCIA Castries	130,000 45,000	238 616	Parliamentary state (C)	Governor-General: Allen Lewis Prime Minister: John G. M. Compton	East Caribbean dollar 0.37	150 1,130
SAINT VINCENT AND THE GRENADINES Kingstown	130,000 32,600	150 388	Parliamentary state (C)	Governor-General: Sir Joseph Lambert Eustace Prime Minister: James Mitchell	East Caribbean dollar 0.37	100 900
SAN MARINO San Marino	22,400 4,400	24 61	Republic	Co-Regents: Renzo Renzi Germano De Biagi	Italian lira 0.0007	NA NA
SÃO TOMÉ AND PRÍNCIPE São Tomé	100,000 35,000	372 964	Republic	President and Prime Minister: Manuel Pinto da Costa	Dobra 0.026	30 320
SAUDI ARABIA Riyadh	11,500,000 1,500,000	830,000 2,149,690	Monarchy	King and Prime Minister: Fahd ibn Abdul-Aziz	Riyal 0.27	116,380 10,740
SENEGAL Dakar	6,900,000 700,000	75,750 196,192	Republic	President: Abdou Diouf Premier: Habib Thiam	CFA franc[4] 0.003	2,440 380
SEYCHELLES Victoria	65,000 23,300	108 280	Republic (C)	President: France Albert René	Rupee 0.16	160 2,430
SIERRA LEONE Freetown	3,700,000 400,000	27,699 71,740	Republic (C)	President: Joseph Momoh	Leone 0.04	1,120 300
SINGAPORE Singapore	2,600,000 2,531,000	224 581	Republic (C)	President: Wee Kim Wee Prime Minister: Lee Kuan Yew	Dollar 0.46	18,390 7,260
SOLOMON ISLANDS Honiara	260,000 20,800	10,983 28,446	Parliamentary state (C)	Governor-General: Sir Baddeley Devesi Prime Minister: Peter Kenilorea	Dollar 0.58	160 608
SOMALIA Mogadisho	7,800,000 400,000	246,201 637,657	Republic	President and Chairman, Council of Ministers: Maj. Gen. Muhammad Siad Barre	Somali 0.03	1,360 260
SOUTH AFRICA,[11] REPUBLIC OF Cape Town Pretoria	33,200,000 790,900 528,400	471,445 1,221,037	Republic	President: Pieter Willem Botha	Rand 0.45	73,970 2,260
SPAIN Madrid	38,800,000 3,188,300	194,897 504,782	Constitutional monarchy	King: Juan Carlos I Prime Minister: Felipe González Márquez	Peseta 0.008	172,360 4,470
SRI LANKA (CEYLON) Colombo	16,600,000 602,000	25,332 65,610	Republic (C)	President: Junius R. Jayewardene Prime Minister: Ranasinghe Premadasa	Rupee 0.04	5,660 360
SUDAN Khartoum	22,900,000 476,200	967,500 2,505,813	Republic	Chairman of the Sovereign Council: Ahmed al-Mirgani Prime Minister: Sadiq al-Mahdi	Pound 0.40	7,360 340
SURINAME Paramaribo	370,000 180,000	63,037 163,265	Republic	President: Dési Bouterse Prime Minister: Pretapnaarian Radhakishun	Guilder 0.57	1,350 3,520
SWAZILAND Mbabane	630,000 38,600	6,704 17,363	Monarchy (C)	King: Mswati III Prime Minister: Sotsha Dlamini	Emala 0.45	590 800

Imports Exports	Revenue Expenditure	Elementary Schools: Teachers Students	Secondary Schools: Teachers Students	Colleges and Universities: Teachers Students
$ 295,000,000	$ 164,600,000	14,105	1,082	NA
83,000,000	187,900,000	761,955	14,761	1,317
51,000,000	27,900,000	357	289	8
17,000,000	27,900,000	8,070	4,060	40
NA	NA	1,084	350	105
NA	79,700,000	32,107	5,314	537
61,000,000	37,200,000	1,184	320	41
32,000,000	61,100,000	21,497	5,123	259
NA	107,100,000	165	155	NA
NA	107,100,000	1,456	1,266	NA
26,000,000	NA	517	325	NA
13,000,000	NA	16,013	6,436	NA
33,696,000,000	55,400,000,000	69,286	32,482	7,928
36,834,000,000	55,400,000,000	1,102,110	419,031	75,110
1,001,000,000	1,030,000,000	12,934	4,980	640
536,000,000	1,330,000,000	533,394	113,561	11,293
88,000,000	82,000,000	679	290	28
20,000,000	91,200,000	14,256	3,889	144
166,000,000	120,980,000	9,472	3,829	270
148,000,000	135,210,000	263,724	81,879	1,809
28,712,000,000	6,650,000,000	9,921	9,704	1,613
24,108,000,000	3,900,000,000	290,800	193,007	14,179
107,000,000	NA	1,199	267	NA
151,000,000	NA	30,246	5,118	NA
109,000,000	324,500,000	9,460	3,018	NA
45,000,000	324,500,000	220,680	63,255	2,899
14,956,000,000	11,788,800,000	190,325[10]	190,325[10]	NA
9,334,000,000	13,656,800,000	4,583,905	1,428,637	159,403
28,812,000,000	25,800,000,000	214,391	190,859	32,838
23,544,000,000	35,500,000,000	3,633,713	4,169,047	543,873
1,845,000,000	1,352,400,000	136,280	NA	2,234
1,454,000,000	1,343,100,000	2,145,343	NA	34,725
1,354,000,000	960,100,000	47,084	20,600	6,081
624,000,000	1,558,900,000	1,579,286	455,969	25,151
346,000,000	147,800,000	NA	NA	165
356,000,000	255,400,000	NA	NA	951
544,000,000	115,200,000	3,922	1,528	113
289,000,000	120,200,000	129,767	27,801	1,064

STATISTICS OF THE WORLD

Nation Capital	Population	Area of Country (sq mi/ sq km)	Type of Government	Heads of State and Government	Currency: Value in U.S. Dollars	GNP (000,000): GNP Per Capita
SWEDEN Stockholm	8,400,000 650,900	173,732 449,964	Constitutional monarchy	King: Carl XVI Gustaf Prime Minister: Ingvar Carlsson	Krona ....$ 0.15	99,060 11,880
SWITZERLAND Bern	6,500,000 143,900	15,941 41,288	Federal republic	President: Alphons Egli	Franc 0.61	105,060 15,990
SYRIA Damascus	10,500,000 2,083,000	71,500 185,180	Socialist republic	President: Hafez al-Assad Prime Minister: Abdel al-Raouf al-Kassem	Pound 0.26	18,540 1,870
TAIWAN or FORMOSA (REPUBLIC OF CHINA) Taipei	19,600,000 2,500,000	13,900 36,000	Republic	President: Chiang Ching-kuo Premier: Yu Kuo-hua	New Taiwan dollar 0.03	38,200 1,989
TANZANIA Dar es-Salaam	22,400,000 279,800	364,900 945,087	Republic (C)	President: Ali Hassan Mwinyi Prime Minister: Joseph Warioba	Shilling 0.02	4,460 210
THAILAND Bangkok	52,800,000 5,500,000	198,456 514,000	Constitutional monarchy	King: Bhumibol Adulyadej Prime Minister: Gen. Prem Tinsulanonda	Baht 0.04	42,760 850
TOGO Lomé	3,000,000 366,500	21,925 56,785	Republic	President: Gen. Gnassingbé Eyadéma	CFA franc[4] 0.003	730 250
TONGA Nukualofa	99,000 20,560	270 699	Constitutional monarchy	King: Taufa'ahau Tupou IV Prime Minister: Prince Fatafehi Tu'ipelehake	Pa'anga 0.66	80 808
TRINIDAD AND TOBAGO Port of Spain	1,200,000 61,200	1,981 5,130	Republic (C)	President: Sir Ellis E. I. Clarke Prime Minister: Arthur N. Robinson	Dollar 0.43	8,350 7,140
TUNISIA Tunis	7,200,000 1,000,000	63,170 163,610	Republic	President: Habib Bourguiba Prime Minister: Rachid Sfar	Dinar 1.19	8,840 1,250
TURKEY Ankara	52,300,000 1,877,800	301,382 780,576	Republic	President: Gen. Kenan Evren Prime Minister: Turgut Özal	Lira 0.001	57,810 1,200
TUVALU (ELLICE ISLANDS) Funafuti	8,200 NA	10 26	Parliamentary state (C)	Governor-General: Tupua Leupena Prime Minister: Tomasi Puapua	Australian dollar 0.66	5 714
UGANDA Kampala	15,200,000 458,000	91,134 236,036	Republic (C)	Head of state: Yoweri Museveni Prime Minister: Samson Kisekka	Shilling 0.0007	3,290 230
UNION OF SOVIET SOCIALIST REPUBLICS Moscow	280,000,000 8,867,000	8,649,538 22,402,200	Federal socialist state	Chairman, Presidium of the Supreme Soviet: Andrei Gromyko Chairman, Council of Ministers (Premier): Nikolai Rhyzkov	Ruble 1.47	1,212,000[1] 4,423
UNITED ARAB EMIRATES Abu Dhabi	1,400,000 316,000	32,278 83,600	Federal state	President: Sheikh Zayed bin Sultan al-Nahayan Prime Minister: Sheikh Rashid bin Saeed al-Maktoum	Dirham 0.27	28,480 22,300
UNITED STATES OF AMERICA Washington, D.C.	241,000,000 626,000	3,618,770 9,372,571	Federal republic	President: Ronald W. Reagan Vice President: George Bush	Dollar *	3,670,490 15,490

Imports Exports	Revenue Expenditure	Elementary Schools: Teachers Students	Secondary Schools: Teachers Students	Colleges and Universities: Teachers Students
$ 26,416,000,000 29,378,000,000	$ 53,122,700,000 55,420,400,000	40,800 658,127	51,397 607,199	NA 223,295
29,469,000,000 25,863,000,000	8,195,100,000 8,233,400,000	NA 398,931	NA 443,427	5,882 66,206
4,116,000,000 1,853,000,000	NA 5,970,000,000	67,057 1,823,684	45,035 755,095	NA 115,229
21,959,000,000 30,456,000,000	14,542,100,000 14,186,800,000	80,808 2,456,717	74,873 1,682,364	19,166 395,153
874,000,000 377,000,000	1,390,000,000 1,390,000,000	85,308 3,552,923	4,162 78,655	974 3,943
10,398,000,000 7,413,000,000	6,169,000,000 7,675,000,000	333,351 7,449,219	NA 2,191,706	16,245 795,970
271,000,000 191,000,000	360,000,000 370,000,000	10,145 457,376	NA 101,989	308 3,734
41,000,000 9,000,000	19,500,000 19,500,000	832 16,329	NA 17,085	13 79
2,101,000,000 2,194,000,000	3,828,200,000 3,828,200,000	7,522 169,853	4,653 90,815	NA 2,503
3,218,000,000 1,797,000,000	NA NA	33,347 198,447	20,493 387,445	4,397 35,426
10,822,000,000 7,086,000,000	9,164,600,000 10,413,400,000	208,891 6,497,308	132,217 2,540,636	20,492 335,080
2,700,000 NA	NA 2,400,000	61 1,349	NA 265	NA NA
NA 399,000,000	555,600,000 805,400,000	44,426 1,616,791	7,022 145,389	369 4,854
80,412,000,000 91,343,000,000	319,000,000,000 319,000,000,000	2,839,200 27,461,900	NA 23,774,400	NA 6,382,300
NA 14,103,000,000	NA 4,694,200,000	5,278 126,726	NA 51,892	279 4,227
345,276,000,000 213,133,000,000	769,100,000,000 989,800,000,000	1,352,000 27,411,000	1,033,000 14,122,000	301,943 7,654,074

Nation Capital	Population	Area of Country (sq mi/ sq km)	Type of Government	Heads of State and Government	Currency: Value in U.S. Dollars	GNP (000,000): GNP Per Capita
UPPER VOLTA (BURKINA FASO) Ouagadougou	7,100,000 300,000	105,869 274,200	Republic	Head of State and Government: Thomas Sankara	CFA franc[4] 0.003	$ 1,040 160
URUGUAY Montevideo	3,000,000 1,500,000	68,037 176,215	Republic	President: Julio María Sanguinetti Cairolo	New peso 0.006	5,900 1,970
VANUATU (NEW HEBRIDES) Vila	100,000 15,000	5,700 14,763	Republic (C)	President: Ati George Sokomanu Prime Minister: Rev. Walter H. Lini	Vatu 0.01	40 400
VENEZUELA Caracas	17,800,000 1,663,000	352,144 912,050	Federal republic	President: Jaime Lusinchi	Bolivar 0.04	57,360 3,220
VIETNAM Hanoi	62,000,000 3,000,000	127,242 329,556	Socialist republic	Chairman, Council of State (President): Truong Chinh Chairman, Council of Ministers (Premier): Pham Van Dong	New dong 0.01	7,750 128
WESTERN SAMOA Apia	160,000 33,200	1,097 2,842	Constitutional monarchy (C)	Head of State: Malietoa Tanumafili II Prime Minister: Va'ai Kolone	Talà 0.46	NA NA
YEMEN, PEOPLE'S DEMOCRATIC REPUBLIC OF Aden	2,300,000 272,000	128,600 333,000	People's republic	President: Haidar Bakr al-Attas Prime Minister: Yasin Said Numan	Dinar 2.92	1,130 560
YEMEN ARAB REPUBLIC Sana	6,300,000 427,200	75,300 195,000	Republic	President: Col. Ali Abdullah Saleh Prime Minister: Abdel Aziz Abdel Ghani	Rial 0.10	3,940 510
YUGOSLAVIA Belgrade	23,200,000 1,470,100[5]	98,766 255,804	Federal socialist republic	President: Sinan Hassani President, Federal Executive Council (Prime Minister): Branko Mikulic	Dinar 0.002	48,690[1] 2,120
ZAIRE Kinshasa	31,300,000 1,700,000	905,568 2,345,409	Republic	President: Mobutu Sese Seko First State Commissioner (Prime Minister): Kengo wa Dondo	Zaire 0.02	4,220 140
ZAMBIA Lusaka	7,100,000 538,800	290,586 752,614	Republic (C)	President: Kenneth D. Kaunda Prime Minister: Kebby Musokotwane	Kwacha 0.12	3,020 470
ZIMBABWE (RHODESIA) Harare	9,000,000 656,000	150,804 390,580	Republic (C)	President: Rev. Canaan S. Banana Prime Minister: Robert G. Mugabe	Dollar 0.60	6,040 740

1. Figures are for gross domestic product.
2. Figure excludes trade with members of the Soviet bloc.
3. Figure includes trade for Luxembourg.
4. "CFA" stands for Communauté Financière Africaine.
5. Figure includes the whole metropolitan area.
6. Information pertains to the Greek sector only. The president of the Turkish sector (Turkish Republic of Northern Cyprus) is Rauf Denktash; the prime minister is Dervis Eroğlu.

Imports Exports	Revenue Expenditure	Elementary Schools: Teachers Students	Secondary Schools: Teachers Students	Colleges and Universities: Teachers Students
$ 288,000,000 ....$ 57,000,000	188,000,000 190,000,000	4,103 276,732	2,037 47,493	333 3,406
776,000,000 925,000,000	989,200,000 1,178,200,000	17,036 350,178	NA 197,890	4,349 50,151
67,000,000 44,000,000	NA .... NA	934 22,244	188 2,480	NA NA
6,676,000,000 4,337,000,000	13,200,000,000 11,500,000,000	100,681 2,660,440	63,303 939,678	24,186 298,483
838,000,000 430,000,000	5,104,400,000 6,697,300,000	204,104 7,887,439	NA .... NA	17,242 114,701
50,000,000 19,000,000	36,200,000 51,700,000	1,502 40,090	NA 21,643	11 134
1,543,000,000 645,000,000	582,500,000 909,100,000	11,281 294,028	1,946 34,807	403 3,645
1,521,000,000 39,000,000	843,000,000 1,200,000,000	13,305 675,402	3,826 60,683	157 4,510
11,538,000,000 9,811,000,000	7,049,400,000 7,118,000,000	61,441 1,460,214	134,360 2,381,378	21,218 294,492
682,000,000 1,004,000,000	677,300,000 622,500,000	NA 3,919,395	NA .... NA	NA 31,643
608,000,000 655,000,000	551,000,000 835,000,000	22,258 1,073,203	4,602 104,859	NA 4,236
959,000,000 1,003,000,000	1,290,000,000 1,820,000,000	54,086 2,130,487	10,440 316,435	342 4,131

7. Entries include data for Greenland and the Faeroe Islands.
8. Figures include data for Northern Ireland.
9. Figures are for peninsular Malaysia only.
10. These are combined figures for elementary and secondary education.
11. Data generally exclude the homelands that have been granted independence. Estimated population of the following homelands, including homeland citizens residing in South Africa, in 1986 was: Bophuthatswana, 1,400,000; Ciskei, 721,000; Transkei, 2,500,000; Venda, 340,000. Presidents of the homelands were: Bophuthatswana, Lucas Mangope; Ciskei, Lennox Sebe; Transkei, Tutor Ndamase; Venda, Patrick Mphephu.

THE STATES AND OUTLYING AREAS OF THE UNITED STATES

State Capital	Population	Area (sq mi/ sq km)	Per Capita Personal Income	Governor Lieutenant-Governor	Revenue Expenditure	Public Roads (Miles)
ALABAMA Montgomery	4,021,000 196,300	51,705 133,915	$10,673	George Wallace (D) William Baxley (D)	$ 6,195,000,000 5,191,000,000	87,798
ALASKA Juneau	521,000 27,000	591,004 1,530,693	18,187	William J. Sheffield (D) Stephen McAlpine (D)	5,463,000,000 3,969,000,000	11,601
ARIZONA Phoenix	3,187,000 881,600	114,000 295,259	12,795	Bruce E. Babbitt (D) *	4,552,000,000 4,046,000,000	76,906
ARKANSAS Little Rock	2,359,000 178,100	53,187 137,754	10,476	Bill Clinton (D) Winston Bryant (D)	2,967,000,000 2,636,000,000	77,029
CALIFORNIA Sacramento	26,365,000 322,500	158,706 411,047	16,065	George Deukmejian (R) Leo T. McCarthy (D)	50,634,000,000 44,716,000,000	174,081
COLORADO Denver	3,231,000 500,000	104,091 269,594	14,812	Richard D. Lamm (D) Nancy Dick (D)	4,878,000,000 4,560,000,000	75,972
CONNECTICUT Hartford	3,174,000 135,700	5,018 12,997	18,089	William A. O'Neill (D) Joseph L. Fauliso (D)	5,514,000,000 4,869,000,000	19,633
DELAWARE Dover	622,000 22,500	2,044 5,295	14,272	Michael N. Castle (R) S. B. Woo (D)	1,494,000,000 1,211,000,000	5,313
DISTRICT OF COLUMBIA *	626,000	67 174	18,168	Mayor: Marion S. Barry, Jr. (D)	3,407,000,000 3,387,000,000	1,102
FLORIDA Tallahassee	11,366,000 116,200	58,664 151,939	13,742	D. Robert Graham (D) Wayne Mixson (D)	11,896,000,000 10,320,000,000	99,071
GEORGIA Atlanta	5,976,000 426,100	58,910 152,576	12,543	Joe Frank Harris (D) Zell B. Miller (D)	7,458,000,000 6,699,000,000	106,257
HAWAII Honolulu	1,054,000 380,000	6,471 16,760	13,814	George R. Ariyoshi (D) John Waihee (D)	2,541,000,000 2,244,000,000	3,939
IDAHO Boise	1,005,000 110,000	83,564 216,430	11,120	John V. Evans (D) David Leroy (R)	1,478,000,000 1,347,000,000	69,169
ILLINOIS Springfield	11,535,000 101,600	56,345 145,933	14,738	James R. Thompson, Jr. (R) George H. Ryan (R)	16,470,000,000 15,050,000,000	134,709
INDIANA Indianapolis	5,499,000 710,300	36,185 93,719	12,446	Robert D. Orr (R) John M. Mutz (R)	7,163,000,000 6,416,000,000	91,396
IOWA Des Moines	2,884,000 190,800	56,275 145,752	12,594	Terry E. Branstad (R) Robert Anderson (D)	4,351,000,000 4,277,000,000	112,478
KANSAS Topeka	2,450,000 118,900	82,277 213,096	13,775	John W. Carlin (D) Tom Docking (D)	3,363,000,000 2,974,000,000	132,409
KENTUCKY Frankfort	3,726,000 26,800	40,409 104,659	10,824	Martha Layne Collins (D) Steven Beshear (D)	5,448,000,000 5,358,000,000	69,460

The material in the following tables is the latest available. As before, it should be noted that the symbol * indicates that the category is not applicable to the area mentioned, and that NA means that the data were not available. The Office of Territorial Affairs was helpful in supplying some data for the table on Outlying Areas.

Railways (Miles)	Aircraft Departures	English-language Daily Newspapers	Public Elementary Schools (K–8): Teachers Students	Public Secondary Schools (9–12): Teachers Students	Colleges and Universities: Institutions Students
3,832	40,312	27	18,534 510,814	14,865 211,087	60 171,381
526	72,344	7	3,400 65,998	2,059 26,920	15 26,045
1,757	119,466	19	18,877 350,961	7,391 152,267	29 213,437
2,712	13,131	32	11,385 304,975	11,856 127,145	35 76,702
6,438	503,103	116	102,865 2,813,524	71,425 1,275,493	273 1,730,847
3,388	183,997	28	16,051 376,775	12,370 165,421	47 172,650
464	28,107	23	11,490 328,574	15,987 149,011	47 164,344
213	415	3	2,461 61,181	2,968 30,225	8 31,945
48	118,751	2	2,953 63,297	2,206 25,546	18 80,367
3,230	329,513	47	40,574 1,044,107	34,966 451,436	85 443,436
5,119	286,401	32	29,564 738,258	19,578 312,601	80 201,453
0	104,291	5	3,809 110,419	2,981 51,822	12 52,065
2,180	20,785	11	4,618 148,363	4,352 57,989	9 42,911
8,380	314,999	83	56,697 1,271,525	29,846 581,791	160 673,084
5,069	61,847	71	22,324 670,440	23,643 313,944	74 256,470
3,646	24,670	36	14,977 333,198	16,156 164,089	60 152,968
7,509	42,123	46	12,911 282,389	10,602 122,833	53 141,709
3,175	31,297	23	21,061 454,931	11,397 192,483	57 146,503

457

State Capital	Population	Area (sq mi/ sq km)	Per Capita Personal Income	Governor Lieutenant-Governor	Revenue Expenditure	Public Roads (Miles)
LOUISIANA	4,481,000	47,752	$11,274	Edwin W. Edwards (D)	$ 7,201,000,000	58,241
Baton Rouge	246,500	123,677		Robert L. Freeman (D)	7,664,000,000	
MAINE	1,164,000	33,265	11,887	Joseph E. Brennan (D)	1,873,000,000	21,955
Augusta	21,100	86,156		*	1,775,000,000	
MARYLAND	4,392,000	10,460	15,864	Harry R. Hughes (D)	7,296,000,000	27,564
Annapolis	31,700	27,091		J. Joseph Curran (D)	6,880,000,000	
MASSACHUSETTS	5,822,000	8,284	16,380	Michael Dukakis (D)	10,253,000,000	33,804
Boston	570,700	21,455		*	9,736,000,000	
MICHIGAN	9,088,000	58,527	13,608	James J. Blanchard (D)	17,071,000,000	117,581
Lansing	128,000	151,584		Martha W. Griffiths (D)	15,368,000,000	
MINNESOTA	4,193,000	84,402	14,087	Rudy Perpich (DFL)	8,826,000,000	131,998
St. Paul	267,800	218,600		Marlene Johnson (DFL)	7,536,000,000	
MISSISSIPPI	2,613,000	47,689	9,187	Bill Allain (D)	3,641,000,000	71,694
Jackson	208,800	123,514		Brad Dye (D)	3,351,000,000	
MISSOURI	5,029,000	69,697	13,244	John Ashcroft (R)	5,964,000,000	119,155
Jefferson City	33,600	180,514		Harriet Woods (D)	5,263,000,000	
MONTANA	826,000	147,046	10,974	Ted Schwinden (D)	1,538,000,000	71,543
Helena	24,300	380,847		George Turman (D)	1,385,000,000	
NEBRASKA	1,606,000	77,355	13,281	Robert Kerrey (D)	2,047,000,000	92,119
Lincoln	180,400	200,349		Don McGinley (D)	1,884,000,000	
NEVADA	936,000	110,561	14,488	Richard Bryan (D)	1,767,000,000	43,830
Carson City	35,400	286,352		Robert Cashell (R)	1,485,000,000	
NEW HAMPSHIRE	998,000	9,279	14,964	John Sununu (R)	1,276,000,000	14,527
Concord	31,900	24,032		*	1,128,000,000	
NEW JERSEY	7,562,000	7,787	17,211	Thomas H. Kean (R)	14,677,000,000	33,883
Trenton	92,200	20,168		*	12,635,000,000	
NEW MEXICO	1,450,000	121,593	10,914	Toney Anaya (D)	3,338,000,000	53,564
Santa Fe	52,300	314,924		Mike Runnels (D)	2,833,000,000	
NEW YORK	17,783,000	49,108	16,050	Mario M. Cuomo (D)	42,412,000,000	110,027
Albany	100,000	127,189		*	35,917,000,000	
NORTH CAROLINA	6,255,000	52,669	11,617	James G. Martin (R)	8,735,000,000	93,214
Raleigh	201,000	136,412		Robert P. Jordan 3rd (D)	7,588,000,000	
NORTH DAKOTA	685,000	70,702	12,052	George Sinner (D)	1,553,000,000	85,980
Bismarck	44,500	183,117		Ruth Meiers (D)	1,440,000,000	
OHIO	10,744,000	41,330	13,226	Richard F. Celeste (D)	18,682,000,000	112,984
Columbus	566,100	107,044		*	16,348,000,000	
OKLAHOMA	3,301,000	69,956	12,232	George Nigh (D)	5,064,000,000	110,674
Oklahoma City	443,200	181,185		Spencer Bernard (D)	4,708,000,000	
OREGON	2,687,000	97,073	12,622	Victor G. Atiyeh (R)	4,981,000,000	94,000
Salem	94,600	251,418		*	4,443,000,000	
PENNSYLVANIA	11,853,000	45,308	13,437	Richard L. Thornburgh (R)	18,985,000,000	115,663
Harrisburg	53,300	117,347		William W. Scranton 3rd (R)	16,601,000,000	
RHODE ISLAND	968,000	1,212	13,906	Edward D. Di Prete (R)	1,987,000,000	5,997
Providence	154,100	3,139		Richard Licht (D)	1,832,000,000	
SOUTH CAROLINA	3,347,000	31,113	10,586	Richard W. Riley (D)	5,017,000,000	63,213
Columbia	98,600	80,582		Michael S. Daniel (D)	4,396,000,000	
SOUTH DAKOTA	708,000	77,116	11,161	William J. Janklow (R)	999,000,000	73,293
Pierre	12,000	199,730		Lowell C. Hansen 2nd (R)	953,000,000	

Railways (Miles)	Aircraft Departures	English-language Daily Newspapers	Public Elementary Schools (K–8): Teachers Students	Public Secondary Schools (9–12): Teachers Students	Colleges and Universities: Institutions Students
3,050	69,402	24	27,168 561,181	15,011 221,253	32 179,647
1,516	8,417	8	7,554 145,814	5,880 63,939	29 53,347
908	55,228	16	15,071 451,716	19,156 231,775	57 239,232
1,077	96,505	46	17,856 578,306	32,703 300,538	117 423,348
3,579	141,658	48	42,515 1,132,701	18,778 603,180	92 515,760
5,592	108,271	25	18,635 466,579	20,757 238,663	67 214,219
1,744	17,931	22	13,528 327,509	11,427 140,235	42 109,728
5,741	222,621	45	23,371 546,155	22,847 249,298	92 248,329
3,326	26,400	10	6,419 108,268	3,060 45,378	16 37,877
4,597	32,980	19	9,321 185,941	8,227 81,057	28 95,162
1,451	83,975	8	3,375 102,358	3,134 48,084	8 43,768
409	408	8	4,796 106,303	5,025 52,727	27 53,143
1,268	127,203	28	37,038 761,194	29,099 386,377	60 314,468
2,062	45,975	18	6,152 191,824	6,349 77,877	20 66,094
3,565	335,423	73	64,836 1,735,517	60,573 939,301	296 1,022,521
3,334	140,592	54	34,981 761,053	19,352 328,553	128 301,675
4,579	13,545	10	4,474 82,321	2,593 34,892	18 37,591
6,238	159,691	89	51,517 1,240,344	45,410 586,956	139 535,592
3,289	57,715	47	15,980 420,913	15,528 170,476	45 174,171
2,889	50,608	20	13,112 307,121	10,510 139,988	45 141,172
5,232	182,246	94	43,897 1,130,767	48,313 607,185	202 545,112
135	9,197	7	3,867 87,789	3,953 48,391	13 70,811
2,579	29,091	17	20,461 423,016	11,862 181,537	62 134,532
1,953	14,659	13	5,667 86,324	2,668 36,736	20 35,015

State Capital	Population	Area (sq mi/ sq km)	Per Capita Personal Income	Governor Lieutenant-Governor	Revenue Expenditure	Public Roads (Miles)
TENNESSEE	4,762,000	42,144	$11,243	Lamar Alexander (R)	$ 5,335,000,000	83,831
Nashville	462,500	109,152		John S. Wilder (D)	4,830,000,000	
TEXAS	16,370,000	266,807	13,483	Mark White (D)	18,912,000,000	282,254
Austin	468,000	691,027		William P. Hobby (D)	16,880,000,000	
UTAH	1,645,000	84,899	10,493	Norman H. Bangerter (R)	2,877,000,000	48,563
Salt Lake City	164,900	219,887		W. Val Oveson (R)	2,446,000,000	
VERMONT	535,000	9,614	12,117	Madeleine Kunin (D)	992,000,000	14,031
Montpelier	8,300	24,900		Peter Smith (R)	941,000,000	
VIRGINIA	5,706,000	40,767	14,542	Gerald Baliles (D)	8,171,000,000	65,492
Richmond	219,100	105,586		L. Douglas Wilder (D)	7,096,000,000	
WASHINGTON	4,409,000	68,139	13,876	Booth Gardner (D)	8,833,000,000	81,074
Olympia	29,000	176,479		John A. Cherberg (D)	8,139,000,000	
WEST VIRGINIA	1,936,000	24,231	10,193	Arch A. Moore, Jr. (R)	3,547,000,000	35,117
Charleston	64,000	62,758		*	3,136,000,000	
WISCONSIN	4,775,000	56,153	13,154	Anthony S. Earl (D)	9,572,000,000	108,507
Madison	175,700	145,436		James T. Flynn (D)	7,530,000,000	
WYOMING	509,000	97,809	13,223	Ed Herschler (D)	1,802,000,000	38,239
Cheyenne	47,300	253,324		*	1,415,000,000	

OUTLYING AREAS OF THE UNITED STATES

Area Capital	Population	Area (sq mi/ sq km)	Status	Governor Lieutenant-Governor	Revenue Expenditure	Roads (Miles)
AMERICAN SAMOA	40,000	76	Unorganized,	A. P. Lutali	$ NA	95
Pago Pago		197	unincorporated territory	Eni Hunkin	91,600,000	
GUAM	120,000	209	Unincorporated	Ricardo J. Bordallo	161,000,000	419
Agaña		541	territory	Edward D. Reyes	178,100,000	
PUERTO RICO	3,300,000	3,515	Commonwealth	Rafael Hernández Colón	4,134,000,000	8,520
San Juan	435,000	9,104		*	3,832,000,000	
TRUST TERRITORY OF THE PACIFIC ISLANDS[1] Capitol Hill, on Saipan Island	156,000	708 1,834	UN trust territory[1]	High Commissioner: Janet J. McCoy[1]	125,137,000 118,869,000	362
VIRGIN ISLANDS	108,000	133	Unincorporated	Juan Luis	259,800,000	641
Charlotte Amalie		344	territory	Julio Brady	252,000,000	

1. The Trust Territory of the Pacific Islands, not yet formally dissolved, comprises four entities. The Northern Mariana Islands became a U.S. commonwealth in 1986; the Federated States of Micronesia and the Republic of the Marshall Islands entered into compacts of free association with the United States in 1986. The Republic of Palau did not enter into a compact or choose otherwise to end the trusteeship.

Railways (Miles)	Aircraft Departures	English-language Daily Newspapers	Public Elementary Schools (K–8): Teachers Students	Public Secondary Schools (9–12): Teachers Students	Colleges and Universities: Institutions Students
2,597	105,915	27	24,713 587,014	14,696 235,043	80 207,777
12,853	518,904	106	75,431 2,155,012	75,996 834,784	157 795,741
1,493	65,034	5	8,313 281,649	5,558 97,416	14 103,324
102	6,028	8	2,794 63,452	3,378 26,964	22 31,306
3,766	51,255	36	31,745 674,016	24,200 292,094	69 288,588
3,927	85,546	25	17,098 503,551	15,353 232,688	50 229,639
3,209	8,401	22	10,965 263,254	8,445 107,997	29 83,202
3,752	60,015	35	21,140 500,778	18,470 273,868	63 277,751
1,993	6,388	9	4,100 73,861	2,085 27,104	8 23,844

Railways (Miles)	Aircraft Departures	Daily Newspapers	Public Elementary and Secondary School Teachers	Public School Students: Elementary Secondary	Higher Education: Institutions Students
0	2,733	0	616	7,535 2,589	1 845
0	5,568	1	1,334	19,331 6,918	2 3,436
60	12,588	4	32,247	582,564 182,782	39 161,215
0	9,301	0	2,539	37,320 6,802	2 909
0	3,799	2	1,683	19,298 6,828	1 2,864

THE PROVINCES AND TERRITORIES OF CANADA

Province Capital	Population	Area (sq mi/ sq km)	Per Capita Personal Income	Premier Lieutenant-Governor
ALBERTA	2,348,800	255,285	$14,652	Donald Getty
Edmonton	560,100	661,185		Helen Hunley
BRITISH COLUMBIA	2,892,500	366,255	14,339	William N. Vander Zalm
Victoria	66,800	948,596		Robert Gordon Rogers
MANITOBA	1,069,600	251,000	12,063	Howard R. Pawley
Winnipeg	535,200	650,087		George Johnson
NEW BRUNSWICK	719,200	28,354	10,040	Richard B. Hatfield
Fredericton	66,800	73,436		George F. G. Stanley
NEWFOUNDLAND	580,400	156,185	9,179	Brian Peckford
St. John's	97,000	404,517		James A. McGrath
NORTHWEST TERRITORIES	50,900	1,304,903	14,282[1]	Commissioner:
Yellowknife	12,500	3,379,684		John H. Parker
NOVA SCOTIA	880,700	21,425	10,889	John M. Buchanan
Halifax	114,600	55,491		Alan R. Abraham
ONTARIO	9,066,200	412,582	14,784	David Peterson
Toronto	600,000	1,068,582		Lincoln Alexander
PRINCE EDWARD ISLAND	127,100	2,184	10,056	Joseph Ghiz
Charlottetown	15,800	5,657		Robert Lloyd George MacPhail
QUÉBEC	6,580,700	594,860	12,531	Robert Bourassa
Québec	176,600	1,540,680		Gilles Lamontagne
SASKATCHEWAN	1,019,500	251,700	12,686	Grant Devine
Regina	174,800	651,900		Frederick Johnson
YUKON TERRITORY	22,800	186,300	14,282[1]	Commissioner:
Whitehorse	17,000	482,515		Kenneth McKinnon

1. Figure is the combined average for the Northwest Territories and Yukon Territory.

462

The material in this table has been prepared with the assistance of Statistics Canada. It should be noted that all dollar figures are in Canadian dollars.

Revenue Expenditure	Motor Vehicle Registrations	Railways (Miles)	Radio and Television Stations	Daily Newspapers	Elementary and Secondary Schools: Teachers Enrollment	Postsecondary Education: Institutions Enrollment
$ 9,765,000,000 10,000,000,000	1,729,287	2,318	90 14	12	25,015 472,170	26 68,680
8,768,000,000 9,643,000,000	2,175,032	3,875	134 12	23	26,066 523,990	26 58,440
3,380,000,000 3,869,000,000	739,488	1,755	31 6	9	12,190 218,740	14 23,720
2,813,000,000 3,120,000,000	416,805	684	34 6	6	7,320 141,300	12 17,850
2,274,000,000 2,591,000,000	257,693	149	48 7	2	8,050 139,900	11 14,570
669,400,000 695,000,000	23,271	0	8 2	0	680 13,630	1 100
2,662,000,000 2,895,000,000	529,267	430	40 6	7	10,360 174,260	25 27,030
29,948,000,000 31,596,000,000	5,179,918	9,349	201 36	54	85,990 1,851,400	52 275,100
486,300,000 509,600,000	76,126	0	6 1	3	1,260 24,935	3 2,790
25,600,000,000 28,700,000,000	2,974,099	2,918	148 54	13	70,630 1,157,000	91 278,700
3,360,000,000 3,750,000,000	697,160	2,497	33 14	5	11,195 215,240	6 22,360
254,000,000 273,000,000	20,479	0	3 1	0	260 4,470	1 350

KEY TO SIGNED ARTICLES

Here is a list of contributors to this Yearbook. The initials at the end of an article are those of the author, or authors, of that article.

A.D., ALASDAIR DRYSDALE, PH.D.
Associate Professor, University of New Hampshire.

A.L.N., A. LIN NEUMANN, B.A.
Free-lance Journalist. Coeditor, *Bayanko: Images of the Philippine Revolt.*

A.L.R., ARTHUR L. ROBINSON, PH.D.
Senior Writer, Research News Section, *Science* Magazine.

A.M.M., ANN M. MARTIN, A.B.
Free-lance Writer and Editor. Author, *Bummer Summer, The Babysitters Club, With You and Without You.*

A.R., ANSIL RAMSAY, A.B., PH.D.
Professor of Government, St. Lawrence University. Editorial Board Member, *Asian Survey.*

A.S., AARON SEGAL, B.A., M.PHIL., PH.D.
Visiting Professor, Air War College, U.S. Air Force. Professor of Political Science, University of Texas at El Paso.

A.T., ALAN TONELSON, B.A.
Associate Editor, *Foreign Policy.*

B.B., BRUCE BOWER, B.A., M.A.
Staff Writer, *Science News.*

B.B.R., BONNIE B. REECE, B.S., M.B.A., PH.D.
Assistant Professor of Advertising, Michigan State University. Member, Editorial Review Board, *Journal of Public Policy and Marketing.*

B.B.S., BONNIE BARRETT STRETCH, A.B., M.S.
Contributing Editor, *Art & Auction.* Columnist, *American Photographer.*

B.D.J., BRIAN D. JOHNSON, B.A.
Senior Writer, *Maclean's.* Author, *Railway Country: Across Canada by Train.*

B.J., BRUCE JUDDERY, A.B.
Canberra Correspondent, *Australian Business.*

B.K., BOB KLAPISCH, B.A.
Baseball Reporter, New York *Post.*

B.R., BEA RIEMSCHNEIDER, A.B., M.A.
Editor in Chief, *Archaeology.*

B.S., BROOKE GRUNDFEST SCHOEPF, PH.D.
Anthropologist. Former Fulbright Senior Research Scholar, Zimbabwe.

B.V., BOB VERDI, A.B.
Columnist, Chicago *Tribune.*

C.B., CHRISTIE BARTER, A.B.
Music Editor, *Stereo Review.*

C.C., CRAIG COVAULT, B.A.
Senior Space Editor, *Aviation Week & Space Technology.*

C.H.A., CALVIN H. ALLEN, JR., A.B., M.A., PH.D.
Associate Professor of History, School of the Ozarks, Mo.

C.J.S., CURTIS J. SITOMER, B.A.
Columnist, *Christian Science Monitor.*

C.S.J.W., CHARLES S. J. WHITE, B.A., M.A., PH.D.
Professor and Chairman, Department of Philosophy and Religion, The American University. Former Director, Center for Asian Studies.

D.D.B., DARALICE D. BOLES, A.B., M.ARCH.
Senior Editor, *Progressive Architecture.*

D.E.S., DONALD E. SCHULZ, B.A., PH.D.
Assistant Professor of Political Science, University of Tampa.

D.F., DON FREEMAN
Television Editor and Columnist, San Diego *Union* and Copley News Service.

D.F.A., DONALD F. ANTHROP, PH.D.
Professor of Environmental Studies, San Jose State University. Author, *Noise Pollution.*

D.G.S., DAVID G. SAVAGE, A.B., M.S.
Education Writer, Los Angeles *Times.*

D.L.L., DAVID L. LEWIS, B.S., M.S., M.A., PH.D.
Professor of Business History, Graduate

School of Business Administration, University of Michigan.

D.M., DALE MITCH, B.A.
Editor, *Skating* Magazine. Director of Publications and Public Relations, United States Figure Skating Association.

D.M.P., DAVID M. PHILIPS, A.B.
Sports Writer, Providence *Journal.*

D.P., DON PERETZ, A.B., M.A., PH.D.
Professor of Political Science, State University of New York at Binghamton. Author, *Middle East Today,* and *The West Bank.*

D.P.W., DAVID P. WERLICH, B.A., M.A., PH.D.
Professor of History, Southern Illinois University. Author, *Peru: A Short History.*

D.R.W., DONALD R. WHITAKER, A.B.
Economist, Office of Industry Services, National Marine Fisheries Service. Contributor, *Fishing Gazette.*

D.S., DAVID STAINES, A.B., A.M., PH.D.
Professor of English, University of Ottawa. Author, *Tennyson's Camelot: The Idylls of the King and Its Medieval Sources.*

D.S.M., DONALD S. MACDONALD, PH.D.
Research Professor of Korean Studies, School of Foreign Service, Georgetown University. Former State Department Foreign Service Officer.

E.C.R., EDWARD C. ROCHETTE
Former Executive Director, American Numismatic Association. Numismatic Writer, Los Angeles *Times* Syndicate.

E.J.F., ERIK J. FRIIS, B.S., M.A.
Editor and Publisher, *The Scandinavian-American Bulletin.* General Editor, *The Library of Nordic Literature.*

E.J.G., ELLEN J. GREENFIELD, A.B., M.A.
Free-lance Writer. Former Textiles Editor, *Women's Wear Daily.* Author, *House Dangerous.*

E.S.K., ELAINE S. KNAPP, B.A.
Editor, Council of State Governments.

E.W., ED WARD
Free-lance Writer, Rolling Stone Press. Coauthor, *Rock of Ages: The Rolling Stone History of Rock & Roll.*

F.B., FOX BUTTERFIELD, B.A., M.A.
Boston Bureau Chief and Former Peking Chief, New York *Times.* Author, *China: Alive in the Bitter Sea.*

F.D.S., FREDERICK D. SCHNEIDER, PH.D.
Professor Emeritus of History, Vanderbilt University.

F.E.H., FREDERICK E. HOXIE, B.A., PH.D.
Director, D'Arcy McNickle Center for the History of the American Indian. Author, *A Final Promise: The Campaign to Assimilate the Indians.*

F.L., FRANK LITSKY, B.S.
Sports Writer, New York *Times.* Author, *The New York Times Official Sports Record Book.*

G.B.H., GARY B. HANSEN, B.S., M.S., PH.D.
Professor of Economics, Utah State University. Director, Utah Center for Productivity and Quality of Working Life.

G.D.W., G. DAVID WALLACE, B.A.
Corporate Strategies Editor, *Business Week.* Author, *Money Basics.*

G.M.H., GEOFFREY M. HORN, A.B., M.A.
Free-lance Writer. Coauthor, *Bible Stories for Children.* Former Executive Editor, *Worldmark Encyclopedia of the Nations.*

H.C.H., HAROLD C. HINTON, PH.D.
Professor of Political Science and International Affairs, George Washington University. Editor, *The People's Republic of China, 1949-1979: A Documentary Survey.*

H.W.H., HARRY W. HENDERSON, A.B.
Free-lance Writer. Former Writer-Economist, U.S. Department of Agriculture.

I.C.B., IRIRANGI COATES BLOOMFIELD, A.B., M.A., PH.D.
Lecturer and Writer. Former Member, New Zealand United Nations Delegation.

I.K., INDULIS KEPARS, B.A.
Chief Reference Librarian, Australian Studies, National Library of Australia.

J.A.P., JOHN A. PETROPULOS, PH.D.
Professor of History, Amherst College. Author, *Politics and Statecraft in the Kingdom of Greece.*

J.A.R., JAMES A. ROTHERHAM, A.B., M.A., M.A.L.D., PH.D.
Staff Director, Nutrition Subcommittee, U.S. House of Representatives.

J.B., JOHN BEAUFORT
Contributing Drama Critic, *Christian Science Monitor.*

J.D., JOHN DAMIS, PH.D.
Visiting Professor of Government, Harvard University. Author, *Conflict in Northwest Africa: The Western Sahara Dispute.*

J.F., JULIE FREDERIKSE, A.B.
Southern Africa Correspondent, National Public Radio. Author, *South Africa: A Different Kind of War.*

J.F., Jr. JOHN FORAN, JR., A.B., M.A.
Graduate Fellow and Doctoral Candidate in Sociology, University of California, Berkeley.

J.F.J., JAMES F. JEKEL, M.D., M.P.H.
Professor of Epidemiology and Public Health, Yale University Medical School.

J.F.S., JOANNE F. SCHNEIDER, A.B., M.A., PH.D.
Assistant Professor of History, Wheaton College.

J.G.D., JOHN G. DEEDY, A.B., M.A.
Former Managing Editor, *Commonweal.* Contributor, New York *Times.* Author, *Catholic Fact Book.*

J.H., JOHN HAY, A.B.
Editorial Board Member, Ottawa *Citizen.*

J.H.B., JAMES H. BUDD
Free-lance Writer Based in Mexico. Correspondent, Murdoch Magazines and Gemini News Service.

J.J., JOHN JENNINGS, B.A.
International Editor, National Underwriter Company. Former Business Reporter, UPI.

J.J.Z., JOSEPH J. ZASLOFF, A.B., M.A., PH.D.
Professor of Political Science, University of Pittsburgh. Specialist in Southeast Asian Affairs.

J.L., JOHN LUTER, A.B.
Professor and Chairman, Journalism Department, University of Hawaii. Former Coordinator, Advanced International Reporting Program, Columbia University Graduate School of Journalism.

J.L.L., JANE L. LEVERE, B.A.
Associate Editor, *Travel Weekly.*

J.M., JOHN MUTTER, B.A.
Senior Associate Editor, *Publishers Weekly.*

J.M.L., JOEL M. LEE, A.B., A.M.
Headquarters Librarian and ALANET System Manager, American Library Association. Associate Editor, *ALA World Encyclopedia of Library and Information Services.*

J.O.S., JAMES O. SAFFORD III, A.B., M.A., PH.D.
Former Instructor of History, The Shipley School, Bryn Mawr, Pa.

J.Q., JOHN QUINN, B.F.A.
Editor, *Tropical Fish Hobbyist* Magazine.

J.S.I., JACQUELINE S. ISMAEL, B.A., M.A., PH.D.
Professor of Social Welfare, University of Calgary; Author, *Kuwait: Social Change in Historical Perspective.*

J.T.S., JAMES T. SHERWIN, A.B., LL.B.
Former New York State, Intercollegiate, and U.S. Speed Chess Champion and International Master.

J.W.K., JOHN W. KAMPA, B.S.
Former Editorial Board Member, *Minkus World-Wide Stamp Catalog* and *New American Stamp Catalog.*

K.F., KARYN FEIDEN, B.A.
Yearbook Staff Editor

K.F.R., KARL F. REULING
American Editor, *Ballet International.*

K.J.B., KIRK J. BEATTIE, A.B., M.A.
Assistant Professor of Government, Simmons College.

K.M., KENT MULLINER, B.S., M.A.
Assistant to the Director, Ohio University Libraries.

K.P., KATHRYN PAULSEN, A.B.
Free-lance Writer and Editor.

K.W.G., KENNETH W. GRUNDY, A.B., M.A., PH.D.
Professor of Political Science, Case Western Reserve University.

L.A.K., LAWRENCE A. KLETTER, A.B., M.A., J.D.

Certificate in Middle Eastern Studies, Columbia University. Associate, Fine & Ambrogne, Boston.

L.D., LARRY DIAMOND, B.A., M.A., PH.D.
Senior Research Fellow, Hoover Institution, Stanford University.

L.G., LOIS GOTTESMAN, A.B., M.A.
Free-lance Writer. Former Research Analyst, American Jewish Committee.

L.G.H., LINDA GIBSON HIEBERT, B.S.
Codirector, Indochina Project.

L.K., LESLIE KANDELL, A.B., M.S.
Free-lance Music Journalist.

L.L.P., LARRY L. PIPPIN, A.B., M.A., PH.D.
Professor of Political Science, University of the Pacific.

L.R.H., LINDLEY R. HIGGINS, P.E., B.S., M.S.
Consulting Engineer. President, Piedmont Publications. Author, *Handbook of Construction Equipment Maintenance, Maintenance Engineering Handbook,* and *Cost Reduction From A to Z.*

L.S.G., LOVETT S. GRAY, A.B.
Free-lance Writer and Consultant. Former Editor, National Council on Crime and Deliquency.

L.W.G., LOWELL W. GUDMUNDSON, A.B., M.A., PH.D.
Assistant Professor of History, University of Oklahoma.

L.Z., LAWRENCE ZIRING, B.S., M.I.A., PH.D.
Director, Institute of Government and Politics, Professor of Political Science, Western Michigan University. Author, *Pakistan: The Enigma of Political Development* and *The Asian Political Dictionary.*

M.C.C., MARY C. CARRAS, B.A., PH.D.
Associate Professor and Chair, Political Science Department, Rutgers University. Author, *Indira Gandhi in the Crucible of Leadership.*

M.C.H., MICHAEL C. HUDSON, A.B., M.A., PH.D.
Professor of International Relations and Government; Director, Center for Contemporary Arab Studies, Georgetown University. President, Middle East Studies Association. Author, *Arab Politics: The Search for Legitimacy.*

M.D., MICHAEL DIRDA, A.B., M.A., PH.D.
Staff Editor, *The Washington Post Book World.*

M.D.H., M. DONALD HANCOCK, PH.D.
Professor of Political Science, Vanderbilt University.

M.G., MURIEL GRINDROD, A.B.
Author, *Italy, Rebuilding of Italy.*

M.Gr., MILTON GREENBERG, A.B., M.A., PH.D.
Provost, The American University. Coauthor, *The American Political Dictionary, Political Science Dictionary.*

M.G.G., M. GRANT GROSS, A.B., M.S., PH.D.
Director, Division of Ocean Sciences, National Science Foundation. Author, *Oceanography: A View of the Earth.*

M.R.B., MARK R. BEISSINGER, B.A., PH.D.
Assistant Professor of Government, Harvard University. Fellow, Harvard Russian Research Center.

M.S.B., MICHAEL S. BAKER, A.B., M.A.
Certificate in East Asian Studies, Columbia University.

M.W., MARGARET WILLY, F.R.S.L.
Former Lecturer, City Literary Institute, London. Lecturer, Morley College, London. Poetry Collected in *The Invisible Sun, Every Star a Tongue.*

N.J.P., NEALE J. PEARSON, B.S., M.S., PH.D.
Professor of Political Science, Texas Tech University. Former Vice Consul, American Embassy in Tegucigalpa.

N.M.R., NATHAN M. REISS, PH.D.
Associate Professor of Meteorology, Cook College, Rutgers University.

N.P.N., NANCY PEABODY NEWELL, A.B.
Coauthor, *The Struggle for Afghanistan.*

P.F., PAMELA FESSLER, B.A., M.P.A.
Economics Reporter, *Congressional Quarterly.* Former Budget Specialist, U.S. Office of Management and Budget.

P.G., PAUL GARDNER
Free-lance Writer. Author, *The Simplest Game, Nice Guys Finish Last.* Commentator, NBC Soccer Telecasts.

P.H.C., PARRIS H. CHANG, PH.D.
Professor of Political Science, Chairman of Asian Area Studies, Pennsylvania State University. Author, *Elite Conflict in the Post-Mao China.*

P.J.M., PAUL J. MAGNARELLA, A.M., PH.D.
Professor of Anthropology, University of Florida. Author, *Tradition and Change in a Turkish Town, The Peasant Venture.* Editor, *Anthropological Diplomacy: Case Studies in the Applications of Anthropology to International Relations.*

P.S., PATRICIA STAMP, B.A., M.SC., PH.D.
Associate Professor and Coordinator, African Studies Program, York University. Free-lance Writer.

P.W., PETER WINN, A.B., PH.D.
Associate Professor of History, Tufts University. Senior Research Fellow, Research Institute on International Change, Columbia University.

R.A., RICHARD AMDUR, B.A.
Yearbook Staff Editor.

R.A.M., ROBERT A. MORTIMER, A.B., M.A., PH.D.
Professor of Political Science, Haverford College. Author, *The Third World Coalition in International Politics.*

R.A.P., RICHARD A. PIERCE, PH.D.
Professor Emeritus of History, Queen's University, Ontario. Author, *Eastward to Empire: Exploration and Conquest on the Russian Open Frontier to 1750.*

R.A.S., ROBERT A. SCHORN, B.S., M.S., PH.D.
Technical Editor, *Sky and Telescope.* Former Chief, Ground-Based Planetary Astronomy, NASA.

R.B., RICHARD E. BISSELL, A.B., M.A., PH.D.
Executive Editor, *Washington Quarterly.* Adjunct Professor of Government, Georgetown University. Coeditor, *Africa in the Post-Decolonization Era.*

R.C., RAY CONLOGUE, B.A., M.A.
Theater Critic, Toronto *Globe and Mail.*

R.C.O., ROBERT C. OBERST, B.A., M.A., PH.D.
Assistant Professor of Political Science, Nebraska Wesleyan University. Author, *Legislation and Representation: The Decentralization of Development Policy in Sri Lanka.*

R.E.B., ROGER E. BILSTEIN, B.A., M.A., PH.D.
Professor of History, University of Houston at Clear Lake City. Author, *Stages to Saturn: A Technological History of the Apollo/Saturn Launch Vehicles* and *Flight in America, 1900-1983.*

R.E.K., ROGER E. KANET, PH.B., A.B., M.A., A.M., PH.D.
Professor and Head, Political Science Department, University of Illinois at Urbana-Champaign. Editor, *Background to Crisis: Policies and Politics in Gierek's Poland.*

R.I.C., ROBERT I. CRANE, B.A., M.A., PH.D.
Ford-Maxwell Professor of South Asian History, Syracuse University. Coauthor, *Self-study Guide on Urban Problems and Urbanism in South Asia.*

R.J.K., ROBERT J. KURSAR, A.B.
News Editor, *Traffic World* Magazine.

R.J.L., ROBERT J. LaMARCHE, A.B.
Senior Editor, *Tennis* Magazine.

R.J.M., R. J. MAY, M.E.C., D. PHIL.
Senior Fellow, Research School of Pacific Studies, Australian National University. Former Director, Institute of Applied Social and Economic Research, Papua New Guinea.

R.J.W., RICHARD J. WILLEY, A.B., M.A., PH.D.
Professor of Political Science, Vassar College. Author, *Democracy in the West German Trade Unions.* Contributor, New York *Times.*

R.L.B., RICHARD L. BUTWELL, A.B., M.A., D. PHIL.
President and Professor of Political Science, California State University, Dominguez Hills. Author, *Southeast Asia, A Political Introduction; U Nu of Burma.*

R.L.F., RANDALL L. FRAME, B.A., M.A.
Associate News Editor, *Christianity Today.*

R.O.F., ROBERT O. FREEDMAN, PH.D.
Dean and Professor of Political Science, School of Graduate Studies, Baltimore Hebrew College. Editor, *Israel in the Begin Era.*

466

R.T., ROBERT TIMBERG, B.S., M.A.
White House Correspondent, Baltimore *Sun.*

S.A.W., STEFI ANN WEISBURD, B.A., M.S.,
Earth Sciences Editor, *Science News.* Former Assistant Project Director, Congressional Office of Technology Assessment.

S.C., STEVE COHEN, B.A.
Executive Editor, *Ski* Magazine.

S.E., SANFORD ELWITT, PH.D.
Professor of History, University of Rochester. Author, *The Making of the Third Republic, The Republic Defended.*

S.G., SHAV GLICK, A.B.
Motor Racing Writer, Los Angeles *Times.*

S.K., SETH KITANGE, B.A., M.S.
Writer, Editor and Researcher, African News Service.

S.M., SIEGFRIED MANDEL, A.B., M.A., PH.D.
Professor of English and Comparative Literature, University of Colorado at Boulder. Author, *Contemporary European Novelists.*

S.M.G., SAM M. GOLDAPER
Sports Reporter, New York *Times.* New York Area Chairman, Pro Basketball Writers' Association.

S.M.H., STEPHEN M. HEAD, M.A., PH.D.
Assistant Professor of Biology, Sultan Qaboos University, Oman.

S.W., SUSAN WALTON, A.B., M.A.
Free-lance Science and Education Writer.

T.D., THOMAS DEFRANK, B.A., M.A.
Deputy Bureau Chief and White House Correspondent, *Newsweek.*

T.H.M., THOMAS H. MAUGH, II, PH.D.
Science Writer, Los Angeles *Times.* Coauthor, *Energy and the Future, Seeds of Destruction: The Science Report on Cancer Research.*

T.I., TAREQ Y. ISMAEL, A.B., M.A., PH.D.
Professor of Political Science, University of Calgary. Author, *The Middle East in World Politics: A Study in Contemporary International Relations.*

T.J.O.H., T.J.O. HICKEY
Former Member, Editorial Staff, *The Times* of London.

T.McC., TOM McCOLLISTER, A.B.
Sports Writer, Atlanta *Constitution.*

W.C.C., WILLIAM C. CROMWELL, A.B., M.A., PH.D.
Professor of International Relations, American University. Visiting Professor, College of Europe, Belgium. Author, *The Eurogroup and NATO.*

W.D.M., WILLIAM D. MARBACH, B.A., M.A.
General Editor, *Newsweek.*

W.E.K., W. ERIC KELLER, B.A.
Assistant Editor, *Smithsonian* Magazine. Editor, *Environment* Magazine.

W.F., WILLIAM FREDERICK, PH.D.
Assistant Professor of History, Ohio University.

W.L., WILLIAM LEGGETT, A.B.
Senior Writer, *Sports Illustrated.*

W.M., WILLIAM MINTER, PH.D.
Contributing Editor, Africa News Service. Author, *King Solomon's Mines Revisited: Western Interests, and the Burdened History of Southern Africa.*

W.N., WILLIAM NEIKIRK, A.B.
Economics Correspondent, Washington Bureau, Chicago *Tribune.*

W.W., WILLIAM WOLF, A.B.
Film Critic, Gannett News Service. Lecturer, New York University and St. John's University. Author, *Landmark Films, The Marx Brothers.*

PICTURE CREDITS

INDEX TO THE
1987 YEARBOOK
EVENTS OF 1986

INTRODUCTION

This Index is a comprehensive listing of persons, organizations, and events that are discussed in the 1987 Yearbook. Entries in **boldface** letters indicate subjects on which the Yearbook has an individual article. Entries in lightface type indicate individual references or sections within articles. In any entry, the letters a and b refer, respectively, to the left and right column of the page cited. If no letter follows a page number, the reference is to text that is printed in a different format. Usually only the first significant mention of a subject in a given article has been included in the Index.

In a main entry such as **Australia:** 82a, the first number refers to the page on which the article begins. The succeeding lightface page numbers refer to other text discussions in the volume. The first number in lightface entries, when not in numerical order, will similarly provide the most extensive information on the subject. Subtitles following major entries refer to further references on the main subject, as in Congress of the United States: 416b; Agriculture, 64b. In the case of comprehensive articles such as the **United States of America,** reference is made to the page location of the beginning of the article. The discussion of foreign relations of the United States in that article may be augmented by reference to separate articles on the countries and international organizations concerned.

When an entry is designated by the abbreviation **illus.,** the reference is to a caption and picture on the page mentioned. When a text mention and an illustration of the same subject fall within the same article, usually only the text location is included in the Index.

LIST OF ABBREVIATIONS USED IN THE INDEX

NATO   North Atlantic Treaty Organization
OPEC   Organization of Petroleum Exporting Countries
PLO   Palestine Liberation Organization
U.N.   United Nations
U.S.   United States
U.S.S.R.   Union of Soviet Socialist Republics

Nobel Prizes: 331b
nonaligned movement: 63a, 200a, 389a, 435b
Norgay, Tenzing: 291b
Noriega, Manuel Antonio: 300a
North, Oliver: 387a, 415b
North Atlantic Treaty Organization: 279b, 258b, 359b
North Carolina: 117a, 150b, 458
North Dakota: 154, 458
Northern Ireland: 181a, 204a
Northern Marianas: 298a, 460
North Korea. *See* KOREA, DEMOCRATIC PEOPLE'S REPUBLIC OF
Northwest Territories: 462
North Yemen. *See* YEMEN ARAB REPUBLIC
Norway: 280b, 34, 55b, 448
Nova Scotia: 71a, 105a, 462
NOW. *See* NATIONAL ORGANIZATION FOR WOMEN
nuclear power: 163a, 170b, 275b, 412b; *See also* CHERNOBYL NUCLEAR ACCIDENT
nuclear ships: 276a, 298a
nuclear tests: 409a
nuclear weapons: 253a, 279b, 344b, 408b, 426b
numismatics. *See* COINS AND COIN COLLECTING
Nureyev, Rudolf: 133a
Nyerere, Julius: 389a

O

OAS. *See* ORGANIZATION OF AMERICAN STATES
OAU. *See* ORGANIZATION OF AFRICAN UNITY
Obando y Bravo, Miguel: 276b
obesity: 191b
Obituaries: 282a
oceanography: 139a
O'Connor, Sandra Day: **illus.** 422
Ohio: 136a, 154, 458
oil. *See* PETROLEUM
O'Keeffe, Georgia: 291b
Okello, Tito: 404a
Oklahoma: 140a, 154, 164a, 383a, 458
older population: 59a, 93b
Oman: 321a, 203b, 297b, 448
O'Neal, Tatum: 304a
O'Neill, Thomas P., Jr.: 150a, 419b
Onizuka, Ellison S.: 39, 357a
Ontario: 105a, 462
OPEC. *See* ORGANIZATION OF PETROLEUM EXPORTING COUNTRIES
opera: 270b
optics: 329b
Order, the: 130b
Oregon: 56a, 153a, 458
Organization of African Unity: 62b, 108a, 405a, 412b
Organization of American States: 296a
Organization of Petroleum Exporting Countries: 296b, 67a, 159b, 202b, 204a, 216b, 225b, 350b
Organization of the Oppressed on Earth: 221a

Orlov, Yuri: 408a
Orr, Kay: 153a, 430a
Ortega Saavedra, Daniel: 276b
Orthodox churches: 344a
Oumar, Acheikh ibn: 108b
Oxford English Dictionary: 182b
Özal, Turgut: 131b, 403b
ozone: 136b

P

Pacific Islands: 297a, 460
Pacific Ocean: 138a
Packwood, Bob: 418a
Pakistan: 298b, 66a, 197b, 448
Palau, Republic of: 298a, 460
Palestine Liberation Organization: 251b, 206a, 213a, 221b, 403b
Palestine National Salvation Front: 251b
Palme, Olof: 292a, 385b
Palmer, Lilli: 292a
Panama: 300a, 448
Pan American Airways: 298b
Papandreou, Andreas: 131b, 183a
paper industry: 245b
Papua New Guinea: 298a, 448
Paraguay: 300b, 239a, 448
Paris: 173a, 248b
Paris Opera Ballet: 133a
particle accelerators: 328a
Pasteur Institute: 188b
Pastora Gómez, Edén: 277a
Pathans: 299a
Pavlof volcano: 137b
Paz Estenssoro, Victor: 97b
Peabody Awards. *See* GEORGE FOSTER PEABODY AWARDS
Peace Prize, Nobel: 332b
Pears, Sir Peter: 292a
Peggy, Typhoon: 56b
Pelotte, Donald E.: 199a
Pelton, Ronald W.: 126b
penicillin: 192a
Pennsylvania: 68b, 116b, 154, 383a, 424a, 458
People Express: 399b
People in the News: 301a
people mover: 402b
Peres, Shimon: 149b, 205a, 251a, 259b
Pérez de Cuéllar, Javier: 75a, 131b, 409b
Perkins, Edward J.: 97a, 427a
Perkins, Marlin: 292a
Perot, H. Ross: 85b, 308b
Persian Gulf States: 321a
Peru: 321b, 138b, 228b, 239a, 448
pesticides: 165a
petroleum: 159b, 140a; Algeria, 67a; Canada, 105a; Colombia, 121a; Egypt, 148b; Iran, 202b; Iraq, 204a; Kuwait, 216b; Libya, 225b; North Yemen, 432b; OPEC, 296b; Persian Gulf States, 321a; Saudi Arabia, 350b; Venezuela, 428a
Pets: 322b
Philip, Prince: 303b
Philippines: 323a, 256a, 343a, 387a, 448; Aquino, Corazon, 308b

Photography: 326a, 334a
Physics: 328a, 333a
Physiology or Medicine, Nobel Prize in: 333a
Picasso, Jacqueline: 292a
Picasso, Pablo: 77b
Pilliod, Charles J., Jr.: 247a
Pinchet Ugarte, Augusto: 111b
Plante, Jacques: 292a
Poindexter, John: 415b
Poland: 330a, 122a, 448
Polanyi, John C.: 332b
Polgar, Judith: **illus.** 110
Polisario Front: 62b, 260a
political prisoners: 122a, 131a, 193b, 330a, 408a
Pollard, Jonathan Jay: 126b, 205a
pollution. *See* ENVIRONMENT
polymers: 108b
population: 436
pornography: 117a, 222b, 337a, 430b
Portland (Ore.): 402a
Portugal: 331a, 56a, 124a, 166b, 448
Powell, Lewis F., Jr.: **illus.** 422
Pran, Dith: 307b
Preminger, Otto L.: 292a
Prem Tinsulanonda: 394b
Prensa, La: 276b
president of the United States. *See* REAGAN, RONALD
press, freedom of the: 422a; Kuwait, 216b; Nicaragua, 276b; Panama, 300a
preventive medicine: 192b
primary elections: 421a
Prince Edward Island: 104b, 462
prisons: 130a, 384a
Prizes and Awards: 331b, 58b, 74a, 234b, 260b, 268b, 360b, 392b, 398b
product tampering: 128b
Prost, Alain: 360a
protectionism: 101b, 144b
Protestant churches: 344a
psychology. *See* BEHAVIORAL SCIENCES
Publishing: 335a, 232a, 334a
Puerto Rico: 339b, 57b, 460
Pulitzer Prizes: 273a, 334a
Punjab (India): 196a
Pym, Barbara: 237b

Q

Qaddafi, Muammar al-: 316b, 63a, 200a, 224b
Qatar: 321a, 203b, 448
Québec: 104b, 462

R

rabies: 193a, 227b
Rabin, Yitzhak: 387b
radio. *See* TELEVISION AND RADIO BROADCASTING
radon: 164a
Rahal, Bobby: 360a
railroads: 400a, 55a, 67a, 433b
Raines, Tim: 361b
Rainwater, James: 292a

477

478